매일 3단계로 푸는 영 어독해

고3

수능기출

시간은 없고 과목은 많은 통합 수능! 절대평가인 영어부터 끝내는 것이 최적의 전략입니다.

수능 기본 단어부터 필수 구문과 유형별 독해 Tip까지, <매3영 고3>으로 단 2주에 완벽 정리하세요!

- 수능 영어에 대한 근거 있는 자신감을 키워주는 책
- 수능+내신 필수 단어/구문을 끝내주는 책
- 친절한 해설로 독학 영어의 길잡이가 되어주는 책

고등 영어 마스터, <매3영>이라면 가능합니다!

STEP 1

모든 영어 공부의 시작은 단어!
수능 필수 단어 & 어구 익히기

❶ 수능 필수 단어 LIST

문제 풀이에 앞서 지문 속 필수 어휘를
완벽하게 정리합니다.

❸ 단어 SELF-TEST

암기한 단어를 확인해 보고, 놓친 단어는
그 자리에서 바로 정리합니다.

❷ 예문 확인 & 빈칸 채우기

지문에 실제로 쓰인 표현에서 단어의
용법을 확인하며 쉽게 암기합니다.

❹ 문장 속 단어 CHECK

외운 단어를 문장 속에서 직접 해석해 보며
단어의 응용력을 기릅니다.

STEP ② 좋은 기출 문제도 풀어야 내 것!

문제 풀이 실전 훈련

❶ 시간 & 난이도 확인

유형 및 난이도에 따른 문제 풀이 제한 시간을 확인하고, 실전처럼 시간 안배를 연습합니다.

❸ 종합 성적표 REVIEW

3일마다 종합 성적표를 작성해 보면서 나의 문제 풀이 습관을 돌아보고, 시간 초과나 실수가 잦은 영역을 확인합니다.

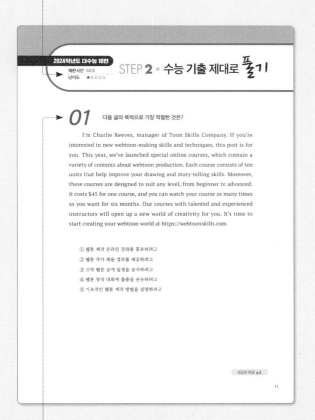

❷ 매일 실전 훈련 연습

매일 유형별 문제풀이로 기출을 빠르게 **1회독**하며 실전 감각을 기릅니다.

❹ 맞춤 솔루션 찾기

오답 이유에 따라 맞춤 솔루션을 찾고, 앞으로의 학습 방향을 설계합니다.

작은 단어, 구문도 놓치지 않는다!
첨삭 해설로 지문 복습하기

❶ 전 문장 직독직해

끊어읽기로 지문을 **2회독**하며, 모든 문장을 직독직해 해보고 정확한 해석 능력을 키웁니다.

❸ 지문 속 단어 복습

STEP 1에서 외웠던 단어가 지문 속에 어떻게 활용되었는지 최종 확인하고, 암기 여부를 재점검합니다.

❷ 구문 첨삭 해설

실제 수능에 자주 나오는 구문을 꼼꼼히 학습하고, 다음 문제 풀이에 적용합니다.

❹ 구문 CHECK-UP

첨삭 해설로 학습한 구문 포인트를 어법 변형 문제로 다시 정리합니다.

기본기를 독해력으로 끌어올린다!
정답 및 해설

❶ 해석
직독직해로 읽은 의미를 매끄러운 말로 확인하며 내용을 정리합니다.

❷ 해설
근거 중심의 자세한 해설로 정답 도출의 과정을 상세히 확인합니다.

❹ 지문 자세히 보기
하이라이트 표시된 정답 근거와 주요 표현을 꼼꼼히 체크하며, 자연스럽게 지문을 **3회독**합니다.

❸ 상세 오답 풀이
선택지 함정과 오답의 근거를 자세히 설명해주는 오답 풀이를 통해 약점을 완벽히 알고 보완합니다.

❺ 구문플러스 & 유형플러스
필수 구문/어법 사항, 문항 유형별 주의 사항을 추가로 확인하며 실전력을 더욱 향상시킵니다.

Contents

단 15일 만에 완성하는 수능 영어독해 전 유형

최신 5개년 출제 경향을 대표하는 좋은 기출 문제와
지문 분석력을 길러주는 영어 공부법의 만남

<매3영>이 제시하는 3단계로

유형3일 훈련

DAY

01~03

공부한 날			출처	페이지
DAY 1	월	일	2024학년도 대수능 18번 2023학년도 대수능 18번 2023학년도 6월 19번 2022학년도 대수능 19번 2022학년도 6월 19번 2021학년도 6월 19번 2020학년도 6월 19번	9
DAY 2	월	일	2024학년도 6월 22번 2023학년도 6월 22번 2022학년도 대수능 20번 2022학년도 9월 22번 2021학년도 9월 20번 2021학년도 6월 22번 2020학년도 대수능 22번	37
DAY 3	월	일	2024학년도 대수능 21번 2024학년도 9월 21번 2024학년도 6월 21번 2023학년도 9월 21번 2022학년도 대수능 21번 2021학년도 대수능 21번 2020학년도 6월 21번	65

01 STEP 1 • 수능에 *진짜* 나오는 *단어*

✔ 문제에 나오는 단어들을 확인하세요.

01	launch	v. 시작하다, 출시하다	(✔ launch) special online courses	특별 온라인 강좌를 출시하다
02	a variety of	다양한	contain (　) (　　　) (　) contents	다양한 콘텐츠를 담다
03	production	n. 제작	webtoon (　　　　)	웹툰 제작
04	consist of	~로 구성되다	(　　　) (　) ten units	10차시로 구성되다
05	suit	v. (~에) 맞다, 적합하다	(　　) any level	어떤 수준에든 맞다
06	advanced	a. (수준이) 고급의	from beginner to (　　　)	초급부터 고급까지
07	talented	a. 재능 있는	(　　　) and experienced	재능 있고 노련한
08	instructor	n. 강사	a skilled (　　　)	숙련된 강사

✚ 본문 문장 속에서 단어들을 확인해 보세요.

Moreover, / these courses are designed to suit any level, / from beginner to advanced.

게다가, / 이 강좌들은 어떤 수준에도 적합하도록 설계되어 있습니다 / 초급에서 고급까지.

문제를 풀기 전에 단어들을 **30초** 동안 다시 확인하세요.

01	launch	✎ 시작하다, 출시하다	launch special online courses	특별 온라인 강좌를 (출시하다)
02	a variety of		contain a variety of contents	( ) 콘텐츠를 담다
03	production		webtoon production	웹툰 ( )
04	consist of		consist of ten units	10차시로 ( )
05	suit		suit any level	어떤 수준에든 ( )
06	advanced		from beginner to advanced	초급부터 ( )까지
07	talented		talented and experienced	( ) 노련한
08	instructor		a skilled instructor	숙련된 ( )

➕ **본문 문장 속에서 단어의 의미를 우리말로 해석해 보세요.**

Moreover, / these courses are designed to suit any level, / from beginner to advanced.

➡ 게다가, / 이 강좌들은 ░░░░░░░░░░░░░ 설계되어 있습니다 / ░░░░░░░░░.

01 다음 글의 목적으로 가장 적절한 것은?

I'm Charlie Reeves, manager of Toon Skills Company. If you're interested in new webtoon-making skills and techniques, this post is for you. This year, we've launched special online courses, which contain a variety of contents about webtoon production. Each course consists of ten units that help improve your drawing and story-telling skills. Moreover, these courses are designed to suit any level, from beginner to advanced. It costs $45 for one course, and you can watch your course as many times as you want for six months. Our courses with talented and experienced instructors will open up a new world of creativity for you. It's time to start creating your webtoon world at https://webtoonskills.com.

① 웹툰 제작 온라인 강좌를 홍보하려고
② 웹툰 작가 채용 정보를 제공하려고
③ 신작 웹툰 공개 일정을 공지하려고
④ 웹툰 창작 대회에 출품을 권유하려고
⑤ 기초적인 웹툰 제작 방법을 설명하려고

정답과 해설 **p.2**

STEP 3 • 수능 지문 제대로 복습하기

01 I'm Charlie Reeves, / manager of Toon Skills Company.
동격

02 If you're interested in new webtoon-making skills and techniques, / this post is for
접속사(~한다면)
you.

03 This year, / we've launched special online courses, / which contain a variety of
선행사   수 일치
contents about webtoon production.
계속적 용법

04 Each course consists of ten units / [that help improve your drawing and story-telling
「help (to) + 동사원형: ~하기를 돕다」
skills].
주격 관계대명사절

05 Moreover, / these courses are designed to suit any level, / from beginner to advanced.
~하도록 설계되다

06 It costs $45 for one course, / and you can watch your course / as many times as you
want for six months.

07 Our courses with talented and experienced instructors / will open up a new world of
주어   전치사구   동사구
creativity for you.

08 It's time to start / creating your webtoon world at https://webtoonskills.com.
~할 때이다

01 저는 Charlie Reeves입니다 / Toon Skills Company의 경영자인.

02 여러분이 새로운 웹툰 제작 기술과 기법에 관심이 있으시다면, / 이 게시물은 여러분을 위한 것입니다.

03 올해, / 저희는 특별 온라인 강좌를 출시했는데launch, / 여기에는 웹툰 제작production에 관한 다양한a variety of
콘텐츠가 담겨 있습니다.

04 각 강좌는 10차시로 구성되어consist of 있습니다 / 여러분의 그리기와 스토리텔링 기술을 향상하는 데 도움이 되는.

05 게다가, / 이 강좌들은 어떤 수준에든 맞게suit 설계되어 있습니다 / 초급에서 고급advanced까지.

06 비용은 한 강좌당 45달러이며 / 여러분은 여러분의 강좌를 보실 수 있습니다 / 6개월 동안 원하는 만큼 여러 번.

07 재능이 있고 노련한 강사들talented and experienced instructors이 담당하는 저희 강좌는 / 여러분에게 창의력의
새로운 세계를 열어줄 것입니다.

08 이제 시작할 때입니다 / https://webtoonskills.com에서 여러분의 웹툰 세계를 창조하는 것을.

구문 Check up

① This year, we've launched special online courses, which contains / contain a variety of contents about webtoon production.

선행사가 special online courses라는 복수명사이므로, 주격 관계대명사절의 동사로 복수형인 contain이 적절하다.

② Each course consists of ten units that help improving / improve your drawing and story-telling skills.

help는 to부정사 또는 원형부정사를 목적어로 취하므로 improve를 쓴다.

정답 ① contain ② improve

12

글의 목적 +

STEP 1 • 수능에 진짜 나오는 단어

✔ 문제에 나오는 단어들을 확인하세요.

01	to whom it may concern	관계자 귀하	(✔ to) (whom) (it) (may) (concern)	관계자 귀하
02	yard	n. 뜰, 마당	watch birds in my ( )	내 뜰에서 새들을 관찰하다
03	happen to	우연히 ~하다	( ) ( ) see you	너를 우연히 만나다
04	article	n. 기사	read an ( ) about your club	당신의 클럽에 관한 기사를 읽다
05	passionate	a. 열정적인	a community of ( ) bird-watchers	열정적인 조류 관찰자들의 공동체
06	annually	ad. 매년, 연마다	travel ( )	매년 여행하다
07	birding	n. 조류 관찰	go ( ) on this weekend	이번 주말에 조류 관찰을 가다
08	under construction	공사 중인, 보수 중인	still ( ) ( )	아직 공사 중인
09	sign up for	~에 등록하다, 가입하다	( ) ( ) ( ) a birding club	조류 관찰 클럽에 가입하다

+ 본문 문장 속에서 단어들을 확인해 보세요.

Yesterday, / I happened to read an article about your club.

어제 / 저는 귀하의 클럽에 대한 기사를 우연히 읽었습니다.

01	to whom it may concern	✎ 관계자 귀하	to whom it may concern	(관계자 귀하)
02	yard		watch birds in my yard	내 ( )에서 새들을 관찰하다
03	happen to		happen to see you	너를 ( )
04	article		read an article about your club	당신의 클럽에 관한 ( )를 읽다
05	passionate		a community of passionate bird-watchers	( ) 조류 관찰자들의 공동체
06	annually		travel annually	( ) 여행하다
07	birding		go birding on this weekend	이번 주말에 ( )을 가다
08	under construction		still under construction	아직 ( )
09	sign up for		sign up for a birding club	조류 관찰 클럽에 ( )

➕ 본문 문장 속에서 단어의 의미를 우리말로 해석해 보세요.

Yesterday, / I happened to read an article about your club.

→ 어제 / 저는 귀하의 클럽에 대한 ██████████████████████.

02   다음 글의 목적으로 가장 적절한 것은?

To whom it may concern,

My name is Michael Brown. I have been a bird-watcher since childhood. I have always enjoyed watching birds in my yard and identifying them by sight and sound. Yesterday, I happened to read an article about your club. I was surprised and excited to find out about a community of passionate bird-watchers who travel annually to go birding. I would love to join your club, but your website appears to be under construction. I could not find any information except for this contact email address. I would like to know how to sign up for the club. I look forward to your reply.

Sincerely,
Michael Brown

① 조류 관찰 클럽에 가입하는 방법을 문의하려고
② 조류 관찰 시 주의해야 할 사항을 전달하려고
③ 조류 관찰 협회의 새로운 규정을 확인하려고
④ 조류 관찰과 관련된 웹 사이트를 소개하려고
⑤ 조류 관찰 시 필요한 장비를 알아보려고

정답과 해설 **p.2**

01 To whom it may concern,

02 My name is Michael Brown. // I have been a bird-watcher since childhood.
동사(현재완료)　기간 부사구(since)

03 I have always enjoyed watching birds in my yard / and identifying them by sight and
동사　목적어1　목적어2(동명사구 병렬)
sound.

04 Yesterday, / I happened to read an article about your club. // I was surprised and
「happen to + 동사원형: 우연히 ~하다」　감정 형용사
excited / to find out about a community of passionate bird-watchers / [who travel
부사적 용법(원인)　선행사　주격 관계대명사절
annually to go birding].

05 I would love to join your club, / but your website appears to be under construction. //
「appear + to부정사: ~인 것 같다」
I could not find any information / except for this contact email address.
~을 제외하고

06 I would like to know how to sign up for the club.
「how + to부정사: ~할 방법」

07 I look forward to your reply.

08 Sincerely, / Michael Brown

01 담당자 귀하to whom it may concern

02 제 이름은 Michael Brown입니다. // 저는 어렸을 때부터 조류 관찰자였습니다.

03 저는 항상 저의 뜰yard에서 새들을 관찰하기를 즐겼습니다 / 그리고 모습과 소리로 그것들을 식별하기를.

04 어제 / 저는 귀하의 클럽에 대한 기사를 우연히 읽었습니다happen to read an article. // 저는 놀라고 신났습니다 /
열정적인passionate 조류 관찰자들의 공동체에 대해 알게 되어서 / 매년annually 조류 관찰birding을 하러 다니는.

05 저는 귀하의 클럽에 가입하기를 몹시 원하지만, / 귀하의 웹 사이트가 공사 중인under construction 것 같습니다. // 저는
다른 정보를 찾을 수가 없었습니다 / 이 이메일 주소를 제외하고는.

06 저는 클럽에 가입하는sign up for 방법을 알고 싶습니다.

07 귀하의 답장을 기다리겠습니다.

08 Michael Brown 드림

구문 Check up

① I have always enjoyed to watch / watching birds in my yard and identifying them by sight and sound.

enjoy는 동명사를 목적어로 취하는 동사이므로 watching이 정답이다.

② I was surprised and excited to find / finding out about a community of passionate bird-watchers who travel annually to go birding.

감정의 형용사 뒤에서 감정의 원인을 설명하는 문맥이므로 to find를 써야 한다.

정답 ① watching ② to find

03 STEP 1 • 수능에 *진짜* 나오는 *단어*

✔ 문제에 나오는 단어들을 확인하세요.

01	cliff	n. 절벽	move toward the ocean (✔ cliff)s	바다에 면한 절벽 쪽으로 움직이다
02	sigh	v. 한숨을 쉬다	(　　　) with relief	안도의 한숨을 쉬다
03	concern	n. 걱정, 우려	with (　　　　)	걱정스럽게
04	sunset	n. 일몰, 노을	miss the (　　　) because of the traffic	교통 때문에 일몰을 놓치다
05	gather	v. (흩어진 것을) 챙기다, 모으다	(　　　) the bag	가방을 챙기다
06	brightly	ad. 밝게	shine (　　　) in the sky	하늘에서 밝게 빛나다
07	glow	n. 빛 v. 빛나다	the (　　　) of the setting sun	지는 해의 빛

⊕ 본문 문장 속에서 단어들을 확인해 보세요.

Jessica sighed with concern, / "I'm going to miss the sunset / because of the traffic."

Jessica는 걱정스럽게 한숨지었다 / "나는 일몰을 놓치게 **될 거야** / 교통 때문에."

01	cliff	✏ 절벽	move toward the ocean cliffs	바다에 면한 (절벽)쪽으로 움직이다
02	sigh		sigh with relief	안도의 ( )
03	concern		with concern	( )스럽게
04	sunset		miss the sunset because of the traffic	교통 때문에 ( )을 놓치다
05	gather		gather the bag	가방을 ( )
06	brightly		shine brightly in the sky	하늘에서 ( ) 빛나다
07	glow		the glow of the setting sun	지는 해의 ( )

➕ 본문 문장 속에서 단어의 의미를 우리말로 해석해 보세요.

Jessica sighed with concern, / "I'm going to miss the sunset / because of the traffic."

➡ Jessica는 ▨▨▨▨▨▨ / "나는 ▨▨▨▨▨ 될 거야 / ▨▨▨▨▨."

03 다음 글에 나타난 Jessica의 심경 변화로 가장 적절한 것은?

The island tour bus Jessica was riding on was moving slowly toward the ocean cliffs. Outside, the sky was getting dark. Jessica sighed with concern, "I'm going to miss the sunset because of the traffic." The bus arrived at the cliffs' parking lot. While the other passengers were gathering their bags, Jessica quickly got off the bus and she ran up the cliff that was famous for its ocean views. She was about to give up when she got to the top. Just then she saw the setting sun and it still shone brightly in the sky. Jessica said to herself, "The glow of the sun is so beautiful. It's even better than I expected."

① worried → delighted

② bored → confident

③ relieved → annoyed

④ joyful → indifferent

⑤ regretful → depressed

정답과 해설 p.3

01 The island tour bus [Jessica was riding on] / was moving slowly toward the ocean cliffs.
주어(선행사)   목적격 관계대명사절   동사(과거진행)

02 Outside, the sky was getting dark.

03 Jessica sighed with concern, / "I'm going to miss the sunset / because of the traffic."
전치사(~ 때문에)

04 The bus arrived at the cliffs' parking lot.

05 While the other passengers were gathering their bags, / Jessica quickly got off the bus
접속사(~ 동안)   주어1   동사1
/ and she ran up the cliff / [that was famous for its ocean views].
주어2   동사2   주격 관계대명사절

06 She was about to give up / when she got to the top.
「be about to + 동사원형: 막 ~할 참이다」

07 Just then she saw the setting sun / and it still shone brightly in the sky.
현재분사   부사

08 Jessica said to herself, / "The glow of the sun is so beautiful. / It's even better than I
비교급 강조(훨씬)
expected."

---

01 Jessica가 타고 있는 섬 관광버스는 / 바다에 면한 절벽cliff 쪽으로 천천히 움직이고 있었다.

02 바깥에서는 하늘이 점점 어두워지고 있었다.

03 Jessica는 걱정스럽게 한숨지었다sigh with concern / "나는 일몰sunset을 놓치게 될 거야 / 교통 때문에."

04 버스가 절벽의 주차장에 도착했다.

05 다른 승객들이 자신들의 가방을 챙기는gather 동안, / Jessica는 재빨리 버스에서 내렸고 / 그녀는 그 절벽으로 뛰어 올라갔다 / 바다 전망으로 유명한.

06 그녀는 막 포기하려 했다 / 그녀가 꼭대기에 도달했을 때.

07 바로 그때 그녀는 지는 해를 보았는데, / 그것은 여전히 하늘에서 밝게brightly 빛나고 있었다.

08 Jessica는 혼잣말했다 / "노을빛glow이 너무 아름다워. / 내가 기대했던 것보다 훨씬 더 좋아."라고.

---

① The island tour bus Jessica was riding on was / to be moving slowly toward the ocean cliffs.

주어 The island tour bus 뒤로 동사가 필요하므로 was가 적절하다. Jessica was riding on은 주어를 꾸미는 관계대명사절이다.

② She was about to give up / giving up when she got to the top.

「be about to + 동사원형(막 ~할 참이다)」 구문이므로 give up이 적절하다.

정답 ① was ② give up

DAY 01
04 STEP 1 • 수능에 *진짜* 나오는 *단어*

심경/분위기 ➕

✔ 문제에 나오는 단어들을 확인하세요.

01	explore	v. 탐험하다	(✔ explore) a new land	새로운 땅을 탐험하다
02	numerous	a. 수많은	( ) dinosaur fossils	수많은 공룡 화석
03	overflow	v. (감정 등으로) 가득 차다, 넘치다	( ) with gratitude	감사로 가득 차다
04	anticipation	n. 기대(감)	filled with ( )	기대에 부푼
05	species	n. (생물) 종	a common dinosaur ( )	어느 흔한 공룡 종
06	rare	a. 희귀한, 드문	( ) fossils of dinosaurs	희귀한 공룡 화석
07	eagerly	ad. 열심히, 열성적으로	( ) search for the truth	열심히 진리를 찾다
08	wander	v. 배회하다	( ) throughout the land	땅을 배회하다
09	deserted	a. 황량한, 버려진, (장소가) 사람이 없는	a ( ) village	버려진 마을
10	unsuccessful	a. 성과 없는, 성공하지 못한	many ( ) attempts	성과 없는 많은 시도
11	beyond one's reach	~의 손이 닿지 않는, 힘이 미치지 않는	still far ( ) your ( )	여전히 네 손이 닿지 않는 먼 곳에

➕ 본문 문장 속에서 단어들을 확인해 보세요.

As a young amateur bone-hunter, / she was overflowing with anticipation.

젊은 아마추어 뼈 발굴자로서 / 그녀는 기대감으로 가득 차 있었다.

21

01	explore	🖉 탐험하다	explore a new land	새로운 땅을 (탐험하다)
02	numerous		numerous dinosaur fossils	( ) 공룡 화석
03	overflow		overflow with gratitude	감사로 ( )
04	anticipation		filled with anticipation	( )에 부푼
05	species		a common dinosaur species	어느 흔한 공룡 ( )
06	rare		rare fossils of dinosaurs	( ) 공룡 화석
07	eagerly		eagerly search for the truth	( ) 진리를 찾다
08	wander		wander throughout the land	땅을 ( )
09	deserted		a deserted village	( ) 마을
10	unsuccessful		many unsuccessful attempts	( ) 많은 시도
11	beyond one's reach		still far beyond your reach	여전히 ( ) 먼 곳에

➕ **본문 문장 속에서 단어의 의미를 우리말로 해석해 보세요.**

As a young amateur bone-hunter, / she was overflowing with anticipation.

➜ 젊은 아마추어 뼈 발굴자로서 / 그녀는 ▨▨▨▨▨▨▨▨▨ 있었다.

04 다음 글에 나타난 Evelyn의 심경 변화로 가장 적절한 것은?

It was Evelyn's first time to explore the Badlands of Alberta, famous across Canada for its numerous dinosaur fossils. As a young amateur bone-hunter, she was overflowing with anticipation. She had not travelled this far for the bones of common dinosaur species. Her life-long dream to find rare fossils of dinosaurs was about to come true. She began eagerly searching for them. After many hours of wandering throughout the deserted lands, however, she was unsuccessful. Now, the sun was beginning to set, and her goal was still far beyond her reach. Looking at the slowly darkening ground before her, she sighed to herself, "I can't believe I came all this way for nothing. What a waste of time!"

① confused → scared
② discouraged → confident
③ relaxed → annoyed
④ indifferent → depressed
⑤ hopeful → disappointed

정답과 해설 p.4

01 It was Evelyn's first time / to explore the Badlands of Alberta, / (which is) famous
선행사
형용사적 용법   계속적 용법
across Canada for its numerous dinosaur fossils.
형용사구(is의 보어)

02 As a young amateur bone-hunter, / she was overflowing with anticipation. // She had
전치사(~로서)
not travelled this far / for the bones of common dinosaur species.
과거완료(~해본 적이 없었다)

03 Her life-long dream to find rare fossils of dinosaurs / was about to come true. // She
주어(단수)   형용사적 용법   「be about to + 동사원형: ~할 참이다」
began eagerly searching for them.
「begin + 동명사: ~하기 시작하다」

04 After many hours of wandering throughout the deserted lands, / however, / she was
unsuccessful. // Now, the sun was beginning to set, / and her goal was still far beyond
her reach.

05 Looking at the slowly darkening ground before her, / she sighed to herself, / "I can't
분사구문
believe I came all this way for nothing. / What a waste of time!"
접속사 that 생략   「what + a/an + 형 + 명: 감탄문(얼마나 ~한가!)」

01 Evelyn에게는 처음이었다 / 앨버타주의 Badlands를 탐험하는explore 것이 / 캐나다 전역에서 수많은numerous 공룡
화석으로 유명한.

02 젊은 아마추어 뼈 발굴자로서 / 그녀는 기대감으로 가득 차overflow with anticipation 있었다. // 그녀는 이렇게 멀리까지
이동해본 적이 없었다 / 흔한 공룡 종species의 뼈 때문에.

03 희귀한rare 공룡 화석을 발견하고자 하는 그녀의 평생의 꿈이 / 막 실현될 참이었다. // 그녀는 열심히eagerly 그것들을
찾기 시작했다.

04 황량한deserted 땅을 여러 시간 배회하고wander 난 후에도, / 하지만 / 그녀는 성과를 얻지 못했다unsuccessful. //
이제 해는 지기 시작하고 있었고, / 그녀의 목표는 여전히 손 닿지 않는beyond one's reach 먼 곳에 있었다.

05 천천히 어두워지는 자기 앞의 땅을 바라보며, / 그녀는 혼자 한숨을 쉬며 말했다. / "이렇게 멀리 와서 아무 성과도 못
내다니 믿을 수가 없네. / 이게 무슨 시간 낭비야!"

구문 Check up

① It was Evelyn's first time to explore the Badlands of
Alberta, famous / famously across Canada for its
numerous dinosaur fossils.

the Badlands of Alberta를 보충 설명하는 관계절 'which is famous ~'에
서 which is가 생략되고 보어만 남은 구조이다. 따라서 famous가 적절하
다.

② Her life-long dream to find rare fossils of dinosaurs
were / was about to come true.

주어가 단수명사인 Her life-long dream이므로 was가 적절하다.

정답 ① famous ② was

24

05 STEP 1 • 수능에 *진짜* 나오는 *단어*

✔ 문제에 나오는 단어들을 확인하세요.

01	session	n. (특정한 활동을 위한) 시간, 기간	an online counseling (✔ session)	온라인 상담 시간
02	wonder	v. 의문을 갖다, 궁금해하다	( ) how I can open my heart	내가 어떻게 마음을 열 수 있을지 궁금해하다
03	save A B	A에게 B를 절약해주다	( ) her a lot of time	그녀에게 많은 시간을 절약해주다
04	in person	직접	meet ( ) ( )	직접 만나다
05	concern	n. 걱정	( )s about online counseling	온라인 상담에 대한 걱정
06	go away	사라지다	your concerns will ( ) ( )	너의 걱정이 사라질 것이다
07	convenient	a. 편리한	more ( ) than expected	기대했던 것보다 더 편리한
08	definitely	ad. 꼭, 분명히	I'll ( ) see you again	당신을 꼭 다시 만날 거예요

✚ 본문 문장 속에서 단어들을 확인해 보세요.

Natalie just wasn't sure / if it would be as helpful / as meeting her counselor in person.

다만 Natalie는 확신할 수 없었다 / 그것이 도움이 될지 / 상담사를 직접 만나는 것만큼.

문제를 풀기 전에 단어들을 **30초** 동안 다시 확인하세요.

01	session	✏️ 시간, 기간	an online counseling session	온라인 상담 (시간)
02	wonder		wonder how I can open my heart	내가 어떻게 마음을 열 수 있을지 (　　　)
03	save A B		save her a lot of time	그녀에게 많은 시간을 (　　　)
04	in person		meet in person	(　　　) 만나다
05	concern		concerns about online counseling	온라인 상담에 대한 (　　　)
06	go away		your concerns will go away	너의 걱정이 (　　　) 것이다
07	convenient		more convenient than expected	기대했던 것보다 더 (　　　)
08	definitely		I'll definitely see you again	당신을 (　　　) 다시 만날 거예요

➕ 본문 문장 속에서 단어의 의미를 우리말로 해석해 보세요.

Natalie just wasn't sure / if it would be as helpful / as meeting her counselor in person.

→ 다만 Natalie는 확신할 수 없었다 / 그것이 도움이 될지 / ███████████████ 만큼.

05 다음 글에 드러난 Natalie의 심경 변화로 가장 적절한 것은?

As Natalie was logging in to her first online counseling session, she wondered, "How can I open my heart to the counselor through a computer screen?" Since the counseling center was a long drive away, she knew that this would save her a lot of time. Natalie just wasn't sure if it would be as helpful as meeting her counselor in person. Once the session began, however, her concerns went away. She actually started thinking that it was much more convenient than expected. She felt as if the counselor were in the room with her. As the session closed, she told him with a smile, "I'll definitely see you online again!"

① doubtful → satisfied

② regretful → confused

③ confident → ashamed

④ bored → excited

⑤ thrilled → disappointed

정답과 해설 p.4

01 As Natalie was logging in to her first online counseling session, / she wondered, /
접속사(~하면서, ~할 때)   주어 동사
"How can I open my heart to the counselor / through a computer screen?"
목적어(직접의문문)

02 Since the counseling center was a long drive away, / she knew / [that this would save
접속사(~이기 때문에)   주어 동사   목적어(명사절)
her a lot of time].

03 Natalie just wasn't sure / if it would be as helpful / as meeting her counselor in person.
접속사(~인지 아닌지)   「as + 원급 + as: ~만큼 …한」

04 Once the session began, / however, / her concerns went away.
접속사(일단 ~하자)

05 She actually started thinking / that it was much more convenient than expected.
「much + 비교급 + than: 훨씬 더 ~한」

06 She felt / as if the counselor were in the room with her.
「as if + 주어 + 과거 동사: 가정법 과거(실제 ~이지 않지만 마치 ~인 것처럼)」

07 As the session closed, / she told him with a smile, / "I'll definitely see you online
접속사(~할 때)   동사 간접목적어   직접목적어
again!"

---

01 Natalie가 자신의 첫 온라인 상담 시간counseling session에 접속하면서, / 그녀는 의문을 가졌다wonder / "내가
상담사에게 어떻게 나의 마음을 열 수 있을까 / 컴퓨터 화면을 통해?"라는.

02 상담 센터가 차로 오래 가야 하는 곳에 있었기 때문에, / 그녀는 알고 있었다 / 이것이 자신에게 많은 시간을 절약해 줄
것임을save her a lot of time.

03 다만 Natalie는 확신할 수 없었다 / 그것이 도움이 될 것인지 / 상담사를 직접in person 만나는 것만큼.

04 일단 (상담) 시간이 시작되자, / 하지만 / 그녀의 걱정concern은 사라졌다go away.

05 그녀는 실제로 생각하기 시작했다 / 그것이 예상했던 것보다 훨씬 더 편리하다고convenient.

06 그녀는 느꼈다 / 마치 상담사가 함께 방 안에 있는 것처럼.

07 (상담) 시간이 끝났을 때, / 그녀는 미소를 지으며 그에게 말했다 / "온라인에서 꼭definitely 다시 만나요!"

구문 Check up

① She actually started thinking that it was much / very
more convenient than expected.

뒤에 비교급 형용사가 나오므로 이를 수식할 수 있는 much가 적절하다.
much 외에 far, even, still, a lot 등을 써도 된다. very는 원급 또는 최상급
을 꾸민다.

② She felt as if the counselor is / were in the room with
her.

실제로 방 안에 함께 있지 않았지만 마치 그런 듯한 기분이 들었다는 의
미를 나타내기 위해 가정법 과거 구문을 써야 한다. 따라서 were가 적절
하다.

정답 ① much ② were

06 STEP 1 · 수능에 *진짜* 나오는 *단어*

✔ 문제에 나오는 단어들을 확인하세요.

01	upcoming	a. 다가오는, 곧 있을	an (✔ upcoming) concert	다가오는 콘서트
02	come across	우연히 마주치다	( ) ( ) a review	리뷰를 우연히 발견하다
03	harsh	a. 가혹한, 혹독한	a ( ) review	혹독한 평가
04	awful	a. 끔찍한	an ( ) performance	끔찍한 공연
05	performance	n. 공연, 연주	a tango ( )	탱고 공연
06	raise	v. (의문을) 제기하다	( ) a question	의문을 제기하다
07	worthwhile	a. 가치 있는	( ) to go	갈 만한 가치가 있는
08	reluctantly	ad. 마지못해	( ) decide	마지못해 결정하다
09	run-down	a. 황폐한, 쇠퇴한	a ( ) hall	황폐한 홀
10	in harmony	조화를 이루는	everything was ( ) ( )	모든 것이 조화로웠다
11	sensational	a. 환상적인	a ( ) concert	환상적인 콘서트
12	expectation	n. 예상, 기대	far beyond her ( )s	그녀의 예상을 훨씬 뛰어넘은

⊕ 본문 문장 속에서 단어들을 확인해 보세요.

That raised in Sharon's mind / the question of whether it was worthwhile to go, / but in the end, / she reluctantly decided to attend the concert.

그것은 Sharon의 마음속에 제기했다 / 그것이 갈 만한 가치가 있을지 하는 의문을 / 하지만 결국 / 그녀는 마지못해 콘서트에 참석하기로 결정했다.

01	upcoming	🖉 다가오는, 곧 있을	an upcoming concert	(다가오는) 콘서트
02	come across		come across a review	리뷰를 ( )
03	harsh		a harsh review	( ) 평가
04	awful		an awful performance	( ) 공연
05	performance		a tango performance	탱고 ( )
06	raise		raise a question	의문을 ( )
07	worthwhile		worthwhile to go	갈 만한 ( )
08	reluctantly		reluctantly decide	( ) 결정하다
09	run-down		a run-down hall	( ) 홀
10	in harmony		everything was in harmony	모든 것이 ( )
11	sensational		a sensational concert	( ) 콘서트
12	expectation		far beyond her expectations	그녀의 ( )을 훨씬 뛰어넘은

➕ **본문 문장 속에서 단어의 의미를 우리말로 해석해 보세요.**

That raised in Sharon's mind / the question of whether it was worthwhile to go, / but in the end, / she reluctantly decided to attend the concert.

➜ 그것은 Sharon의 마음속에 제기했다 /   하는 의문을 / 하지만 결국 / 그녀는   .

06 다음 글에 드러난 Sharon의 심경 변화로 가장 적절한 것은?

Sharon received a ticket to an upcoming tango concert from her friend. While surfing the Internet, she came across a review for the concert. The reviewer was harsh, calling it "an awful performance." That raised in Sharon's mind the question of whether it was worthwhile to go, but in the end, she reluctantly decided to attend the concert. The hall located in the old town was ancient and run-down. Looking around, Sharon again wondered what kind of show she could expect. But as soon as the tango started, everything changed. The piano, guitar, flute, and violin magically flew out in harmony. The audience cheered. "Oh my goodness! What fantastic music!" Sharon shouted. The rhythm and tempo were so energetic and sensational that they shook her body and soul. The concert was far beyond her expectations.

① excited → bored

② doubtful → amazed

③ calm → upset

④ ashamed → grateful

⑤ envious → indifferent

정답과 해설 **p.5**

01 Sharon received a ticket to an upcoming tango concert / from her friend.

02 While surfing the Internet, / she came across a review for the concert. // The reviewer
분사구문(접속사+분사)
was harsh, / calling it "an awful performance."
분사구문(~하면서)

03 That raised (in Sharon's mind) / the question [of whether it was worthwhile to go], /
주어1   동사1   부사구   목적어   접속사(~인지 아닌지)
but in the end, / she reluctantly decided to attend the concert.
주어2   동사2

04 The hall located in the old town / was ancient and run-down. // Looking around, /
주어   과거분사구   동사   분사구문(~하면서)
Sharon again wondered / what kind of show she could expect.
주어   동사   목적어(간접의문문)

05 But as soon as the tango started, / everything changed. // The piano, guitar, flute, and
접속사(~하자마자)
violin / magically flew out in harmony.

06 The audience cheered. // "Oh my goodness! What fantastic music!" / Sharon shouted.
감탄문(what+(a/an)+형+명)
// The rhythm and tempo were so energetic and sensational / that they shook her body
「so ~ that : 너무 ~해서 …하다」
and soul.

07 The concert was far beyond her expectations.

01 Sharon은 다가오는upcoming 탱고 콘서트 표를 받았다 / 자신의 친구로부터.

02 인터넷을 검색하던 중 / 그녀는 그 콘서트에 관한 리뷰를 우연히 발견하게 되었다come across a review. // 리뷰를 쓴
사람은 가혹했다harsh / 그것을 '끔찍한 공연awful performance'이라고 부르며.

03 그것은 Sharon의 마음속에 제기했다raise / 그것이 갈 만한 가치가 있을지worthwhile to go 하는 의문을 / 하지만 결국 /
그녀는 마지못해reluctantly 콘서트에 참석하기로 결정했다.

04 구시가지에 위치한 홀은 / 아주 오래되고 황폐했다run-down. // 주위를 둘러보며 / Sharon은 또다시 궁금했다 / 어떤
쇼를 기대할 수 있을지.

05 그러나 탱고가 시작되자마자 / 모든 것이 바뀌었다. // 피아노, 기타, 플루트, 바이올린이 / 마법처럼 조화를 이루며in
harmony 흘러나왔다.

06 청중은 환호성을 질렀다. // "어머나! 얼마나 환상적인 음악인가!" / Sharon은 소리쳤다. // 리듬과 박자가 너무 활기차고
환상적이어서sensational / 그녀의 몸과 마음을 뒤흔들었다.

07 그 콘서트는 그녀의 예상을 훨씬 뛰어넘었다beyond her expectations.

구문 Check up

① That raised / was raised in Sharon's mind the question of whether it was worthwhile to go, but in the end, she reluctantly decided to attend the concert.

주어인 That이 목적어인 the question을 '제기하는' 주체이므로 능동태인 raised를 쓰는 것이 적절하다.

② Looking / Looked around, Sharon again wondered what kind of show she could expect.

분사구문의 의미상 주어인 Sharon이 '보는' 주체이므로 Looking이 적절하다.

정답 ① raised ② Looking

STEP 1 • 수능에 *진짜* 나오는 *단어*

✔ **문제에 나오는 단어들을 확인하세요.**

01	submission	n. 제출	the paper (✔ submission)	논문 제출
02	at hand	(시간·공간상) 가까운	close (　　) (　　　　)	가까이에(눈앞에) 닥친
03	struggle with	~로 고심하다, 분투하다	(　　　　) (　　) her writing	그녀의 글로 고심하다
04	pressed	a. 압박을 받는, (시간이나 돈이) 충분치 않은	(　　　　) for time	시간 압박을 받는
05	deadlock	n. 막다른 상태, 교착 상태	stuck in a (　　　　　)	막다른 상태에 처한
06	on time	제때에	submit it (　　) (　　　　)	그것을 제때 제출하다
07	seemingly	ad. 겉보기에	(　　　　　) strange	겉보기에 이상한
08	disjointed	a. 일관성이 없는	(　　　　　) ideas	일관성이 없는 생각
09	make sense	의미가 통하다	nothing (　　)s (　　　)	아무것도 의미가 통하지 않다
10	ticking	n. (시계의) 똑딱거리는 소리	the (　　　　) of the clock	시계의 똑딱거리는 소리
11	grab	v. 움켜쥐다, 잡다	(　　　　) a pencil	연필을 움켜잡다

➕ **본문 문장 속에서 단어들을 확인해 보세요.**

Pressed for time and stuck in a deadlock, / she had no idea / how to finish the paper.

시간 압박을 받고 막다른 상태에 처해, / 그녀는 몰랐다 / 그 논문을 어떻게 끝마쳐야 할지.

01	submission	제출	the paper submission	논문 (제출)
02	at hand		close at hand	( ) 닥친
03	struggle with		struggle with her writing	그녀의 글로 ( )
04	pressed		pressed for time	시간 ( )
05	deadlock		stuck in a deadlock	( )에 처한
06	on time		submit it on time	그것을 ( ) 제출하다
07	seemingly		seemingly strange	( ) 이상한
08	disjointed		disjointed ideas	( ) 생각
09	make sense		nothing makes sense	아무것도 ( ) 않다
10	ticking		the ticking of the clock	시계의 ( )
11	grab		grab a pencil	연필을 ( )

➕ **본문 문장 속에서 단어의 의미를 우리말로 해석해 보세요.**

Pressed for time and stuck in a deadlock, / she had no idea / how to finish the paper.

➔ ▬▬▬▬▬▬▬▬▬▬▬▬▬, / 그녀는 몰랐다 / 그 논문을 어떻게 끝마쳐야 할지.

07 다음 글에 드러난 Claire의 심경 변화로 가장 적절한 것은?

It was two hours before the paper submission. With the deadline close at hand, Claire was still struggling with her writing. Pressed for time and stuck in a deadlock, she had no idea how to finish the paper. She wasn't even sure whether she could submit it on time. What she found in her paper was scribbled words, half sentences, and a pile of seemingly strange and disjointed ideas. "Nothing makes sense," she said to herself. She looked at her writing and began reading it over and over. All of a sudden and unexpectedly, something was found in that pile of thoughts: the flow and connection of ideas she had not considered while she was writing. From this moment, the ticking of the clock sounded encouraging to her. "Yes, I can do it!" Claire said as she grabbed her pencil again.

*scribble: 휘갈겨 쓰다

① delighted → ashamed

② relieved → worried

③ nervous → confident

④ indifferent → excited

⑤ bored → embarrassed

정답과 해설 **p.6**

STEP 3 • 수능 지문 제대로 복습하기

01 It was two hours before the paper submission. // With the deadline close at hand, /
비인칭주어(시간)
Claire was still struggling with her writing.

02 Pressed for time and stuck in a deadlock, / she had no idea / how to finish the paper. //
분사구문1   분사구문2   「how + to부정사: ~하는 방법」
She wasn't even sure / whether she could submit it on time.
접속사(~인지 아닌지)   주격보어(명사구 병렬)

03 What she found in her paper / was / scribbled words, / half sentences, / and a pile of
주어(명사절)   동사(단수)
seemingly strange and disjointed ideas. // "Nothing makes sense," / she said to herself.
// She looked at her writing / and began reading it over and over.

04 All of a sudden and unexpectedly, / something was found / in that pile of thoughts: /
주어   동사(수동태)
the flow and connection of ideas / [she had not considered while she was writing].
동격(=something)   목적격 관계대명사절

05 From this moment, / the ticking of the clock / sounded encouraging to her. // "Yes, I
주어   동사   주격보어(현재분사)
can do it!" / Claire said / as she grabbed her pencil again.
접속사(~하면서)

---

01 논문 제출submission 2시간 전이었다. // 마감 시간이 눈앞에 닥쳤는데close at hand, / Claire는 여전히 자신의 글로 고심하고 있었다struggle with her writing.

02 시간 압박을 받고pressed for time 막다른 상태deadlock에 처해, / 그녀는 몰랐다 / 그 논문을 어떻게 끝마쳐야 할지. // 그녀는 심지어 확신하지 못했다 / 그녀가 그것을 제때on time 제출할 수 있을지.

03 그녀가 자신의 논문에서 발견한 것은 ~였다 / 휘갈겨 쓴 단어, / 불완전한 문장, / 겉보기에seemingly 이상하고 일관성이 없는disjointed 생각의 무더기. // "어느 것도 의미가 통하지make sense 않아."라고 / 그녀는 혼잣말했다. // 그녀는 자신의 글을 살펴보고 / 그것을 반복해서 읽기 시작했다.

04 문득 예기치 않게 / 뭔가가 발견되었는데 / 그 생각의 무더기에서 / 생각의 흐름과 연결이었다 / 그녀가 쓰는 동안에는 고려하지 않았던.

05 이때부터 / 시계의 똑딱거리는 소리ticking는 / 그녀에게 힘을 북돋아 주는 것처럼 들렸다. // "그래, 난 할 수 있어!" / Claire는 말했다 / 다시 연필을 움켜쥐며grab.

구문 Check up

① That / What she found in her paper was scribbled words, half sentences, and a pile of seemingly strange and disjointed ideas.

앞에 선행사가 없고 뒤에 found의 목적어가 없는 불완전한 문장이 나오므로 선행사를 포함한 관계대명사 What이 적절하다.

② From this moment, the ticking of the clock sounded encouraging / encouraged to her.

주어인 the ticking of the clock이 그녀에게 '힘을 주는' 주체이므로 현재분사 encouraging이 적절하다.

정답 ① What ② encouraging

✔️ **문제에 나오는 단어들을 확인하세요.**

01	reside	v. (~에) 있다, 살다	all that (✔️ reside)s on the Internet	인터넷에 있는 모든 것
02	sensible	a. 합리적인, 분별 있는	a ( ) person	합리적인 사람
03	validity	n. 타당성	question the ( )	타당성에 의문을 제기하다
04	instinct	n. 본능	our natural ( )	우리의 자연스러운 본능
05	protective	a. 방어적인	place oneself in a ( ) position	스스로 방어적인 자세를 취하다
06	acquaintance	n. 지인	a common ( )	공통 지인
07	cognitive	a. 인지적인	go through a ( ) validation	인지적 검증을 통과하다
08	trustworthy	a. 믿을 만한	accept someone as more ( )	누군가 더 믿을 만하다고 받아들이다
09	defense mechanism	방어 기제	a natural ( ) ( )	자연스러운 방어 기제
10	threat	n. 위협	a physical ( ) to our well-being	우리의 행복에 대한 물리적인 위협

➕ **본문 문장 속에서 단어들을 확인해 보세요.**

Given the level of anonymity with all / that resides on the Internet, / it's sensible to question the validity of any data / that you may receive.

모든 것의 익명성 수준을 고려할 때, / 인터넷에 있는 / 어떤 데이터든 그것의 타당성에 대해 의문을 제기하는 것이 합리적이다 / 여러분이 받을지도 모르는.

01	reside	✎ (~에) 있다, 살다	all that resides on the Internet	인터넷에 (있는) 모든 것
02	sensible		a sensible person	( ) 사람
03	validity		question the validity	( )에 의문을 제기하다
04	instinct		our natural instinct	우리의 자연스러운 ( )
05	protective		place oneself in a protective position	스스로 ( ) 자세를 취하다
06	acquaintance		a common acquaintance	공통 ( )
07	cognitive		go through a cognitive validation	( ) 검증을 통과하다
08	trustworthy		accept someone as more trustworthy	누군가 더 ( )고 받아들이다
09	defense mechanism		a natural defense mechanism	자연스러운 ( )
10	threat		a physical threat to our well-being	우리의 행복에 대한 물리적인 ( )

➕ **본문 문장 속에서 단어의 의미를 우리말로 해석해 보세요.**

Given the level of anonymity with all / that resides on the Internet, / it's sensible to question the validity of any data / that you may receive.

➡ 모든 것의 익명성 수준을 고려할 때, / ▨▨▨▨▨▨▨ / 어떤 데이터든 그것의 타당성에 대해 ▨▨▨▨▨▨▨▨▨▨이다 / 여러분이 받을지도 모르는.

08 다음 글의 요지로 가장 적절한 것은?

When it comes to the Internet, it just pays to be a little paranoid (but not a lot). Given the level of anonymity with all that resides on the Internet, it's sensible to question the validity of any data that you may receive. Typically it's to our natural instinct when we meet someone coming down a sidewalk to place yourself in some manner of protective position, especially when they introduce themselves as having known you, much to your surprise. By design, we set up challenges in which the individual must validate how they know us by presenting scenarios, names or acquaintances, or evidence by which to validate (that is, photographs). Once we have received that information and it has gone through a cognitive validation, we accept that person as more trustworthy. All this happens in a matter of minutes but is a natural defense mechanism that we perform in the real world. However, in the virtual world, we have a tendency to be less defensive, as there appears to be no physical threat to our well-being.

*paranoid: 편집성의 **anonymity: 익명

① 가상 세계 특유의 익명성 때문에 표현의 자유가 남용되기도 한다.

② 인터넷 정보의 신뢰도를 검증하는 기술은 점진적으로 향상되고 있다.

③ 가상 세계에서는 현실 세계와 달리 자유로운 정보 공유가 가능하다.

④ 안전한 인터넷 환경 구축을 위해 보안 프로그램을 설치하는 것이 좋다.

⑤ 방어 기제가 덜 작동하는 가상 세계에서는 신중한 정보 검증이 중요하다.

정답과 해설 p.8

01   When it comes to the Internet, / it just pays / to be a little paranoid (but not a lot). //

Given the level of anonymity with all / [that resides on the Internet], / it's sensible to
분사구문(~을 고려하면)   명사구   주격 관계대명사절   가주어
question the validity of any data / [that you may receive].
진주어   목적격 관계대명사(any data 수식)

02   Typically it's to our natural instinct / when we meet someone coming down a sidewalk
가주어   현재분사구
/ to place yourself in some manner of protective position, / especially when they
진주어
introduce themselves as having known you, / much to your surprise.
전치사   완료동명사(introduce보다 더 이전)

03   By design, / we set up challenges / [in which the individual must validate how they
선행사   = where
know us / by presenting scenarios, names or acquaintances, or evidence by which to
                                            = by which they should validate
validate / (that is, photographs)]. // Once we have received that information / and it
접속사(일단 ~하면)
has gone through a cognitive validation, / we accept that person as more trustworthy.
                                       「accept A as B: A를 B라고 받아들이다」

04   All this happens in a matter of minutes / but is a natural defense mechanism / [that we
동사1   동사2   선행사
perform in the real world]. // However, / in the virtual world, / we have a tendency to
목적격 관계대명사절
be less defensive, / as there appears to be no physical threat to our well-being.
             접속사(이유)   「appear + to부정사: ~인 것 같다」

01 인터넷에 관한 한, / 이득이 될 따름이다 / (많이는 아니어도) 약간 편집적이 되는 것. // 모든 것의 익명성 수준을 고려할 때, / 인터넷에 있는reside / 어떤 데이터든 그것의 타당성validity에 대해 의문을 제기하는 것이 합리적이다sensible / 여러분이 받을지도 모르는.

02 일반적으로 우리의 자연스러운 본능instinct이다 / 우리가 인도를 따라 내려오는 누군가를 만날 때, / 여러분이 스스로 일종의 방어적인protective 자세를 취하는 것은 / 특히 그들이 여러분을 알고 있었다고 자신을 소개할 때 / 여러분에게는 너무 놀랍게도.

03 일부러 / 우리는 과제를 설정한다 / 그 사람이 우리를 어떻게 아는지 입증해야만 하는 / 시나리오, 이름, 지인acquaintance, 혹은 입증할 증거를 제시해서 / (말하자면, 사진). // 일단 우리가 그 정보를 받고 / 그것이 인지적cognitive 검증을 통과하면, / 우리는 그 사람을 더 믿을 만하다trustworthy고 받아들인다.

04 이 모든 것이 몇 분 안에 일어나지만, / 자연스러운 방어 기제defense mechanism이다 / 우리가 현실 세계에서 수행하는. // 하지만, / 가상 세계에서는 / 우리는 덜 방어적인 경향이 있다 / 우리의 안녕에 물리적인 위협threat이 없는 것처럼 보이기 때문에.

<table>
<tr><td>구문 Check up</td><td>① By design, we set up challenges which / in which the individual must validate how they know us.

뒤에 완전한 3형식 문장이 나오므로 「전치사 + 관계대명사」 형태의 in which가 적절하다.</td><td>② Once we have received that information and it has gone through a cognitive validation, we accept that person as more trustworthy / trustworthily .

문맥상 목적어 that person의 상태를 설명하는 것이므로 형용사 trustworthy를 써야 한다.</td></tr>
</table>

정답 ① in which ② trustworthy

✔ 문제에 나오는 단어들을 확인하세요.

01	overlook	v. 간과하다, 못 보고 넘어가다	(✔ overlook) a factor	한 가지 요인을 간과하다
02	engagement	n. 참여, 몰입	consumer ( ) levels	소비자의 참여 수준
03	explode	v. 폭발적으로 증가하다	the ( )ing world population	폭발적으로 증가하는 세계 인구
04	awareness	n. 인식, 앎	a growing ( ) among consumers	소비자들 사이에서의 인식 증가
05	conflicted	a. 갈등을 겪는	feel ( )	갈등을 겪는다고 느끼다
06	armed with	~으로 무장한	( ) ( ) high-end tools	최신의 도구로 무장한
07	passive	a. 수동적인	play a ( ) role	수동적인 역할을 하다
08	bystander	n. 방관자	passive ( )s	수동적인 방관자

⊕ 본문 문장 속에서 단어들을 확인해 보세요.

Consumer engagement levels / in all manner of digital experiences and communities / have simply exploded / — and they show little or no signs of slowing.

소비자의 참여 수준은 / 모든 방식의 디지털 경험과 공동체에서 / 그야말로 폭발적으로 증가해 왔으며 / 그것들은 둔화될 기미가 거의 또는 전혀 보이지 않는다.

문제를 풀기 전에 단어들을 **30초** 동안 다시 확인하세요.

01	overlook	✎ 간과하다	overlook a factor	한 가지 요인을 (간과하다)
02	engagement		consumer engagement levels	소비자의 ( ) 수준
03	explode		the exploding world population	( ) 세계 인구
04	awareness		a growing awareness among consumers	소비자들 사이에서의 ( ) 증가
05	conflicted		feel conflicted	( )고 느끼다
06	armed with		armed with high-end tools	최신의 도구로 ( )
07	passive		play a passive role	( ) 역할을 하다
08	bystander		passive bystanders	수동적인 ( )

➕ 본문 문장 속에서 단어의 의미를 우리말로 해석해 보세요.

Consumer engagement levels / in all manner of digital experiences and communities / have simply exploded / — and they show little or no signs of slowing.

➜ ▓▓▓▓▓▓▓▓은 / 모든 방식의 디지털 경험과 공동체에서 / ▓▓▓▓▓▓▓▓▓▓▓ / 그것들은 둔화될 기미가 거의 또는 전혀 보이지 않는다.

09 다음 글의 요지로 가장 적절한 것은?

Often overlooked, but just as important a stakeholder, is the consumer who plays a large role in the notion of the privacy paradox. Consumer engagement levels in all manner of digital experiences and communities have simply exploded — and they show little or no signs of slowing. There is an awareness among consumers, not only that their personal data helps to drive the rich experiences that these companies provide, but also that sharing this data is the price you pay for these experiences, in whole or in part. Without a better understanding of the what, when, and why of data collection and use, the consumer is often left feeling vulnerable and conflicted. "I love this restaurant-finder app on my phone, but what happens to my data if I press 'ok' when asked if that app can use my current location?" Armed with tools that can provide them options, the consumer moves from passive bystander to active participant.

*stakeholder: 이해관계자 **vulnerable: 상처를 입기 쉬운

① 개인정보 제공의 속성을 심층적으로 이해하면 주체적 소비자가 된다.
② 소비자는 디지털 시대에 유용한 앱을 적극 활용하는 자세가 필요하다.
③ 현명한 소비자가 되려면 다양한 디지털 데이터를 활용해야 한다.
④ 기업의 디지털 서비스를 이용하면 상응하는 대가가 뒤따른다.
⑤ 타인과의 정보 공유로 인해 개인정보가 유출되기도 한다.

정답과 해설 p.8

01 Often overlooked, but just as important a stakeholder, / is the consumer / [who plays a
　　주격보어1　　　　　　　　　　주격보어2(도치)　　　　　　　　　동사　　주어　　　　　　주격 관계대명사절
large role in the notion of the privacy paradox].

02 Consumer engagement levels / in all manner of digital experiences and communities /
　　주어1　　　　　　　　　　　　전치사구
have simply exploded / — and they show little or no signs of slowing.
　　동사1(현재완료)　　　　　　　　　　주어2　동사2

03 There is an awareness among consumers, / not only [that their personal data helps to
　　동사　주어(추상명사)　　　　　　　　　　　　　　　동격절1
drive the rich experiences / [that these companies provide]], / but also [that sharing
　　　　　　　　　　　　　목적격 관계대명사절　　　　　　　　　　　　　　동격절2
this data is the price / [you pay for these experiences, / in whole or in part]].
　　　　　　　　　　목적격 관계대명사절

04 Without a better understanding / of the what, when, and why of data collection and
　　　　　　　　　　　　　　　　　전치사구
use, / the consumer is often left / feeling vulnerable and conflicted. // "I love this
　　　　　　　　　　　　　5형식 수동태(be p.p. + 현재분사)
restaurant-finder app on my phone, / but what happens to my data if I press 'ok' /
when asked if that app can use my current location?"
접속사가 있는 분사구문(= when I am asked ~)

05 Armed with tools / [that can provide them options], / the consumer moves from
　　분사구문(수동)　　주격 관계대명사절(tools 수식)
passive bystander to active participant.

---

01 흔히 간과되지만overlook 못지않게 중요한 이해관계자는 / 소비자이다 / 개인정보 역설이라는 개념에서 큰 역할을 하는.

02 소비자의 참여engagement 수준은 / 모든 방식의 디지털 경험과 공동체에서의 / 그야말로 폭발적으로 증가해explode
왔으며 / 그것들은 둔화될 기미가 거의 또는 전혀 보이지 않는다.

03 소비자들 사이에서는 인식awareness이 있다 / 자신들의 개인 정보가 풍부한 경험을 추진하는 데 도움이 된다는 것뿐만
아니라, / 이러한 회사들이 제공하는 / 이 정보를 공유하는 것이 대가이기도 하다는 / 여러분이 이러한 경험에 대해
지불하는 / 전체로든 부분으로든.

04 더 나은 이해 없이는 / 정보 수집 및 이용의 내용과 시기, 이유에 관한 / 소비자는 흔히 남겨진다 / 취약하고 갈등을
겪는다conflicted고 느끼는 상태로. // '내 전화기에 있는 이 식당 검색 앱이 마음에 드는데, / 'ok'를 누르면 내 정보는
어떻게 되는 걸까 / 그 앱이 내 현재 위치를 이용할 수 있느냐고 물을 때?'

05 도구로 무장한armed with / 그들에게 선택권을 제공할 수 있는 / 소비자는 수동적 방관자passive bystander에서 능동적
참여자로 이동한다.

구문 Check up

① Without a better understanding of the what, when, and
　why of data collection and use, the consumer is often
　leaving / left feeling vulnerable and conflicted.

the consumer가 '(~한 기분을 느끼는 상태로) 남겨지는' 대상이므로 left
를 써야 한다.

② "What happens to my data if I press 'ok' when asking /
asked if that app can use my current location?"

분사구문의 의미상 주어인 I가 '질문을 받는' 대상이므로 asked가 적절하
다.

정답 ① left ② asked

10

STEP 1 • 수능에 진짜 나오는 단어

✔ 문제에 나오는 단어들을 확인하세요.

01	experiment	v. 실험하다	(✔ experiment) with social media	소셜 미디어로 실험하다
02	objective	n. 목표	business ( )s	사업 목표
03	thorough	a. 철저한	a ( ) understanding	철저한 이해
04	merely	ad. 그저, ~만	not ( ) talented but also hardworking	그저 재능만 있는 것이 아니라 성실한
05	fulfillment	n. 이행, 성취	the ( ) of a need	필요의 이행
06	vague	a. 막연한, 모호한	a ( ) meaning	모호한 의미
07	presence	n. 존재	have a ( )	존재하다
08	purpose	n. 목적	serve a ( )	목적을 수행하다(도움이 되다)
09	in and of itself	그 자체로	important ( ) ( ) ( ) ( )	그 자체로 중요한
10	result in	(결과적으로) ~을 낳다	( ) ( ) an improvement	개선이라는 결과를 낳다
11	measurable	a. 측정 가능한	a ( ) improvement	측정 가능한 향상

➕ 본문 문장 속에서 단어들을 확인해 보세요.

A social media program / is not merely the fulfillment of a vague need / to manage a "presence" on popular social networks / because "everyone else is doing it."

소셜 미디어 프로그램은 / 그저 막연한 필요의 이행이 아니다 / 인기 소셜 네트워크상에서 '존재'를 관리해야 할 / '다른 모든 이가 하고 있다'는 이유로.

01	experiment	✏️ 실험하다	experiment with social media	소셜 미디어로 (실험하다)
02	objective		business objectives	사업 ( )
03	thorough		a thorough understanding	( ) 이해
04	merely		not merely talented but also hardworking	( ) 재능만 있는 것이 아니라 성실한
05	fulfillment		the fulfillment of a need	필요의 ( )
06	vague		a vague meaning	( ) 의미
07	presence		have a presence	( )하다
08	purpose		serve a purpose	( )을 수행하다
09	in and of itself		important in and of itself	( ) 중요한
10	result in		result in an improvement	개선이라는 결과를 ( )
11	measurable		a measurable improvement	( ) 향상

➕ **본문 문장 속에서 단어의 의미를 우리말로 해석해 보세요.**

A social media program / is not merely the fulfillment of a vague need / to manage a "presence" on popular social networks / because "everyone else is doing it."

➡️ 소셜 미디어 프로그램은 / ▨▨▨▨▨▨▨▨▨▨▨ / 인기 소셜 네트워크상에서 ▨▨▨▨▨▨▨▨ 할 / '다른 모든 이가 하고 있다'는 이유로.

10

다음 글에서 필자가 주장하는 바로 가장 적절한 것은?

One of the most common mistakes made by organizations when they first consider experimenting with social media is that they focus too much on social media tools and platforms and not enough on their business objectives. The reality of success in the social web for businesses is that creating a social media program begins not with insight into the latest social media tools and channels but with a thorough understanding of the organization's own goals and objectives. A social media program is not merely the fulfillment of a vague need to manage a "presence" on popular social networks because "everyone else is doing it." "Being in social media" serves no purpose in and of itself. In order to serve any purpose at all, a social media presence must either solve a problem for the organization and its customers or result in an improvement of some sort (preferably a measurable one). In all things, purpose drives success. The world of social media is no different.

① 기업 이미지에 부합하는 소셜 미디어를 직접 개발하여 운영해야 한다.
② 기업은 사회적 가치와 요구를 반영하여 사업 목표를 수립해야 한다.
③ 기업은 소셜 미디어를 활용할 때 사업 목표를 토대로 해야 한다.
④ 소셜 미디어로 제품을 홍보할 때는 구체적인 정보를 제공해야 한다.
⑤ 소비자의 의견을 수렴하기 위해 소셜 미디어를 적극 활용해야 한다.

정답과 해설 p.9

01 One of the most common mistakes / made by organizations / when they first consider
주어(one of the + 최상급 + 복수명사)　　　　　과거분사구(the ~ mistakes 수식)
experimenting with social media / is / [that they focus too much on social media tools
동사(단수)　주격보어
and platforms / and not enough on their business objectives].

02 The reality of success / in the social web for businesses / is / [that creating a social
주어　　　전치사구　　　　동사(단수)　　주어(동명사구)
media program begins / not with insight into the latest social media tools and
동사(단수)
channels / but with a thorough understanding of the organization's own goals and
「not A but B: A가 아니라 B인」
objectives].

형용사적 용법(a vague need 수식)
03 A social media program / is not merely the fulfillment of a vague need / to manage a
주어　　　동사　　주격보어
"presence" on popular social networks / because "everyone else is doing it." // "Being
접속사(~이기 때문에)　　　주어(동명사구)
in social media" / serves no purpose in and of itself.
동사(단수)

04 In order to serve any purpose at all, / a social media presence must either solve a
「in order to + 동사원형: ~하기 위해서」　　　　「either A or B: A 또는 B 둘 중 하나」
problem / for the organization and its customers / or result in an improvement of
some sort / (preferably a measurable one).

05 In all things, / purpose drives success. // The world of social media is no different.

01 가장 일반적인 실수 중 하나는 / 조직이 범하는 / 그들이 소셜 미디어로 실험하는experiment 것을 처음 고려할 때 / ~이다 / 그들이 소셜 미디어 도구와 플랫폼에 너무 지나치게 중점을 두고 / 조직의 사업 목표objective에는 충분히 중점을 두지 않는다는 것.

02 성공의 실제는 / 기업을 위한 소셜 웹에서의 / ~이다 / 소셜 미디어 프로그램을 고안하는 것이 시작된다는 것 / 최신 소셜 미디어 도구와 채널에 대한 통찰력이 아니라 / 조직 자체의 목적과 목표에 대한 철저한thorough 이해와 더불어.

03 소셜 미디어 프로그램은 / 그저 막연한 필요의 이행이 아니다not merely the fulfillment of a vague need / 인기 소셜 네트워크상에서 '존재presence'를 관리해야 할 / '다른 모든 이가 하고 있다'는 이유로. // '소셜 미디어에 있다는 것'은 / 그 자체로는 아무 쓸모도 없다serve no purpose in and of itself.

04 조금이라도 어떤 쓸모가 있으려면, / 소셜 미디어상의 존재는 문제를 해결하거나 / 조직과 조직의 고객을 위해 / 어떤 종류의 개선이라는 결과를 가져와야result in 한다 / (될 수 있으면 측정 가능한measurable 결과).

05 어떤 일이든, / 목적이 성공을 이끌어낸다. // 소셜 미디어의 세계도 다르지 않다.

구문 Check up

① One of the most common mistakes made by organizations when they first consider experimenting with social media is / are that they focus too much on social media tools and platforms.

주어가 「one of the + 최상급 + 복수명사(가장 ~한 … 중 하나)」이므로 단수형 동사인 is가 적절하다.

② The reality of success in the social web for businesses is that / what creating a social media program begins with a thorough understanding of the organization's own goals and objectives.

뒤에 'creating ~ begins ~'의 완전한 1형식 구조가 나오는 것으로 보아 접속사 that이 적절하다.

11

STEP 1 • 수능에 *진짜* 나오는 *단어*

✔ 문제에 나오는 단어들을 확인하세요.

01	**profession**	n. 전문직, 직업	the relationship between the (✔ profession)s and society	전문직과 사회의 관계
02	**negotiate**	v. 협상하다	a ( )ing process	협상 과정
03	**accountability**	n. 책임성	the public's demand for ( )	책임성에 대한 공공의 요구
04	**willingness**	n. 자발성, ~하려는 마음	the ( ) to contribute to social well-being	사회 복지에 기여하려는 자발성
05	**consistent**	a. 일치하는	( ) with social values	사회적 가치와 일치하는
06	**expertise**	n. 전문지식	his ( ) in finance	재정에 관한 그의 전문지식
07	**confer**	v. 주다, 수여하다	( ) authority and power	권위와 권한을 주다
08	**readily**	ad. 쉽게	can ( ) be used	쉽게 이용될 수 있다
09	**at the expense of**	~을 희생하여	( ) ( ) ( ) ( ) others	다른 사람들을 희생하여
10	**qualify**	v. 자격을 부여하다	be ( )ied for liberty	자유를 누릴 자격이 부여되다
11	**proportion**	n. 비례, 비율	in exact ( ) to their disposition	그들의 성향에 정확히 비례하여
12	**disposition**	n. 성향	our ( ) to make moral judgments	도덕적 결정을 하려는 우리의 성향
13	**irreversibly**	ad. 뒤집을 수 없게, 되돌릴 수 없게	( ) damaged	되돌릴 수 없게 손상된

✚ 본문 문장 속에서 단어들을 확인해 보세요.

At the heart of this process / is / the tension / between the professions' pursuit of autonomy / and the public's demand for accountability.

이 과정의 핵심에는 / 있다 / 긴장이 / 전문직의 자율성 추구와 / 책임성에 대한 공공의 요구 사이의.

문제를 풀기 전에 단어들을 **30초** 동안 다시 확인하세요.

01	profession	✏ 전문직, 직업	the relationship between the professions and society	(전문직)과 사회의 관계
02	negotiate		a negotiating process	( ) 과정
03	accountability		the public's demand for accountability	( )에 대한 공공의 요구
04	willingness		the willingness to contribute to social well-being	사회 복지에 기여하려는 ( )
05	consistent		consistent with social values	사회적 가치와 ( )
06	expertise		his expertise in finance	재정에 관한 그의 ( )
07	confer		confer authority and power	권위와 권한을 ( )
08	readily		can readily be used	( ) 이용될 수 있다
09	at the expense of		at the expense of others	다른 사람들을 ( )
10	qualify		be qualified for liberty	자유를 누릴 ( )
11	proportion		in exact proportion to their disposition	그들의 성향에 정확히 ( ) 하여
12	disposition		our disposition to make moral judgments	도덕적 결정을 하려는 우리의 ( )
13	irreversibly		irreversibly damaged	( ) 손상된

➕ **본문 문장 속에서 단어의 의미를 우리말로 해석해 보세요.**

At the heart of this process / is / the tension / between the professions' pursuit of autonomy / and the public's demand for accountability.

➜ 이 과정의 핵심에는 / 있다 / 긴장이 / 전문직의 자율성 추구와 /   사이의.

11 다음 글의 요지로 가장 적절한 것은?

Historically, the professions and society have engaged in a negotiating process intended to define the terms of their relationship. At the heart of this process is the tension between the professions' pursuit of autonomy and the public's demand for accountability. Society's granting of power and privilege to the professions is premised on their willingness and ability to contribute to social well-being and to conduct their affairs in a manner consistent with broader social values. It has long been recognized that the expertise and privileged position of professionals confer authority and power that could readily be used to advance their own interests at the expense of those they serve. As Edmund Burke observed two centuries ago, "Men are qualified for civil liberty in exact proportion to their disposition to put moral chains upon their own appetites." Autonomy has never been a one-way street and is never granted absolutely and irreversibly.

*autonomy: 자율성 **privilege: 특권 ***premise: 전제로 말하다

① 전문직에 부여되는 자율성은 그에 상응하는 사회적 책임을 수반한다.
② 전문직의 권위는 해당 집단의 이익을 추구하는 데 이용되어 왔다.
③ 전문직의 사회적 책임을 규정할 수 있는 제도 정비가 필요하다.
④ 전문직이 되기 위한 자격 요건은 사회 경제적 요구에 따라 변화해 왔다.
⑤ 전문직의 업무 성과는 일정 수준의 자율성과 특권이 부여될 때 높아진다.

정답과 해설 p.10

01 Historically, / the professions and society have engaged in a negotiating process / intended to define the terms of their relationship. // At the heart of this process / is / 과거분사구   장소 부사구(도치)   동사(단수)
the tension / between the professions' pursuit of autonomy / and the public's demand 주어   「between A and B: A와 B 사이(의)」
for accountability.

02 Society's granting of power and privilege to the professions / is premised / on their 주어   동사(수동태)
willingness and ability / to contribute to social well-being / and to conduct their 형용사적 용법1   형용사적 용법2
affairs / in a manner consistent with broader social values. 형용사구

03 가주어-진주어 구문
It has long been recognized / that the expertise and privileged position of 가주어   동사(현재완료 수동태)
professionals / confer authority and power / [that could readily be used / to advance 선행사   주격 관계대명사절   부사적 용법(목적)
their own interests / at the expense of those they serve].

04 As Edmund Burke observed two centuries ago, / "Men are qualified for civil liberty / 접속사(~듯이, ~대로)
in exact proportion to their disposition / to put moral chains upon their own 형용사적 용법
appetites."

05 Autonomy has never been a one-way street / and is never granted absolutely and 동사구1   동사구2   부사구
irreversibly.

---

01 역사적으로 / 전문직profession과 사회는 협상 과정negotiating process에 참여해 왔다 / 그들의 관계의 조건을 규정하고자 의도된. // 이 과정의 핵심에는 / 있다 / 긴장이 / 전문직의 자율성 추구와 / 책임성accountability에 대한 공공의 요구 사이의.

02 사회가 전문직에 권한과 특권을 부여한 것은 / 전제로 한다 / 그들의 자발성willingness과 능력을 / 사회 복지에 기여하고 / 자신의 일을 수행하려는 / 더 넓은 사회적 가치와 일치하는consistent 방식으로.

03 오랫동안 인식되어 왔다 / 전문직의 전문지식expertise과 특권적 지위는 / 권위와 권한을 준다confer는 것이 / 쉽게readily 이용될 수 있는 / 그들 자신의 이익을 향상시키기 위해 / 그들이 봉사하는 사람들을 희생시키고서at the expense of those they serve.

04 Edmund Burke가 두 세기 전에 말했듯이, / "인간은 시민적 자유를 누릴 자격이 부여된다qualify / 그들의 성향에 정확히 비례해서in exact proportion to their disposition / 자신의 욕구를 도덕적으로 구속하는."

05 자율성은 일방통행로였던 적이 없었으며 / 결코 절대적이고 뒤집을 수 없게irreversibly 주어지지 않는다.

구문 Check up

① Historically, the professions and society have engaged in a negotiating process intend / intended to define the terms of their relationship.

a negotiating process가 '의도되는' 대상이므로 과거분사 intended를 사용해 꾸미는 것이 적절하다.

② At the heart of this process is / are the tension between the professions' pursuit of autonomy and the public's demand for accountability.

「장소 부사구 + 동사 + 주어」 어순의 도치 구문이다. 즉 주어가 단수명사인 the tension이므로 동사로는 is가 적절하다.

정답 ① intended ② is

12

필자의 주장 ➕

✔️ 문제에 나오는 단어들을 확인하세요.

01	entrepreneurship	n. 기업가 정신	promote (✔️ entrepreneurship)	기업가 정신을 증진하다
02	weave A into B	A를 B에 짜 넣다	( ) ourselves ( ) the fabric of everyday life	우리 자신을 일상 속에 짜 넣다
03	expand	v. 확장하다	( ) its reach	범위를 확장하다
04	act on	~에 따라 행동하다	( ) ( ) opportunities	기회에 따라 행동하다
05	catch a bug	병에 걸리다	prone to ( ) ( ) ( )	병에 걸리기 쉬운
06	varied	a. 다양한	( ) educational backgrounds	다양한 교육 배경
07	concentrate	v. 집중하다	( ) on my study	내 공부에 집중하다
08	cultivate	v. 배양하다, 구축하다	( ) a culture	문화를 배양하다
09	position	v. (~할) 위치에 두다	be uniquely ( )ed to do this	이것을 할 독특한 위치에 있다

➕ 본문 문장 속에서 단어들을 확인해 보세요.

One study showed / that, within the workplace, / peers influence each other / to spot opportunities and act on them: / the more entrepreneurs you have working together in an office, / the more likely their colleagues will catch the bug.

한 연구는 보여주었다 / 직장 내에서 / 동료들은 서로에게 영향을 미친다고 / 기회를 포착하고 그에 따라 행동하도록 / 여러분이 사무실에서 함께 일하는 기업가들을 더 많이 둘수록, / 그들의 동료들이 병에 걸릴 가능성이 더 크다.

문제를 풀기 전에 단어들을 **30초** 동안 다시 확인하세요.

01	entrepreneurship	🖉 기업가 정신	promote entrepreneurship	(기업가 정신)을 증진하다
02	weave A into B		weave ourselves into the fabric of everyday life	우리 자신을 일상 속에 ( )
03	expand		expand its reach	범위를 ( )
04	act on		act on opportunities	기회에 ( )
05	catch a bug		prone to catch a bug	( ) 쉬운
06	varied		varied educational backgrounds	( ) 교육 배경
07	concentrate		concentrate on my study	내 공부에 ( )
08	cultivate		cultivate a culture	문화를 ( )
09	position		be uniquely positioned to do this	이것을 할 독특한 ( )

➕ **본문 문장 속에서 단어의 의미를 우리말로 해석해 보세요.**

One study showed / that, within the workplace, / peers influence each other / to spot opportunities and act on them: / the more entrepreneurs you have working together in an office, / the more likely their colleagues will catch the bug.

➜ 한 연구는 보여주었다 / 직장 내에서 / 동료들은 서로에게 영향을 미친다고 / ▓▓▓▓▓▓▓▓▓▓▓▓ / 여러분이 사무실에서 함께 일하는 기업가들을 더 많이 둘수록, / 그들의 동료들이 ▓▓▓▓▓▓ 가능성이 더 크다.

12 다음 글에서 필자가 주장하는 바로 가장 적절한 것은?

Given the right conditions, entrepreneurship can be fully woven into the fabric of campus life, greatly expanding its educational reach. One study showed that, within the workplace, peers influence each other to spot opportunities and act on them: the more entrepreneurs you have working together in an office, the more likely their colleagues will catch the bug. A study of Stanford University alumni found that those "who have varied work and educational backgrounds are much more likely to start their own businesses than those who have focused on one role at work or concentrated in one subject at school." To cultivate an entrepreneurial culture, colleges and universities need to offer students a broad choice of experiences and wide exposure to different ideas. They are uniquely positioned to do this by combining the resources of academic programming, residential life, student groups, and alumni networks.

*entrepreneur: 기업가 **alumni: 졸업생

① 훌륭한 기업가가 되기 위해서 관심 있는 한 분야에 집중해야 한다.
② 대학은 학생들이 기업가 정신을 함양하도록 환경을 조성해야 한다.
③ 좋은 직장을 얻기 위해서 학업과 대외 활동에 충실해야 한다.
④ 기업은 대학생들의 다양한 소모임 활동을 적극 지원해야 한다.
⑤ 대학생은 학업 성취를 위하여 경험과 생각의 폭을 넓혀야 한다.

정답과 해설 p.11

01 Given the right conditions, / entrepreneurship can be fully woven into the fabric of
　　분사구문　　　　　　　　　　　　주어　　　　　　　조동사 수동태(조동사 + be p.p.)
campus life, / greatly expanding its educational reach.
　　　　　　　　분사구문(그리고 ~하다)

02 One study showed / that, within the workplace, / peers influence each other / to spot
　　　　　　　　　　　　접속사　　　　　　　　　　　　동사　　　　목적어　　　　　목적격보어
opportunities and act on them: / the more entrepreneurs you have working together
　　　　　　　　　　　　　　　　　　「the + 비교급 ~ the + 비교급 …: ~할수록 더 …하다」
in an office, / the more likely their colleagues will catch the bug.

03 A study of Stanford University alumni found / that those ["who have varied work
　　　　　　　　　　　　　　　　　　　　　　　　接속사　주어　　　주격 관계대명사절
and educational backgrounds] / are much more likely to start their own businesses /
　　　　　　　　　　　　　　　　　　동사구(be likely to + 동사원형: ~할 가능성이 있다)
than those [who have focused on one role at work / or concentrated in one subject at
　　　　　　　주격 관계대명사절
school]."

04 To cultivate an entrepreneurial culture, / colleges and universities need to offer
　　부사적 용법(목적)　　　　　　　　　　　　　　　　　　　　　　　　　　　　　동사구
students / a broad choice of experiences and wide exposure to different ideas.
　간접목적어　　직접목적어

05 They are uniquely positioned to do this / by combining the resources / of academic
　　　　　　　　　　　　　　　　　　　　　　　　「by + 동명사: ~함으로써」　　　전치사구
programming, residential life, student groups, and alumni networks.

01 적절한 환경이 주어지면, / 기업가 정신entrepreneurship은 캠퍼스 생활의 구조로 완전히 짜여 들어가be woven into
the fabric of campus life / 그것의 교육적 범위를 크게 확장할expand 수 있다.

02 한 연구는 보여주었다 / 직장 내에서 / 동료들은 서로에게 영향을 미친다고 / 기회를 포착하고 그에 따라 행동하도록act on
/ 여러분이 사무실에서 함께 일하는 기업가들을 더 많이 둘수록, / 그들의 동료들이 (기업가 정신이라는) 병에 걸릴catch
the bug 가능성이 더 크다.

03 스탠퍼드대학교 졸업생들을 대상으로 한 연구는 발견했다 / '다양한varied 업무 및 교육 배경을 가진 사람들이 / 자기
자신의 사업을 시작할 가능성이 훨씬 더 크다는 것을 / 직장에서 한 가지 역할에 집중한concentrate 사람들보다 / 혹은
학교에서 한 가지 과목에 집중했던'.

04 기업가적 문화를 배양하기cultivate 위해, / 단과대학과 종합대학에서는 학생들에게 제공할 필요가 있다 / 폭넓은 경험의
선택지와 다양한 아이디어를 널리 접할 기회를.

05 그것들은 이것을 할 수 있는 독특한 위치에 있다position / 자원을 결합하여 / 학업 프로그램 기획, 주거 생활, 학생 집단,
동창회 네트워크의.

구문 Check up

① Cultivate / To cultivate an entrepreneurial culture,
colleges and universities need to offer students a
broad choice of experiences and wide exposure to
different ideas.

'colleges and universities need to offer ~'라는 주절 앞에 부사구가 나오
는 문맥이므로 To cultivate가 적절하다.

② They are uniquely positioned to do this by combining /
combination the resources of academic programming,
residential life, student groups, and alumni networks.

뒤에 명사구가 나오는 것으로 보아 이를 목적어로 취할 수 있는 동명사
combining이 적절하다. 명사는 자신만의 목적어를 취할 수 없다.

정답 ① To cultivate ② combining

13

STEP 1 • 수능에 *진짜* 나오는 *단어*

✔ **문제에 나오는 단어들을 확인하세요.**

01	**definition**	n. 정의	an official (✔ definition) of sport		스포츠의 공식적 정의
02	**implication**	n. 함의, 영향	have important ( )s		중요한 함의를 갖다
03	**emphasize**	v. 강조하다	( ) rules and competition		규칙과 경쟁을 강조하다
04	**performance**	n. 수행, 기량, 성과	high ( )		높은 기량
05	**exclusive**	a. (아무나 이용할 수 없는) 상류의, 배타적인	an ( ) club soccer team		상위 클럽 축구팀
06	**recreational**	a. 오락의	( ) activity rather than a real sport		진정한 스포츠라기보다는 오락 활동
07	**inactive**	a. 활동적이지 않은	physically ( )		신체적으로 활동적이지 않은
08	**relatively**	ad. 상대적으로, 비교적	perform at ( ) high levels		상대적으로 높은 수준으로 경기하다
09	**negatively**	ad. 부정적으로	( ) impact health		건강에 부정적으로 영향을 주다
10	**integrate**	v. 융합하다, 통합하다	physical activities that are ( )d into social life		사회생활에 융합된 신체 활동

⊕ **본문 문장 속에서 단어들을 확인해 보세요.**

For example, / when a 12-year-old is cut from an exclusive club soccer team, / she may not want to play in the local league / because she sees it as "recreational activity" / rather than a real sport.

예를 들어 / 12세의 선수가 상위 클럽 축구팀에서 잘리면 / 그 선수는 지역 리그에서 뛰고 싶지 않을 수도 있는데, / 그 이유는 그 선수가 그것을 '오락 활동'으로 보기 때문이다 / 진정한 스포츠라기보다는.

문제를 풀기 전에 단어들을 **30초** 동안 다시 확인하세요.

01	definition	✎ 정의	an official definition of sport	스포츠의 공식적 (정의)
02	implication		have important implications	중요한 ( )를 갖다
03	emphasize		emphasize rules and competition	규칙과 경쟁을 ( )
04	performance		high performance	높은 ( )
05	exclusive		an exclusive club soccer team	( ) 클럽 축구팀
06	recreational		recreational activity rather than a real sport	진정한 스포츠라기보다는 ( ) 활동
07	inactive		physically inactive	신체적으로 ( )
08	relatively		perform at relatively high levels	( ) 높은 수준으로 경기하다
09	negatively		negatively impact health	건강에 ( ) 영향을 주다
10	integrate		physical activities that are integrated into social life	사회생활에 ( ) 신체 활동

➕ **본문 문장 속에서 단어의 의미를 우리말로 해석해 보세요.**

For example, / when a 12-year-old is cut from an exclusive club soccer team, / she may not want to play in the local league / because she sees it as "recreational activity" / rather than a real sport.

➔ 예를 들어 / 12세의 선수가 ▨▨▨▨▨▨▨▨▨▨▨에서 잘리면 / 그 선수는 지역 리그에서 뛰고 싶지 않을 수도 있는데, / 그 이유는 그 선수가 ▨▨▨▨▨▨▨▨▨▨▨▨▨ 때문이다 / 진정한 스포츠라기보다는.

13 다음 글의 요지로 가장 적절한 것은?

Official definitions of sport have important implications. When a definition emphasizes rules, competition, and high performance, many people will be excluded from participation or avoid other physical activities that are defined as "second class." For example, when a 12-year-old is cut from an exclusive club soccer team, she may not want to play in the local league because she sees it as "recreational activity" rather than a real sport. This can create a situation in which most people are physically inactive at the same time that a small number of people perform at relatively high levels for large numbers of fans — a situation that negatively impacts health and increases health-care costs in a society or community. When sport is defined to include a wide range of physical activities that are played for pleasure and integrated into local expressions of social life, physical activity rates will be high and overall health benefits are likely.

① 운동선수의 기량은 경기 자체를 즐길 때 향상된다.
② 공정한 승부를 위해 합리적인 경기 규칙이 필요하다.
③ 스포츠의 대중화는 스포츠 산업의 정의를 바꾸고 있다.
④ 스포츠의 정의는 신체 활동 참여와 건강에 영향을 미친다.
⑤ 활발한 여가 활동은 원만한 대인 관계 유지에 도움이 된다.

정답과 해설 p.12

01 <u>Official definitions of sport</u> / <u>have important implications.</u>
　　주어　　　　　　　　　　　　　　동사(복수)

02 <u>When</u> a definition <u>emphasizes</u> rules, competition, and high performance, / <u>many people</u>
　　접속사(시간)　　　　　동사(현재)　　　　　　　　　　　　　　　　　　　　　　　주어
<u>will be excluded</u> from participation / or <u>avoid</u> other physical activities / [that are
　　동사1　　　　　　　　　　　　　　　　　　　　　동사2　목적어(선행사)
defined as "second class]."
주격 관계대명사절

03 For example, / when a 12-year-old is cut from an exclusive club soccer team, / she may
not want to play in the local league / because she sees it as "recreational activity" /
　　　　　　　　　　　　　　　　　　　　　　　　　　　　「see A as B: A를 B로 보다」
rather than a real sport.
「A rather than B: B라기보다 A인」

04 This <u>can create</u> a <u>situation</u> / [<u>in which</u> most people are physically inactive / at the
　　　　　동사　　　　　목적어　　　　　= where
same time / that a small number of people perform at relatively high levels / for large
numbers of fans] / — a <u>situation</u> / [that negatively impacts health / and increases
　　　　　　　　　　　목적어 동격　　　주격 관계대명사절
health-care costs in a society or community].

05 <u>When</u> sport <u>is defined</u> / to include a <u>wide range of physical activities</u> / [that are played
　　　　　　　　동사1 is　　　　　　　　　　　선행사　　　　　　　　　주격 관계대명사절
for pleasure] / and <u>integrated</u> into local expressions of social life, / <u>physical activity</u>
　　　　　　　　　　동사2　　　　　　　　　　　　　　　　　　　　　　주어1
<u>rates</u> <u>will be</u> <u>high</u> / and overall health benefits are likely.
　　　　동사1　주격보어1　주어2　　　　　　　　　　　　동사2 주격보어2

01 스포츠에 대한 공식적인 정의definition는 / 중요한 함의implication를 갖는다.

02 정의가 규칙, 경쟁, 높은 기량performance을 강조할emphasize 때 / 많은 사람이 참여에서 배제되거나 / 다른 신체
활동을 피하게 될 것이다 / '이류'로 정의되는.

03 예를 들어 / 12세의 선수가 상위exclusive 클럽 축구팀에서 잘리면 / 그 선수는 지역 리그에서 뛰고 싶지 않을 수도
있는데, / 그 이유는 그 선수가 그것을 '오락recreational 활동'으로 보기 때문이다 / 진정한 스포츠라기보다는.

04 이것은 상황을 만들 수 있다 / 대부분의 사람이 신체적으로 활동적이지 않은inactive / (~하는) 동시에 / 소수의 사람이
상대적으로relatively 높은 수준의 시합을 하는 / 많은 수의 팬을 위해 / 즉 상황 / 건강에 부정적으로negatively 영향을
끼치고 / 사회나 지역 사회에 의료비를 증가시키는.

05 스포츠가 정의되고 / 광범위한 신체 활동을 포함하도록 / 즐거움을 위해 행해지는 / 사회생활의 지역적인 표현들로
융합될integrate 때 / 신체 활동 비율이 높을 것이고 / 전반적인 건강상의 이점이 있을 수 있다.

구문 Check up

① When a definition emphasizes rules, competition, and high performance, many people will be excluded from participation or avoid / be avoided other physical activities that are defined as "second class."

뒤에 목적어 other physical activities가 나오는 것으로 보아 능동태 동사 avoid가 적절하다.

② This can create a situation which / in which most people are physically inactive at the same time that a small number of people perform at relatively high levels for large numbers of fans.

앞에 추상적 공간 선행사인 a situation이 있고 뒤에 완전한 2형식 문장이 오는 것으로 보아 where와 같은 기능의 in which가 적절하다.

정답 ① avoid ② in which

14 STEP 1 • 수능에 *진짜* 나오는 *단어*

✔ 문제에 나오는 단어들을 확인하세요.

01	retrospect	n. 되돌아봄, 회고	in (✔ retrospect)	돌이켜 보면
02	driving force	원동력	the ( ) ( ) for an advance	진보의 원동력
03	fundamental	a. 근본적인	as ( ) as written language	문자 언어만큼 근본적인
04	accompany	v. 수반하다, 동반하다	( ) economic activity	경제 활동을 수반하다
05	transaction	n. 거래	a ( ) between friends	친구끼리의 거래
06	keep track of	~을 기억하다, 기록하다	( ) ( ) ( ) who owns what	누가 무엇을 소유하고 있는지 기억하다
07	contract	n. 계약(서)	draw up a ( )	계약서를 작성하다
08	leave behind	~을 뒤에 남기다	( ) the great works ( )	위대한 작품을 뒤에 남기다
09	literary	a. 문학의	the world's greatest ( ) works	가장 위대한 세계 문학 작품들
10	associate	v. 연관 짓다	( ) the works with the history of culture	작품들을 문화의 역사와 연관 짓다

⊕ 본문 문장 속에서 단어들을 확인해 보세요.

In retrospect, / it might seem surprising / that something as mundane as the desire to count sheep / was the driving force for an advance / as fundamental as written language.

돌이켜 보면 / 놀라운 일로 보일지도 모른다 / 양의 수를 세고자 하는 욕구만큼 세속적인 것이 / 진보의 원동력이었다는 것은 / 문자 언어처럼 근본적인.

문제를 풀기 전에 단어들을 **30초** 동안 다시 확인하세요.

01	retrospect	🖉 되돌아봄, 회고	in retrospect	(돌이켜 보면)
02	driving force		the driving force for an advance	진보의 ( )
03	fundamental		as fundamental as written language	문자 언어만큼 ( )
04	accompany		accompany economic activity	경제 활동을 ( )
05	transaction		a transaction between friends	친구끼리의 ( )
06	keep track of		keep track of who owns what	누가 무엇을 소유하고 있는지 ( )
07	contract		draw up a contract	( )를 작성하다
08	leave behind		leave the great works behind	위대한 작품을 ( )
09	literary		the world's greatest literary works	가장 위대한 세계 ( ) 작품들
10	associate		associate the works with the history of culture	작품들을 문화의 역사와 ( )

➕ **본문 문장 속에서 단어의 의미를 우리말로 해석해 보세요.**

In retrospect, / it might seem surprising / that something as mundane as the desire to count sheep / was the driving force for an advance / as fundamental as written language.

➡ ▓▓▓▓▓▓▓▓▓ / 놀라운 일로 보일지도 모른다 / 양의 수를 세고자 하는 욕구만큼 세속적인 것이 / ▓▓▓▓▓▓▓ 이었다는 것은 / 문자 언어처럼 ▓▓▓▓▓▓.

14   다음 글의 요지로 가장 적절한 것은?

In retrospect, it might seem surprising that something as mundane as the desire to count sheep was the driving force for an advance as fundamental as written language. But the desire for written records has always accompanied economic activity, since transactions are meaningless unless you can clearly keep track of who owns what. As such, early human writing is dominated by wheeling and dealing: a collection of bets, bills, and contracts. Long before we had the writings of the prophets, we had the writings of the profits. In fact, many civilizations never got to the stage of recording and leaving behind the kinds of great literary works that we often associate with the history of culture. What survives these ancient societies is, for the most part, a pile of receipts. If it weren't for the commercial enterprises that produced those records, we would know far, far less about the cultures that they came from.

*mundane: 세속의 **prophet: 예언자

① 고대 사회에서 경제 활동은 문자 기록의 원동력이었다.
② 고전 문학을 통해 당대의 경제 활동을 파악할 수 있다.
③ 경제 발전의 정도가 문명의 발달 수준을 결정한다.
④ 종교의 역사는 상업의 역사보다 먼저 시작되었다.
⑤ 모든 문명이 위대한 작가를 배출한 것은 아니다.

정답과 해설 p.12

01 In retrospect, / it might seem surprising / that something [as mundane as the desire
가주어-진주어 구문
주어   [ ]:「as + 원급 + as: ~만큼 …한」
to count sheep] / was the driving force for an advance / [as fundamental as written
동사(단수)   주격보어
language].

02 But / the desire for written records / has always accompanied economic activity, / since
주어   전치사구   동사(현재완료)   접속사(~ 때문에)
transactions are meaningless / unless you can clearly keep track of [who owns what].
접속사(~하지 않는 한)   의문사절(of의 목적어)

03 As such, / early human writing is dominated by wheeling and dealing: / a collection of
동격
bets, bills, and contracts. // Long before we had the writings of the prophets, / we had
접속사(~하기 오래전에)
the writings of the profits.

04 In fact, / many civilizations never got to the stage / of recording and leaving behind
the kinds of great literary works / [that we often associate with the history of culture].
선행사   목적격 관계대명사절

05 [What survives these ancient societies] / is, (for the most part), a pile of receipts. //
주어(명사절)   동사(단수)   주격보어
If it weren't for the commercial enterprises / that produced those records, / we would
가정법 과거(현재 사실과 반대)
know far, far less about the cultures / that they came from.

01 돌이켜 보면in retrospect, / 놀라운 일로 보일지도 모른다 / 양의 수를 세고자 하는 욕구만큼 세속적인 것이 / 진보의
원동력driving force이었다는 것은 / 문자 언어처럼 근본적인fundamental.

02 그러나 / 문자 기록에 대한 욕구는 / 언제나 경제 활동을 수반해accompany 왔는데, / 그 이유는 거래transaction는
무의미하기 때문이다 / 여러분이 누가 무엇을 소유하고 있는지 명확하게 기억할keep track of 수 없는 한.

03 따라서 / 인간의 초기 글쓰기는 목적을 위해서는 수단을 가리지 않는 것에 의해 지배된다 / 내기, 계산서,
계약서contract의 모음과 같이. // 우리가 예언자들에 관한 기록을 갖기 훨씬 이전에 / 우리는 이익에 대한 기록을 가졌다.

04 사실, / 많은 문명이 단계에 결코 이르지 못했다 / 그런 종류의 위대한 문학literary 작품을 기록하고 그것을 후세에
남기는leave behind / 우리가 흔히 문화의 역사와 연관 짓는associate.

05 이런 고대 사회에서 살아남은 것은 / 대부분 영수증 더미이다. // 만약 상업적 기업이 없다면 / 그런 기록을 만들어냈던 /
우리는 문화에 대해 아주 훨씬 더 적게 알 것이다 / 그런 기록이 생겨난.

구문 Check up

① What survives these ancient societies is / are , for the
most part, a pile of receipts.

What이 이끄는 명사절 주어는 일반적으로 단수 취급하므로 단수동사 is
가 적절하다.

② If it weren't for the commercial enterprises that
produced those records, we would know / would have
known far, far less about the cultures that they came
from.

If it weren't for는 '~이 없다면'이라는 뜻의 가정법 과거 구문이다. 따라서
「조동사 과거형 + 동사원형」 형태의 would know가 적절하다.

정답 ① is ② would know

15

STEP **1** • 수능에 *진짜* 나오는 *단어*

함축 의미 ⊕

✔ 문제에 나오는 단어들을 확인하세요.

01	critical	a. 중요한	play a (✔ critical) role	중요한 역할을 하다
02	scatter	v. 분산시키다	( )ed attention	분산된 주의
03	narrowly	ad. 좁게	( ) focused	좁게 집중된
04	fixate on	~에 집착하다	( ) ( ) the stressful parts	스트레스가 되는 부분에 집착하다
05	put ~ in perspective	~을 균형 있게 보다	( ) things ( ) ( )	상황을 균형 있게 보다
06	get locked into	~에 갇히다	( ) ( ) ( ) one part	한 부분에 갇히다
07	tie down to	~에 옭아매다	Don't ( ) yourself ( ) ( ) a single path of life.	한 가지 삶의 길에 여러분 자신을 옭아매지 말라.
08	superficial	a. 피상적인	a ( ) anaylsis	피상적인 분석
09	anxiety	n. 불안, 걱정	( )-provoking levels of attention	불안을 유발하는 주의 수준
10	heighten	v. 높이다	( ) the risk	위험을 높이다
11	turn down	낮추다, 약하게 하다	( ) ( ) the stress level	스트레스 수준을 낮추다
12	nonstick	a. (음식이) 눌어붙지 않는	a ( ) frying pan	눌어붙지 않는 프라이팬
13	stick to	~에 달라붙다, ~을 고수하다	( ) ( ) the pan	팬에 달라붙다

⊕ 본문 문장 속에서 단어들을 확인해 보세요.

It's like transforming yourself into a nonstick frying pan.

그것은 여러분 자신을 (음식이) 눌어붙지 않는 프라이팬으로 변형시키는 것과 같다.

01	critical	✏ 중요한	play a critical role	(중요한) 역할을 하다
02	scatter		scattered attention	( ) 주의
03	narrowly		narrowly focused	( ) 집중된
04	fixate on		fixate on the stressful parts	스트레스가 되는 부분에 ( )
05	put ~ in perspective		put things in perspective	상황을 ( )
06	get locked into		get locked into one part	한 부분에 ( )
07	tie down to		Don't tie yourself down to a single path of life.	한 가지 삶의 길에 여러분 자신을 ( ) 말라.
08	superficial		a superficial anaylsis	( ) 분석
09	anxiety		anxiety-provoking levels of attention	( )을 유발하는 주의 수준
10	heighten		heighten the risk	위험을 ( )
11	turn down		turn down the stress level	스트레스 수준을 ( )
12	nonstick		a nonstick frying pan	( ) 프라이팬
13	stick to		stick to the pan	팬에 ( )

➕ **본문 문장 속에서 단어의 의미를 우리말로 해석해 보세요.**

It's like transforming yourself into a nonstick frying pan.

→ 그것은 여러분 자신을 ⬛⬛⬛⬛⬛⬛⬛⬛⬛⬛ 으로 변형시키는 것과 같다.

15

밑줄 친 a nonstick frying pan이 다음 글에서 의미하는 바로 가장 적절한 것은?

How you focus your attention plays a critical role in how you deal with stress. Scattered attention harms your ability to let go of stress, because even though your attention is scattered, it is narrowly focused, for you are able to fixate only on the stressful parts of your experience. When your attentional spotlight is widened, you can more easily let go of stress. You can put in perspective many more aspects of any situation and not get locked into one part that ties you down to superficial and anxiety-provoking levels of attention. A narrow focus heightens the stress level of each experience, but a widened focus turns down the stress level because you're better able to put each situation into a broader perspective. One anxiety-provoking detail is less important than the bigger picture. It's like transforming yourself into a nonstick frying pan. You can still fry an egg, but the egg won't stick to the pan.

*provoke: 유발시키다

① never being confronted with any stressful experiences in daily life

② broadening one's perspective to identify the cause of stress

③ rarely confining one's attention to positive aspects of an experience

④ having a larger view of an experience beyond its stressful aspects

⑤ taking stress into account as the source of developing a wide view

정답과 해설 **p.14**

01 How you focus your attention / plays a critical role in how you deal with stress.
　　　　　　　　　　　　　　명사절(~하는 방식)

02 Scattered attention harms your ability to let go of stress, / because even though your
　　　　　　　　　　　　　　　　　　　　형용사적 용법
attention is scattered, / it is narrowly focused, / for you are able to fixate only on the
　　　　　　　　　　　　　　　　　　　　　등위접속사(왜냐하면 ~이다)
stressful parts of your experience.

03 When your attentional spotlight is widened, / you can more easily let go of stress. //
　　　　　　　　　　　　　　　　　　　　　　　비교급 부사(동사 수식)
You can put in perspective many more aspects of any situation / and not get locked
　　　　　동사원형1　　　　　　　　　　　　　　　　　　　　　　동사원형2
into one part / [that ties you down to superficial and anxiety-provoking levels of
　　　선행사　　　　주격 관계대명사절
attention].

04 A narrow focus heightens the stress level of each experience, / but a widened focus
turns down the stress level / because you're better able to put each situation into a
broader perspective. // One anxiety-provoking detail is less important than the bigger
　　　　　　　　　　　　　　　　　　　　　　　　　　　　= not so important as
picture.

05 It's like transforming yourself into a nonstick frying pan. // You can still fry an egg, /
　　　　　동명사구(전치사의 목적어)
but the egg won't stick to the pan.

01 여러분이 여러분의 주의를 집중하는 방식은 / 여러분이 스트레스에 대처하는 방식에 중요한critical 역할을 한다.

02 주의가 분산되면scattered attention 스트레스를 해소하는 능력이 손상되는데, / 왜냐하면 여러분의 주의가
분산되더라도, / 그것이 좁게narrowly 집중되기 때문이다 / 여러분은 여러분의 경험 중 스트레스가 많은 부분에만
집착할fixate on 수 있으므로.

03 여러분의 주의 초점 범위가 넓어지면, / 여러분은 스트레스를 더 쉽게 해소할 수 있다. // 여러분은 어떤 상황이라도 그
상황의 더 많은 측면을 균형 있는 시각으로 볼put in perspective 수 있으며, / 어느 한 부분에 갇히지get locked into one
part 않을 수 있다 / 피상적이고 불안을 유발하는superficial and anxiety-provoking 주의 수준에 여러분을 옭아매는tie
down to.

04 초점이 좁으면 각 경험의 스트레스 수준이 높아지지만heighten, / 초점이 넓으면 스트레스 수준이 낮아진다turn down /
여러분이 각 상황을 더 넓은 시각으로 더 잘 볼 수 있기 때문에. // 불안감을 유발하는 하나의 세부 사항은 더 큰 그림보다 덜
중요하다.

05 그것은 여러분 자신을 (음식이) 눌어붙지 않는nonstick 프라이팬으로 변모시키는 것과 같다. // 여러분은 여전히 달걀을
부칠 수 있지만, / 그 달걀은 팬에 들러붙지stick to 않을 것이다.

구문 Check up	① When your attentional spotlight is widened, you can easier / more easily let go of stress.	② One anxiety-provoking detail is less important as / than the bigger picture.
	동사구인 can let go of를 꾸미는 비교급 부사 자리이므로 more easily가 적절하다.	「less + 원급 + than(~보다 덜 …한)」 구문으로, 「not so + 원급 + as」와 같은 의미이다.

정답 ① more easily ② than

16

STEP 1 • 수능에 *진짜* 나오는 *단어*

✔️ 문제에 나오는 단어들을 확인하세요.

01	**needlessly**	ad. 불필요하게	(✔️ needlessly) = unnecessarily	불필요하게
02	**enhance**	v. 향상하다	( ) the expected results	예상되는 결과를 향상하다
03	**characteristic**	n. 특징	( )s that are costly	비용이 많이 드는 특징
04	**with respect to**	~와 관련해서	( ) ( ) ( ) the targets	목표와 관련해서
05	**justification**	n. 명분, (합당한) 이유	with no real ( )	실질적 명분 없이
06	**marked**	a. 뚜렷한, 눈에 띄는	a ( ) professional component	뚜렷한 전문적 요소
07	**specialist**	n. 전문가	( )s with proven experience	검증된 경험을 갖춘 전문가들
08	**extensive**	a. 폭넓은, 광범위한	( ) professional autonomy	폭넓은 전문적 자율성
09	**enrich**	v. 강화하다, 풍부하게 하다	( ) their skill sets	그들의 다양한 기술을 강화하다
10	**in good faith**	선의에서	( ) all ( ) ( )	전적으로 선의에서
11	**desirable**	a. 바람직한	a ( ) outcome	바람직한 결과
12	**overqualified**	a. 필요 이상의 자격을 갖춘	( ) specialists	필요 이상의 자격을 갖춘 전문가들
13	**ensure**	v. 보장하다, 반드시 ~하게 하다	( ) success	성공을 보장하다

➕ **본문 문장 속에서 단어들을 확인해 보세요.**

Gold plating in the project / means needlessly enhancing the expected results, / namely, adding characteristics that are costly, not required, / and that have low added value with respect to the targets.

프로젝트에서 금도금이란 / 예상되는 결과를 불필요하게 향상하는 것을 뜻한다 / 즉 필수는 아니면서 비용이 많이 드는 특징을 더하는 것 / 그리고 목표와 관련해서는 부가 가치가 낮은.

01	needlessly	✎ 불필요하게	needlessly = unnecessarily	(불필요하게)
02	enhance		enhance the expected results	예상되는 결과를 ( )
03	characteristic		characteristics that are costly	비용이 많이 드는 ( )
04	with respect to		with respect to the targets	목표와 ( )
05	justification		with no real justification	실질적 ( ) 없이
06	marked		a marked professional component	( ) 전문적 요소
07	specialist		specialists with proven experience	검증된 경험을 갖춘 ( )들
08	extensive		extensive professional autonomy	( ) 전문적 자율성
09	enrich		enrich their skill sets	그들의 다양한 기술을 ( )
10	in good faith		in all good faith	전적으로 ( )
11	desirable		a desirable outcome	( ) 결과
12	overqualified		overqualified specialists	( ) 전문가들
13	ensure		ensure success	성공을 ( )

➕ **본문 문장 속에서 단어의 의미를 우리말로 해석해 보세요.**

Gold plating in the project / means needlessly enhancing the expected results, / namely, adding characteristics that are costly, **not required,** / and that have low added value with respect to the targets.

➡ 프로젝트에서 금도금이란 / ▓▓▓▓▓▓▓▓▓▓▓▓▓▓▓▓▓▓ 을 뜻한다 / 즉 필수는 아니면서 ▓▓▓▓▓▓▓▓▓▓▓▓ 을 더하는 것 / 그리고 ▓▓▓▓▓▓▓▓ 부가 가치가 낮은.

16

밑줄 친 "The best is the enemy of the good."이 다음 글에서 의미하는 바로 가장 적절한 것은?

Gold plating in the project means needlessly enhancing the expected results, namely, adding characteristics that are costly, not required, and that have low added value with respect to the targets — in other words, giving more with no real justification other than to demonstrate one's own talent. Gold plating is especially interesting for project team members, as it is typical of projects with a marked professional component — in other words, projects that involve specialists with proven experience and extensive professional autonomy. In these environments specialists often see the project as an opportunity to test and enrich their skill sets. There is therefore a strong temptation, in all good faith, to engage in gold plating, namely, to achieve more or higher-quality work that gratifies the professional but does not add value to the client's requests, and at the same time removes valuable resources from the project. As the saying goes, "The best is the enemy of the good."

*autonomy: 자율성 **gratify: 만족시키다

① Pursuing perfection at work causes conflicts among team members.

② Raising work quality only to prove oneself is not desirable.

③ Inviting overqualified specialists to a project leads to bad ends.

④ Responding to the changing needs of clients is unnecessary.

⑤ Acquiring a range of skills for a project does not ensure success.

정답과 해설 p.14

01 Gold plating in the project / means needlessly enhancing the expected results, /
「mean+동명사: ~하는 것을 의미하다」
namely, adding characteristics [that are costly, not required], / and [that have low
주격 관계대명사절1   주격 관계대명사절2
added value with respect to the targets] / — in other words, / giving more with no real
justification / other than to demonstrate one's own talent.
~ 외에는

02 Gold plating is especially interesting for project team members, / as it is typical of
접속사(= because)
projects with a marked professional component / — in other words, / projects [that
선행사(복수)
involve specialists / with proven experience and extensive professional autonomy]. //
주격 관계대명사절   전치사구
In these environments / specialists often see the project as an opportunity / to test
「see A as B: A를 B라고 여기다」
and enrich their skill sets.
형용사적 용법

03 There is therefore a strong temptation, / in all good faith, / to engage in gold plating, /
형용사적 용법1
namely, to achieve more or higher-quality work / [that gratifies the professional / but
형용사적 용법2   동사1
does not add value to the client's requests, / and at the same time removes valuable
동사2   동사3
resources from the project]. // As the saying goes, / "The best is the enemy of the
good."

01 프로젝트에서 금도금이란 / 예상되는 결과를 불필요하게 향상하는needlessly enhance 것을 뜻한다 / 즉 필수는 아니면서
비용이 많이 드는 특징characteristic을 더하는 것 / 그리고 목표와 관련해서는with respect to 부가 가치가 낮은. / 다시
말해, / 실질적인 명분justification이 없이 더 많이 주는 것을 뜻한다 / 본인의 재능을 입증한다는 것 외에는.

02 금도금은 특히 프로젝트 팀원들에게 있어 흥미로운데, / 이는 전문적 요소가 뚜렷한marked 프로젝트에서 흔하기 때문이다
/ 다시 말해 / 전문가specialist가 참여하는 프로젝트 / 검증된 경험과 폭넓은extensive 전문적 자율성을 갖춘. // 이런
환경에서 / 전문가들은 흔히 프로젝트가 기회라고 본다 / 자신의 다양한 기술을 테스트하고 강화할enrich.

03 따라서 강한 유혹이 있다 / 전적으로 선의에서in all good faith / 금도금에 참여하려는 / 즉, 더 많고 더 질 높은 성과를
달성하려는 / 전문가는 만족시키지만 / 고객의 요청에는 가치를 더하지 않으면서, / 동시에 프로젝트의 귀중한 자원을
없애는 (성과). // 속담에서 말하듯이, / '최고는 좋음의 적'이다.

구문 Check up

① Gold plating in the project means adding characteristics that are costly, not required, and that has / have low added value with respect to the targets.

that절의 선행사인 복수명사 characteristics에 수 일치하여 have를 쓴다.

② There is therefore a strong temptation, in all good faith, engages / to engage in gold plating.

a strong temptation을 꾸미는 수식어가 필요하므로 to engage가 적절하다.

정답 ① have ② to engage

17 STEP 1 · 수능에 *진짜* 나오는 *단어*

✔ 문제에 나오는 단어들을 확인하세요.

01	ownership	n. 소유권	the definition of (✔ ownership)	소유권의 정의
02	bundle	n. 다발	a ( ) of sticks	막대의 다발
03	metaphor	n. 비유, 은유	a ( ) for ownership	소유권에 대한 비유
04	interpersonal	a. 대인 관계적인, 사람 간의	( ) intimacy	사람들 간의 친밀함
05	put together	합치다, 모으다	be ( ) back ( )	다시 합쳐지다
06	in reference to	~에 관해서	( ) ( ) ( ) a resource	어떤 자원에 관해서
07	license	v. 허가하다, 인가하다 n. 면허	a ( ) to enter the land	토지 진입 면허
08	give away	증여하다, 거저 주다	( ) ( ) the rest	나머지를 증여하다
09	split up	~을 쪼개다, 나누다	( ) the sticks ( )	막대들을 쪼개다
10	as for	~에 관해 말하자면	( ) ( ) a piece of land	토지 한 면에 관해 말하자면
11	lease	n. 임대차 계약	a tenant with a ( )	임대차 계약을 맺은 임차인
12	plumber	n. 배관공	hire a ( )	배관공을 고용하다
13	mineral	n. 광물	an oil company with ( ) rights	광물에 대한 권리를 가진 석유 회사
14	party	n. 당사자	each ( )	각각의 이해 당사자

⊕ 본문 문장 속에서 단어들을 확인해 보세요.

The metaphor is useful / because it helps us see ownership as a grouping of interpersonal rights / that can be separated and put back together.

그 비유는 유용한데, / 그것이 우리가 소유권을 대인 관계적인 권리의 모음으로 보는 것을 도와주기 때문이다 / 분리되고 다시 합쳐질 수 있는.

01	ownership	✏️ 소유권	the definition of ownership	(소유권)의 정의
02	bundle		a bundle of sticks	막대의 ( )
03	metaphor		a metaphor for ownership	소유권에 대한 ( )
04	interpersonal		interpersonal intimacy	( ) 친밀함
05	put together		be put back together	다시 ( )
06	in reference to		in reference to a resource	어떤 자원에 ( )
07	license		a license to enter the land	토지 진입 ( )
08	give away		give away the rest	나머지를 ( )
09	split up		split the sticks up	막대들을 ( )
10	as for		as for a piece of land	토지 한 면에 ( )
11	lease		a tenant with a lease	( )을 맺은 임차인
12	plumber		hire a plumber	( )을 고용하다
13	mineral		an oil company with mineral rights	( )에 대한 권리를 가진 석유 회사
14	party		each party	각각의 ( )

➕ **본문 문장 속에서 단어의 의미를 우리말로 해석해 보세요.**

The metaphor is useful / because it helps us see ownership as a grouping of interpersonal rights / that can be separated and put back together.

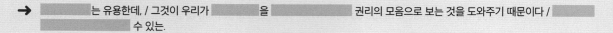

➡️ _____는 유용한데, / 그것이 우리가 _____을 _____ 권리의 모음으로 보는 것을 도와주기 때문이다 / _____ 수 있는.

17

밑줄 친 a stick in the bundle이 다음 글에서 의미하는 바로 가장 적절한 것은?

Lawyers sometimes describe ownership as *a bundle of sticks*. This metaphor was introduced about a century ago, and it has dramatically transformed the teaching and practice of law. The metaphor is useful because it helps us see ownership as a grouping of interpersonal rights that can be separated and put back together. When you say *It's mine* in reference to a resource, often that means you own a lot of the sticks that make up the full bundle: the sell stick, the rent stick, the right to mortgage, license, give away, even destroy the thing. Often, though, we split the sticks up, as for a piece of land: there may be a landowner, a bank with a mortgage, a tenant with a lease, a plumber with a license to enter the land, an oil company with mineral rights. Each of these parties owns a stick in the bundle.

*mortgage: 저당잡히다   **tenant: 임차인

① a legal obligation to develop the resource

② a priority to legally claim the real estate

③ a right to use one aspect of the property

④ a building to be shared equally by tenants

⑤ a piece of land nobody can claim as their own

정답과 해설 p.15

01 Lawyers sometimes describe ownership as *a bundle of sticks*. // This metaphor was
「describe A as B: A를 B라고 묘사하다」
introduced about a century ago, / and it has dramatically transformed the teaching
부사(약, 대략)
and practice of law.

02 The metaphor is useful / because it helps us see ownership as a grouping of
「help + 목적어 + 원형부정사: ~이 …하도록 돕다」
interpersonal rights / [that can be separated and put back together].
주격 관계대명사절

03 When you say *It's mine* in reference to a resource, / often that means you own a lot of
지시대명사(= It's mine)   선행사(복수)
the sticks / [that make up the full bundle]: / the sell stick, / the rent stick, / the right to
주격 관계대명사절
mortgage, license, give away, even destroy the thing.
형용사적 용법

04 Often, though, we split the sticks up, / as for a piece of land: / there may be a landowner,
주어1
/ a bank with a mortgage, / a tenant with a lease, / a plumber with a license to enter
주어2   주어3   주어4
the land, / an oil company with mineral rights. // Each of these parties owns a stick in
주어5   주어(each of + 복수명사)   동사(단수)
the bundle.

01 변호사들은 때때로 소유권ownership을 '막대 다발bundle'로 묘사한다. // 이 비유metaphor는 약 1세기 전에 도입되었고 / 그것은 법학 교육과 실무를 극적으로 변화시켰다.

02 그 비유는 유용한데, / 그것이 우리가 소유권을 대인 관계적인interpersonal 권리의 모음으로 보는 것을 도와주기 때문이다 / 분리되고 다시 합쳐질put back together 수 있는.

03 어떤 자원에 관해in reference to '그건 내 거다'라고 말할 때, / 흔히 그것은 여러분이 많은 막대를 소유한다는 뜻이다 / 전체 다발을 구성하는 / 즉 판매 막대, / 임대 막대, / 저당잡히고 허가하고license 증여하고give away 심지어 그것을 파괴할 권리.

04 그러나 우리는 흔히 그 막대들을 쪼갠다split up, / 토지 한 면에 대해서 보자면as for (다음과 같다) / 땅 주인이 있을 수 있고 / 저당권을 가진 은행, / 임대차 계약lease을 맺은 임차인, / 토지 진입 면허를 가진 배관공plumber, / 광물mineral에 대한 권리를 가진 석유 회사가 있을 수 있다. // 이 당사자party 각각은 그 다발의 막대 하나를 소유한다.

① The metaphor is useful because it helps us see / seeing ownership as a grouping of interpersonal rights that can be separated and put back together.

help는 원형부정사 또는 to부정사를 목적격보어로 취하므로, see가 알맞다.

② When you say *It's mine* in reference to a resource, often that means you own a lot of the sticks that makes / make up the full bundle.

주격 관계대명사절의 동사는 선행사에 수 일치한다. 여기서는 the sticks 가 복수명사이므로 make가 적절하다.

18

STEP 1 • 수능에 *진짜* 나오는 *단어*

✔ **문제에 나오는 단어들을 확인하세요.**

01	scary	*a.* 무서운	something (✔ scary)	뭔가 무서운 것
02	by oneself	혼자서, 스스로	eat (　　) (　　　　)	혼자서 먹다
03	get stuck	갇히다	(　　) (　　　　) in a routine	틀에 박힌 일상에 갇히다
04	suited	*a.* 적합한, 잘 맞는	seem (　　　　) to the position	그 자리에 적합해 보이다
05	drive A into B	A를 B로 몰아가다	(　　　) me (　　　) a corner	나를 궁지로 몰아가다
06	convergence	*n.* 수렴	the (　　　　　) of opinions	의견의 수렴
07	taste	*n.* 취향	a man of refined (　　　)s	세련된 취향의 사람
08	nonlinear	*a.* 비선형적인	(　　　　　) mathematics	비선형적 수학
09	chaotic	*a.* 불규칙한, 혼돈의	a (　　　　) age in the history of Europe	유럽 역사에서 혼돈의 시대

✚ **본문 문장 속에서 단어들을 확인해 보세요.**

My worry originally about such algorithms / was / that they might drive everyone into certain parts of the library, / leaving others lacking listeners.

원래 그런 알고리즘에 대한 나의 걱정은 / ~였다 / 그것이 모든 사람을 라이브러리의 특정 부분으로 몰아넣을지도 모른다는 것 / 나머지 부분은 청취자가 부족한 채로 남겨놓고.

문제를 풀기 전에 단어들을 **30초** 동안 다시 확인하세요.

No.	단어	뜻	예문	해석
01	scary	✏ 무서운	something scary	뭔가 (무서운) 것
02	by oneself		eat by oneself	(　　　　) 먹다
03	get stuck		get stuck in a routine	틀에 박힌 일상에 (　　　　)
04	suited		seem suited to the position	그 자리에 (　　　　) 보이다
05	drive A into B		drive me into a corner	나를 궁지로 (　　　　)
06	convergence		the convergence of opinions	의견의 (　　　　)
07	taste		a man of refined tastes	세련된 (　　　　)의 사람
08	nonlinear		nonlinear mathematics	(　　　　) 수학
09	chaotic		a chaotic age in the history of Europe	유럽 역사에서 (　　　　) 시대

➕ **본문 문장 속에서 단어의 의미를 우리말로 해석해 보세요.**

My worry originally about such algorithms / was / that they might drive everyone into certain parts of the library, / leaving others lacking listeners.

➡ 원래 그런 알고리즘에 대한 나의 걱정은 / ~였다 / 그것이 ▮▮▮▮▮▮▮▮▮▮▮▮▮▮▮▮▮▮▮▮▮▮ 지도 모른다는 것 / 나머지 부분은 청취자가 부족한 채로 남겨놓고.

18

밑줄 친 send us off into different far corners of the library가 다음 글에서 의미하는 바로 가장 적절한 것은?

You may feel there is something scary about an algorithm deciding what you might like. Could it mean that, if computers conclude you won't like something, you will never get the chance to see it? Personally, I really enjoy being directed toward new music that I might not have found by myself. I can quickly get stuck in a rut where I put on the same songs over and over. That's why I've always enjoyed the radio. But the algorithms that are now pushing and pulling me through the music library are perfectly suited to finding gems that I'll like. My worry originally about such algorithms was that they might drive everyone into certain parts of the library, leaving others lacking listeners. Would they cause a convergence of tastes? But thanks to the nonlinear and chaotic mathematics usually behind them, this doesn't happen. A small divergence in my likes compared to yours can send us off into different far corners of the library.

*rut: 관습, 틀 **gem: 보석 ***divergence: 갈라짐

① lead us to music selected to suit our respective tastes

② enable us to build connections with other listeners

③ encourage us to request frequent updates for algorithms

④ motivate us to search for talented but unknown musicians

⑤ make us ignore our preferences for particular music genres

정답과 해설 p.16

01 You may feel / there is <u>something scary about an algorithm</u> / <u>deciding what you might</u>
형용사구   현재분사구(an algorithm 수식)
<u>like</u>. // Could it mean / that, if computers <u>conclude</u> you won't like something, / you
시간과 조건의 부사절에서는 현재가 미래를 대신함
<u>will never get</u> the chance to see it?

02 Personally, / I really enjoy <u>being directed</u> toward new music / that I <u>might not have</u>
동명사의 수동태(being p.p.)   「might have p.p.: ~했을지도 모른다」
<u>found</u> by myself. // I can quickly get stuck in a rut / [where I put on the same songs
관계부사절
over and over]. // That's why I've always enjoyed the radio.
이것이 ~한 이유다

03 But the algorithms / [that are now pushing and pulling me through the music library]
주어   주격 관계대명사절
/ are perfectly suited to finding gems / [that I'll like]. // My worry originally about such
동사(복수)   전치사 동명사   목적격 관계대명사절
algorithms / was / [that they might drive everyone into certain parts of the library, /
주격보어(~것)
<u>leaving</u> others lacking listeners]. // Would they cause a convergence of tastes?
분사구문(= and leave ~)

04 But thanks to the nonlinear and chaotic mathematics usually behind them, / this
~ 덕분에
doesn't happen. // A small divergence in my likes / compared to yours / can send us off
into different far corners of the library.

---

01 여러분은 느낄 수도 있다 / 알고리즘에 대해 뭔가 무서운**scary** 것이 있다고 / 여러분이 좋아할지도 모를 것을 판단하는.
// 그것은 ~하다는 뜻일까 / 만일 컴퓨터가 여러분이 뭔가를 좋아하지 않을 것이라고 결론 짓는다면 / 여러분은 그것을 볼
기회를 영영 얻지 못한다는?

02 개인적으로, / 나는 새로운 음악 쪽으로 안내받는 것을 정말 좋아한다 / 내가 혼자서는**by oneself** 발견하지 못했을지도
모르는. // 나는 틀에 빨리 갇힐**get stuck** 수 있다 / 내가 같은 노래를 계속 반복해서 틀어놓는. // 이것이 내가 항상
라디오를 즐겨 듣는 이유다.

03 그러나 알고리즘은 / 지금 뮤직 라이브러리를 통해 나를 밀고 당기고 있는 / 보석을 찾는 데 완벽하게 적합하다**suited**
/ 내가 좋아할. // 원래 그런 알고리즘에 대한 나의 걱정은 ~였다 / 그것이 모든 사람을 라이브러리의 특정 부분으로
몰아넣을지도**drive everyone into certain parts of the library** 모른다는 것 / 나머지 부분은 청취자가 부족한 채로
남겨놓고. // 그것은 취향의 수렴**a convergence of tastes**을 일으킬 것인가?

04 그러나 일반적으로 그 배후에 있는 비선형적이고 불규칙한**nonlinear and chaotic** 수학 덕분에 / 이런 일은 발생하지
않는다. // 내가 좋아하는 것에서의 작은 갈라짐이(차이가) / 여러분이 좋아하는 것과 비교하여 / <u>우리를 뮤직 라이브러리의</u>
<u>저 멀리 떨어진 구석으로 보낼</u> 수 있다.

구문 Check up

① Could it mean that, if computers conclude / will
conclude you won't like something, you will never get
the chance to see it?

시간과 조건의 부사절에서는 현재시제가 미래시제 대신 쓰이므로
conclude가 적절하다.

② My worry originally about such algorithms was that
they might drive everyone into certain parts of the
library, leaving / leaves others lacking listeners.

콤마 앞의 문장이 완전하므로 콤마 뒤는 분사구문으로서 앞을 보충 설명
해야 한다. 따라서 leaving이 적절하다.

정답 ① conclude ② leaving

19 STEP 1 • 수능에 *진짜* 나오는 *단어*

✔ 문제에 나오는 단어들을 확인하세요.

01	purchase	n. 강점, 유리한 입장	have no special (✔ purchase)	특별한 강점이 없다
02	collapse	n. 붕괴	bee colony ( )	꿀벌 집단의 붕괴
03	feature	n. 특징	an interesting ( )	흥미로운 특징
04	specialize	v. 전문적으로 다루다, 전공하다	a ( )d domain	전문화된 분야
05	ignorance	n. 무지	( ) in many other fields	여러 다른 분야의 영역에서의 무지
06	relevant	a. 관련된, 적절한	( ) experiences	관련 경험
07	gather	v. 수집하다, 모으다	( ) observations	관찰을 수집하다
08	designate	v. 지정하다	a ( )d area	지정 구역
09	devote A to B	A를 B에 바치다	( ) their lives ( ) research	연구에 그들의 일생을 바치다
10	sort out	처리하다, 해결하다	( ) ( ) tough questions	어려운 문제를 처리하다
11	in effect	사실상	be ( ) ( ) identical	사실상 동일하다

➕ 본문 문장 속에서 단어들을 확인해 보세요.

The very features / that create expertise in a specialized domain / lead to ignorance in many others.

바로 그 특징이 / 전문화된 영역에서의 전문지식을 만들어내는 / 여러 다른 영역에서의 무지로 이어진다.

문제를 풀기 전에 단어들을 **30초** 동안 다시 확인하세요.

01	purchase	🖉 강점, 유리한 입장	have no special purchase	특별한 (강점)이 없다
02	collapse		bee colony collapse	꿀벌 집단의 ( )
03	feature		an interesting feature	흥미로운 ( )
04	specialize		a specialized domain	( ) 분야
05	ignorance		ignorance in many other fields	여러 다른 분야의 영역에서의 ( )
06	relevant		relevant experiences	( ) 경험
07	gather		gather observations	관찰을 ( )
08	designate		a designated area	( ) 구역
09	devote A to B		devote their lives to research	연구에 그들의 일생을 ( )
10	sort out		sort out tough questions	어려운 문제를 ( )
11	in effect		be in effect identical	( ) 동일하다

➕ **본문 문장 속에서 단어의 의미를 우리말로 해석해 보세요.**

The very features / that create expertise in a specialized domain / lead to ignorance in many others.

➡ ▢▢▢▢▢▢▢이 / ▢▢▢▢▢▢에서의 전문지식을 만들어내는 / ▢▢▢▢▢▢▢로 이어진다.

19

밑줄 친 whether to make ready for the morning commute or not
이 다음 글에서 의미하는 바로 가장 적절한 것은?

Scientists have no special purchase on moral or ethical decisions; a climate scientist is no more qualified to comment on health care reform than a physicist is to judge the causes of bee colony collapse. The very features that create expertise in a specialized domain lead to ignorance in many others. In some cases lay people — farmers, fishermen, patients, native peoples — may have relevant experiences that scientists can learn from. Indeed, in recent years, scientists have begun to recognize this: the Arctic Climate Impact Assessment includes observations gathered from local native groups. So our trust needs to be limited, and focused. It needs to be very *particular*. Blind trust will get us into at least as much trouble as no trust at all. But without some degree of trust in our designated experts — the men and women who have devoted their lives to sorting out tough questions about the natural world we live in — we are paralyzed, in effect not knowing whether to make ready for the morning commute or not.

*lay: 전문가가 아닌   **paralyze: 마비시키다   ***commute: 통근

① questionable facts that have been popularized by non-experts

② readily applicable information offered by specialized experts

③ common knowledge that hardly influences crucial decisions

④ practical information produced by both specialists and lay people

⑤ biased knowledge that is widespread in the local community

정답과 해설 p.17

01 Scientists have no special purchase on moral or ethical decisions; / a climate scientist
「A is no more B ~ than C is D: A가 B가 아니듯 C도 D가 아니다」
is **no more** qualified / to comment on health care reform / **than** a physicist is / to judge
대동사(= is qualified)
the causes of bee colony collapse.

02 The very features / [that create expertise in a specialized domain] / lead to ignorance
주어(선행사) 　주격 관계대명사절　　　　　　　　　　동사(복수)
in many others.

03 In some cases / lay people / — (farmers, fishermen, patients, native peoples) — / may
주어　　　　　　삽입구(주어 보충 설명)　　　　　　　동사
have relevant experiences / [that scientists can learn from]. // Indeed, in recent years,
목적어(선행사)　　목적격 관계대명사절
/ scientists have begun to recognize this: / the Arctic Climate Impact Assessment
includes observations / gathered from local native groups.
　　　　　　　　　과거분사구

04 So our trust needs to be limited, and focused. // It needs to be very *particular*. // Blind
trust will get us into at least **as** much trouble / **as** no trust at all.
「as + 원급 + as: ~만큼 …한」

05 But without some degree of trust in our designated experts / — the men and women /
「devote A to B: A를 B에 바치다」　　　　　　동격
[who **have devoted** their lives **to** sorting out tough questions / about the natural world
주격 관계대명사절(the men and women 수식)
we live in] — / we are paralyzed, / in effect not knowing **whether to make** ready for the
「whether to-V or not: ~할지 말지」
morning commute or not.

01 과학자들은 도덕적 혹은 윤리적 결정에 대한 특별한 강점purchase이 없으며, / 기후 과학자가 자격이 없는 것처럼 / 의료 개혁에 대해 견해를 밝힐 / 물리학자도 자격이 없다 / 꿀벌 집단의 붕괴collapse 원인을 판단할.

02 바로 그 특징feature이 / 전문화된specialize 영역에서의 전문지식을 만들어내는 / 여러 다른 영역의 무지ignorance로 이어진다.

03 어떤 경우에는, / 전문가가 아닌 사람들이 / 농부, 어부, 환자, 토착민 등 / 관련relevant 경험을 지니고 있을 수 있다 / 과학자들이 배울 수 있는. // 실제로 최근 들어 / 과학자들은 이 점을 인식하기 시작하여, / 북극 기후 영향 평가는 관찰을 포함한다 / 지역 토착 집단에게서 수집된gather.

04 그러므로 우리의 신뢰는 한정되고 초점이 맞춰질 필요가 있다. // 그것은 매우 '특정할' 필요가 있다. // 맹목적 신뢰는 최소한 우리를 문제에 봉착하게 할 것이다 / 전적인 불신만큼이나.

05 하지만 우리의 지정된designate 전문가들에 대한 어느 정도의 신뢰가 없으면 / 남자와 여자 / 어려운 질문들을 처리하는 데 자신의 생애를 바쳐온devote their lives to sorting out / 우리가 사는 자연 세계에 관한 / 우리는 마비되고, / 사실상in effect 아침 통근을 위해 준비해야 할지 말아야 할지도 모를 것이다.

구문 Check up

① The very features that create expertise in a specialized domain **lead / leads** to ignorance in many others.

주어가 복수명사인 The very features이므로 동사도 복수형인 lead가 적절하다. 주어와 동사 사이 that절은 주어를 꾸민다.

② In some cases lay people — farmers, fishermen, patients, native peoples — may have relevant experiences **that / what** scientists can learn from.

선행사 relevant experiences가 있으므로 관계대명사 that이 적절하다. what은 선행사가 없을 때 쓴다.

정답 ① lead ② that

20

STEP 1 • 수능에 *진짜* 나오는 *단어*

함축 의미 ➕

✔ 문제에 나오는 단어들을 확인하세요.

01	proverb	n. 속담	an African (✔ proverb)	아프리카 속담
02	historian	n. 역사가	the role of ( )s	역사가의 역할
03	glorify	v. 미화하다	( ) the past	과거를 미화하다
04	put across	~을 이해시키다, ~에게 전달하다	( ) ( ) the point of view	관점을 이해시키다
05	consumption	n. 소비	the present rate of human ( )	현재 인간 소비의 비율
06	unsustainable	a. 지속 불가한	( ) growth	(자원·환경적으로) 지속 불가한 성장
07	wasteland	n. 황무지, 불모지	desert and ( )	사막과 황무지
08	disposable	a. (마음대로) 이용 가능한, 처분 가능한	( ) for the demands of human population	인류의 필요를 위해 이용 가능한
09	accelerate	v. 가속화되다	the ( )ing demands	가속화되는 필요
10	cut down on	~을 줄이다	( ) ( ) ( ) consumption	소비를 줄이다
11	alter	v. 바꾸다	( ) lifestyles	생활 방식을 바꾸다
12	violation	n. 침해, 위반	a ( ) of human rights	인권 침해

➕ 본문 문장 속에서 단어들을 확인해 보세요.

But to ask for any change in human behaviour / — whether it be / to cut down on consumption, / alter lifestyles / or decrease population growth — / is seen as a violation of human rights.

하지만 인간의 행동에 그 어떤 변화라도 요구하는 것은 / 그것이 ~이든 간에 / 소비를 줄이는 것, / 생활 방식을 바꾸는 것, / 또는 인구 증가를 줄이는 것, / 인권 침해로 간주된다.

01	proverb	🖉 속담	an African proverb	아프리카 (속담)
02	historian		the role of historians	( )의 역할
03	glorify		glorify the past	과거를 ( )
04	put across		put across the point of view	관점을 ( )
05	consumption		the present rate of human consumption	현재 인간 ( )의 비율
06	unsustainable		unsustainable growth	( ) 성장
07	wasteland		desert and wasteland	사막과 ( )
08	disposable		disposable for the demands of human population	인류의 필요를 위해 ( )
09	accelerate		the accelerating demands	( ) 필요
10	cut down on		cut down on consumption	소비를 ( )
11	alter		alter lifestyles	생활 방식을 ( )
12	violation		a violation of human rights	인권 ( )

➕ 본문 문장 속에서 단어의 의미를 우리말로 해석해 보세요.

But to ask for any change in human behaviour / — whether it be / to cut down on consumption, / alter lifestyles / or decrease population growth — / is seen as a violation of human rights.

➔ 하지만 인간의 행동에 그 어떤 변화라도 요구하는 것은 / 그것이 ~이든 간에 / ▨▨▨▨▨▨▨▨▨▨, / ▨▨▨▨▨▨▨, / 또는 인구 증가를 줄이는 것, / ▨▨▨▨▨▨▨▨로 간주된다.

20 밑줄 친 the role of the 'lion's historians'가 다음 글에서 의미하는 바로 가장 적절한 것은?

There is an African proverb that says, 'Till the lions have their historians, tales of hunting will always glorify the hunter'. The proverb is about power, control and law making. Environmental journalists have to play the role of the 'lion's historians'. They have to put across the point of view of the environment to people who make the laws. They have to be the voice of wild India. The present rate of human consumption is completely unsustainable. Forest, wetlands, wastelands, coastal zones, eco-sensitive zones, they are all seen as disposable for the accelerating demands of human population. But to ask for any change in human behaviour — whether it be to cut down on consumption, alter lifestyles or decrease population growth — is seen as a violation of human rights. But at some point human rights become 'wrongs'. It's time we changed our thinking so that there is no difference between the rights of humans and the rights of the rest of the environment.

① uncovering the history of a species' biological evolution

② urging a shift to sustainable human behaviour for nature

③ fighting against widespread violations of human rights

④ rewriting history for more underrepresented people

⑤ restricting the power of environmental lawmakers

정답과 해설 p.18

01 There is an African proverb / [that says, / 'Till the lions have their historians, / tales of
  hunting will always glorify the hunter']. // The proverb is about power, control and law
  making.

02 Environmental journalists have to play the role of the 'lion's historians'. // They have
  to put across the point of view of the environment / to people [who make the laws]. //
  They have to be the voice of wild India.

03 The present rate of human consumption / is completely unsustainable. // Forest,
  wetlands, wastelands, coastal zones, eco-sensitive zones, / they are all seen as
  disposable / for the accelerating demands of human population.

04 But to ask for any change in human behaviour / — (whether it be / to cut down on
  consumption, / alter lifestyles / or decrease population growth) — / is seen as a
  violation of human rights.

05 But at some point / human rights become 'wrongs'. // It's time we changed our
  thinking / so that there is no difference / between the rights of humans and the rights
  of the rest of the environment.

01 아프리카 속담proverb이 있다 / ~라고 말하는 / '사자가 자신의 역사가historian를 둘 때까지, / 사냥 이야기는 항상
  사냥꾼을 미화한다glorify'. // 이 속담은 권력과 통제와 법 제정에 관한 것이다.

02 환경 저널리스트들은 '사자의 역사가' 역할을 해야 한다. // 그들은 환경의 관점을 이해시켜야put across 한다 / 법을
  만드는 사람들에게. // 그들은 인도 야생 자연의 목소리가 되어야 한다.

03 현재 인간 소비consumption의 비율은 / 완전히 지속 불가하다unsustainable. // 숲, 습지, 황무지wasteland, 해안 지대,
  환경 민감 지역, / 이것들은 모두 마음대로 쓰일 수 있다disposable고 여겨진다 / 인류의 가속화되는accelerate 필요를
  위해.

04 하지만 인간의 행동에 그 어떤 변화라도 요구하는 것은 / 그것이 ~이든 간에 / 소비를 줄이는 것cut down on, / 생활
  방식을 바꾸는 것alter, / 또는 인구 증가를 줄이는 것, / 인권 침해violation로 간주된다.

05 그러나 어느 지점에 이르면 / 인권은 '잘못된 것'이 된다. // 우리가 우리 생각을 바꿔야 할 때이다 / 차이가 없도록 / 인간의
  권리와 나머지 환경의 권리 사이에.

구문 Check up	① There is an African proverb that says, 'Till the lions have / will have their historians, tales of hunting will always glorify the hunter'.	② But ask / to ask for any change in human behaviour — whether it be to cut down on consumption, alter lifestyles or decrease population growth — is seen as a violation of human rights.
	시간과 조건의 부사절에서는 현재시제가 미래시제를 대신하므로 have가 적절하다.	동사 is seen 앞에 주어가 필요하므로 to ask가 적절하다.

정답 ① have ② to ask

21

STEP 1 • 수능에 *진짜* 나오는 *단어*

함축 의미 +

✔ 문제에 나오는 단어들을 확인하세요.

01	consequence	n. 결과	as a (✔ consequence)	그 결과
02	set out	제시하다, 착수하다	( ) ( ) milestones	획기적인 일을 제시하다
03	carry out	수행하다	( ) ( ) activities	활동을 수행하다
04	genius	n. 비범한 재능, 천재(성)	have a ( ) for selling things	물건을 파는 데 비범한 재능이 있다
05	compensate	v. 보상하다	do what's ( )d	보상받는 일을 하다
06	cold call	(주로 상품 구입을 위한) 권유 전화	make ( ) ( )	(물건을 사 달라고) 권유 전화를 걸다
07	inappropriate	a. 부적절한	( ) information	부적절한 정보
08	garbage	n. 쓰레기	throw out the ( )	쓰레기를 버리다
09	delight	v. 기뻐하다, 즐기다 n. 기쁨	( ) in communicating with people	사람들과 소통하기를 즐기다
10	dumb	a. 바보 같은, 멍청한	a ( ) process	바보 같은 과정

➕ 본문 문장 속에서 단어들을 확인해 보세요.

As a consequence, / they make the mistake of designing a process / that sets out milestones in the form of activities / that must be carried out during the sales cycle.

그 결과, / 그들은 과정을 기획하는 실수를 범한다 / 활동의 형태로 획기적인 일을 제시하는 / 판매 주기 동안 수행되어야 하는.

문제를 풀기 전에 단어들을 **30초** 동안 다시 확인하세요.

01	consequence	🖉 결과	as a consequence	그 (결과)
02	set out		set out milestones	획기적인 일을 ( )
03	carry out		carry out activities	활동을 ( )
04	genius		have a genius for selling things	물건을 파는 데 ( ) 이 있다
05	compensate		do what's compensated	( ) 일을 하다
06	cold call		make cold call	( )를 걸다
07	inappropriate		inappropriate information	( )정보
08	garbage		throw out the garbage	( )를 버리다
09	delight		delight in communicating with people	사람들과 소통하기를 ( )
10	dumb		a dumb process	( )과정

➕ 본문 문장 속에서 단어의 의미를 우리말로 해석해 보세요.

As a consequence, / they make the mistake of designing a process / that sets out milestones in the form of activities / that must be carried out during the sales cycle.

→ 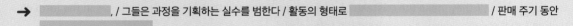 , / 그들은 과정을 기획하는 실수를 범한다 / 활동의 형태로   / 판매 주기 동안   .

21 밑줄 친 Garbage in, garbage out이 다음 글에서 의미하는 바로 가장 적절한 것은?

Many companies confuse activities and results. As a consequence, they make the mistake of designing a process that sets out milestones in the form of activities that must be carried out during the sales cycle. Salespeople have a genius for doing what's compensated rather than what's effective. If your process has an activity such as "submit proposal" or "make cold call," then that's just what your people will do. No matter that the calls were to the wrong customer or went nowhere. No matter that the proposal wasn't submitted at the right point in the buying decision or contained inappropriate information. The process asked for activity, and activity was what it got. Salespeople have done what was asked for. "Garbage in, garbage out" they will delight in telling you. "It's not our problem, it's this dumb process."

① In seeking results, compensation is the key to quality.

② Salespeople should join in a decision-making process.

③ Shared understanding does not always result in success.

④ Activities drawn from false information produce failure.

⑤ Processes focused on activities end up being ineffective.

정답과 해설 p.19

01 Many companies confuse activities and results. // As a consequence, / they make the mistake of designing a process / [that sets out milestones in the form of activities / {that 선행사(단수) ↑·········· 주격 관계대명사절 ↑·········· must be carried out during the sales cycle}]. 주격 관계대명사절

「A rather than B: B라기보다 A인(명사절 병렬)」

02 Salespeople have a genius / for doing [what's compensated] rather than [what's effective]. // If your process has an activity / such as "submit proposal" or "make cold call," / then that's just [what your people will do]. 명사절(주격보어)

03 No matter / that the calls were to the wrong customer or went nowhere. // No matter 접속사(~것) / that the proposal wasn't submitted at the right point in the buying decision / or 접속사(~것) 동사1 contained inappropriate information. 동사2

04 The process asked for activity, / and activity was what it got. // Salespeople have done 주어1 동사1 주어2 동사2 what was asked for. 관계대명사(~것)

05 "Garbage in, garbage out" / they will delight in telling you. // "It's not our problem, / 직접목적어 동명사 간접목적어 it's this dumb process."

01 많은 회사가 활동과 성과를 혼동한다. // 그 결과as a consequence, / 그들은 과정을 기획하는 실수를 범한다 / 활동의 형태로 획기적인 일을 제시하는set out / 판매 주기 동안 수행되어야 하는carry out.

02 판매원들은 비범한 재능genius이 있다 / 보상받는compensate 일을 하는 데 / 효과적인 일보다는. // 만약 당신의 과정에 활동이 있다면 / '제안 제출하기'나 '임의의 권유 전화 걸기make cold call'와 같은 / 그러면 그것이 바로 당신의 아랫사람들이 할 일이다.

03 문제가 아니다 / 전화가 잘못된 고객에게 갔거나 아무 성과를 보지 못했어도. // 문제가 아니다 / 제안이 구매 결정의 적절한 시점에 제출되지 않았거나 / 부적절한inappropriate 정보를 포함했더라도.

04 과정이 활동을 요구했을 뿐이고, / 활동은 그것으로 인한 것이었다. // 판매원들은 요구받은 일을 한 것이다.

05 "쓰레기를 넣으니 쓰레기가 나오지요Garbage in, garbage out"라고 / 그들은 당신에게 말하기를 즐길delight 것이다. // "그것은 우리의 문제가 아니라 / 이 바보 같은dumb 과정 때문이에요."

구문 Check up

① As a consequence, they make the mistake of designing a process that set / sets out milestones in the form of activities that must be carried out ~.

주격 관계대명사절의 동사는 선행사와 수일치시킨다. 여기서 that절의 선행사는 단수명사인 a process이므로, that 뒤에는 단수동사인 sets가 적절하다.

② Salespeople have done that / what was asked for.

have done의 목적어와 was asked for의 주어를 동시에 할 수 있는 단어가 필요하므로 선행사를 포함한 관계대명사 what이 적절하다.

정답 ① sets ② what

 Review

☑ 종합 성적표

구분	공부한 날 ❶	결과 분석			
		출처	풀이 시간 ❷	채점 결과 (O, X)	틀린 이유 ❸
Day 1 글의 목적 + 심경/분위기	월 일	2024학년도 대수능 18번	분 초		
		2023학년도 대수능 18번	분 초		
		2023학년도 6월 19번	분 초		
		2022학년도 대수능 19번	분 초		
		2022학년도 6월 19번	분 초		
		2021학년도 6월 19번	분 초		
		2020학년도 6월 19번	분 초		
Day 2 필자의 주장 + 글의 요지	월 일	2024학년도 6월 22번	분 초		
		2023학년도 6월 22번	분 초		
		2022학년도 대수능 20번	분 초		
		2022학년도 9월 22번	분 초		
		2021학년도 9월 20번	분 초		
		2021학년도 6월 22번	분 초		
		2020학년도 대수능 22번	분 초		
Day 3 함축 의미	월 일	2024학년도 대수능 21번	분 초		
		2024학년도 9월 21번	분 초		
		2024학년도 6월 21번	분 초		
		2023학년도 9월 21번	분 초		
		2022학년도 대수능 21번	분 초		
		2021학년도 대수능 21번	분 초		
		2020학년도 6월 21번	분 초		

3일간
공부한 내용을
다시 보니,
……

❶ **매일 지문을 하루 계획에 맞춰 풀었다. vs. 내가 한 약속을 못 지켰다.**

<매3영 수능기출>은 단순 문제풀이를 위한 책이 아니라, 매일 규칙적으로 영어를 공부하는 습관을 잡는 책입니다. 따라서 푸는 문제 개수는 상황에 따라 다르더라도 '매일' 학습하는 것이 중요합니다.

❷ **주어진 시간을 자꾸 넘긴다?**

풀이 시간이 계속해서 권장 시간을 넘긴다면 실전 훈련이 부족하다는 신호이므로, 매일의 훈련을 실전처럼 긴장감 있게 해야 합니다. 한편으로, 오답의 이유를 철저히 분석하고 맞춤 공부법을 찾아갑니다.

❸ ⭐**틀린 이유 맞춤 솔루션:** 오답 이유에 따라 다음 해결책을 참고하세요.

(1) 해석이 잘 안 돼서
  ▶ <STEP 1 단어>, <STEP 3 지문 복습>을 정독하며 단어/구문 실력을 길러보세요.

(2) 해석은 되는데, 지문 이해가 안 돼서
  ▶ [정답 및 해설]의 <지문 자세히 보기>를 정독하며 수능 지문의 논리 전개 방식을 익혀보세요.

(3) 이해는 했는데, 선택지로 연결을 못 해서
  ▶ [정답 및 해설]의 <오답풀이>, <유형플러스>를 통해 함정에 주의하는 방법을 숙지하세요.

❗ **결론적으로,** 내가 **취약한 부분**은 [   ] 이다.
취약점을 보완하기 위해서 나는 [   ] 을/를 해야겠다.
복습 때 다시 봐야 할 문항과, 다시 점검할 사항이 있는 페이지는 지금 바로 접어 두세요.

<매3영>이 제시하는 3단계로

유형 3일 훈련

DAY

04~06

공부한 날		출처	페이지
DAY 4	월 일	2024학년도 9월 23번 2023학년도 대수능 23번 2022학년도 6월 23번 2021학년도 대수능 23번 2021학년도 9월 23번 2020학년도 대수능 23번 2020학년도 6월 23번	95
DAY 5	월 일	2024학년도 6월 24번 2023학년도 대수능 24번 2023학년도 9월 24번 2022학년도 대수능 24번 2021학년도 대수능 24번 2021학년도 9월 24번 2020학년도 9월 24번	123
DAY 6	월 일	2024학년도 6월 26번 2023학년도 9월 26번 2022학년도 대수능 25번 2021학년도 9월 26번 2021학년도 6월 27번 2020학년도 대수능 28번 2020학년도 6월 26번	151

22

STEP 1 • 수능에 *진짜* 나오는 *단어*

✔ 문제에 나오는 단어들을 확인하세요.

01	commercial	a. 민영의, 상업적인	a (✔ commercial) radio station	민영 라디오 방송국
02	advertiser	n. 광고주	a group of ( )s	광고주 집단
03	demographic	a. 인구 통계적인	( ) profile	인구 통계적인 개요
04	quantity	n. 양, 크기	the ( ) of an audience	관객의 크기
05	mass	n. 집단, 대중, 대규모	aggregated as a ( )	집단으로 모인
06	metric	n. 측정 기준, 미터법	the most significant ( )	가장 중요한 측정 기준
07	profitable	a. 수익성 있는	( ) ends	수익성 있는 목적
08	attempt	v. 시도하다, 노력하다	( ) to increase their profits	수익을 극대화하려고 노력하다
09	rely (up)on ~ to ...	~가 …할 것이라 믿다	( ) ( ) you ( ) finish the job	네가 그 일을 끝마칠 거라고 믿다
10	mark out	~을 구별 짓다, 표시하다	What ( )s her ( ) from the other students?	그녀를 다른 학생들과 구별 짓는 게 뭐니?
11	restricted	a. (규모나 수량이) 제한된	a ( ) number of stations	제한된 수의 방송국
12	feature	n. 특징	the core ( )s	핵심 특징
13	attract	v. 매혹시키다, 끌다	( ) large audiences	많은 청중을 매혹시키다

⊕ 본문 문장 속에서 단어들을 확인해 보세요.

The primary purpose of commercial music radio broadcasting / is to deliver an audience to a group of advertisers and sponsors.

민영 음악 라디오 방송의 주된 목적은 / 청취자를 광고주와 후원자 집단으로 인도하는 것이다.

문제를 풀기 전에 단어들을 **30초** 동안 다시 확인하세요.

01	commercial	✎ 민영의, 상업적인	a commercial radio station	(민영) 라디오 방송국
02	advertiser		a group of advertisers	( ) 집단
03	demographic		demographic profile	( ) 개요
04	quantity		the quantity of an audience	관객의 ( )
05	mass		aggregated as a mass	( )으로 모인
06	metric		the most significant metric	가장 중요한 ( )
07	profitable		profitable ends	( ) 목적
08	attempt		attempt to increase their profits	수익을 극대화하려고 ( )
09	rely (up)on ~ to ...		rely upon you to finish the job	네가 그 일을 끝마칠 거라고 ( )
10	mark out		What marks her out from the other students?	그녀를 다른 학생들과 ( )게 뭐니?
11	restricted		a restricted number of stations	( ) 수의 방송국
12	feature		the core features	핵심 ( )
13	attract		attract large audiences	많은 청중을 ( )

⊕ **본문 문장 속에서 단어의 의미를 우리말로 해석해 보세요.**

The primary purpose of commercial music radio broadcasting / is to deliver an audience to a group of advertisers and sponsors.

➜ ▨▨▨ 음악 라디오 방송의 주된 목적은 / 청취자를 ▨▨▨▨▨▨▨▨▨으로 인도하는 것이다.

22 다음 글의 주제로 가장 적절한 것은?

The primary purpose of commercial music radio broadcasting is to deliver an audience to a group of advertisers and sponsors. To achieve commercial success, that audience must be as large as possible. More than any other characteristics (such as demographic or psychographic profile, purchasing power, level of interest, degree of satisfaction, quality of attention or emotional state), the quantity of an audience aggregated as a mass is the most significant metric for broadcasters seeking to make music radio for profitable ends. As a result, broadcasters attempt to maximise their audience size by playing music that is popular, or — at the very least — music that can be relied upon not to cause audiences to switch off their radio or change the station. Audience retention is a key value (if not the key value) for many music programmers and for radio station management. In consequence, a high degree of risk aversion frequently marks out the 'successful' radio music programmer. Playlists are restricted, and often very small.

*aggregate: 모으다   **aversion: 싫어함

① features of music playlists appealing to international audiences

② influence of advertisers on radio audiences' musical preferences

③ difficulties of increasing audience size in radio music programmes

④ necessity of satisfying listeners' diverse needs in the radio business

⑤ outcome of music radio businesses' attempts to attract large audiences

정답과 해설 p.21

01 The primary purpose of commercial music radio broadcasting / is to deliver an
주어   동사(단수)
audience to a group of advertisers and sponsors.   주격보어(~것)

02 To achieve commercial success, / that audience must be as large as possible. // More
부사적 용법(목적)   「as + 원급 + as possible: 가급적 ~한/하게」
than any other characteristics / (such as demographic or psychographic profile, /
purchasing power, / level of interest, / degree of satisfaction, / quality of attention /
or emotional state), / the quantity of an audience aggregated as a mass / is the most
                        주어   과거분사구   「the + 최상급: 가장 ~한」
significant metric for broadcasters / seeking to make music radio for profitable ends.
                                        현재분사구   동사(단수)

03 As a result, / broadcasters attempt to maximise their audience size / by playing music
[that is popular], / or — at the very least — music / [that can be relied upon / not to
주격 관계대명사절   동격   주격 관계대명사절
cause audiences to switch off their radio or change the station]. // Audience retention
                                              to
「cause + 목적어 + to부정사: ~이 …하게 하다」
is a key value / (if not the key value) / for many music programmers and for radio
삽입구
station management.

04 In consequence, / a high degree of risk aversion / frequently marks out the 'successful'
                    주어   동사(단수)
radio music programmer. // Playlists are restricted, and often very small.

01 민영commercial 음악 라디오 방송의 주된 목적은 / 청취자를 광고주advertiser와 후원자 집단으로 인도하는 것이다.

02 상업적 성공을 달성하려면, / 그 청취자는 가능한 한 대규모여야 한다. // 다른 어떤 특성보다도, / (인구 통계학적
demographic 또는 심리 통계학적 개요, / 구매력, / 관심 수준, / 만족도, / 주목의 질, / 또는 정서 상태 같은) /
집단mass으로 모인 청취자의 크기quantity는 / 방송 진행자에게 가장 중요한 측정 기준metric이다 / 음악 라디오가 수익
목적profitable end에 맞게 만들려는.

03 결과적으로 / 방송 진행자는 청취자의 규모를 극대화하려고 애쓴다attempt / 인기 있는 음악을 틀어줘서 / 혹은 적어도
음악 / 여겨질 수 있는be relied upon / 청취자가 라디오를 끄거나 채널을 바꾸게 하지 않을 거라고. // 청취자 보유는
하나의 핵심 가치이다 / (유일한 핵심 가치까지는 아니더라도) / 많은 음악 프로그램 제작자와 라디오 방송국 경영진에.

04 그 결과 / 높은 수준의 모험 회피는 / 흔히 '성공한' 라디오 음악 프로그램 제작자를 구분 짓는다mark out. // 방송 목록은
제한적restricted이고, 흔히 매우 적다.

구문 Check up

① To achieve commercial success, that audience must be largely / large as possible.

② More than any other characteristics, the quantity of an audience aggregated / is aggregated as a mass is the most significant metric for broadcasters.

must be의 보어 역할을 할 형용사 large가 적절하다.

an audience의 수식어구로 과거분사 aggregated가 적절하다. 문장 전체의 술어는 뒤에 나오는 is이다.

정답 ① large ② aggregated

23

STEP 1 · 수능에 *진짜* 나오는 *단어*

✔ 문제에 나오는 단어들을 확인하세요.

01	disclosure	n. 공개, 폭로	the (✔ disclosure) of secret information	비밀 정보의 공개
02	aggressive	a. 공격적인, 공세의, 대단히 적극적인	( ) forms of regulation	공격적인 형태의 규제
03	flexibility	n. 유연성	the ( ) of labor market	노동 시장의 유연성
04	operation	n. 작용	the ( ) of free markets	자유 시장의 작용
05	blunt	a. (끝이) 무딘, 뭉툭한	a ( ) sword	무딘 칼
06	neglect	v. 무시하다, 소홀히 하다	( ) diversity	다양성을 무시하다
07	unintended	a. 의도하지 않은	( ) adverse effects	의도하지 않은 역효과
08	efficiency	n. 효율	energy ( ) requirements	에너지 효율 요건
09	publicize	v. 공개하다, 알리다	( ) the safety characteristics of cars	자동차의 안전 특성을 공개하다
10	attribute	n. 속성, 특성	three ( )s of color	색의 3가지 속성
11	inform A of B	A에게 B를 알리다	( ) customers ( ) the calories in their meals	소비자들에게 식사에 들어 있는 칼로리를 알려주다
12	unconcerned	a. 신경 쓰지 않는	those who are ( ) about calories	칼로리에 신경 쓰지 않는 사람들
13	interfere with	~을 방해하다	( ) ( ) the decision-making process	의사 결정 과정을 방해하다

➕ 본문 문장 속에서 단어들을 확인해 보세요.

Regulatory mandates are blunt swords; / they tend to neglect diversity / and may have serious unintended adverse effects.

규제하는 명령은 무딘 칼이다 / 그것들은 다양성을 무시하는 경향이 있으며, / 의도하지 않은 심각한 역효과를 발생시킬 수도 있다.

문제를 풀기 전에 단어들을 **30초** 동안 다시 확인하세요.

01	disclosure	✏ 공개, 폭로	the disclosure of secret information	비밀 정보의 (공개)
02	aggressive		aggressive forms of regulation	( ) 형태의 규제
03	flexibility		the flexibility of labor market	노동 시장의 ( )
04	operation		the operation of free markets	자유 시장의 ( )
05	blunt		a blunt sword	( ) 칼
06	neglect		neglect diversity	다양성을 ( )
07	unintended		unintended adverse effects	( ) 역효과
08	efficiency		energy efficiency requirements	에너지 ( ) 요건
09	publicize		publicize the safety characteristics of cars	자동차의 안전 특성을 ( )
10	attribute		three attributes of color	색의 3가지 ( )
11	inform A of B		inform customers of the calories in their meals	소비자들에게 식사에 들어 있는 칼로리를 ( )
12	unconcerned		those who are unconcerned about calories	칼로리에 ( ) 사람들
13	interfere with		interfere with the decision-making process	의사 결정 과정을 ( )

➕ **본문 문장 속에서 단어의 의미를 우리말로 해석해 보세요.**

Regulatory mandates are blunt swords; / they tend to neglect diversity / and may have serious unintended adverse effects.

→ 규제하는 명령은 _____ 이다 / 그것들은 _____ 경향이 있으며, / _____ 를 발생시킬 수도 있다.

23 다음 글의 주제로 가장 적절한 것은?

An important advantage of disclosure, as opposed to more aggressive forms of regulation, is its flexibility and respect for the operation of free markets. Regulatory mandates are blunt swords; they tend to neglect diversity and may have serious unintended adverse effects. For example, energy efficiency requirements for appliances may produce goods that work less well or that have characteristics that consumers do not want. Information provision, by contrast, respects freedom of choice. If automobile manufacturers are required to measure and publicize the safety characteristics of cars, potential car purchasers can trade safety concerns against other attributes, such as price and styling. If restaurant customers are informed of the calories in their meals, those who want to lose weight can make use of the information, leaving those who are unconcerned about calories unaffected. Disclosure does not interfere with, and should even promote, the autonomy (and quality) of individual decision-making.

*mandate: 명령 **adverse: 거스르는 ***autonomy: 자율성

① steps to make public information accessible to customers

② benefits of publicizing information to ensure free choices

③ strategies for companies to increase profits in a free market

④ necessities of identifying and analyzing current industry trends

⑤ effects of diversified markets on reasonable customer choices

정답과 해설 **p.21**

01 An important advantage of disclosure, / as opposed to more aggressive forms of
주어(단수)　　　　　　　　　「as opposed to + (동)명사: ~와는 반대로」
regulation, / is its flexibility and respect for the operation of free markets.
　　　　　동사　　주격보어　　　　　　전치사구

02 Regulatory mandates are blunt swords; / they tend to neglect diversity / and may have
　　　　　　　　　　　　　　　　　동사구1　　　　　　　　　동사구2
serious unintended adverse effects. // For example, / energy efficiency requirements
for appliances / may produce goods / [that work less well] / or [that have characteristics
　　　　　　　　선행사(복수)　　　　　　　　　주격 관계대명사절
that consumers do not want].

03 Information provision, / by contrast, / respects freedom of choice. // If automobile
manufacturers are required to measure and publicize the safety characteristics of cars,
　　　　　「be required + to부정사: ~하도록 요구받다」
/ potential car purchasers can trade safety concerns against other attributes, / such as
price and styling. // If restaurant customers are informed of the calories in their meals,
주어(~한 사람들)　　접속사(조건)　　　　「A be informed of B: A가 B를 통지받다」
/ those [who want to lose weight] / can make use of the information, / leaving those
　　　　　　　　　　　　　　　　　　동사구　　　　목적어　　　　　분사구문　　목적어
who are unconcerned about calories unaffected.
　　　　　　　　　　　목적격보어(형용사)

04 Disclosure does not interfere with, / and should even promote, / the autonomy (and
　　　　　　　　동사구1　　　　　　　동사구2(삽입구)　　　　　공통 목적어
quality) of individual decision-making.

01 공개disclosure의 중요한 이점은 / 더 공격적인aggressive 형태의 규제와는 반대로 / 자유 시장의 작용operation에 대한 유연성flexibility과 존중이다.

02 규제하는 명령은 무딘blunt 칼이다 / 그것들은 다양성을 무시하는neglect 경향이 있으며, / 의도하지 않은unintended 심각한 역효과를 발생시킬 수도 있다. // 예를 들어, / 가전제품에 대한 에너지 효율efficiency 요건은 / 제품을 만들어 낼 수도 있다 / 덜 잘 작동하거나 / 소비자가 원하지 않는 특성을 가진.

03 정보 제공은 / 반대로 / 선택의 자유를 존중한다. // 자동차 제조업체가 자동차의 안전 특성을 측정하고 공개하기를publicize 요구받는다면 / 잠재적인 자동차 구매자는 안전에 대한 우려를 다른 속성attribute과 맞바꿀 수 있다 / 가격과 스타일 같은. // 식당 손님들이 식사에 들어 있는 칼로리를 안내받는다면be informed of the calories, / 살을 빼고 싶은 사람들은 / 그 정보를 이용할 수 있다 / 칼로리에 신경 쓰지 않는unconcerned 사람들을 영향 받지 않은 상태로 두면서.

04 공개는 방해하지interfere with 않으며 / 심지어 촉진할 것이다 / 개인 의사 결정의 자율성(과 품질)을.

구문 Check up	① For example, energy efficiency requirements for appliances may produce goods that work less well or that has / have characteristics that consumers do not want.	② If restaurant customers inform / are informed of the calories in their meals, those who want to lose weight can make use of the information.
	or로 연결된 2개의 관계대명사 that절의 선행사가 복수명사인 goods이므로, have가 답으로 적절하다.	주어인 restaurant customers가 칼로리에 관해 '통지받는' 대상이므로, 수동태인 are informed가 적절하다.

정답 ① have ② are informed

24

STEP 1 • 수능에 진짜 나오는 단어

글의 주제 ⊕

✔ 문제에 나오는 단어들을 확인하세요.

01	effortlessly	*ad.* 쉽게	move (✔ effortlessly)	쉽게 이동하다
02	absorption	*n.* 몰입, 흡수	( ) in a story	이야기로의 몰입
03	narratively	*ad.* 이야기식으로	( ) structured	이야기식으로 구조화된
04	identify with	~와 동일시하다	( ) ( ) characters in the movie	영화 속 등장인물과 동일시하다
05	adolescence	*n.* 청소년기, 사춘기	grow towards ( )	청소년기로 성장하다
06	regress	*v.* 퇴행하다	( ) to our childhood	아동기로 퇴행하다
07	derive from	~에서 기인하다, 얻다	( ) ( ) experience	경험에서 기인하다
08	metaphorical	*a.* 은유적인	( ) expressions	은유적 표현
09	transformation	*n.* 변신	( )s of our selves	우리 자아의 변신

⊕ 본문 문장 속에서 단어들을 확인해 보세요.

The taking of roles in a narratively structured game of pirates / is not very different / than the taking of roles in identifying with characters / as one watches a movie.

이야기식으로 구조화된 해적 게임에서 역할을 맡는 것은 / 크게 다르지 않다 / 등장인물과 동일시하며 역할을 맡는 것과 / 영화를 감상하면서.

01	effortlessly	✏️ 쉽게	move effortlessly	(쉽게) 이동하다
02	absorption		absorption in a story	이야기로의 ( )
03	narratively		narratively structured	( ) 구조화된
04	identify with		identify with characters in the movie	영화 속 등장인물과 ( )
05	adolescence		grow towards adolescence	( )로 성장하다
06	regress		regress to our childhood	아동기로 ( )
07	derive from		derive from experience	경험에서 ( )
08	metaphorical		metaphorical expressions	( ) 표현
09	transformation		transformations of our selves	우리 자아의 ( )

➕ **본문 문장 속에서 단어의 의미를 우리말로 해석해 보세요.**

The taking of roles in a narratively structured game of pirates / is not very different / than the taking of roles in identifying with characters / as one watches a movie.

→ ▓▓▓▓▓▓▓▓▓▓ 해적 게임에서 역할을 맡는 것은 / 크게 다르지 않다 / ▓▓▓▓▓▓▓▓▓▓ 역할을 맡는 것과 / 영화를 감상하면서.

24 다음 글의 주제로 가장 적절한 것은?

Children can move effortlessly between play and absorption in a story, as if both are forms of the same activity. The taking of roles in a narratively structured game of pirates is not very different than the taking of roles in identifying with characters as one watches a movie. It might be thought that, as they grow towards adolescence, people give up childhood play, but this is not so. Instead, the bases and interests of this activity change and develop to playing and watching sports, to the fiction of plays, novels, and movies, and nowadays to video games. In fiction, one can enter possible worlds. When we experience emotions in such worlds, this is not a sign that we are being incoherent or regressed. It derives from trying out metaphorical transformations of our selves in new ways, in new worlds, in ways that can be moving and important to us.

*pirate: 해적 **incoherent: 일관되지 않은

① relationship between play types and emotional stability

② reasons for identifying with imaginary characters in childhood

③ ways of helping adolescents develop good reading habits

④ continued engagement in altered forms of play after childhood

⑤ effects of narrative structures on readers' imaginations

정답과 해설 **p.22**

01 Children can move effortlessly / between play and absorption in a story, / as if both are
「between A and B: A와 B 사이」　　　　　　　　　　　접속사(마치 ~인 것처럼)
forms of the same activity. // The taking of roles in a narratively structured game of
　　　　　　　　　　　　　　주어
pirates / is not very different / than the taking of roles in identifying with characters /
　　　　동사(단수)
as one watches a movie.
접속사(~하면서)

가주어-진주어 구문
02 It might be thought / [that, (as they grow towards adolescence), / people give up
　　　　　　　　　　　　　　　　　　부사절
childhood play], / but this is not so.

03 Instead, / the bases and interests of this activity change and develop / to playing and
　　　　　주어　　　　　　　　　↑　　　　　　　　동사구(복수)　　　　　　전치사구1
watching sports, / to the fiction of plays, novels, and movies, / and nowadays to video
　　　　　　　　전치사구2　　　　　　　　　　　　　　　　　　　　　　　　　부사구3
games.

04 In fiction, / one can enter possible worlds. // When we experience emotions in such
worlds, / this is not a sign / [that we are being incoherent or regressed].
　　　　　　　　　　　동격

05 It derives from trying out metaphorical transformations of our selves / in new ways, /
in new ways, / in ways [that can be moving and important to us].
　　　　　선행사　　　주격 관계대명사절

01 아이들은 쉽게effortlessly 이동한다 / (역할) 놀이와 이야기로의 몰입absorption 사이를 / 그 둘이 같은 활동의
　　형태인 것처럼. // 이야기식으로narratively 구조화된 해적 게임에서 역할을 맡는 것은 / 크게 다르지 않다 / 등장인물과
　　동일시하며identify with characters 역할을 맡는 것과 / 영화를 감상할 때.

02 여겨질 수도 있겠지만 / 그들이 청소년기adolescence로 성장하면서 / 사람들은 아동기의 놀이를 그만둔다고 / 이는
　　그렇지 않다.

03 대신에, / 이런 활동의 기반과 흥미가 바뀌고 발전한다 / 스포츠 활동과 관람으로 / 연극, 소설, 영화의 허구로, / 그리고
　　최근에는 비디오 게임으로.

04 허구에서 / 사람들은 있을법한 세계로 들어갈 수 있다. // 우리가 그런 세계에서 감정들을 경험하면, / 이는 신호가 아니다 /
　　우리가 일관되지 않다거나 퇴행하고regress 있다는.

05 그것은 우리 자아의 은유적 변신metaphorical transformation을 시도하는 것에서 기인한다derive from / 새로운
　　방식으로, / 새로운 세계에서, / 우리에게 감동적이고 중요할 수 있는 방식으로.

구문 Check up

① The taking of roles in a narratively structured game of
pirates is / are not very different than the taking of
roles in identifying with characters as one watches a
movie.

주어가 The taking이라는 단수명사이므로 is가 적절하다.

② When we experience emotions in such worlds, this is
not a sign that / which we are being incoherent or
regressed.

we are being incoherent or regressed는 앞에 나오는 a sign과 내용상 같
은 완전한 명사절이다. 따라서 동격의 접속사 that이 적절하다.

정답 ① is ② that

25 STEP 1 · 수능에 진짜 나오는 단어

✔️ 문제에 나오는 단어들을 확인하세요.

01	arise	v. 발생하다	when difficulties (✔️ arise)	어려움이 발생할 때
02	think of A as B	A를 B로 생각하다	( ) ( ) her ( ) one of the family	그녀를 가족의 일원으로 생각하다
03	assign	v. 할당하다	( ) tasks to people	사람들에게 작업을 할당하다
04	automate	v. 자동화하다	tasks that can be ( )d	자동화될 수 있는 작업
05	end up	결국 ~이 되다	( ) ( ) behaving like a machine	결국 기계처럼 행동하게 되다
06	capability	n. 능력	human ( )ies	인간의 능력
07	precision	n. 정밀함	with ( )	정밀하게
08	accuracy	n. 정확성	with ( )	정확하게
09	take advantage of	~을 이용하다	( ) ( ) ( ) human strengths and capabilities	인간의 강점과 능력을 이용하다
10	rely upon	~에 의존하다	( ) ( ) machines	기계에 의존하다
11	genetically	ad. 유전적으로	( ) modified	유전적으로 변형된
12	unsuited	a. 부적합한	( ) for the task	그 과업에 부적합한

➕ 본문 문장 속에서 단어들을 확인해 보세요.

This ends up requiring people / to behave in machine-like fashion, / in ways that differ from human capabilities.

이것은 결국 사람들에게 요구하게 된다 / 기계와 똑같이 행동할 것을 / 즉 인간의 능력과는 다른 방식으로.

문제를 풀기 전에 단어들을 **30초** 동안 다시 확인하세요.

01	arise	✎ 발생하다	when difficulties arise	어려움이 (발생할) 때
02	think of A as B		think of her as one of the family	그녀를 가족의 일원으로 ( )
03	assign		assign tasks to people	사람들에게 작업을 ( )
04	automate		tasks that can be automated	( ) 수 있는 작업
05	end up		end up behaving like a machine	( ) 기계처럼 행동하게 ( )
06	capability		human capabilities	인간의 ( )
07	precision		with precision	( )하게
08	accuracy		with accuracy	( )하게
09	take advantage of		take advantage of human strengths and capabilities	인간의 강점과 능력을 ( )
10	rely upon		rely upon machines	기계에 ( )
11	genetically		genetically modified	( ) 변형된
12	unsuited		unsuited for the task	그 과업에 ( )

➕ 본문 문장 속에서 단어의 의미를 우리말로 해석해 보세요.

This ends up requiring people / to behave in machine-like fashion, / in ways that differ from human capabilities.

➔ 이것은 ▓▓▓▓▓▓▓▓▓▓▓▓▓ / 기계와 똑같이 행동할 것을 / 즉 ▓▓▓▓▓▓▓▓▓▓▓▓▓ 방식으로.

25 다음 글의 주제로 가장 적절한 것은?

Difficulties arise when we do not think of people and machines as collaborative systems, but assign whatever tasks can be automated to the machines and leave the rest to people. This ends up requiring people to behave in machine-like fashion, in ways that differ from human capabilities. We expect people to monitor machines, which means keeping alert for long periods, something we are bad at. We require people to do repeated operations with the extreme precision and accuracy required by machines, again something we are not good at. When we divide up the machine and human components of a task in this way, we fail to take advantage of human strengths and capabilities but instead rely upon areas where we are genetically, biologically unsuited. Yet, when people fail, they are blamed.

① difficulties of overcoming human weaknesses to avoid failure

② benefits of allowing machines and humans to work together

③ issues of allocating unfit tasks to humans in automated systems

④ reasons why humans continue to pursue machine automation

⑤ influences of human actions on a machine's performance

정답과 해설 **p.23**

01 Difficulties arise / when we do not think of people and machines as collaborative
　　주어　　　　　　　동사　　접속사(~할 때)　　동사1
systems, / but assign [whatever tasks can be automated to the machines] / and leave
　　　　　　동사2　　　목적어(복합관계형용사: 어떤 ~이든지)　　　　　　　　　　　동사3
the rest to people.

02 This **ends up requiring** people / to behave in machine-like fashion, / in ways [that
　　　「end up + 동명사: 결국 ~이 되다」
differ from human capabilities].
주격 관계대명사절

03 We expect people to monitor machines, / which means keeping alert for long periods, /
　　　　　　　　　　　　선행사　　　　　계속적 용법　　동명사구(목적어)
something [we are bad at].
선행사　　　　　　목적격 관계대명사절

04 We require people to do repeated operations / with the extreme precision and accuracy
　　　　　　　　　　　　　　　　　　　　　　　　= extremely precisely and accurately
/ required by machines, / again something [we are not good at].
과거분사구　　　　　선행사　　　　　목적격 관계대명사절

05 When we divide up the machine and human components of a task / in this way, / we
fail to take advantage of human strengths and capabilities / but instead rely upon
동사1　　　　　　　　　　　　　　　　　　　　　　　　　　　　　　동사2
areas / [where we are genetically, biologically unsuited].
선행사　　　　　　　관계부사절

06 Yet, / when people fail, / they are blamed.

---

01 어려움이 발생한다arise / 우리가 사람과 기계를 협업 시스템으로 생각하지think of people and machines as collaborative systems 않고 / 자동화될automate 수 있는 작업은 무엇이든 기계에 할당하고assign / 그 나머지를 사람들에게 맡길 때.

02 이것은 결국 사람들에게 요구하게 된다end up requiring people / 기계와 똑같이 행동할 것을 / 즉 인간의 능력capability과는 다른 방식으로.

03 우리는 사람들이 기계를 감시하기를 기대하는데, / 이는 오랫동안 경계를 게을리하지 않는 것을 의미한다 / 우리가 잘하지 못하는 것인.

04 우리는 사람들에게 반복적인 작업을 할 것을 요구하는데 / 몹시 정밀하고 정확하게with precision and accuracy / 기계에 의해 요구되는 (정도의) / 이 또한 우리가 잘하지 못하는 것이다.

05 우리가 어떤 과제의 기계적 구성요소와 인간적 구성요소를 나눌 때 / 이런 식으로 / 우리는 인간의 강점과 능력을 이용하take advantage of 못하고, / 그 대신 영역에 의존하게rely upon 되는 것이다 / 우리가 유전적으로genetically, 생물학적으로 부적합한unsuited.

06 하지만, / 사람들이 실패할 때, / 그들은 비난을 받는다.

구문 Check up

① Difficulties arise when we assign whatever / however tasks can be automated to the machines and leave the rest to people.

뒤에 관사 없는 명사로 시작하는 완전한 절이 나오는 것으로 보아 복합관계형용사 whatever(어떤 ~이든지)가 적절하다. however는 「however + 형/부 + 주어 + 동사」 어순으로 쓰인다.

② This ends up requiring people to behave in machine-like fashion, in ways how / that differ from human capabilities.

뒤에 주어 없는 불완전한 절이 이어지는 것으로 보아 주격 관계대명사 that이 적절하다.

정답 ① whatever ② that

26

STEP 1 • 수능에 진짜 나오는 단어

✔ 문제에 나오는 단어들을 확인하세요.

01	philosopher	n. 철학자	influenced by (✔ philosopher)s	철학자들에 의해 영향을 받은
02	credit A with B	A에게 B가 있다고 믿다	( ) individuals ( ) creativity	개인에게 창의력이 있다고 믿다
03	genius	n. 천재	a mathematical ( )	수학 천재
04	originality	n. 독창성	people with ( )	독창성을 가진 사람들
05	eliminate	v. 배제하다, 없애다	be ( )d from consideration	고려로부터 배제되다
06	trace	v. (기원이나 원인을) 추적하다	be ( )d to their genes	유전자에서 그 기원을 추적하다
07	embody	v. 구현하다	( ) the variety of social and cultural influences	사회적 및 문화적 영향의 다양성을 구현하다
08	individuality	n. 개인성, 개성	express your ( )	당신의 개성을 표현하다
09	religious	a. 종교적인	( ) belief	종교적 믿음
10	grammatical	a. 문법적인, 문법에 맞는	( ) errors	문법적 오류

✚ 본문 문장 속에서 단어들을 확인해 보세요.

Thoughts, / original and conventional, / are identified with individuals, / and the special things / that individuals are and do / are traced to their genes and their brains.

사상은, / 독창적이든 종래의 것이든 / 개인과 동일시되며, / 특별한 것은 / 개인이 ~이고 개인이 행하는 / 그 사람의 유전자와 두뇌에서 그 기원을 찾는다.

문제를 풀기 전에 단어들을 **30초** 동안 다시 확인하세요.

01	philosopher	🖊 철학자	influenced by philosophers	(철학자)들에 의해 영향을 받은
02	credit A with B		credit individuals with creativity	개인에게 창의력이 있다고 ( )
03	genius		a mathematical genius	수학 ( )
04	originality		people with originality	( )을 가진 사람들
05	eliminate		be eliminated from consideration	고려로부터 ( )
06	trace		be traced to their genes	유전자에서 그 기원을 ( )
07	embody		embody the variety of social and cultural influences	사회적 및 문화적 영향의 다양성을 ( )
08	individuality		express your individuality	당신의 ( )을 표현하다
09	religious		religious belief	( ) 믿음
10	grammatical		grammatical errors	( ) 오류

➕ **본문 문장 속에서 단어의 의미를 우리말로 해석해 보세요.**

Thoughts, / original and conventional, / are identified with individuals, / and the special things / that individuals are and do / are traced to their genes and their brains.

➡ 사상은, / 독창적이든 종래의 것이든 / 개인과 동일시되며, / 특별한 것은 / 개인이 ~이고 개인이 행하는 / ▨▨▨▨▨▨▨▨▨▨ ▨▨▨▨▨▨.

26 다음 글의 주제로 가장 적절한 것은?

Conventional wisdom in the West, influenced by philosophers from Plato to Descartes, credits individuals and especially geniuses with creativity and originality. Social and cultural influences and causes are minimized, ignored, or eliminated from consideration at all. Thoughts, original and conventional, are identified with individuals, and the special things that individuals are and do are traced to their genes and their brains. The "trick" here is to recognize that individual humans are social constructions themselves, embodying and reflecting the variety of social and cultural influences they have been exposed to during their lives. Our individuality is not denied, but it is viewed as a product of specific social and cultural experiences. The brain itself is a social thing, influenced structurally and at the level of its connectivities by social environments. The "individual" is a legal, religious, and political fiction just as the "I" is a grammatical illusion.

① recognition of the social nature inherent in individuality

② ways of filling the gap between individuality and collectivity

③ issues with separating original thoughts from conventional ones

④ acknowledgment of the true individuality embodied in human genes

⑤ necessity of shifting from individualism to interdependence

정답과 해설 **p.24**

01 Conventional wisdom in the West, / influenced by philosophers from Plato to
주어　　　　　　　　　　　　　　　분사구문
Descartes, / credits individuals and especially geniuses / with creativity and originality.
------- 「credit A with B: A에게 B가 있다고 믿다」 -------
// Social and cultural influences and causes / are minimized, ignored, or eliminated
주어　　　　　　　　　　　　　　　　　　　　동사(수동태: 과거분사 A, B, or C 병렬)
from consideration at all.

02 Thoughts, / (original and conventional), / are identified with individuals, / and the
주어1　　　　삽입구(주어 보충)　　　　　동사1
special things / [that individuals are and do] / are traced to their genes and their
주어2　　　　　　　　　　　　　　　　　　　동사2
brains.

03 The "trick" here is to recognize / [that individual humans are social constructions
　　　　　　　　　　　　　　　　접속사(~것)　　　주어
themselves, / embodying and reflecting the variety of social and cultural influences /
재귀대명사(주어 강조)　분사구문　　　　　　　　　　　　　　　목적어(선행사)
{they have been exposed to during their lives}].
목적격 관계대명사절

04 Our individuality is not denied, / but it is viewed / as a product of specific social and
　　　　　　　　　　　　　　　　　　「A be viewed as B: A가 B라고 여겨지다」
cultural experiences. // The brain itself is a social thing, / influenced structurally and
　　　　　　　　　　　　　　　　　　　　　　　　　　　분사구문(수동)
at the level of its connectivities by social environments.

05 The "individual" is a legal, religious, and political fiction / just as the "I" is a
　　　　　　　　　　　　　　　　　　　　　　　　접속사(~와 마찬가지로)
grammatical illusion.

01 서양의 통념은 / 플라톤에서 데카르트에 이르는 철학자philosopher들의 영향을 받은 / 개인, 특히 천재들을 믿는다credit individuals and especially geniuses / 창의력과 독창성이 있다고with creativity and originality. // 사회적, 문화적 영향과 원인은 / 최소화되거나 무시되거나 고려로부터 완전히 배제된다eliminate.

02 사상은, / 독창적이든 종래의 것이든 / 개인과 동일시되며, / 특별한 것은 / 개인이 ~이고 개인이 행하는 / 그 사람의 유전자와 두뇌에서 그 기원을 찾는다trace.

03 여기서 '요령'은 인식하는 것이다 / 개개의 인간이 바로 사회적 구성이며 / 사회적, 문화적 영향의 다양성을 구현하고embody 반영한다는 것을 / 그들이 생애 동안 접해온.

04 우리의 개인성individuality이 부인되는 것이 아니라, / 그것은 여겨지는 것이다 / 특정한 사회적, 문화적 경험의 산물로. // 뇌 그 자체가 사회적인 것이며, / 구조적으로, 그리고 그것의 사회 환경에 의한 연결성 수준에서 영향을 받는다.

05 '개인'은 법적, 종교적religious, 그리고 정치적 허구이다 / '나'가 문법적grammatical 환상인 것과 마찬가지로.

구문 Check-up

① The special things that individuals are and do are / to be traced to their genes and their brains.

주어 the special things 뒤로 동사가 필요하므로 are가 적절하다. that individuals are and do는 the special things를 꾸미는 관계대명사절이다.

② The brain itself is a social thing, influenced / influencing structurally and at the level of its connectivities by social environments.

분사의 의미상 주어 The brain이 '영향받는' 대상이므로 과거분사 influenced가 적절하다.

정답 ① are ② influenced

27

STEP 1 • 수능에 *진짜* 나오는 *단어*

✔ 문제에 나오는 단어들을 확인하세요.

01	competent	a. 유능한	(✔ competent) employees	유능한 직원
02	agent	n. 행위자	moral ( )s	도덕적 행위자
03	acquire	v. 습득하다, 얻다	( ) a bit of decency	얼마간의 예의를 습득하다
04	qualify	v. 자격을 주다	( ) them for membership	그들에게 구성원 자격을 주다
05	decent	a. 예의 바른, 품위 있는	become a ( ) human being	예의 바른 사람이 되다
06	nurture	n. 양육	nature and ( )	천성과 양육
07	grasp	v. 이해하다	( ) the complex concept	그 복잡한 개념을 이해하다
08	oversimplify	v. 지나치게 단순화하다	an ( )ied view	지나치게 단순화된 견해
09	nonsensical	a. 무의미한	( ) thoughts	무의미한 생각
10	evolution	n. 진화, 발전	the ( ) of the human species	인류의 진화

✚ 본문 문장 속에서 단어들을 확인해 보세요.

Human beings do not enter the world / as competent moral agents.

인간은 세상에 들어오지 않는다 / 유능한 도덕적 행위자로서.

01	competent	유능한	competent employees	(유능한)직원
02	agent		moral agents	도덕적 ( )
03	acquire		acquire a bit of decency	얼마간의 예의를 ( )
04	qualify		qualify them for membership	그들에게 구성원 ( )
05	decent		become a decent human being	( ) 사람이 되다
06	nurture		nature and nurture	천성과 ( )
07	grasp		grasp the concept	그 복잡한 개념을 ( )
08	oversimplify		an oversimplified view	( ) 견해
09	nonsensical		nonsensical thoughts	( ) 생각
10	evolution		the evolution of the human species	인류의 ( )

➕ 본문 문장 속에서 단어의 의미를 우리말로 해석해 보세요.

Human beings do not enter the world / as competent moral agents.

➡ 인간은 세상에 들어오지 않는다 / ⬛⬛⬛⬛⬛⬛⬛ 로서.

27 다음 글의 주제로 가장 적절한 것은?

Human beings do not enter the world as competent moral agents. Nor does everyone leave the world in that state. But somewhere in between, most people acquire a bit of decency that qualifies them for membership in the community of moral agents. Genes, development, and learning all contribute to the process of becoming a decent human being. The interaction between nature and nurture is, however, highly complex, and developmental biologists are only just beginning to grasp just how complex it is. Without the context provided by cells, organisms, social groups, and culture, DNA is inert. Anyone who says that people are "genetically programmed" to be moral has an oversimplified view of how genes work. Genes and environment interact in ways that make it nonsensical to think that the process of moral development in children, or any other developmental process, can be discussed in terms of nature *versus* nurture. Developmental biologists now know that it is really both, or nature *through* nurture. A complete scientific explanation of moral evolution and development in the human species is a very long way off.

*decency: 예의   **inert: 비활성의

① evolution of human morality from a cultural perspective

② difficulties in studying the evolutionary process of genes

③ increasing necessity of educating children as moral agents

④ nature versus nurture controversies in developmental biology

⑤ complicated gene-environment interplay in moral development

정답과 해설 **p.24**

01 Human beings do not enter the world / as competent moral agents. // Nor does
전치사(~로서)   「부정어+조동사+
everyone leave the world in that state.
주어+동사원형: 도치 구문」

02 But somewhere in between, / most people acquire a bit of decency / [that qualifies
선행사   주격 관계대명사절
them for membership / in the community of moral agents]. // Genes, development, and
주어(가산+불가산명사)
learning / all contribute to the process of becoming a decent human being.
동사(복수)

03 The interaction between nature and nurture / is, however, highly complex, / and
주어1   동사(단수)   주격보어
developmental biologists are only just beginning to grasp / just how complex it is. //
주어2   동사2   간접의문문(how+형/부+주어+동사)
Without the context / provided by cells, organisms, social groups, and culture, / DNA
과거분사구
is inert. // Anyone / [who says that people are "genetically programmed" to be moral] /
주어   주격 관계대명사절
has an oversimplified view of how genes work.
동사(단수)

04 Genes and environment interact in ways / [that make it nonsensical to think / {that
주격 관계대명사
선행사   5형식 가목적어 구문(make it+보어+to부정사 ~)
the process of moral development in children, / or any other developmental process, /
{ }: 명사절(to think의 목적어)
can be discussed in terms of nature versus nurture}]. // Developmental biologists now
know / that it is really both, or nature through nurture.
대명사(= the process)

05 A complete scientific explanation of moral evolution and development in the human
주어
species / is a very long way off.
동사(단수)

01 인간은 세상에 들어오지 않는다 / 유능한 도덕적 행위자competent moral agents로서. // 또한 모든 이가 그 상태로
세상을 떠나지도 않는다.

02 하지만 그 사이 어딘가에서, / 대부분의 사람들은 얼마간의 예의를 습득한다acquire / 그들에게 구성원 자격을
주는qualify / 도덕적 행위자 공동체의. // 유전자, 발달, 그리고 학습은 / 모두 예의 바른decent 인간이 되는 과정에
기여한다.

03 천성과 양육nurture 사이의 상호 작용은 / 하지만 매우 복잡하며, / 발달 생물학자들은 간신히 이해하기grasp 시작하고
있을 뿐이다 / 그저 그것이 얼마나 복잡한지를. // 맥락이 없으면 / 세포, 유기체, 사회 집단, 그리고 문화에 의해 제공되는 /
DNA는 비활성이다. // 누구든 / 사람들은 도덕적이도록 '유전적으로 프로그램이 짜여 있다'고 말하는 / 유전자가 작동하는
방식에 대한 지나치게 단순화된oversimplify 견해를 가지고 있다.

04 유전자와 환경은 방식으로 상호 작용한다 / 생각하는 것을 무의미하게nonsensical 만드는 / 아이들의 도덕적 발달 과정, /
또는 다른 어떤 발달 과정이든 / 천성 '대' 양육이라는 견지에서 논의될 수 있다고. // 발달 생물학자들은 이제 안다 / 그것이
진정 둘 다, 즉 양육을 '통한' 천성이라는 것을.

05 인간 종의 도덕적 진화evolution와 발달에 대한 완전한 과학적 설명은 / 까마득히 멀다.

구문 Check up

① Human beings do not enter the world as competent moral agents. Nor everyone leaves / does everyone leave the world in that state.

부정어인 Nor가 문장 맨 앞에 나온 도치 구문이므로 뒤에 나오는 주어와 동사는 의문문 어순으로 쓴다. 따라서 does everyone leave가 적절하다.

② Anyone who / whoever says that people are "genetically programmed" to be moral has an oversimplified view of how genes work.

앞에 선행사 Anyone이 나오므로 관계대명사 who를 쓴다. 복합관계대명사 whoever(~하는 누구든)는 what처럼 선행사를 포함하므로 선행사 뒤에 쓰지 않는다.

정답 ① does everyone leave ② who

28

STEP 1 • 수능에 *진짜* 나오는 *단어*

✔️ **문제에 나오는 단어들을 확인하세요.**

01	offspring	*n.* 자녀, 후손	the (✔️ offspring) of aristocrats	귀족의 자녀
02	subsequently	*ad.* 그 이후, 나중에	( ) have a great success	그 이후 엄청난 성공을 거두다
03	define	*v.* 규정하다, 정의하다	( ) who I am	내가 누구인지 규정하다
04	distinguish	*v.* 구별하다	( ) who is in from who is out	누가 내부자이고 외부자인지 구별하다
05	separate	*v.* 분리하다	( ) us from them	우리를 그들과 분리하다
06	address	*v.* ~을 대상으로 하다	the manual ( )ed to students	학생들을 대상으로 한 매뉴얼
07	reference	*n.* 언급	have a negative ( ) to the peasant	소작농을 부정적으로 언급하다
08	peasant	*n.* 소작농	( ) farmers	소작농들
09	exclude	*v.* 배제하다	be ( )d from membership	회원에서 배제되다 (제명되다)
10	lordly	*a.* 귀족의, 귀족다운	the ( ) table	귀족의 식탁

➕ **본문 문장 속에서 단어들을 확인해 보세요.**

It is for this reason / that manuals of "good manners" addressed to the aristocracy / always have a negative reference to the peasant / who behaves badly, / who "doesn't know" what the rules are, / and for this reason is excluded from the lordly table.

바로 이런 이유에서인데 / 귀족 계층을 대상으로 한 '좋은 예절'의 교범이 / 항상 소작농을 부정적으로 언급하는 것은 / 예의범절이 좋지 않은 / 그들은 규칙이 무엇인지를 '알지 못하며', / 이런 이유로 귀족의 식탁에서 배제된다.

01	offspring	🖉 자녀, 후손	the offspring of aristocrats	귀족의 (자녀)
02	subsequently		subsequently have a great success	( ) 엄청난 성공을 거두다
03	define		define who I am	내가 누구인지 ( )
04	distinguish		distinguish who is in from who is out	누가 내부자이고 외부자인지 ( )
05	separate		separate us from them	우리를 그들과 ( )
06	address		the manual addressed to students	학생들을 ( ) 매뉴얼
07	reference		have a negative reference to the peasant	소작농을 부정적으로 ( )하다
08	peasant		peasant farmers	( )들
09	exclude		be excluded from membership	회원에서 ( )
10	lordly		the lordly table	( ) 식탁

➕ **본문 문장 속에서 단어의 의미를 우리말로 해석해 보세요.**

It is for this reason / that manuals of "good manners" addressed to the aristocracy / always have a negative reference to the peasant / who behaves badly, / who "doesn't know" what the rules are, / and for this reason is excluded from the lordly table.

➔ 바로 이런 이유에서인데 / 귀족 계층을 ⬛⬛⬛⬛⬛ '좋은 예절'의 교범이 / 항상 ⬛⬛⬛⬛⬛⬛⬛⬛ 것은 / 예의 범절이 좋지 않은 / 그들은 규칙이 무엇인지를 '알지 못하며', / 이런 이유로 ⬛⬛⬛⬛⬛⬛⬛.

28 다음 글의 주제로 가장 적절한 것은?

In the twelfth to thirteenth centuries there appeared the first manuals teaching "table manners" to the offspring of aristocrats. It was a genre that subsequently had a great success in the early modern period with *The Courtier* by Baldassare Castiglione, *The Galateo* by Monsignor Della Casa, and many others produced in different European countries. In a variety of ways and meanings, these are all instruments intended to define or distinguish who is *in* from who is *out*, separating the participants from the ostracized. It is for this reason that manuals of "good manners" addressed to the aristocracy always have a negative reference to the peasant who behaves badly, who "doesn't know" what the rules are, and for this reason is excluded from the lordly table. Food etiquette had become a sign of social barriers and of the impossibility of breaking them down.

*aristocrat: 귀족 **ostracize: 추방하다

① table manners as a marker for class distinction

② publications to bring about equality between classes

③ unintended effects of distinguishing insiders from outsiders

④ attempts to elaborate food etiquette for educational purposes

⑤ roles of manners in uniting people from different backgrounds

정답과 해설 p.26

01 In the twelfth to thirteenth centuries / there appeared the first manuals / teaching
동사   주어   현재분사구
"table manners" to the offspring of aristocrats.

02 It was a genre / [that subsequently had a great success in the early modern period /
선행사   주격 관계대명사절
with *The Courtier* by Baldassare Castiglione, / *The Galateo* by Monsignor Della Casa, /
전치사 명사구1   명사구2
and many others produced in different European countries].
명사구3   과거분사구

03 In a variety of ways and meanings, / these are all instruments / intended to define
주어   동사   주격보어   과거분사구
or distinguish who is *in* from who is *out*, / separating the participants from the
분사구문(~하면서)
ostracized.

04 「it is[was] ~ that … 강조구문: …한 것은 바로 ~이다[였다]」
It is for this reason / that manuals of "good manners" addressed to the aristocracy /
주어   과거분사구
always have a negative reference to the peasant / [who behaves badly], / [who "doesn't
동사(복수)   선행사   동사1
know" what the rules are, / and for this reason is excluded from the lordly table].
동사2

05 Food etiquette had become a sign / of social barriers / and of the impossibility of
주어   동사(과거완료)   주격보어   전치사구 병렬(보어 수식)
breaking them down.

01   12세기부터 13세기에 / 최초의 교범이 등장했다 / 귀족의 자녀**offspring**에게 '식탁 예절'을 가르치는.

02   그것은 장르였다 / 그 이후**subsequently** 근대 초기에 큰 성공을 거둔 / Baldassare Castiglione가 쓴 〈The Courtier〉, / Monsignor Della Casa가 쓴 〈The Galateo〉 / 그리고 다양한 유럽 국가에서 제작된 많은 다른 책들과 함께.

03   다양한 방식과 의미로, / 이 책들은 모두 도구들이다 / 누가 '내부자'이고 '외부자'인지를 규정하거나 구별하기**define or distinguish** 위하여 의도된 / 참여하는 자들을 추방되는 자들로부터 분리하면서**separate**.

04   바로 이런 이유에서인데 / 귀족 계층을 대상으로 한**address** '좋은 예절'의 교범이 / 소작농을 항상 부정적으로 언급하는 것은**have a negative reference to the peasant** / 예의범절이 좋지 않은 / 그들은 규칙이 무엇인지를 '알지 못하며', / 이런 이유로 귀족의 식탁에서 배제된다**be excluded from the lordly table**.

05   음식 예절은 표시가 되어 버렸다 / 사회적 장벽의 / 그리고 그 장벽 타파의 불가능성에 대한.

구문 Check up

① These are all instruments intended to define or distinguish who is *in* from who is *out*, separating / separated the participants from the ostracized.

분사구문의 의미상 주어 These가 '분리하는' 주체이므로 separating이 적절하다.

② It is for this reason that / which manuals of "good manners" addressed to the aristocracy always have a negative reference to the peasant.

「it is[was] ~ that …(…한 것은 바로 ~이다[였다])」 강조구문이므로 that이 적절하다.

29 STEP **1** 수능에 *진짜* 나오는 *단어*

✔ 문제에 나오는 단어들을 확인하세요.

01	generate	v. 만들어내다	(✔ generate) economic success	경제적 성공을 만들어 내다
02	distinguishing	a. 두드러진, 특징적인	a ( ) feature of urban areas	도시 지역의 두드러진 특징
03	approximately	ad. 대략	( ) 7.5 billion trips	대략 75억 건의 이동
04	infrastructure	n. 사회 기반 시설	the associated ( )	관련 사회 기반 시설
05	threefold	a. 세 배의 ad. 세 배로	rise more than ( )	세 배 넘게 오르다
06	urbanization	n. 도시화	a key dynamic of ( )	도시화의 핵심 동력
07	invariably	ad. 변함없이, 늘	( ) suffer	변함없이 고생하다
08	constitute	v. 구성하다	( ) the core of urban form	도시 형태의 핵심을 구성하다
09	backbone	n. 중추	the ( ) of the urban economy	도시 경제의 중추
10	externality	n. 외부 효과	a number of negative ( )ies	많은 부정적 외부 효과
11	unprecedented	a. 전례 없는	an ( ) economic crisis	전례 없는 경제 위기
12	winding	a. 구불구불한, 복잡한	a long and ( ) road	길고 구불구불한 길
13	inevitable	a. 불가피한	( ) conflicts	불가피한 갈등

⊕ **본문 문장 속에서 단어들을 확인해 보세요.**

Hyper-mobility / — the notion / that more travel at faster speeds covering longer distances / generates greater economic success — / seems to be a distinguishing feature of urban areas.

하이퍼 모빌리티는 / 개념 / 더 먼 거리를 더 빠른 속도로 더 많이 이동하는 것이 / 더 큰 경제적 성공을 만든다는 / 도시 지역의 두드러진 특징인 것으로 보인다.

01	generate	✎ 만들어내다	generate economic success	경제적 성공을 (만들어내다)
02	distinguishing		a distinguishing feature of urban areas	도시 지역의 (　　　) 특징
03	approximately		approximately 7.5 billion trips	(　　　) 75억 건의 이동
04	infrastructure		the associated infrastructure	관련 (　　　　　)
05	threefold		rise more than threefold	(　　　) 넘게 오르다
06	urbanization		a key dynamic of urbanization	(　　　)의 핵심 동력
07	invariably		invariably suffer	(　　　) 고생하다
08	constitute		constitute the core of urban form	도시 형태의 핵심을 (　　　)
09	backbone		the backbone of the urban economy	도시 경제의 (　　　)
10	externality		a number of negative externalities	많은 부정적 (　　　)
11	unprecedented		an unprecedented economic crisis	(　　　) 경제 위기
12	winding		a long and winding road	길고 (　　　) 길
13	inevitable		inevitable conflicts	(　　　) 갈등

➕ **본문 문장 속에서 단어의 의미를 우리말로 해석해 보세요.**

Hyper-mobility / — the notion / that more travel at faster speeds covering longer distances / generates greater economic success — / seems to be a distinguishing feature of urban areas.

➡ 하이퍼 모빌리티는 / 개념 / 더 먼 거리를 더 빠른 속도로 더 많이 이동하는 것이 / 　　　　　　　　　는 / 　　　　　　　　인 것으로 보인다.

29 다음 글의 제목으로 가장 적절한 것은?

Hyper-mobility — the notion that more travel at faster speeds covering longer distances generates greater economic success — seems to be a distinguishing feature of urban areas, where more than half of the world's population currently reside. By 2005, approximately 7.5 billion trips were made each day in cities worldwide. In 2050, there may be three to four times as many passenger-kilometres travelled as in the year 2000, infrastructure and energy prices permitting. Freight movement could also rise more than threefold during the same period. Mobility flows have become a key dynamic of urbanization, with the associated infrastructure invariably constituting the backbone of urban form. Yet, despite the increasing level of urban mobility worldwide, access to places, activities and services has become increasingly difficult. Not only is it less convenient — in terms of time, cost and comfort — to access locations in cities, but the very process of moving around in cities generates a number of negative externalities. Accordingly, many of the world's cities face an unprecedented accessibility crisis, and are characterized by unsustainable mobility systems.

*freight: 화물

① Is Hyper-mobility Always Good for Cities?

② Accessibility: A Guide to a Web of Urban Areas

③ A Long and Winding Road to Economic Success

④ Inevitable Regional Conflicts from Hyper-mobility

⑤ Infrastructure: An Essential Element of Hyper-mobility

정답과 해설 p.27

01 Hyper-mobility / — the notion / [that more travel at faster speeds covering longer
주어   동격   동격
distances / generates greater economic success] — / seems to be a distinguishing
                                                    동사
feature of urban areas, / where more than half of the world's population currently
       선행사   계속적 용법(보충 설명)
reside.

02 By 2005, / approximately 7.5 billion trips / were made each day in cities worldwide. //
In 2050, / there may be three to four times as many passenger-kilometres travelled /
                              배수 표현(배수사 + as + 원급 + as: 몇 배 더 ~한)
as in the year 2000, / infrastructure and energy prices permitting. // Freight movement
                     독립분사구문(의미상 주어 + 현재분사)
could also rise more than threefold / during the same period. // Mobility flows have
become a key dynamic of urbanization, / with the associated infrastructure invariably
                                      「with + 명사 + 현재분사: ~이 …한 채로」
constituting the backbone of urban form.

03 Yet, / despite the increasing level of urban mobility worldwide, / access to places,
         전치사(~에도 불구하고)   주어(불가산)
activities and services has become increasingly difficult. // Not only is it less convenient
                        동사(단수)   부정어구의 도치(be + 가주어)
/ — in terms of time, cost and comfort — / to access locations in cities, / but the very
                                          진주어
process of moving around in cities / generates a number of negative externalities. //
Accordingly, / many of the world's cities face an unprecedented accessibility crisis, /
              주어(부분 + of + 전체)   동사1(복수)
and are characterized by unsustainable mobility systems.
    동사2(복수)

01 하이퍼 모빌리티는 / 개념 / 더 먼 거리를 더 빠른 속도로 더 많이 이동하는 것이 / 더 큰 경제적 성공을 만든다generate는
/ 도시 지역의 두드러진distinguishing 특징인 것으로 보이는데 / 도시에는 현재 세계 인구의 절반이 넘는 사람이 산다.

02 2005년까지 / 대략approximately 75억 건의 이동이 / 전 세계 도시에서 매일 이루어졌다. // 2050년에는 / 이동된
인킬로미터가 서너 배 더 될지도 모른다 / 2000년보다 / 사회 기반 시설infrastructure 및 에너지 가격이 허락한다면. //
화물 이동도 세 배threefold 넘게 증가할 수 있다 / 같은 기간에. // 이동성 흐름은 도시화urbanization의 핵심 동력이
되었다 / 관련 사회 기반 시설이 변함없이invariably 도시 형태의 중추를 구성하면서constitute the backbone of urban
form.

03 그러나 / 전 세계적으로 증가하는 도시 이동성 수준에도 불구하고, / 장소, 활동 및 서비스에 대한 접근은 점점 더
어려워졌다. // 덜 편리할 뿐만 아니라, / 시간, 비용 및 편안함 측면에서 보면, / 도시에서 장소에 접근하는 것이 / 도시에서
돌아다니는 바로 그 과정은 / 많은 부정적인 외부 효과externality를 발생시킨다. // 그에 따라 / 세계의 많은 도시는 전례
없는unprecedented 접근성 위기에 직면해 있으며 / 지속 불가능한 이동성 시스템을 특징으로 한다.

구문 Check up

① In 2050, there may be three to four times as many passenger-kilometres travelled as in the year 2000, infrastructure and energy prices permit / permitting .

콤마 이하로 접속사 없이 「의미상 주어 + 분사구문」이 이어지는 것이므로 permitting을 쓴다.

② Mobility flows have become a key dynamic of urbanization, with the associated infrastructure invariably constituted / constituting the backbone of urban form.

「with + 명사 + 분사」 구문인데, 의미상 주어 the associated infrastructure가 '구성하는' 주체이므로 능동을 나타내는 constituting이 적절하다.

정답 ① permitting ② constituting

30

STEP 1 • 수능에 *진짜* 나오는 *단어*

글의 제목 ⊕

✔ **문제에 나오는 단어들을 확인하세요.**

01	visual	*a.* 시각적인	the brain's (✓ visual) system	뇌 시각 체계
02	on a need-to-know basis	필요할 때 필요한 것만 알려주는 방식으로	( ) ( ) ( ) ( )	필요할 때 필요한 것만 알려주는 방식으로
03	cell	*n.* 세포	every ( ) of the body	체내 모든 세포
04	reach out to	~에 닿다	( ) ( ) ( ) an object	어떤 물체에 닿다
05	location	*n.* 위치, 장소	know the size and ( ) of the object	물체의 크기와 위치를 알다
06	sensitive	*a.* 예민한, 민감한	( ) to details of shape	모양의 세부 사항에 예민한
07	detect	*v.* 감지하다, 알아내다	( ) the current location	현재 위치를 감지하다
08	perceive	*v.* 인식하다	( ) movement	움직임을 인식하다
09	localized	*a.* 국부적인	( ) brain damage	국부적인 뇌 손상

⊕ **본문 문장 속에서 단어들을 확인해 보세요.**

Cells that help your hand muscles reach out to an object / need to know the size and location of the object, / but they don't need to know about color.

여러분의 손 근육이 어떤 물체에 닿을 수 있도록 돕는 세포들은 / 그 물체의 크기와 위치를 알아야 하지만 / 그들은 색깔에 대해 알 필요는 없다.

문제를 풀기 전에 단어들을 **30초** 동안 다시 확인하세요.

01	visual	✎ 시각적인	the brain's visual system	뇌 (시각) 체계
02	on a need-to-know basis		on a need-to-know basis	( )
03	cell		every cell of the body	체내 모든 ( )
04	reach out to		reach out to an object	어떤 물체에 ( )
05	location		know the size and location of the object	물체의 크기와 ( )를 알다
06	sensitive		sensitive to details of shape	모양의 세부 사항에 ( )
07	detect		detect the current location	현재 위치를 ( )
08	perceive		perceive movement	움직임을 ( )
09	localized		localized brain damage	( ) 뇌 손상

➕ 본문 문장 속에서 단어의 의미를 우리말로 해석해 보세요.

Cells that help your hand muscles reach out to an object / need to know the size and location of the object, / but they don't need to know about color.

➡️ 여러분의 손 근육이 ▓▓▓▓▓▓ 수 있도록 돕는 ▓▓▓▓은 / ▓▓▓▓▓▓▓를 알아야 하지만 / 그들은 색깔에 대해 알 필요는 없다.

30 다음 글의 제목으로 가장 적절한 것은?

Different parts of the brain's visual system get information on a need-to-know basis. Cells that help your hand muscles reach out to an object need to know the size and location of the object, but they don't need to know about color. They need to know a little about shape, but not in great detail. Cells that help you recognize people's faces need to be extremely sensitive to details of shape, but they can pay less attention to location. It is natural to assume that anyone who sees an object sees everything about it — the shape, color, location, and movement. However, one part of your brain sees its shape, another sees color, another detects location, and another perceives movement. Consequently, after localized brain damage, it is possible to see certain aspects of an object and not others. Centuries ago, people found it difficult to imagine how someone could see an object without seeing what color it is. Even today, you might find it surprising to learn about people who see an object without seeing where it is, or see it without seeing whether it is moving.

① Visual Systems Never Betray Our Trust!

② Secret Missions of Color-Sensitive Brain Cells

③ Blind Spots: What Is Still Unknown About the Brain

④ Why Brain Cells Exemplify Nature's Recovery Process

⑤ Separate and Independent: Brain Cells' Visual Perceptions

정답과 해설 **p.27**

01 Different parts of the brain's visual system / get information on a need-to-know basis.
주어(선행사)
// Cells [that help your hand muscles reach out to an object] / need to know the size
주격 관계대명사절   동사구(복수)
and location of the object, / but they don't need to know about color. // They need to
know a little about shape, / but not in great detail. // Cells [that help you recognize
주어(선행사)   주격 관계대명사절
people's faces] / need to be extremely sensitive to details of shape, / but they can pay
동사구(복수)
less attention to location.

02 It is natural to assume / [that anyone who sees an object sees everything about it / —
가주어   진주어   명사절(to assume의 목적어)
the shape, color, location, and movement]. // However, / one part of your brain sees
부정대명사(여럿 중 하나)
its shape, / another sees color, / another detects location, / and another perceives
부정대명사(또 다른 하나)
movement.

03 Consequently, / after localized brain damage, / it is possible / to see certain aspects
가주어   진주어
of an object and not others. // Centuries ago, / people found it difficult / to imagine
가목적어   진목적어
how someone could see an object / without seeing what color it is. // Even today, / you
might find it surprising / to learn about people / [who see an object without seeing
가목적어   진목적어   선행사   동사1
where it is, / or see it without seeing whether it is moving].
동사2

01 뇌 시각 체계visual system의 다양한 부분들은 / 필요할 때 필요한 것만 알려주는 방식으로on a need-to-know basis
정보를 얻는다. // 여러분의 손 근육이 어떤 물체에 닿을reach out to 수 있도록 돕는 세포cell들은 / 그 물체의 크기와
위치location를 알아야 하지만 / 그들은 색깔에 대해 알 필요는 없다. // 그것들은 모양에 대해 약간 알아야 하지만, / 매우
자세히는 아니다. // 여러분이 사람의 얼굴을 인식하도록 돕는 세포는 / 모양의 세부 사항에 극도로 예민해야sensitive 할
필요가 있지만, / 그들은 위치에는 신경을 덜 쓸 수 있다.

02 추정하는 것은 당연하다 / 어떤 물체를 보는 사람이라면 그것에 관한 모든 것을 보고 있다고 / 모양, 색깔, 위치, 움직임
등. // 하지만, / 여러분 뇌의 한 부분은 그것의 모양을 보고, / 다른 한 부분은 색깔을 보며, / 또 다른 부분은 위치를
감지하고detect, / 또 다른 한 부분은 움직임을 인식한다perceive.

03 따라서 / 국부적localized 뇌 손상 후 / 가능하다 / 물체의 특정한 측면은 볼 수 있으면서 다른 측면은 보지 못하는 것이. //
수 세기 전, / 사람들은 어렵다고 생각했다 / 어떻게 누군가가 물체를 볼 수 있는지 상상하는 것이 / 그것이 무슨 색깔인지
못 보면서. // 심지어 오늘날에도, / 여러분은 놀랍다고 여길 수 있다 / 사람들에 대해 알게 되는 것을 / 어떤 물체가 어디에
있는지 못 보면서 그 물체를 보거나, / 또는 그것이 움직이고 있는지 보지 못하면서 물체를 보는.

구문 Check up

① Cells that help your hand muscles reach out to an object needs / need to know the size and location of the object, but they don't need to know about color.

주어가 복수명사인 Cells이므로 복수형인 need가 적절하다.

② Centuries ago, people found that / it difficult to imagine how someone could see an object without seeing what color it is.

「find + 가목적어 + 형용사 + to부정사(진목적어) ~」 구문이다. 가주어 또는 가목적어는 원칙상 it으로만 쓴다.

정답 ① need ② it

31

STEP 1 • 수능에 진짜 나오는 단어

✔ 문제에 나오는 단어들을 확인하세요.

01	committed	a. 열성적인, 헌신적인	a very (✔ committed) artist	매우 열성적인 예술가
02	enthusiast	n. 애호가	music ( )s and experts	음악 애호가와 전문가
03	gain in	~을 얻다	( ) ( ) attraction	매력을 얻다
04	score	n. 악보	printed in the ( )	악보에 인쇄된
05	variation	n. 변주, 변화	a wide potential of ( )s	광범위한 변주 가능성
06	tonal	a. 음색의, 음조의	( ) quality	음색의 질
07	intonation	n. 인토네이션(음정의 높낮이), 억양	accurate ( ) and rhythm	정확한 억양과 리듬
08	composition	n. 작품, 구성	based on the ( )	작품에 기초하여
09	diverge	v. 갈라지다	( ) from the same ancestor	똑같은 조상에서 갈라지다
10	individually	ad. 개별적으로	speak to them ( )	그들에게 개별적으로 말하다
11	expressivity	n. 표현성, 표현 능력	( ) in music performance	음악 공연에서의 표현성
12	worthwhile	a. 가치 있는	why it is ( ) to repeat the same repertoire	왜 똑같은 레퍼토리를 반복하는 것이 가치 있는지
13	enrich	v. 풍부하게 하다	( ) the contents	내용을 풍부하게 하다
14	animate	v. 활기[힘, 생기]를 불어넣다	( ) the music scene	음악계에 활기를 불어넣다

✚ 본문 문장 속에서 단어들을 확인해 보세요.

New, inspiring interpretations / help us to expand our understanding, / which serves to enrich and animate the music scene.

새롭고 영감을 주는 해석은 / 우리가 이해를 넓히는 데 도움을 주는데, / 이것은 음악계를 풍부하게 하고 활기를 불어넣는 역할을 한다.

01	committed	🖉 열성적인, 헌신적인	a very committed artist	매우 (열성적인) 예술가
02	enthusiast		music enthusiasts and experts	음악 ( )와 전문가
03	gain in		gain in attraction	매력을 ( )
04	score		printed in the score	( )에 인쇄된
05	variation		a wide potential of variations	광범위한 ( ) 가능성
06	tonal		tonal quality	( )질
07	intonation		accurate intonation and rhythm	정확한 ( )과 리듬
08	composition		based on the composition	( )에 기초하여
09	diverge		diverge from the same ancestor	똑같은 조상에서 ( )
10	individually		speak to them individually	그들에게 ( ) 말하다
11	expressivity		expressivity in music performance	음악 공연에서의 ( )
12	worthwhile		why it is worthwhile to repeat the same repertoire	왜 똑같은 레퍼토리를 반복하는 것이 ( )지
13	enrich		enrich the contents	내용을 ( )
14	animate		animate the music scene	음악계에 ( )

✛ **본문 문장 속에서 단어의 의미를 우리말로 해석해 보세요.**

New, inspiring interpretations / help us to expand our understanding, / which serves to enrich and animate the music scene.

→ 새롭고 영감을 주는 해석은 / 우리가 이해를 넓히는 데 도움을 주는데, / 이것은 ▨▨▨▨▨▨▨▨▨▨▨ 역할을 한다.

31 다음 글의 제목으로 가장 적절한 것은?

Not only musicians and psychologists, but also committed music enthusiasts and experts often voice the opinion that the beauty of music lies in an expressive deviation from the exactly defined score. Concert performances become interesting and gain in attraction from the fact that they go far beyond the information printed in the score. In his early studies on musical performance, Carl Seashore discovered that musicians only rarely play two equal notes in exactly the same way. Within the same metric structure, there is a wide potential of variations in tempo, volume, tonal quality and intonation. Such variation is based on the composition but diverges from it individually. We generally call this 'expressivity'. This explains why we do not lose interest when we hear different artists perform the same piece of music. It also explains why it is worthwhile for following generations to repeat the same repertoire. New, inspiring interpretations help us to expand our understanding, which serves to enrich and animate the music scene.

*deviation: 벗어남

① How to Build a Successful Career in Music Criticism

② Never the Same: The Value of Variation in Music Performance

③ The Importance of Personal Expression in Music Therapy

④ Keep Your Cool: Overcoming Stage Fright When Playing Music

⑤ What's New in the Classical Music Industry?

정답과 해설 p.28

01 Not only musicians and psychologists, / but also committed music enthusiasts and
「not only A but also B: A뿐 아니라 B도」
experts / often voice the opinion / [that the beauty of music / lies in an expressive
동격
deviation from the exactly defined score]. // Concert performances become interesting
현재분사(become의 보어)
and gain in attraction / from the fact / [that they go far beyond the information printed
동격
in the score].
과거분사구

02 In his early studies on musical performance, / Carl Seashore discovered /
[that musicians only rarely play two equal notes in exactly the same way]. // Within
명사절(discovered의 목적어)
the same metric structure, / there is a wide potential of variations / in tempo, volume,
tonal quality and intonation.

03 Such variation is based on the composition / but diverges from it individually. // We
동사1(~에 근거를 두다)   동사2
generally call this 'expressivity'. // This explains (the reason) [why we do not lose
선행사 생략   관계부사
interest / when we hear different artists perform the same piece of music].

04 It also explains why it is worthwhile / for following generations to repeat the same
가주어   의미상 주어   진주어
repertoire. // New, inspiring interpretations / help us to expand our understanding, /
which serves to enrich and animate the music scene.
계속적 용법(콤마 앞 부연)

01 음악가와 심리학자뿐만 아니라, / 열성적인 음악 애호가committed music enthusiasts와 전문가도 / 흔히 의견을 표한다
/ 음악의 아름다움은 / 정확히 정해진 악보로부터 표현상 벗어나는 데 있다는. // 콘서트 공연은 흥미로워지고 매력을
얻는다gain in attraction / 사실로부터 / 그것이 악보score에 인쇄된 정보를 훨씬 뛰어넘는다는.

02 음악 연주에 관한 그의 초기 연구에서, / Carl Seashore는 발견했다 / 음악가가 같은 두 음을 정확히 똑같이 연주하는
경우가 거의 없다는 것을. // 같은 미터 구조 내에서, / 광범위한 변주variation 가능성이 있다 / 박자, 음량, 음질tonal
quality 및 인토네이션intonation에 있어.

03 이러한 변주는 작품composition에 기초하지만 / 그로부터 개별적으로 갈라진다diverge from it individually. // 우리는
일반적으로 이것을 '표현성expressivity'이라고 부른다. // 이것은 우리가 흥미를 잃지 않는 이유를 설명해 준다 / 우리가
서로 다른 예술가가 같은 음악을 연주하는 것을 들을 때.

04 이것은 또한 가치 있는worthwhile 이유이기도 하다 / 다음 세대가 같은 레퍼토리를 반복하는 것이. // 새롭고 영감을 주는
해석은 / 우리가 이해를 넓히는 데 도움을 주는데, / 이것은 음악계를 풍부하게 하고 활기를 불어넣는enrich and animate
역할을 한다.

구문 Check up

① Not only musicians and psychologists, but also committed music enthusiasts and experts often voice / voices the opinion ~

주어가 「not only A but also B」 형태일 때 동사는 B에 수일치한다. 여기서는 B에 해당하는 committed music enthusiasts and experts가 복수명사구이므로 voice를 쓴다.

② This explains what / why we do not lose interest when we hear different artists perform the same piece of music.

뒤에 나오는 'we do not lose interest ~'가 완전한 3형식 문장이므로 관계부사 why가 적절하다. 일반적인 선행사 the reason은 생략되었다.

정답 ① voice ② why

32

STEP 1 • 수능에 진짜 나오는 단어

✔ **문제에 나오는 단어들을 확인하세요.**

01	mend	v. 고치다	(✔ mend) objects	물건을 고치다
02	restore	v. 복원하다, 복구하다	( ) old paintings	옛날 그림을 복원하다
03	preindustrial	a. 산업화 이전의	the ( ) era	산업화 이전의 시대
04	blacksmith	n. 대장장이	a ( ) making a sword	칼을 만들고 있는 대장장이
05	immediate	a. 가까이에 있는	in his ( ) community	그와 가까이에 사는 마을 사람들
06	customize	v. 주문 제작하다	( ) the product	물건을 주문 제작하다
07	modify	v. 수정하다	( ) the product	물건을 수정하다
08	fabrication	n. 제작	an extension of ( )	제작의 연장
09	province	n. (개인의 특정 지식, 관심, 책임) 영역, 분야	the ( ) of management	경영진의 영역
10	tender	n. 관리자, 감시인	machine ( )s	기계 관리자
11	grasp	n. 이해	a ( ) of design and materials	설계와 재료에 대한 이해
12	comprehension	n. 이해	a ( ) of the designer's intentions	설계자의 의도에 대한 이해
13	vast	a. 방대한	a ( ) area of forest	방대한 삼림 지대
14	subdivision	n. 세분, 다시 나눔	the ( ) of labour	노동의 세분(분업)

⊕ **본문 문장 속에서 단어들을 확인해 보세요.**

But repair continued / to require a larger grasp of design and materials, / an understanding of the whole and a comprehension of the designer's intentions.

그러나 수리는 계속했다 / 설계와 재료에 대한 더 큰 이해를 요구하기를 / 즉 전체에 대한 이해와 설계자의 의도에 대한 이해를.

01	mend	✎ 고치다	mend objects	물건을 (고치다)
02	restore		restore old paintings	옛날 그림을 ( )
03	preindustrial		the preindustrial era	( ) 시대
04	blacksmith		a blacksmith making a sword	칼을 만들고 있는 ( )
05	immediate		in his immediate community	그와 ( ) 마을 사람들
06	customize		customize the product	물건을 ( )
07	modify		modify the product	물건을 ( )
08	fabrication		an extension of fabrication	( )의 연장
09	province		the province of management	경영진의 ( )
10	tender		machine tenders	기계 ( )
11	grasp		a grasp of design and materials	설계와 재료에 대한 ( )
12	comprehension		a comprehension of the designer's intentions	설계자의 의도에 대한 ( )
13	vast		a vast area of forest	( ) 삼림 지대
14	subdivision		the subdivision of labour	노동의 ( )

➕ 본문 문장 속에서 단어의 의미를 우리말로 해석해 보세요.

But repair continued / to require a larger grasp of design and materials, / an understanding of the whole and a comprehension of the designer's intentions.

➜ 그러나 수리는 계속했다 / ＿＿＿＿＿＿＿＿＿＿＿＿＿＿＿를 요구하기를 / 즉 전체에 대한 이해와 ＿＿＿＿＿＿＿＿＿＿＿＿＿를.

32 다음 글의 제목으로 가장 적절한 것은?

Mending and restoring objects often require even more creativity than original production. The preindustrial blacksmith made things to order for people in his immediate community; customizing the product, modifying or transforming it according to the user, was routine. Customers would bring things back if something went wrong; repair was thus an extension of fabrication. With industrialization and eventually with mass production, making things became the province of machine tenders with limited knowledge. But repair continued to require a larger grasp of design and materials, an understanding of the whole and a comprehension of the designer's intentions. "Manufacturers all work by machinery or by vast subdivision of labour and not, so to speak, by hand," an 1896 *Manual of Mending and Repairing* explained. "But all repairing *must* be done by hand. We can make every detail of a watch or of a gun by machinery, but the machine cannot mend it when broken, much less a clock or a pistol!"

① Still Left to the Modern Blacksmith: The Art of Repair

② A Historical Survey of How Repairing Skills Evolved

③ How to Be a Creative Repairperson: Tips and Ideas

④ A Process of Repair: Create, Modify, Transform!

⑤ Can Industrialization Mend Our Broken Past?

정답과 해설 p.29

01 Mending and restoring objects / often require even more creativity / than original
주어(동명사구: A and B)   동사(복수)   「비교급 + than: ~보다 더 …한」
production.

02 The preindustrial blacksmith made things to order / for people in his immediate
community; / customizing the product, / modifying or transforming it according to the
                동격(동명사구 주어)
user, / was routine. // Customers would bring things back / if something went wrong; /
    동사(단수)   조동사: 과거 습관(~하곤 했다)
repair was thus an extension of fabrication.

03 With industrialization and eventually with mass production, / making things became
부사구1   부사구2   주어(동명사구)   동사
the province of machine tenders with limited knowledge.
주격보어   형용사구(machine tenders 수식)

04 But repair continued / to require a larger grasp of design and materials, / an
                                명사구 동격
understanding of the whole and a comprehension of the designer's intentions.

05 "Manufacturers all work / by machinery or by vast subdivision of labour / and not, so
                                                            전치사구 병렬
to speak, by hand," / an 1896 *Manual of Mending and Repairing* explained. // "But all
repairing *must* be done by hand. / We can make every detail of a watch or of a gun by
        조동사 수동태(~돼야 하다)   대명사 it is
machinery, / but the machine cannot mend it when broken, / much less a clock or a
pistol!"

01 물건을 고치고 복원하는 것mend and restore objects은 / 흔히 훨씬 더 많은 창의력이 필요하다 / 최초 제작보다.

02 산업화 이전의 대장장이preindustrial blacksmith는 주문에 따라 물건을 만들었기에 / 가까이에 사는immediate 마을 사람들을 위해 / 제품을 주문 제작하는customize 것, / 즉 사용자에게 맞게 그것을 수정하거나modify 변형하는 일이 / 일상적이었다. // 고객들은 물건을 다시 가져다주곤 했고, / 뭔가 잘못되면 / 따라서 수리는 제작fabrication의 연장이었다.

03 산업화와 결국 대량 생산이 이루어지면서, / 물건을 만드는 것은 제한된 지식을 지닌 기계 관리자의 영역the province of machine tenders이 되었다.

04 그러나 수리는 계속했다 / 설계와 재료에 대한 더 큰 이해grasp를 요구하기를 / 즉 전체에 대한 이해와 설계자의 의도에 대한 이해comprehension를.

05 "제조업자들은 모두 일하고, / 기계나 방대한 분업vast subdivision of labour으로 / 말하자면 수작업으로 일하지는 않는다." / 1896년의 〈Manual of Mending and Repairing〉은 설명한다. // "그러나 모든 수리는 손으로 '해야 한다'. / 우리는 기계로 손목시계나 총의 모든 세부적인 것을 만들 수 있지만, / 기계는 그게 고장 났을 때 고칠 수 없으며, / 시계나 권총은 말할 것도 없다!"

---

① The preindustrial blacksmith made things to order for people in his immediate community; customize / customizing the product, modifying or transforming it according to the user, was routine.

세미콜론(;) 뒤로 새로운 절이 연결된다. 동사 was 앞에 주어가 필요하므로 동명사 customizing이 적절하다.

② We can make every detail of a watch or of a gun by machinery, but the machine cannot mend it when breaking / broken, much less a clock or a pistol!"

when절의 생략된 주어 it이 앞의 a watch or a gun을 받는 대명사인데, 이는 '고장 나는' 대상이므로 과거분사 broken을 써야 한다.

정답 ① customizing ② broken

33

STEP 1 • 수능에 진짜 나오는 단어

✔ 문제에 나오는 단어들을 확인하세요.

01	temporal	*a.* 시간적인	(✔ temporal) dimensions	시간적 차원
02	phenomenon	*n.* 현상	a cultural ( )	문화적 현상
03	spatial	*a.* 공간적인	( ) ability	공간 능력
04	identify	*v.* (신원 등을) 알아맞히다, 인정하다	( ) an object	물건을 알아맞히다
05	perception	*n.* 지각	the sensory ( ) of touch	촉각이라는 감각적 지각
06	acuity	*n.* (감각의) 예리함	have high ( )	몹시 예리하다
07	make use of	~을 사용하다	( ) complex ( ) ( ) touch	촉각을 복잡하게 사용하다
08	unlock	*v.* 열다	( ) your front door	현관문을 열다
09	continuous	*a.* 지속적인	( ) patterns	지속적인 패턴
10	sensation	*n.* 느낌, 감각	touch ( )	촉각적 감각(촉감)

➕ 본문 문장 속에서 단어들을 확인해 보세요.

People don't usually think of touch as a temporal phenomenon, / but it is every bit as time-based as it is spatial.

사람들은 보통 촉각을 시간의 현상으로 생각하지 않지만, / 그것은 공간적인 만큼 전적으로 시간에 기반을 두고 있다.

01	temporal	🖉 시간적인	temporal dimensions	(시간적)차원
02	phenomenon		a cultural phenomenon	문화적 ( )
03	spatial		spatial ability	( )능력
04	identify		identify an object	물건을 ( )
05	perception		the sensory perception of touch	촉각이라는 감각적 ( )
06	acuity		have high acuity	몹시 ( )
07	make use of		make complex use of touch	촉각을 복잡하게 ( )
08	unlock		unlock your front door	현관문을 ( )
09	continuous		continuous patterns	( )패턴
10	sensation		touch sensation	촉각적 ( )

➕ **본문 문장 속에서 단어의 의미를 우리말로 해석해 보세요.**

People don't usually think of touch as a temporal phenomenon, / but it is every bit as time-based as it is spatial.

➡ 사람들은 보통 ▨▨▨▨▨▨▨▨▨▨▨▨▨▨ 않지만, / 그것은 ▨▨▨▨▨▨▨▨ 만큼 전적으로 시간에 기반을 두고 있다.

33 다음 글의 제목으로 가장 적절한 것은?

People don't usually think of touch as a temporal phenomenon, but it is every bit as time-based as it is spatial. You can carry out an experiment to see for yourself. Ask a friend to cup his hand, palm face up, and close his eyes. Place a small ordinary object in his palm — a ring, an eraser, anything will do — and ask him to identify it without moving any part of his hand. He won't have a clue other than weight and maybe overall size. Then tell him to keep his eyes closed and move his fingers over the object. He'll most likely identify it at once. By allowing the fingers to move, you've added time to the sensory perception of touch. There's a direct analogy between the fovea at the center of your retina and your fingertips, both of which have high acuity. Your ability to make complex use of touch, such as buttoning your shirt or unlocking your front door in the dark, depends on continuous time-varying patterns of touch sensation.

*analogy: 유사 **fovea: (망막의) 중심와(窩) ***retina: 망막

① Touch and Movement: Two Major Elements of Humanity

② Time Does Matter: A Hidden Essence of Touch

③ How to Use the Five Senses in a Timely Manner

④ The Role of Touch in Forming the Concept of Time

⑤ The Surprising Function of Touch as a Booster of Knowledge

정답과 해설 p.30

01 People don't usually think of touch as a temporal phenomenon, / but it is every bit
「think of A as B: A를 B로 여기다」
as time-based as it is spatial.
「as + 원급 + as: ~만큼 …한」

02 You can carry out an experiment / to see for yourself.
부사적 용법(목적)

03 Ask a friend / to cup his hand, / palm face up, / and close his eyes. // Place a small
동사(명령문)   목적격보어1   목적격보어2   목적격보어3   명령문 병렬
ordinary object in his palm / — (a ring, an eraser, anything will do) — / and ask him to
삽입절
identify it / without moving any part of his hand. // He won't have a clue / other than
「without + 동명사: ~하지 않으면서」
weight and maybe overall size.

04 Then tell him / to keep his eyes closed / and move his fingers over the object. // He'll
동사 목적어 목적격보어1   목적격보어2
most likely identify it at once. // By allowing the fingers to move, / you've added time
「by + 동명사: ~함으로써」
to the sensory perception of touch.

05 There's a direct analogy / between the fovea at the center of your retina and your
주어   전치사구
fingertips, / both of which have high acuity. // Your ability to make complex use
계속적 용법   주어   형용사적 용법
of touch, / such as buttoning your shirt or unlocking your front door in the dark, /
동명사1   동명사2
depends on continuous time-varying patterns of touch sensation.
동사(단수)

---

01 사람들은 보통 촉각을 시간의 현상temporal phenomenon으로 생각하지 않지만, / 그것은 공간적인spatial 만큼
전적으로 시간에 기반을 두고 있다.

02 여러분은 실험을 해볼 수 있다 / 직접 알아보려면.

03 친구에게 요청해 보라 / 손을 컵 모양으로 동그랗게 모아 쥐고, / 손바닥이 위로 향하게 해서, / 눈을 감으라고. // 그의
손바닥에 작은 평범한 물건을 올려놓고 / ― 반지, 지우개, 무엇이든 괜찮다 ― / 그것이 무엇인지 알아맞혀identify 보라고
요청해 보라 / 손의 어떤 부분도 움직이지 말고. // 그는 아무것도 모를 것이다 / 무게와 아마 전체적인 크기 외에.

04 그런 다음 그에게 말하라 / 눈을 감은 채로 있으면서 / 그 물건 위로 손가락을 움직여보라고. // 그는 거의 틀림없이 그것이
무엇인지 즉시 알아낼 것이다. // 손가락이 움직이게 함으로써 / 여러분은 촉각이라는 감각적 지각perception에 시간을
더했다.

05 직접적인 유사함이 있는데 / 망막의 중심에 있는 중심와(窩)와 손가락 끝 사이에 / 둘 다 몹시 예민하다have high acuity는
것이다. // 촉각을 복잡하게 사용하는make complex use of touch 능력은 / 어둠 속에서 셔츠 단추를 잠그거나 현관문을
여는unlock 것과 같이 / 지속적이고도continuous 시간에 따라 달라지는 촉각touch sensation의 패턴에 의존한다.

구문 Check up

① Then tell him to keep his eyes closed and move /
moved his fingers over the object.

tell의 목적격보어인 to keep과 병렬을 이루는 두 번째 목적격보어가 필
요하므로 (to) move가 적절하다.

② There's a direct analogy between the fovea at the
center of your retina and your fingertips, both of which
/ them have high acuity.

콤마 앞뒤로 절이 연결되는 것으로 보아, 접속사와 대명사 역할을 동시에
수행하는 관계대명사 which가 적절하다. 선행사는 'the fovea ~ and your
fingertips'이다.

정답 ① move ② which

34

STEP 1 • 수능에 *진짜* 나오는 *단어*

✔ **문제에 나오는 단어들을 확인하세요.**

01	humbling	a. 겸손해지게 하는	a (✔ humbling) experience	겸손해지게 하는 경험
02	calming	a. 진정시키는	a ( ) effect	진정시키는 효과
03	observe	v. 목격하다, 관찰하다	( ) the effect	효과를 관찰하다
04	absolutely	ad. 완전히, 절대적으로	( ) impossible	완전히 불가능한
05	adjust	v. 조정하다	( ) the limit to satisfy our needs	우리의 필요를 충족시키기 위해 한계를 조정하다
06	uncertainty	n. 불확실성	the level of ( )	불확실성의 수준
07	emerge	v. 나타나다, 생기다	goals that suddenly ( )	갑자기 생기는 목표
08	attainable	a. 달성 가능한	( ) goals	달성 가능한 목표
09	inherently	ad. 본질적으로	our ( ) incomplete knowledge	우리의 본질적으로 불완전한 지식
10	precisely	ad. 정확히	know ( ) how high is the highest mountain	가장 높은 산이 얼마나 높은지 정확히 알다

➕ **본문 문장 속에서 단어들을 확인해 보세요.**

We know within limits, / not absolutely, / even if the limits can usually be adjusted to satisfy our needs.

우리는 한계 내에서 알며, / 완전히는 아니다 / 비록 그 한계가 보통 우리의 필요를 충족시키기 위해 조정될 수 있을지라도.

문제를 풀기 전에 단어들을 30초 동안 다시 확인하세요.

01	humbling	🖊 겸손해지게 하는	a humbling experience	(겸손해지게 하는)경험
02	calming		a calming effect	( )효과
03	observe		observe the effect	효과를 ( )
04	absolutely		absolutely impossible	( )불가능한
05	adjust		adjust the limit to satisfy our needs	우리의 필요를 충족시키기 위해 한계를 ( )
06	uncertainty		the level of uncertainty	( )의 수준
07	emerge		goals that suddenly emerge	갑자기 ( )목표
08	attainable		attainable goals	( )목표
09	inherently		our inherently incomplete knowledge	우리의 ( )불완전한 지식
10	precisely		know precisely how high is the highest mountain	가장 높은 산이 얼마나 높은지 ( )알다

➕ 본문 문장 속에서 단어의 의미를 우리말로 해석해 보세요.

We know within limits, / not absolutely, / even if the limits can usually be adjusted to satisfy our needs.

➔ 우리는 한계 내에서 알며, / ⬛⬛⬛⬛⬛ 는 아니다 / 비록 그 한계가 보통 ⬛⬛⬛⬛⬛⬛⬛⬛⬛⬛⬛ 수 있을지라도.

34 다음 글의 제목으로 가장 적절한 것은?

The discovery that man's knowledge is not, and *never has been*, perfectly accurate has had a humbling and perhaps a calming effect upon the soul of modern man. The nineteenth century, as we have observed, was the last to believe that the world, as a whole as well as in its parts, could ever be perfectly known. We realize now that this is, and always was, impossible. We know within limits, not absolutely, even if the limits can usually be adjusted to satisfy our needs. Curiously, from this new level of uncertainty even greater goals emerge and appear to be attainable. Even if we cannot know the world with absolute precision, we can still control it. Even our inherently incomplete knowledge seems to work as powerfully as ever. In short, we may never know precisely how high is the highest mountain, but we continue to be certain that we can get to the top nevertheless.

① Summits Yet to Be Reached: An Onward Journey to Knowledge

② Over the Mountain: A Single But Giant Step to Success

③ Integrating Parts into a Whole: The Road to Perfection

④ How to Live Together in an Age of Uncertainty

⑤ The Two Faces of a Knowledge-Based Society

정답과 해설 **p.31**

01 The discovery / [that man's knowledge is not, and *never has been*, perfectly accurate] /
주어　　　동격
has had a humbling and perhaps a calming effect / upon the soul of modern man.
동사(단수)

02 The nineteenth century, / (as we have observed), / was the last to believe / [that the
주어　　　　　　　삽입절　　　　　　주격보어　형용사적 용법　　동사　　　접속사(~것)　주어
world, / (as a whole as well as in its parts), / could ever be perfectly known].
삽입구　　　　　　　　　　　　　동사(조동사 수동태)

03 We realize now / [that this is, and always was, impossible]. // We know within limits, /
접속사(~것)
(not absolutely), / even if the limits can usually be adjusted to satisfy our needs.
삽입구　　　　　　　　　동사(조동사 수동태)　　　부사적 용법(목적)

04 Curiously, / from this new level of uncertainty / even greater goals emerge / and appear
비교급 수식(훨씬)
to be attainable. // Even if we cannot know the world with absolute precision, / we can
= absolutely precisely
still control it.
(with + 추상명사=부사)

05 Even our inherently incomplete knowledge / seems to work as powerfully as ever.
「as + 원급 + as ever: 그 어느 때만큼이나 ~한」

06 In short, / we may never know precisely / how high is the highest mountain, / but we
주어1　동사1　　　　　　　　　　　　　　　　　　　　주어2
continue to be certain / that we can get to the top nevertheless.
동사2

01 발견은 / 인간의 지식이 완벽하게 정확하지 않고, 그랬던 적이 '결코 없다'는 / 겸손해지게 하는humbling, 그리고 아마도 진정시키는calming 효과를 가져다주었다 / 현대 인간의 영혼에.

02 19세기는 / 우리가 목격했듯이observe, / 믿은 마지막 시기였다 / 세계가 / 그것의 부분들뿐만 아니라 전체로서, / 언제나 완벽하게 알려질 수 있다고.

03 우리는 이제 깨닫는다 / 이것이 불가능하며, 언제나 불가능했다는 것을. // 우리는 한계 내에서 알며, / 완전히absolutely는 아니다 / 비록 그 한계가 보통 우리의 필요를 충족시키기 위해 조정될adjust 수 있을지라도.

04 의아스럽게도 / 이 새로운 수준의 불확실성uncertainty으로부터 / 훨씬 더 위대한 목표가 나타나고emerge / 달성 가능해attainable 보인다. // 비록 우리가 세계를 절대적으로 정확하게 알 수 없을지라도, / 우리는 여전히 그것을 제어할 수 있다.

05 심지어 우리의 본질적으로inherently 불완전한 지식조차도 / 그 어느 때만큼이나 강력하게 작동하는 듯 보인다.

06 간단히 말해, / 우리는 결코 정확하게precisely 알 수 없을 테지만, / 가장 높은 산이 얼마나 높은지 / 우리는 계속 확신한다 / 그런데도 우리가 정상에 도달할 수 있다는 것을.

구문 Check up

① The discovery that / which man's knowledge is not, and *never has been*, perfectly accurate has had a humbling and perhaps a calming effect upon the soul of modern man.

뒤에 The discovery의 내용을 설명하는 완전한 2형식 문장(man's knowledge ~ accurate)이 나오므로 동격의 접속사 that을 써야 한다.

② Curiously, from this new level of uncertainty very / even greater goals emerge and appear to be attainable.

뒤에 비교급 형용사 greater가 있으므로 비교급을 수식할 수 있는 even이 적절하다. very는 원급 또는 최상급을 꾸민다.

정답 ① that ② even

STEP 1 · 수능에 진짜 나오는 단어

글의 제목 ⊕

✔ 문제에 나오는 단어들을 확인하세요.

01	withdrawal	n. 위축, 움츠리기	social (✔ withdrawal)	사회적 위축
02	cling to	~에 집착하다, 매달리다	( ) ( ) the past	과거에 집착하다
03	characteristically	ad. 특징적으로	be ( ) represented	특징적으로 기술되다
04	represent	v. 기술하다, 묘사하다	( ) him as evil	그를 악으로 묘사하다
05	symptom	n. 증상	the ( )s of depression	우울증의 증상
06	inevitable	a. 필연적인, 불가피한	the ( ) result	필연적인 결과
07	involuntary	a. 비자발적인, 원치 않는	( ) unemployment	비자발적 실업
08	retirement	n. 퇴직, 은퇴	early ( )	조기 퇴직
09	strip A of B	A에게서 B를 빼앗다	( ) him ( ) his title	그에게서 직함을 빼앗다
10	deprive A of B	A에게서 B를 박탈하다	( ) elderly people ( ) their social roles	노인들에게서 사회적 역할을 박탈하다
11	occupy	v. ~의 마음을 사로잡다	the activities that ( ) them	그들의 마음을 사로잡는 흥미와 활동

⊕ 본문 문장 속에서 단어들을 확인해 보세요.

The location of senile mental deterioration / was no longer the aging brain / but a society / that, through involuntary retirement, social isolation, and the loosening of traditional family ties, / stripped the elderly of the roles / that had sustained meaning in their lives.

노쇠한 이들의 정신적 노화의 장소는 / 더 이상 노화한 뇌가 아니라 / 사회였다 / 비자발적 퇴직, 사회적 고립, 그리고 전통적인 가족 유대감의 해체를 통해 / 노인들에게서 역할을 빼앗아 버린 / 그들의 삶에서 의미를 유지했던.

01	withdrawal	✎ 위축, 움츠리기	social withdrawal	사회적 (위축)
02	cling to		cling to the past	과거에 ( )
03	characteristically		be characteristically represented	( ) 기술되다
04	represent		represent him as evil	그를 악으로 ( )
05	symptom		the symptoms of depression	우울증의 ( )
06	inevitable		the inevitable result	( ) 결과
07	involuntary		involuntary unemployment	( ) 실업
08	retirement		early retirement	조기 ( )
09	strip A of B		strip him of his title	그에게서 직함을 ( )
10	deprive A of B		deprive elderly people of their social roles	노인들에게서 사회적 역할을 ( )
11	occupy		the activities that occupy them	그들의 마음을 ( ) 흥미와 활동

➕ 본문 문장 속에서 단어의 의미를 우리말로 해석해 보세요.

The location of senile mental deterioration / was no longer the aging brain / but a society / that, through involuntary retirement, social isolation, and the loosening of traditional family ties, / stripped the elderly of the roles / that had sustained meaning in their lives.

➜ 노쇠한 이들의 정신적 노화의 장소는 / 더 이상 노화한 뇌가 아니라 / 사회였다 / ▓▓▓▓▓▓▓▓, ▓▓▓▓▓▓, 그리고 전통적인 가족 유대감의 해체를 통해 / ▓▓▓▓▓▓▓▓▓▓▓▓▓▓▓ / 그들의 삶에서 의미를 유지했던.

35 다음 글의 제목으로 가장 적절한 것은?

From the late nineteenth century on, the dullness found in the senile, their isolation and withdrawal, their clinging to the past and lack of interest in worldly affairs were characteristically represented as the *symptoms* of senility — the social shame of the inevitable deterioration of the brain. Following World War II, academic discourse on aging typically represented these as the *causes* of senility. The location of senile mental deterioration was no longer the aging brain but a society that, through involuntary retirement, social isolation, and the loosening of traditional family ties, stripped the elderly of the roles that had sustained meaning in their lives. When elderly people were deprived of these meaningful social roles, when they became increasingly isolated and were cut off from the interests and activities that had earlier occupied them, not surprisingly their mental functioning deteriorated. The elderly did not so much lose their minds as lose their place.

*senile: 노쇠한 **deterioration: 노화

① Aged Mind in Concert with Aged Body: An Unfailing Truth

② No Change from Past to Present: Social Images of Old Age

③ No Country for Old Men: Age Discrimination Intensified

④ What Makes the Elderly Decline: Being Left Out Socially

⑤ Not Disabled But Differently Abled: New Faces of Old Age

정답과 해설 p.32

01 From the late nineteenth century on, / the dullness found in the senile, / their
　　주어1　　　　　　↑　　　　　과거분사구　　　주어2
isolation and withdrawal, / their clinging to the past and lack of interest in worldly
　　　　　　　　　　　주어3
affairs / were characteristically represented / as the *symptoms* of senility / — the social
　　　　동사(복수)　　　　　　　　　　　　　　　　　↓　　　　동격
shame of the inevitable deterioration of the brain.

02 Following World War II, / academic discourse on aging / typically represented these as
　　　　　　　　　　　　　　　　　　　　　　　　　「represent A as B: A를 B라고 기술하다」
the *causes* of senility.

「no longer A but B: 더 이상 A가 아니라 B인」

03 The location of senile mental deterioration / was no longer the aging brain / but
a society / [that, (through involuntary retirement, social isolation, and the loosening
　선행사　↑　　　주격 관계대명사절　　　　　　　삽입구
of traditional family ties), / stripped the elderly of the roles / {that had sustained
　　　　　　　　　　　　　　「strip A of B: A에게서 B를 빼앗다」　　　　↑　　　주격 관계대명사절
meaning in their lives}].

04 When elderly people were deprived of these meaningful social roles, / when they
　　　　　　　　「A be deprived of B: A가 B를 박탈당하다」　　　　　접속사(~할 때)
became increasingly isolated / and were cut off from the interests and activities / [that
　　　　　　　　　　　　　　　　　　　　　　　　　　선행사　　　　↑
had earlier occupied them], / not surprisingly their mental functioning deteriorated.
　주격 관계대명사절　　　　　　　　　　　　주어　　　　　　　　　　동사

05 The elderly did not so much lose their minds / as lose their place.
　　　　　　　　└──── 「not so much A as B: A라기보다 B인」────┘

01 19세기 후반부터 줄곧, / 노쇠한 이들에게서 발견되는 활기 부족, / 그들의 고립과 위축withdrawal, / 그들의 과거에 대한 집착their clinging to the past과 세상사에 대한 관심 결여는 / 특징적으로 기술되었다be characteristically represented / 노쇠의 '증상'symptom이라고, / 즉 뇌의 필연적인inevitable 노화의 사회적 수치로서.

02 제2차 세계 대전 후에 / 노화에 대한 학술적 담론은 / 이것들을 전형적으로 노쇠의 '원인'으로 기술했다.

03 노쇠한 이들의 정신적 노화의 장소는 / 더 이상 노화한 뇌가 아니라 / 사회였다 / 비자발적 퇴직involuntary retirement, 사회적 고립, 그리고 전통적인 가족 유대감의 해체를 통해 / 노인들에게서 역할을 빼앗아 버린strip the elderly of the roles / 그들의 삶에서 의미를 유지했던.

04 노인들이 이 의미 있는 사회적 역할을 박탈당했을 때be deprived of these meaningful social roles, / 그들이 점점 더 고립되고 / 흥미와 활동으로부터 단절되었을 때 / 예전에 그들의 마음을 사로잡았던occupy / 당연하게도 그들의 정신이 노화했다.

05 그 노인들은 그들의 정신을 잃었다기보다는 / 그들의 위치를 잃었다.

구문 Check up

① The location of senile mental deterioration was a society that / where , through involuntary retirement, stripped the elderly of the roles that had sustained meaning in their lives.

선행사 a society를 수식하는 'stripped the elderly ~'가 주어 없이 불완전한 절이므로 주격 관계대명사 that이 적절하다.

② The elderly did not so much lose their minds as lose / losing their place.

「not so much A as B(A라기보다는 B인)」 구문에서 A, B는 병렬구조를 이루므로, lose와 마찬가지로 동사인 lose가 적절하다.

정답 ① that ② lose

36

STEP 1 • 수능에 *진짜* 나오는 *단어*

✔ **문제에 나오는 단어들을 확인하세요.**

01	director	n. 감독	a French film (✔ director)	프랑스 영화감독
02	painter	n. 화가	the son of the famous ( )	유명 화가의 아들
03	outbreak	n. 발발	at the ( ) of World War I	제1차 세계대전의 발발
04	serve in the army	군에서 복무하다	( ) ( ) ( ) French ( )	프랑스 군에서 복무하다
05	wound	v. 부상 입히다	be ( )ed in the leg	다리에 부상을 입다
06	enormously	ad. 엄청나게, 대단히	( ) successful	엄청나게 성공적인
07	invade	v. 침공하다	The Nazis ( )d France in 1940.	나치는 1940년 프랑스를 침공했다.
08	numerous	a. 수많은	be awarded ( ) honors and awards	수많은 명예상과 상을 받다
09	throughout	prep. ~ 내내, ~을 통틀어	( ) his career	그의 경력 내내
10	endure	v. 지속되다	His influence as an artist ( )s.	예술가로서 그의 영향력은 지속되고 있다.

⊕ **본문 문장 속에서 단어들을 확인해 보세요.**

At the outbreak of World War I, / Jean Renoir was serving in the French army / but was wounded in the leg.

제1차 세계대전이 발발했을 때, / Jean Renoir는 프랑스 군에서 복무하는 중이었는데 / 다리에 부상을 입었다.

문제를 풀기 전에 단어들을 **30초** 동안 다시 확인하세요.

01	director ✏ 감독	a French film director	프랑스 영화(감독)
02	painter	the son of the famous painter	유명( )의 아들
03	outbreak	at the outbreak of World War I	제1차 세계대전의 ( )
04	serve in the army	serve in the French army	프랑스 ( )
05	wound	be wounded in the leg	다리에 ( )
06	enormously	enormously successful	( ) 성공적인
07	invade	The Nazis invaded France in 1940.	나치는 1940년 프랑스를 ( ).
08	numerous	be awarded numerous honors and awards	( ) 명예상과 상을 받다
09	throughout	throughout his career	그의 경력 ( )
10	endure	His influence as an artist endures.	예술가로서 그의 영향력은 ( ) 있다.

➕ **본문 문장 속에서 단어의 의미를 우리말로 해석해 보세요.**

At the outbreak of World War I, / Jean Renoir was serving in the French army / but was wounded in the leg.

→ ⬚⬚⬚⬚⬚⬚⬚⬚⬚⬚⬚, / Jean Renoir는 ⬚⬚⬚⬚⬚⬚⬚⬚⬚ 중이었는데 / ⬚⬚⬚⬚⬚⬚⬚⬚⬚.

36 다음 글의 내용과 일치하지 <u>않는</u> 것은?

Jean Renoir (1894—1979), a French film director, was born in Paris, France. He was the son of the famous painter Pierre-Auguste Renoir. He and the rest of the Renoir family were the models of many of his father's paintings. At the outbreak of World War I, Jean Renoir was serving in the French army but was wounded in the leg. In 1937, he made *La Grande Illusion*, one of his better-known films. It was enormously successful but was not allowed to show in Germany. During World War II, when the Nazis invaded France in 1940, he went to Hollywood in the United States and continued his career there. He was awarded numerous honors and awards throughout his career, including the Academy Honorary Award in 1975 for his lifetime achievements in the film industry. Overall, Jean Renoir's influence as a film-maker and artist endures.

① 유명 화가의 아들이었다.
② 제1차 세계대전이 발발했을 때 프랑스 군에 복무 중이었다.
③ *La Grande Illusion*을 1937년에 만들었다.
④ 제2차 세계대전 내내 프랑스에 머물렀다.
⑤ Academy Honorary Award를 수상하였다.

정답과 해설 p.33

01 Jean Renoir (1894—1979), a French film director, / was born in Paris, France. // He was
주어   주어 동격(직위, 신분 등 보충 설명)
the son of the famous painter Pierre-Auguste Renoir. // He and the rest of the Renoir
                                                                                    주어
family / were the models of many of his father's paintings.
            동사(복수)

02 At the outbreak of World War I, / Jean Renoir was serving in the French army / but was
시간 부사구(역사적 과거)   동사1(과거진행)   동사2(과거)
wounded in the leg.

03 In 1937, / he made *La Grande Illusion*, / one of his better-known films. // It was
                                              동격
enormously successful / but was not allowed to show in Germany.

04 During World War II, / when the Nazis invaded France in 1940, / he went to Hollywood
전치사(~동안)   접속사(~할 때)
in the United States / and continued his career there. // He was awarded numerous
                                                                      4형식 수동태   목적어(~을)
honors and awards throughout his career, / including the Academy Honorary Award in
                                                          전치사(~을 포함해)
1975 / for his lifetime achievements in the film industry.

주어-동사 수 일치
05 Overall, / Jean Renoir's influence as a film-maker and artist / endures.
                                            전치사(~로서)

01 프랑스 영화감독**film director**인 Jean Renoir(1894~1979)는 / 프랑스 파리에서 태어났다. // 그는 유명 화가**painter**
Pierre-Auguste Renoir의 아들이었다. // 그와 나머지 Renoir 가족은 / 아버지의 그림 중 다수의 모델이었다.

02 제1차 세계대전이 발발**outbreak**했을 때, / Jean Renoir는 프랑스 군에서 복무하다가**serve in the army** / 다리에 부상을
입었다**be wounded**.

03 1937년에 / 그는 <La Grande Illusion>을 만들었다 / 그의 더 잘 알려진 영화 중 하나인. // 그것은 엄청나게**enormously**
흥행했지만, / 독일에서는 상영이 허용되지 않았다.

04 제2차 세계대전 중, / 1940년에 나치가 프랑스를 침공했을**invade** 때 / 그는 미국 할리우드로 가서 / 거기서 경력을
이어갔다. // 그는 경력 내내**throughout** 수많은**numerous** 명예상과 상을 받았다 / 1975년 아카데미 공로상을 포함해 /
영화계에서의 평생의 업적에 대한.

05 전반적으로, / 영화 제작자이자 예술가로서의 Jean Renoir의 영향력은 / 지속되고 있다**endure**.

구문 Check up	① During World War II, which / when the Nazis invaded France in 1940, he went to Hollywood in the United States and continued his career there.	② Overall, Jean Renoir's influence as a film-maker and artist enduring / endures.
	과거의 한때를 설명하는 부사절 접속사로 when을 쓴다. when 뒤에는 완전한 절이 온다.	주어 Jean Renoir's influence 다음 동사가 필요하므로 endures를 써야 한다.

정답 ① when ② endures

37

STEP 1 • 수능에 *진짜* 나오는 *단어*

✔ 문제에 나오는 단어들을 확인하세요.

01	**psychologist**	n. 심리학자	a social (✔ psychologist)	사회 심리학자
02	**immigrant**	n. 이민자	born to a Russian ( ) family	러시아인 이민자 가정에서 태어난
03	**leading**	a. 선도적인, 가장 중요한	a ( ) researcher	선도적인 연구자
04	**comparison**	n. 비교	his theory of social ( )	그의 사회 비교 이론
05	**earn**	v. (~에게 …을) 얻게 해주다	( ) him a trophy	그에게 트로피를 얻게 해주다
06	**reputation**	n. 명성	build a great ( )	대단한 명성을 쌓다
07	**cite**	v. 인용하다	one of the most ( )d psychologists	가장 많이 인용된 심리학자들 중 한 명

✚ 본문 문장 속에서 단어들을 확인해 보세요.

His theory of social comparison / earned him a good reputation.

그의 사회 비교 이론은 / 그에게 훌륭한 명성을 얻게 해주었다.

단어 다시보기 문제를 풀기 전에 단어들을 30초 동안 다시 확인하세요.

01	psychologist	심리학자	a social psychologist	사회 (심리학자)
02	immigrant		born to a Russian immigrant family	러시아인 ( ) 가정에서 태어난
03	leading		a leading researcher	( ) 연구자
04	comparison		his theory of social comparison	그의 사회 ( ) 이론
05	earn		earn him a trophy	그에게 트로피를 ( )
06	reputation		build a great reputation	대단한 ( )을 쌓다
07	cite		one of the most cited psychologists	가장 많이 ( ) 심리학자 들 중 한 명

⊕ 본문 문장 속에서 단어의 의미를 우리말로 해석해 보세요.

His theory of social comparison / earned him a good reputation.

→ 그의 ______ 이론은 / ______.

37 Leon Festinger에 관한 다음 글의 내용과 일치하지 <u>않는</u> 것은?

Leon Festinger was an American social psychologist. He was born in New York City in 1919 to a Russian immigrant family. As a graduate student at the University of Iowa, Festinger was influenced by Kurt Lewin, a leading social psychologist. After graduating from there, he became a professor at the Massachusetts Institute of Technology in 1945. He later moved to Stanford University, where he continued his work in social psychology. His theory of social comparison earned him a good reputation. Festinger actively participated in international scholarly cooperation. In the late 1970s, he turned his interest to the field of history. He was one of the most cited psychologists of the twentieth century. Festinger's theories still play an important role in psychology today.

① 러시아인 이민자 가정에서 태어났다.

② 사회 심리학자 Kurt Lewin에게 영향을 받았다.

③ Stanford University에서 사회 심리학 연구를 중단했다.

④ 국제 학술 협력에 활발하게 참여했다.

⑤ 1970년대 후반에 역사 분야로 관심을 돌렸다.

정답과 해설 p.33

01 Leon Festinger was an American social psychologist. // He was born in New York City in 1919 / to a Russian immigrant family.

02 As a graduate student at the University of Iowa, / Festinger was influenced by
전치사(~로서)
Kurt Lewin, / a leading social psychologist. // After graduating from there, / he became
└─── 동격 ───┘   접속사가 있는 분사구문(= After he graduated ~)
a professor / at the Massachusetts Institute of Technology / in 1945.

03 He later moved to Stanford University, / where he continued his work in social
선행사(장소)   계속적 용법
psychology. // His theory of social comparison / earned him a good reputation.
                                                동사   간접목적어   직접목적어

04 Festinger actively participated in international scholarly cooperation.

05 In the late 1970s, / he turned his interest to the field of history. // He was one of the
시간 부사구(연도)   동사(과거)   「one of the + 최상급 + 복수명사:
most cited psychologists of the twentieth century.   가장 ~한 … 중 하나」

06 Festinger's theories still play an important role / in psychology today.

---

01 Leon Festinger는 미국의 사회 심리학자psychologist였다. // 그는 1919년 뉴욕에서 태어났다 / 러시아인 이민자immigrant 가정에서.

02 아이오와대학교의 대학원생으로서, / Festinger는 Kurt Lewin의 영향을 받았다 / 선도적인leading 사회 심리학자인. // 그곳을 졸업한 후 / 그는 교수가 되었다 / 매사추세츠 공과대학에서 / 1945년에.

03 이후 그는 스탠퍼드대학교로 옮겼고 / 그곳에서 그는 사회 심리학 연구를 계속했다. // 그의 사회 비교social comparison 이론은 / 그에게 훌륭한 명성을 얻게 해주었다earn him a good reputation.

04 Festinger는 국제 학술 협력에 적극적으로 참여했다.

05 1970년대 후반, / 그는 역사 분야로 관심을 돌렸다. // 그는 20세기에 가장 많이 인용된cite 심리학자 중 한 명이었다.

06 Festinger의 이론은 여전히 중요한 역할을 한다 / 현대 심리학에서도.

구문 Check up

① As a graduate student at the University of Iowa, Festinger influenced / was influenced by Kurt Lewin, a leading social psychologist.

주어 Festinger가 'Kurt Lewin에 의해 영향을 받는' 대상이므로 was influenced가 적절하다.

② He later moved to Stanford University, which / where he continued his work in social psychology.

앞에 장소 선행사 Stanford University가 있고 뒤에 'he continued his work ~'라는 완전한 3형식 문장이 나오므로 관계부사 where가 적절하다.

정답 ① was influenced ② where

38

STEP 1 • 수능에 진짜 나오는 단어

✔ **문제에 나오는 단어들을 확인하세요.**

01	share	n. 몫, 점유율 v. 공유하다	Korea's market (✔ share)	한국의 시장 점유율
02	middle class	중산층	the global ( ) ( )	세계 중산층
03	region	n. 지역	by ( )	지역별로
04	project	v. 예상하다	the ( )ed share of the world population	예상되는 세계 인구 점유율
05	Pacific	n. 태평양 a. 태평양의	countries in Asia ( )	아시아 태평양 (지역)의 국가들
06	among	prep. ~ 중에서	the largest ( ) the six regions	여섯 개 지역 중에서 가장 큰
07	sub-Saharan	a. 사하라 사막 이남의	( ) Africa	사하라 사막 이남의 아프리카

✚ **본문 문장 속에서 단어들을 확인해 보세요.**

It is projected / that the share of the global middle class in Asia Pacific / will increase / from 46 percent in 2015 / to 60 percent in 2025.

예상된다 / 아시아 태평양의 세계 중산층 점유율은 / 증가할 것으로 / 2015년에 46퍼센트로부터 / 2025년에는 60퍼센트로.

01	share	🖉 몫, 점유율	Korea's market share	한국의 시장 (점유율)
02	middle class		the global middle class	세계 ( )
03	region		by region	( )별로
04	project		the projected share of the world population	( ) 세계 인구 점유율
05	Pacific		countries in Asia Pacific	아시아 ( )의 국가들
06	among		the largest among the six regions	여섯 개 지역 ( ) 가장 큰
07	sub-Saharan		sub-Saharan Africa	( ) 아프리카

➕ **본문 문장 속에서 단어의 의미를 우리말로 해석해 보세요.**

It is projected / that the share of the global middle class in Asia Pacific / will increase / from 46 percent in 2015 / to 60 percent in 2025.

➡   /   은 / 증가할 것으로 / 2015년에 46퍼센트로부터 / 2025년에는 60퍼센트로.

38 다음 도표의 내용과 일치하지 않는 것은?

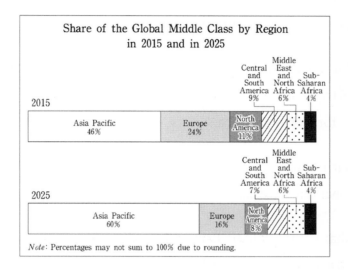

The above graphs show the percentage share of the global middle class by region in 2015 and its projected share in 2025. ① It is projected that the share of the global middle class in Asia Pacific will increase from 46 percent in 2015 to 60 percent in 2025. ② The projected share of Asia Pacific in 2025, the largest among the six regions, is more than three times that of Europe in the same year. ③ The shares of Europe and North America are both projected to decrease, from 24 percent in 2015 to 16 percent in 2025 for Europe, and from 11 percent in 2015 to 8 percent in 2025 for North America. ④ Central and South America is not expected to change from 2015 to 2025 in its share of the global middle class. ⑤ In 2025, the share of the Middle East and North Africa will be larger than that of sub-Saharan Africa, as it was in 2015.

정답과 해설 **p.34**

161

01 The above graphs / show / the percentage share of the global middle class by region in 2015 / and its projected share in 2025.

02 It is projected / [that the share of the global middle class in Asia Pacific / will increase / from 46 percent in 2015 / to 60 percent in 2025].
접속사(진주어절)
가주어   주어   동사
「from A to B: A부터 B까지」

03 The projected share of Asia Pacific in 2025, / (the largest among the six regions), / is more than three times that of Europe in the same year.
주어(선행사)   삽입구(주어 동격)   동사(단수)
배수사   지시대명사(= the projected share)

04 The shares of Europe and North America / are both projected to decrease, / from 24 percent in 2015 to 16 percent in 2025 for Europe, / and from 11 percent in 2015 to 8 percent in 2025 for North America.
주어   「be projected to-V: ~할 거라고 예상되다」
「from A to B: A부터 B까지」

05 Central and South America / is not expected to change / from 2015 to 2025 / in its share of the global middle class.
「be expected to-V: ~할 거라고 예상되다」

06 In 2025, / the share of the Middle East and North Africa / will be larger than that of sub-Saharan Africa, / as it was in 2015.
지시대명사(=the share)
접속사(~듯이)

01 위의 그래프들은 / 보여준다 / 2015년 지역별 세계 중산층의 점유율the percentage share of the global middle class by region과 / 2025년에 그것의 예상되는project 점유율을.

02 예상된다 / 아시아 태평양Asia Pacific의 세계 중산층 점유율은 / 증가할 것으로 / 2015년에 46퍼센트로부터 / 2025년에는 60퍼센트로.

03 2025년의 아시아 태평양 지역의 예상 점유율은 / 여섯 개의 지역 중에서 가장 크며the largest among the six regions, / 같은 해 유럽의 예상 점유율의 세 배보다 더 많다.

04 유럽과 북미 지역의 점유율은 / 둘 다 감소할 것으로 예상된다 / 유럽의 경우 2015년 24퍼센트에서 2025년 16퍼센트로, / 북미 지역의 경우 2015년 11퍼센트에서 2025년 8퍼센트로.

05 중남미 지역은 / 변하지 않을(→ 변할) 것으로 예상된다 / 2015년에서 2025년까지 / 세계 중산층 점유율에 있어서.

06 2025년에 / 중동 및 북아프리카의 점유율은 / 사하라 사막 이남의 아프리카sub-Saharan Africa의 점유율보다 더 클 것이다 / 2015년에 그랬듯이.

구문 Check up	① The above graphs show the percentage share of the global middle class by region in 2015 and its projecting / projected share in 2025.	② In 2025, the share of the Middle East and North Africa will be larger than that of sub-Saharan Africa, as it did / was in 2015.
	분사의 꾸밈을 받는 share가 '예측되는' 대상이므로 과거분사 projected를 쓰는 것이 적절하다.	주절의 동사가 will be이므로 as 뒤의 대동사 또한 be동사인 was가 적절하다.

STEP 1 • 수능에 *진짜* 나오는 *단어*

✔️ **문제에 나오는 단어들을 확인하세요.**

01	construction	n. 건설	known for the (✔️ construction) of the tunnel	터널의 건설로 알려진
02	originally	ad. 원래	(　　　　) born in France	원래 프랑스에서 태어난
03	revolution	n. 혁명	during the (　　　　　)	혁명 중에
04	height	n. 최고조, 절정	at the (　　　) of the war	전쟁이 절정에 있을 때 (한창일 때)
05	go out of business	폐업하다	(　) (　　) (　) (　　　　　)	폐업하다
06	imprison	v. 수감시키다, 투옥하다	be (　　　　)ed for several months	몇 달 동안 수감되다
07	debt	n. 빚	pay the (　　　)	빚을 갚다
08	divide	v. 나누다	the region (　　　)d by the river	강에 의해 나뉜 지역
09	officially	ad. 정식으로, 공식적으로	be (　　　　) opened in March	3월에 정식으로 개장하다

⊕ **본문 문장 속에서 단어들을 확인해 보세요.**

After the Wars ended, / however, / the government stopped buying his boots / and he went out of business.

전쟁이 끝난 후, / 그러나 / 정부는 그의 부츠를 더 이상 사지 않았고 / 그는 파산했다.

01	construction	🖉 건설	known for the construction of the tunnel	터널의 (건설)로 알려진
02	originally		originally born in France	( ) 프랑스에서 태어난
03	revolution		during the revolution	( ) 중에
04	height		at the height of the war	전쟁이 ( )에 있을 때
05	go out of business		go out of business	( )
06	imprison		be imprisoned for several months	몇 달 동안 ( )
07	debt		pay the debt	( )을 갚다
08	divide		the region divided by the river	강에 의해 ( ) 지역
09	officially		be officially opened in March	3월에 ( ) 개장하다

➕ **본문 문장 속에서 단어의 의미를 우리말로 해석해 보세요.**

After the Wars ended, / however, / the government stopped buying his boots / and he went out of business.

➡ 전쟁이 끝난 후, / 그러나 / 정부는 그의 부츠를 더 이상 사지 않았고 / 그는   .

39 Marc Isambard Brunel에 관한 다음 글의 내용과 일치하지 <u>않는</u> 것은?

Marc Isambard Brunel (1769—1849) is best known for the design and construction of the Thames Tunnel. Originally born in France, Brunel escaped to the United States during the French Revolution. He later moved to London. When the Napoleonic Wars were at their height, he invented machines for making boots. During the Napoleonic Wars, Brunel's factory supplied British troops with boots. After the Wars ended, however, the government stopped buying his boots and he went out of business. A few years later, Brunel was imprisoned for several months because of his debt. At that time, London was very much divided by the River Thames and needed more ways for people and goods to move across it. In 1825, Brunel designed a tunnel under the river. The Thames Tunnel officially opened on 25 March 1843, and Brunel, despite being in ill health, attended the opening ceremony.

① 프랑스 혁명 중에 미국으로 달아났다.
② 부츠를 만드는 기계를 발명하였다.
③ 그의 공장은 영국 군대에 부츠를 공급한 적이 있다.
④ 빚 때문에 감옥에 수감되었다.
⑤ Thames Tunnel 개통식에 아파서 참석하지 못했다.

정답과 해설 p.35

01 Marc Isambard Brunel (1769—1849) is best known / for the design and construction of
「A be known for B: A는 B로 알려지다, 유명하다」
the Thames Tunnel.

02 Originally born in France, / Brunel escaped to the United States / during the French
분사구문(수동)   전치사(~ 동안에)
Revolution. // He later moved to London.

03 When the Napoleonic Wars were at their height, / he invented machines for making
boots. // During the Napoleonic Wars, / Brunel's factory supplied British troops with
「supply A with B: A에게 B를 공급하다」
boots.

04 After the Wars ended, / however, / the government stopped buying his boots / and he
접속사(~한 후에)   주어1   동사1   목적어(~하기를 멈추다)   주어2
went out of business. // A few years later, / Brunel was imprisoned for several months /
동사2
because of his debt.
전치사(~ 때문에)

05 At that time, / London was very much divided by the River Thames / and needed more
ways / for people and goods / to move across it. // In 1825, / Brunel designed a tunnel
의미상 주어   형용사적 용법
under the river.

06 The Thames Tunnel officially opened on 25 March 1843, / and Brunel, / (despite being
주어1   동사1   주어2   삽입구
in ill health), / attended the opening ceremony.
동사2

01 Marc Isambard Brunel(1769~1849)은 가장 잘 알려져 있다 / Thames Tunnel의 설계와 건설construction로.

02 원래originally 프랑스에서 태어나 / Brunel은 미국으로 달아났다 / 프랑스 혁명French Revolution 중에. // 그는 후에
런던으로 거처를 옮겼다.

03 나폴레옹 전쟁이 한창일at the height 때, / 그는 부츠를 만드는 기계를 발명했다. // 나폴레옹 전쟁 중에, / Brunel의
공장은 영국 군대에 부츠를 공급했다.

04 전쟁이 끝난 후, / 그러나 / 정부는 그의 부츠를 더 이상 사지 않았고 / 그는 파산했다go out of business. // 몇 년 후, /
Brunel은 몇 달 동안 감옥에 수감되었다imprison / 빚debt 때문에.

05 그 당시, / 런던은 템스강에 의해 매우 많이 나뉘어divide 있었고 / 더 많은 방법을 필요로 했다 / 사람과 상품이 / 강을
가로질러 건널. // 1825년, / Brunel은 강 밑의 터널을 설계했다.

06 Thames Tunnel은 1843년 3월 25일에 정식으로officially 개통했고, / Brunel은 / 건강이 좋지 않았음에도 불구하고 /
개통식에 참석했다.

구문 Check up

① At that time, London was very much divided by the River Thames and needed more ways for people and goods moved / to move across it.

문맥상 ways를 꾸미는 수식어가 필요하므로 to move가 적절하다. 2개의 술어(was ~ divided, needed) 뒤로 접속사가 없어 동사를 추가할 수 없음에 유의한다.

② The Thames Tunnel officially opened on 25 March 1843, and Brunel, despite being in ill health, attending / attended the opening ceremony.

and 뒤로 주어 Brunel이 나온 후 동사가 이어져야 하므로 attended가 적절하다. 주어와 동사 사이에 「despite + 동명사」가 삽입되었다.

정답 ① to move ② attended

40 STEP 1 • 수능에 *진짜* 나오는 *단어*

✔ 문제에 나오는 단어들을 확인하세요.

01	instruction	n. 지시, 설명(서)	read the (✔ instruction)s	(사용) 설명서를 읽다
02	care for	~을 돌보다	(　　) (　　) the baby	아기를 돌보다
03	connection	n. 연결	an Internet (　　　　)	인터넷 연결
04	protective	a. 보호의	remove the (　　　　) film	보호 필름을 제거하다
05	insert	v. 넣다, 삽입하다	(　　　　) the battery	배터리를 넣다
06	skip	v. 건너뛰다	(　　　　) to the next song	다음 노래로 건너뛰다
07	waterproof	a. 방수의	(　　　　) clothing	방수복

⊕ 본문 문장 속에서 단어들을 확인해 보세요.

Read these instructions / to learn how to play with and care for him.

이 사용 설명서를 읽으세요 / 그와 함께 놀고 그를 돌보는 방법을 배우기 위해.

문제를 풀기 전에 단어들을 30초 동안 다시 확인하세요.

01	instruction	🖉 지시, 설명(서)	read the instructions	(설명서)를 읽다
02	care for		care for the baby	아기를 ( )
03	connection		an Internet connection	인터넷 ( )
04	protective		remove the protective film	( ) 필름을 제거하다
05	insert		insert the battery	배터리를 ( )
06	skip		skip to the next song	다음 노래로 ( )
07	waterproof		waterproof clothing	( )복

➕ 본문 문장 속에서 단어의 의미를 우리말로 해석해 보세요.

Read these instructions / to learn how to play with and care for him.

➜ ▨▨▨▨▨▨▨▨▨▨▨ / 그와 함께 놀고 ▨▨▨▨▨▨▨▨▨▨ 방법을 배우기 위해.

40

Singing Tommy 사용에 관한 다음 안내문의 내용과 일치하지 <u>않는</u> 것은?

Singing Tommy

Congratulations! Tommy is now your singing friend. Read these instructions to learn how to play with and care for him. Tommy sings to you anytime, anywhere. An Internet connection is not required to play the songs!

Before Use

1. Remove the protective film covering Tommy's eyes.
2. Insert two AA batteries into the battery box and press the power button.
3. Choose your volume setting: LOW volume or HIGH volume.

Operation

1. Play
   - Touch Tommy's right ear to start a song.
2. Stop
   - Press Tommy's hat to stop the song.
3. Control
   - Choose from five songs.
   - Push Tommy's badge to skip to the next song.

Caution

Tommy is not waterproof. Be careful not to get Tommy wet!

---

① 인터넷에 연결되지 않아도 노래를 재생할 수 있다.

② 사용 전에 두 개의 AA 건전지를 넣어야 한다.

③ 모자를 누르면 노래가 시작된다.

④ 다섯 곡의 노래 중에 선택할 수 있다.

⑤ 방수가 되지 않는다.

정답과 해설 p.36

01 Singing Tommy

02 Congratulations! // Tommy is now your singing friend. // Read these instructions /
동사(명령문)
to learn how to play with and care for him. // Tommy sings to you anytime, anywhere.
부사적 용법(목적)
// An Internet connection is not required / to play the songs!
동사(수동태)   부사적 용법(목적)

03 Before Use // 1. Remove the protective film / covering Tommy's eyes.
현재분사구

04 2. Insert two AA batteries into the battery box / and press the power button.
명령문 병렬(~하고 …하라)

05 3. Choose your volume setting: LOW volume or HIGH volume.

06 Operation // 1. Play // Touch Tommy's right ear to start a song.
부사적 용법(~하려면)

07 2. Stop // Press Tommy's hat to stop the song.

08 3. Control // Choose from five songs. // Push Tommy's badge to skip to the next song.

09 Caution // Tommy is not waterproof. // Be careful not to get Tommy wet!
~하지 않도록 주의하라

---

01 노래하는 Tommy

02 축하합니다! // 이제 Tommy는 여러분의 노래하는 친구입니다. // 이 사용 설명서instruction를 읽으세요 / 그와 함께
놓고 그를 돌보는care for him 방법을 배우기 위해. // Tommy는 언제 어디서나 여러분에게 노래를 불러 줍니다. // 인터넷
연결Internet connection이 필요 없습니다 / 노래를 재생하기 위해!

03 사용 전 // 1. Tommy의 눈을 덮고 있는 보호 필름protective film을 제거하세요.

04 2. 배터리 칸에 AA 건전지 두 개를 넣고insert / 전원 단추를 누르세요.

05 3. 소리 크기 설정을 선택하세요: '낮은' 소리 크기 또는 '높은' 소리 크기

06 작동 // 1. 재생 // 노래를 시작하려면 Tommy의 오른쪽 귀를 만지세요.

07 2. 중지 // 노래를 멈추려면 Tommy의 모자를 누르세요.

08 3. 조절 // 다섯 곡의 노래 중에 선택하세요. // 다음 노래로 건너뛰려면skip Tommy의 배지를 누르세요.

09 주의사항 // Tommy는 방수가 되지waterproof 않습니다. // Tommy가 물에 젖지 않게 조심하세요!

구문 Check up

① Read these instructions to learn / learn how to play with and care for him.

명령문인 주절 뒤에 '~하기 위해'라는 뜻의 부사구가 이어지는 문맥이므로 to learn이 적절하다.

② Be careful to not get / not to get Tommy wet!

to부정사의 부정은 to 앞에 부정어를 써서 표현하는 것이 원칙이다. 따라서 not to get이 적절하다.

41

STEP 1 • 수능에 진짜 나오는 단어

✔ **문제에 나오는 단어들을 확인하세요.**

01	charity	n. 자선	attend a (✔ charity) event	자선 행사에 참여하다
02	tournament	n. 토너먼트	join the (　　　) event	토너먼트 경기에 참가하다
03	host	v. 주최하다	(　　　) an event	경기(행사)를 주최하다
04	support	v. 지원하다, 지지하다	(　　　) the children's hospital	아동병원을 지원하다
05	entry	n. 참가, 입장	pay the (　　　) fee	참가비를 내다
06	donation	n. 기부(금)	as a (　　　)	기부금으로
07	challenge	v. 도전하다	(　　　) last year's champion team	작년 우승팀에 도전하다
08	additional	a. 추가적인	with an (　　　) donation	추가적인 기부금으로
09	professional	a. 프로의, 전문적인	(　　　) badminton players	프로 배드민턴 선수들
10	register	v. 등록하다	(　　　) now	지금 등록하다

➕ **본문 문장 속에서 단어들을 확인해 보세요.**

Join the charity tournament event / hosted by Cliffield Community Center!

자선 토너먼트 행사에 참가하세요 / Cliffield 커뮤니티 센터에 의해 주최되는!

01	charity	자선	attend a charity event	(자선) 행사에 참여하다
02	tournament		join the tournament event	( ) 경기에 참가하다
03	host		host an event	경기를 ( )
04	support		support the children's hospital	아동병원을 ( )
05	entry		pay the entry fee	( )비를 내다
06	donation		as a donation	( )으로
07	challenge		challenge last year's champion team	작년 우승팀에 ( )
08	additional		with an additional donation	( ) 기부금으로
09	professional		professional badminton players	( ) 배드민턴 선수들
10	register		register now	지금 ( )

➕ **본문 문장 속에서 단어의 의미를 우리말로 해석해 보세요.**

Join the charity tournament event / hosted by Cliffield Community Center!

→ ▬▬▬▬▬▬▬▬▬▬ 에 참가하세요 / Cliffield 커뮤니티 센터에 의해 ▬▬▬▬▬▬ !

41 2019 Badminton Challenge for Charity에 관한 다음 안내문의 내용과 일치하는 것은?

2019 Badminton Challenge for Charity

Join the charity tournament event hosted by Cliffield Community Center! This event supports Salke Children's Hospital.

When & Where
- Saturday, November 23, 2:00 p.m.
- Cliffield Sports Center

How to Join the Tournament
- Make a two-member team.
- Pay your team's $100 entry fee as a donation.

Activities
- Challenge last year's champion team to a 3-point match.
- With an additional $20 donation, you can learn badminton skills from professional players.

※ Rackets and shuttlecocks will be provided.

Click here to register now!

---

① Salke Children's Hospital이 주최한다.

② 3명이 한 팀을 구성해서 참가해야 한다.

③ 참가비는 한 사람당 100달러이다.

④ 20달러 추가 기부 시 배드민턴 기술을 배울 수 있다.

⑤ 라켓과 셔틀콕은 제공되지 않는다.

정답과 해설 **p.37**

STEP 3 • 수능 지문 제대로 복습하기

01 2019 Badminton Challenge for Charity

02 Join the charity tournament event / hosted by Cliffield Community Center! // This
　　동사(명령문)　목적어　　　　　　　과거분사구
event supports Salke Children's Hospital.

03 When & Where // Saturday, November 23, 2:00 p.m. // Cliffield Sports Center

04 How to Join the Tournament // Make a two-member team. // Pay your team's $100
　　「how + to부정사: ~하는 방법」　　　　　　　복합형용사(수사 + 단수명사)　동사(명령문)
entry fee / as a donation.
　　　　　　전치사(~로서)

05 Activities // Challenge last year's champion team to a 3-point match.

06 With an additional $20 donation, / you can learn badminton skills from professional
players.

07 Rackets and shuttlecocks will be provided.
　　　　　　　　　　　　　　동사(조동사 수동태)

08 *Click here to register now!*
　　　부사적 용법(목적)

01 2019 자선 배드민턴 경기

02 자선 토너먼트charity tournament 경기에 참가하세요 / Cliffield 커뮤니티 센터에 의해 주최되는host! // 이 행사는
Salke 아동병원을 지원합니다support.

03 시간 및 장소 // 11월 23일 토요일 오후 2시 // Cliffield 스포츠 센터

04 토너먼트에 참가하는 방법 // 두 명이 한 팀을 구성하세요. // 팀 참가비entry fee 100달러를 내세요 /
기부금donation으로.

05 활동 // 작년 우승팀과의 3점 내기 시합에 도전하세요challenge.

06 20달러 추가additional 기부 시 / 여러분은 프로professional 선수들에게서 배드민턴 기술을 배울 수 있습니다.

07 라켓과 셔틀콕은 제공됩니다.

08 여기를 클릭하셔서 지금 등록하세요register!

구문 Check up

① Join the charity tournament event hosting / hosted by Cliffield Community Center!

꾸밈 받는 명사인 the charity tournament event가 '주최되는' 대상이므로 hosted가 적절하다.

② Make a two-member / two-members team.

「수사 + 명사」가 결합되어 한 단어가 된 복합형용사에서 수사 뒤 명사는 항상 단수형으로 쓴다. 따라서 two-member가 적절하다.

정답 ① hosted ② two-member

174

42

STEP 1 • 수능에 *진짜* 나오는 *단어*

✔ **문제에 나오는 단어들을 확인하세요.**

01	sparkling	*a.* 반짝이는	a land of (✔ sparkling) blue	반짝이는 파란색 지대
02	measure	*v.* (치수, 면적, 길이, 양 등이) ~에 이르다	( ) 6.4 million hectares	면적이 640만 헥타르에 이르다
03	wildlife	*n.* 야생 동물	a wide variety of ( )	매우 다양한 야생 동물
04	rare	*a.* 희귀한	a ( ) kind of bear	희귀종 곰
05	mammal	*n.* 포유류	the world's slowest ( )	세계에서 제일 느린 포유류
06	vital	*a.* 매우 중요한	play a ( ) role in our lives	우리 삶에서 매우 중요한 역할을 하다
07	ecosystem	*n.* 생태계	the ocean ( )	해양 생태계
08	lightweight	*a.* 가벼운	a strong, ( ) wood	견고하고 가벼운 목재
09	rot-resistant	*a.* 방부성이 있는, 썩지 않는	naturally ( )	본래 썩지 않는

⊕ **본문 문장 속에서 단어들을 확인해 보세요.**

They play a vital role in this area's ecosystem / as a wide range of animals, / as well as humans, / consume them.

그것은 이 지역의 생태계에서 매우 중요한 역할을 한다 / 매우 다양한 동물들이 / 인간뿐만 아니라 / 그것을 먹기 때문에.

문제를 풀기 전에 단어들을 **30초** 동안 다시 확인하세요.

01	sparkling	✏ 반짝이는	a land of sparkling blue	(반짝이는) 파란색 지대
02	measure		measure 6.4 million hectares	면적이 640만 헥타르에 ( )
03	wildlife		a wide variety of wildlife	매우 다양한 ( )
04	rare		a rare kind of bear	( ) 종 곰
05	mammal		the world's slowest mammal	세계에서 제일 느린 ( )
06	vital		play a vital role in our lives	우리 삶에서 ( ) 역할을 하다
07	ecosystem		the ocean ecosystem	해양 ( )
08	lightweight		a strong, lightweight wood	견고하고 ( ) 목재
09	rot-resistant		naturally rot-resistant	본래 ( )

➕ **본문 문장 속에서 단어의 의미를 우리말로 해석해 보세요.**

They play a vital role in this area's ecosystem / as a wide range of animals, / as well as humans, / consume them.

➔ 그것은 ▇▇▇▇▇▇▇▇▇▇▇▇▇▇▇▇▇▇▇ / 매우 다양한 동물들이 / 인간뿐만 아니라 / 그것을 먹기 때문에.

42 Great Bear Rainforest에 관한 다음 글의 내용과 일치하지 <u>않는</u> 것은?

Along the coast of British Columbia lies a land of forest green and sparkling blue. This land is the Great Bear Rainforest, which measures 6.4 million hectares — about the size of Ireland or Nova Scotia. It is home to a wide variety of wildlife. One of the unique animals living in the area is the Kermode bear. It is a rare kind of bear known to be the official mammal of British Columbia. Salmon are also found here. They play a vital role in this area's ecosystem as a wide range of animals, as well as humans, consume them. The Great Bear Rainforest is also home to the Western Red Cedar, a tree that can live for several hundred years. The tree's wood is lightweight and rot-resistant, so it is used for making buildings and furniture.

① British Columbia의 해안가를 따라 위치한다.
② Ireland와 Nova Scotia를 합친 크기이다.
③ Kermode 곰이 살고 있다.
④ 연어는 이 지역 생태계에서 중요한 역할을 한다.
⑤ Western Red Cedar의 서식지이다.

정답과 해설 p.38

01 Along the coast of British Columbia / lies / a land of forest green and sparkling blue. //
장소 부사구(도치)　　　　　　　　　　　　　동사(단수)　　주어
This land is the Great Bear Rainforest, / which measures 6.4 million hectares / — about
　　　　　선행사　　　　　　　　　계속적 용법
the size of Ireland or Nova Scotia.

02 It is home to a wide variety of wildlife.

03 One of the unique animals / living in the area / is the Kermode bear. // It is a rare kind
주어(one of the + 복수명사)　　현재분사구(the unique animals 수식)　　동사(단수)
of bear / known to be the official mammal of British Columbia.
　　　　과거분사구

04 Salmon are also found here. // They play a vital role in this area's ecosystem / as a wide
　　　　　　　　　　　　　　　　　　　　　　　　　　　　　　　　　　　접속사(~ 때문에)
range of animals, / (as well as humans), / consume them.
주어　　　　　　　삽입구　　　　　　동사(복수)

05 The Great Bear Rainforest / is also home to the Western Red Cedar, / a tree / [that can
　　　　　　　　　　　　　　　　　　　　　　　　　　　　　　　　　동격　　　　　　　
live for several hundred years]. // The tree's wood is lightweight and rot-resistant, / so
주격 관계대명사절
it is used for making buildings and furniture.

01 British Columbia의 해안가를 따라서 / 있다 / 짙은 황록색과 반짝이는**sparkling** 파란색 지대가. // 이 지대는 Great Bear Rainforest인데, / 이것은 면적이 640만 헥타르이다**measure** / 즉 Ireland나 Nova Scotia 정도의 크기.

02 그것은 매우 다양한 야생 동물**wildlife**의 서식지이다.

03 독특한 동물 중 하나는 / 그 지역에 서식하는 / Kermode 곰이다. // 그것은 희귀종**a rare kind** 곰이다 / British Columbia의 공식 포유류**mammal**로 알려져 있는.

04 연어 또한 이곳에서 발견된다. // 그것은 이 지역의 생태계**ecosystem**에서 매우 중요한**vital** 역할을 한다 / 매우 다양한 동물들이 / 인간뿐만 아니라 / 그것을 먹기 때문에.

05 Great Bear Rainforest는 / 또한 Western Red Cedar의 서식지이기도 하다 / 나무인 / 수백 년 동안 살 수 있는. // 그 나무의 목재는 가볍고 방부성이 있어**lightweight and rot-resistant** / 그것은 건축물을 짓고 가구를 만드는 데 사용된다.

구문 Check up

① One of the unique animals living in the area is / are the Kermode bear.

「one of the + 복수명사」가 주어이므로 단수동사 is가 적절하다.

② They play a vital role in this area's ecosystem as a wide range of animals, as well as humans, consume / consuming them.

접속사 as(~ 때문에)가 이끄는 부사절의 주어 a wide range of animals 뒤로 동사가 필요하므로 consume이 적절하다.

정답 ① is ② consume

☑ **종합 성적표**

구분	공부한 날 ❶	결과 분석			
		출처	풀이 시간 ❷	채점 결과 (O, ×)	틀린 이유 ❸
Day 4 글의 주제	월 일	2024학년도 9월 23번	분 초		
		2023학년도 대수능 23번	분 초		
		2022학년도 6월 23번	분 초		
		2021학년도 대수능 23번	분 초		
		2021학년도 9월 23번	분 초		
		2020학년도 대수능 23번	분 초		
		2020학년도 6월 23번	분 초		
Day 5 글의 제목	월 일	2024학년도 6월 24번	분 초		
		2023학년도 대수능 24번	분 초		
		2023학년도 9월 24번	분 초		
		2022학년도 대수능 24번	분 초		
		2021학년도 대수능 24번	분 초		
		2021학년도 9월 24번	분 초		
		2020학년도 9월 24번	분 초		
Day 6 내용 일치/불일치	월 일	2024학년도 6월 26번	분 초		
		2023학년도 9월 26번	분 초		
		2022학년도 대수능 25번	분 초		
		2021학년도 9월 26번	분 초		
		2021학년도 6월 27번	분 초		
		2020학년도 대수능 28번	분 초		
		2020학년도 6월 26번	분 초		

3일간
공부한 내용을
다시 보니,
……

❶ **매일 지문을 하루 계획에 맞춰 풀었다. vs. 내가 한 약속을 못 지켰다.**

<매3영 수능기출>은 단순 문제풀이를 위한 책이 아니라, 매일 규칙적으로 영어를 공부하는 습관을 잡는 책입니다. 따라서 푸는 문제 개수는 상황에 따라 다르더라도 '매일' 학습하는 것이 중요합니다.

❷ **주어진 시간을 자꾸 넘긴다?**

풀이 시간이 계속해서 권장 시간을 넘긴다면 실전 훈련이 부족하다는 신호이므로, 매일의 훈련을 실전처럼 긴장감 있게 해야 합니다. 한편으로, 오답의 이유를 철저히 분석하고 맞춤 공부법을 찾아갑니다.

❸ ⭐**틀린 이유 맞춤 솔루션**: 오답 이유에 따라 다음 해결책을 참고하세요.

(1) 해석이 잘 안 돼서
▶ <STEP 1 단어>, <STEP 3 지문 복습>을 정독하며 단어/구문 실력을 길러보세요.

(2) 해석은 되는데, 지문 이해가 안 돼서
▶ [정답 및 해설]의 <지문 자세히 보기>를 정독하며 수능 지문의 논리 전개 방식을 익혀보세요.

(3) 이해는 했는데, 선택지로 연결을 못 해서
▶ [정답 및 해설]의 <오답풀이>, <유형플러스>를 통해 함정에 주의하는 방법을 숙지하세요.

!

결론적으로, 내가 **취약한 부분**은 [   ] 이다.
취약점을 보완하기 위해서 나는 [   ] 을/를 해야겠다.

복습 때 다시 봐야 할 문항과, 다시 점검할 사항이 있는 페이지는 지금 바로 접어 두세요.

<매3영>이 제시하는 3단계로

유형3일 훈련

DAY

07~09

공부한 날			출처	페이지
DAY 7	월	일	2024학년도 9월 29번 2023학년도 9월 29번 2022학년도 9월 29번 2022학년도 6월 29번 2021학년도 9월 29번 2020학년도 9월 29번 2020학년도 6월 29번	181
DAY 8	월	일	2024학년도 대수능 30번 2023학년도 6월 30번 2022학년도 대수능 30번 2022학년도 6월 30번 2021학년도 대수능 30번 2021학년도 6월 30번 2020학년도 6월 30번	209
DAY 9	월	일	2024학년도 9월 31번 2023학년도 9월 32번 2023학년도 6월 32번 2022학년도 대수능 31번 2022학년도 9월 32번 2021학년도 대수능 31번 2020학년도 9월 31번	237

43 STEP 1 • 수능에 *진짜* 나오는 *단어*

✔ 문제에 나오는 단어들을 확인하세요.

01	transform	v. 변화시키다, 바꾸다	(✔ transform) fear into courage	두려움을 용기로 바꾸다
02	turn A into B	A를 B로 바꾸다	( ) a threat ( ) a challenge	위협을 도전으로 바꾸다
03	as in the case of	~의 경우처럼	( ) ( ) ( ) ( ) ( ) stress	스트레스의 경우처럼
04	anxiety	n. 불안	feel ( ) for no reason	아무 이유 없이 불안을 느끼다
05	confidence	n. 자신감	more ( )	더 많은 자신감
06	willingness	n. 기꺼이 ~하려는 의지, 마음	a ( ) to take action	행동을 취하려는 의지
07	quicken	v. 빨라지다	feel my breath ( )ing	내 호흡이 빨라지는 것을 느끼다
08	tension	n. 긴장	notice ( ) in your body	당신의 몸에서 긴장을 감지하다
09	remind	v. 상기시키다	( ) yourself that stress can help you.	스트레스가 도움이 될 수 있다는 점을 상기하라.
10	sweaty	a. 땀이 난	( ) palms	땀이 난 손바닥

➕ 본문 문장 속에서 단어들을 확인해 보세요.

It can turn a threat into a challenge / and can help you do your best under pressure.

그것은 위협을 도전으로 바꿀 수 있고, / 여러분이 압박감 속에서도 최선을 다하도록 도울 수 있다.

01	transform	변화시키다, 바꾸다	transform fear into courage	두려움을 용기로 (바꾸다)
02	turn A into B		turn a threat into a challenge	위협을 도전으로 ( )
03	as in the case of		as in the case of stress	스트레스의 ( )
04	anxiety		feel anxiety for no reason	아무 이유 없이 ( )을 느끼다
05	confidence		more confidence	더 많은 ( )
06	willingness		a willingness to take action	행동을 취하려는 ( )
07	quicken		feel my breath quickening	내 호흡이 ( ) 것을 느끼다
08	tension		notice tension in your body	당신의 몸에서 ( )을 감지하다
09	remind		Remind yourself that stress can help you.	스트레스가 도움이 될 수 있다는 점을 ( ).
10	sweaty		sweaty palms	( ) 손바닥

➕ **본문 문장 속에서 단어의 의미를 우리말로 해석해 보세요.**

It can turn a threat into a challenge / and can help you do your best under pressure.

→ 그것은 [   ] 수 있고, / 여러분이 압박감 속에서도 최선을 다하도록 도울 수 있다.

43 다음 글의 밑줄 친 부분 중, 어법상 틀린 것은?

Viewing the stress response as a resource can transform the physiology of fear into the biology of courage. It can turn a threat into a challenge and can help you ① do your best under pressure. Even when the stress doesn't feel helpful — as in the case of anxiety — welcoming it can transform ② it into something that is helpful: more energy, more confidence, and a greater willingness to take action. You can apply this strategy in your own life anytime you notice signs of stress. When you feel your heart beating or your breath quickening, ③ realizing that it is your body's way of trying to give you more energy. If you notice tension in your body, remind yourself ④ that the stress response gives you access to your strength. Sweaty palms? Remember what it felt like ⑤ to go on your first date — palms sweat when you're close to something you want.

*physiology: 생리 기능

정답과 해설 **p.39**

01 Viewing the stress response as a resource / can transform the physiology of fear / into
주어(동명사구)　　　　　　　　　　　　　　　　「transform A into B: A를 B로 바꾸다」
the biology of courage. // It can turn a threat into a challenge / and can help you do
　　　　　　　　　　　　　동사구 병렬　　　　　　　　　　　　　「help + 목적어 + 원형부정사:
your best under pressure.　　　　　　　　　　　　　　　　　　　　　~이 …하는 것을 돕다」

02 Even when the stress doesn't feel helpful / — (as in the case of anxiety) — / welcoming
심지어 ~할 때도　　　　　　　　　　　　　　　　삽입구　　　　　　주어(동명사구)
it can transform it / into something [that is helpful]: / more energy, more confidence,
= the stress　선행사　　　주격 관계대명사절　something that is helpful의 예시
and a greater willingness to take action. // You can apply this strategy in your own life
/ anytime you notice signs of stress.
~할 때마다(= whenever)

03 When you feel your heart beating or your breath quickening, / realize that it is your
지각동사　목적어1　　　목적격보어1　　　목적어2　　　목적격보어2　　동사(명령문: ~하라)
body's way of trying / to give you more energy. // If you notice tension in your body, /
remind yourself / [that the stress response gives you access to your strength].
명령문(주어 you 생략)　접속사(뒤에 완전한 문장)

04 Sweaty palms? // Remember [what it felt like to go on your first date] / — palms sweat
가주어　　　진주어
when you're close to something you want.
that 생략

01 스트레스 반응을 자원으로 보는 것은 / 두려움이라는 생리 기능을 바꿀transform 수 있다 / 용기라는 생명 작용으로. // 그것은 위협을 도전으로 바꿀turn a threat into a challenge 수 있고, / 여러분이 압박감 속에서도 최선을 다하도록 도울 수 있다.

02 스트레스가 도움이 되지 않는다고 느껴질 때조차도 / 불안감의 경우처럼as in the case of anxiety / 그것을 기꺼이 받아들이는 것은 그것을 바꿀 수 있다 / 유용한 것으로 / 더 많은 에너지, 더 많은 자신감confidence, 더 기꺼이 행동을 취하려는 의지willingness 등. // 여러분은 이 전략을 삶에 적용할 수 있다 / 여러분이 스트레스의 징후를 알아차릴 때마다.

03 여러분이 심장이 두근거리거나 숨이 가빠지는quicken 것을 느낄 때 / 그것은 여러분의 몸이 노력하는 방식임을 깨달으라 / 여러분에게 더 많은 에너지를 주려고. // 여러분이 몸에서 긴장tension을 감지한다면 / 스스로에게 상기시키라remind / 스트레스 반응이 여러분의 힘을 이용할 기회를 준다는 것을.

04 손바닥에 땀이 나는가sweaty palm? // 첫 데이트에 나갔을 때 어떤 기분이었는지 기억해 보라. / 여러분이 원하는 것에 가까이 있을 때 손바닥에 땀이 난다.

구문 Check-up

① View / Viewing the stress response as a resource can transform the physiology of fear into the biology of courage.

can transform 앞에 주어가 필요하므로 동명사 Viewing을 써야 한다.

② Remember that / what it felt like to go on your first date.

뒤에 전치사 like에 연결될 명사가 없으므로 불완전한 명사절을 이끄는 what이 적절하다. that이 불완전한 절을 이끌 때는 앞에 선행사가 필요하다.

정답 ① Viewing ② what

44

STEP 1 • 수능에 *진짜* 나오는 *단어*

✔ **문제에 나오는 단어들을 확인하세요.**

01	identifiable	*a.* 식별 가능한	an (✔ identifiable) problem	식별 가능한 문제
02	evaluate	*v.* 평가하다	( ) actions	행동을 평가하다
03	unethical	*a.* 비윤리적인	ethical or ( )	윤리적 또는 비윤리적인
04	alternative	*n.* 대안 *a.* 대안의	choose from ( )s	대안들 중에서 고르다
05	competence	*n.* 역량, 능력, 능숙도	knowledge ( )	지식 역량
06	area of concern	관심 영역	the business ( ) ( ) ( )	관심 사업 영역
07	code of ethics	윤리 강령	draw up a ( ) ( ) ( )	윤리 강령을 작성하다
08	conduct	*n.* 행동, 행위 *v.* 수행하다	appropriate ( )	적절한 행동
09	gray area	애매한 영역, (이도 저도 아닌) 중간 영역	the ( ) ( ) where good and evil overlap	선과 악이 겹치는 애매한 영역
10	time theft	시간 절도(업무 시간을 낭비해 피해를 주는 행위)	engage in ( ) ( )	시간 절도 행위를 하다
11	leave out	~을 생략하다, 빠뜨리다	( ) ( ) some facts	몇 가지 사실을 생략하다

✛ **본문 문장 속에서 단어들을 확인해 보세요.**

An ethical issue is an identifiable problem, situation, or opportunity / that requires a person to choose from among several actions / that may be evaluated as right or wrong, ethical or unethical.

윤리적 문제는 식별 가능한 문제, 상황 또는 기회이다 / 여러 가지 행동들 중에서 한 사람이 선택하기를 요구하는 / 옳거나 그르다고, 즉 윤리적 또는 비윤리적이라고 평가될 수도 있는.

01	identifiable	식별 가능한	an identifiable problem	(식별 가능한) 문제
02	evaluate		evaluate actions	행동을 ( )
03	unethical		ethical or unethical	윤리적 또는 ( )
04	alternative		choose from alternatives	( )들 중에서 고르다
05	competence		knowledge competence	지식 ( )
06	area of concern		the business area of concern	( ) 사업 ( )
07	code of ethics		draw up a code of ethics	( )을 작성하다
08	conduct		appropriate conduct	적절한 ( )
09	gray area		the gray area where good and evil overlap	선과 악이 겹치는 ( )
10	time theft		engage in time theft	( ) 행위를 하다
11	leave out		leave out some facts	몇 가지 사실을 ( )

➕ 본문 문장 속에서 단어의 의미를 우리말로 해석해 보세요.

An ethical issue is an identifiable problem, situation, or opportunity / that requires a person to choose from among several actions / that may be evaluated as right or wrong, ethical or unethical.

→ 윤리적 문제는 ▓▓▓▓▓▓ 문제, 상황 또는 기회이다 / 여러 가지 행동들 중에서 한 사람이 선택하기를 요구하는 / 옳거나 그르다고, 즉 윤리적 또는 ▓▓▓▓▓▓ 수도 있는.

44 다음 글의 밑줄 친 부분 중, 어법상 틀린 것은?

Recognizing ethical issues is the most important step in understanding business ethics. An ethical issue is an identifiable problem, situation, or opportunity that requires a person to choose from among several actions that may ① be evaluated as right or wrong, ethical or unethical. ② Learn how to choose from alternatives and make a decision requires not only good personal values, but also knowledge competence in the business area of concern. Employees also need to know when to rely on their organizations' policies and codes of ethics or ③ have discussions with co-workers or managers on appropriate conduct. Ethical decision making is not always easy because there are always gray areas ④ that create dilemmas, no matter how decisions are made. For instance, should an employee report on a co-worker engaging in time theft? Should a salesperson leave out facts about a product's poor safety record in his presentation to a customer? Such questions require the decision maker to evaluate the ethics of his or her choice and decide ⑤ whether to ask for guidance.

정답과 해설 **p.39**

01 Recognizing ethical issues is the most important step / in understanding business ethics.
　　　　주어-동사 수 일치

02 An ethical issue is an identifiable problem, situation, or opportunity / [that requires
　　　　　　　　　선행사(단수)　　　　　　　　　　　　　　　　　　　　주격 관계대명사절
a person to choose from among several actions / [that may be evaluated as right or
　　　　　　　　　　　　　　　　　선행사　　　　　주격 관계대명사절
wrong, ethical or unethical]]. // Learning how to choose from alternatives and make a
　　　　　　　　　　　　　　　　　주어(동명사구)
decision / requires not only good personal values, / but also knowledge competence in
　　　　　동사(단수)　　　　　　A뿐만 아니라 B도(명사구 병렬)
the business area of concern.

03 Employees also need to know / when to rely on their organizations' policies and codes
　　　　　　　　　동사구
of ethics / or have discussions with co-workers or managers / on appropriate conduct.
　　　　　　　　　목적어(when + to부정사: 언제 ~할지)

04 Ethical decision making is not always easy / because there are always gray areas / [that
　　　　　　　　　　　　　　　　　　　　　　　　　　　　　　　선행사(복수)
create dilemmas], / no matter how decisions are made. // For instance, / should an
주격 관계대명사절　　= however(어떻게 ~하든 간에)
employee report on a co-worker / engaging in time theft? // Should a salesperson leave
out facts / about a product's poor safety record / in his presentation to a customer?

05 Such questions require the decision maker / to evaluate the ethics of his or her choice
　　　　　　　　　　동사　　　　목적어　　　　　　목적격보어1
/ and decide whether to ask for guidance.
목적격보어2　　「whether + to부정사: ~할지 말지」

01 윤리적 문제를 인식하는 것은 가장 중요한 단계이다 / 비즈니스 윤리를 이해하는 데.

02 윤리적 문제는 식별 가능한identifiable 문제, 상황 또는 기회이다 / 여러 가지 행동들 중에서 한 사람이 선택하기를 요구하는 / 옳거나 그르다고, 즉 윤리적 또는 비윤리적unethical이라고 평가될evaluate 수도 있는. // 대안alternative 중에서 선택하고 결정을 내리는 방법을 배우는 것은 / 훌륭한 개인적 가치관뿐만 아니라 (~도) 요구한다 / 관심 사업 영역the business area of concern에 대한 지식 역량competence도.

03 직원들은 또한 알아야 한다 / 언제 자신이 속한 조직의 정책과 윤리 강령code of ethics에 의존할지 / 혹은 동료나 관리자와 논의할지 / 적절한 행동conduct에 대해.

04 윤리적 의사결정이 항상 쉬운 것은 아닌데 / 왜냐하면 애매한 영역gray area이 늘 있기 때문이다 / 딜레마를 만들어내는 / 어떤 결정이 내려지든. // 예를 들어, / 직원은 동료에 대해 보고해야 하는가 / 시간 절도time theft 행위를 하는? // 판매원은 사실을 생략해야leave out 하는가 / 어떤 제품의 형편없는 안전 상태에 대한 기록을 / 고객을 대상으로 한 그의 프레젠테이션에서?

05 그러한 질문은 의사결정자에게 요구한다 / 자신이 선택한 윤리를 평가하도록 / 그리고 지침을 요청할 것인지를 결정하도록.

구문 Check up

① Ethical decision making is not always easy because there are always gray areas that create dilemmas, no matter **how / however** decisions are made.

no matter how가 합쳐서 however가 되는 것이므로 how가 적절하다.

② Such questions require the decision maker **to evaluate / evaluating** the ethics of his or her choice and decide whether to ask for guidance.

require는 to부정사를 목적격보어로 취하는 동사이므로, to evaluate가 적절하다.

정답 ① how ② to evaluate

45

STEP 1 • 수능에 *진짜* 나오는 *단어*

✔ **문제에 나오는 단어들을 확인하세요.**

01	communicate	v. 전달하다, 소통하다	(✔ communicate) a message	메시지를 전달하다
02	pay off	성공하다, 결실을 맺다	( ) ( ) in the end	결국 결실을 맺다
03	correspond to	~와 일치하다	( ) ( ) the reality	현실과 일치하다
04	commonality	n. 공통성	the ( ) of interests	관심사의 공통성
05	pregnant	a. 임신한	a ( ) mother	임신한 어머니(임산부)
06	mistrust	v. 믿지 못하다, 불신하다	( ) the chemical signals	화학적 신호를 믿지 못하다
07	chase	v. 쫓다, 추구하다	( ) a prey	사냥감을 쫓다
08	guarantee	n. 보장 v. 보장하다	strong ( )s that it is worthy of trust	그것이 믿을 가치가 있다는 강력한 보장
09	well off	잘 사는, (형편이) 좋은	nations that are ( ) ( )	잘 사는 국가들
10	cognitive	a. 인지적인	a set of ( ) mechanisms	일련의 인지 기제
11	harmful	a. 해로운	reject ( ) messages	해로운 메시지를 거부하다

➕ **본문 문장 속에서 단어들을 확인해 보세요.**

Accepting whatever others are communicating / only pays off / if their interests correspond to ours / — think cells in a body, / bees in a beehive.

다른 사람들이 전달하고 있는 어떤 것이든 받아들이는 것은 / 오로지 성공하는데 / 그들의 관심사가 우리의 것과 일치할 때, / 체내의 세포를 생각해 보라 / 벌집 속의 벌을.

01	communicate	✐ 전달하다, 소통하다	communicate a message	메시지를 (전달하다)
02	pay off		pay off in the end	결국 ( )
03	correspond to		correspond to the reality	현실과 ( )
04	commonality		the commonality of interests	관심사의 ( )
05	pregnant		a pregnant mother	( ) 어머니
06	mistrust		mistrust the chemical signals	화학적 신호를 ( )
07	chase		chase a prey	사냥감을 ( )
08	guarantee		strong guarantees that it is worthy of trust	그것이 믿을 가치가 있다는 강력한 ( )
09	well off		nations that are well off	( ) 국가들
10	cognitive		a set of cognitive mechanisms	일련의 ( ) 기제
11	harmful		reject harmful messages	( ) 메시지를 거부하다

➕ **본문 문장 속에서 단어의 의미를 우리말로 해석해 보세요.**

Accepting whatever others are communicating / only pays off / if their interests correspond to ours / — think cells in a body, / bees in a beehive.

➡ ▓▓▓▓▓▓▓▓▓▓▓▓▓▓▓▓▓▓ 받아들이는 것은 / 오로지 ▓▓▓▓▓▓▓▓ / 그들의 관심사가 ▓▓▓▓▓▓▓ 때, / 체내의 세포를 생각해 보라 / 벌집 속의 벌을.

45 다음 글의 밑줄 친 부분 중, 어법상 틀린 것은?

Accepting whatever others are communicating only pays off if their interests correspond to ours — think cells in a body, bees in a beehive. As far as communication between humans is concerned, such commonality of interests ① is rarely achieved; even a pregnant mother has reasons to mistrust the chemical signals sent by her fetus. Fortunately, there are ways of making communication work even in the most adversarial of relationships. A prey can convince a predator not to chase ② it. But for such communication to occur, there must be strong guarantees ③ which those who receive the signal will be better off believing it. The messages have to be kept, on the whole, ④ honest. In the case of humans, honesty is maintained by a set of cognitive mechanisms that evaluate ⑤ communicated information. These mechanisms allow us to accept most beneficial messages — to be open — while rejecting most harmful messages — to be vigilant.

*fetus: 태아 **adversarial: 반대자의 ***vigilant: 경계하는

정답과 해설 **p.40**

01 Accepting [whatever others are communicating] / only pays off / if their interests
     주어(동명사)   복합관계대명사(~하는 무엇이든)   동사(단수)
    correspond to ours / — think cells in a body, / bees in a beehive.
                  소유대명사(= our interests)

02 As far as communication between humans is concerned, / such commonality of
    「as far as A be concerned: A에 관한 한」
    interests is rarely achieved; / even a pregnant mother has reasons / to mistrust the
                                                                reasons   to mistrust the
                                                                          형용사적 용법
    chemical signals / sent by her fetus.
                            과거분사구

03 Fortunately, / there are ways of making communication work / even in the most
                                  동명사구(사역동사 + 목적어 + 원형부정사)
    adversarial of relationships.

04 A prey can convince a predator / not to chase it. // But for such communication
                                                                          의미상 주어
    to occur, / there must be strong guarantees / [that those {who receive the signal} /
    부사적 용법(목적)   동격   주어   주격 관계대명사절
    will be better off believing it].
    동사

05 The messages have to be kept, / (on the whole), / honest.
                동사(5형식 수동태)   삽입구   주격보어

06 In the case of humans, / honesty is maintained by a set of cognitive mechanisms / [that
                                                                  선행사
    evaluate communicated information]. // These mechanisms allow us / to accept most
    주격 관계대명사절
    beneficial messages / — to be open — / while rejecting most harmful messages / — to
                            동격   동격
    be vigilant.

---

01 다른 사람들이 전달하고 있는communicate 어떤 것이든 받아들이는 것은 / 오로지 성공하는데pay off / 그들의 관심사가
    우리의 것과 일치할correspond to ours 때, / 체내의 세포를 생각해 보라 / 벌집 속의 벌을.

02 인간 사이의 의사소통에 관한 한, / 관심사의 그런 공통성commonality은 좀처럼 이루어지지 않는데, / 심지어
    임산부pregnant mother에게도 이유가 있다 / 화학적 신호를 믿지 못할mistrust / 태아가 보내는.

03 다행히도, / 의사소통이 이루어지게 할 수 있는 방법이 있다 / 가장 적대적인 관계에서도.

04 먹잇감은 포식자를 설득할 수 있다 / 자신을 쫓지chase 말도록. // 그러나 그러한 의사소통이 일어나기 위해서는, / 강력한
    보장guarantee이 있어야 한다 / 신호를 받는 자가 / 그것을 믿는 것이 더 좋을well off 것이라는.

05 메시지는 유지되어야 한다 / 전체적으로 / 정직한 상태로.

06 인간의 경우, / 정직성은 일련의 인지cognitive 기제에 의해 유지된다 / 전달된 정보를 평가하는. // 이러한 기제는 우리가
    ~할 수 있게 해준다 / 가장 유익한 메시지를 받아들이게 / 즉 개방적이게 / 가장 해로운harmful 메시지를 거부하는 반면에
    / 즉 경계하는.

구문 Check up

① Accepting whatever others are communicating only pays off if their interests correspond to us / ours — think cells in a body, bees in a beehive.

문맥상 our interests를 대신하는 소유대명사가 필요하므로 ours가 적절하다.

② The messages have to keep / be kept , on the whole, honest.

주어 The messages가 '유지되어야' 하는 대상이므로 be kept가 적절하다.

정답 ① ours ② be kept

46

STEP 1 • 수능에 *진짜* 나오는 *단어*

✔️ 문제에 나오는 단어들을 확인하세요.

01	reliable	a. 신뢰할 만한	the need for a (✔️ reliable) calendar	신뢰할 만한 달력의 필요성
02	regulate	v. 규제하다, 통제하다	( ) industry	산업을 규제하다
03	agricultural	a. 농업의	( ) activity	농업 활동
04	astronomy	n. 천문학	early ( )	초기 천문학
05	regularity	n. 규칙성	the discovery of ( )	규칙성의 발견
06	predictability	n. 예측 가능성	the ( ) of an event	어떤 사건의 예측 가능성
07	inhabit	v. 살다, 거주하다	the world we ( )	우리가 사는 세계
08	existence	n. 존재	the ( ) of life after death	사후 세계의 존재
09	immediate	a. 눈앞의	see behind ( ) appearances	눈앞의 모습의 이면을 보고

➕ 본문 문장 속에서 단어들을 확인해 보세요.

Most historians of science / point to the need for a reliable calendar / to regulate agricultural activity / as the motivation / for learning about what we now call astronomy, / the study of stars and planets.

대부분의 과학 역사가들은 / 신뢰할 만한 달력의 필요성을 지적한다 / 농업 활동을 규제하기 위한 / 동기로 / 우리가 현재 천문학이라 부르는 것에 대해 배우고자 하는 / 즉 별과 행성에 대한 연구.

문제를 풀기 전에 단어들을 **30초** 동안 다시 확인하세요.

01	reliable	🖉 신뢰할 만한	the need for a reliable calendar	(신뢰할 만한)달력의 필요성
02	regulate		regulate industry	산업을 ( )
03	agricultural		agricultural activity	( )활동
04	astronomy		early astronomy	초기 ( )
05	regularity		the discovery of regularity	( )의 발견
06	predictability		the predictability of an event	어떤 사건의 ( )
07	inhabit		the world we inhabit	우리가 ( ) 세계
08	existence		the existence of life after death	사후 세계의 ( )
09	immediate		see behind immediate appearances	( ) 모습의 이면을 보고

➕ **본문 문장 속에서 단어의 의미를 우리말로 해석해 보세요.**

Most historians of science / point to the need for a reliable calendar / to regulate agricultural activity / as the motivation / for learning about what we now call astronomy, / the study of stars and planets.

→ 대부분의 과학 역사가들은 /   을 지적한다 /   위한 / 동기로 /   에 대해 배우고자 하는 / 즉 별과 행성에 대한 연구.

46 다음 글의 밑줄 친 부분 중, 어법상 틀린 것은?

Most historians of science point to the need for a reliable calendar to regulate agricultural activity as the motivation for learning about what we now call astronomy, the study of stars and planets. Early astronomy provided information about when to plant crops and gave humans ① their first formal method of recording the passage of time. Stonehenge, the 4,000-year-old ring of stones in southern Britain, ② is perhaps the best-known monument to the discovery of regularity and predictability in the world we inhabit. The great markers of Stonehenge point to the spots on the horizon ③ where the sun rises at the solstices and equinoxes — the dates we still use to mark the beginnings of the seasons. The stones may even have ④ been used to predict eclipses. The existence of Stonehenge, built by people without writing, bears silent testimony both to the regularity of nature and to the ability of the human mind to see behind immediate appearances and ⑤ discovers deeper meanings in events.

*monument: 기념비   **eclipse: (해·달의) 식(蝕)
***testimony: 증언

정답과 해설 **p.41**

01 Most historians of science / point to the need for a reliable calendar / to regulate
agricultural activity / as the motivation for learning about what we now call
astronomy, / the study of stars and planets. // Early astronomy provided information
　　　　　動격　　　　　　　　　　　　　　　　　　　　　　　　　　　　　　　　동사1
about when to plant crops / and gave humans their first formal method of recording
　　「when + to부정사: 언제 ~할지」　　동사2　간접목적어　직접목적어
the passage of time.

02 Stonehenge, / (the 4,000-year-old ring of stones in southern Britain), / is perhaps the
　주어　　　　　삽입구(주어 동격)　　　　　　　　　　　　　　　　　　동사(단수)
best-known monument / to the discovery of regularity and predictability / in the world
we inhabit.

03 The great markers of Stonehenge / point to the spots on the horizon / [where the sun
　　　　　　　　　　　　　　　　　　　　　　선행사　　　　　　　　　　　　　관계부사절
rises at the solstices and equinoxes] / — the dates / [we still use to mark the beginnings
　　　　　　동격　　　　　　　　　　　　　　　목적격 관계대명사절
of the seasons]. // The stones may even have been used / to predict eclipses.
　　　　　　　　　　　　　「may have p.p.: ~했을지도 모른다」

04 The existence of Stonehenge, / (built by people without writing), / bears silent
　주어　　　　　　　　　　　삽입구(Stonehenge 보충 설명)　　　　　　　동사(단수)
testimony / both to the regularity of nature / and to the ability of the human mind / to
　　　　　　A와 B 둘 다(전치사구 병렬)
see behind immediate appearances / and (to) discover deeper meanings in events.
형용사적 용법

01 대부분의 과학 역사가들은 / 신뢰할 만한reliable 달력의 필요성을 지적한다 / 농업 활동을 규제하기regulate agricultural
activity 위한 / 우리가 현재 천문학astronomy이라 부르는 것에 대해 배우고자 하는 동기로 / 즉 별과 행성에 대한 연구.
// 초기 천문학은 언제 작물을 심어야 하는지에 대한 정보를 제공했고 / 인간에게 시간의 흐름을 기록하는 그들 최초의
공식적인 방법을 제공했다.

02 스톤헨지는 / 영국 남부에 있는, 4,000년 된 고리 모양의 돌들인 / 아마도 가장 잘 알려진 기념비일 것이다 /
규칙성regularity과 예측 가능성predictability의 발견에 대한 / 우리가 살고 있는inhabit 세계의.

03 스톤헨지의 커다란 표식은 / 지평선의 장소를 가리킨다 / 지점(至點)과 분점(分點)에서 태양이 뜨는 / 날짜인 / 우리가
계절의 시작을 표시하기 위해 여전히 사용하는. // 그 돌들은 심지어 사용되었을지도 모른다 / (해·달의) 식(蝕)을 예측하기
위해.

04 스톤헨지의 존재existence는 / 글이 없던 시절 사람들이 세운 / 말없이 증언해 준다 / 자연의 규칙성뿐만 아니라 / 인간의
정신적 능력에 대해 / 눈앞에 보이는immediate 모습의 이면을 보고 / 사건에서 더 깊은 의미를 발견할 수 있는.

구문 Check up

① Most historians of science point to the need for a reliable calendar to regulate agricultural activity as the motivation for learning about that / what we now call astronomy, the study of stars and planets.

앞에 about의 목적어가 없고 뒤에 call의 목적어가 없는 불완전한 문장이 나오는 것으로 보아 what이 적절하다.

② The great markers of Stonehenge point to the spots on the horizon where the sun rises / is risen at the solstices and equinoxes — the dates we still use to mark the beginnings of the seasons.

rise는 수동태로 만들 수 없는 1형식 동사이므로 rises가 적절하다.

정답 ① what ② rises

47

STEP 1 • 수능에 *진짜* 나오는 *단어*

✔ 문제에 나오는 단어들을 확인하세요.

01	overlook	v. 무시하다, 간과하다	(✔ overlook) the rest	나머지를 무시하다
02	provision	n. 제공	the ( ) of feedback	피드백의 제공
03	constructive	a. 건설적인	timely and ( ) feedback	시기 적절하고 건설적인 피드백
04	asset	n. 자산	a valuable ( )	가치 있는 자산
05	restrict	v. 국한하다, 제한하다	( )ed to negative comments	부정적 코멘트에 국한된
06	emphasis	n. 강조점, 역점	shift the ( ) to other issues	강조점을 다른 문제로 옮기다
07	superior	a. 우월한, 우수한	demonstrate ( ) performance	우월한 수행 기량을 보여주다
08	place	v. 입상하다	the participant who does not win or ( )	우승하거나 입상하지 못하는 참가자

➕ 본문 문장 속에서 단어들을 확인해 보세요.

For many, / this is restricted to information / about whether the participant is an award- or prizewinner.

많은 경우에, / 이것은 정보에 국한된다 / 참가자가 수상자 또는 입상자인지에 관한.

문제를 풀기 전에 단어들을 **30초** 동안 다시 확인하세요.

01	overlook	🖉 무시하다, 간과하다	overlook the rest	나머지를 (무시하다)
02	provision		the provision of feedback	피드백의 ( )
03	constructive		timely and constructive feedback	시기 적절하고 ( ) 피드백
04	asset		a valuable asset	가치 있는 ( )
05	restrict		restricted to negative comments	부정적 코멘트에 ( )
06	emphasis		shift the emphasis to other issues	( )을 다른 문제로 옮기다
07	superior		demonstrate superior performance	( ) 수행 기량을 보여주다
08	place		the participant who does not win or place	우승하거나 ( ) 못하는 참가자

➕ **본문 문장 속에서 단어의 의미를 우리말로 해석해 보세요.**

For many, / this is restricted to information / about whether the participant is an award- or prizewinner.

➡ 많은 경우에, / 이것은 ▓▓▓▓▓▓▓▓▓▓▓ / 참가자가 수상자 또는 입상자인지에 관한.

47 다음 글의 밑줄 친 부분 중, 어법상 틀린 것은?

Competitive activities can be more than just performance showcases ① which the best is recognized and the rest are overlooked. The provision of timely, constructive feedback to participants on performance ② is an asset that some competitions and contests offer. In a sense, all competitions give feedback. For many, this is restricted to information about whether the participant is an award- or prizewinner. The provision of that type of feedback can be interpreted as shifting the emphasis to demonstrating superior performance but not ③ necessarily excellence. The best competitions promote excellence, not just winning or "beating" others. The emphasis on superiority is what we typically see as ④ fostering a detrimental effect of competition. Performance feedback requires that the program go beyond the "win, place, or show" level of feedback. Information about performance can be very helpful, not only to the participant who does not win or place but also to those who ⑤ do.

*foster: 조장하다 **detrimental: 유해한

정답과 해설 p.42

01 Competitive activities / can be more than just performance showcases / [where the
best is recognized and the rest are overlooked]. // The provision of timely, constructive
feedback to participants on performance / is an asset / [that some competitions and
contests offer].

선행사　관계부사절
주격보어　목적격 관계대명사절

02 In a sense, / all competitions give feedback. // For many, / this is restricted to
information / about [whether the participant is an award- or prizewinner]. //
The provision of that type of feedback / can be interpreted / as shifting the emphasis
to demonstrating superior performance / but not necessarily excellence.

전치사　명사절(~인지 아닌지)
동사(조동사 수동태)　전치사(~로서)
「B, but not A: A가 아니라 B인」

03 The best competitions promote excellence, / not just winning or "beating" others. //
The emphasis on superiority is / [what we typically see / as fostering a detrimental
effect of competition].

전치사(~로서)　동명사

04 Performance feedback requires / [that the program go beyond the "win, place, or show"
level of feedback]. // Information about performance can be very helpful, / not only to
the participant [who does not win or place] / but also to those [who do].

'요구' 동사
should
'~해야 한다'라는 의미일 때 should 생략 가능
A뿐만 아니라 B도(to + 명사 병렬)
대동사(= win or place)

01 경쟁을 벌이는 활동은 / 단지 수행 기량을 보여주는 공개 행사 그 이상일 수 있다 / 최고는 인정받고 나머지는
무시되는overlook. // 참가자에게 수행 기량에 대한 시기적절하고 건설적인constructive 피드백을 제공provision하는
것은 / 자산asset이다 / 일부 대회와 경연이 제공하는.

02 어떤 의미에서는, / 모든 대회가 피드백을 제공한다. // 많은 경우에, / 이것은 정보에 국한된다restrict / 참가자가 수상자
또는 입상자인지에 관한. // 그런 유형의 피드백의 제공은 / 해석될 수 있다 / 우월한superior 수행 기량을 보여주는 것으로
강조점emphasis을 옮기는 것이라고 / 꼭 탁월함은 아니더라도.

03 최고의 대회는 탁월함을 장려한다 / 단순히 이기는 것 또는 다른 사람을 '패배시키는 것'만이 아니라. // 우월성에 대한
강조는 ~이다 / 우리가 일반적으로 간주하는 것 / 유해한 경쟁 효과를 조장하는 것이라고.

04 수행 기량에 대한 피드백은 요구한다 / 프로그램이 '이기거나, 입상하거나, 또는 보여주는' 수준의 피드백을 넘어서야
한다는 것을. // 수행 기량에 관한 정보는 매우 도움이 될 수 있다 / 우승 또는 입상하지place 못하는 참가자뿐만 아니라 /
그렇게 하는 참가자에게도.

구문 Check up

① For many, this is restricted to information about that /
whether the participant is an award- or prizewinner.

전치사 about의 목적어인 명사절을 이끌 접속사로 whether(~인지 아닌
지)가 적절하다. 접속사 that은 전치사 뒤에 쓸 수 없다.

② Performance feedback requires that the program
goes / go beyond the "win, place, or show" level of
feedback.

주장, 요구, 명령, 제안 등의 동사 뒤에 당위(~해야 한다)의 that절이 목적
어로 나오면 that절의 동사 자리에는 「(should) + 동사원형」을 쓴다. 따라
서 go가 적절하다.

48 STEP 1 • 수능에 *진짜* 나오는 *단어*

✔️ 문제에 나오는 단어들을 확인하세요.

01	psychological	a. 심리적인	a (✔️ psychological) reason	심리적인 이유
02	tempt	v. 부추기다, 유혹하다	(　　　) him to repeat the information	그에게 정보를 반복하라고 부추기다
03	possessor	n. 소유자	the (　　　) of information	정보의 소유자
04	unrevealed	a. 숨겨진, 드러나지 않은	(　　　) information	숨겨진 정보
05	keep to oneself	남에게 말하지 않다, 혼자 알다	(　　) his information (　) (　　　)	자신의 정보를 남에게 말하지 않다
06	superiority	n. 우월함, 우세	the feeling of (　　　)	우월함의 감정
07	actualize	v. 실현하다	(　　　) your ideas	당신의 생각을 실현하다
08	disclosure	n. 폭로	at the moment of (　　　)	폭로의 순간
09	well-known	a. 유명한, 잘 알려진	(　　　) figures	유명한 인물들
10	fame	n. 명성	the (　　) of an artist	예술가의 명성
11	rub off on	~에게 옮겨지다, 영향을 미치다	(　) (　) (　) others	다른 사람에게 영향을 주다

➕ 본문 문장 속에서 단어들을 확인해 보세요.

This is the main motive / for gossiping about well-known figures and superiors.

이것이 주요 동기이다 / 유명한 인물들과 윗사람들에 대해 뒷공론을 하는.

문제를 풀기 전에 단어들을 30초 동안 다시 확인하세요.

01	psychological	✎ 심리적인	a psychological reason	(심리적인) 이유
02	tempt		tempt him to repeat the information	그에게 정보를 반복하라고 ( )
03	possessor		the possessor of information	정보의 ( )
04	unrevealed		unrevealed information	( ) 정보
05	keep to oneself		keep his information to himself	자신의 정보를 ( )
06	superiority		the feeling of superiority	( )의 감정
07	actualize		actualize your ideas	당신의 생각을 ( )
08	disclosure		at the moment of disclosure	( )의 순간
09	well-known		well-known figures	( ) 인물들
10	fame		the fame of an artist	예술가의 ( )
11	rub off on		rub off on others	다른 사람에게 ( )

➕ **본문 문장 속에서 단어의 의미를 우리말로 해석해 보세요.**

This is the main motive / for gossiping about well-known figures and superiors.

→ 이것이 주요 동기이다 / _____과 윗사람들에 대해 뒷공론을 하는.

48 다음 글의 밑줄 친 부분 중, 어법상 틀린 것은?

To begin with a psychological reason, the knowledge of another's personal affairs can tempt the possessor of this information ① to repeat it as gossip because as unrevealed information it remains socially inactive. Only when the information is repeated can its possessor ② turn the fact that he knows something into something socially valuable like social recognition, prestige, and notoriety. As long as he keeps his information to ③ himself, he may feel superior to those who do not know it. But knowing and not telling does not give him that feeling of "superiority that, so to say, latently contained in the secret, fully ④ actualizing itself only at the moment of disclosure." This is the main motive for gossiping about well-known figures and superiors. The gossip producer assumes that some of the "fame" of the subject of gossip, as ⑤ whose "friend" he presents himself, will rub off on him.

*prestige: 명성 **notoriety: 악명
***latently: 잠재적으로

정답과 해설 **p.43**

01 To begin with a psychological reason, / the knowledge of another's personal affairs / can tempt the possessor of this information / to repeat it as gossip / because (as
동사   목적어   목적격보어   접속사(~ 때문에)
unrevealed information) it remains socially inactive.
주어   동사   주격보어

02 Only when the information is repeated / can its possessor turn the fact / [that he
only 부사절(오로지 ~할 때)   도치(의문문 어순)   동격절(=the fact)
knows something] / into something socially valuable / like social recognition, prestige,
전치사(~처럼)
and notoriety.

03 As long as he keeps his information to himself, / he may feel superior to those / [who
접속사(~하는 한)   ~한 사람들
do not know it]. // But / knowing and not telling / does not give him that feeling of
주격 관계대명사절   주어(동명사)   동사   간접목적어   직접목적어
"superiority / [that, (so to say, latently contained in the secret), / fully actualizes itself
삽입구   동사(단수)
only at the moment of disclosure]."

04 This is the main motive / for gossiping about well-known figures and superiors.
전치사구

05 The gossip producer assumes / [that some of the "fame" of the subject of gossip, / (as
whose의 선행사
whose "friend" he presents himself), / will rub off on him].
소유격 관계대명사   주어   동사구   목적어(= the gossip producer)

01 심리적인psychological 이유부터 시작하자면, / 다른 사람의 개인적인 일에 대한 지식은 / 이 정보의 소유자possessor를 부추길tempt 수 있는데 / 그것을 뒷공론으로 반복하도록 / 왜냐하면 숨겨진unrevealed 정보로서는 그것이 사회적으로 비활동적인 상태로 남기 때문이다.

02 오로지 그 정보가 반복될 때만 / 그 정보를 소유한 사람은 사실을 바꿀 수 있다 / 그가 무언가를 알고 있다는 / 사회적으로 가치 있는 어떤 것으로 / 사회적 인지, 명성 그리고 악명과 같은.

03 그가 자신의 정보를 남에게 말하지 않는keep his information to himself 동안은, / 그는 사람들보다 우월감을 느낄 수도 있다 / 그것을 알지 못하는. // 그러나 / 알면서 말하지 않는 것은 / 그에게 그런 우월함superiority의 감정을 주지 못한다 / '말하자면 그 비밀 속에 보이지 않게 들어 있다가 / 폭로disclosure의 순간에만 완전히 실현되는actualize'.

04 이것이 주요 동기이다 / 유명한well-known 인물들과 윗사람들에 대해 뒷공론을 하는.

05 뒷공론을 만들어 내는 사람은 생각한다 / 그 뒷공론 대상의 '명성fame' 일부가 / 자신이 그의 '친구'라고 소개하는 / 자신에게 옮겨질rub off on 것이라고.

구문 Check up

① As long as he keeps his information to himself, he may feel superior to that / those who do not know it.

주격 관계대명사 who가 이끄는 절의 수식을 받는 대명사(~한 사람들)로 those를 쓴다.

② The gossip producer assumes that some of the "fame" of the subject of gossip, as whose "friend" he presents himself, will rub off on him / himself .

will rub off on에 연결되는 주어는 some of the "fame"인데, 이는 목적어인 him과 동일하지 않으므로 재귀대명사를 쓸 필요가 없다. 따라서 him이 적절하다.

정답 ① those ② him

49 STEP 1 · 수능에 *진짜* 나오는 *단어*

✔ 문제에 나오는 단어들을 확인하세요.

01	appealing	a. 매력적인	find the song (✔ appealing)	그 노래를 매력적이라고 여기다
02	obvious	a. 분명한, 명백한	things that were not ( )	분명하지 않았던 것들
03	certainly	ad. 분명히, 확실히	( ) true	분명히 사실인
04	lyric	n. 가사	hear a ( )	가사를 듣다
05	emerge	v. 나타나다, 드러나다	( ) with each listening	매번 들을 때 나타나다
06	fond	a. 좋아하는	( ) of each other	서로 좋아하는
07	architecture	n. 건축	major in ( )	건축을 전공하다

➕ 본문 문장 속에서 단어들을 확인해 보세요.

An interesting aspect of human psychology / is / that we tend to like things more / and find them more appealing / if everything about those things is not obvious / the first time we experience them.

인간 심리의 흥미로운 일면은 / ~이다 / 우리가 어떤 것을 더 좋아하는 경향이 있다는 것 / 그리고 그것을 더 매력적으로 여기는 / 만약 그것에 관한 모든 것이 분명하지 않다면 / 우리가 처음으로 어떤 것을 경험할 때.

문제를 풀기 전에 단어들을 **30초** 동안 다시 확인하세요.

01	appealing	🖉 매력적인	find the song appealing	그 노래를 (매력적)이라고 여기다
02	obvious		things that were not obvious	( )않았던 것들
03	certainly		certainly true	( ) 사실인
04	lyric		hear a lyric	( )를 듣다
05	emerge		emerge with each listening	매번 들을 때( )
06	fond		fond of each other	서로 ( )
07	architecture		major in architecture	( )을 전공하다

➕ **본문 문장 속에서 단어의 의미를 우리말로 해석해 보세요.**

An interesting aspect of human psychology / is / that we tend to like things more / and find them more appealing / if everything about those things is not obvious / the first time we experience them.

→ 인간 심리의 흥미로운 일면은 / ~이다 / 우리가 어떤 것을 더 좋아하는 경향이 있다는 것 / 그리고 ▨▨▨▨▨▨▨▨▨▨▨▨▨▨ / 만약 그것에 관한 모든 것이 ▨▨▨▨▨▨▨▨ 면 / 우리가 처음으로 어떤 것을 경험할 때.

49

다음 글의 밑줄 친 부분 중, 어법상 틀린 것은?

An interesting aspect of human psychology is that we tend to like things more and find them more ① appealing if everything about those things is not obvious the first time we experience them. This is certainly true in music. For example, we might hear a song on the radio for the first time that catches our interest and ② decide we like it. Then the next time we hear it, we hear a lyric we didn't catch the first time, or we might notice ③ what the piano or drums are doing in the background. A special harmony ④ emerges that we missed before. We hear more and more and understand more and more with each listening. Sometimes, the longer ⑤ that takes for a work of art to reveal all of its subtleties to us, the more fond of that thing — whether it's music, art, dance, or architecture — we become.

*subtleties: 중요한 세부 요소[사항]들

정답과 해설 **p.44**

01   An interesting aspect of human psychology / is / [that we tend to like things more /
주어   동사(단수) 접속사(~것)
and find them more appealing / if everything about those things is not obvious / the
「find + 목적어 + 형용사: ~이 …한 것을 깨닫다」
first time we experience them].

02   This is certainly true in music. // For example, / we might hear a song on the radio for
동사1   동사1   목적어(선행사)
the first time / [that catches our interest] / and (might) decide we like it.
주격 관계대명사절   동사2

03   Then the next time we hear it, / we hear a lyric / [we didn't catch the first time], / or
목적격 관계대명사절
we might notice / [what piano or drums are doing in the background]. // A special
간접의문문   주어
harmony emerges / [that we missed before].
  동사   목적격 관계대명사절

04   We hear more and more and understand more and more / with each listening.

05   Sometimes, / the longer it takes for a work of art / to reveal all of its subtleties to us, /
가주어-진주어 구문
the more fond of that thing / — whether it's music, art, dance, or architecture — / we
「the + 비교급 ~, the + 비교급 …: ~할수록 더 …하다」   주어
become.
동사

---

01   인간 심리의 흥미로운 일면은 / ~이다 / 우리가 어떤 것을 더 좋아하는 경향이 있다는 것 / 그리고 그것을 더
     매력적으로appealing 여기는 / 만약 그것에 관한 모든 것이 분명하지obvious 않다면 / 우리가 처음으로 어떤 것을 경험할
     때.

02   이것은 음악에 있어서 분명히certainly 사실이다. // 예를 들어 / 우리는 라디오에서 노래를 처음 듣고, / 우리의 관심을
     끄는 / 그 노래가 마음에 든다고 판단할 수 있다.

03   그리고 나서 우리가 다음에 그것을 들을 때, / 우리는 가사lyric를 듣거나 / 우리가 처음에 알아차리지 못한 / 아니면 알아챌
     수 있다 / 배경에서 피아노나 드럼이 무엇을 하고 있는지. // 특별한 화음이 나타난다emerge / 우리가 전에 놓쳤던.

04   우리는 점점 더 많은 것을 듣고 점점 더 많이 이해하게 된다 / 매번 들으면서.

05   때때로 / 예술 작품이 ~하는 데 걸리는 시간이 길어질수록 / 우리에게 그것의 중요한 세부 요소들을 모두 드러내는 데 /
     그것을 더 좋아하게fond (된다) / 그것이 음악이든, 미술이든, 춤이든, 또는 건축architecture이든 간에 / 우리는 (~하게)
     된다.

구문 Check up

① For example, we might hear a song on the radio for the first time that catch / catches our interest and decide we like it.

선행사가 단수명사 a song이므로 관계대명사 that 뒤의 동사는 단수형인 catches로 써야 한다.

② Sometimes, the longer it takes for a work of art to reveal all of its subtleties to us, the more fond / fondly of that thing we become.

뒤에 나오는 we become으로 보아, become의 보어인 비교급 형용사가 「the + 비교급」 구문으로 강조된 것임을 알 수 있다. 따라서 형용사인 fond가 적절하다.

정답 ① catches ② fond

50 STEP 1 • 수능에 *진짜* 나오는 *단어*

어휘 추론 ✚

✔ 문제에 나오는 단어들을 확인하세요.

01	bazaar	n. 상점가	(✔ bazaar) economies	상점가 경제	
02	feature	v. ~을 특징으로 하다	( ) a unique mechanism	독특한 메커니즘을 특징으로 하다	
03	flexible	a. 유연한	apparently ( )	겉보기에 유연한	
04	enduring	a. 지속적인, 오래가는	more ( ) ties	더 지속적인 유대	
05	restriction	n. 제약	aware of each other's ( )s	서로의 제약을 알고 있는	
06	assess	v. 평가하다, 가늠하다	( ) the financial constraints	재정적 제약을 평가하다	
07	to a large extent	대체로, 상당 부분	( ) ( ) ( ) ( )	대체로	
08	necessity	n. 필수품, 필수 사항	a ( ) and a luxury	필수품과 사치품	
09	possession	n. 소유	( ) of video games	비디오 게임의 소유	
10	absolute	a. 절대적인	an ( ) necessity	절대적인 필수 사항	
11	establish	v. 형성하다, 세우다	( ) a price consensus	가격 일치를 형성하다	
12	relate to	~을 관련 짓다	( ) ( ) each other's preferences and limitations	서로의 선호와 한계를 관련 짓다	

✚ 본문 문장 속에서 단어들을 확인해 보세요.

In Delhi's bazaars, / buyers and sellers can assess to a large extent the financial constraints / that other actors have in their everyday life.

델리의 상점가에서, / 구매자와 판매자는 대체로 재정적인 제약을 평가할 수 있다 / 다른 행위자들이 그들의 일상생활에서 가지는.

01	bazaar	상점가	bazaar economies	(상점가)경제
02	feature		feature a unique mechanism	독특한 메커니즘을 ( )
03	flexible		apparently flexible	겉보기에 ( )
04	enduring		more enduring ties	더 ( ) 유대
05	restriction		aware of each other's restrictions	서로의 ( )을 알고 있는
06	assess		assess the financial constraints	재정적 제약을 ( )
07	to a large extent		to a large extent	( )
08	necessity		a necessity and a luxury	( )과 사치품
09	possession		possession of video games	비디오 게임의 ( )
10	absolute		an absolute necessity	( ) 필수 사항
11	establish		establish a price consensus	가격 일치를 ( )
12	relate to		relate to each other's preferences and limitations	서로의 선호와 한계를 ( )

⊕ **본문 문장 속에서 단어의 의미를 우리말로 해석해 보세요.**

In Delhi's bazaars, / buyers and sellers can assess to a large extent the financial constraints / that other actors have in their everyday life.

➜ 델리의 상점가에서, / 구매자와 판매자는   재정적인 제약을   수 있다 / 다른 행위자들이 그들의 일상생활에서 가지는.

50 다음 글의 밑줄 친 부분 중, 문맥상 낱말의 쓰임이 적절하지 <u>않은</u> 것은?

Bazaar economies feature an apparently flexible price-setting mechanism that sits atop more enduring ties of shared culture. Both the buyer and seller are aware of each other's ① <u>restrictions</u>. In Delhi's bazaars, buyers and sellers can ② <u>assess</u> to a large extent the financial constraints that other actors have in their everyday life. Each actor belonging to a specific economic class understands what the other sees as a necessity and a luxury. In the case of electronic products like video games, they are not a ③ <u>necessity</u> at the same level as other household purchases such as food items. So, the seller in Delhi's bazaars is careful not to directly ask for very ④ <u>low</u> prices for video games because at no point will the buyer see possession of them as an absolute necessity. Access to this type of knowledge establishes a price consensus by relating to each other's preferences and limitations of belonging to a ⑤ <u>similar</u> cultural and economic universe.

*constraint: 압박   **consensus: 일치

정답과 해설 p.45

211

01 Bazaar economies feature an apparently flexible price-setting mechanism / [that sits
선행사(단수)   주격 관계대명사절
atop more enduring ties of shared culture]. // Both the buyer and seller are aware of
                                              주어(both A and B: 복수)
each other's restrictions.

02 In Delhi's bazaars, / buyers and sellers can assess (to a large extent) the financial
                                               동사   목적어
constraints / [that other actors have in their everyday life]. // Each actor belonging to a
           목적격 관계대명사절   현재분사구
specific economic class / understands [what the other sees as a necessity and a luxury].
                                                    목적어(의문사절)

03 In the case of electronic products like video games, / they are not a necessity at
the same ~ as …: …와 같은 ~
the same level / as other household purchases such as food items. // So, / the seller

in Delhi's bazaars is careful / not to directly ask for very low prices for video games /
                                to부정사의 부정(not + to + 동사원형)
because at no point will the buyer see possession of them as an absolute necessity.
         부정어구   도치 구문(조동사 + 주어 + 동사원형)   = video games

04 Access to this type of knowledge establishes a price consensus / by relating to each
   주어(불가산명사)   수 일치(단수)
other's preferences and limitations / of belonging to a similar cultural and economic
                                전치사구
universe.

01 상점가 경제bazaar economy는 겉으로 보기에 유연한apparently flexible 가격 설정 메커니즘을 특징으로 한다feature
/ 공유되는 문화라는 더 지속적인enduring 유대 위에 자리 잡은. // 구매자와 판매자 둘 다 서로의 제약restriction을 알고
있다.

02 델리의 상점가에서, / 구매자와 판매자는 대체로to a large extent 재정적인 제약을 평가할assess 수 있다 / 다른
행위자들이 그들의 일상생활에서 가지는. // 특정 경제 계층에 속하는 각 행위자는 / 상대방이 무엇을 필수품으로 여기고
무엇을 사치품으로 여기는지를 이해한다.

03 비디오 게임과 같은 전자 제품의 경우, / 그것들은 동일한 수준의 필수품이 아니다 / 식품과 같은 다른 가정 구매품과. //
따라서 / 델리의 상점가에 있는 판매자는 주의한다 / 비디오 게임에 대해 직접적으로 매우 낮은(→ 높은) 가격을 요구하지
않으려고 / 왜냐하면 구매자가 비디오 게임의 소유possession를 절대적인 필수 사항absolute necessity으로 볼 이유가
전혀 없기 때문이다.

04 이러한 유형의 지식에 대한 접근은 가격 일치를 형성한다establish / 서로의 선호와 한계를 관련지어relate to / 비슷한
문화 및 경제 세계에 속하여 생기는.

구문 Check up

① In Delhi's bazaars, buyers and sellers can assess / be
assessed to a large extent the financial constraints
that other actors have in their everyday life.

주어가 '평가하는' 주체이고 뒤에 목적어(the financial constraints)가 나
오는 것으로 보아 능동태가 적절하다.

② At no point the buyer will / will the buyer see
possession of them as an absolute necessity.

At no point가 부정어구이므로 「조동사 + 주어 + 동사원형」 어순의 도치
구문이 이어져야 한다.

정답 ① assess ② will the buyer

51

STEP 1 • 수능에 *진짜* 나오는 *단어*

✔ 문제에 나오는 단어들을 확인하세요.

01	automobile	n. 자동차	(✔ automobile) demand in cities	도시에서의 자동차 수요
02	accommodate	v. (필요에) 부응하다, 맞추다	( ) the demand	수요에 부응하다
03	inevitably	ad. 불가피하게, 필히	( ) lead to increases in price	필히 가격 증가로 이어지다
04	motorization	n. 자동차 보급	increases in ( )	자동차 보급의 증가
05	densely	ad. 밀집하여, 빽빽이	( ) inhabited cities	(사람들이) 밀집하여 거주하는 도시
06	corresponding	a. 상응하는, 해당하는	bring a ( ) change	상응하는 변화를 가져오다
07	accessibility	n. 접근성	( ) of public transportation	대중 교통 접근성
08	livability	n. 거주 적합성	urban ( )	도시 거주 적합성
09	prosperous	a. 부유한, 번성한	( ) cities	부유한 도시
10	restrict	v. 제한하다	( ) motorized travel	자동차 여행을 제한하다
11	administrative	a. 행정의	( ) rules	행정 규칙
12	contribution	n. 원인이 됨, 기여	the ( ) of motorized travel to climate change	자동차 여행이 기후 변화의 원인이 되는 것
13	reinforce	v. 강화하다	( ) the existing belief	기존의 믿음을 강화하다

⊕ 본문 문장 속에서 단어들을 확인해 보세요.

In recent years / urban transport professionals globally / have largely acquiesced to the view / that automobile demand in cities needs to be managed / rather than accommodated.

최근 몇 년 동안 / 전 세계적으로 도시 교통 전문가들은 / 견해를 대체로 따랐다 / 도시의 자동차 수요가 관리되어야 한다는 / (그것이) 맞춰지기보다는.

단어 다시보기 문제를 풀기 전에 단어들을 30초 동안 다시 확인하세요.

01	automobile	자동차	automobile demand in cities	도시에서의 (자동차) 수요
02	accommodate		accommodate the demand	수요에 ( )
03	inevitably		inevitably lead to increases in price	( ) 가격 증가로 이어지다
04	motorization		increases in motorization	( )의 증가
05	densely		densely inhabited cities	( ) 거주하는 도시
06	corresponding		bring a corresponding change	( ) 변화를 가져오다
07	accessibility		accessibility of public transportation	대중 교통 ( )
08	livability		urban livability	도시 ( )
09	prosperous		prosperous cities	( ) 도시
10	restrict		restrict motorized travel	자동차 여행을 ( )
11	administrative		administrative rules	( ) 규칙
12	contribution		the contribution of motorized travel to climate change	자동차 여행이 기후 변화의 ( )
13	reinforce		reinforce the existing belief	기존의 믿음을 ( )

⊕ 본문 문장 속에서 단어의 의미를 우리말로 해석해 보세요.

In recent years / urban transport professionals globally / have largely acquiesced to the view / that automobile demand in cities needs to be managed / rather than accommodated.

→ 최근 몇 년 동안 / 전 세계적으로 도시 교통 전문가들은 / 견해를 대체로 따랐다 / ______________가 관리되어야 한다는 / (그것이) ______________.

51

다음 글의 밑줄 친 부분 중, 문맥상 낱말의 쓰임이 적절하지 <u>않은</u> 것은?

In recent years urban transport professionals globally have largely acquiesced to the view that automobile demand in cities needs to be managed rather than accommodated. Rising incomes inevitably lead to increases in motorization. Even without the imperative of climate change, the physical constraints of densely inhabited cities and the corresponding demands of accessibility, mobility, safety, air pollution, and urban livability all ① <u>limit</u> the option of expanding road networks purely to accommodate this rising demand. As a result, as cities develop and their residents become more prosperous, ② <u>persuading</u> people to choose *not* to use cars becomes an increasingly key focus of city managers and planners. Improving the quality of ③ <u>alternative</u> options, such as walking, cycling, and public transport, is a central element of this strategy. However, the most direct approach to ④ <u>accommodating</u> automobile demand is making motorized travel more expensive or restricting it with administrative rules. The contribution of motorized travel to climate change ⑤ <u>reinforces</u> this imperative.

*acquiesce: 따르다　**imperative: 불가피한 것
***constraint: 압박

정답과 해설 **p.45**

01 In recent years / urban transport professionals globally have largely acquiesced to
    기간 부사구   주어   동사(현재완료)
the view / [that automobile demand in cities needs to be managed / rather than
              동격
accommodated].

02 Rising incomes inevitably lead to increases in motorization. // Even without the
imperative of climate change, / the physical constraints of densely inhabited cities
                                  주어1
/ and the corresponding demands of accessibility, mobility, safety, air pollution,
    주어2
and urban livability / all limit the option of expanding road networks / purely to
                         동사(복수)
accommodate this rising demand.
부사적 용법(목적)

03 As a result, / as cities develop and their residents become more prosperous, /
                  접속사(~함에 따라)
persuading people to choose *not* to use cars / becomes an increasingly key focus of
주어(동명사구)   동사(단수)
city managers and planners. // Improving the quality of alternative options, / (such as
                                  주어(동명사구)   삽입구
walking, cycling, and public transport), / is a central element of this strategy.
                                             동사(단수)

04 However, / the most direct approach / to accommodating automobile demand / is
               주어   동사
making motorized travel more expensive / or restricting it with administrative rules. //
                주격 보어(동명사구 병렬)
The contribution of motorized travel to climate change / reinforces this imperative.
주어   동사(단수)

01 최근 몇 년 동안 / 전 세계적으로 도시 교통 전문가들은 견해를 대체로 따랐다 / 도시의 자동차automobile 수요가
   관리되어야 한다는 / (그것이) 맞춰지기accommodate보다는.

02 소득 증가는 필연적으로 자동차 보급의 증가로 이어진다inevitably lead to increases in motorization. // 기후
   변화로 인한 불가피성이 없다 하더라도, / 인구가 밀집한densely inhabited 도시의 물리적 제약 / 그리고 그에
   상응하는corresponding 접근성accessibility, 이동성, 안전, 대기 오염, 그리고 도시 거주 적합성urban livability에 대한
   요구는 / 모두 도로망을 확장한다는 선택권을 제한한다 / 단지 이러한 증가하는 수요에 부응하기 위해.

03 결과적으로, / 도시가 발전하고 도시의 거주자들이 더 부유해짐prosperous에 따라, / 사람들이 자동차를 사용하지
   '않기로' 결정하도록 설득하는 것이 / 점점 더 도시 관리자와 계획 설계자들의 핵심 중점 사항이 된다. // 대안적인 선택
   사항의 질을 향상하는 것이 / 걷기, 자전거 타기, 대중교통과 같은 / 이 전략의 핵심 요소이다.

04 하지만 / 가장 직접적인 접근 방법은 / 자동차 수요를 맞추는(→ 관리하는) / 자동차 여행을 더 비싸게 만들거나 / 행정
   규정administrative rule으로 그것을 제한하는restrict 것이다. // 자동차로 하는 이동이 기후 변화의 원인이 된다는
   점contribution이 / 이런 불가피성을 강화한다reinforce.

구문 Check up

① In recent years urban transport professionals globally have largely acquiesced to the view which / that automobile demand in cities needs to be managed rather than accommodated.

추상명사 the view 뒤로 '견해'의 내용을 설명하는 완전한 명사절이 이어지므로 동격 접속사인 that이 적절하다.

② As a result, as cities develop and their residents become more prosperous, persuading / persuade people to choose *not* to use cars becomes an increasingly key focus of city managers and planners.

콤마 앞은 부사절이고, 문장의 동사인 becomes 앞에는 주어가 필요하므로 동명사인 persuading이 적절하다.

정답 ① that ② persuading

52

STEP 1 • 수능에 *진짜* 나오는 *단어*

✔ 문제에 나오는 단어들을 확인하세요.

01	organic	a. 유기농의	(✔ organic) farming methods	유기농 농법
02	biosphere	n. 생물권	damaging to the ( )	생물권에 해가 되는
03	adoption	n. 채택, 선정	the ( ) of organic farming methods	유기농 농법의 채택
04	essential	a. 필수적인	( ) ingredients	필수 요소
05	moderate	a. 중간의	from ( ) to high levels	중간에서 상위 수준
06	productivity	n. 생산성	increase ( )	생산성을 늘리다
07	extensive	a. 광범위한	the ( ) use of chemicals	화학물질의 광범위한 사용
08	weed	n. 잡초	( ) control	잡초 방제
09	wealthy	a. 부유한	become ( )	부유해지다
10	sensible	a. 합리적인, 분별 있는	a ( ) use of resources	자원의 합리적 사용
11	livestock	n. 가축	( ) enterprises	가축 경영
12	sustainability	n. 지속 가능성	the ( ) of rural ecosystems	농촌 생태계의 지속 가능성

+ 본문 문장 속에서 단어들을 확인해 보세요.

It has been suggested / that "organic" methods, / defined as those / in which only natural products can be used as inputs, / would be less damaging to the biosphere.

시사되어 왔다 / '유기농' 방식은 / 방식이라 정의되는 / 천연 제품들만 투입물로 사용될 수 있는 / 생물권에 해를 덜 끼칠 것이라는 점이.

01	organic	✏ 유기농의	organic farming methods	(유기농)농법
02	biosphere		damaging to the biosphere	( )에 해가 되는
03	adoption		the adoption of organic farming methods	유기농 농법의 ( )
04	essential		essential ingredients	( )요소
05	moderate		from moderate to high levels	( )에서 상위 수준
06	productivity		increase productivity	( )을 늘리다
07	extensive		the extensive use of chemicals	화학물질의 ( )사용
08	weed		weed control	( )방제
09	wealthy		become wealthy	( )지다
10	sensible		a sensible use of resources	자원의 ( )사용
11	livestock		livestock enterprises	( )경영
12	sustainability		the sustainability of rural ecosystems	농촌 생태계의 ( )

➕ **본문 문장 속에서 단어의 의미를 우리말로 해석해 보세요.**

It has been suggested / that "organic" methods, / defined as those / in which only natural products can be used as inputs, / would be less damaging to the biosphere.

➡ 시사되어 왔다 /   은 / 방식이라 정의되는 / 천연 제품들만 투입물로 사용될 수 있는 /   것이라는 점이.

52 다음 글의 밑줄 친 부분 중, 문맥상 낱말의 쓰임이 적절하지 않은 것은?

It has been suggested that "organic" methods, defined as those in which only natural products can be used as inputs, would be less damaging to the biosphere. Large-scale adoption of "organic" farming methods, however, would ① reduce yields and increase production costs for many major crops. Inorganic nitrogen supplies are ② essential for maintaining moderate to high levels of productivity for many of the non-leguminous crop species, because organic supplies of nitrogenous materials often are either limited or more expensive than inorganic nitrogen fertilizers. In addition, there are ③ benefits to the extensive use of either manure or legumes as "green manure" crops. In many cases, weed control can be very difficult or require much hand labor if chemicals cannot be used, and ④ fewer people are willing to do this work as societies become wealthier. Some methods used in "organic" farming, however, such as the sensible use of crop rotations and specific combinations of cropping and livestock enterprises, can make important ⑤ contributions to the sustainability of rural ecosystems.

*nitrogen fertilizer: 질소 비료　**manure: 거름
***legume: 콩과(科) 식물

정답과 해설 **p.46**

01 It has been suggested / that "organic" methods, / defined as those [in which only
natural products can be used as inputs], / would be less damaging to the biosphere. //
Large-scale adoption of "organic" farming methods, / however, / would reduce yields
and increase production costs / for many major crops.

02 Inorganic nitrogen supplies are essential / for maintaining moderate to high levels
of productivity / for many of the non-leguminous crop species, / because organic
supplies of nitrogenous materials / often are either limited or more expensive / than
inorganic nitrogen fertilizers.

03 In addition, / there are benefits / to the extensive use of either manure or legumes / as
"green manure" crops. // In many cases, / weed control can be very difficult or require
much hand labor / if chemicals cannot be used, / and fewer people are willing to do
this work / as societies become wealthier.

04 Some methods used in "organic" farming, / (however), / (such as the sensible use of
crop rotations / and specific combinations of cropping and livestock enterprises), / can
make important contributions / to the sustainability of rural ecosystems.

---

01 시사되어 왔다 / '유기농organic' 방식은 / 천연 제품들만 투입물로 사용될 수 있는 방식이라 정의되는 /
생물권biosphere에 해를 덜 끼칠 것이라는 점이. // '유기농' 경작 방식의 대규모 채택adoption은 / 그러나 / 산출량을
감소시키고 생산비를 증가시킬 것이다 / 많은 주요 작물에 있어.

02 무기질 질소 공급은 필수적essential인데 / 생산성productivity을 중간moderate에서 상급 수준으로 유지하는 데 / 많은
비(非)콩과 작물 종에 있어 / 질소성 물질의 유기적 공급이 / 흔히 제한적이거나 더 비싸기 때문이다 / 무기 질소 비료보다.

03 게다가, / 이점(→ 제약)이 있다 / 거름이나 콩과 식물의 광범위한extensive 사용에는 / '친환경 거름' 작물로서의. // 많은
경우, / 잡초weed 방제가 매우 어렵거나 많은 손일이 필요할 수 있는데 / 화학 물질이 사용될 수 없으면 / 이 작업을 기꺼이
하려는 사람이 더 적을 것이다 / 사회가 부유해짐wealthy에 따라.

04 '유기농' 경작에서 사용되는 몇몇 방식들은 / 그러나 / 윤작의 합리적인sensible 사용과 / 경작과 가축livestock 경영의
특정한 조합과 같은 / 중요하게 기여할 수 있다 / 농촌 생태계의 지속 가능성sustainability에.

구문 Check up

① It has been suggested that "organic" methods, defined
as those which / in which only natural products can
be used as inputs, would be less damaging to the
biosphere.

only natural products can be used as inputs가 완전한 수동태 문장이므
로, 관계부사와 같은 기능을 하는 「전치사 + 관계대명사」 형태의 in which
가 적절하다.

② Inorganic nitrogen supplies are essential for many of
the non-leguminous crop species, because / because
of organic supplies of nitrogenous materials often are
either limited or more expensive.

뒤에 'organic supplies ~ are ~'라는 절이 나오므로 접속사 because가 적
절하다. because of 뒤에는 명사구가 나온다.

정답 ① in which ② because

53 STEP 1 • 수능에 *진짜* 나오는 *단어*

어휘 추론 ⊕

✔ 문제에 나오는 단어들을 확인하세요.

01	trigger	v. 촉발하다	(✔ trigger) an emotional response		정서적 반응을 촉발하다
02	loyalty	n. 충성심	show ( )		충성심을 보이다
03	passionate	a. 열정적인	( ) about players and teams		선수와 팀에 매우 열정적인
04	border on	~에 가깝다	( ) ( ) obsession		집착에 가깝다
05	addiction	n. 중독	( ) to online games		온라인 게임에 대한 중독
06	intensity	n. 격렬함, 강도	emotional ( )		정서적 격렬함
07	attachment	n. 애착	strong ( )s to the past		과거에 대한 강한 애착
08	nostalgia	n. 향수	a sense of ( )		향수의 감정
09	project	v. 투사하다	( ) a more attractive image		더 매력적인 이미지를 투사하다
10	defeat	v. 무산시키다, 패배시키다	a ( )ed proposal		무산된 제안

⊕ 본문 문장 속에서 단어들을 확인해 보세요.

While most managers can only dream of having customers / that are as passionate about their products / as sport fans, / the emotion triggered by sport / can also have a negative impact.

대부분의 관리자는 고객을 가지기를 오직 꿈꾸지만 / 그들 제품에 열정적인 / 스포츠팬만큼 / 스포츠로 인해 촉발되는 감정은 / 또한 부정적인 영향을 미칠 수 있다.

01	trigger	✐ 촉발하다	trigger an emotional response	정서적 반응을 (촉발하다)
02	loyalty		show loyalty	( )을 보이다
03	passionate		passionate about players and teams	선수와 팀에 매우 ( )
04	border on		border on obsession	집착에 ( )
05	addiction		addiction to online games	온라인 게임에 대한 ( )
06	intensity		emotional intensity	정서적 ( )
07	attachment		strong attachments to the past	과거에 대한 강한 ( )
08	nostalgia		a sense of nostalgia	( )의 감정
09	project		project a more attractive image	더 매력적인 이미지를 ( )
10	defeat		a defeated proposal	( ) 제안

➕ **본문 문장 속에서 단어의 의미를 우리말로 해석해 보세요.**

While most managers can only dream of having customers / that are as passionate about their products / as sport fans, / the emotion triggered by sport / can also have a negative impact.

→ 대부분의 관리자는 고객을 가지기를 오직 꿈꾸지만 / ▨▨▨▨▨▨▨▨▨ / 스포츠팬만큼 / ▨▨▨▨▨▨▨▨▨▨▨▨은 / 또한 부정적인 영향을 미칠 수 있다.

53

다음 글의 밑줄 친 부분 중, 문맥상 낱말의 쓰임이 적절하지 <u>않은</u> 것은?

Sport can trigger an emotional response in its consumers of the kind rarely brought forth by other products. Imagine bank customers buying memorabilia to show loyalty to their bank, or consumers ① <u>identifying</u> so strongly with their car insurance company that they get a tattoo with its logo. We know that some sport followers are so ② <u>passionate</u> about players, teams and the sport itself that their interest borders on obsession. This addiction provides the emotional glue that binds fans to teams, and maintains loyalty even in the face of on-field ③ <u>failure</u>. While most managers can only dream of having customers that are as passionate about their products as sport fans, the emotion triggered by sport can also have a negative impact. Sport's emotional intensity can mean that organisations have strong attachments to the past through nostalgia and club tradition. As a result, they may ④ <u>increase</u> efficiency, productivity and the need to respond quickly to changing market conditions. For example, a proposal to change club colours in order to project a more attractive image may be ⑤ <u>defeated</u> because it breaks a link with tradition.

*memorabilia: 기념품   **obsession: 집착

정답과 해설 **p.47**

223

01 Sport can trigger an emotional response in its consumers / of the kind rarely brought
과거분사구
forth by other products. // Imagine bank customers buying memorabilia / to show
명령문(~하라)   목적어-목적격보어 병렬
loyalty to their bank, / or consumers identifying so strongly with their car insurance
company / that they get a tattoo with its logo.
「so ~ that …: 너무 ~해서 …하다」

02 We know / that some sport followers are so passionate / about players, teams and the
sport itself / that their interest borders on obsession. // This addiction provides the
동사1
emotional glue / [that binds fans to teams], / and maintains loyalty even in the face of
목적어1(선행사)   주격 관계대명사절   동사2   목적어2
on-field failure.

03 While most managers can only dream of having customers / [that are as passionate
접속사(~한 반면)   선행사   「as + 원급 + as: ~만큼 …한」
about their products / as sport fans], / the emotion triggered by sport / can also have a
과거분사구
negative impact.

04 Sport's emotional intensity can mean / that organisations have strong attachments
접속사(~것)
to the past / through nostalgia and club tradition. // As a result, / they may increase
동사
efficiency, productivity and the need / to respond quickly to changing market
목적어(A, B, and C)   형용사적 용법
conditions.

05 For example, / a proposal to change club colours / in order to project a more attractive
주어   형용사적 용법   부사적 용법(목적)
image / may be defeated / because it breaks a link with tradition.
동사(조동사 수동태)

01 스포츠는 그것의 소비자에게 정서적 반응을 촉발시킬trigger 수 있다 / 다른 제품이 좀처럼 일으키지 못하는 종류의. //
은행 고객이 기념품을 구입한다고 상상해 보라 / 그들 은행에 대한 충성심loyalty을 보여주기 위해 / 혹은 고객이 그들
자동차 보험 회사에 매우 강한 동질감을 가져서 / 그들이 회사 로고로 문신을 한다고.

02 우리는 알고 있다 / 일부 스포츠 추종자들이 매우 열정적이어서passionate / 선수, 팀, 그리고 그 스포츠 자체에 / 그들의
관심이 집착에 아주 가깝다border on는 것을. // 이런 중독addiction은 정서적 접착제를 제공하고 / 팬을 팀과 묶어주는 /
구장에서 일어나는 실패에도 불구하고 충성심을 유지하게 한다.

03 대부분의 관리자는 고객을 가지기를 오직 꿈꾸지만 / 그들 제품에 열정적인 / 스포츠팬만큼 / 스포츠로 인해 촉발되는
감정은 / 또한 부정적인 영향을 미칠 수 있다.

04 스포츠의 정서적 격렬함intensity은 의미할 수 있다 / 조직이 과거에 대한 강한 애착attachment을 가지고 있다는 것을 /
향수nostalgia와 클럽 전통을 통해. // 그 결과, / 조직은 효율성, 생산성 및 필요성을 늘릴(→ 무시할) 수도 있다 / 변화하는
시장 상황에 신속하게 대응해야 할.

05 예를 들어, / 클럽 색깔을 바꾸자는 제안은 / 더 매력적인 이미지를 투사하기project 위해 / 무산될defeat 수도 있다 /
그것이 전통과의 관계를 끊기 때문에.

구문 Check up

① Sport can trigger an emotional response in its consumers of the kind rarely bringing / brought forth by other products.

꾸밈 받는 명사 the kind가 '일으켜지는' 대상이므로 과거분사 brought이 적절하다.

② We know that some sport followers are so passionate about players, teams and the sport itself that / which their interest borders on obsession.

「so ~ that …(너무 ~해서 …하다)」 구문이므로 접속사 that이 적절하다.

정답 ① brought ② that

54

어휘 추론 +

STEP 1 • 수능에 진짜 나오는 단어

✔ 문제에 나오는 단어들을 확인하세요.

01	demonstrate	v. 입증하다	(✔ demonstrate) the effect	효과를 입증하다
02	measurement	n. 측정	( )s of the speed of light	빛의 속도의 측정
03	relativity	n. 상대성	the theory of ( )	상대성 이론
04	quantity	n. (일정한 단위로 측정되는) 양	the most frequently measured ( )ies	가장 자주 측정된 양
05	opposite	n. 정반대	the ( ) of the previous results	이전 결과의 정반대
06	bias	n. 편향	a cognitive ( )	인지적 편향
07	subconsciously	ad. 잠재의식적으로	( ) adjust their results	잠재의식적으로 그들의 결과를 조정하다
08	intentionally	ad. 고의로, 의도적으로	( ) hurt someone	고의로 누군가를 상처 주다
09	dishonest	a. 부정직한	( ) behavior in experiments	실험에서의 부정직한 행동
10	lack	v. 부족하다, 결여하다	( ) the courage	용기가 부족하다

+ 본문 문장 속에서 단어들을 확인해 보세요.

How the bandwagon effect occurs / is demonstrated / by the history of measurements of the speed of light.

편승 효과가 어떻게 발생하는지는 / 입증된다 / 빛의 속도의 측정의 역사로.

문제를 풀기 전에 단어들을 **30초** 동안 다시 확인하세요.

01	demonstrate	✏️ 입증하다	demonstrate the effect	효과를 (입증하다)
02	measurement		measurements of the speed of light	빛의 속도의 ( )
03	relativity		the theory of relativity	( ) 이론
04	quantity		the most frequently measured quantities	가장 자주 측정된 ( )
05	opposite		the opposite of the previous results	이전 결과의 ( )
06	bias		a cognitive bias	인지적 ( )
07	subconsciously		subconsciously adjust their results	( ) 그들의 결과를 조정하다
08	intentionally		intentionally hurt someone	( ) 누군가를 상처 주다
09	dishonest		dishonest behavior in experiments	실험에서의 ( ) 행동
10	lack		lack the courage	용기가 ( )

➕ **본문 문장 속에서 단어의 의미를 우리말로 해석해 보세요.**

How the bandwagon effect occurs / is demonstrated / by the history of measurements of the speed of light.

➡️ 편승 효과가 어떻게 발생하는지는 / _____ / _____ 의 역사로.

54 다음 글의 밑줄 친 부분 중, 문맥상 낱말의 쓰임이 적절하지 <u>않은</u> 것은?

How the bandwagon effect occurs is demonstrated by the history of measurements of the speed of light. Because this speed is the basis of the theory of relativity, it's one of the most frequently and carefully measured ① <u>quantities</u> in science. As far as we know, the speed hasn't changed over time. However, from 1870 to 1900, all the experiments found speeds that were too high. Then, from 1900 to 1950, the ② <u>opposite</u> happened — all the experiments found speeds that were too low! This kind of error, where results are always on one side of the real value, is called "bias." It probably happened because over time, experimenters subconsciously adjusted their results to ③ <u>match</u> what they expected to find. If a result fit what they expected, they kept it. If a result didn't fit, they threw it out. They weren't being intentionally dishonest, just ④ <u>influenced</u> by the conventional wisdom. The pattern only changed when someone ⑤ <u>lacked</u> the courage to report what was actually measured instead of what was expected.

*bandwagon effect: 편승 효과

정답과 해설 **p.48**

01 How the bandwagon effect occurs / is demonstrated / by the history of measurements
주어(간접의문문)　　　　　　　　　　동사(단수)
of the speed of light. // Because this speed is the basis of the theory of relativity, / it's /
　　　　　　　　　　접속사(~ 때문에)
one of the most frequently and carefully measured quantities in science.
주격보어(one of the + 최상급 + 복수명사)

02 As far as we know, / the speed hasn't changed over time. // However, / from 1870 to
　　　　　　　　　　　　　동사(현재완료)　　기간 부사구
1900, / all the experiments found speeds / [that were too high]. // Then, / from 1900 to
　　　　　　　　　　　　　　　　　　↑⋯⋯⋯⋯⋯ 주격 관계대명사절
1950, / the opposite happened / — all the experiments found speeds / [that were too
　　　　　　　　　　　　　　　　　　　　　　　　　　　　　　　↑⋯⋯⋯⋯⋯ 주격 관계대명사절
low]!

03 This kind of error, / [where results are always on one side of the real value], / is called
주어　　　　　↑⋯⋯⋯⋯⋯ 관계부사절　　　　　　　　　　　　　　　　　　　동사(수동태)
"bias." // It probably happened / because over time, / experimenters subconsciously
주격보어　　　　　　　　　　接속사(~ 때문에)
adjusted their results / to match what they expected to find.
　　　　　　　　　부사적 용법(~하도록)

04 If a result fit [what they expected], / they kept it. // If a result didn't fit, / they
　　　　　　　명사절(목적어)
threw it out. // They weren't being intentionally dishonest, / just influenced by the
　　　　　　　　　　　　　　　　　　　　　　　　　　　　　분사구문(수동)
conventional wisdom.

05 The pattern only changed / when someone lacked the courage / to report what was
　　　　　　　　　　　　　　　　　　　　　　　　　　↑⋯⋯⋯⋯ 형용사적 용법
actually measured / instead of what was expected.

01 편승 효과가 어떻게 발생하는지는 / 입증된다demonstrate / 빛의 속도 측정measurement의 역사로. // 이 속도는
상대성relativity 이론의 기초이기 때문에, / 이것은 ~이다 / 과학에서 가장 자주 면밀하게 측정된 물리량quantity 중 하나.

02 우리가 아는 한, / 그 속도는 시간이 흐르는 동안 변함이 없었다. // 하지만 / 1870년부터 1900년까지 / 모든 실험에서
속도를 발견했다 / 너무 빠른. // 그러고 나서, / 1900년부터 1950년까지는 / 정반대opposite가 일어났다 / — 모든
실험에서 속도를 발견했다 / 너무 느린!

03 이런 오류는 / 결과가 항상 실제 값의 어느 한쪽에 있는 / '편향bias'이라 불린다. // 그것은 아마 생겨났을 것이다 / 시간이
지나면서 / 실험자들이 결과를 잠재의식적으로subconsciously 조정했기 때문에 / 자신들이 발견하리라 예상했던 것과
일치하도록.

04 결과가 그들이 예상한 것과 부합하면, / 그들은 그것을 취했다. // 결과가 부합하지 않으면, / 그들은 그것을 버렸다. //
그들은 고의로 부정직했던intentionally dishonest 것이 아니고, / 그저 통념에 영향을 받았을 뿐이다.

05 그 패턴은 비로소 바뀌었다 / 누군가가 용기가 부족했을lacked(→ 있었을) 때에야 / 실제로 측정된 것을 보고할 / 예상된 것
대신에.

구문 Check up

① How the bandwagon effect occurs is / are demonstrated
by the history of measurements of the speed of light.

How가 이끄는 명사절이 주어이므로 단수동사인 is를 쓰는 것이 적절하다.

② This kind of error, which / where results are always
on one side of the real value, is called "bias."

results are always on one side of the real value가 완전한 1형식 문장이므로 관계부사 where가 적절하다.

정답 ① is ② where

55

STEP 1 • 수능에 *진짜* 나오는 *단어*

✔ 문제에 나오는 단어들을 확인하세요.

01	encode	v. 부호화하다	(✔ encode) the information	정보를 부호화하다
02	note	n. (음악의) 음	( ) by ( )	한 음 한 음
03	make sense of	~을 이해하다	( ) ( ) ( ) anything	어떤 것이든 이해하다
04	composition	n. (음악, 미술의) 작품	play ( )s	작품을 연주하다
05	out of place	틀린, 제자리에 있지 않은	without a note ( ) ( ) ( )	한 음도 틀리지 않고
06	improbable	a. 일어날 것 같지 않은	an ( ) event	일어날 것 같지 않은 사건
07	mentally	ad. 머릿속으로, 정신적으로	( ) replay the music	머릿속으로 음악을 재생하다
08	recite	v. 열거하다, 암송하다	( ) the names of roads	길의 이름을 열거하다
09	abstract	a. 추상적인	an ( ) list	추상적인 목록
10	retrace	v. (갔던 길을) 되짚어가다	( ) the route	경로를 되짚어가다
11	wind back	(~로) 되돌아가다	( ) ( ) to the start	시작부로 되돌아가다

➕ 본문 문장 속에서 단어들을 확인해 보세요.

If we had to encode it in our brains / note by note, / we'd struggle to make sense of anything / more complex than the simplest children's songs.

만일 우리가 그것을 우리의 뇌에서 부호화해야 한다면 / 한 음 한 음 / 우리는 어느 것이든 이해하려면 악전고투하게 될 것이다 / 가장 간단한 동요보다 더 복잡한.

01	encode	✐ 부호화하다	encode the information	정보를 (부호화하다)
02	note		note by note	한 ( ) 한 ( )
03	make sense of		make sense of anything	어떤 것이든 ( )
04	composition		play compositions	( ) 을 연주하다
05	out of place		without a note out of place	한 음도 ( ) 않고
06	improbable		an improbable event	( ) 사건
07	mentally		mentally replay the music	( ) 음악을 재생하다
08	recite		recite the names of roads	길의 이름을 ( )
09	abstract		an abstract list	( ) 목록
10	retrace		retrace the route	경로를 ( )
11	wind back		wind back to the start	시작부로 ( )

➕ **본문 문장 속에서 단어의 의미를 우리말로 해석해 보세요.**

If we had to encode it in our brains / note by note, / we'd struggle to make sense of anything / more complex than the simplest children's songs.

➡ 만일 우리가 그것을 우리의 뇌에서 _____한다면 / _____ / 우리는 _____ 악전고투하게 될 것이다 / 가장 간단한 동요보다 더 복잡한.

55 다음 글의 밑줄 친 부분 중, 문맥상 낱말의 쓰임이 적절하지 <u>않은</u> 것은?

Chunking is vital for cognition of music. If we had to encode it in our brains note by note, we'd ① <u>struggle</u> to make sense of anything more complex than the simplest children's songs. Of course, most accomplished musicians can play compositions containing many thousands of notes entirely from ② <u>memory</u>, without a note out of place. But this seemingly awesome accomplishment of recall is made ③ <u>improbable</u> by remembering the musical *process*, not the individual notes as such. If you ask a pianist to start a Mozart sonata from bar forty-one, she'll probably have to ④ <u>mentally</u> replay the music from the start until reaching that bar — the score is not simply laid out in her mind, to be read from any random point. It's rather like describing how you drive to work: you don't simply recite the names of roads as an abstract list, but have to construct your route by mentally retracing it. When musicians make a mistake during rehearsal, they wind back to the ⑤ <u>start</u> of a musical phrase ('let's take it from the second verse') before restarting.

*chunking: 덩어리로 나누기 **bar: (악보의) 마디

정답과 해설 p.49

01 Chunking is vital for cognition of music. // If we had to encode it in our brains / note
「if + 주어 + 과거 동사 ~
by note, / we'd struggle to make sense of anything / more complex than the simplest
주어 + 조동사 과거형 + 동사원형: 가정법 과거」   형용사구
children's songs.

02 Of course, / most accomplished musicians can play compositions / containing many
                                                         현재분사구
thousands of notes / entirely from memory, / without a note out of place. // But / this
seemingly awesome accomplishment of recall / is made improbable / by remembering
주어(단수)   5형식 수동태(be p.p. + 형용사)
the musical *process*, / not the individual notes as such.

03 If you ask a pianist / to start a Mozart sonata from bar forty-one, / she'll probably have
                  ─── 시간과 조건의 부사절에서는 현재가 미래를 대신함 ───
to mentally replay the music from the start / until reaching that bar / — the score is
not simply laid out in her mind, / to be read from any random point.
                                  부사적 용법(목적)

04 It's rather like describing [how you drive to work]: / you don't simply recite the names
         전치사(~처럼) 동명사   간접의문문   동사구1
of roads / as an abstract list, / but have to construct your route / by mentally retracing
        전치사(~로서)   동사구2
it.

05 When musicians make a mistake during rehearsal, / they wind back to the start of a
musical phrase / ('let's take it from the second verse') / before restarting.

01 덩어리로 나누는 것은 음악의 인식에서 필수적이다. // 만일 우리가 그것을 우리의 뇌에서 부호화해야encode 한다면 / 한 음 한 음note by note / 우리는 어느 것이든 이해하려면make sense of 악전고투하게 될 것이다 / 가장 간단한 동요보다 더 복잡한.

02 물론, / 기량이 뛰어난 대부분의 음악가들은 작품composition을 연주할 수 있다 / 수천 개의 음을 포함하는 / 완전히 외워서 / 한 음도 틀리지out of place 않고. // 그렇지만 / 겉보기에는 굉장한 것 같은 이러한 기억의 성취는 / 일어날 것 같지 않게improbable(→ 가능하게) 되는 것이다 / 음악적인 '과정'을 기억함으로써 / 보통 말하는 그런 개별적인 음을 기억하는 것이 아니라.

03 만일 여러분이 피아니스트에게 요청하면 / 모차르트 소나타를 41번 마디로부터 시작해 달라고 / 그녀는 아마도 그 음악을 처음부터 머릿속으로mentally 재생해야 할 것이다 / 그 마디에 올 때까지 / 악보는 그저 그녀의 머릿속에 펼쳐져 있지 않다 / 어떤 임의의 지점부터 읽히기 위해.

04 그것은 흡사 여러분이 어떻게 운전해서 직장까지 가는지 설명하는 것과 같다 / 여러분은 길의 이름을 열거하는recite 것이 아니고 / 추상적인abstract 목록으로 / 여러분의 경로를 구성해야 한다 / 마음속에서 그것을 되짚어감으로써retrace.

05 음악가들이 리허설 중에 실수한다면, / 그들은 한 악구의 시작부로 되돌아간다wind back / ('2절부터 다시 합시다') / 다시 시작하기 전에.

구문 Check up	① If we had to encode it in our brains note by note, we'd **struggle / have struggled** to make sense of anything more complex than the simplest children's songs.	② But this seemingly awesome accomplishment of recall is made **improbable / improbably** by remembering the musical process, not the individual notes as such.
	「if + 주어 + 과거 동사 ~」 형태의 종속절로 보아 가정법 과거 구문이므로, 조동사 would(')d 뒤에는 struggle이 적절하다.	형용사를 목적격보어로 취하는 5형식 동사 make를 수동태로 쓰면 「be made + 형용사」가 되므로, improbable이 적절하다.

정답 ① struggle ② improbable

56

STEP 1 · 수능에 *진짜* 나오는 *단어*

✔ 문제에 나오는 단어들을 확인하세요.

01	awareness	n. 인식, 자각	(✔ awareness) of the fact	사실에 대한 인식
02	trust A with B	A에게 B를 믿고 맡기다	( ) her ( ) shared responsibilities	그녀에게 공유된 책무를 믿고 맡기다
03	consistently	ad. 지속적으로, 계속해서	( ) disappointing	지속적으로 실망스러운
04	let down	실망시키다	( ) others ( )	다른 사람들을 실망시키다
05	follow through on	~을 이행하다, 완수하다	( ) ( ) ( ) promises	약속을 이행하다
06	commitment	n. 약속, 책임	previous ( )s	이전의 약속
07	worthy of	~할 자격이 있는, ~을 받을 만한	( ) ( ) their trust	그들의 신임을 받을 만한
08	dependable	a. 믿을 만한	a trustworthy and ( ) person	신뢰할 만하고 믿을 만한 사람
09	disorienting	a. 혼란스러운	a ( ) dilemma	혼란스러운 딜레마
10	doubt	v. 의심하다	( ) the idea	생각을 의심하다
11	suspicious	a. 의심하는	with a ( ) look	의심하는 표정으로
12	undermine	v. 손상시키다, 약화시키다	( ) her confidence	그녀의 자신감을 약화시키다
13	deceit	n. 속임수	( ) and betrayal	속임수와 배신

⊕ 본문 문장 속에서 단어들을 확인해 보세요.

But distrust of one / who is sincere in her efforts / to be a trustworthy and dependable person / can be disorienting / and might cause her / to doubt her own perceptions / and to distrust herself.

하지만 사람에 대한 불신은 / 자신의 노력에 진실한 / 신뢰할 만하고 믿을 만한 사람이 되려는 / 혼란스러울 수 있고, / 그녀로 하여금 ~하게 할 수 있다 / 자신의 인식을 의심하고 / 자신을 불신하게.

01	awareness	✎ 인식	awareness of the fact	사실에 대한 (인식)
02	trust A with B		trust her with shared responsibilities	그녀에게 공유된 책무를 ( )
03	consistently		consistently disappointing	( ) 실망스러운
04	let down		let others down	다른 사람들을 ( )
05	follow through on		follow through on promises	약속을 ( )
06	commitment		previous commitments	이전의 ( )
07	worthy of		worthy of their trust	그들의 신임을 ( )
08	dependable		a trustworthy and dependable person	신뢰할 만하고 ( ) 사람
09	disorienting		a disorienting dilemma	( ) 딜레마
10	doubt		doubt the idea	생각을 ( )
11	suspicious		with a suspicious look	( ) 표정으로
12	undermine		undermine her confidence	그녀의 자신감을 ( )
13	deceit		deceit and betrayal	( )와 배신

➕ **본문 문장 속에서 단어의 의미를 우리말로 해석해 보세요.**

But distrust of one / who is sincere in her efforts / to be a trustworthy and dependable person / can be disorienting / and might cause her / to doubt her own perceptions / and to distrust herself.

➜ 하지만 사람에 대한 불신은 / 자신의 노력에 진실한 / ⬜⬜⬜⬜ 이 되려는 / ⬜⬜⬜⬜ 수 있고, / 그녀로 하여금 ~하게 할 수 있다 / ⬜⬜⬜⬜ / 자신을 불신하게.

56 다음 글의 밑줄 친 부분 중, 문맥상 낱말의 쓰임이 적절하지 <u>않은</u> 것은?

Sometimes the awareness that one is distrusted can provide the necessary incentive for self-reflection. An employee who ① <u>realizes</u> she isn't being trusted by her co-workers with shared responsibilities at work might, upon reflection, identify areas where she has consistently let others down or failed to follow through on previous commitments. Others' distrust of her might then ② <u>forbid</u> her to perform her share of the duties in a way that makes her more worthy of their trust. But distrust of one who is ③ <u>sincere</u> in her efforts to be a trustworthy and dependable person can be disorienting and might cause her to doubt her own perceptions and to distrust herself. Consider, for instance, a teenager whose parents are ④ <u>suspicious</u> and distrustful when she goes out at night; even if she has been forthright about her plans and is not ⑤ <u>breaking</u> any agreed-upon rules, her identity as a respectable moral subject is undermined by a pervasive parental attitude that expects deceit and betrayal.

*forthright: 솔직한, 거리낌 없는   **pervasive: 널리 스며 있는

정답과 해설 **p.50**

01　Sometimes / the awareness [that one is distrusted] / can provide the necessary incentive for self-reflection.

（동격 / 주어）

02　An employee / [who realizes / she isn't being trusted by her co-workers with shared responsibilities at work] / might, (upon reflection), identify areas / [where she has consistently let others down / or failed to follow through on previous commitments].

（주어 / 주격 관계대명사절 / 동사구 / 관계부사절）

03　Others' distrust of her / might then forbid her / to perform her share of the duties / in a way [that makes her more worthy of their trust].

（「forbid + 목적어 + to부정사: ~이 …하지 못하게 하다」 / 주격 관계대명사절）

04　But distrust of one / [who is sincere in her efforts / to be a trustworthy and dependable person] / can be disorienting / and might cause her / to doubt her own perceptions / and to distrust herself.

（주어 / 주격 관계대명사절 / 「cause + 목적어 + to부정사: ~이 …하게 하다」）

05　Consider, for instance, a teenager / [whose parents are suspicious and distrustful / when she goes out at night]; / even if she has been forthright about her plans / and is not breaking any agreed-upon rules, / her identity as a respectable moral subject / is undermined by a pervasive parental attitude / [that expects deceit and betrayal].

（동사(명령문) / 목적어 / 소유격 관계대명사절 / 접속사(비록 ~일지라도) / 주어 / 동사(수동태) / 선행사 / 주격 관계대명사절）

01　때로는 / 신임을 얻지 못한다는 인식awareness이 / 자기 성찰에 필요한 동기를 제공할 수 있다.

02　직원은 / 깨달은 / 직장에서 동료들이 자신에게 공유된 책무를 믿고 맡기지be trusted with shared responsibilities 않고 있다는 사실을 / 성찰을 통해 분야를 찾아낼 수 있다 / 자신이 지속적으로 다른 사람들을 실망하게 했거나consistently let others down / 이전의 약속들을 이행하지 못했던follow through on previous commitments.

03　그녀에 대한 다른 사람들의 불신은, / 그러면 그녀를 막을(→ 동기부여할) 수 있다 / 자기 몫의 직무를 수행하는 것을 / 그녀가 그들의 신임을 더 받을 만하게worthy of their trust 해 주는 방식으로.

04　하지만 사람에 대한 불신은 / 자신의 노력에 진실한 / 신뢰할 만하고 믿을 만한dependable 사람이 되려는 / 혼란스러울disorienting 수 있고, / 그녀로 하여금 ~하게 할 수 있다 / 자신의 인식을 의심하고doubt / 자신을 불신하게.

05　예를 들어 십 대 아이를 생각해 보라 / 부모가 의심하고suspicious 믿어주지 않는 / 그녀가 밤에 외출할 때 / 비록 그녀가 자신의 계획에 대해 솔직해 왔고 / 합의된 규칙은 어떤 것도 어기고 있지 않을지라도, / 존경할 만한 도덕적 주체로서의 그녀의 정체성은 / 널리 스며 있는 부모의 태도에 의해 손상된다undermine / 속임수deceit와 배신을 예상하는.

구문 Check up

① Sometimes the awareness that / which one is distrusted can provide the necessary incentive for self-reflection.

추상명사 the awareness 뒤로 '인식한' 내용을 보충 설명하는 완전한 문장이 나오므로, 동격의 접속사 that이 적절하다.

② Consider, for instance, a teenager whose / whom parents are suspicious and distrustful when she goes out at night; ~

뒤에 나오는 parents가 문맥상 선행사 a teenager의 부모이므로, 선행사의 소유격을 나타내는 whose가 적절하다.

정답 ① that ② whose

✔ 문제에 나오는 단어들을 확인하세요.

01	fuel	v. 부추기다	(✔ fuel) a building boom	건축 붐을 부추기다
02	massive	a. 대규모의	( ) damage	대규모의 피해
03	migration	n. 이주	( ) from big cities to countryside	큰 도시에서 시골로의 이주
04	suburban	a. 교외의	new ( ) areas	새로운 교외 지역
05	shift	n. 전환 v. 바꾸다	the ( ) to private cars	자가용으로의 전환
06	decline	n. 감소	the ( ) of public transportation	대중교통의 감소
07	leisure	n. 여가	( ) time	여가 시간
08	recreation	n. 휴양, 오락	enlarge the ( ) area	휴양 공간을 확장하다
09	neighborhood	n. 인근, 이웃	in my ( )	우리 인근에서
10	entertainment	n. 오락, 예능	new forms of ( )	새로운 형태의 오락
11	downfall	n. 몰락	the ( ) of an empire	제국의 몰락
12	uniformity	n. 획일성	promote ( )	획일성을 증진하다
13	privatization	n. 사유화, 민영화	the ( ) of public utilities	공공 시설의 사유화

➕ 본문 문장 속에서 단어들을 확인해 보세요.

In the post-World War II years after 1945, / unparalleled economic growth fueled a building boom and a massive migration / from the central cities to the new suburban areas.

1945년 이후 제2차 세계대전 이후 / 유례없는 경제 성장은 건축 붐과 대규모 이주를 부추겼다 / 중심 도시에서 새로운 교외 지역으로의.

단어 다시보기 문제를 풀기 전에 단어들을 30초 동안 다시 확인하세요.

01	fuel	부추기다	fuel a building boom	건축 붐을 (부추기다)
02	massive		massive damage	( ) 피해
03	migration		migration from big cities to countryside	큰 도시에서 시골로의 ( )
04	suburban		new suburban areas	새로운 ( ) 지역
05	shift		the shift to private cars	자가용으로의 ( )
06	decline		the decline of public transportation	대중교통의 ( )
07	leisure		leisure time	( ) 시간
08	recreation		enlarge the recreation area	( ) 공간을 확장하다
09	neighborhood		in my neighborhood	우리 ( )에서
10	entertainment		new forms of entertainment	새로운 형태의 ( )
11	downfall		the downfall of an empire	제국의 ( )
12	uniformity		promote uniformity	( )을 증진하다
13	privatization		the privatization of public utilities	공공 시설의 ( )

⊕ 본문 문장 속에서 단어의 의미를 우리말로 해석해 보세요.

In the post-World War II years after 1945, / unparalleled economic growth fueled a building boom and a massive migration / from the central cities to the new suburban areas.

→ 1945년 이후 제2차 세계대전 이후 / 유례없는 경제 성장은 ________ / 중심 도시에서 ________ 으로의.

57 다음 빈칸에 들어갈 말로 가장 적절한 것은?

In the post-World War II years after 1945, unparalleled economic growth fueled a building boom and a massive migration from the central cities to the new suburban areas. The suburbs were far more dependent on the automobile, signaling the shift from primary dependence on public transportation to private cars. Soon this led to the construction of better highways and freeways and the decline and even loss of public transportation. With all of these changes came a _____ of leisure. As more people owned their own homes, with more space inside and lovely yards outside, their recreation and leisure time was increasingly centered around the home or, at most, the neighborhood. One major activity of this home-based leisure was watching television. No longer did one have to ride the trolly to the theater to watch a movie; similar entertainment was available for free and more conveniently from television.

*unparalleled: 유례없는

① downfall

② uniformity

③ restoration

④ privatization

⑤ customization

정답과 해설 p.52

01 In the post-World War II years after 1945, / unparalleled economic growth fueled
a building boom and a massive migration / from the central cities to the new suburban
areas.
목적어1　　　　　목적어2

02 The suburbs were far more dependent on the automobile, / signaling the shift from
비교급 수식　　　　　　　　　　　　　　　　　　　　　　　분사구문(= and it signaled ~)
primary dependence on public transportation to private cars. // Soon this led to the
동사
construction of better highways and freeways / and the decline and even loss of public
목적어1　　　　　　　　　　　　　　　　　　　　목적어2
transportation.

03 With all of these changes / came a privatization of leisure. // As more people owned
전치사구　　　　　　　　　　　도치 구문(동사 + 주어)　　　　접속사(~함에 따라)
their own homes, / with more space inside and lovely yards outside, / their recreation
and leisure time / was increasingly centered around the home / or, at most, the
neighborhood.

04 One major activity of this home-based leisure / was watching television. // No
주격 보어(동명사구)　　　　　부정어구
longer did one have to ride the trolly to the theater / to watch a movie; / similar
도치 구문(의문문 어순)　　　　　　　　　　　　　부사적 용법(목적)
entertainment was available for free and more conveniently from television.

01 1945년 이후 제2차 세계대전 이후 / 유례없는 경제 성장은 건축 붐과 대규모 이주massive migration를 부추겼다fuel /
중심 도시에서 새로운 교외suburban 지역으로의.

02 교외 지역은 자동차에 훨씬 더 많이 의존했고, / 이는 주로 대중교통에 의존하던 것에서 자가용으로의 전환shift을 알렸다.
// 이것은 곧 더 나은 고속도로와 초고속도로의 건설로 이어졌다 / 그리고 대중교통의 감소decline와 심지어 쇠퇴까지로.

03 이러한 모든 변화와 함께 / 여가leisure의 사유화privatization가 이뤄졌다. // 더 많은 사람이 자기 집을 갖게 됨에 따라 /
내부 공간이 더 넓어지고 아름다운 외부 정원이 딸린 / 그들의 휴양recreation과 여가 시간은 / 점점 더 집에 집중되었다 /
또는 기껏해야 인근 지역neighborhood에.

04 이러한 집 중심의 여가에서 주요한 활동 한 가지는 / TV 시청이었다. // 사람들은 더 이상 전차를 타고 극장까지 갈 필요가
없었고, / 영화를 보러 / 유사한 오락entertainment이 텔레비전을 통해 무료로 더 편리하게 이용 가능해졌다.

구문 Check up

① The suburbs were far more dependent on the automobile, signaled / signaling the shift from primary dependence on public transportation to private cars.

주절을 보충하는 분사구문 자리이므로 signaling이 적절하다.

② No longer one had / did one have to ride the trolly to the theater to watch a movie

부정어구가 문장 맨 앞에 있으면 주어와 동사가 의문문 어순(조동사 + 주어 + 동사원형)으로 도치된다. 따라서 did one have가 정답이다.

정답 ① signaling ② did one have

58 STEP 1 • 수능에 *진짜* 나오는 *단어*

✔ 문제에 나오는 단어들을 확인하세요.

01	for one's own sake	그 자체로	feel (✓ for) feeling's (own) (sake)	감정을 그 자체로 느끼다
02	identity	n. 정체성	build an ( )	정체성을 만들다
03	artistic	a. 예술적인	make ( ) creations of their own	그들만의 예술적 창작물을 만들다
04	idealize	v. 이상화하다	an ( )d view of married life	결혼 생활에 대한 이상화된 관점
05	nostalgia	n. 향수, 그리움	strong feelings of memory and ( )	강한 추억과 향수의 감정
06	attachment	n. 애착	other people with shared ( )s	공유된 애착을 지닌 다른 사람들
07	affection	n. 애정	the object of their ( )s	그들의 애정의 대상
08	attendance	n. 참석(률)	high ( )s	높은 참석률
09	differentiation	n. 구별, 분화, 차이	( )s from one another	서로 간의 구별
10	afford	v. (격식) 제공하다, 주다	( ) no explanation	아무런 설명도 제공하지 않다

➕ 본문 문장 속에서 단어들을 확인해 보세요.

They build identities and experiences, / and make artistic creations of their own / to share with others.

그들은 정체성과 경험을 만들고, / 그들만의 예술적 창작물을 만든다 / 다른 사람들과 공유하기 위해.

01	for one's own sake *그 자체로*	feel for feeling's own sake	감정을 (그 자체로) 느끼다	
02	identity	build an identity	( )을 만들다	
03	artistic	make artistic creations of their own	그들만의 ( ) 창작물을 만들다	
04	idealize	an idealized view of married life	결혼 생활에 대한 ( ) 관점	
05	nostalgia	strong feelings of memory and nostalgia	강한 추억과 ( )의 감정	
06	attachment	other people with shared attachments	공유된 ( )을 지닌 다른 사람들	
07	affection	the object of their affections	그들의 ( )의 대상	
08	attendance	high attendances	높은 ( )	
09	differentiation	differentiations from one another	서로 간의 ( )	
10	afford	afford no explanation	아무런 설명도 ( ) 않다	

➕ **본문 문장 속에서 단어의 의미를 우리말로 해석해 보세요.**

They build identities and experiences, / and make artistic creations of their own / to share with others.

→ 그들은 ▢▢▢▢▢▢▢▢▢▢▢▢▢▢▢▢▢, / ▢▢▢▢▢▢▢▢▢▢▢▢▢▢▢▢ / 다른 사람들과 공유하기 위해.

58 다음 빈칸에 들어갈 말로 가장 적절한 것은?

Fans feel for feeling's own sake. They make meanings beyond what seems to be on offer. They build identities and experiences, and make artistic creations of their own to share with others. A person can be an individual fan, feeling an "idealized connection with a star, strong feelings of memory and nostalgia," and engaging in activities like "collecting to develop a sense of self." But, more often, individual experiences are embedded in social contexts where other people with shared attachments socialize around the object of their affections. Much of the pleasure of fandom _____. In their diaries, Bostonians of the 1800s described being part of the crowds at concerts as part of the pleasure of attendance. A compelling argument can be made that what fans love is less the object of their fandom than the attachments to (and differentiations from) one another that those affections afford.

*embed: 끼워 넣다 **compelling: 강력한

① is enhanced by collaborations between global stars

② results from frequent personal contact with a star

③ deepens as fans age together with their idols

④ comes from being connected to other fans

⑤ is heightened by stars' media appearances

정답과 해설 p.52

01 Fans feel for feeling's own sake. // They make meanings / beyond [what seems to be on offer]. // They build identities and experiences, / and make artistic creations of their own / to share with others. // A person can be an individual fan, / feeling an "idealized connection with a star, / strong feelings of memory and nostalgia," / and engaging in activities / like "collecting to develop a sense of self."

02 But, more often, / individual experiences are embedded in social contexts / [where other people with shared attachments / socialize around the object of their affections]. // Much of the pleasure of fandom / comes from being connected to other fans. // In their diaries, / Bostonians of the 1800s described / being part of the crowds at concerts / as part of the pleasure of attendance.

03 A compelling argument can be made / [that what fans love is less the object of their fandom / than the attachments to (and differentiations from) one another / that those affections afford].

01 팬은 감정을 그 자체로for one's own sake 느낀다. // 그들은 의미를 만든다 / 제공된다고 보이는 것 이상의. // 그들은 정체성identity과 경험을 만들고, / 그들만의 예술적artistic 창작물을 만든다 / 다른 사람들과 공유하기 위해. // 한 사람은 개인적인 팬이 되어, / '어떤 스타와 이상화된idealize 관계'를 느낀다 / 즉 '강한 추억과 향수nostalgia의 감정'을 / 그리고 활동에 참여한다 / '자아감을 형성하기 위한 수집하기' 같은.

02 그러나 더 흔히 / 개인적인 경험은 사회적 상황에 끼워 넣어져 있다 / 공유된 애착attachment을 지닌 다른 사람들이 / 그들의 애정affection의 대상을 중심으로 교제하는. // 팬덤의 많은 즐거움은 / 다른 팬들과 관계를 맺는 데서 온다. // 그들의 일기에서 / 1800년대의 보스턴 사람들은 묘사했다 / 콘서트에 모인 군중의 일부가 되는 것이 / 참석attendance의 즐거움의 일부라고.

03 강력한 주장이 제기될 수 있다 / 팬이 사랑하는 것은 그들의 팬덤의 대상이라기보다 / 서로에 대한 애착(그리고 서로 간의 차이differentiation)이라는 / 그 애정이 제공하는afford.

구문 Check up

① They build identities and experiences, and make artistic creations of their own share / to share with others.

문맥상 '예술품을 만드는' 행위의 목적을 설명하는 부사구가 필요하므로, to share가 적절하다. make를 사역동사로 오해하지 않도록 주의한다.

② Much of the pleasure of fandom come / comes from being connected to other fans.

「much of + 불가산명사」가 주어이므로 동사는 단수형인 comes로 쓰는 것이 적절하다.

정답 ① to share ② comes

59

STEP 1 · 수능에 *진짜* 나오는 *단어*

✔ 문제에 나오는 단어들을 확인하세요.

01	literature	*n.* 문학, 문헌	write about (✔ literature)	문학에 관해 글을 쓰다
02	examine	*v.* 검토하다	(　　　) all the elements of a text	한 작품의 모든 요소를 검토하다
03	autonomy	*n.* 자율성	the (　　　) of art	예술의 자율성
04	historical	*a.* 역사의, 역사적인	various (　　　) periods	다양한 역사적 시기
05	biography	*n.* 일대기, 전기	author (　　　)ies	작가 일대기
06	assumption	*n.* 추정, 상정	the (　　　) that all people are equal	모든 사람이 다 동등하다는 추정
07	self-contained	*a.* 자족적인, 자립하는	a (　　　) community	자족적인 공동체
08	correspondence	*n.* 연관성, 유사함	a close (　　　) between sounds and letters	소리와 글자의 밀접한 연관성
09	relevant	*a.* 적절한, 관련 있는	(　　　) information	관련 있는 정보

➕ 본문 문장 속에서 단어들을 확인해 보세요.

The critic / who wants to write about literature from a formalist perspective / must first be a close and careful reader / who examines all the elements of a text individually / and questions how they come together to create a work of art.

비평가는 / 형식주의의 관점에서 문학에 관해 글을 쓰고 싶어 하는 / 먼저 면밀하고도 주의 깊은 독자가 되어야 한다 / 글의 모든 요소를 개별적으로 검토하고 / 그것들이 모여서 하나의 예술 작품을 만드는 방식에 대해 질문하는.

01	literature	문학, 문헌	write about literature	(문학)에 관해 글을 쓰다
02	examine		examine all the elements of a text	한 작품의 모든 요소를 ( )
03	autonomy		the autonomy of art	예술의 ( )
04	historical		various historical periods	다양한 ( ) 시기
05	biography		author biographies	작가 ( )
06	assumption		the assumption that all people are equal	모든 사람이 다 동등하다는 ( )
07	self-contained		a self-contained community	( ) 공동체
08	correspondence		a close correspondence between sounds and letters	소리와 글자의 밀접한 ( )
09	relevant		relevant information	( ) 정보

➕ **본문 문장 속에서 단어의 의미를 우리말로 해석해 보세요.**

The critic / who wants to write about literature from a formalist perspective / must first be a close and careful reader / who examines all the elements of a text individually / and questions how they come together to create a work of art.

➡️ 비평가는 / 형식주의의 관점에서 ▨▨▨▨▨▨▨▨▨ 싶어 하는 / 먼저 면밀하고도 주의 깊은 독자가 되어야 한다 / ▨▨▨▨▨▨▨▨▨ / 그것들이 모여서 하나의 예술 작품을 만드는 방식에 대해 질문하는.

59 다음 빈칸에 들어갈 말로 가장 적절한 것은?

The critic who wants to write about literature from a formalist perspective must first be a close and careful reader who examines all the elements of a text individually and questions how they come together to create a work of art. Such a reader, who respects the autonomy of a work, achieves an understanding of it by _____. Instead of examining historical periods, author biographies, or literary styles, for example, he or she will approach a text with the assumption that it is a self-contained entity and that he or she is looking for the governing principles that allow the text to reveal itself. For example, the correspondences between the characters in James Joyce's short story "Araby" and the people he knew personally may be interesting, but for the formalist they are less relevant to understanding how the story creates meaning than are other kinds of information that the story contains within itself.

*entity: 실체

① putting himself or herself both inside and outside it

② finding a middle ground between it and the world

③ searching for historical realities revealed within it

④ looking inside it, not outside it or beyond it

⑤ exploring its characters' cultural relevance

정답과 해설 p.53

01 The critic / [who wants to write about literature from a formalist perspective] /
주어   주격 관계대명사절
must first be a close and careful reader / [who examines all the elements of a text
동사   주격보어   동사1
individually / and questions {how they come together to create a work of art}].
동사2   목적어

02 Such a reader, / (who respects the autonomy of a work), / achieves an understanding of
주어   주어 보충   동사
it / by looking inside it, not outside it or beyond it.
「by + 동명사: ~함으로써」

03 Instead of examining historical periods, author biographies, or literary styles, / for
example, / he or she will approach a text with the assumption / {that it is a self-
                                              추상명사   동격 명사절1
contained entity} / and {that he or she is looking for the governing principles / [that
              동격 명사절2   선행사
allow the text to reveal itself]}.
주격 관계대명사절

04 For example, / the correspondences / between the characters in James Joyce's short
                                      A와 B 사이(명사구 병렬)
story "Araby" and the people he knew personally / may be interesting, / but for the
formalist they are less relevant to understanding / how the story creates meaning /
         「less + 원급 + than: ~보다 덜 ···한」
than are other kinds of information / [that the story contains within itself].
대동사(= are relevant)   목적격 관계대명사절

01 비평가는 / 형식주의의 관점에서 문학literature에 관해 글을 쓰고 싶어 하는 / 먼저 면밀하고도 주의 깊은 독자가 되어야
   한다 / 글의 모든 요소를 개별적으로 검토하고examine / 그것들이 모여서 하나의 예술 작품을 만드는 방식에 대해
   질문하는.

02 그러한 독자는 / 작품의 자율성autonomy을 존중하는 / 그것에 대한 이해를 달성한다 / 그것의 외부나 너머가 아니라
   내부를 들여다봄으로써.

03 역사적historical 시대, 작가의 일대기biography, 또는 문학적 양식을 검토하는 대신, / 가령 / 그 사람은
   추정assumption을 가지고 글에 접근할 것이다 / 그것이 자족적인self-contained 실체이며, / 자신은 지배적인 원칙을
   찾고 있다는 / 그 글이 스스로를 드러내도록 해주는.

04 예를 들어, / 연관성correspondence은 / James Joyce의 단편 소설인 'Araby' 속의 등장인물들과 그가 개인적으로 알았던
   사람들 사이의 / 흥미로울 수도 있다 / 하지만 형식주의자에게 그것들은 이해하는 데 덜 적절하다relevant / 이야기가
   어떻게 의미를 만들어내는지를 / 다른 종류의 정보보다 / 그 이야기가 안에 포함하고 있는.

구문 Check up

① The critic who writes about literature from a formalist perspective must first be a close and careful reader who examines all the elements of a text individually and questions / to question how they come together.

who 뒤의 동사 examines와 병렬 연결되는 동사로 questions를 써야 한다.

② For the formalist they are less relevant to understanding how the story creates meaning as / than are other kinds of information that the story contains within itself.

앞에 「less + 원급(덜 ~한)」이 있으므로 '~보다'에 해당하는 than이 적절하다.

정답 ① questions ② than

248

60 STEP 1 • 수능에 *진짜* 나오는 *단어*

✔ 문제에 나오는 단어들을 확인하세요.

01	practical	a. 실제적인	(✔ practical) solutions	실제적인 해결책
02	disengagement	n. 이탈, 해방	cognitive ( )	인식의 이탈
03	be concerned with	~에 관심[관련]이 있다	( ) ( ) ( ) the rumor	그 소문에 관심을 두다
04	for the moment	잠깐	be closed ( ) ( ) ( )	잠깐 닫다
05	fictional	a. 허구적인	real or ( )	진짜인지 허구인지
06	considerable	a. 상당한	( ) freedom	상당한 자유
07	exaggerate	v. 과장하다	( ) the silliness of a situation	상황의 어리석음을 과장하다
08	make up	꾸며내다, 만들어내다	( ) ( ) a few details	몇 가지 세부사항을 꾸며내다
09	licence	n. (문학의) 허용, 파격, (행동의) 자유	poetic ( )	시적 허용
10	spill	v. 쏟다	( ) the spaghetti on the keyboard	스파게티를 키보드에 쏟다
11	interrupt	v. 방해하다, 끼어들다	stop ( )ing	방해하는 것을 중단하다

➕ 본문 문장 속에서 단어들을 확인해 보세요.

If they are getting extra laughs / by exaggerating the silliness of a situation / or even by making up a few details, / we are happy to grant them comic licence, / a kind of poetic licence.

만약 그들이 추가 웃음을 얻고 있다면 / 상황의 어리석음을 과장함으로써 / 혹은 심지어 몇 가지 세부 사항을 꾸며냄으로써 / 우리는 기꺼이 그들에게 희극적 허용을 허락한다 / 일종의 시적 허용.

01	practical	✎ 실제적인	practical solutions	(실제적인)해결책
02	disengagement		cognitive disengagement	인식의 ( )
03	be concerned with		be concerned with the rumor	그 소문에 ( )
04	for the moment		be closed for the moment	( ) 닫다
05	fictional		real or fictional	진짜인지 ( )인지
06	considerable		considerable freedom	( ) 자유
07	exaggerate		exaggerate the silliness of a situation	상황의 어리석음을 ( )
08	make up		make up a few details	몇 가지 세부사항을 ( )
09	licence		poetic licence	시적 ( )
10	spill		spill the spaghetti on the keyboard	스파게티를 키보드에 ( )
11	interrupt		stop interrupting	( )것을 중단하다

➕ **본문 문장 속에서 단어의 의미를 우리말로 해석해 보세요.**

If they are getting extra laughs / by exaggerating the silliness of a situation / or even by making up a few details, / we are happy to grant them comic licence, / a kind of poetic licence.

➜ 만약 그들이 추가 웃음을 얻고 있다면 / ▮▮▮▮▮▮▮▮▮▮▮▮으로써 / 혹은 심지어 ▮▮▮▮▮▮▮▮▮▮▮▮으로써 / 우리는 기꺼이 그들에게 희극적 허용을 허락한다 / ▮▮▮▮▮▮▮▮.

60 다음 빈칸에 들어갈 말로 가장 적절한 것은?

Humour involves not just practical disengagement but cognitive disengagement. As long as something is funny, we are for the moment not concerned with whether it is real or fictional, true or false. This is why we give considerable leeway to people telling funny stories. If they are getting extra laughs by exaggerating the silliness of a situation or even by making up a few details, we are happy to grant them comic licence, a kind of poetic licence. Indeed, someone listening to a funny story who tries to correct the teller — 'No, he didn't spill the spaghetti on the keyboard and the monitor, just on the keyboard' — will probably be told by the other listeners to stop interrupting. The creator of humour is putting ideas into people's heads for the pleasure those ideas will bring, not to provide _____ information.

*cognitive: 인식의   **leeway: 여지

① accurate

② detailed

③ useful

④ additional

⑤ alternative

정답과 해설 **p.54**

01 Humour involves not just practical disengagement but cognitive disengagement. //
「not just[only] A but (also) B: A뿐만 아니라 B도」
As long as something is funny, / we are for the moment not concerned / with [whether
접속사(~하는 한)   접속사(~인지 아닌지)
it is real or fictional, true or false].

02 This is why we give considerable leeway to people / telling funny stories.
「this[that] is why + 주어 + 동사: 이것이 ~한 이유다」   현재분사구

03 If they are getting extra laughs / by exaggerating the silliness of a situation / or even
「by+동명사: ~함으로써」
by making up a few details, / we are happy to grant them comic licence, / a kind of
poetic licence.

04 Indeed, / someone listening to a funny story / [who tries to correct the teller] / — ('No,
주어   현재분사구   주격 관계대명사절   삽입절
he didn't spill the spaghetti on the keyboard and the monitor, / just on the keyboard')
/ — will probably be told by the other listeners / to stop interrupting.
「be told + to부정사: ~하라는 말을 듣다」

05 The creator of humour / is putting ideas into people's heads / for the pleasure [those
선행사
ideas will bring], / not to provide accurate information.
목적격 관계대명사절   부사적 용법(목적: ~하지 않기 위해서)

---

01 유머는 실제적인 이탈practical disengagement뿐만 아니라 인식의 이탈을 포함한다. // 어떤 것이 재미있기만 하면, / 우리는 잠깐 관심을 두지 않는다be for the moment not concerned with / 그것이 진짜인지 허구인지fictional, 진실인지 거짓인지에 관해.

02 이것이 우리가 사람들에게 상당한considerable 여지를 주는 이유이다 / 재미있는 이야기를 하는.

03 만약 그들이 추가 웃음을 얻고 있다면 / 상황의 어리석음을 과장함exaggerate으로써 / 혹은 심지어 몇 가지 세부 사항을 꾸며냄make up a few details으로써 / 우리는 기꺼이 그들에게 희극적 허용licence을 허락한다 / 일종의 시적 허용.

04 실제로, / 재미있는 이야기를 듣고 있는 누군가는 / 말하는 사람을 바로잡으려고 하는 / '아니야, 그는 스파게티를 키보드와 모니터에 쏟은spill 것이 아니라 / 키보드에만 쏟았어.' / 아마 듣고 있는 다른 사람들에게서 들을 것이다 / 방해하지interrupt 말라는 말을.

05 유머를 만드는 사람은 / 사람들의 머릿속에 생각을 집어넣고 있다 / 그 생각이 가져올 재미를 위해서 / 정확한 정보를 제공하기 위해서가 아니라.

구문 Check up

① As long as something is funny, we are for the moment not concerned with that / whether it is real or fictional, true or false.

that이 이끄는 명사절은 전치사의 목적어 역할을 할 수 없다. 따라서 whether가 적절하다.

② This is why we give / are given considerable leeway to people telling funny stories.

「give A to B(A를 B에게 주다)」 형태의 3형식 문장이다.

STEP 1 • 수능에 *진짜* 나오는 *단어*

✔ 문제에 나오는 단어들을 확인하세요.

01	performance	n. 성과, 수행	test (✔ performance)	시험 성과(성적)
02	experimenter	n. 실험자	a group of (　　　　)s	실험자 집단
03	exclaim	v. 소리치다, 외치다	(　　　) with admiration	감탄하여 소리치다
04	supposedly	ad. 아마도	(　　　　) correct	아마도 맞는
05	distraction	n. 주의를 딴 데로 돌리는 것	(　　　) through television viewing	텔레비전 시청을 통해 주의를 딴 데로 돌리는 것
06	discomfort	n. 불편함	relieve the (　　　　)	불편함을 완화하다
07	mismatch	n. 불일치, 부조화	a (　　　　) between the self-image and the true self	자아상과 실제 자아 간의 부조화
08	self-related	a. 자기 자신과 관련된	(　　　　) thoughts	자기 자신과 관련된 생각

+ 본문 문장 속에서 단어들을 확인해 보세요.

The researchers concluded / that distraction through television viewing / can effectively relieve the discomfort / associated with painful failures or mismatches between the self and self-guides.

연구자들은 결론지었다 / 텔레비전 시청을 통해 주의를 딴 데로 돌리는 것이 / 효과적으로 불편함을 완화할 수 있다고 / 고통스러운 실패 또는 자신과 자기 안내 지침 사이의 불일치와 관련된.

01	performance	✎ 성과, 수행	test performance	시험 (성과)
02	experimenter		a group of experimenters	(　　) 집단
03	exclaim		exclaim with admiration	감탄하여 (　　　)
04	supposedly		supposedly correct	(　　) 맞는
05	distraction		distraction through television viewing	텔레비전 시청을 통해 (　　　　　)
06	discomfort		relieve the discomfort	(　　) 을 완화하다
07	mismatch		a mismatch between the self-image and the true self	자아상과 실제 자아 간의 (　　)
08	self-related		self-related thoughts	(　　　) 생각

➕ **본문 문장 속에서 단어의 의미를 우리말로 해석해 보세요.**

The researchers concluded / that distraction through television viewing / can effectively relieve the discomfort / associated with painful failures or mismatches between the self and self-guides.

➜ 연구자들은 결론지었다 / ▮▮▮▮▮▮▮▮▮▮▮▮▮▮ 이 / 효과적으로 ▮▮▮▮▮▮▮ 수 있다고 / 고통스러운 실패 또는 자신과 자기 안내 지침 사이의 ▮▮▮▮▮▮ 와 관련된.

61

다음 빈칸에 들어갈 말로 가장 적절한 것은?

Even as mundane a behavior as watching TV may be a way for some people to _____. To test this idea, Sophia Moskalenko and Steven Heine gave participants false feedback about their test performance, and then seated each one in front of a TV set to watch a video as the next part of the study. When the video came on, showing nature scenes with a musical soundtrack, the experimenter exclaimed that this was the wrong video and went supposedly to get the correct one, leaving the participant alone as the video played. The participants who had received failure feedback watched the video much longer than those who thought they had succeeded. The researchers concluded that distraction through television viewing can effectively relieve the discomfort associated with painful failures or mismatches between the self and self-guides. In contrast, successful participants had little wish to be distracted from their self-related thoughts!

*mundane: 보통의

① ignore uncomfortable comments from their close peers

② escape painful self-awareness through distraction

③ receive constructive feedback from the media

④ refocus their divided attention to a given task

⑤ engage themselves in intense self-reflection

정답과 해설 p.55

STEP 3 • 수능 지문 제대로 복습하기

01 ┌─────「as+원급+as: ~만큼 …한」─────┐
Even <u>as mundane a behavior</u> as watching TV / may be a way / for some people
　　　주어　　　　　　　　　　　　　　　　　　　　　　　　주격보어　　　의미상 주어
to escape painful self-awareness through distraction.
형용사적 용법(보어 수식)

02 To test this idea, / Sophia Moskalenko and Steven Heine / gave participants false
　　　　　　　　　　　　　　　　　　　　　　　　　　　　　　　동사1　간접목적어　　　직접목적어
<u>feedback</u> about their test performance, / and then seated each one in front of a TV set
　　　　　　　　　　　　　　　　　　　　　　　　　　　　동사2
to watch a video / as the next part of the study. // When the video came on, / showing
　　　　　　　　　전치사(~로서)
nature scenes with a musical soundtrack, / the experimenter exclaimed / [that this
　　　　　　　　　　　　　　　　　　　　　　　　　　　　　　　　　　　명사절(exclaimed의 목적어)
was the wrong video] / and went supposedly to get the correct one, / leaving the
　　　　　　　　　　　　　　　　　　　　　　　　　　　　　　　　　　분사구문
participant alone as the video played.
　　　　　　　　　接속사(~할 때)

03 <u>The participants</u> / [who had received failure feedback] / <u>watched</u> the video much
주어　　　　　　↑┈┈┈┈┈ 주격 관계대명사절　　　　　　동사　　　　　　　비교급 강조(훨씬)
longer / than those [who thought they had succeeded].
　　　　　　　선행사 ↑┈┈┈┈ 주격 관계대명사절

04 The researchers concluded / [that distraction through television viewing / can
　　　　　　　　　　　　　　　　　　　接속사
effectively relieve <u>the discomfort</u> / associated with painful failures or mismatches
　　　　　　　　　　　↑┈┈┈┈┈┈┈┈┈┈┈ 과거분사구
between the self and self-guides]. // In contrast, / successful participants had little
<u>wish</u> / to be distracted from their self-related thoughts!
↑┈┈┈┈┈ 부정사의 수동태(to be p.p.)

---

01 심지어 TV를 보는 것처럼 평범한 행동도 / 방법이 될 수 있다 / 어떤 사람들이 <u>주의를 딴 데로 돌려 고통스러운 자각에서</u> <u>벗어나는</u>.

02 이 생각을 검증하기 위해, / Sophia Moskalenko와 Steven Heine은 / 참가자들에게 그들의 시험 성적**test performance**에 관한 거짓 피드백을 주었고 / 그런 다음 각각을 TV 앞에 앉혀 비디오를 시청하게 했다 / 연구의 다음 부분으로서. // 비디오가 나오자 / 음악 사운드트랙과 함께 자연의 장면을 보여주는 / 실험자**experimenter**는 소리쳤고**exclaim** / 이것이 잘못된 비디오라고 / 아마도**supposedly** 제대로 된 것을 가지러 가면서, / 비디오가 재생될 때 참가자를 홀로 남겨두었다.

03 참가자들은 / 낙제라는 피드백을 받았던 / 훨씬 더 오래 비디오를 시청했다 / 자신이 성공했다고 생각하는 참가자들보다.

04 연구자들은 결론지었다 / 텔레비전 시청을 통해 주의를 딴 데로 돌리는 것**distraction**이 / 불편함**discomfort**을 효과적으로 완화할 수 있다고 / 고통스러운 실패 또는 자신과 자기 안내 지침 간의 불일치**mismatch**와 관련된. // 이와 대조적으로, / 성공한 참가자들은 거의 바라지 않았다 / 자기 자신과 관련된**self-related** 생각에서 주의가 딴 데로 돌려지기를!

구문 Check up

① The participants who had received failure feedback watched the video very / much longer than those who thought they had succeeded.

비교급 부사 longer를 꾸미는 말로 much(훨씬)가 적절하다. very는 비교급을 수식하지 않는다.

② In contrast, successful participants had little wish to distract / to be distracted from their self-related thoughts!

participants가 '산만하게 만들어지는' 대상이므로 부정사의 수동태인 to be distracted가 적절하다.

정답 ① much ② to be distracted

256

62 STEP 1 · 수능에 *진짜* 나오는 *단어*

✔ 문제에 나오는 단어들을 확인하세요.

01	function as	~로 기능하다	(✔ function)(as) a government	정부로서 기능하다
02	administrative	a. 행정의	( ) work	행정 사무
03	authority	n. 당국, 권위	the proper ( )ies	관계 당국
04	commodity	n. 상품	( ) production	상품 생산
05	redistribution	n. 재분배	the ( ) of wealth	부의 재분배
06	centralize	v. 중앙 집권화하다	( )d economic governance	중앙 집권화된 경제 지배
07	domestic	a. 가정집의, 국내의	( ) sites	가정집의 터
08	widespread	a. 널리 퍼진, 광범위한	how ( ) writing was	글쓰기가 얼마나 널리 퍼져 있었는지
09	literacy	n. 읽고 쓰는 능력	basic ( ) skills	기본적으로 글을 읽고 쓰는 능력
10	identifiable	a. 식별 가능한	the use of ( ) symbols	식별 가능한 기호의 사용
11	pictogram	n. 상형 문자	( )s that explain the life of ancient people	고대 사람들의 삶을 설명해 주는 상형 문자
12	consistent	a. 일치하는, 부합하는	( ) with the facts	사실과 일치하는
13	mutually	ad. 상호, 서로	( ) acceptable	상호 수락할 수 있는
14	intelligible	a. 이해되는, 알 수 있는	( ) to all the parties involved	모든 관련 당사자들에게 이해되는
15	abstract	a. 추상적인	become more ( )	더 추상적이 되다

✚ 본문 문장 속에서 단어들을 확인해 보세요.

For that matter, / it is not clear / how widespread literacy was at its beginnings.

그 문제와 관련하여, / 명확하지 않다 / 초기에 읽고 쓰는 능력이 얼마나 널리 퍼져 있었는지.

01	function as	✎ ~로 기능하다	function as a government	정부로서 (기능하다)
02	administrative		administrative work	( ) 사무
03	authority		the proper authorities	관계 ( )
04	commodity		commodity production	( ) 생산
05	redistribution		the redistribution of wealth	부의 ( )
06	centralize		centralized economic governance	( ) 경제 지배
07	domestic		domestic sites	( ) 터
08	widespread		how widespread writing was	글쓰기가 얼마나 ( ) 있었는지
09	literacy		basic literacy skills	기본적으로 ( )
10	identifiable		the use of identifiable symbols	( ) 기호의 사용
11	pictogram		pictograms that explain the life of ancient people	고대 사람들의 삶을 설명해 주는 ( )
12	consistent		consistent with the facts	사실과 ( )
13	mutually		mutually acceptable	( ) 수락할 수 있는
14	intelligible		intelligible to all the parties involved	모든 관련 당사자들에게 ( )
15	abstract		become more abstract	더 ( )이 되다

➕ 본문 문장 속에서 단어의 의미를 우리말로 해석해 보세요.

For that matter, / it is not clear / how widespread literacy was at its beginnings.

→ 그 문제와 관련하여, / 명확하지 않다 / 초기에 ⬛⬛⬛⬛⬛⬛⬛⬛⬛⬛⬛⬛.

62 다음 빈칸에 들어갈 말로 가장 적절한 것은?

In the classic model of the Sumerian economy, the temple functioned as an administrative authority governing commodity production, collection, and redistribution. The discovery of administrative tablets from the temple complexes at Uruk suggests that token use and consequently writing evolved as a tool of centralized economic governance. Given the lack of archaeological evidence from Uruk-period domestic sites, it is not clear whether individuals also used the system for _____. For that matter, it is not clear how widespread literacy was at its beginnings. The use of identifiable symbols and pictograms on the early tablets is consistent with administrators needing a lexicon that was mutually intelligible by literate and nonliterate parties. As cuneiform script became more abstract, literacy must have become increasingly important to ensure one understood what he or she had agreed to.

*archaeological: 고고학적인   **lexicon: 어휘 목록
***cuneiform script: 쐐기 문자

① religious events

② personal agreements

③ communal responsibilities

④ historical records

⑤ power shifts

정답과 해설 p.56

259

01 In the classic model of the Sumerian economy, / the temple functioned as
전치사(~로서)
an administrative authority / governing commodity production, collection, and
현재분사구
redistribution.

02 The discovery of administrative tablets / from the temple complexes at Uruk / suggests
주어 · · · · · · · · 전치사구 · · · · · · · 동사(단수)
/ [that token use and consequently writing evolved / as a tool of centralized economic
목적어 전치사(~로서)
governance].

03 분사구문(~을 고려하면)
Given the lack of archaeological evidence / from Uruk-period domestic sites, / it is not
· · · · · · · · · · · · · · · 가주어-진주어 구문 · · · · · · · · · · · · · · ·
clear / whether individuals also used the system for personal agreements.

04 For that matter, / it is not clear / how widespread literacy was at its beginnings.
· · · 가주어-진주어 구문 · · ·

05 The use of identifiable symbols and pictograms / on the early tablets / is consistent
주어 현재분사구 전치사구 동사(단수)
with administrators / needing a lexicon / [that was mutually intelligible by literate and
현재분사구 주격 관계대명사절(a lexicon 수식)
nonliterate parties].

06 As cuneiform script became more abstract, / literacy must have become increasingly
접속사(~하면서, ~함에 따라) 「must have p.p.: ~했음에 틀림없다」
that
important / to ensure one understood / [what he or she had agreed to].
주격보어(형용사) 부사적 용법(목적) 명사절

01 수메르 경제의 전형적 모델에서 / 사원은 행정 당국으로서 기능했다 function as an administrative authority / 상품의 생산 commodity production, 수집, 그리고 재분배 redistribution를 관장하는.

02 행정용 판의 발견은 / Uruk의 사원 단지에서의 / 시사한다 / 상징의 사용, 그리고 결과적으로 글자가 발달했음을 / 중앙 집권화된 centralize 경제 지배의 도구로.

03 고고학적 증거의 부족을 고려하면 / Uruk 시기 가정집의 domestic 터에서 나온 / 명확하지 않다 / 개인들이 사적인 합의를 위해서도 그 체계를 사용했는지는.

04 그 문제와 관련하여, / 명확하지 않다 / 초기에 읽고 쓰는 능력 literacy이 얼마나 널리 퍼져 widespread 있었는지.

05 식별 가능한 기호와 그림 문자 identifiable symbols and pictograms의 사용은 / 초기 판에서의 / 행정가들과 일치한다 consistent / 어휘 목록이 필요했던 / 읽고 쓸 줄 아는 측과 읽고 쓸 수 없는 측이 서로 이해할 수 있는 mutually intelligible.

06 쐐기 문자가 더욱 추상적이 되면서 abstract, / 읽고 쓰는 능력이 점점 더 중요해졌음이 틀림없다 / 사람들이 안다는 것을 확실히 하고자 / 자신이 뭐에 합의했는지.

구문 Check up	① Giving / Given the lack of archaeological evidence from Uruk-period domestic sites, it is not clear whether individuals also used the system for personal agreements.	② As cuneiform script became more abstract, literacy must have become increasing / increasingly important to ensure one understood what he or she had agreed to.
	'~을 고려하면'이라는 뜻의 분사구문으로는 Given을 쓴다.	become의 형용사 보어인 important를 수식하는 말로 부사인 increasingly 를 쓰는 것이 적절하다.

정답 ① Given ② increasingly

63 STEP 1 • 수능에 *진짜* 나오는 *단어*

✔ 문제에 나오는 단어들을 확인하세요.

01	index	n. 지표	the (✔ index) to the story	이야기의 지표
02	standardize	v. 표준화하다	become ( )d	표준화되다
03	variation	n. 변형, 변화	show little ( )	변형을 거의 보이지 않다
04	regardless of	~와 관계없이	( ) ( ) its origin	그것의 기원과 관계없이
05	add A to B	A를 B에 더하다	( ) details ( ) their stories	세부 사항을 이야기에 더하다
06	recall	v. 기억해 내다, 회상하다	( ) stories	이야기를 기억해 내다
07	reconstruct	v. 재구성하다	( ) details	세부 사항을 재구성하다
08	validity	n. 타당성	the ( ) of an argument	주장의 타당성
09	permanent	a. 영구적인	ensure its ( ) place	영구적 입지를 보장하다
10	relate	v. (말이나 글로) ~에 대하여 전달하다	the events that the story ( )s	이야기가 전달하는 사건들

✚ 본문 문장 속에서 단어들을 확인해 보세요.

An old man's story / that he has told hundreds of times / shows little variation, / and any variation that does exist / becomes part of the story itself, / regardless of its origin.

한 노인의 이야기는 / 그가 수백 번 말한 / 변형을 거의 보이지 않으며, / 실제로 존재하는 어떤 변형이든 / 이야기 자체의 일부가 된다 / 그것의 기원과 관계없이.

문제를 풀기 전에 단어들을 **30초** 동안 다시 확인하세요.

01	index	지표	the index to the story	이야기의 (지표)
02	standardize		become standardized	( )되다
03	variation		show little variation	( )을 거의 보이지 않다
04	regardless of		regardless of its origin	그것의 기원과 ( )
05	add A to B		add details to their stories	세부 사항을 이야기에 ( )
06	recall		recall stories	이야기를 ( )
07	reconstruct		reconstruct details	세부 사항을 ( )
08	validity		the validity of an argument	주장의 ( )
09	permanent		ensure its permanent place	( )입지를 보장하다
10	relate		the events that the story relates	이야기가 ( ) 사건들

➕ **본문 문장 속에서 단어의 의미를 우리말로 해석해 보세요.**

An old man's story / that he has told hundreds of times / shows little variation, / and any variation that does exist / becomes part of the story itself, / regardless of its origin.

➡ 한 노인의 이야기는 / 그가 수백 번 말한 / ▓▓▓▓▓▓▓▓▓▓▓▓▓, / 실제로 존재하는 어떤 변형이든 / 이야기 자체의 일부가 된다 / ▓▓▓▓▓▓▓▓▓▓.

63 다음 빈칸에 들어갈 말로 가장 적절한 것은?

When you begin to tell a story again that you have retold many times, what you retrieve from memory is the index to the story itself. That index can be embellished in a variety of ways. Over time, even the embellishments become standardized. An old man's story that he has told hundreds of times shows little variation, and any variation that does exist becomes part of the story itself, regardless of its origin. People add details to their stories that may or may not have occurred. They are recalling indexes and reconstructing details. If at some point they add a nice detail, not really certain of its validity, telling the story with that same detail a few more times will ensure its permanent place in the story index. In other words, the stories we tell time and again are _____ to the memory we have of the events that the story relates.

*retrieve: 회수하다   **embellish: 윤색하다

① identical

② beneficial

③ alien

④ prior

⑤ neutral

정답과 해설 p.56

01 When you begin to tell a story again / [that you have retold many times], / [what
선행사   목적격 관계대명사절   주어(명사절)
you retrieve from memory] / is the index to the story itself. // That index can be
동사(단수)   재귀대명사(the story 강조)
embellished in a variety of ways.

02 Over time, / even the embellishments become standardized. // An old man's story / [that
주어1
he has told hundreds of times] / shows little variation, / and any variation [that does
목적격 관계대명사절   동사1(단수)   주어2   주격 관계대명사절
exist] / becomes part of the story itself, / regardless of its origin.
동사2

03 People add details to their stories / [that may or may not have occurred]. // They are
선행사   「may have p.p.: ~했을지도 모른다」
recalling indexes and reconstructing details.

04 If at some point they add a nice detail, / not really certain of its validity, / telling the
분사구문 being 생략
story with that same detail a few more times / will ensure its permanent place in the
주어(동명사)   동사
story index.

05 In other words, / the stories [we tell time and again] / are identical to the memory / [we
주어(복수)   목적격 관계대명사절   선행사
have of the events {that the story relates}].
목적격 관계대명사절

---

01 여러분이 이야기를 다시 말하기 시작할 때 / 여러분이 여러 번 반복하여 말했던 / 여러분이 기억에서 되찾는 것은 / 이야기 자체에 대한 지표index이다. // 그 지표는 다양한 방식으로 윤색될 수 있다.

02 시간이 흐르면서, / 그 윤색된 것들조차도 표준화된다standardize. // 한 노인의 이야기는 / 그가 수백 번 말한 / 변형variation을 거의 보이지 않으며, / 실제로 존재하는 어떤 변형이든 / 이야기 자체의 일부가 된다 / 그것의 기원과 관계없이regardless of its origin.

03 사람들은 세부 사항을 자신들의 이야기에 덧붙인다add details to their stories / 일어났을 수도, 또는 일어나지 않았을 수도 있는. // 그들은 지표들을 기억해 내고recall 세부 사항들을 재구성하고reconstruct 있다.

04 만약 어떤 시점에 그들이 멋진 세부 사항을 덧붙인다면, / 그것의 타당성validity에 대해 정말로 확신하지 못한 채 / 바로 그 세부 사항을 붙여 몇 번 더 그 이야기를 말하는 것은 / 이야기 지표에서 그것의 영구적인permanent 입지를 보장해줄 것이다.

05 다시 말해 / 우리가 되풀이해서 말하는 이야기는 / 기억과 동일하다 / 우리가 그 이야기가 전달하는relate 사건들에 대해 가지고 있는.

구문 Check up

① When you begin to tell a story again that you have retold many times, what / that you retrieve from memory is the index to the story itself.

앞에 선행사가 없고, 뒤의 you retrieve from memory가 불완전한 절이므로 what이 적절하다.

② An old man's story that he has told hundreds of times shows little variation, and any variation that does exist becomes / becoming part of the story itself, regardless of its origin.

and 뒤의 주어 any variation에 이어 동사가 필요하므로 becomes가 적절하다. that does exist는 주어를 꾸민다.

정답 ① what ② becomes

☑ 종합 성적표

구분	공부한 날 ❶	결과 분석			
		출처	풀이 시간 ❷	채점 결과 (O, ×)	틀린 이유 ❸
Day **7** 어법성 판단	월 일	2024학년도 9월 29번	분 초		
		2023학년도 9월 29번	분 초		
		2022학년도 9월 29번	분 초		
		2022학년도 6월 29번	분 초		
		2021학년도 9월 29번	분 초		
		2020학년도 9월 29번	분 초		
		2020학년도 6월 29번	분 초		
Day **8** 어휘 추론	월 일	2024학년도 대수능 30번	분 초		
		2023학년도 6월 30번	분 초		
		2022학년도 대수능 30번	분 초		
		2022학년도 6월 30번	분 초		
		2021학년도 대수능 30번	분 초		
		2021학년도 6월 30번	분 초		
		2020학년도 6월 30번	분 초		
Day **9** 빈칸 추론 (1)	월 일	2024학년도 9월 31번	분 초		
		2023학년도 9월 32번	분 초		
		2023학년도 6월 32번	분 초		
		2022학년도 대수능 31번	분 초		
		2022학년도 9월 32번	분 초		
		2021학년도 대수능 31번	분 초		
		2020학년도 9월 31번	분 초		

3일간
공부한 내용을
다시 보니,
……

❶ **매일 지문을 하루 계획에 맞춰 풀었다. vs. 내가 한 약속을 못 지켰다.**

<매3영 수능기출>은 단순 문제풀이를 위한 책이 아니라, 매일 규칙적으로 영어를 공부하는 습관을 잡는 책입니다. 따라서 푸는 문제 개수는 상황에 따라 다르더라도 '매일' 학습하는 것이 중요합니다.

❷ **주어진 시간을 자꾸 넘긴다?**

풀이 시간이 계속해서 권장 시간을 넘긴다면 실전 훈련이 부족하다는 신호이므로, 매일의 훈련을 실전처럼 긴장감 있게 해야 합니다. 한편으로, 오답의 이유를 철저히 분석하고 맞춤 공부법을 찾아갑니다.

❸ **틀린 이유 맞춤 솔루션**: 오답 이유에 따라 다음 해결책을 참고하세요.

(1) 해석이 잘 안 돼서
  ▶ <STEP 1 단어>, <STEP 3 지문 복습>을 정독하며 단어/구문 실력을 길러보세요.

(2) 해석은 되는데, 지문 이해가 안 돼서
  ▶ [정답 및 해설]의 <지문 자세히 보기>를 정독하며 수능 지문의 논리 전개 방식을 익혀보세요.

(3) 이해는 했는데, 선택지로 연결을 못 해서
  ▶ [정답 및 해설]의 <오답풀이>, <유형플러스>를 통해 함정에 주의하는 방법을 숙지하세요.

!

결론적으로, 내가 **취약한 부분**은 [   ] 이다.
취약점을 보완하기 위해서 나는 [   ] 을/를 해야겠다.

복습 때 다시 봐야 할 문항과, 다시 점검할 사항이 있는 페이지는 지금 바로 접어 두세요.

<매3영>이 제시하는 3단계로

유형 3일 훈련

DAY

10~12

64

STEP 1 · 수능에 진짜 나오는 단어

✔️ 문제에 나오는 단어들을 확인하세요.

01	lift out of	~에서 들어올리다, 벗어나게 하다	(✔️ lift) nations (out) (of) poverty	나라들을 빈곤에서 벗어나게 하다
02	dwelling	n. 거처, 주택	an old ( )	오래된 주택
03	time-consuming	a. 시간이 많이 걸리는	( ) to produce	제작에 시간이 많이 걸리는
04	one-of-a-kind	a. 단품 수주의, 독특한	( ) production	단품 수주 생산
05	multiplication	n. 증가	the ( ) of photographs	사진의 증가
06	reproduction	n. 복제, 재생	mechanical ( )	기계적 복제
07	periodical	n. 정기 간행물	newspapers and ( )s	신문과 정기 간행물
08	limitless	a. 무한한	in ( ) quantities	무한한 양으로
09	landscape	n. 풍경	the beautiful ( )	아름다운 풍경
10	circulation	n. 유통, 순환	the ( ) of representations	표현물의 유통
11	inescapable	a. 피할 수 없는	virtually ( )	사실상 피할 수 없는
12	democratised	a. 대중화된, 민주화된	( ) images	대중화된 이미지들
13	mass-produced	a. 대량 생산된	( ) objects	대량 생산된 물건들
14	hold up	~을 떠받치다	( ) ( ) a mirror	거울을 떠받치다

➕ 본문 문장 속에서 단어들을 확인해 보세요.

While painters have always lifted particular places out of their 'dwelling' / and transported them elsewhere, / paintings were time-consuming to produce, / relatively difficult to transport / and one-of-a-kind.

화가들이 항상 특정 장소를 그 '거처'에서 벗어나게 해 / 다른 곳으로 이동시키긴 했지만, / 그림은 제작에 시간이 많이 걸렸고, / 상대적으로 운반이 어려웠으며, / 단품 수주 생산이었다.

01	lift out of	~에서 들어올리다, 벗어나게 하다	lift nations out of poverty	나라들을 빈곤에서 (벗어나게 하다)
02	dwelling		an old dwelling	오래된 ( )
03	time-consuming		time-consuming to produce	제작에 ( )
04	one-of-a-kind		one-of-a-kind production	( ) 생산
05	multiplication		the multiplication of photographs	사진의 ( )
06	reproduction		mechanical reproduction	기계적 ( )
07	periodical		newspapers and periodicals	신문과 ( )
08	limitless		in limitless quantities	( ) 양으로
09	landscape		the beautiful landscape	아름다운 ( )
10	circulation		the circulation of representations	표현물의 ( )
11	inescapable		virtually inescapable	사실상 ( )
12	democratised		democratised images	( ) 이미지들
13	mass-produced		mass-produced objects	( ) 물건들
14	hold up		hold up a mirror	거울을 ( )

⊕ 본문 문장 속에서 단어의 의미를 우리말로 해석해 보세요.

While painters have always lifted particular places out of their 'dwelling' / and transported them elsewhere, / paintings were time-consuming to produce, / relatively difficult to transport / and one-of-a-kind.

➔ 화가들이 항상 _____ / 다른 곳으로 이동시키긴 했지만, / 그림은 _____, / 상대적으로 운반이 어려웠으며, / _____ 생산이었다.

64 다음 빈칸에 들어갈 말로 가장 적절한 것은?

Prior to photography, _____. While painters have always lifted particular places out of their 'dwelling' and transported them elsewhere, paintings were time-consuming to produce, relatively difficult to transport and one-of-a-kind. The multiplication of photographs especially took place with the introduction of the half-tone plate in the 1880s that made possible the mechanical reproduction of photographs in newspapers, periodicals, books and advertisements. Photography became coupled to consumer capitalism and the globe was now offered 'in limitless quantities, figures, landscapes, events which had not previously been utilised either at all, or only as pictures for one customer'. With capitalism's arrangement of the world as a 'department store', 'the proliferation and circulation of representations ... achieved a spectacular and virtually inescapable global magnitude'. Gradually photographs became cheap mass-produced objects that made the world visible, aesthetic and desirable. Experiences were 'democratised' by translating them into cheap images. Light, small and mass-produced photographs became dynamic vehicles for the spatiotemporal circulation of places.

*proliferation: 확산 **magnitude: (큰) 규모 ***aesthetic: 미적인

① paintings alone connected with nature

② painting was the major form of art

③ art held up a mirror to the world

④ desire for travel was not strong

⑤ places did not travel well

정답과 해설 p.58

01 Prior to photography, / places did not travel well. // While painters have always lifted particular places out of their 'dwelling' / and transported them elsewhere, / paintings were time-consuming to produce, / relatively difficult to transport / and one-of-a-kind.

02 The multiplication of photographs especially took place / with the introduction of the half-tone plate in the 1880s / [that made possible the mechanical reproduction of photographs / in newspapers, periodicals, books and advertisements]. // Photography became coupled to consumer capitalism / and the globe was now offered ('in limitless quantities), / figures, landscapes, events / [which had not previously been utilised either at all, / or only as pictures for one customer'].

03 With capitalism's arrangement of the world as a 'department store', / 'the proliferation and circulation of representations … / achieved a spectacular and virtually inescapable global magnitude'. // Gradually photographs became cheap mass-produced objects / [that made the world visible, aesthetic and desirable]. // Experiences were 'democratised' by translating them into cheap images. // Light, small and mass-produced photographs / became dynamic vehicles for the spatiotemporal circulation of places.

---

01 사진 이전에는 / 장소들이 잘 이동하지 않았다. // 화가들이 특정 장소를 그 '거처dwelling'에서 벗어나게 해lift out of / 그것들을 다른 곳으로 이동시켰지만, / 그림은 제작에 시간이 많이 걸렸고time-consuming, / 상대적으로 운반이 어려웠으며, / 단품 수주one-of-a-kind 생산이었다.

02 사진의 증가multiplication는 특히 이루어졌다 / 1880년대 하프톤 판의 도입과 함께 / 사진의 기계적인 복제reproduction를 가능하게 한 / 신문, 정기 간행물periodical, 광고, 책, 광고에서. // 사진은 소비자 자본주의와 결합했고, / 이제 세계는 '무한한limitless 양으로' 제공받았다 / '인물, 풍경landscape, 사건들을 / 이전에는 전혀 사용되지 않았거나 / 단 한 명의 고객을 위한 그림으로만 사용되었던'.

03 자본주의가 세계를 '백화점'으로 정리하면서 / '표현물의 확산과 유통circulation은… / 극적이고 사실상 피할 수 없는inescapable 세계적 (대)규모를 달성했다'. // 점차 사진은 값싼 대량생산품mass-produced object이 되었다 / 세계를 눈에 보이고 미적이고 바람직한 것으로 만드는. // 경험들은 '대중화'되었다democratised / 그것을 저렴한 이미지로 바꾸어서. // 가볍고 작고 대량으로 제작된 사진은 / 장소의 시공간적 순환을 위한 역동적인 수단이 되었다.

구문 Check up

① The introduction of the half-tone plate made possible / possibly the mechanical reproduction of photographs in newspapers, periodicals, books and advertisements.

「make + 목적격보어 + 목적어」 어순이므로, 보어로 형용사 possible이 알맞다.

② The globe was now offered in limitless quantities, figures, landscapes, events what / which had not previously been utilised at all.

앞에 선행사 figures, landscapes, events가 있으므로 which가 적절하다. 이를 that으로 바꿔도 된다.

정답 ① possible ② which

65

STEP 1 • 수능에 *진짜* 나오는 *단어*

✔ 문제에 나오는 단어들을 확인하세요.

01	oddly	ad. 이상하게도, 희한하게도	an (✔ oddly) self-referential framework	희한하게 자기 지시적인 틀
02	conventional	a. 전통적인, 관례적인	in this ( ) manner	이러한 전통적인 방식으로
03	division	n. 나눔, 분할, 구분	the sharp ( )	분명한 구분
04	desperately	ad. 극심하게, 절박하게	feel ( ) nervous inside	내면에서 극심하게 초조함을 느끼다
05	misleading	a. (사실을) 오도하는, 오해의 소지가 있는	( ) data	오해의 소지가 있는 데이터
06	smooth the way	(~하는) 길을 닦다, 장애물을 제거하다	( ) ( ) ( ) for a great change	위대한 변화를 위한 길을 닦다
07	divorce A from B	A를 B로부터 단절시키다	( ) ourselves ( ) responsibility	우리를 책임으로부터 단절시키다
08	partition	v. 나누다, 분할하다	( ) a country	국가를 분할하다
09	arise	v. 생기다	( ) naturally over time	시간이 흐르며 자연스럽게 생기다

⊕ 본문 문장 속에서 단어들을 확인해 보세요.

The narrowing of our consciousness of time / smooths the way to divorcing ourselves from responsibility / for developments in the past and the future / with which our lives are in fact deeply intertwined.

시간에 대한 우리의 의식을 좁히는 것은 / 책임으로부터 우리를 단절시키는 길을 닦는다 / 과거와 미래의 발전에 대한 / 사실은 우리의 삶이 깊이 뒤얽혀 있는.

01	oddly	✎ 이상하게도, 희한하게도	an oddly self-referential framework	(희한하게) 자기 지시적인 틀
02	conventional		in this conventional manner	이러한 ( ) 방식으로
03	division		the sharp division	분명한 ( )
04	desperately		feel desperately nervous inside	내면에서 ( ) 초조함을 느끼다
05	misleading		misleading data	( ) 데이터
06	smooth the way		smooth the way for a great change	위대한 변화를 위한 ( )
07	divorce A from B		divorce ourselves from responsibility	우리를 책임으로부터 ( )
08	partition		partition a country	국가를 ( )
09	arise		arise naturally over time	시간이 흐르며 자연스럽게 ( )

➕ **본문 문장 속에서 단어의 의미를 우리말로 해석해 보세요.**

The narrowing of our consciousness of time / smooths the way to divorcing ourselves from responsibility / for developments in the past and the future / with which our lives are in fact deeply intertwined.

→ 시간에 대한 우리의 의식을 좁히는 것은 / ▬▬▬▬▬▬▬▬▬▬▬ / 과거와 미래의 발전에 대한 / 사실은 우리의 삶이 깊이 뒤얽혀 있는.

65 다음 빈칸에 들어갈 말로 가장 적절한 것은?

We understand that the segregation of our consciousness into present, past, and future is both a fiction and an oddly self-referential framework; your present was part of your mother's future, and your children's past will be in part your present. Nothing is generally wrong with structuring our consciousness of time in this conventional manner, and it often works well enough. In the case of climate change, however, the sharp division of time into past, present, and future has been desperately misleading and has, most importantly, hidden from view the extent of the responsibility of those of us alive now. The narrowing of our consciousness of time smooths the way to divorcing ourselves from responsibility for developments in the past and the future with which our lives are in fact deeply intertwined. In the climate case, it is not that _____. It is that the realities are obscured from view by the partitioning of time, and so questions of responsibility toward the past and future do not arise naturally.

*segregation: 분리 **intertwine: 뒤얽히게 하다
***obscure: 흐릿하게 하다

① all our efforts prove to be effective and are thus encouraged

② sufficient scientific evidence has been provided to us

③ future concerns are more urgent than present needs

④ our ancestors maintained a different frame of time

⑤ we face the facts but then deny our responsibility

정답과 해설 p.58

01 We understand / [that the segregation of our consciousness into present, past, and
　　　　　　　　　　　명사절(understand의 목적어)
future / is both a fiction and an oddly self-referential framework]; / your present was
　　　　　　　「both A and B: A이자 B인」
part of your mother's future, / and your children's past will be in part your present.

02 Nothing is generally wrong / with structuring our consciousness of time in this
　　부정 주어(아무것도 ~않다)
conventional manner, / and it often works well enough. // In the case of climate

change, however, / the sharp division of time into past, present, and future / has been
　　　　　　　　　　　　주어(단수)　　　　　　　　　　전치사구　　　　　　　　동사1
desperately misleading / and has, most importantly, hidden (from view) / the extent of
주격보어　　　　　　　　　　　동사2　　　　　　　　　　　　부사구　　　　　목적어
the responsibility of those of us alive now.

03 The narrowing of our consciousness of time / smooths the way to divorcing ourselves
　　　　　　　　　　　　　　　　　　　　　　　　　　　　동명사구(전치사 to의 목적어)
from responsibility / for developments in the past and the future / [with which our
　　　　　　　　　　　　　　　　　　전치사구　　　　　　　　　　　　　「전치사+관계대명사」
lives are in fact deeply intertwined].

04 In the climate case, / it is not that we face the facts but then deny our responsibility.
　　　　　　　　　　　　　　「not A (but) B: A가 아니라 B이다(문장이 나눠져서 but을 생략함)」
// It is that the realities are obscured from view / by the partitioning of time, / and so
　　　주어1　　　　　　동사(수동태)
questions of responsibility toward the past and future / do not arise naturally.
주어2(복수)　　　　　　　　　　전치사구　　　　　　　　　동사2

01 우리는 이해한다 / 우리의 의식을 현재, 과거, 미래로 분리하는 것이 / 허구이자 희한하게도oddly 자기 지시적인 틀이라는
것을 / 여러분의 현재는 여러분 어머니 미래의 일부였고 / 여러분 자녀의 과거는 여러분 현재의 일부가 될 것이다.

02 일반적으로 잘못된 것이 없다 / 시간에 대한 우리의 의식을 이러한 전통적인conventional 방식으로 구조화하는
것에 / 그리고 이것은 흔히 충분히 효과적이다. // 그러나 기후 변화의 경우, / 시간을 과거, 현재, 미래로 분명하게
구분division하는 것은 / 심하게 (사실을) 오도해왔다desperately misleading / 그리고 가장 중요하게는 시야로부터
숨겨왔다 / 지금 살아 있는 우리들의 책임 범위를.

03 시간에 대한 우리의 의식을 좁히는 것은 / 책임으로부터 우리를 단절시키는divorce ourselves from responsibility 길을
닦는다smooth the way / 과거와 미래의 발전에 대한 / 사실은 우리의 삶이 깊이 뒤얽혀 있는.

04 기후의 경우, / 우리가 사실을 직면하면서도 책임을 부인하는 것이 문제가 아니다. // 문제는 현실이 시야로부터
흐릿해진다는 것이다 / 시간을 나눔partition으로써 / 그리고 그리하여 과거와 현재의 책임에 관한 질문이 / 자연스럽게
생겨나지arise 않는다는 것.

구문 Check up	① The sharp division of time into past, present, and future has, most importantly, hidden / been hidden from view the extent of the responsibility of those of us alive now.	② The narrowing of our consciousness of time divorces ourselves from responsibility for developments in the past and the future which / with which our lives are deeply intertwined.
	목적어인 'the extent ~'가 뒤에 나오는 것으로 보아 현재완료 능동태를 완성하는 hidden을 써야 한다. most importantly는 삽입구로, 문장 구조에 영향을 미치지 않는다.	'our lives ~ intertwined'가 완전한 수동태 문장이므로 '전치사+관계대명사' 형태의 with which를 써야 한다.

정답 ① hidden ② with which

66 STEP 1 • 수능에 *진짜* 나오는 *단어*

✔ 문제에 나오는 단어들을 확인하세요.

01	entrance	n. 입구	the (✔ entrance) to a honeybee colony	꿀벌 군집의 입구
02	refer to A as B	A를 B라고 일컫다	( ) ( ) him ( ) a genius	그를 천재라고 일컫다
03	state	n. 상태	the ( ) of the colony	군집의 상태
04	hive	n. 벌집	the environment outside the ( )	벌집 밖의 환경
05	illustrative	a. 분명히 보여주는	a number of ( ) examples	분명히 보여주는 여러 예시들
06	unload	v. (짐을) 내리다	( ) the luggage	짐을 내리다
07	recruit	v. 모집하다	( ) new members	새 회원을 모집하다
08	pass on	~을 전해주다	( ) ( ) their water to other bees	자기 물을 다른 벌들에게 넘겨주다
09	correlate	v. 서로 연관시키다, 상관관계를 보여주다	( ) smoking with lung cancer	흡연을 폐암과 연관시키다
10	regulate	v. 조절하다, 통제하다	( ) the flow of water	물의 흐름을 조절하다

➕ 본문 문장 속에서 단어들을 확인해 보세요.

The entrance to a honeybee colony, / often referred to as the dancefloor, / is a market place for information / about the state of the colony and the environment outside the hive.

꿀벌 군집의 입구는 / 흔히 댄스 플로어라고 불리는 / 정보를 교환하는 시장이다 / 군집의 상태와 벌집 밖의 환경에 관한.

문제를 풀기 전에 단어들을 **30초** 동안 다시 확인하세요.

01	entrance	✎ 입구	the entrance to a honeybee colony	꿀벌 군집의 (입구)
02	refer to A as B		refer to him as a genius	그를 천재라고 (　　　)
03	state		the state of the colony	군집의 (　　　)
04	hive		the environment outside the hive	(　　　) 밖의 환경
05	illustrative		a number of illustrative examples	(　　　　　　) 여러 예시들
06	unload		unload the luggage	짐을 (　　　　)
07	recruit		recruit new members	새 회원을 (　　　　)
08	pass on		pass on their water to other bees	자기 물을 다른 벌들에게 (　　　　)
09	correlate		correlate smoking with lung cancer	흡연을 폐암과 (　　　　　)
10	regulate		regulate the flow of water	물의 흐름을 (　　　　)

➕ 본문 문장 속에서 단어의 의미를 우리말로 해석해 보세요.

The entrance to a honeybee colony, / often referred to as the dancefloor, / is a market place for information / about the state of the colony and the environment outside the hive.

➡ 꿀벌 군집의 　　　　　는 / 흔히 　　　　　　　　　　 / 정보를 교환하는 시장이다 / 　　　　　　　와 　　　　　　에 관한.

66 다음 빈칸에 들어갈 말로 가장 적절한 것은?

The entrance to a honeybee colony, often referred to as the dancefloor, is a market place for information about the state of the colony and the environment outside the hive. Studying interactions on the dancefloor provides us with a number of illustrative examples of how individuals changing their own behavior in response to local information _____. For example, upon returning to their hive honeybees that have collected water search out a receiver bee to unload their water to within the hive. If this search time is short then the returning bee is more likely to perform a waggle dance to recruit others to the water source. Conversely, if this search time is long then the bee is more likely to give up collecting water. Since receiver bees will only accept water if they require it, either for themselves or to pass on to other bees and brood, this unloading time is correlated with the colony's overall need of water. Thus the individual water forager's response to unloading time (up or down) regulates water collection in response to the colony's need.

*brood: 애벌레   **forager: 조달자

① allow the colony to regulate its workforce

② search for water sources by measuring distance

③ decrease the colony's workload when necessary

④ divide tasks according to their respective talents

⑤ train workers to acquire basic communication patterns

정답과 해설 p.59

01
The entrance to a honeybee colony, / often referred to as the dancefloor, / is a market
　　　　　　　　　　　　　　　　　　　　which is 생략
주어　　　　　　전치사구　　　　　　　　　　과거분사구　　　　　　　　　　　　　동사(단수)
place for information / about the state of the colony and the environment outside
the hive. // Studying interactions on the dancefloor / provides us with a number of
　　　　　주어(동명사구)　　　　　　　　　　　　　동사(단수)
illustrative examples / of [how individuals changing their own behavior in response to
　　　　　　　　　　　　　　　　　　　주어　　　　　　　현재분사구
local information allow the colony to regulate its workforce].
　　　　　　　　　「allow + 목적어 + to부정사: ~이 …하게 하다」

02
For example, / upon returning to their hive / honeybees [that have collected water] /
　　　　　　　~하자마자　　　　　　　　　　주어
search out a receiver bee to unload their water to within the hive. // If this search time
　　　　　목적어　　　　　　형용사적 용법(~할)
is short / then the returning bee is more likely to perform a waggle dance / to recruit
　　　　　　　　　　　　　　　~할 가능성이 더 크다　　　　　　　　　　　　　　부사적 용법(~하려고)
others to the water source.

03
Conversely, / if this search time is long / then the bee is more likely to give up
collecting water. // Since receiver bees will only accept water / if they require it, /
　　　　　　　　　　接続詞(이유)
either for themselves or to pass on to other bees and brood, / this unloading time is
「either A or B: A 아니면 B(부사구 병렬)」
correlated with the colony's overall need of water.
~와 상관관계가 있다

04
Thus / the individual water forager's response to unloading time (up or down) /
　　　　주어　　　　　　　　　　　　　　　　　　　　　전치사구
regulates water collection in response to the colony's need.
동사(단수)

01 꿀벌 군집의 입구entrance는 / 흔히 댄스 플로어라고 불리는referred to as the dancefloor / 정보를 교환하는 시장이다 / 군집의 상태state와 벌집hive 밖의 환경에 관한. // 댄스 플로어에서의 상호 작용을 연구하는 것은 / 여러 분명한illustrative 사례를 우리에게 제공한다 / 국지적 정보에 반응해 행동을 바꾸는 개체들이 어떻게 군집에서 그 노동력을 조절하게 하는지에 관한.

02 예를 들어, / 벌집으로 돌아오자마자 / 물을 모아온 꿀벌들은 / 자기 물을 넘겨줄unload 벌집 안의 수신자 벌을 찾는다. // 만약 찾는 시간이 짧으면, / 그 돌아온 벌은 8자 춤을 출 가능성이 크다 / 그 물의 출처까지 갈 다른 벌들을 모집하려고recruit.

03 반대로, / 찾는 시간이 길다면 / 그 벌은 물을 가지러 가는 것을 포기할 가능성이 더 크다. // 물을 받는 벌들은 오로지 넘겨받을 것이므로 / 그들이 물을 필요로 하는 경우에만 / 자기 자신을 위해서든, 아니면 다른 벌과 애벌레에게 전해주기pass on 위해서든, / 물을 넘겨주는 데 들어가는 이런 시간은 군집의 전반적인 물 수요와 상관관계가 있다be correlated with.

04 따라서 / (시간이 늘든 줄든 간에) 물을 넘겨주는 시간에 대한 물 조달자 개체의 반응은 / 군집의 수요에 맞춰 물의 수집량을 조절한다regulate.

구문 Check up

① The entrance to a honeybee colony, often referred / is referred to as the dancefloor, is a market place for information about the state of the colony and the environment outside the hive.

뒤에 술어인 is가 나오므로 주어를 보충하는 수식어구 자리임을 알 수 있다. 따라서 분사인 referred를 쓴다.

② For example, upon returning to their hive honeybees that have collected water search out a receiver bee unload / to unload their water to within the hive.

a receiver bee를 꾸미는 수식어 자리이므로 to unload를 쓴다.

67

STEP 1 • 수능에 *진짜* 나오는 *단어*

✔ **문제에 나오는 단어들을 확인하세요.**

01	precision	n. 정확성	(✔ precision) in calculation	계산의 정확성
02	determinacy	n. 확정성	absolute ( )	절대적 확정성
03	requirement	n. 필요(조건), 요구	a necessary ( ) for debate	토론을 위한 필요조건
04	ongoing	a. 진행 중인	the ( ) process	진행 중인 과정
05	representation	n. 진술, 표현	historical ( )	역사적 진술
06	put a premium on	~을 중시하다	( ) ( ) ( ) ( ) precision	정확성을 중시하다
07	refinement	n. 정제, 개선	the ( ) of a hypothesis	가설의 정제
08	approximation	n. 근접, 접근	an ( ) of the truth	진리에 대한 근접
09	explosion	n. 폭발(적 증가)	an ( ) of possible points of view	가능한 관점들의 폭발적 증가
10	illusion	n. 환상	the unmasking of previous ( )s	이전의 환상을 드러내는 것

➕ **본문 문장 속에서 단어들을 확인해 보세요.**

Historical insight is / not a matter of a continuous "narrowing down" of previous options, / not of an approximation of the truth, / but, on the contrary, / is an "explosion" of possible points of view.

역사적 통찰은 / 이전에 선택한 것들을 지속해서 '좁혀 가는' 것의 문제가 아니라 / 즉 진리에 대한 근접의 문제 / 반대로 / 가능한 관점들의 '폭발적 증가'이다.

01	precision	✎ 정확성	precision in calculation	계산의 (정확성)
02	determinacy		absolute determinacy	절대적 ( )
03	requirement		a necessary requirement for debate	토론을 위한 ( )
04	ongoing		the ongoing process	( ) 과정
05	representation		historical representation	역사적 ( )
06	put a premium on		put a premium on precision	정확성을 ( )
07	refinement		the refinement of a hypothesis	가설의 ( )
08	approximation		an approximation of the truth	진리에 대한 ( )
09	explosion		an explosion of possible points of view	가능한 관점들의 ( )
10	illusion		the unmasking of previous illusions	이전의 ( )을 드러내는 것

➕ **본문 문장 속에서 단어의 의미를 우리말로 해석해 보세요.**

Historical insight is / not a matter of a continuous "narrowing down" of previous options, / not of an approximation of the truth, / but, on the contrary, / is an "explosion" of possible points of view.

➡️ 역사적 통찰은 / 이전에 선택한 것들을 지속해서 '좁혀 가는' 것의 문제가 아니라 / 즉 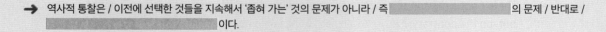의 문제 / 반대로 / 이다.

67 다음 빈칸에 들어갈 말로 가장 적절한 것은?

Precision and determinacy are a necessary requirement for all meaningful scientific debate, and progress in the sciences is, to a large extent, the ongoing process of achieving ever greater precision. But historical representation puts a premium on a proliferation of representations, hence not on the refinement of one representation but on the production of an ever more varied set of representations. Historical insight is not a matter of a continuous "narrowing down" of previous options, not of an approximation of the truth, but, on the contrary, is an "explosion" of possible points of view. It therefore aims at the unmasking of previous illusions of determinacy and precision by the production of new and alternative representations, rather than at achieving truth by a careful analysis of what was right and wrong in those previous representations. And from this perspective, the development of historical insight may indeed be regarded by the outsider as a process of creating ever more confusion, a continuous questioning of _____, rather than, as in the sciences, an ever greater approximation to the truth.

*proliferation: 증식

① criteria for evaluating historical representations

② certainty and precision seemingly achieved already

③ possibilities of alternative interpretations of an event

④ coexistence of multiple viewpoints in historical writing

⑤ correctness and reliability of historical evidence collected

정답과 해설 p.60

01 Precision and determinacy are a necessary requirement / for all meaningful scientific
주어1(A and B) 동사1(복수) 주격보어1
debate, / and progress in the sciences / is, (to a large extent), / the ongoing process of
주어2(불가산) 동사2(단수) 주격보어2
achieving ever greater precision.

02 But historical representation puts a premium / on a proliferation of representations, /
hence not on the refinement of one representation / but on the production of an ever
「not A but B: A가 아니라 B인(on + 명사 병렬)」
more varied set of representations.

03 Historical insight is / not a matter of a continuous "narrowing down" of previous
「not A ~, not A' ~ but B: A도 아니고 A'도 아니고 B인」
options, / not (a matter) of an approximation of the truth, / but, on the contrary, /
is an "explosion" of possible points of view. // It therefore aims / at the unmasking
of previous illusions of determinacy and precision / by the production of new and
alternative representations, / rather than at achieving truth / by a careful analysis of
「A rather than B: B라기보다 A인(at + 명사 병렬)」
[what was right and wrong in those previous representations].
명사절(of의 목적어)

04 And from this perspective, / the development of historical insight / may indeed be
「A be regarded as B: A가 B로 여겨지다」
regarded by the outsider / as a process of creating ever more confusion, / a continuous
동격
questioning of certainty and precision / seemingly achieved already, / rather than, as
과거분사구
in the sciences, / an ever greater approximation to the truth.

---

01 정확성과 확정성precision and determinacy은 필요조건requirement이며, / 모든 의미 있는 과학 토론을 위한 /
과학에서의 발전은 / 상당 부분, / 훨씬 더 높은 정확성을 달성하는 계속 진행 중인ongoing 과정이다.

02 그러나 역사적 진술은 중요시한다put a premium on / 진술representation의 증식을 / 따라서 한 가지 진술의
정제refinement가 아닌 / 훨씬 더 다양한 진술 집합의 생성에.

03 역사적 통찰은 / 이전에 선택한 것들을 지속해서 '좁혀 가는' 것의 문제가 아니라 / 즉 진리에 대한 근접approximation의
문제 / 반대로 / 가능한 관점들의 '폭발적 증가explosion'이다. // 그러므로 그것은 목표로 한다 / 확정성과 정확성에 대한
이전의 환상illusion을 드러내는 것을 / 새롭고 대안적인 진술의 생성에 의해 / 진리를 획득하는 것이 아니라 / 이전의
진술에서 무엇이 옳고 틀렸는지에 대한 신중한 분석에 의해.

04 그리고 이러한 관점에서 보면, / 역사적 통찰의 발전은 / 외부인에게는 진정 여겨질 수도 있다 / 훨씬 더 큰 혼란을
만들어내는 과정으로 / 즉 확실성과 정확성에 대한 지속적인 의문 제기 / 이미 획득한 것처럼 보이는 / 과학에서처럼
~이라기보다는 / 진리에 훨씬 근접해가는 것.

구문 Check up

① Historical insight is not a matter of a continuous "narrowing down" of previous options, not of an approximation of the truth, but **is / are** an "explosion" of possible points of view.

공통 주어 Historical insight에 동사가 「not A, not A', but B」로 연결되는 것이므로 is가 적절하다.

② It therefore aims at achieving truth by a careful analysis of **that / what** was right and wrong in those previous representations.

of의 목적어이면서 뒤에 나오는 동사 was의 주어 역할을 할 수 있는 말로 what이 적절하다.

정답 ① is ② what

68

STEP 1 • 수능에 *진짜* 나오는 *단어*

✔ 문제에 나오는 단어들을 확인하세요.

01	interdependence	n. 상호의존성	recognize the (✔ interdependence)	상호의존성을 인식하다
02	integration	n. 통합	cultural ( )	문화적 통합
03	contradictory	a. 모순되는	( ) patterns	모순되는 패턴
04	implication	n. 영향, 함의	the logical ( )s of the ideas	그 사상들의 논리적 영향
05	consequence	n. 결과	the natural ( )s of an action	어떤 행동의 당연한 결과
06	inherent	a. 내재된	( ) in human nature	인간 본성에 내재된
07	integral	a. 내장된, 필수적인	( ) to the conceptual system	개념 체계에 내장된
08	premise	n. 전제	the acceptance of its ( )s	전제의 수용
09	prime number	(수학) 소수	the discoveries of new ( ) ( )s	새로운 소수의 발견
10	cumulative	a. 축적된, 누적된	the ( ) work of many individuals	많은 개인의 축적된 작업
11	ripe	a. (시기가) 무르익은, 적합한	( ) for development	(시기상) 개발에 적합한

➕ 본문 문장 속에서 단어들을 확인해 보세요.

New ideas are discovered through logical reasoning, / but such discoveries are inherent in and integral to the conceptual system / and are made possible / only because of the acceptance of its premises.

새로운 사상은 논리적 추론을 통해 발견되지만, / 그러한 발견은 개념 체계에 내재 및 내장되어 있고, / 가능해진다 / 오직 그 전제의 수용으로 인해.

문제를 풀기 전에 단어들을 30초 동안 다시 확인하세요.

01	interdependence	상호의존성	recognize the interdependence	(상호의존성)을 인식하다
02	integration		cultural integration	문화적 ( )
03	contradictory		contradictory patterns	( ) 패턴
04	implication		the logical implications of the ideas	그 사상들의 논리적 ( )
05	consequence		the natural consequences of an action	어떤 행동의 당연한 ( )
06	inherent		inherent in human nature	인간 본성에 ( )
07	integral		integral to the conceptual system	개념 체계에 ( )
08	premise		the acceptance of its premises	( )의 수용
09	prime number		the discoveries of new prime numbers	새로운 ( )의 발견
10	cumulative		the cumulative work of many individuals	많은 개인의 ( ) 작업
11	ripe		ripe for development	개발에 ( )

➕ 본문 문장 속에서 단어의 의미를 우리말로 해석해 보세요.

New ideas are discovered through logical reasoning, / but such discoveries are inherent in and integral to the conceptual system / and are made possible / only because of the acceptance of its premises.

➔ 새로운 사상은 논리적 추론을 통해 발견되지만, / 그러한 발견은 ▒▒▒▒▒▒▒▒▒▒▒▒ 있고, / 가능해진다 / 오직 ▒▒▒▒▒▒ ▒▒▒▒▒▒ 으로 인해.

68 다음 빈칸에 들어갈 말로 가장 적절한 것은?

It is important to recognise the interdependence between individual, culturally formed actions and the state of cultural integration. People work within the forms provided by the cultural patterns that they have internalised, however contradictory these may be. Ideas are worked out as logical implications or consequences of other accepted ideas, and it is in this way that cultural innovations and discoveries are possible. New ideas are discovered through logical reasoning, but such discoveries are inherent in and integral to the conceptual system and are made possible only because of the acceptance of its premises. For example, the discoveries of new prime numbers are 'real' consequences of the particular number system employed. Thus, cultural ideas show 'advances' and 'developments' because they _____. The cumulative work of many individuals produces a corpus of knowledge within which certain 'discoveries' become possible or more likely. Such discoveries are 'ripe' and could not have occurred earlier and are also likely to be made simultaneously by numbers of individuals.

*corpus: 집적(集積) **simultaneously: 동시에

① are outgrowths of previous ideas

② stem from abstract reasoning ability

③ form the basis of cultural universalism

④ emerge between people of the same age

⑤ promote individuals' innovative thinking

정답과 해설 p.61

01 It is important / to recognise the interdependence / between individual, culturally
가주어   진주어

formed actions and the state of cultural integration. // People work within the

forms / provided by the cultural patterns / [that they have internalised], / however
     과거분사구   목적격 관계대명사절

contradictory these may be.
「however + 형/부 + 주어 + 동사: 아무리 ~하더라도」

02 Ideas are worked out / as logical implications or consequences of other accepted ideas,
     전치사(~로서)

/ and it is in this way / that cultural innovations and discoveries are possible.
     「it is[was] ~ that …: …한 것은 바로 ~이다[였다]」

03 New ideas are discovered through logical reasoning, / but such discoveries are inherent

in and integral to the conceptual system / and are made possible / only because of the
     5형식 수동태(be p.p. + 형용사)

acceptance of its premises. // For example, / the discoveries of new prime numbers /
     주어

are 'real' consequences of the particular number system employed.
동사(복수)   과거분사

04 Thus, / cultural ideas show 'advances' and 'developments' / because they are

outgrowths of previous ideas.

05 The cumulative work of many individuals / produces a corpus of knowledge / [within
     선행사   = where

which certain 'discoveries' become possible or more likely]. // Such discoveries are 'ripe'

/ and could not have occurred earlier / and are also likely to be made simultaneously /
     「could not have p.p.: ~할 수 없었을 것이다」

by numbers of individuals.

---

01 중요하다 / 상호의존성interdependence을 인식하는 것은 / 개별적이고 문화적으로 형성된 행동과 문화적
통합integration의 상태 사이의. // 사람들은 형태 내에서 일한다 / 문화적 패턴에 의해 제공되는 / 자신이 내면화한 /
이것들이 아무리 모순되더라도contradictory.

02 사상은 도출되고 / 다른 수용된 사상의 논리적 영향이나 결과logical implications or consequences로 / 바로 이러한
방식이다 / 문화적 혁신과 발견이 가능한 것은.

03 새로운 사상은 논리적 추론을 통해 발견되지만, / 그러한 발견은 개념 체계에 내재inherent 및 내장되어integral 있고, /
가능해진다 / 오직 그 전제premise의 수용으로 인해. // 예를 들어, / 새로운 소수prime number의 발견은 / 사용되고
있는 특정 숫자 체계의 '실제' 결과이다.

04 따라서, / 문화적 사상은 '진보'와 '발전'을 보여 준다 / 그것들이 이전 사상의 결과물이기 때문에.

05 많은 개인의 축적된cumulative 작업은 / 집적된 지식을 생산한다 / 특정 '발견'이 가능해지거나 가능성이 높아지는. //
그러한 발견은 '무르익었고ripe', / 더 일찍 발생할 수 없었을 것이며, / 또한 동시에 이루어질 가능성이 있다 / 다수의
개인에 의해.

구문 Check up	
① People work within the forms provided by the cultural patterns that they have internalised, whatever / however contradictory these may be.	② Such discoveries are inherent in and integral to the conceptual system and are made possibly / possible only because of the acceptance of its premises.
'아무리 ~하더라도'라는 의미의 「however + 형/부 + 주어 + 동사」 구문이 므로 however를 쓴다.	5형식 수동태 are made 뒤로 보어가 필요하므로 형용사 possible이 적절 하다.

정답 ① however ② possible

69

STEP 1 • 수능에 진짜 나오는 단어

✔ 문제에 나오는 단어들을 확인하세요.

01	destination	n. 목적지, 행선지	reach the (✔ destination)	목적지에 도착하다
02	stem from	~에서 비롯되다	( ) ( ) an accident	사고에서 비롯되다
03	subtle	a. 미묘한	a ( ) progress	미묘한 진보
04	dramatic	a. 극적인	a ( ) improvement	극적인 향상
05	generate	v. 발생시키다	( ) many new problems	많은 새로운 문제를 발생시키다
06	circular	a. 순환적인	the ( ) flow	순환적 흐름
07	expansion	n. 팽창, 확장	the ( ) of the universe	우주의 팽창
08	enlightenment	n. (18세기) 계몽(주의), 깨우침, 이해	ever since the European ( )	유럽 계몽주의 이래로 줄곧
09	star in	~에서 주연을 맡다	( ) ( ) movies	영화에서 주연을 맡다

➕ 본문 문장 속에서 단어들을 확인해 보세요.

The "pro" in protopian / stems from the notions of process and progress.

프로토피아적이라는 말에서 '프로'는 / 과정과 진보라는 개념에서 비롯된다.

01	destination	🖉 목적지, 행선지	reach the destination	(목적지)에 도착하다
02	stem from		stem from an accident	사고에서 ( )
03	subtle		a subtle progress	( ) 진보
04	dramatic		a dramatic improvement	( ) 향상
05	generate		generate many new problems	많은 새로운 문제를 ( )
06	circular		the circular flow	( ) 흐름
07	expansion		the expansion of the universe	우주의 ( )
08	enlightenment		ever since the European enlightenment	유럽 ( ) 이래로 줄곧
09	star in		star in movies	영화에서 ( )

➕ **본문 문장 속에서 단어의 의미를 우리말로 해석해 보세요.**

The "pro" in protopian / stems from the notions of process and progress.

➡ 프로토피아적이라는 말에서 '프로'는 / 과정과 진보라는 개념에서 　　　　　　.

69 다음 빈칸에 들어갈 말로 가장 적절한 것은?

Protopia is a state of becoming, rather than a destination. It is a process. In the protopian mode, things are better today than they were yesterday, although only a little better. It is incremental improvement or mild progress. The "pro" in protopian stems from the notions of process and progress. This subtle progress is not dramatic, not exciting. It is easy to miss because a protopia generates almost as many new problems as new benefits. The problems of today were caused by yesterday's technological successes, and the technological solutions to today's problems will cause the problems of tomorrow. This circular expansion of both problems and solutions _____. Ever since the Enlightenment and the invention of science, we've managed to create a tiny bit more than we've destroyed each year. But that few percent positive difference is compounded over decades into what we might call civilization. Its benefits never star in movies.

*incremental: 증가의 **compound: 조합하다

① conceals the limits of innovations at the present time

② makes it difficult to predict the future with confidence

③ motivates us to quickly achieve a protopian civilization

④ hides a steady accumulation of small net benefits over time

⑤ produces a considerable change in technological successes

정답과 해설 p.62

STEP 3 ● 수능 지문 제대로 복습하기

01 Protopia is a state of becoming, / rather than a destination. // It is a process.
「A rather than B: B라기보다 A인」

02 In the protopian mode, / things are better today than they were yesterday, / although
they are
only a little better. // It is incremental improvement or mild progress.
주격보어
접속사(비록 ~하더라도)

03 The "pro" in protopian / stems from the notions of process and progress. // This
subtle progress is not dramatic, / not exciting. // It is easy to miss / because a protopia
가주어   진주어
generates almost as many new problems as new benefits.
「as + 원급 + as: ~만큼 …한」

04 The problems of today / were caused by yesterday's technological successes, / and the
주어1   동사1(복수)   주어2
technological solutions to today's problems / will cause the problems of tomorrow. //
                                            동사2
This circular expansion of both problems and solutions / hides a steady accumulation
주어   동사(단수)
of small net benefits / over time.

05 Ever since the Enlightenment and the invention of science, / we've managed to create
전치사(~이래로 줄곧) 명사구(과거)   동사(현재완료)
a tiny bit more / than we've destroyed each year. // But that few percent positive
difference / is compounded over decades into [what we might call civilization]. // Its
                                              명사절(into의 목적어)
benefits never star in movies.

01 프로토피아는 생성의 상태이다 / 목적지destination라기보다는. // 그것은 과정이다.

02 프로토피아적인 방식에서는 / 어제보다 오늘 상황이 더 낫다 / 비록 그저 약간 더 낫다고 하더라도. // 그것은 점진적인
개선이나 가벼운 진보이다.

03 프로토피아적이라는 말에서 '프로'는 / 과정과 진보라는 개념에서 비롯된다stem from. // 이 미묘한subtle 진보는
극적dramatic이지도 않고 / 자극적이지도 않다. // 그것은 놓치기 쉽다 / 프로토피아가 거의 새로운 이점만큼 많은 새로운
문제를 발생시키기generate 때문에.

04 오늘의 문제는 / 어제의 기술적 성공이 가져온 것이고, / 오늘의 문제에 대한 기술적 해결책은 / 내일의 문제를 유발할
것이다. // 문제와 해결책의 이런 순환적 팽창circular expansion은 / 작은 순이익의 꾸준한 축적을 보이지 않게 한다 /
시간이 지남에 따라.

05 계몽주의enlightenment와 과학의 발명 이래로 줄곧, / 우리는 조금 더 많은 것을 만들어냈다 / 매년 우리가 파괴해 온
것보다. // 그러나 그 얼마 안 되는 비율의 긍정적인 차이는 / 수십 년에 걸쳐 우리가 문명이라고 부를 수 있는 것으로
조합된다. // 그것의 장점은 영화에서 주연을 맡는star in movies 법이 없다.

구문 Check up	
① In the protopian mode, things are better today than they were yesterday, despite / although only a little better.	② That few percent positive difference is compounded over decades into that / what we might call civilization.
뒤에 명사구가 아닌 형용사구가 나오는 것으로 보아 「대명사 주어 + be동사」가 생략된 부사절이므로, 접속사 although가 적절하다.	앞에 선행사가 없고 뒤에 call의 목적어가 없는 불완전한 절이 나오는 것으로 보아 선행사를 포함한 관계대명사 what이 적절하다.

정답 ① although ② what

70

STEP 1 • 수능에 *진짜* 나오는 *단어*

✔ 문제에 나오는 단어들을 확인하세요.

01	accelerate	v. 가속화하다	(✓ accelerate) the process	과정을 가속화하다
02	dematerialization	n. 비물질화	the ( ) of goods	재화의 비물질화
03	hasten	v. 앞당기다, 재촉하다	( ) the growth	성장을 앞당기다
04	migration	n. 이동, 이주	the ( ) from products to services	제품에서 서비스로의 이동
05	solid	a. 고체의, 단단한	( ) physical goods	고체의 물리적 상품
06	deliver	v. (결과 등을) 내놓다, 산출하다	( ) more benefits	더 많은 이익을 내놓다
07	substitute	v. 대체하다	( ) oil for butter	버터를 기름으로 대체하다
08	weightless	a. 무게가 없는, 무중력의	in a ( ) state	무중력 상태에서
09	tangible	a. 유형의, 만질 수 있는	( ) goods	유형의 재화
10	embed	v. (단단히) 박아 넣다, 끼워넣다	( )ded in his memory	그의 기억 속에 깊이 박힌
11	infuse	v. 주입하다, 불어넣다	( )d with new hope	새로운 희망이 주입된

⊕ 본문 문장 속에서 단어들을 확인해 보세요.

Digital technology accelerates dematerialization / by hastening the migration from products to services.

디지털 기술은 비물질화를 가속한다 / 제품에서 서비스로의 이동을 앞당김으로써.

01	accelerate	🖉 가속화하다	accelerate the process	과정을 (가속화하다)
02	dematerialization		the dematerialization of goods	재화의 ( )
03	hasten		hasten the growth	성장을 ( )
04	migration		the migration from products to services	제품에서 서비스로의 ( )
05	solid		solid physical goods	( ) 물리적 상품
06	deliver		deliver more benefits	더 많은 이익을 ( )
07	substitute		substitute oil for butter	버터를 기름으로 ( )
08	weightless		in a weightless state	( ) 상태에서
09	tangible		tangible goods	( ) 재화
10	embed		embedded in his memory	그의 기억 속에 깊이 ( )
11	infuse		infused with new hope	새로운 희망이 ( )

➕ **본문 문장 속에서 단어의 의미를 우리말로 해석해 보세요.**

Digital technology accelerates dematerialization / by hastening the migration from products to services.

➡ 디지털 기술은 ▨▨▨▨▨▨▨▨▨▨▨▨ / ▨▨▨▨▨▨▨▨▨▨▨▨▨▨▨▨▨▨으로써.

70 다음 빈칸에 들어갈 말로 가장 적절한 것은?

Digital technology accelerates dematerialization by hastening the migration from products to services. The liquid nature of services means they don't have to be bound to materials. But dematerialization is not just about digital goods. The reason even solid physical goods — like a soda can — can deliver more benefits while inhabiting less material is because their heavy atoms are substituted by weightless bits. The tangible is replaced by intangibles — intangibles like better design, innovative processes, smart chips, and eventually online connectivity — that do the work that more aluminum atoms used to do. Soft things, like intelligence, are thus embedded into hard things, like aluminum, that make hard things behave more like software. Material goods infused with bits increasingly act as if _____. Nouns morph to verbs. Hardware behaves like software. In Silicon Valley they say it like this: "Software eats everything."

*morph: 변화하다

① they were intangible services

② they replaced all digital goods

③ hardware could survive software

④ digital services were not available

⑤ software conflicted with hardware

정답과 해설 p.63

01 Digital technology accelerates dematerialization / by hastening the migration from
「by + 동명사: ~함으로써」
products to services. // The liquid nature of services means / they don't have to
접속사 that 생략
be bound to materials.
「be bound to + 명사: ~에 얽매이다」

02 But dematerialization is not just about digital goods. // The reason / [(why) even solid
주어   주어
physical goods — (like a soda can) — can deliver more benefits / while inhabiting less
삽입구   동사   접속사가 있는 분사구문(= while they inhabit ~)
material] / is [because their heavy atoms are substituted by weightless bits].
동사(단수)   주격보어(부사절이 명사절처럼 쓰임)

03 The tangible is replaced by intangibles — / intangibles like better design, innovative
동격   전치사구
processes, smart chips, and eventually online connectivity — / [that do the work /
주격 관계대명사절(intangibles 수식)
that more aluminum atoms used to do]. // Soft things, / (like intelligence), / are thus
선행사
embedded into hard things, / (like aluminum), / [that make hard things behave more
사역동사 목적어   목적격보어(원형부정사)
like software].

04 Material goods infused with bits increasingly act / as if they were intangible services.
주어   과거분사구   동사(복수)
「as if + 주어 + 과거 동사: (실제로 ~이지 않지만) 마치 ~인 것처럼」
// Nouns morph to verbs. // Hardware behaves like software. // In Silicon Valley they
대명사(일반 사람들)
say it like this: / "Software eats everything."

---

01 디지털 기술은 비물질화를 가속한다**accelerate dematerialization** / 제품에서 서비스로의 이동을 앞당김**hasten the migration**으로써. // 서비스의 유동적인 특성은 의미한다 / 그것들이 물질에 얽매일 필요가 없다는 것을.

02 그러나 비물질화는 단지 디지털 상품에 관련된 것만은 아니다. // 이유는 / 탄산음료 캔과 같은 고체의**solid** 물리적 상품조차도 더 많은 이익을 내놓을**deliver** 수 있는 / 더 적은 양의 물질을 가지고 있으면서도 / 그것들의 무거운 원자가 무게가 없는**weightless** 비트로 대체되기**substitute** 때문이다.

03 유형의**tangible** 것들은 무형의 것들로 대체된다 / 더 나은 설계, 혁신적인 과정, 스마트 칩, 그리고 궁극적으로 온라인 연결성과 같은 무형의 것들 / 일을 하는 / 더 많은 알루미늄 원자들이 하던. // 부드러운 것들이 / 지능과 같이 / 따라서 단단한 물건에 삽입된다**embed**, / 알루미늄과 같은 / 딱딱한 물건들을 더 소프트웨어처럼 작용하게 만드는.

04 비트가 주입된**infuse** 물질적 상품들은 점점 행동한다 / 마치 그것들이 무형의 서비스인 것처럼. // 명사가 동사로 변한다. // 하드웨어가 소프트웨어처럼 동작한다. // Silicon Valley에서 사람들은 이렇게 말한다 / "소프트웨어가 모든 것을 먹는다."

구문 Check up

① Soft things, like intelligence, are thus embedded into hard things, like aluminum, that make / makes hard things behave more like software.

관계대명사 that의 선행사가 문맥상 Soft things라는 복수명사이므로, that절의 동사 자리에는 복수동사인 make가 적절하다.

② Material goods infused with bits increasingly act as if they were / are intangible services.

물질적 상품은 '실제로는 비물질적이지 않음에도 마치 비물질적인 것처럼' 행동한다는 의미이므로, 가정법 과거 구문의 동사 were가 적절하다.

정답 ① make ② were

DAY 11
71 STEP 1 • 수능에 진짜 나오는 단어

✔ 문제에 나오는 단어들을 확인하세요.

01	suffer	v. 고생하다, 고통받다	(✔ suffer) as much as beginners		초보자만큼 고생하다
02	extensive	a. 엄청난, 광범위한	( ) practice		엄청난 연습
03	component	n. 구성 요소	the key ( ) skills		핵심 구성 요소 기술
04	automated	a. 자동화된	highly practiced and ( )		고도로 숙련되고 자동화된
05	demand	v. 필요로 하다, 요구하다	( ) physical strength		체력을 필요로 하다
06	cognitive	a. 인지적인	( ) resources		인지적 자원
07	load	n. 부하, 짐	lower the total cognitive ( )		총 인지 부하를 낮추다
08	isolate	v. 분리시키다, 고립시키다	when the tasks are divided and ( )d		과제가 분할되고 분리될 때
09	fluency	n. 능숙함, 유창성	the high level of ( )		높은 수준의 능숙함
10	efficiency	n. 효율성	ease and ( )		용이함과 효율성

⊕ 본문 문장 속에서 단어들을 확인해 보세요.

Because experts have extensive practice within a limited domain, / the key component skills in their domain / tend to be highly practiced and more automated.

전문가는 제한된 영역 내에서 엄청난 연습을 하기 때문에, / 자기 분야에서의 핵심 구성 요소 기술은 / 고도로 숙련되고 더 자동화되어 있는 경향이 있다.

01	suffer	✏️ 고생하다, 고통받다	suffer as much as beginners	초보자만큼 (고생하다)
02	extensive		extensive practice	( ) 연습
03	component		the key component skills	핵심 ( ) 기술
04	automated		highly practiced and automated	고도로 숙련되고 ( )
05	demand		demand physical strength	체력을 ( )
06	cognitive		cognitive resources	( ) 자원
07	load		lower the total cognitive load	총 인지 ( ) 를 낮추다
08	isolate		when the tasks are divided and isolated	과제가 분할되고 ( ) 때
09	fluency		the high level of fluency	높은 수준의 ( )
10	efficiency		ease and efficiency	용이함과 ( )

➕ 본문 문장 속에서 단어의 의미를 우리말로 해석해 보세요.

Because experts have extensive practice within a limited domain, / the key component skills in their domain / tend to be highly practiced and more automated.

➡️ 전문가는 제한된 영역 내에서 　　　　　　　을 하기 때문에, / 자기 분야에서의 　　　　　　　은 / 　　　　　　　경향이 있다.

71

다음 글에서 전체 흐름과 관계 <u>없는</u> 문장은?

Interestingly, experts do not suffer as much as beginners when performing complex tasks or combining multiple tasks. Because experts have extensive practice within a limited domain, the key component skills in their domain tend to be highly practiced and more automated. ① Each of these highly practiced skills then demands relatively few cognitive resources, effectively lowering the total cognitive load that experts experience. ② Thus, experts can perform complex tasks and combine multiple tasks relatively easily. ③ Furthermore, beginners are excellent at processing the tasks when the tasks are divided and isolated. ④ This is not because they necessarily have more cognitive resources than beginners; rather, because of the high level of fluency they have achieved in performing key skills, they can do more with what they have. ⑤ Beginners, on the other hand, have not achieved the same degree of fluency and automaticity in each of the component skills, and thus they struggle to combine skills that experts combine with relative ease and efficiency.

정답과 해설 p.65

01 Interestingly, / experts do not suffer as much as beginners / when performing complex tasks or combining multiple tasks.
「not as + 원급 + as: ~만큼 …하지 않은」
접속사가 있는 분사구문
(= when they perform ~ or combine ~)

02 Because experts have extensive practice within a limited domain, / the key component skills in their domain / tend to be highly practiced and more automated. // Each of these highly practiced skills / then demands relatively few cognitive resources, / effectively lowering the total cognitive load / [that experts experience]. // Thus, / experts can perform complex tasks / and combine multiple tasks relatively easily.
접속사(이유)
주어
동사구(복수)
주어(each of + 복수명사)
동사(단수)
분사구문
선행사
목적격 관계대명사절

03 Furthermore, / beginners are excellent at processing the tasks / when the tasks are divided and isolated.
「be excellent at + 동명사: ~에 탁월하다」

04 This is not because they necessarily have more cognitive resources than beginners; / rather, / because of the high level of fluency / [they have achieved in performing key skills], / they can do more with what they have. // Beginners, on the other hand, / have not achieved the same degree of fluency and automaticity / in each of the component skills, / and thus they struggle to combine skills / [that experts combine with relative ease and efficiency].
「not A ~. rather, B: A가 아니라 오히려 B이다(A, B 자리에 '이유')」
선행사
목적격 관계대명사절(관계사 생략)
선행사
목적격 관계대명사절
「with + 추상명사: 부사 역할(= relatively easily and efficiently)」

01 흥미롭게도, / 전문가들은 초보자만큼 고생하지suffer 않는다 / 복잡한 과제를 수행하거나 많은 과제를 결합할 때.

02 전문가는 제한된 영역 내에서 엄청난extensive 연습을 하기 때문에, / 자기 분야에서의 핵심 구성 요소component 기술은 / 고도로 숙련되고 더 자동화되어automated 있는 경향이 있다. // 고도로 숙련된 이러한 각각의 기술은 / 그래서 비교적 적은 인지 자원을 필요로 하여demand, / 총 인지 부하cognitive load를 효과적으로 낮춘다 / 전문가가 경험하는. // 따라서 전문가는 비교적 쉽게 복잡한 과제를 수행하고 / 많은 과제를 결합할 수 있다.

03 (게다가, / 초보자는 그것을 처리하는 데 탁월하다 / 과제가 분할되고 분리될isolate 때.)

04 이것은 그들이 반드시 초보자보다 더 많은 인지적 자원을 가지고 있기 때문인 것은 아니다 / 오히려 / 높은 수준의 능숙함fluency 때문에 / 핵심 기술을 수행하면서 그들이 달성한 / 그들은 자신들이 가지고 있는 것으로 더 많은 것을 할 수 있다. // 반면에 초보자는 / 동일한 수준의 능숙함과 자동성을 달성하지 못했으며, / 각각의 구성 기술에서 / 따라서 그들은 기술들을 결합하려고 애쓴다 / 전문가가 비교적 쉽고 효율적으로with relative ease and efficiency 결합하는.

구문 Check up

① Each of these highly practiced skills then demands / demand relatively few cognitive resources, effectively lowering the total cognitive load that experts experience.

「each of + 복수명사」가 주어이므로 단수동사 demands가 적절하다.

② Rather, because / because of the high level of fluency they have achieved in performing key skills, they can do more with what they have.

뒤에 명사구 the high level of fluency가 나오므로 전치사 because of가 적절하다. 'they ~ key skills'는 관계사가 생략된 목적격 관계대명사절이다.

정답 ① demands ② because of

72 · STEP 1 · 수능에 *진짜* 나오는 *단어*

✔ 문제에 나오는 단어들을 확인하세요.

01	countless	a. 수없이 많은	(✔ countless) others	수없이 많은 다른 사람들
02	means of communication	의사소통 수단	as a ( ) ( ) ( )	의사소통 수단으로서
03	decoding	n. (암호 등의) 해독	the ( ) of secret messages	비밀 메시지의 해독
04	confidently	ad. 자신 있게	talk ( )	자신 있게 말하다
05	instruction	n. 수업, 설명, 지도	give ( )s	수업을 하다
06	address	v. (문제 등에) 대처하다, 다루다	( ) serious noise issues	심각한 소음 문제에 대처하다
07	incredibly	ad. 놀라울 만큼	( ) lucky	놀라울 만큼 운이 좋은
08	sparingly	ad. 드물게, 조금만	Use your loudest voice ( ).	제일 큰 목소리는 조금만 쓰라.
09	authoritative	a. 권위적인	a quiet and ( ) voice	조용하고도 권위적인 목소리
10	measured	a. 신중한, 침착한	in a ( ) tone	신중한 어조로
11	panicked	a. 당황한, 겁에 질린	( ) shouting	당황한 고함 소리

➕ 본문 문장 속에서 단어들을 확인해 보세요.

Actors, singers, politicians and countless others / recognise the power of the human voice as a means of communication / beyond the simple decoding of the words that are used.

배우, 가수, 정치가, 그리고 수없이 많은 다른 사람은 / 의사소통 수단으로서의 사람 목소리의 힘을 인정한다 / 사용된 단어의 단순한 해독을 넘어서는.

01	countless	✎ 수없이 많은	countless others	(수없이 많은) 다른 사람들
02	means of communication		as a means of communication	( )으로서
03	decoding		the decoding of secret messages	비밀 메시지의 ( )
04	confidently		talk confidently	( ) 말하다
05	instruction		give instructions	( )을 하다
06	address		address serious noise issues	심각한 소음 문제에 ( )
07	incredibly		incredibly lucky	( ) 운이 좋은
08	sparingly		Use your loudest voice sparingly.	제일 큰 목소리는 ( ) 쓰라.
09	authoritative		a quiet and authoritative voice	조용하고도 ( ) 목소리
10	measured		in a measured tone	( ) 어조로
11	panicked		panicked shouting	( ) 고함 소리

➕ **본문 문장 속에서 단어의 의미를 우리말로 해석해 보세요.**

Actors, singers, politicians and countless others / recognise the power of the human voice as a means of communication / beyond the simple decoding of the words that are used.

→ 배우, 가수, 정치가, 그리고   은 /   사람 목소리의 힘을 인정한다 / 사용된 단어의 단순한   을 넘어서는.

72 다음 글에서 전체 흐름과 관계 없는 문장은?

Actors, singers, politicians and countless others recognise the power of the human voice as a means of communication beyond the simple decoding of the words that are used. Learning to control your voice and use it for different purposes is, therefore, one of the most important skills to develop as an early career teacher. ① The more confidently you give instructions, the higher the chance of a positive class response. ② There are times when being able to project your voice loudly will be very useful when working in school, and knowing that you can cut through a noisy classroom, dinner hall or playground is a great skill to have. ③ In order to address serious noise issues in school, students, parents and teachers should search for a solution together. ④ However, I would always advise that you use your loudest voice incredibly sparingly and avoid shouting as much as possible. ⑤ A quiet, authoritative and measured tone has so much more impact than slightly panicked shouting.

정답과 해설 **p.65**

01 Actors, singers, politicians and countless others / recognise the power of the human voice **as** a means of communication / beyond the simple decoding of the words [that are used]. // Learning to control your voice and use it for different purposes **is**, / therefore, / one of the most important skills / to develop as an early career teacher.

전치사(~로서)   주격 관계대명사절   주어(동명사)   동사(단수)   형용사적 용법

02 「the + 비교급 ~, the + 비교급 …: ~할수록 더 …하다」
The more confidently you give instructions, / the higher the chance of a positive class response. // There are times / [**when** being able to project your voice loudly will be very useful] / when working in school, / and knowing [that you can cut through a noisy classroom, dinner hall or playground] / **is** a great skill to have.

관계부사   접속사가 있는 분사구문(= when you work ~)   주어(동명사)   knowing의 목적어   동사(단수)

03 In order to address serious noise issues in school, / students, parents and teachers should search for a solution together.

목적의 부사구(= So as to address ~)

04 should
However, / I **would** always **advise** / that you **use** your loudest voice incredibly sparingly / and **avoid** shouting as much as possible. // A quiet, authoritative and measured tone / has so much more impact than slightly panicked shouting.

'충고' 동사   '~해야 한다'라는 의미일 때 should 생략 가능

01 배우, 가수, 정치가, 그리고 수없이 많은**countless** 다른 사람은 / 의사소통 수단**means of communication** 으로서의 사람 목소리의 힘을 인정한다 / 사용된 단어의 단순한 해독**decoding**을 넘어서는. // 여러분의 목소리를 통제하고 다양한 목적을 위해 사용하는 법을 배우는 것은 / 따라서 / 가장 중요한 기술 중 하나이다 / 경력 초기의 교사로서 개발해야 할.

02 여러분이 더 자신 있게**confidently** 수업할수록**give instructions**, / 긍정적인 학급의 반응이 나올 확률은 더 높다. // 경우가 있다 / 여러분의 목소리를 크게 낼 수 있는 것이 매우 유용할 / 학교에서 일할 때 / 그래서 여러분이 시끄러운 교실, 구내식당이나 운동장을 (목소리로) 가를 수 있다는 것을 아는 것은 / 갖춰야 할 훌륭한 기술이다.

03 (학교 내의 심각한 소음 문제에 대처하려면**address** / 학생, 학부모, 교사가 함께 해결책을 찾아야 한다.)

04 하지만 / 나는 늘 조언코자 한다 / 여러분이 가장 큰 목소리는 놀라울 만큼 드물게**incredibly sparingly** 써야 한다고 / 그리고 소리치는 것을 최대한 피하라고. // 조용하고도 권위 있으며**authoritative** 침착한**measured** 어조는 / 약간 당황한**panicked** 고함 소리보다 훨씬 더 큰 효과를 지닌다.

구문 Check up

① The more confident / confidently you give instructions, the higher the chance of a positive class response.

「the + 비교급」 뒤의 동사 give를 꾸밀 수 있도록 부사 confidently를 써야 한다. confident를 쓰려면 뒤에 보어가 빠져 있거나 수식받을 명사가 있어야 한다.

② However, I would always advise that you use your loudest voice incredibly sparingly and avoid / to avoid shouting as much as possible.

use와 and로 병렬 연결되는 동사원형으로 avoid를 써야 한다. 'use ~ and avoid ~' 앞에는 should가 생략되어 있다.

정답 ① confidently ② avoid

73

STEP 1 • 수능에 *진짜* 나오는 *단어*

✔ 문제에 나오는 단어들을 확인하세요.

01	theoretical	*a.* 이론적인	(✔ theoretical) perspectives		이론적 관점
02	immigration	*n.* 이주, 이민	restrict ( )		이민을 제한하다
03	utility	*n.* 효용, 이용	a high ( ) value		높은 효용 가치
04	maximization	*n.* 극대화, 최대화	engage in utility ( )		효용 극대화에 참여하다
05	represent	*v.* 제시하다, 나타내다	( ) a framework		틀을 제시하다
06	rational	*a.* 합리적인	individuals as ( ) actors		합리적 행위자로서의 개인
07	assessment	*n.* 평가, 사정	the ( ) of the costs		비용에 대한 평가
08	monetary	*a.* 금전적인	( ) gains		금전적 혜택
09	show off	과시하다	( ) ( ) their social status		사회적 지위를 과시하다
10	luxurious	*a.* 사치스러운	purchase ( ) items		사치스러운 물건을 구입하다
11	expense	*n.* 비용	the ( ) of travel		여행(이동) 비용
12	uncertainty	*n.* 불확실성	( ) about a different culture		다른 문화에 대한 불확실성
13	separation	*n.* 이별, 분리	( ) from family		가족과의 이별
14	unknown	*a.* 미지의	the fear of the ( )		미지의 것에 대한 두려움

⊕ 본문 문장 속에서 단어들을 확인해 보세요.

Economics, / which assumes that actors engage in utility maximization, / represents one framework.

경제학은 / 행위자들이 효용 극대화에 참여한다고 상정하는 / 하나의 틀을 제시한다.

01	theoretical	🖉 이론적인	theoretical perspectives	(이론적)관점
02	immigration		restrict immigration	( )을 제한하다
03	utility		a high utility value	높은 ( ) 가치
04	maximization		engage in utility maximization	효용 ( )에 참여하다
05	represent		represent a framework	틀을 ( )
06	rational		individuals as rational actors	( ) 행위자로서의 개인
07	assessment		the assessment of the costs	비용에 대한 ( )
08	monetary		monetary gains	( ) 혜택
09	show off		show off their social status	사회적 지위를 ( )
10	luxurious		purchase luxurious items	( ) 물건을 구입하다
11	expense		the expense of travel	여행 ( )
12	uncertainty		uncertainty about a different culture	다른 문화에 대한 ( )
13	separation		separation from family	가족과의 ( )
14	unknown		the fear of the unknown	( ) 것에 대한 두려움

➕ 본문 문장 속에서 단어의 의미를 우리말로 해석해 보세요.

Economics, / which assumes that actors engage in utility maximization, / represents one framework.

➔ 경제학은 / 행위자들이 ▨▨▨▨▨▨▨▨▨▨▨▨▨고 상정하는 / ▨▨▨▨▨▨▨▨▨▨▨.

73 다음 글에서 전체 흐름과 관계 <u>없는</u> 문장은?

A variety of theoretical perspectives provide insight into immigration. Economics, which assumes that actors engage in utility maximization, represents one framework. ① From this perspective, it is assumed that individuals are rational actors, i.e., that they make migration decisions based on their assessment of the costs as well as benefits of remaining in a given area versus the costs and benefits of leaving. ② Benefits may include but are not limited to short-term and long-term monetary gains, safety, and greater freedom of cultural expression. ③ People with greater financial benefits tend to use their money to show off their social status by purchasing luxurious items. ④ Individual costs include but are not limited to the expense of travel, uncertainty of living in a foreign land, difficulty of adapting to a different language, uncertainty about a different culture, and the great concern about living in a new land. ⑤ Psychic costs associated with separation from family, friends, and the fear of the unknown also should be taken into account in cost-benefit assessments.

*psychic: 심적인

정답과 해설 p.66

01　A variety of theoretical perspectives / provide insight into immigration. // Economics, 주어(선행사) / (which assumes that actors engage in utility maximization), / represents one 삽입절(주어 보충 설명) 동사(단수) framework.

02　From this perspective, / it is assumed / [that individuals are rational actors], / i.e., 가주어-진주어 구문 [that they make migration decisions / based on their assessment of the costs as well as benefits of remaining in a given area / versus the costs and benefits of leaving]. 전치사 of의 목적어 // Benefits may include but are not limited to / short-term and long-term monetary 동사구(A but B) gains, safety, and greater freedom of cultural expression. 목적어(A, B, and C)

03　People with greater financial benefits / tend to use their money / to show off their 주어 　전치사구 동사구(복수) 부사적 용법(목적) social status / by purchasing luxurious items. 「by + 동명사: ~함으로써」

04　Individual costs include but are not limited to / the expense of travel, / uncertainty of 목적어1 목적어2 living in a foreign land, / difficulty of adapting to a different language, / uncertainty 목적어3 목적어4 about a different culture, / and the great concern about living in a new land. // Psychic 목적어5 costs associated with separation from family, friends, / and the fear of the unknown / 　과거분사 주어(A and B) also should be taken into account in cost-benefit assessments. 구동사 take into account의 수동태

01　다양한 이론적theoretical 관점은 / 이주immigration에 대한 통찰을 제공한다. // 경제학은 / 행위자들이 효용 극대화utility maximization에 참여한다고 상정하는 / 하나의 틀을 제시한다represent.

02　이런 관점에서는 / 추정된다 / 개인은 합리적인rational 행위자라고 / 즉 그들은 이주 결정을 내린다고 / 특정한 지역에 남는 것의 편익뿐 아니라 비용에 대한 자신의 평가assessment에 근거하여 / 떠나는 것의 비용과 편익에 대비하여. / 편익은 포함할 수도 있지만 ~에 국한되지는 않는다 / 단기적 및 장기적인 금전적monetary 이득, 안전, 문화적 표현의 더 큰 자유에.

03　(더 큰 금전적 혜택이 있는 사람들은 / 돈을 쓰는 경향이 있다 / 자신의 사회적 지위를 과시하기 위해show off their social status / 사치품luxurious item을 구입함으로써.)

04　개인적 비용은 포함하지만 ~에 국한되지는 않는다 / 이동 비용expense / 타지에서 사는 것의 불확실성uncertainty, / 다른 언어에 적응하는 것의 어려움, / 다른 문화에 대한 불확실성, / 그리고 새로운 지역에서 사는 것에 대한 큰 염려. // 가족, 친구와의 이별separation과 관련된 심리적 비용 / 그리고 미지의unknown 것에 대한 두려움도 / 비용-편익 평가에서 또한 고려되어야 한다.

구문 Check up

① Economics, that / which assumes that actors engage in utility maximization, represents one framework.

콤마 뒤에는 원칙적으로 관계대명사 that을 쓸 수 없으므로 which가 보다 적절하다.

② Psychic costs associate / associated with separation from family, friends, and the fear of the unknown also should be taken into account.

주어 Psychic costs와 동사 should be taken 사이의 수식어구 자리이므로 과거분사 associated가 적절하다.

74

STEP 1 • 수능에 진짜 나오는 단어

✔ 문제에 나오는 단어들을 확인하세요.

01	kinship	n. 친족	(✔ kinship) ties	친족 유대 관계
02	get-together	n. 모임	family ( )s	가족 모임
03	refer to A as B	A를 B라고 언급하다	( ) ( ) her ( ) my partner	그녀를 내 파트너라고 언급하다
04	extended family	확대가족	the modified ( ) ( )	수정확대가족
05	multigenerational	a. 다세대의	( ) ties	다세대의 유대 관계
06	rest on	~에 기초를 두다	( ) ( ) co-residence	공동 거주에 기초를 두다
07	corporate	a. 공동의	act as ( ) groups	공동 집단으로서 기능하다
08	geographical	a. 지리적인	require ( ) proximity	지리적 근접을 필요로 하다
09	considerable	a. 상당한	( ) distances	상당한 거리
10	occupational	a. 직업상의	( ) advancement	직업상의 발전

✛ 본문 문장 속에서 단어들을 확인해 보세요.

It is an extended family structure / because multigenerational ties are maintained, / but it is modified / because it does not usually rest on co-residence between the generations / and most extended families do not act as corporate groups.

그것은 확대가족 구조이지만, / 다세대의 유대 관계가 유지되기 때문에 / 그것은 수정되었다 / 일반적으로 그것이 세대 간의 공동 거주에 기초를 두지 않고 / 대부분의 확대가족이 공동 집단으로서 기능하지는 않기 때문에.

문제를 풀기 전에 단어들을 30초 동안 다시 확인하세요.

01	kinship	🖊 친족	kinship ties	(친족) 유대 관계
02	get-together		family get-togethers	가족 ( )
03	refer to A as B		refer to her as my partner	그녀를 내 파트너라고 ( )
04	extended family		the modified extended family	수정( )
05	multigenerational		multigenerational ties	( ) 유대 관계
06	rest on		rest on co-residence	공동 거주에 ( )
07	corporate		act as corporate groups	( ) 집단으로서 기능하다
08	geographical		require geographical proximity	( ) 근접을 필요로 하다
09	considerable		considerable distances	( ) 거리
10	occupational		occupational advancement	( ) 발전

➕ 본문 문장 속에서 단어의 의미를 우리말로 해석해 보세요.

It is an extended family structure / because multigenerational ties are maintained, / but it is modified / because it does not usually rest on co-residence between the generations / and most extended families do not act as corporate groups.

→ 그것은 확대가족 구조이지만, / ▓▓▓▓▓▓▓▓▓▓▓▓▓▓▓▓▓▓▓▓▓ 때문에 / 그것은 수정되었다 / 일반적으로 그것이 세대 간의 ▓▓▓▓▓▓▓▓ ▓▓▓▓▓▓▓▓ 않고 / 대부분의 확대가족이 ▓▓▓▓▓▓▓▓▓▓▓▓▓▓▓ 않기 때문에.

74 다음 글에서 전체 흐름과 관계 <u>없는</u> 문장은?

Kinship ties continue to be important today. In modern societies such as the United States people frequently have family get-togethers, they telephone their relatives regularly, and they provide their kin with a wide variety of services. ① Eugene Litwak has referred to this pattern of behaviour as the 'modified extended family'. ② It is an extended family structure because multigenerational ties are maintained, but it is modified because it does not usually rest on co-residence between the generations and most extended families do not act as corporate groups. ③ Although modified extended family members often live close by, the modified extended family does not require geographical proximity and ties are maintained even when kin are separated by considerable distances. ④ The oldest member of the family makes the decisions on important issues, no matter how far away family members live from each other. ⑤ In contrast to the traditional extended family where kin always live in close proximity, the members of modified extended families may freely move away from kin to seek opportunities for occupational advancement.

*kin: 친족   **proximity: 근접

정답과 해설 p.67

01 Kinship ties continue to be important today. // In modern societies / such as the United States / [people frequently have family get-togethers], / they telephone their
선행사
관계부사절(where 생략)   주어1 동사1
relatives regularly, / and they provide their kin with a wide variety of services.
주어2 동사2

02 Eugene Litwak has referred to this pattern of behaviour / as the 'modified extended
「refer to A as B: A를 B라고 언급하다」
family'. // It is an extended family structure / because multigenerational ties are maintained, / but it is modified / because it does not usually rest on co-residence between the generations / and most extended families do not act as corporate groups.

03 Although modified extended family members often live close by, / the modified
접속사(비록 ~일지라도)   주어1
extended family does not require geographical proximity / and ties are maintained /
동사1   주어2 동사2
even when kin are separated by considerable distances.
접속사(심지어 ~할 때)

04 The oldest member of the family / makes the decisions on important issues, /
no matter how far away family members live from each other.
「no matter how + 형/부 + 주어 + 동사: 아무리 ~할지라도」

05 In contrast to the traditional extended family / [where kin always live in close
선행사   관계부사절
proximity], / the members of modified extended families / may freely move away from
주어   동사
kin / to seek opportunities for occupational advancement.
부사적 용법(목적)

01 친족kinship 유대 관계는 오늘날에도 계속 중요하다. // 현대 사회에서 / 미국과 같은 / 사람들이 자주 가족 모임family get-together을 갖는 / 그들은 친척에게 자주 전화하고, / 친척에게 아주 다양한 도움을 제공한다.

02 Eugene Litwak은 이 행동 패턴을 언급했다refer to this pattern of behaviour / '수정확대가족'이라고as the 'modified extended family'. // 그것은 확대가족 구조이지만, / 다세대의multigenerational 유대 관계가 유지되기 때문에 / 그것은 수정되었다 / 일반적으로 그것이 세대 간 공동 거주에 기초를 두지rest on co-residence 않고 / 대부분의 확대가족이 공동corporate 집단으로서 기능하지는 않기 때문에.

03 비록 수정확대가족의 구성원들이 흔히 가까이 살기는 하지만, / 수정확대가족은 지리적geographical 근접이 필요치 않으며, / 유대 관계는 유지된다 / 심지어 친척이 상당한considerable 거리로 떨어져 있더라도.

04 (가족의 최고 연장자가 / 중요한 문제에 관해서 결정을 내린다 / 가족 구성원들이 서로 아무리 멀리 떨어져 살지라도.)

05 전통적인 확대가족과는 대조적으로 / 친척이 항상 아주 가까이서 사는 / 수정확대가족의 구성원들은 / 친척에게서 자유로이 멀리 이주할 수도 있다 / 직업상의occupational 발전을 위한 기회를 추구하기 위해.

구문 Check up

① The oldest member of the family makes the decisions on important issues, no matter what / how far away family members live from each other.

「no matter how + 형/부 + 주어 + 동사(아무리 ~하더라도)」 구문이므로 how가 적절하다.

② In contrast to the traditional extended family which / where kin always live in close proximity, the members of modified extended families may freely move away from kin.

kin always live in close proximity가 완전한 1형식 문장이므로 관계부사 where가 적절하다.

정답 ① how ② where

310

75 STEP 1 · 수능에 *진짜* 나오는 *단어*

✔ **문제에 나오는 단어들을 확인하세요.**

01	commercialize	v. 상업화하다	in a (✔ commercialize)d society	상업화된 사회에서
02	landscape	n. 경관, 풍경	the beautiful ( )	아름다운 경관
03	commodity	n. 상품	see landscapes as ( )ies	경관을 상품으로 여기다
04	identity	n. 정체성	develop an ( )	정체성을 발전시키다
05	generate	v. 창출하다, 만들어내다	( ) income	소득을 창출하다
06	conversion	n. 전환	the ( ) of waste into fuels	쓰레기를 연료로 전환하는 것
07	take on	(색이나 형태를) 띠다	( ) ( ) the form of a commodity	상품의 형태를 띠다
08	wilderness	n. 황무지	areas of ( )	황무지 지역
09	mountainous	a. 산악의, 산이 많은	( ) regions	산악 지대
10	evolve	v. 발전하다, 진화하다	( ) into a complex creature	복잡한 생명체로 진화하다

⊕ **본문 문장 속에서 단어들을 확인해 보세요.**

The landscape itself, / including the people and their sense of self, / takes on the form of a commodity.

경관 자체가 / 사람들과 그들의 자아의식을 포함하여 / 상품의 형태를 띤다.

01	commercialize	상업화하다	in a commercialized society	(상업화된) 사회에서
02	landscape		the beautiful landscape	아름다운 ( )
03	commodity		see landscapes as commodities	경관을 ( )으로 여기다
04	identity		develop an identity	( )을 발전시키다
05	generate		generate income	소득을 ( )
06	conversion		the conversion of waste into fuels	쓰레기를 연료로 ( )하는 것
07	take on		take on the form of a commodity	상품의 형태를 ( )
08	wilderness		areas of wilderness	( ) 지역
09	mountainous		mountainous regions	( ) 지대
10	evolve		evolve into a complex creature	복잡한 생명체로 ( )

➕ 본문 문장 속에서 단어의 의미를 우리말로 해석해 보세요.

The landscape itself, / including the people and their sense of self, / takes on the form of a commodity.

➔ ⬛⬛⬛⬛⬛⬛⬛ 가 / 사람들과 그들의 자아의식을 포함하여 / ⬛⬛⬛⬛⬛⬛⬛⬛⬛⬛⬛.

75

다음 글에서 전체 흐름과 관계 <u>없는</u> 문장은?

In a highly commercialized setting such as the United States, it is not surprising that many landscapes are seen as commodities. In other words, they are valued because of their market potential. Residents develop an identity in part based on how the landscape can generate income for the community. ① This process involves more than the conversion of the natural elements into commodities. ② The landscape itself, including the people and their sense of self, takes on the form of a commodity. ③ Landscape protection in the US traditionally focuses on protecting areas of wilderness, typically in mountainous regions. ④ Over time, the landscape identity can evolve into a sort of "logo" that can be used to sell the stories of the landscape. ⑤ Thus, California's "Wine Country," Florida's "Sun Coast," or South Dakota's "Badlands" shape how both outsiders and residents perceive a place, and these labels build a set of expectations associated with the culture of those who live there.

정답과 해설 **p.68**

01 In a highly commercialized setting / such as the United States, / it is not surprising /
가주어-진주어 구문
[that many landscapes are seen as commodities]. // In other words, / they are valued
because of their market potential.
전치사(~ 때문에)

02 Residents develop an identity / in part based on [how the landscape can generate
분사구문   간접의문문   전치사구
income for the community]. // This process involves / more than the conversion of the
동사   목적어
natural elements into commodities. // The landscape itself, / (including the people and
재귀대명사(주어 강조)
their sense of self), / takes on the form of a commodity.
삽입구

03 Landscape protection in the US / traditionally focuses on protecting areas of
주어   동사(단수)   목적어(동명사)
wilderness, / typically in mountainous regions.

04 Over time, / the landscape identity can evolve into a sort of "logo" / [that can be used /
선행사   주격 관계대명사절
to sell the stories of the landscape].
부사적 용법(목적)

05 Thus, / California's "Wine Country," Florida's "Sun Coast," or South Dakota's
주어1(A, B, or C)
"Badlands" / shape [how both outsiders and residents perceive a place], / and these
동사1   목적어1(간접의문문)   주어2
labels build a set of expectations / associated with the culture of those / [who live
동사2 목적어2   과거분사구   주격 관계대명사절
there].

01 고도로 상업화commercialize된 환경에서는 / 미국처럼 / 놀랍지 않다 / 많은 경관landscape이 상품commodity으로
    여겨지는 것이. // 다시 말해 / 경관은 그것들의 시장 잠재력 때문에 가치 있게 여겨진다.

02 주민들은 정체성identity을 발전시킨다 / 경관이 지역 사회를 위해 어떻게 소득을 창출할generate 수 있는지에
    부분적으로 기초하여. // 이 과정은 포함한다 / 자연의 요소를 상품으로 전환conversion하는 것 그 이상이. // 경관 자체가
    / 사람들과 그들의 자아의식을 포함하여 / 상품의 형태를 띤다take on the form of a commodity.

03 (미국에서 경관 보호는 / 전통적으로 황무지wilderness 지역을 보호하는 데 초점을 두고 있다 / 일반적으로
    산악지대mountainous region에 있는.)

04 시간이 흐르면서 / 경관 정체성은 일종의 '로고'로 발전할evolve 수 있다 / 사용될 수 있는 / 경관에 대한 이야기를
    판매하기 위해.

05 따라서 / California의 'Wine Country', Florida의 'Sun Coast', 혹은 South Dakota의 'Badlands'는 / 외지인과 거주자가
    모두 장소를 인식하는 방식을 형성하며, / 이런 호칭들은 일련의 기대치를 형성한다 / 사람들의 문화와 관련된 / 그곳에
    사는.

구문 Check up	① The landscape itself, including the people and their sense of self, take / takes on the form of a commodity.	② Over time, the landscape identity can evolve into a sort of "logo" that can be used to sell / selling the stories of the landscape.
	주어가 단수명사인 The landscape이므로 takes가 적절하다.	a sort of "logo"가 '~하기 위해 사용될' 수 있는 대상이므로, 「be used to + 동사원형(~하기 위해 사용되다)」 구문을 완성하는 sell이 적절하다.

76

STEP 1 • 수능에 *진짜* 나오는 *단어*

✔ 문제에 나오는 단어들을 확인하세요.

01	commonsense	a. 상식적인	(✔ commonsense) knowledge	상식적 지식
02	merit	n. 장점, 이득	have ( )	장점이 있다
03	contradict	v. ~와 모순되다	( ) oneself	스스로 모순되다
04	feather	n. 깃털	birds of a ( )	같은 깃털의 새들
05	flock	v. 모이다	( ) together	함께 모이다
06	dissimilar	a. 닮지 않은, 비슷하지 않은	persons who are ( )	닮지 않은 사람들
07	inevitably	ad. 필연적으로, 불가피하게	( ) produce poor results	필연적으로 좋지 않은 결과를 만들다
08	broth	n. 국, (걸쭉한) 수프	spoil the ( )	국을 망치다
09	statement	n. 말, 진술	a clear ( )	명확한 진술
10	heavily	ad. 매우, 몹시	( ) depend on what others say	남들이 하는 말에 매우 의존하다
11	venture	v. 모험하다, 도전하다	( ) a voyage	항해에 도전하다

⊕ 본문 문장 속에서 단어들을 확인해 보세요.

Although commonsense knowledge may have merit, / it also has weaknesses, / not the least of which is that it often contradicts itself.

상식적 지식에 장점이 있을 수도 있지만, / 그것에는 약점도 있는데, / 그중 중요한 것은 그것이 흔히 모순된다는 것이다.

01	commonsense	✎ 상식적인	commonsense knowledge	(상식적)지식
02	merit		have merit	( )이 있다
03	contradict		contradict oneself	스스로 ( )
04	feather		birds of a feather	같은 ( )의 새들
05	flock		flock together	함께 ( )
06	dissimilar		persons who are dissimilar	( )사람들
07	inevitably		inevitably produce poor results	( ) 좋지 않은 결과를 만들다
08	broth		spoil the broth	( )을 망치다
09	statement		a clear statement	명확한 ( )
10	heavily		heavily depend on what others say	남들이 하는 말에 ( ) 의존하다
11	venture		venture a voyage	항해에 ( )

➕ **본문 문장 속에서 단어의 의미를 우리말로 해석해 보세요.**

Although commonsense knowledge may have merit, / it also has weaknesses, / not the least of which is that it often contradicts itself.

➡   에   수도 있지만, / 그것에는 약점도 있는데, / 그중 중요한 것은   는 것이다.

76 다음 글에서 전체 흐름과 관계 <u>없는</u> 문장은?

Although commonsense knowledge may have merit, it also has weaknesses, not the least of which is that it often contradicts itself. For example, we hear that people who are similar will like one another ("Birds of a feather flock together") but also that persons who are dissimilar will like each other ("Opposites attract"). ① We are told that groups are wiser and smarter than individuals ("Two heads are better than one") but also that group work inevitably produces poor results ("Too many cooks spoil the broth"). ② Each of these contradictory statements may hold true under particular conditions, but without a clear statement of when they apply and when they do not, aphorisms provide little insight into relations among people. ③ That is why we heavily depend on aphorisms whenever we face difficulties and challenges in the long journey of our lives. ④ They provide even less guidance in situations where we must make decisions. ⑤ For example, when facing a choice that entails risk, which guideline should we use — "Nothing ventured, nothing gained" or "Better safe than sorry"?

*aphorism: 격언, 경구(警句) **entail: 수반하다

정답과 해설 **p.69**

01 Although commonsense knowledge may have merit, / it also has weaknesses, / not the
접속사(비록 ~이지만)　　　　　　　　　　　　　　　　선행사　　　　계속적 용법
least of which is that it often contradicts itself.　　　　　　　　　　　　　　(그중 중요한 것은)

02 For example, / we hear / that people who are similar will like one another / ("Birds
　　　　　　　　　　　接속사 that 병렬(hear의 목적절)
of a feather flock together") / but also that persons who are dissimilar will like each
other / ("Opposites attract"). // We are told / that groups are wiser and smarter than
　　　　　　　　　　　　　　4형식 tell의 수동태　　　　　接속사 that 병렬(are told의 목적절)
individuals / ("Two heads are better than one") / but also that group work inevitably
produces poor results / ("Too many cooks spoil the broth").

03 Each of these contradictory statements / may hold true under particular conditions, /
주어1(each of + 복수명사: 각각의 ~)　　　　　　　　동사1　　　주격보어
but without a clear statement / of when they apply and when they do not, / aphorisms
　　　　　　　　　　　　　　　　　　　　　　　　　　　　　　　　　　주어2
provide little insight into relations among people.
동사2

04 That is why we heavily depend on aphorisms / whenever we face difficulties and
「that[this] is why + 주어 + 동사: 이것이 ~한 이유이다」　　복합관계부사(~할 때마다)
challenges / in the long journey of our lives.

05 They provide even less guidance in situations / [where we must make decisions]. // For
　　　　接속사가 있는 분사구문(= when we face ~)　　関係부사절
example, / when facing a choice [that entails risk], / which guideline should we use / —
　　　　　　　　　　　　　　　주격 관계대명사절　　의문사(어떤)
"Nothing ventured, nothing gained" or "Better safe than sorry"?

01 상식적 지식commonsense knowledge에 장점merit이 있을 수도 있지만, / 그것에는 약점도 있는데, / 그중 중요한 것은
그것이 흔히 모순된다contradict는 것이다.

02 예를 들어, / 우리는 듣지만 / 비슷한 사람들이 서로 좋아하기 마련이라는 말을 / ('같은 깃털feather의 새가 함께
모인다flock: 유유상종') / 닮지 않은dissimilar 사람들이 서로 좋아하기 마련이라는 말도 듣는다 / ('정반대되는 사람들은
서로에게 끌린다'). // 우리는 듣지만 / 집단이 개인보다 더 현명하고 더 똑똑하다는 말을 / ('머리 둘이 하나보다 낫다:
백지장도 맞들면 낫다') / 집단 작업이 필연적으로inevitably 좋지 않은 결과를 만든다는 말도 듣는다 / ('요리사가 많으면
국broth을 망친다: 사공이 많으면 배가 산으로 간다').

03 이런 모순된 말들 각각은 / 특정한 상황에서는 사실일 수도 있지만, / 명확한 진술statement이 없으면 / 그것이 언제
적용되는지와 언제 적용되지 않는지에 관한 / 격언은 사람들 사이의 관계에 대한 통찰력을 거의 제공하지 못한다.

04 (그것이 우리가 격언에 매우heavily 의존하는 이유이다 / 우리가 어려움과 도전에 직면할 때마다 / 삶의 긴 여정에서.)

05 그것들은 그야말로 거의 아무런 지침도 제공하지 못한다 / 우리가 결정을 내려야 하는 상황에서는. // 예를 들어, / 위험을
수반하는 선택에 직면할 때 / 우리는 어느 지침을 이용해야 하는가 / '모험하지venture 않으면 아무것도 얻을 수 없다'
또는 '나중에 후회하는 것보다 조심하는 것이 낫다' 중에?

구문 Check up

① Although commonsense knowledge may have merit, it also has weaknesses, not the least of them / which is that it often contradicts itself.

weaknesses를 대신하는 동시에 콤마 앞뒤로 절을 연결해야 하므로, 접속사이자 대명사인 which가 적절하다.

② That is why we heavily depend on aphorisms however / whenever we face difficulties and challenges in the long journey of our lives.

문맥상 '~할 때마다'라는 의미의 whenever가 적절하다. however(아무리 ~하더라도)는 주로 「however + 형/부 + 주어 + 동사」로 쓴다.

정답 ① which ② whenever

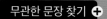
STEP 1 • 수능에 *진짜* 나오는 *단어*

✔ **문제에 나오는 단어들을 확인하세요.**

01	automatic	*a.* 자동적인	(✔ automatic) behavior	자동적인 행동
02	awareness	*n.* 인식, 의식	conscious ( )	의식적인 인식
03	relieve	*v.* (고통이나 부담을) 덜어주다	( ) our minds from stress	우리 마음의 스트레스를 덜어주다
04	come up	발생하다, 생기다	as new problems ( ) ( )	새로운 문제가 발생할 때
05	conversation	*n.* 대화	focus on a ( )	대화에 집중하다
06	disaster	*n.* 엉망진창, 재앙	a total ( )	완전한 엉망진창
07	attract	*v.* 끌다, 매혹하다	( ) a more diverse audience	더 다양한 청중을 끌다
08	varying	*a.* 다양한, (연속적으로) 바뀌는	( ) backgrounds	다양한 배경
09	accomplish	*v.* 성취하다	( ) the goal	목표를 성취하다

➕ **본문 문장 속에서 단어들을 확인해 보세요.**

We need to relieve our conscious minds / so we can solve new problems / as they come up.

우리는 의식적인 마음의 부담을 덜어주어야 한다 / 우리가 새로운 문제를 해결할 수 있도록 / 그것이 발생할 때.

문제를 풀기 전에 단어들을 30초 동안 다시 확인하세요.

01	automatic	🖉 자동적인	automatic behavior	(자동적인) 행동
02	awareness		conscious awareness	의식적인 ( )
03	relieve		relieve our minds from stress	우리 마음의 스트레스를 ( )
04	come up		as new problems come up	새로운 문제가 ( ) 때
05	conversation		focus on a conversation	( )에 집중하다
06	disaster		a total disaster	완전한 ( )
07	attract		attract a more diverse audience	더 다양한 청중을 ( )
08	varying		varying backgrounds	( ) 배경
09	accomplish		accomplish the goal	목표를 ( )

➕ 본문 문장 속에서 단어의 의미를 우리말로 해석해 보세요.

We need to relieve our conscious minds / so we can solve new problems / as they come up.

➙ 우리는 _____ 한다 / 우리가 새로운 문제를 해결할 수 있도록 / 그것이 _____ 때.

77 다음 글에서 전체 흐름과 관계 <u>없는</u> 문장은?

Much of what we do each day is automatic and guided by habit, requiring little conscious awareness, and that's not a bad thing. As Duhigg explains, our habits are necessary mental energy savers. ① We need to relieve our conscious minds so we can solve new problems as they come up. ② Once we've solved the puzzle of how to ballroom dance, for example, we can do it by habit, and so be mentally freed to focus on a conversation while dancing instead. ③ But try to talk when first learning to dance the tango, and it's a disaster — we need our conscious attention to focus on the steps. ④ Tango musicians bring different genres of music together to attract a more diverse audience from varying backgrounds. ⑤ Imagine how little we'd accomplish if we had to focus consciously on every behavior — e.g., on where to place our feet for each step we take.

정답과 해설 p.70

01 Much of what we do each day / is automatic and guided by habit, / requiring little
주어(부분 + of + 전체: 전체에 수 일치)　　　　　동사(단수)　　　　　　　　　분사구문
conscious awareness, / and that's not a bad thing. // As Duhigg explains, / our habits
　　　　　　　　　　　　　　　　　　　　　　접속사(~듯이, ~대로)
are necessary mental energy savers.

02 We need to relieve our conscious minds / so (that) we can solve new problems / as
　　　　　　　　　　　　　　　　　　　접속사(~하도록)　　　　　　　　접속사(~할 때)
they come up.

03 Once we've solved the puzzle of how to ballroom dance, / for example, / we can do it by
접속사(일단 ~하면)　can　　　　　「how + to부정사: ~하는 방법」
habit, / and so be mentally freed to focus on a conversation / while dancing instead. //
　　　　　　　　　　　　　　　　　　　　　　　　　접속사가 있는 분사구문(= while we dance)
But try to talk / when first learning to dance the tango, / and it's a disaster / — we need
　　「명령문 ~ and …: ~하라, 그러면 …」
our conscious attention / to focus on the steps.
　　　　　　　　　부사적 용법(목적)

04 Tango musicians bring different genres of music together / to attract a more diverse
　　　　　　　　　　　　　　　　　　　　　　　　　　　부사적 용법(목적)
audience / from varying backgrounds.

05 Imagine how little we'd accomplish / if we had to focus consciously on every behavior
　　　　　「주어 + 조동사 과거형 + 동사원형 ~ if + 주어 + 과거 동사: 가정법 과거」
/ — e.g., on where to place our feet / for each step [we take].
　　　　　　　　　　　　　　　　　　　　목적격 관계대명사절

01 우리가 매일 하는 일의 많은 부분은 / 자동적이고automatic 습관에 의해 좌우되며, / 의식적인 인식awareness을 거의
필요로 하지 않는데, / 그것은 나쁜 것이 아니다. // Duhigg가 설명하듯이, / 우리의 습관은 꼭 필요한 정신 에너지 절약
장치이다.

02 우리는 의식적인 마음의 부담을 덜어주어야relieve 한다 / 우리가 새로운 문제를 해결할 수 있도록 / 그것이 발생할come
up 때.

03 우리가 사교댄스를 추는 방법에 대한 문제를 해결하고 나면, / 예를 들어, / 우리는 그것을 습관적으로 할 수 있어서 /
정신적으로 자유로워져 대화conversation에 집중할 수 있다 / 춤을 추는 동안 그 대신. // 하지만 말을 하려고 해보라 /
탱고를 처음 배울 때 / 그러면 그것은 엉망진창disaster이 된다 / 우리는 의식적인 주의가 필요하다 / 스텝에 집중하려면.

04 (탱고 음악가는 각기 다른 장르의 음악을 한데 모은다 / 더 다양한 청중을 끌어모으기attract 위해 / 다양한varying
배경의.)

05 우리가 성취할accomplish 수 있는 것이 얼마나 적을지 상상해 보라 / 만약 우리가 모든 행동에 의식적으로 초점을
맞추어야 한다면 / 예를 들어 발을 어디에 두어야 할지에 / 우리가 딛는 모든 스텝에서.

구문 Check up

① Much of what we do each day is / are automatic and
guided by habit, requiring little conscious awareness,
and that's not a bad thing.

주어가 「부분 + of + 전체」 형태이면 동사는 전체 표현에 수일치한다. 여기
서는 전체에 해당하는 말이 절이므로 단수동사 is가 적절하다.

② Imagine how little we'd accomplish if we had / had
had to focus consciously on every behavior — e.g., on
where to place our feet for each step we take.

how 간접의문문의 동사 would(='d) accomplish가 「조동사 과거형 + 동사
원형」의 형태이므로, 가정법 과거 구문임을 알 수 있다. 따라서 if절 동사
로는 과거시제인 had가 적절하다.

정답 ① is ② had

DAY 12
78 STEP 1 • 수능에 진짜 나오는 단어

✔ 문제에 나오는 단어들을 확인하세요.

01	blush	v. 얼굴이 붉어지다	see (✔ blush)ing as uniquely human	얼굴이 붉어지는 것을 특별나게 인간적인 것으로 보다
02	involuntary	a. 무의식적인, 자기도 모르게 하는	an ( ) physical reaction	무의식적인 신체 반응
03	embarrassment	n. 당혹(감)	a feeling of ( )	당혹감
04	self-consciousness	n. 자의식, 남을 의식함	excessive ( )	과도한 자의식
05	loss of face	체면 손상	our brief ( ) ( ) ( )	잠깐 일어나는 우리의 체면 손상
06	cohesion	n. 결속, 응집성	the ( ) of a group	집단의 결속
07	awkward	a. 어색한	feel ( )	어색한 기분이 들다
08	concern	n. 우려, 걱정 v. 걱정하다	( )s about the future	미래에 대한 걱정
09	bring on	~을 초래하다	( ) ( ) a crisis	위기를 초래하다
10	as though	(마치) ~인 것처럼	feel ( ) ( ) it is real	마치 진짜인 것처럼 느끼다
11	norm	n. 규범	social ( )s	사회적 규범

✚ 본문 문장 속에서 단어들을 확인해 보세요.

Darwin saw blushing as uniquely human, / representing an involuntary physical reaction / caused by embarrassment and self-consciousness in a social environment.

다윈은 얼굴이 붉어지는 것을 특별나게 인간적인 것으로 여겨, / 사회적 환경에서 무의식적인 신체 반응을 나타낸다고 보았다 / 당혹감과 자의식에 의한.

01	blush	✏ 얼굴이 붉어지다	see blushing as uniquely human	(얼굴이 붉어지는 것)을 특별나게 인간적인 것으로 보다
02	involuntary		an involuntary physical reaction	( )신체 반응
03	embarrassment		a feeling of embarrassment	( )감
04	self-consciousness		excessive self-consciousness	과도한 ( )
05	loss of face		our brief loss of face	잠깐 일어나는 우리의 ( )
06	cohesion		the cohesion of a group	집단의 ( )
07	awkward		feel awkward	( )기분이 들다
08	concern		concerns about the future	미래에 대한 ( )
09	bring on		bring on a crisis	위기를 ( )
10	as though		feel as though it is real	( )진짜인 것처럼 느끼다
11	norm		social norms	사회적 ( )

➕ **본문 문장 속에서 단어의 의미를 우리말로 해석해 보세요.**

Darwin saw blushing as uniquely human, / representing an involuntary physical reaction / caused by embarrassment and self-consciousness in a social environment.

→ 다윈은 ▨▨▨▨▨▨▨을 특별나게 인간적인 것으로 여겨, / 사회적 환경에서 ▨▨▨▨▨▨▨▨▨을 나타낸다고 보았다 / ▨▨▨▨▨▨▨▨▨에 의한.

78 주어진 글 다음에 이어질 글의 순서로 가장 적절한 것은?

Darwin saw blushing as uniquely human, representing an involuntary physical reaction caused by embarrassment and self-consciousness in a social environment.

(A) Maybe our brief loss of face benefits the long-term cohesion of the group. Interestingly, if someone blushes after making a social mistake, they are viewed in a more favourable light than those who don't blush.

(B) If we feel awkward, embarrassed or ashamed when we are alone, we don't blush; it seems to be caused by our concern about what others are thinking of us. Studies have confirmed that simply being told you are blushing brings it on. We feel as though others can see through our skin and into our mind.

(C) However, while we sometimes want to disappear when we involuntarily go bright red, psychologists argue that blushing actually serves a positive social purpose. When we blush, it's a signal to others that we recognize that a social norm has been broken; it is an apology for a faux pas.

*faux pas: 실수

① (A) — (C) — (B) 　　　　② (B) — (A) — (C)

③ (B) — (C) — (A) 　　　　④ (C) — (A) — (B)

⑤ (C) — (B) — (A)

정답과 해설 p.71

01 Darwin saw blushing as uniquely human, / representing an involuntary physical
「see A as B: A를 B로 여기다」   = which represents ~   수식받는 명사
reaction / caused by embarrassment and self-consciousness in a social environment.
과거분사구

02 If we feel awkward, embarrassed or ashamed when we are alone, / we don't blush; / it
감각동사   주격보어(형용사구)
seems to be caused by our concern / about [what others are thinking of us]. // Studies
부정사의 수동태(to be p.p.)   명사절(about의 목적어)
have confirmed / that simply being told you are blushing brings it on. // We feel /
주어(동명사구)   동사구(단수)
as though others can see through our skin and into our mind.
접속사(마치 ~인 것처럼)

03 However, / while we sometimes want to disappear / when we involuntarily go bright
「go + 형용사: ~하게 되다(상태 변화)」
red, / psychologists argue / that blushing actually serves a positive social purpose.
// When we blush, / it's a signal to others / [that we recognize that a social norm has
대명사(그것)   동격절(= a signal)
been broken]; / it is an apology for a faux pas.
현재완료 수동태

04 Maybe our brief loss of face / benefits the long-term cohesion of the group. //
Interestingly, / if someone blushes after making a social mistake, / they are viewed in a
전치사 명사구   대명사(= someone)
more favourable light / than those [who don't blush].
~한 사람들

01 다원은 얼굴이 붉어지는blush 것을 특별나게 인간적인 것으로 여겨, / 사회적 환경에서 무의식적인involuntary 신체 반응을 나타낸다고 보았다 / 당혹감embarrassment과 자의식self-consciousness에 의한.

02 우리가 혼자 있을 때는 어색하거나awkward 부끄럽거나 창피하다고 느끼더라도 / 얼굴이 붉어지지 않는다. / 이것은 우리의 염려concern 때문인 듯하다 / 우리가 다른 사람들이 우리를 어떻게 생각할지에 대한. // 연구에서는 확인했다 / 단지 얼굴이 붉어진다는 말을 듣는 것만으로도 그것이 초래된다bring on는 것이. // 우리는 느낀다 / 다른 사람들이 우리 피부를 꿰뚫어 우리 마음을 들여다볼 수 있는 것처럼as though.

03 하지만, / 우리가 때로 사라지고 싶어 하기는 해도 / 우리가 자신도 모르는 사이에 얼굴이 새빨개질 때, / 심리학자들은 주장한다 / 얼굴이 붉어지는 것이 실제로는 긍정적인 사회적 목적에 부합한다고. // 우리가 얼굴이 붉어질 때, / 이것은 다른 사람에게 알리는 신호다 / 우리가 사회적 규범social norm이 깨졌음을 인정한다는 / 그것은 실수에 대한 사과이다.

04 아마도 잠깐 일어나는 우리의 체면 손상loss of face은 / 집단의 장기적인 결속cohesion에는 도움이 된다. // 흥미롭게도 / 누군가가 사회적 실수를 저지른 후 얼굴을 붉히면, / 그 사람은 더 호의적인 시각으로 여겨지게 된다 / 얼굴을 붉히지 않는 사람보다.

구문 Check up

① Darwin saw blushing as uniquely human, representing / represented an involuntary physical reaction caused by embarrassment and self-consciousness in a social environment.

콤마 앞이 완전한 문장이고, 콤마 뒤가 blushing을 보충하는 분사구문이므로 representing이 적절하다.

② Studies have confirmed that simply being told you are blushing brings / bringing it on.

that절의 동명사구 주어 'simply being told ~' 뒤로 동사가 필요하므로 단수동사 brings가 적절하다.

정답 ① representing ② brings

79 STEP 1 • 수능에 *진짜* 나오는 *단어*

✔ 문제에 나오는 단어들을 확인하세요.

01	pricing	*n.* 가격 책정	competitive (✔ pricing)	경쟁력 있는 가격 책정
02	outcome	*n.* 결과	an ( ) in the client's favor	고객에게 유리한 결과
03	compensate	*v.* 보수를 지불하다, 보상하다	( ) for hard work	노고에 보상하다
04	in part	부분적으로	( ) ( ) because they are afraid of failure	부분적으로는 그들이 실패를 두려워하기 때문에
05	unfamiliar	*a.* 익숙지 않은	( ) with law firms	법률 사무소에 익숙지 않은
06	fee	*n.* 요금, 수수료	high ( )s for a case	소송에 대한 높은 수수료
07	settle	*v.* 해결하다, 합의하다	take years to ( )	해결하는 데 몇 년이 걸리다
08	bill	*v.* (비용을) 청구하다	the way the case is ( )ed	그 사건의 비용이 청구되는 방식

➕ 본문 문장 속에서 단어들을 확인해 보세요.

Their biggest fears are high fees for a case / that may take years to settle.

그들의 가장 큰 두려움은 소송에 대한 높은 수수료**이다** / 해결하는 데 몇 년이 걸릴**지도 모르는.**

문제를 풀기 전에 단어들을 30초 동안 다시 확인하세요.

01	pricing	🖉 가격 책정	competitive pricing	경쟁력 있는 (가격 책정)
02	outcome		an outcome in the client's favor	고객에게 유리한 ( )
03	compensate		compensate for hard work	노고에 ( )
04	in part		in part because they are afraid of failure	( )는 그들이 실패를 두려워하기 때문에
05	unfamiliar		unfamiliar with law firms	법률 사무소에 ( )
06	fee		high fees for a case	소송에 대한 높은 ( )
07	settle		take years to settle	( ) 데 몇 년이 걸리다
08	bill		the way the case is billed	그 사건의 비용이 ( ) 방식

⊕ **본문 문장 속에서 단어의 의미를 우리말로 해석해 보세요.**

Their biggest fears are high fees for a case / that may take years to settle.

➜ 그들의 가장 큰 두려움은 ＿＿＿＿＿＿＿＿＿＿＿＿＿ 이다 / ＿＿＿＿＿＿＿＿＿＿＿＿＿ 지도 모르는.

79 주어진 글 다음에 이어질 글의 순서로 가장 적절한 것은?

The most commonly known form of results-based pricing is a practice called *contingency pricing,* used by lawyers.

(A) Therefore, only an outcome in the client's favor is compensated. From the client's point of view, the pricing makes sense in part because most clients in these cases are unfamiliar with and possibly intimidated by law firms. Their biggest fears are high fees for a case that may take years to settle.

(B) By using contingency pricing, clients are ensured that they pay no fees until they receive a settlement. In these and other instances of contingency pricing, the economic value of the service is hard to determine before the service, and providers develop a price that allows them to share the risks and rewards of delivering value to the buyer.

(C) Contingency pricing is the major way that personal injury and certain consumer cases are billed. In this approach, lawyers do not receive fees or payment until the case is settled, when they are paid a percentage of the money that the client receives.

*intimidate: 위협하다

① (A) — (C) — (B) 　　② (B) — (A) — (C)

③ (B) — (C) — (A) 　　④ (C) — (A) — (B)

⑤ (C) — (B) — (A)

정답과 해설 p.71

01 The most commonly known form of results-based pricing / is a practice / called
「the + 최상급(가장 ~한)」　　　　　　　　　　　주격보어　　과거분사구
contingency pricing, / used by lawyers.

02 Contingency pricing is the major way / [that personal injury and certain consumer
선행사(방법)　　　관계부사 역할
cases are billed]. // In this approach, / lawyers do not receive fees or payment / until
선행사
the case is settled, / when they are paid a percentage of the money / [that the client
동사(4형식 수동태)　　　목적어　　　　　목적격 관계대명사절
receives].

03 Therefore, / only an outcome in the client's favor / is compensated. // From the client's
point of view, / the pricing makes sense / in part because most clients in these cases
부분적으로 ~하기 때문에
/ are unfamiliar with and possibly intimidated by law firms. // Their biggest fears are
「take + 시간 + to부정사: ~하는 데 (시간)이 걸리다」
high fees for a case / [that may take years to settle].
선행사　　　주격 관계대명사절

04 By using contingency pricing, / clients are ensured / that they pay no fees until they
「by + 동명사: ~함으로써」
receive a settlement. // In these and other instances of contingency pricing, /
the economic value of the service / is hard to determine before the service, / and
목적어 상승 구문(= it is hard to determine the economic value of the service ~)
providers develop a price / [that allows them to share the risks and rewards of
선행사　　　주격 관계대명사절
delivering value to the buyer].

01 결과 기반 가격 책정pricing 중 가장 일반적으로 알려진 형태는 / 관행이다 / '승소 시 보수 약정'이라고 불리는 /
변호사들에 의해 이용되는.

02 승소 시 보수 약정은 주요 방식이다 / 개인 상해 및 특정 소비자 소송에 대해 비용이 청구되는bill. // 이 방식에서 /
변호사는 수수료나 지불금을 받지 않는다 / 소송이 해결될 때까지 / 그리고 이때 그들은 금액의 일정 비율을 받는다 /
의뢰인이 받는.

03 따라서 / 의뢰인에게 유리한 결과outcome만 / 보상이 이뤄진다compensate. // 의뢰인의 관점에서 보면 / 이러한 가격
책정은 타당한데, / 부분적으로in part 이러한 소송의 의뢰인 대부분이 / 법률 사무소에 익숙지 않고unfamiliar 어쩌면
겁먹을 수 있기 때문이다. // 그들의 가장 큰 두려움은 소송에 대한 높은 수수료fee이다 / 해결하는settle 데 몇 년이
걸릴지도 모르는.

04 승소 시 보수 약정을 사용함으로써 / 의뢰인은 보장받는다 / 그들이 합의금을 받을 때까지 수수료를 지불하지 않도록. //
이런 식의 승소 시 보수 약정 사례에서 / 서비스의 경제적 가치는 / 서비스 전에 결정하기 어렵고, / 공급자는 가격을
형성한다 / 그들이 구매자에게 가치를 전달하는 위험과 보상을 나눌 수 있게 하는.

구문 Check up

① The most commonly known form of results-based pricing is a practice is called / called *contingency pricing,* used by lawyers.

앞에 동사 is가 나오는 것으로 보아 주격보어 a practice를 꾸미는 수식어구 자리이다. 따라서 과거분사 called를 써야 한다.

② The economic value of the service is hard to determine / to determine it before the service.

'it is hard to determine ~'에서 to determine의 목적어를 문장의 주어로 올린 목적어 상승 구문이다. 이 경우 to determine은 목적어 없이 그대로 남는다.

정답 ① called ② to determine

80 STEP 1 • 수능에 *진짜* 나오는 *단어*

☑ 문제에 나오는 단어들을 확인하세요.

01	drive	v. 추진하다, 몰아가다	(✓ drive) providers to search for new sources	공급자가 새로운 공급원을 찾도록 추진하다
02	substitute	v. 대체하다, 대용하다	(　　　　) for the existing product	기존의 상품을 대체하다
03	conserve	v. 아껴 쓰다, 보존하다	(　　　) energy	에너지를 아껴 쓰다
04	landfill	n. 쓰레기 매립(지)	(　　　) costs	쓰레기 매립 비용
05	provision	n. 준비, 공급	the (　　　) of garbage disposal	쓰레기 처리 준비
06	dispose of	~을 처리하다, 없애다	(　　　) (　　) all waste	모든 쓰레기를 처리하다
07	result in	~을 낳다, 야기하다	(　　　) (　　) the decreased use	사용 감소를 낳다
08	raise	v. (자금을) 조성하다, 모으다	(　　　) money through the tax	세금을 통해 자금을 조성하다
09	internalize	v. (사상, 태도 등을) 내면화하다, 자기 것으로 만들다	(　　　　) capitalism	자본주의를 내면화하다

⊕ 본문 문장 속에서 단어들을 확인해 보세요.

According to the market response model, / it is increasing prices / that drive providers to search for new sources, / innovators to substitute, / consumers to conserve, / and alternatives to emerge.

시장 반응 모형에 따르면, / 바로 가격의 인상이다 / 공급자가 새로운 공급원을 찾게 추진하는 것은 / 혁신가가 대용하게, / 소비자가 아껴 쓰게 / 그리고 대안이 생기게.

문제를 풀기 전에 단어들을 **30초** 동안 다시 확인하세요.

01	drive	🖊 추진하다, 몰아가다	drive providers to search for new sources	공급자가 새로운 공급원을 찾도록 (추진하다)
02	substitute		substitute for the existing product	기존의 상품을 ( )
03	conserve		conserve energy	에너지를 ( )
04	landfill		landfill costs	( ) 비용
05	provision		the provision of garbage disposal	쓰레기 처리 ( )
06	dispose of		dispose of all waste	모든 쓰레기를 ( )
07	result in		result in the decreased use	사용 감소를 ( )
08	raise		raise money through the tax	세금을 통해 자금을 ( )
09	internalize		internalize capitalism	자본주의를 ( )

➕ **본문 문장 속에서 단어의 의미를 우리말로 해석해 보세요.**

According to the market response model, / it is increasing prices / that drive providers to search for new sources, / innovators to substitute, / consumers to conserve, / and alternatives to emerge.

➡ 시장 반응 모형에 따르면, / 바로 가격의 인상이다 / ▓▓▓▓▓▓▓▓▓▓▓▓▓▓▓▓▓▓ 것은 / ▓▓▓▓▓▓▓▓▓▓▓▓, / ▓▓▓▓▓▓▓▓▓▓▓▓▓▓ / 그리고 대안이 생기게.

80 주어진 글 다음에 이어질 글의 순서로 가장 적절한 것은?

According to the market response model, it is increasing prices that drive providers to search for new sources, innovators to substitute, consumers to conserve, and alternatives to emerge.

(A) Many examples of such "green taxes" exist. Facing landfill costs, labor expenses, and related costs in the provision of garbage disposal, for example, some cities have required households to dispose of all waste in special trash bags, purchased by consumers themselves, and often costing a dollar or more each.

(B) Taxing certain goods or services, and so increasing prices, should result in either decreased use of these resources or creative innovation of new sources or options. The money raised through the tax can be used directly by the government either to supply services or to search for alternatives.

(C) The results have been greatly increased recycling and more careful attention by consumers to packaging and waste. By internalizing the costs of trash to consumers, there has been an observed decrease in the flow of garbage from households.

① (A) — (C) — (B)   ② (B) — (A) — (C)

③ (B) — (C) — (A)   ④ (C) — (A) — (B)

⑤ (C) — (B) — (A)

정답과 해설 p.72

01 According to the market response model, / it is increasing prices / that drive providers

「it is[was] ~ that …: …한 것은 바로 ~이다[였다]」
동사 목적어1

to search for new sources, / innovators to substitute, / consumers to conserve, / and

목적격보어1   목적어2   목적격보어2   목적어3   목적격보어3

alternatives to emerge.

목적어4   목적격보어4

02 Taxing certain goods or services, / and so increasing prices, / should result in / either

주어(동명사구)   동사구

decreased use of these resources / or creative innovation of new sources or options. //

「either A or B: A와 B 둘 중 하나」

The money raised through the tax / can be used directly by the government / either

주어   과거분사구   동사(조동사 수동태)

to supply services or to search for alternatives.

부정사구(목적) 병렬

03 Many examples of such "green taxes" exist. // Facing landfill costs, labor expenses,

분사구문(= As some cities faced ~)

and related costs in the provision of garbage disposal, / for example, / some cities

주어

have required households / to dispose of all waste in special trash bags, / purchased by

동사   목적어   목적격보어

consumers themselves, / and often costing a dollar or more each.

분사구 병렬 연결

04 The results have been / greatly increased recycling / and more careful attention by

주격보어1   주격보어2(명사구 병렬)

consumers to packaging and waste. // By internalizing the costs of trash to consumers,

「by + 동명사: ~함으로써」

/ there has been an observed decrease / in the flow of garbage from households.

동사   주어   전치사구

---

01 시장 반응 모형에 따르면, / 바로 가격의 인상이다 / 공급자가 새로운 공급원을 찾게 추진하는drive 것은 / 혁신가가 대용하게substitute, / 소비자가 아껴 쓰게conserve / 그리고 대안이 생기게.

02 특정 재화나 서비스에 과세하는 것은 / 그리하여 가격을 인상하는 것은 / ~을 낳을result in 것이다 / 이러한 자원 사용의 감소나 / 새로운 공급원 또는 선택사항의 창조적 혁신을. // 세금을 통해 조성된raise 돈은 / 직접 정부에 의해 사용될 수 있다 / 서비스를 공급하거나 대안을 모색하기 위해.

03 그러한 '환경세'의 많은 예가 존재한다. // 쓰레기 매립 비용landfill costs, 인건비, 그리고 쓰레기 처리를 준비provision 하는 데 관련된 비용에 직면해서 / 예를 들어, / 일부 도시는 가정에 요구했다 / 모든 폐기물을 특별 쓰레기 봉투에 담아서 처리하도록dispose of all waste / 소비자에 의해 직접 구입되는 / 그리고 흔히 한 장당 1달러 이상의 비용이 드는.

04 그 결과는 ~였다 / 크게 증가한 재활용 / 그리고 포장과 폐기물에 대한 소비자의 더 세심한 주의. // 소비자에게 쓰레기 비용을 자기 것으로 만들게internalize 함으로써, / 관찰된 감소가 있었다 / 가정에서 나오는 쓰레기 흐름의.

구문 Check up

① It is increasing prices that / what drive providers to search for new sources, innovators to substitute, consumers to conserve, and alternatives to emerge.

명사구 increasing prices를 강조하는 「it is[was] ~ that …」 강조구문이므로 that이 적절하다.

② The money raised / was raised through the tax can be used directly by the government either to supply services or to search for alternatives.

뒤에 동사 can be used가 나오는 것으로 보아 주어를 수식하는 자리이므로 과거분사 raised가 적절하다.

81

STEP 1 • 수능에 *진짜* 나오는 *단어*

✔ **문제에 나오는 단어들을 확인하세요.**

01	spatial	a. 공간적인	(✔ spatial) reasoning	공간 추론
02	reference	n. 기준, 준거	( ) points	기준점
03	landmark	n. 랜드마크, 주요 지형지물	a list of campus ( )s	캠퍼스의 랜드마크 목록
04	paradigm	n. 전형적인 예, 모범	a ( ) for us to copy	우리가 따라야 할 전형적인 예
05	estimate	v. 추정하다 n. 추정치	( ) the distances	거리를 추정하다
06	violate	v. 위배하다, 위반하다	( ) the rule	규칙을 위반하다
07	elementary	a. 기초적인, 초급의	the most ( ) principles	가장 기초적인 원칙
08	coherent	a. 일관성이 있는	a ( ) explanation	일관성 있는 설명
09	remarkable	a. 주목할 만한	the ( ) finding	주목할 만한 결과

➕ **본문 문장 속에서 단어들을 확인해 보세요.**

In a paradigm / that has been repeated on many campuses, / researchers first collect a list of campus landmarks from students.

한 전형적인 예에서 / 많은 대학 캠퍼스에서 반복되어 온 / 연구원들은 먼저 학생들에게서 캠퍼스 랜드마크의 목록을 수집한다.

01	spatial	✏ 공간적인	spatial reasoning	(공간) 추론
02	reference		reference points	( ) 점
03	landmark		a list of campus landmarks	캠퍼스의 ( ) 목록
04	paradigm		a paradigm for us to copy	우리가 따라야 할 ( )
05	estimate		estimate the distances	거리를 ( )
06	violate		violate the rule	규칙을 ( )
07	elementary		the most elementary principles	가장 ( ) 원칙
08	coherent		a coherent explanation	( ) 설명
09	remarkable		the remarkable finding	( ) 결과

➕ **본문 문장 속에서 단어의 의미를 우리말로 해석해 보세요.**

In a paradigm / that has been repeated on many campuses, / researchers first collect a list of campus landmarks from students.

➡ _____ 에서 / 많은 대학 캠퍼스에서 반복되어 온 / 연구원들은 먼저 학생들에게서 _____ .

81 주어진 글 다음에 이어질 글의 순서로 가장 적절한 것은?

Spatial reference points are larger than themselves. This isn't really a paradox: landmarks are themselves, but they also define neighborhoods around themselves.

(A) In a paradigm that has been repeated on many campuses, researchers first collect a list of campus landmarks from students. Then they ask another group of students to estimate the distances between pairs of locations, some to landmarks, some to ordinary buildings on campus.

(B) This asymmetry of distance estimates violates the most elementary principles of Euclidean distance, that the distance from A to B must be the same as the distance from B to A. Judgments of distance, then, are not necessarily coherent.

(C) The remarkable finding is that distances from an ordinary location to a landmark are judged shorter than distances from a landmark to an ordinary location. So, people would judge the distance from Pierre's house to the Eiffel Tower to be shorter than the distance from the Eiffel Tower to Pierre's house. Like black holes, landmarks seem to pull ordinary locations toward themselves, but ordinary places do not.

*asymmetry: 비대칭

① (A) — (C) — (B) ② (B) — (A) — (C) ③ (B) — (C) — (A)
④ (C) — (A) — (B) ⑤ (C) — (B) — (A)

정답과 해설 **p.73**

01 Spatial reference points are larger than themselves. // This isn't really a paradox: / landmarks are themselves, / but they also define neighborhoods around themselves.

02 In a paradigm / [that has been repeated on many campuses], / researchers first collect
　　선행사　　　동사(현재완료 수동태)
a list of campus landmarks from students. // Then they ask another group of students
　　　　　　　　　　　　　　　　　　　　　　　　　　　　　　　　동사　　목적어
/ to estimate the distances between pairs of locations, / some to landmarks, / some to
목적격보어　　　　　　　　　　　　　　　　　　　　　　　　　distances　　　　　　　distances
ordinary buildings on campus.

03 The remarkable finding is / [that distances from an ordinary location to a landmark
/ are judged shorter / than distances from a landmark to an ordinary location]. // So,
5형식 수동태(be p.p. + 형용사)
/ people would judge / the distance from Pierre's house to the Eiffel Tower / to be
　　동사　　　　　　　목적어　　　　　　　　　　　　　　　　　　　　　　　　목적격보어
shorter / than the distance from the Eiffel Tower to Pierre's house. // Like black holes,
　　　　　　　　　　　　　　　　　　　　　　　　　　　　　　　　　　　　　전치사(~처럼)
/ landmarks seem to pull ordinary locations toward themselves, / but ordinary places
do not.
대동사(= do not pull locations toward themselves)

04 This asymmetry of distance estimates / violates the most elementary principles of
Euclidean distance, / [that the distance from A to B / must be the same as the distance
　　　　　　　　　　　동격 명사절(the most ~ principles)　　　　　　　　「the same (A) as B: B와 같은 (A)」
from B to A]. // Judgments of distance, then, are not necessarily coherent.

01 공간 기준점spatial reference point은 자기 자신보다 더 크다. // 이것은 그다지 역설적이지 않은데, / 랜드마크landmark는 그 자체이기도 하지만, / 또한 그것은 자기 자신 주변 지역을 규정하기도 한다.

02 한 전형적인 예paradigm에서 / 많은 대학 캠퍼스에서 반복되어 온 / 연구원들은 먼저 학생들에게서 캠퍼스 랜드마크의 목록을 수집한다. // 그런 다음, 그들은 다른 학생 집단에게 요청한다 / 쌍으로 이루어진 장소 사이의 거리를 추정하라고estimate / 일부는 랜드마크까지 / 일부는 캠퍼스의 평범한 건물까지.

03 주목할 만한remarkable 결과는 ~이다 / 평범한 장소에서 랜드마크까지의 거리가 / 더 짧다고 추정된다는 것이다 / 랜드마크에서 평범한 장소까지의 거리보다. // 그래서 / 사람들은 추정할 것이다 / Pierre의 집에서 에펠탑까지의 거리가 / 더 짧다고 / 에펠탑에서 Pierre의 집까지의 거리보다. // 블랙홀처럼, / 랜드마크는 평범한 장소를 자기 자신 방향으로 끌어들이는 것처럼 보이지만, / 평범한 장소들은 그렇지 않다.

04 거리 추정에 관한 이 비대칭은, / 가장 기초적인 유클리드 거리 법칙에 위배된다violate the most elementary principles / A에서부터 B까지의 거리는 / B에서부터 A까지의 거리와 같아야 한다는. // 그렇다면 거리에 관한 추정은 반드시 일관성이 있는coherent 것은 아니다.

구문 Check up

① In a paradigm that has repeated / has been repeated on many campuses, researchers first collect a list of campus landmarks from students.

선행사 a paradigm이 '반복되는' 대상이므로 현재완료 수동태인 has been repeated가 적절하다.

② Like / Alike black holes, landmarks seem to pull ordinary locations toward themselves, but ordinary places do not.

뒤에 명사구를 동반하여 '~처럼'이라는 의미를 나타내는 말은 전치사 Like이다.

정답 ① has been repeated ② Like

82

STEP 1 • 수능에 진짜 나오는 단어

✔ 문제에 나오는 단어들을 확인하세요.

01	pronounce	v. 선언하다	(✔ pronounce) an opinion	의견을 선언하다
02	measure	n. 척도	man as the ( ) of all things	만물의 척도로서의 사람
03	entitled	a. (~할) 자격이 있는	( ) to ask a question	질문을 할 자격이 있는
04	empathy	n. 공감	( ) for others	다른 사람들에 대한 공감
05	grief	n. 슬픔	feelings of ( )	슬픔의 감정
06	amphibian	n. 양서류	( )s such as frogs	개구리와 같은 양서류
07	reptile	n. 파충류	( )s such as lizards	도마뱀과 같은 파충류
08	organ	n. (신체) 장기, 기관	donate an ( )	장기를 기증하다
09	assumption	n. 추정, 가정	support the ( )	가정을 뒷받침하다
10	overlook	v. 간과하다	( ) important details	중요한 세부사항을 간과하다
11	automobile	n. 자동차	different models of ( )s	다양한 자동차 모델
12	naive	a. (부정적 의미로) 순진한	young and ( )	어리고 순진한
13	exterior	n. 겉모습, 외관 a. 외부의	animals' varied ( )s	동물의 다양한 겉모습

⊕ 본문 문장 속에서 단어들을 확인해 보세요.

In other words, / we feel entitled to ask the world, / "What good are you?"

다시 말해서, / 우리는 세상에게 물어볼 자격이 있다고 느낀다 / "당신은 무슨 쓸모가 있는가?"라고.

01	pronounce	선언하다	pronounce an opinion	의견을 (선언하다)
02	measure		man as the measure of all things	만물의 ( )로서의 사람
03	entitled		entitled to ask a question	질문을 할 ( )
04	empathy		empathy for others	다른 사람들에 대한 ( )
05	grief		feelings of grief	( )의 감정
06	amphibian		amphibians such as frogs	개구리와 같은 ( )
07	reptile		reptiles such as lizards	도마뱀과 같은 ( )
08	organ		donate an organ	( )를 기증하다
09	assumption		support the assumption	( )을 뒷받침하다
10	overlook		overlook important details	중요한 세부사항을 ( )
11	automobile		different models of automobiles	다양한 ( ) 모델
12	naive		young and naive	어리고 ( )
13	exterior		animals' varied exteriors	동물의 다양한 ( )

➕ **본문 문장 속에서 단어의 의미를 우리말로 해석해 보세요.**

In other words, / we feel entitled to ask the world, / "What good are you?"

➡ 다시 말해서, / 우리는 ▨▨▨▨▨▨▨▨▨▨고 느낀다 / "당신은 무슨 쓸모가 있는가?"라고.

82

주어진 글 다음에 이어질 글의 순서로 가장 적절한 것은?

In the fifth century *B.C.E.*, the Greek philosopher Protagoras pronounced, "Man is the measure of all things." In other words, we feel entitled to ask the world, "What good are you?"

(A) Abilities said to "make us human" — empathy, communication, grief, toolmaking, and so on — all exist to varying degrees among other minds sharing the world with us. Animals with backbones (fishes, amphibians, reptiles, birds, and mammals) all share the same basic skeleton, organs, nervous systems, hormones, and behaviors.

(B) We assume that we are the world's standard, that all things should be compared to us. Such an assumption makes us overlook a lot.

(C) Just as different models of automobiles each have an engine, drive train, four wheels, doors, and seats, we differ mainly in terms of our outside contours and a few internal tweaks. But like naive car buyers, most people see only animals' varied exteriors.

*contour: 윤곽, 외형   **tweak: 조정, 개조

① (A) — (C) — (B)
② (B) — (A) — (C)
③ (B) — (C) — (A)
④ (C) — (A) — (B)
⑤ (C) — (B) — (A)

정답과 해설 p.74

01 In the fifth century *B.C.E.*, / the Greek philosopher Protagoras pronounced, / "Man is the measure of all things." // In other words, / we feel entitled to ask the world, / "What good are you?"

「entitled to + 동사원형: ~할 자격이 있는」

02 We assume / [that we are the world's standard], / [that all things should be compared to us]. // Such an assumption makes us overlook a lot.

동격(명사절)

사역동사 목적어 원형부정사

03 Abilities said to "make us human" / — (empathy, communication, grief, toolmaking, and so on) — / all exist to varying degrees / among other minds sharing the world with us. // Animals with backbones / (fishes, amphibians, reptiles, birds, and mammals) / all share the same basic skeleton, organs, nervous systems, hormones, and behaviors.

주어 과거분사구 삽입구(주어 동격) 동사(복수) 현재분사구 주어 동사(복수)

04 Just as different models of automobiles / each have an engine, drive train, four wheels, doors, and seats, / we differ / mainly in terms of our outside contours and a few internal tweaks. // But like naive car buyers, / most people see only animals' varied exteriors.

접속사(~와 마찬가지로) 전치사(~처럼)

01 기원전 5세기에, / 그리스의 철학자 Protagoras는 선언했다**pronounce** / "인간이 만물의 척도**measure**이다."라고. // 다시 말해서, / 우리는 세상을 향해 물어볼 자격이 있다**entitled**고 느낀다 / "당신은 무슨 쓸모가 있는가?"라고.

02 우리는 추정한다 / 우리가 세상의 기준이라고, 즉 모든 것이 우리와 비교되어야 한다고. // 그런 추정**assumption**은 우리로 하여금 많은 것을 간과하게**overlook** 한다.

03 '우리를 인간답게 만들어 준다고' 일컬어지는 능력들, / 즉 공감**empathy**, 의사소통, 슬픔**grief**, 도구 만들기 등은 / 모두 다양한 정도로 존재한다 / 우리와 세상을 공유하는, 지력을 지닌 다른 존재들에게도. // 척추동물은 / (어류, 양서류**amphibian**, 파충류**reptile**, 조류, 포유류) / 모두 동일한 기본 골격, 장기**organ**, 신경계, 호르몬, 행동을 공유한다.

04 다양한 자동차**automobile** 모델들이 ~한 것과 마찬가지로 / 각각 엔진, 동력 전달 체계, 네 바퀴, 문, 좌석을 가지고 있는 / 우리는 다르다 / 주로 우리의 외부 윤곽과 몇몇 내부적인 조정 면에서. // 하지만 순진한**naive** 자동차 구매자들처럼, / 대부분의 사람들은 오직 동물들의 다양한 겉모습**exterior**만을 본다.

구문 Check up

① We assume that we are the world's standard, that / which all things should be compared to us.

첫 번째 that절과 동격인 완전한 명사절이 연결되는 문맥이므로 접속사 that이 적절하다.

② Abilities said to "make us human" exist to varying degrees among other minds shared / sharing the world with us.

other minds가 '공유하는' 주체이므로 능동의 의미로 수식하는 현재분사 sharing이 적절하다.

정답 ① that ② sharing

83

STEP 1 • 수능에 *진짜* 나오는 *단어*

✔ 문제에 나오는 단어들을 확인하세요.

01	struggle with	~로 고생하다	(✔ struggle) (with) health problems	건강 문제로 고생하다
02	majority	n. 대다수	the ( ) of respondents	대다수의 응답자
03	derive A from B	B에서 A를 얻다	( ) benefits ( ) the business	사업에서 이익을 얻다
04	adversity	n. 역경	experience little ( )	역경을 거의 겪지 않다
05	priority	n. 우선순위	reevaluate ( )ies	우선순위를 재평가하다
06	intermediate	a. 중간의, 중급의	( ) levels of adversity	중간 수준의 역경
07	moderate	a. 적당한, 온건한	a ( ) amount of stress	적당한 양의 스트레스
08	foster	v. 촉진하다, 기르다	( ) the ability to manage stress	스트레스를 관리하는 능력을 기르다
09	subject	n. 실험 대상	the ( )s of the study	연구의 실험 대상
10	predictive of	~을 예측하는	be ( ) ( ) future outcomes	미래 결과를 예측하다
11	deal with	~을 해결하다, 다루다	( ) ( ) stress	스트레스를 해결하다
12	in the face of	~에 직면하여	( ) ( ) ( ) ( ) stress	스트레스에 직면하여
13	adaptation	n. 적응	the ( ) process	적응 과정

✚ 본문 문장 속에서 단어들을 확인해 보세요.

Studies of people / struggling with major.health problems / show / that the majority of respondents report / they derived benefits from their adversity.

사람들에 대한 연구는 / 중대한 건강 문제로 고생하는 / 보여준다 / 대다수의 응답자가 보고한다는 것을 / 자신의 역경에서 이익을 얻었다고.

문제를 풀기 전에 단어들을 **30초** 동안 다시 확인하세요.

01	struggle with 🖉 ~로 고생하다	struggle with health problems	건강 문제로 (고생하다)
02	majority	the majority of respondents	( )의 응답자
03	derive A from B	derive benefits from the business	사업에서 이익을 ( )
04	adversity	experience little adversity	( )을 거의 겪지 않다
05	priority	reevaluate priorities	( )를 재평가하다
06	intermediate	intermediate levels of adversity	( ) 수준의 역경
07	moderate	a moderate amount of stress	( ) 양의 스트레스
08	foster	foster the ability to manage stress	스트레스를 관리하는 능력을 ( )
09	subject	the subjects of the study	연구의 ( )
10	predictive of	be predictive of future outcomes	미래 결과를 ( )
11	deal with	deal with stress	스트레스를 ( )
12	in the face of	in the face of stress	스트레스에 ( )
13	adaptation	the adaptation process	( ) 과정

➕ **본문 문장 속에서 단어의 의미를 우리말로 해석해 보세요.**

Studies of people / struggling with major health problems / show / that the majority of respondents report / they derived benefits from their adversity.

➡️ 사람들에 대한 연구는 / ⬜⬜⬜⬜⬜⬜⬜ / 보여준다 / ⬜⬜⬜⬜⬜ 가 보고한다는 것을 / ⬜⬜⬜⬜⬜
⬜⬜⬜⬜ 고.

83 주어진 글 다음에 이어질 글의 순서로 가장 적절한 것은?

Studies of people struggling with major health problems show that the majority of respondents report they derived benefits from their adversity. Stressful events sometimes force people to develop new skills, reevaluate priorities, learn new insights, and acquire new strengths.

(A) High levels of adversity predicted poor mental health, as expected, but people who had faced intermediate levels of adversity were healthier than those who experienced little adversity, suggesting that moderate amounts of stress can foster resilience. A follow-up study found a similar link between the amount of lifetime adversity and subjects' responses to laboratory stressors.

(B) Intermediate levels of adversity were predictive of the greatest resilience. Thus, having to deal with a moderate amount of stress may build resilience in the face of future stress.

(C) In other words, the adaptation process initiated by stress can lead to personal changes for the better. One study that measured participants' exposure to thirty-seven major negative events found a curvilinear relationship between lifetime adversity and mental health.

*resilience: 회복력

① (A) — (C) — (B) ② (B) — (A) — (C) ③ (B) — (C) — (A)

④ (C) — (A) — (B) ⑤ (C) — (B) — (A)

정답과 해설 **p.75**

01 Studies of people / struggling with major health problems / show / [that the majority
　　주어　　　　　　　　　현재분사구(people 수식)　　　　　　　동사(복수)　목적어
of respondents report / (that) they derived benefits from their adversity]. // Stressful

events sometimes force people / to develop new skills, / reevaluate priorities, / learn

new insights, / and acquire new strengths.
　　　　　　　　　　　　　force의 목적격보어 병렬

02 In other words, / the adaptation process initiated by stress / can lead to personal
　　　　　　　　　　　주어　　　　　　　　　　과거분사구　　　　　　동사
changes for the better. // One study / [that measured participants' exposure to thirty-
　　　　　　　　　　　　　　주어　　　　　　주격 관계대명사절
seven major negative events] / found a curvilinear relationship / between lifetime
　　　　　　　　　　　　　　　　동사　　목적어　　　　　　　　　　　　전치사구
adversity and mental health.

03 High levels of adversity predicted poor mental health, / (as expected), / but people /
　　주어1　　　　　　　　　　동사1　　　　　　　　　　　삽입구　　　　　　　주어2
[who had faced intermediate levels of adversity] / were healthier than those / [who
　주격 관계대명사절　　　　　　　　　　　　　　　　　　동사2　　　　　　　선행사
experienced little adversity], / suggesting that moderate amounts of stress can foster
　주격 관계대명사절　　　　　　　　분사구문(그리고 ~하다)
resilience. // A follow-up study found a similar link / between the amount of lifetime

adversity / and subjects' responses to laboratory stressors.

04 Intermediate levels of adversity / were predictive of the greatest resilience. // Thus, /
　　주어　　　　　　　　　　　　　동사(복수)
having to deal with a moderate amount of stress / may build resilience / in the face of
　주어(동명사구)　　　　　　　　　　　　　　　　　　동사
future stress.

01 사람들에 대한 연구는 / 중대한 건강 문제로 고생하는struggle with / 보여준다 / 대다수majority의 응답자가 보고한다는
것을 / 자신의 역경에서 이익을 얻었다derive benefits from their adversity고. // 스트레스를 주는 사건들은 때때로
사람들이 ~하게 한다 / 새로운 기술을 개발하고, / 우선순위priority를 재평가하고, / 새로운 통찰을 배우고, / 새로운
강점을 얻게.

02 다시 말해, / 스트레스에 의해 시작된 적응adaptation 과정은 / 더 나은 쪽으로의 개인적 변화를 가져올 수 있다. // 한
연구는 / 참가자들의 서른일곱 가지 주요 부정적인 사건 경험을 측정한 / 곡선 관계를 발견했다 / 생애에서 겪은 역경과
정신 건강 사이의.

03 높은 수준의 역경은 나쁜 정신 건강을 예측했지만, / 예상대로 / 사람들은 / 중간intermediate 수준의 역경에
직면했던 / 사람들보다 더 건강했는데 / 역경을 거의 경험하지 않았던, / 이것은 적당한moderate 양의 스트레스가
회복력을 촉진할foster 수 있음을 보여준다. // 후속 연구는 비슷한 관계를 발견했다 / 생애에서 겪은 역경의 양과 /
피실험자subject들이 실험 중 주어진 스트레스 요인에 반응하는 것 사이의.

04 중간 수준의 역경이 / 가장 큰 회복력을 예측했다predictive of. // 따라서 / 적당한 양의 스트레스를 해결해야deal with
하는 것은 / 회복력을 기를 수도 있다 / 미래에 스트레스를 직면할 때의in the face of future stress.

구문 Check up

① Studies of people struggled / struggling with major
health problems show that the majority of respondents
report they derived benefits from their adversity.

people이 '고생하는' 주체이므로 현재분사 struggling을 이용해 수식한다.

② Thus, have / having to deal with a moderate amount
of stress may build resilience in the face of future
stress.

동사 may build 앞에 주어가 필요하므로 동명사 having이 적절하다.

정답 ① struggling ② having

84 STEP **1** • 수능에 *진짜* 나오는 *단어*

✔ 문제에 나오는 단어들을 확인하세요.

01	dominant	*a.* 지배적인	support the (✔ dominant) culture		지배적인 문화를 지지하다
02	reproduction	*n.* 재생산	cultural ( )		문화적 재생산
03	punish	*v.* 처벌하다	( ) the bad guys		나쁜 사람들을 처벌하다
04	obstacle	*n.* 장애물	despite the ( )s and difficulties		장애물과 어려움에도 불구하고
05	encounter	*v.* 만나다, 접하다	( ) the difficulties		어려움을 만나다
06	more often than not	대개, 자주	( ) ( ) ( ) ( )		대개
07	wind up	결국 ~에 처하다	( ) ( ) being left out		결국 소외된 상태에 처하다
08	editorial	*n.* 사설	( )s on responsible behavior		책임 있는 행동에 관한 사설
09	directive	*n.* 지시	give a ( )		지시를 내리다
10	prescription	*n.* 처방	( )s for happiness		행복을 위한 처방
11	proper	*a.* 적절한	( ) living		적절한 삶
12	propaganda	*n.* (정치적) 선전	a ( ) campaign		선전 캠페인

➕ 본문 문장 속에서 단어들을 확인해 보세요.

Movies may be said / to support the dominant culture / and to serve as a means for its reproduction over time.

영화는 이야기될 수도 있다 / 지배적인 문화를 지지하고 / 시간이 지남에 따라 그것의 재생산을 위한 수단의 역할을 한다고

문제를 풀기 전에 단어들을 30초 동안 다시 확인하세요.

01	dominant	✎ 지배적인	support the dominant culture	(지배적인) 문화를 지지하다
02	reproduction		cultural reproduction	문화적 ( )
03	punish		punish the bad guys	나쁜 사람들을 ( )
04	obstacle		despite the obstacles and difficulties	( )과 어려움에도 불구하고
05	encounter		encounter the difficulties	어려움을 ( )
06	more often than not		more often than not	( )
07	wind up		wind up being left out	( ) 소외된 상태에 ( )
08	editorial		editorials on responsible behavior	책임 있는 행동에 관한 ( )
09	directive		give a directive	( )를 내리다
10	prescription		prescriptions for happiness	행복을 위한 ( )
11	proper		proper living	( ) 삶
12	propaganda		a propaganda campaign	( ) 캠페인

➕ 본문 문장 속에서 단어의 의미를 우리말로 해석해 보세요.

Movies may be said / to support the dominant culture / and to serve as a means for its reproduction over time.

➔ 영화는 이야기될 수도 있다 / ▨▨▨▨▨▨▨▨▨▨ / 시간이 지남에 따라 ▨▨▨▨▨▨▨▨▨▨ 의 역할을 한다고

84 주어진 글 다음에 이어질 글의 순서로 가장 적절한 것은?

Movies may be said to support the dominant culture and to serve as a means for its reproduction over time.

(A) The bad guys are usually punished; the romantic couple almost always find each other despite the obstacles and difficulties they encounter on the path to true love; and the way we wish the world to be is how, in the movies, it more often than not winds up being. No doubt it is this utopian aspect of movies that accounts for why we enjoy them so much.

(B) The simple answer to this question is that movies do more than present two-hour civics lessons or editorials on responsible behavior. They also tell stories that, in the end, we find satisfying.

(C) But one may ask why audiences would find such movies enjoyable if all they do is give cultural directives and prescriptions for proper living. Most of us would likely grow tired of such didactic movies and would probably come to see them as propaganda, similar to the cultural artwork that was common in the Soviet Union and other autocratic societies.

*didactic: 교훈적인   **autocratic: 독재적인

① (A) — (C) — (B)   ② (B) — (A) — (C)   ③ (B) — (C) — (A)

④ (C) — (A) — (B)   ⑤ (C) — (B) — (A)

정답과 해설 **p.76**

01 Movies may be said / to support the dominant culture / and to serve as a means for its
= It may be said that movies support ~ and serve ~
reproduction over time.

02 But one may ask / [why audiences would find such movies enjoyable / if all they do
to 생략   간접의문문   = the only thing
is / give cultural directives and prescriptions for proper living]. // Most of us would
주격보어   동사1
likely grow tired of such didactic movies / and would probably come to see them as
동사2   「see A as B: A를 B로 보다」
propaganda, / similar to the cultural artwork / [that was common in the Soviet Union
선행사   주격 관계대명사절
and other autocratic societies].

03 The simple answer to this question is / [that movies do more / than present two-hour
접속사(~것)
civics lessons or editorials on responsible behavior]. // They also tell stories / [that, in
선행사   목적격
목적어 생략   관계대명사절
the end, we find satisfying].

04 The bad guys are usually punished; / the romantic couple almost always find each
other / despite the obstacles and difficulties / [they encounter on the path to true
전치사(~에도 불구하고)   명사구   목적격 관계대명사절
love]; / and the way [we wish the world to be] / is [how, in the movies, it more often
주어   동사(단수) 주격 보어
than not winds up being]. // No doubt / it is this utopian aspect of movies / that
「it is[was] ~ that …: …한 것은 바로 ~이다[였다]」
accounts for why we enjoy them so much.

01 영화는 이야기될 수 있다 / 지배적인dominant 문화를 지지하고 / 시간이 지남에 따라 그것의 재생산reproduction을 위한
수단의 역할을 한다고.

02 그러나 사람들은 물을 수도 있다 / 관객들이 왜 그러한 영화가 즐겁다고 느끼는지 / 그것들이 하는 일이 오로지 /
적절한proper 삶에 대한 문화적 지시directive와 처방prescription을 주는 것이라면. // 우리 중 대부분은 그러한
교훈적인 영화에 싫증이 나게 될 것이고, / 아마도 그것들을 선전propaganda으로 보게 될 것이다 / 문화적 예술 작품과
유사한 / 소련과 다른 독재 사회에서 흔했던.

03 이 질문에 대한 간단한 답은 ~이다 / 영화가 ~ 이상을 한다는 것 / 책임 있는 행동에 관한 두 시간짜리 국민 윤리 교육이나
사설editorial을 제시하는 것. // 그것들은 또한 이야기를 한다 / 우리가 결국 만족스럽다고 느끼는.

04 나쁜 사람들은 보통 벌을 받고punish, / 낭만적인 커플은 거의 항상 서로를 만나게 되며 / 장애물obstacle과 어려움에도
불구하고 / 진정한 사랑에 이르는 길에서 그들이 만나는encounter / 그리고 우리가 소망하는 세상의 모습은 / 영화
속에서 대개 결국more often than not wind up being 세상의 모습이 된다. // 틀림없다 / 바로 영화의 이 이상적인
측면임이 / 우리가 왜 그렇게 많이 영화를 즐기는지를 설명해 주는 것.

구문 Check up

① No doubt it is this utopian aspect of movies that /
where accounts for why we enjoy them so much.

「it is[was] ~ that …(…한 것은 바로 ~이다[였다])」 강조구문이므로 that
이 적절하다.

② But one may ask why audiences would find such
movies enjoyable if all they do is give / gives cultural
directives and prescriptions for proper living.

주어가 「all/what ~ do」이고 술어가 be동사이면 주격보어로 to부정사 대
신 원형부정사를 쓸 수 있다. 이때 all은 the only thing의 의미이다.

정답 ① give ② that

☑ **종합 성적표**

구분	공부한 날 ❶	결과 분석			
		출처	풀이 시간 ❷	채점 결과 (O, ✕)	틀린 이유 ❸
Day 10 빈칸 추론 (2)	월 일	2024학년도 9월 34번	분 초		
		2023학년도 대수능 34번	분 초		
		2023학년도 대수능 33번	분 초		
		2022학년도 대수능 34번	분 초		
		2022학년도 9월 33번	분 초		
		2021학년도 9월 34번	분 초		
		2020학년도 6월 33번	분 초		
Day 11 무관한 문장 찾기	월 일	2024학년도 6월 35번	분 초		
		2023학년도 대수능 35번	분 초		
		2022학년도 9월 35번	분 초		
		2022학년도 6월 35번	분 초		
		2021학년도 9월 35번	분 초		
		2020학년도 대수능 35번	분 초		
		2020학년도 9월 35번	분 초		
Day 12 글의 순서	월 일	2024학년도 6월 37번	분 초		
		2023학년도 대수능 37번	분 초		
		2022학년도 대수능 36번	분 초		
		2022학년도 6월 36번	분 초		
		2021학년도 9월 36번	분 초		
		2021학년도 6월 36번	분 초		
		2020학년도 대수능 36번	분 초		

3일간 공부한 내용을 다시 보니, ...

❶ **매일 지문을 하루 계획에 맞춰 풀었다. vs. 내가 한 약속을 못 지켰다.**

<매3영 수능기출>은 단순 문제풀이를 위한 책이 아니라, 매일 규칙적으로 영어를 공부하는 습관을 잡는 책입니다. 따라서 푸는 문제 개수는 상황에 따라 다르더라도 '매일' 학습하는 것이 중요합니다.

❷ **주어진 시간을 자꾸 넘긴다?**

풀이 시간이 계속해서 권장 시간을 넘긴다면 실전 훈련이 부족하다는 신호이므로, 매일의 훈련을 실전처럼 긴장감 있게 해야 합니다. 한편으로, 오답의 이유를 철저히 분석하고 맞춤 공부법을 찾아갑니다.

❸ ⭐**틀린 이유 맞춤 솔루션:** 오답 이유에 따라 다음 해결책을 참고하세요.

(1) 해석이 잘 안 돼서

▶ <STEP 1 단어>, <STEP 3 지문 복습>을 정독하며 단어/구문 실력을 길러보세요.

(2) 해석은 되는데, 지문 이해가 안 돼서

▶ [정답 및 해설]의 <지문 자세히 보기>를 정독하며 수능 지문의 논리 전개 방식을 익혀보세요.

(3) 이해는 했는데, 선택지로 연결을 못 해서

▶ [정답 및 해설]의 <오답풀이>, <유형플러스>를 통해 함정에 주의하는 방법을 숙지하세요.

❗

결론적으로, 내가 **취약한 부분**은 [   ] 이다.

취약점을 보완하기 위해서 나는 [   ] 을/를 해야겠다.

복습 때 다시 봐야 할 문항과, 다시 점검할 사항이 있는 페이지는 지금 바로 접어 두세요.

<매3영>이 제시하는 3단계로

유형 3일 훈련

DAY

13~15

85

STEP 1 • 수능에 *진짜* 나오는 *단어*

✔ 문제에 나오는 단어들을 확인하세요.

01	identification	n. 확인, 식별	(✔ identification) of an atom	원자의 확인
02	particle	n. 입자	tiny ( )s of matter	물질의 미세 입자
03	winner-take-all	a. 승자 독식의 (이긴 사람이 모든 이익을 차지하는)	a ( ) contest	승자 독식 대회
04	extreme	a. 극단적인	an ( ) view	극단적인 견해
05	nature	n. 본질	the ( ) of scientific contests	과학 대회의 본질
06	note	v. 말하다, 언급하다	( ) that it is not accurate	그것이 정확하지 않다고 말하다
07	inaccurate	a. 부정확한	a somewhat ( ) description	다소 부정확한 설명
08	a handful of	소수의	only ( ) ( ) ( ) contests	단지 소수의 대회
09	by way of example	예를 들어	( ) ( ) ( ) ( )	예를 들어
10	cure	n. 치료법 v. 치료하다	a ( ) for cancer	암을 위한 치료법

➕ 본문 문장 속에서 단어들을 확인해 보세요.

Science is sometimes described as a winner-take-all contest, / meaning that there are no rewards for being second or third.

과학은 때때로 승자 독식 대회로 묘사되는데, / 이는 2등이나 3등을 하는 데 보상이 없다는 의미다.

01	identification	✎ 확인, 식별	identification of an atom	원자의 (확인)
02	particle		tiny particles of matter	물질의 미세( )
03	winner-take-all		a winner-take-all contest	( ) 대회
04	extreme		an extreme view	( ) 견해
05	nature		the nature of scientific contests	과학 대회의 ( )
06	note		note that it is not accurate	그것이 정확하지 않다고 ( )
07	inaccurate		a somewhat inaccurate description	다소 ( ) 설명
08	a handful of		only a handful of contests	단지 ( ) 대회
09	by way of example		by way of example	( )
10	cure		a cure for cancer	암을 위한 ( )

➕ **본문 문장 속에서 단어의 의미를 우리말로 해석해 보세요.**

Science is sometimes described as a winner-take-all contest, / meaning that there are no rewards for being second or third.

➡ 과학은 때때로 ▓▓▓▓▓▓▓로 묘사되는데, / 이는 2등이나 3등을 하는 데 보상이 없다는 의미다.

85 글의 흐름으로 보아, 주어진 문장이 들어가기에 가장 적절한 곳은?

Yes, some contests are seen as world class, such as identification of the Higgs particle or the development of high temperature superconductors.

Science is sometimes described as a winner-take-all contest, meaning that there are no rewards for being second or third. This is an extreme view of the nature of scientific contests. (①) Even those who describe scientific contests in such a way note that it is a somewhat inaccurate description, given that replication and verification have social value and are common in science. (②) It is also inaccurate to the extent that it suggests that only a handful of contests exist. (③) But many other contests have multiple parts, and the number of such contests may be increasing. (④) By way of example, for many years it was thought that there would be "one" cure for cancer, but it is now realized that cancer takes multiple forms and that multiple approaches are needed to provide a cure. (⑤) There won't be one winner — there will be many.

*replication: 반복 **verification: 입증

정답과 해설 p.78

355

01 Science is sometimes described as a winner-take-all contest, / meaning that there
분사구문(= and it means ~)
are no rewards for being second or third. // This is an extreme view of the nature of
scientific contests.

주어(~한 사람들)
02 Even those [who describe scientific contests in such a way] / note that it is a somewhat
주격 관계대명사절   동사(복수)
inaccurate description, / given that replication and verification have social value and
~을 고려하면
are common in science. // It is also inaccurate / to the extent that it suggests / that
~할 경우에, ~할 정도로
only a handful of contests exist.

03 Yes, / some contests are seen as world class, / such as identification of the Higgs
particle / or the development of high temperature superconductors. // But many other
contests have multiple parts, / and the number of such contests may be increasing.
「the number of + 복수명사: ~의 수」

04 By way of example, / for many years it was thought / [that there would be "one" cure
가주어-진주어 구문
for cancer], / but it is now realized / [that cancer takes multiple forms] / and [that
multiple approaches are needed to provide a cure]. // There won't be one winner —
there will be many.

01 과학은 때때로 승자 독식 대회winner-take-all contest로 묘사되는데, / 이는 2등이나 3등을 하는 데 보상이 없다는
의미다. // 이는 과학 대회의 본질nature에 대한 극단적인extreme 견해이다.

02 과학 대회를 그렇게 설명하는 사람들조차도 / 그것이 다소 부정확한inaccurate 설명이라고 말한다note, / 반복과 입증이
사회적 가치를 지니고 있으며 과학에서는 일반적이라는 것을 감안할 때. // 또한 그것은 부정확하다 / 그것이 시사하는
경우에 / 단지 소수의a handful of 대회만 존재한다고.

03 물론, / 몇몇 대회는 세계적인 수준으로 여겨진다 / 힉스 입자particle의 확인identification / 또는 고온 초전도체 개발과
같은. // 하지만 다른 많은 대회에는 다양한 부문이 있고, / 그런 대회의 수는 증가하고 있을 것이다.

04 예를 들어by way of example, / 여러 해 동안 생각되었지만 / 암에는 '하나'의 치료법cure만 있다고 / 이제는 인식된다 /
암이 여러 가지 형태를 띠고 있으며 / 치료를 제공하려면 다양한 접근법이 필요하다고. // 승자는 한 명이 아니라, 여러 명이
있을 것이다.

구문 Check up	① Science is sometimes described as a winner-take-all contest, means / meaning that there are no rewards for being second or third.	② Even those who describe scientific contests in such a way notes / note that it is a somewhat inaccurate description,
	콤마 앞 문장의 의미를 설명하는 분사구문으로 meaning(= and it means ~)을 써야 한다.	주어가 those(~한 사람들)이므로 복수형이 적절하다.

정답 ① meaning ② note

356

86

STEP 1 • 수능에 *진짜* 나오는 *단어*

✔️ 문제에 나오는 단어들을 확인하세요.

01	specialist	n. 전문가	an fine art (✔️ specialist)	순수 미술품 전문가
02	critic	n. 비평가	art ( )s	예술 비평가
03	familiarity	n. 친숙함	a deeper ( ) with materials	재료에 대한 더 깊은 친숙함
04	informed	a. 잘 알고 (판단)한, 정보에 근거한	an ( ) judgement	잘 알고 내린 판단
05	acknowledge	v. 안다는 표시를 하다	( ) the making of artworks	예술 작품의 제작에 대해 안다는 표시를 하다
06	technical	a. 전문적인, 기술적인	a detailed, ( ) knowledge	상세한 전문 지식
07	sense	n. 느낌, 의식	a general ( )	일반적인 느낌
08	artistic	a. 예술적인	( ) creation	예술 창작
09	embody	v. 구현하다	( )ied in the artwork	예술 작품에 구현된

➕ 본문 문장 속에서 단어들을 확인해 보세요.

Acknowledging the making of artworks / does not require a detailed, technical knowledge / of, say, how painters mix different kinds of paint, / or how an image editing tool works.

예술 작품의 제작에 대해 안다는 표시를 하는 것은 / 상세한 전문 지식을 필요로 하지 않는다 / 가령 화가가 다양한 종류의 물감을 섞는 방법이나 / 이미지 편집 도구가 작동하는 방식에 관한.

문제를 풀기 전에 단어들을 **30초** 동안 다시 확인하세요.

01	specialist	✎ 전문가	an fine art specialist	순수 미술품 (전문가)
02	critic		art critics	예술 ( )
03	familiarity		a deeper familiarity with materials	재료에 대한 더 깊은 ( )
04	informed		an informed judgement	( ) 판단
05	acknowledge		acknowledge the making of artworks	예술 작품의 제작에 대해 ( )
06	technical		a detailed, technical knowledge	상세한 ( ) 지식
07	sense		a general sense	일반적인 ( )
08	artistic		artistic creation	( ) 창작
09	embody		embodied in the artwork	예술 작품에 ( )

➕ **본문 문장 속에서 단어의 의미를 우리말로 해석해 보세요.**

Acknowledging the making of artworks / does not require a detailed, technical knowledge / of, say, how painters mix different kinds of paint, / or how an image editing tool works.

➡ 예술 작품의 제작에 대해 ▨▨▨▨▨▨▨▨▨은 / ▨▨▨▨▨▨▨▨▨을 필요로 하지 않는다 / 가령 화가가 다양한 종류의 물감을 섞는 방법이나 / 이미지 편집 도구가 작동하는 방식에 관한.

86 글의 흐름으로 보아, 주어진 문장이 들어가기에 가장 적절한 곳은?

In the case of specialists such as art critics, a deeper familiarity with materials and techniques is often useful in reaching an informed judgement about a work.

Acknowledging the making of artworks does not require a detailed, technical knowledge of, say, how painters mix different kinds of paint, or how an image editing tool works. (①) All that is required is a general sense of a significant difference between working with paints and working with an imaging application. (②) This sense might involve a basic familiarity with paints and paintbrushes as well as a basic familiarity with how we use computers, perhaps including how we use consumer imaging apps. (③) This is because every kind of artistic material or tool comes with its own challenges and affordances for artistic creation. (④) Critics are often interested in the ways artists exploit different kinds of materials and tools for particular artistic effect. (⑤) They are also interested in the success of an artist's attempt — embodied in the artwork itself — to push the limits of what can be achieved with certain materials and tools.

*affordance: 행위유발성 **exploit: 활용하다

정답과 해설 p.78

01 Acknowledging the making of artworks / does not require a detailed, technical
주어(동명사구)   동사(단수)   목적어
knowledge / of, say, [how painters mix different kinds of paint], / or [how an image
of의 목적어 병렬
editing tool works].

02 All that is required / is a general sense of a significant difference / between working
전치사구
with paints and working with an imaging application. // This sense might involve a
basic familiarity with paints and paintbrushes / as well as a basic familiarity with how
「A as well as B: B뿐 아니라 A도」
we use computers, / perhaps including [how we use consumer imaging apps].
전치사(~을 포함해)   명사절

03 In the case of specialists such as art critics, / a deeper familiarity with materials and
techniques / is often useful / in reaching an informed judgement about a work. // This
~하는 데   이것은 ~ 때문이다
is because every kind of artistic material or tool comes / with its own challenges and
주어(every + 단수명사)   동사(단수)
affordances for artistic creation.

04 Critics are often interested in the ways / [artists exploit different kinds of materials
how 생략
and tools for particular artistic effect]. // They are also interested in the success of an
artist's attempt / — (embodied in the artwork itself) — / to push the limits of what can
삽입구(분사구문)   형용사적 용법
be achieved with certain materials and tools.

01 예술 작품의 제작에 대해 안다는 표시를 하는acknowledge 것은 / 상세한 전문 지식technical knowledge을 필요로 하지
않는다 / 가령 화가가 다양한 종류의 물감을 섞는 방법이나 / 이미지 편집 도구가 작동하는 방식에 관한.

02 필요한 것이라고는 / 중대한 차이에 대한 일반적인 느낌sense일 뿐이다 / 물감으로 작업하는 것과 이미징 앱을 사용해
작업하는 것 사이의. // 이런 느낌은 물감과 붓에 대한 기본적인 친숙함familiarity을 포함할 수도 있다 / 컴퓨터 사용법에
대한 기본적인 친숙함뿐 아니라 / 아마도 소비자 이미징 앱을 사용하는 방법을 포함해서.

03 예술 비평가critic와 같은 전문가specialist의 경우, / 재료와 기법에 대한 더 깊은 친숙함은 / 흔히 유용하다 / 작품에 관해
잘 알고 내린 판단informed judgement에 이르는 데. // 이것은 모든 종류의 예술 재료나 도구가 오기 때문이다 / 예술
창작artistic creation에 있어 그것만의 도전과 행위유발성과 함께.

04 비평가들은 흔히 방식에 관심이 있다 / 예술가들이 특정한 예술적 효과를 위해 다양한 종류의 재료와 도구를 활용하는.
// 그들은 또한 예술가의 시도가 성공적인지에 관심이 있다 / 예술 작품 그 자체로 구현된embody / 특정 재료와 도구로
달성할 수 있는 것의 한계를 뛰어넘으려는.

구문 Check up	① This is because of / because every kind of artistic material or tool comes with its own challenges.	② Critics are often interested in the ways that / how artists exploit different kinds of materials and tools for particular artistic effect.
	뒤에 절이 나오므로 접속사 because가 적절하다.	that은 방법 또는 이유의 선행사 뒤에서 관계부사 역할을 할 수 있다.

정답 ① because ② that

STEP 1 • 수능에 *진짜* 나오는 *단어*

 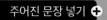
✔ 문제에 나오는 단어들을 확인하세요.

01	reliability	n. 신뢰성	information (✔ reliability)	정보 신뢰성
02	dynamics	n. 역학 (관계)	the (　　　　) of politics	정치의 역학
03	feature	n. 특징 v. ~을 특징으로 하다	have an interesting (　　　　)	흥미로운 특징을 갖다
04	detect	v. 감지하다, 탐지하다	(　　　　) a predator	포식자를 탐지하다
05	shelter	n. 피신, 대피	seek (　　　　)	피신하다
06	departure	n. 출발, 이탈	the moment of (　　　　)	출발의 순간
07	coordinate	v. 조직화하다, 조정하다	develop a (　　　　)d approach	조직화된 접근법을 개발하다
08	attend to	~에 주목하다	(　　) (　) the non-verbal cues	비언어적인 신호에 주목하다
09	multiple	a. 여럿의, 다수의	the departure of (　　　　) individuals	여러 개체의 이탈
10	have little to do with	~와 거의 관련이 없다	(　　) (　　) (　) (　) (　　　) predation threat	포식 위험과 거의 관련이 없다
11	present	a. 존재하는, 있는	the level of threat (　　　　)	존재하는 위협의 수준

➕ 본문 문장 속에서 단어들을 확인해 보세요.

This makes sense / from the perspective of information reliability.

이것은 이치에 맞는다 / 정보 신뢰성의 관점에서.

01	reliability	🖉 신뢰성	information reliability	정보 (신뢰성)
02	dynamics		the dynamics of politics	정치의 ( )
03	feature		have an interesting feature	흥미로운 ( )을 갖다
04	detect		detect a predator	포식자를 ( )
05	shelter		seek shelter	( )하다
06	departure		the moment of departure	( )의 순간
07	coordinate		develop a coordinated approach	( ) 접근법을 개발하다
08	attend to		attend to the non-verbal cues	비언어적인 신호에 ( )
09	multiple		the departure of multiple individuals	( ) 개체의 이탈
10	have little to do with		have little to do with predation threat	포식 위험과 ( )
11	present		the level of threat present	( ) 위협의 수준

➕ **본문 문장 속에서 단어의 의미를 우리말로 해석해 보세요.**

This makes sense / from the perspective of information reliability.

➡ 이것은 이치에 맞는다 / ▭▭▭▭▭▭ 에서.

87 글의 흐름으로 보아, 주어진 문장이 들어가기에 가장 적절한 곳은?

This makes sense from the perspective of information reliability.

The dynamics of collective detection have an interesting feature. Which cue(s) do individuals use as evidence of predator attack? In some cases, when an individual detects a predator, its best response is to seek shelter. (①) Departure from the group may signal danger to nonvigilant animals and cause what appears to be a coordinated flushing of prey from the area. (②) Studies on dark-eyed juncos (a type of bird) support the view that nonvigilant animals attend to departures of individual group mates but that the departure of multiple individuals causes a greater escape response in the nonvigilant individuals. (③) If one group member departs, it might have done so for a number of reasons that have little to do with predation threat. (④) If nonvigilant animals escaped each time a single member left the group, they would frequently respond when there was no predator (a false alarm). (⑤) On the other hand, when several individuals depart the group at the same time, a true threat is much more likely to be present.

*predator: 포식자 **vigilant: 경계하는 ***flushing: 날아오름

정답과 해설 p.79

01 The dynamics of collective detection / have an interesting feature. // Which cue(s) do
　　　주어　　　　　　　　　　　　　　　동사(복수)
individuals use / as evidence of predator attack?
　　　　　　　전치사(~로서)

02 In some cases, / when an individual detects a predator, / its best response is to seek
　　　　　　　　접속사(~할 때)　　　　　　　　　　　　　주어　　　　　　동사 주격보어(~것)
shelter. // Departure from the group / may signal danger to nonvigilant animals / and
　　　　　　　주어　　　　　　　　　　　　동사1　　목적어1
cause [what appears to be a coordinated flushing of prey from the area].
동사2　　목적어2(명사절)

03 Studies on dark-eyed juncos (a type of bird) / support the view / [that nonvigilant
　　주어　　　　　　　　　　　　　　　　　　　　　동사　　목적어　　동격절1
animals attend to departures of individual group mates] / but [that the departure of
　　　　　　　　　　　　　　　　　　　　　　　　　　　　　　　동격절2(=the view)
multiple individuals causes a greater escape response / in the nonvigilant individuals].
// This makes sense / from the perspective of information reliability.

04 If one group member departs, / it might have done so / for a number of reasons / [that
　　　　　　　　　　　　　　　　~했을 수도 있다(과거에 대한 추측)　　　　선행사
have little to do with predation threat]. // If nonvigilant animals escaped / each time
주격 관계대명사절
a single member left the group, / they would frequently respond / when there was no
　　　　　　　　　　　　　　　　「if + 주어 + 과거 동사 ~ 주어 + 조동사 과거형 + 동사원형: 가정법 과거」
predator (a false alarm). // On the other hand, / when several individuals depart the
group at the same time, / a true threat is much more likely to be present.

01 집단적 탐지의 역학dynamics은 / 흥미로운 특징feature이 있다. // 개체들은 어떤 단서를 사용하는가 / 포식자 공격의 증거로?

02 어떤 경우에는 / 개체가 포식자를 탐지할detect 때 / 그것의 최선의 반응은 피신하는seek shelter 것이다. // 무리로부터의 이탈departure은 / 경계하지 않는 동물들에게 위험 신호를 보내서 / 먹잇감 동물이 그 구역에서 조직화되어coordinate 쏟아져 나가는 것처럼 보이게 할 수도 있다.

03 (새의 한 종류인) 검은 눈 검은방울새에 관한 연구는 / 견해를 뒷받침해준다 / 경계하지 않는 동물들이 무리 친구들의 개별적 이탈에 주목한다attend to는 / 하지만 여러multiple 개체의 이탈은 더 큰 도망 반응을 일으킬 수 있다는 / 경계하지 않는 동물에게서. // 이것은 이치에 맞는다 / 정보 신뢰성reliability의 관점에서.

04 무리 구성원 하나가 이탈하는 경우, / 그것은 그렇게 했을 수 있다 / 여러 이유로 / 포식 위험과 관계가 거의 없는have little to do with predation threat. // 경계하지 않는 동물들이 도망한다면, / 단 하나의 구성원이 무리를 떠날 때마다 / 그것들은 자주 반응할 것이다 / 포식자가 전혀 없는 (가짜 경보인) 때에도. // 반면에 / 여러 개체가 동시에 무리를 이탈할 때, / 진짜 위험이 존재할present 가능성이 훨씬 더 크다.

구문 Check up

① Studies support the view that nonvigilant animals attend to departures of individual group mates but that / which the departure of multiple individuals causes a greater escape response.

but 앞뒤로 the view의 내용을 보충 설명하는 2개의 동격 명사절이 병렬 구조로 연결되는 문맥이다. 따라서 접속사 that이 적절하다.

② If one group member departs, it might have done so for a number of reasons that / why have little to do with predation threat.

뒤에 주어가 없는 불완전한 절이 연결되는 것으로 보아 관계대명사 that 이 적절하다. reasons만 보고 기계적으로 why를 고르면 안 된다.

정답 ① that ② that

88 STEP 1 • 수능에 *진짜* 나오는 *단어*

✔ 문제에 나오는 단어들을 확인하세요.

01	structural	a. 구조적인	the (✔ structural) elements of materials	물질의 구조적 요소
02	property	n. 특성	the ( )ies of water	물의 특성
03	have access to	~에 접근하다	( ) ( ) ( ) materials	물질에 접근하다
04	pottery	n. 도자기	( ) from ancient times	고대 도자기
05	alter	v. 바꾸다	be ( )ed by heat treatments	열처리에 의해 바뀌다
06	substance	n. 물질	the addition of other ( )s	다른 물질의 첨가
07	utilization	n. 이용, 활용	materials ( )	물질 이용
08	suited	a. 적합한	best ( ) for an application	용도에 가장 적합한
09	characteristic	n. 특성	the ( )s of materials	물질의 특성
10	empower	v. 권한을 주다	( ) him to manage projects	그가 프로젝트를 관리하도록 권한을 주다
11	fashion	v. 형성하다, 만들다	( ) a vase	꽃병을 만들다

⊕ 본문 문장 속에서 단어들을 확인해 보세요.

This knowledge, / acquired over approximately the past 100 years, / has empowered them to fashion, / to a large degree, / the characteristics of materials.

이 지식은 / 대략 지난 100년 동안 획득된 / 그들이 형성할 수 있게 해주었다 / 상당한 정도로 / 물질의 특성을.

01	structural	✏ 구조적인	the structural elements of materials	물질의 (구조적) 요소
02	property		the properties of water	물의 ( )
03	have access to		have access to materials	물질에 ( )
04	pottery		pottery from ancient times	고대 ( )
05	alter		be altered by heat treatments	열처리에 의해 ( )
06	substance		the addition of other substances	다른 ( )의 첨가
07	utilization		materials utilization	물질 ( )
08	suited		best suited for an application	용도에 가장 ( )
09	characteristic		the characteristics of materials	물질의 ( )
10	empower		empower him to manage projects	그가 프로젝트를 관리하도록 ( )
11	fashion		fashion a vase	꽃병을 ( )

➕ **본문 문장 속에서 단어의 의미를 우리말로 해석해 보세요.**

This knowledge, / acquired over approximately the past 100 years, / has empowered them to fashion, / to a large degree, / the characteristics of materials.

➡ 이 지식은 / 대략 지난 100년 동안 획득된 / ▓▓▓▓▓▓▓▓▓▓ / 상당한 정도로 / ▓▓▓▓▓▓▓을.

88 글의 흐름으로 보아, 주어진 문장이 들어가기에 가장 적절한 곳은?

It was not until relatively recent times that scientists came to understand the relationships between the structural elements of materials and their properties.

The earliest humans had access to only a very limited number of materials, those that occur naturally: stone, wood, clay, skins, and so on. (①) With time, they discovered techniques for producing materials that had properties superior to those of the natural ones; these new materials included pottery and various metals. (②) Furthermore, it was discovered that the properties of a material could be altered by heat treatments and by the addition of other substances. (③) At this point, materials utilization was totally a selection process that involved deciding from a given, rather limited set of materials, the one best suited for an application based on its characteristics. (④) This knowledge, acquired over approximately the past 100 years, has empowered them to fashion, to a large degree, the characteristics of materials. (⑤) Thus, tens of thousands of different materials have evolved with rather specialized characteristics that meet the needs of our modern and complex society, including metals, plastics, glasses, and fibers.

정답과 해설 p.80

01 The earliest humans had access / to only a very limited number of materials, / those
[that occur naturally]: / stone, wood, clay, skins, and so on.
　　주격 관계대명사절　　　　　　　　　　　　　　　동격

02 With time, / they discovered techniques for producing materials / [that had properties
　　　　　　　　　　　　　　　　　　　　　　　　　　　　　선행사
/ superior to those of the natural ones]; / these new materials included pottery and
　형용사구(properties 수식)
various metals. // Furthermore, / it was discovered / [that the properties of a material
　　　　　　　　　　　　　　　가주어-진주어 구문　　　　　주어
could be altered / by heat treatments and by the addition of other substances].
동사(조동사 수동태)

03 At this point, / materials utilization was totally a selection process / [that involved
　　　　　　　　　　　　　　　　　　　　　　　　　선행사
deciding (from a given, rather limited set of materials), / the one best suited for an
동명사　　　　　　　　　　부사구　　　　　　　　deciding의 목적어　　　형용사구
application / based on its characteristics].

04 ┌──「it is[was] not until A that B: A하고 나서야 비로소 B하다」──┐
It was not until relatively recent times / that scientists came to understand the
relationships / between the structural elements of materials and their properties. //
This knowledge, / (acquired over approximately the past 100 years), / has empowered
주어　　　　　　　삽입구(주어 보충 설명)　　　　　　　　　「empower +
them to fashion, / to a large degree, / the characteristics of materials.
목적어+to부정사: ~이 …하게 권한을 주다」

05 Thus, / tens of thousands of different materials have evolved / with rather specialized
　　　　　　　　　　　　　　　　　　　　　　　　　　　　　선행사
characteristics / [that meet the needs of our modern and complex society], / including
　　　　　　　　　　　　　주격 관계대명사절
metals, plastics, glasses, and fibers.

01 초기 인류는 접근할have access to 수 있었다 / 매우 제한된 수의 물질에만 / 즉 자연적으로 존재하는 물질 / 돌, 나무, 찰흙, 가죽 등.

02 시간이 흐르면서 / 그들은 물질을 만들어 내는 기술을 발견했는데 / 특성을 가진 / 자연적인 특성의 물질보다 더 우수한 / 이 새로운 물질에는 도자기pottery와 다양한 금속이 포함되었다. // 게다가, / 발견되었다 / 물질의 특성이 바뀔alter 수 있다는 것이 / 열처리와 다른 물질substance의 첨가로.

03 이 시기에, / 물질 이용utilization은 전적으로 선택의 과정이었다 / 주어진 상당히 제한된 물질 집합 중에서 결정하는 것을 수반하는 / 용도에 가장 적합한suited 물질을 / 물질의 특성characteristic에 근거하여.

04 비교적 최근에 이르러서였다 / 비로소 과학자들이 관계를 이해하게 된 것은 / 물질의 구조적structural 요소와 물질 특성property의. // 이 지식은 / 대략 지난 100년 동안 획득된 / 그들이 형성할 수 있게 해주었다empower them to fashion / 상당한 정도로 / 물질의 특성을.

05 따라서 / 수만 가지의 다양한 물질이 발달했다 / 상당히 특화된 특성을 가진 / 복잡한 우리 현대 사회의 요구를 충족하는 / 금속, 플라스틱, 유리, 섬유를 포함하여.

구문 Check up

① Materials utilization was totally a selection process that involved deciding / being decided from a given, rather limited set of materials, the one best suited for an application.

'from ~ materials' 뒤에 목적어 'the one ~'이 나오는 것으로 보아 능동태 동명사가 필요하므로, deciding이 적절하다.

② This knowledge, acquired over approximately the past 100 years, has / have empowered them to fashion, to a large degree, the characteristics of materials.

주어가 불가산명사인 This knowledge이므로 has가 적절하다.

✔ 문제에 나오는 단어들을 확인하세요.

01	pinpoint	v. 지적하다	exactly (✔ pinpoint)	정확히 지적하다
02	wickedness	n. 사악함	( ) that takes many forms	많은 형태를 띠는 사악함
03	infer	v. 추론하다	( ) the speaker's intention	화자의 의도를 추론하다
04	intonation	n. 억양	( ) patterns	억양 패턴
05	morally	ad. 도덕적으로	( ) bad	도덕적으로 나쁜
06	disapprove of	~을 못마땅해하다, ~에 찬성하지 않다	( ) ( ) those who are dishonest	부정직한 사람들을 못마땅해하다
07	linguistic	a. 언어적인, 언어학의	( ) barriers	언어적 장벽
08	convention	n. 관행, 관습	typical linguistic ( )s	일반적인 언어 관행
09	trait	n. 특성	character ( )s	성격 특성
10	specific	a. 구체적인	( ) descriptions	구체적인 묘사

⊕ 본문 문장 속에서 단어들을 확인해 보세요.

I have still not exactly pinpointed Maddy's character / since wickedness takes many forms.

나는 여전히 Maddy의 성격을 정확하게 지적한 게 아니다 / 사악함은 많은 형태를 띠기 때문에.

문제를 풀기 전에 단어들을 **30초** 동안 다시 확인하세요.

01	pinpoint	🖉 지적하다	exactly pinpoint	정확히 (지적하다)
02	wickedness		wickedness that takes many forms	많은 형태를 띠는 ( )
03	infer		infer the speaker's intention	화자의 의도를 ( )
04	intonation		intonation patterns	( ) 패턴
05	morally		morally bad	( ) 나쁜
06	disapprove of		disapprove of those who are dishonest	부정직한 사람들을 ( )
07	linguistic		linguistic barriers	( ) 장벽
08	convention		typical linguistic conventions	일반적인 언어 ( )
09	trait		character traits	성격 ( )
10	specific		specific descriptions	( ) 묘사

➕ **본문 문장 속에서 단어의 의미를 우리말로 해석해 보세요.**

I have still not exactly pinpointed Maddy's character / since wickedness takes many forms.

➜ 나는 여전히 Maddy의 성격을 ⬜⬜⬜⬜⬜⬜ 게 아니다 / ⬜⬜⬜⬜⬜⬜⬜ 때문에.

89 글의 흐름으로 보아, 주어진 문장이 들어가기에 가장 적절한 곳은?

I have still not exactly pinpointed Maddy's character since wickedness takes many forms.

Imagine I tell you that Maddy is bad. Perhaps you infer from my intonation, or the context in which we are talking, that I mean morally bad. Additionally, you will probably infer that I am disapproving of Maddy, or saying that I think you should disapprove of her, or similar, given typical linguistic conventions and assuming I am sincere. (①) However, you might not get a more detailed sense of the particular sorts of way in which Maddy is bad, her typical character traits, and the like, since people can be bad in many ways. (②) In contrast, if I say that Maddy is wicked, then you get more of a sense of her typical actions and attitudes to others. (③) The word 'wicked' is more specific than 'bad'. (④) But there is more detail nevertheless, perhaps a stronger connotation of the sort of person Maddy is. (⑤) In addition, and again assuming typical linguistic conventions, you should also get a sense that I am disapproving of Maddy, or saying that you should disapprove of her, or similar, assuming that we are still discussing her moral character.

*connotation: 함축

정답과 해설 **p.81**

01 Imagine / I tell you [that Maddy is bad]. // Perhaps you infer / from my intonation, or the context [in which we are talking], / [that I mean morally bad]. // Additionally, / you will probably infer / [that I am disapproving of Maddy, / or saying that I think you should disapprove of her, or similar], / given typical linguistic conventions / and assuming I am sincere.

02 However, / you might not get a more detailed sense / of the particular sorts of way [in which Maddy is bad], / her typical character traits, / and the like, / since people can be bad in many ways.

03 In contrast, / if I say that Maddy is wicked, / then you get more of a sense of her typical actions and attitudes to others. // The word 'wicked' is more specific than 'bad'.

04 I have still not exactly pinpointed Maddy's character / since wickedness takes many forms. // But there is more detail nevertheless, / perhaps a stronger connotation of the sort of person [Maddy is].

05 In addition, / and again assuming typical linguistic conventions, / you should also get a sense / [that I am disapproving of Maddy, / or saying that you should disapprove of her, or similar], / assuming that we are still discussing her moral character.

01 생각해 보라 / 내가 여러분에게 Maddy가 나쁘다고 말한다고. // 아마 여러분은 추론한다infer / 나의 억양intonation 혹은 우리가 말하고 있는 맥락으로부터 / 내가 도덕적으로morally 나쁘다는 뜻을 의도하고 있음을. // 게다가 / 여러분은 아마도 추론할 것이다 내가 Maddy를 못마땅해하고disapprove of 있다고, / 또는 내 생각에 여러분이 그녀를 못마땅해하든 해야 한다고 말하고 있는 것이라고 / 일반적인 언어 관행linguistic convention을 고려하고 / 내가 진심이라고 상정한다면.

02 하지만 / 여러분은 더 자세하게 인식하지 못할 수도 있는데 / Maddy가 나쁜 특정한 방식에 대해 / 그녀의 일반적인 성격 특성character trait / 그리고 기타 등등 / 사람들은 여러 방면에서 나쁠 수 있기 때문이다.

03 그에 반해서, / 만일 내가 Maddy는 사악하다고 말한다면, / 여러분은 다른 사람들에 대한 그녀의 일반적인 행동과 태도에 대해 더 알게 된다. // '사악한'이라는 낱말은 '나쁜'보다 더 구체적specific이다.

04 나는 여전히 Maddy의 성격을 정확하게 지적한pinpoint 게 아니다 / 사악함wickedness은 많은 형태를 띠기 때문에. // 하지만 그럼에도 불구하고 더 많은 세부사항이 있다 / 아마도 Maddy가 어떤 사람인지에 관한 더 강한 함축적 의미.

05 게다가 / 다시 한번 일반적인 언어 관행을 상정하면, / 여러분은 또한 파악할 것이다 / 내가 Maddy를 못마땅해하고 있다고 / 혹은 여러분이 그녀를 못마땅해하든지 해야 한다고 말하고 있다고 / 우리가 여전히 그녀의 도덕적 성격을 논하고 있다고 가정할 때.

구문 Check up

① Perhaps you infer from my intonation, or the context in which we are talking, that / which I mean morally bad.

infer의 목적어인 명사절을 이끌 수 있는 접속사 that이 적절하다. 'from my intonation, or the context ~'는 동사와 목적어 사이에 삽입된 부사구이다.

② Additionally, you will probably infer that I am disapproving of Maddy, or saying / to say that I think you should disapprove of her, or similar, given typical linguistic conventions.

문맥상 that절 안의 현재진행 동사 am disapproving과 병렬 연결되는 동사가 필요하므로 (am) saying이 적절하다.

정답 ① that ② saying

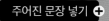
STEP 1 • 수능에 진짜 나오는 단어

☑ 문제에 나오는 단어들을 확인하세요.

01	workable	a. 운용 가능한	a (✓ workable) device	운용 가능한 장치
02	grammar	n. 문법	English ( )	영어 문법
03	vaguely	ad. 어렴풋이, 희미하게	some ( ) defined rules	어렴풋이 정의된 몇 가지 규칙
04	cinematic	a. 영화의	( ) language	영화 언어
05	syntax	n. 문법, 구문론	the ( ) of film	영화의 문법
06	arrangement	n. 처리 방식, 배열	the systematic ( ) of film	영화의 체계적인 처리 방식
07	determinant	n. 결정 요인	( )s of language use	언어 사용의 결정 요인
08	organic	a. 자연스러운, 유기적인	an ( ) development	자연스러운 발전
09	prescriptive	a. 규범적인	( ) grammar	규범 문법(한 언어의 올바른 용법을 지시하는 문법)
10	considerably	ad. 상당히	change ( ) over the years	여러 해에 걸쳐 상당히 변화하다
11	laughable	a. 웃기는, 터무니없는	sound ( )	웃기게 들리다

➕ 본문 문장 속에서 단어들을 확인해 보세요.

As with written and spoken languages, / it is important to remember / that the syntax of film is a result of its usage, / not a determinant of it.

문어와 구어에서와 마찬가지로, / 기억하는 것이 중요하다 / 영화의 문법은 영화에서의 사용의 결과물이지 / 그것의 결정 요인은 아니라는 것을.

01	workable	✎ 운용 가능한	a workable device	(운용 가능한)장치
02	grammar		English grammar	영어 ( )
03	vaguely		some vaguely defined rules	( ) 정의된 몇 가지 규칙
04	cinematic		cinematic language	( ) 언어
05	syntax		the syntax of film	영화의 ( )
06	arrangement		the systematic arrangement of film	영화의 체계적인 ( )
07	determinant		determinants of language use	언어 사용의 ( )
08	organic		an organic development	( ) 발전
09	prescriptive		prescriptive grammar	( ) 문법
10	considerably		change considerably over the years	여러 해에 걸쳐 ( ) 변화하다
11	laughable		sound laughable	( ) 들리다

➕ **본문 문장 속에서 단어의 의미를 우리말로 해석해 보세요.**

As with written and spoken languages, / it is important to remember / that the syntax of film is a result of its usage, / not a determinant of it.

➔ 문어와 구어에서와 마찬가지로, / 기억하는 것이 중요하다 / ⬛⬛⬛⬛⬛ 은 영화에서의 사용의 결과물이지 / ⬛⬛⬛⬛⬛ 은 아니라는 것을.

374

90 글의 흐름으로 보아, 주어진 문장이 들어가기에 가장 적절한 곳은?

Rather, it evolved naturally as certain devices were found in practice to be both workable and useful.

Film has no grammar. (①) There are, however, some vaguely defined rules of usage in cinematic language, and the syntax of film — its systematic arrangement — orders these rules and indicates relationships among them. (②) As with written and spoken languages, it is important to remember that the syntax of film is a result of its usage, not a determinant of it. (③) There is nothing preordained about film syntax. (④) Like the syntax of written and spoken language, the syntax of film is an organic development, descriptive rather than prescriptive, and it has changed considerably over the years. (⑤) "Hollywood Grammar" may sound laughable now, but during the thirties, forties, and early fifties it was an accurate model of the way Hollywood films were constructed.

*preordained: 미리 정해진

정답과 해설 **p.82**

01 Film has no grammar. // There are, / however, / some vaguely defined rules of usage in cinematic language / and the syntax of film / — (its systematic arrangement) — / 주어   삽입구
orders these rules and indicates relationships among them.
동사1   동사2

02 As with written and spoken languages, / it is important to remember / [that the 가주어   진주어   접속사(~것)
syntax of film is a result of its usage, / not a determinant of it]. // There is nothing preordained about film syntax.
과거분사구

03 Rather, / it evolved naturally / as certain devices were found in practice / to be both 접속사(~함에 따라)   5형식 수동태(be p.p. + to부정사)
workable and useful. // Like the syntax of written and spoken language, / the syntax of 전치사(~처럼)   선행사
film is an organic development, / (which is) descriptive rather than prescriptive, / and it has changed considerably over the years.
현재완료   기간 부사구

04 "Hollywood Grammar" may sound laughable now, / but during the thirties, forties, and 감각동사   주격보어(형용사)   how 생략
early fifties / it was an accurate model of the way / [Hollywood films were constructed].
선행사   관계부사절

01 영화에는 문법grammar이 없다. // ~이 있다 / 그러나 / 영화cinematic 언어 사용에 관한 어렴풋이vaguely 정의된 몇 가지 규칙이 / 그리고 영화의 문법syntax은 / 즉 그것의 체계적인 처리 방식arrangement / 이러한 규칙들을 정리하고 그것들 사이의 관계를 보여준다.

02 문어와 구어에서와 마찬가지로, / 기억하는 것이 중요하다 / 영화의 문법은 영화에서의 사용의 결과물이지 / 그것의 결정 요인determinant은 아니라는 것을. // 영화 문법에 관해 미리 정해진 것은 아무것도 없다.

03 오히려, / 그것은 자연스럽게 발전했다 / 특정 방법이 실제로 밝혀지면서 / 운용할 수 있고workable 유용하다고. // 문어와 구어의 문법처럼, / 영화의 문법은 자연스러운organic 발전으로 / 규범적이지prescriptive 않고 기술적이며, / 그것은 여러 해에 걸쳐 상당히considerably 변화했다.

04 '할리우드 문법'은 지금은 웃기게laughable 들릴지 모르지만, / 30년대, 40년대, 50년대 초반에는 / 그것은 방식의 정확한 모델이었다 / 할리우드 영화가 구성되던.

구문 Check up

① Rather, it evolved naturally as certain devices found / were found in practice to be both workable and useful.

접속사 as(~함에 따라)가 이끄는 부사절의 주어인 certain devices가 '여겨지는' 대상이므로 were found가 적절하다.

② "Hollywood Grammar" may sound laughable / laughably now, but it was an accurate model of the way Hollywood films were constructed.

may sound가 보어를 필요로 하는 2형식 동사이므로 형용사인 laughable이 적절하다.

정답 ① were found ② laughable

91

STEP 1 • 수능에 *진짜* 나오는 *단어*

✔ 문제에 나오는 단어들을 확인하세요.

01	confront	v. 마주하다, 직면하다	be (✔ confront)ed with change	변화와 마주하다
02	fitness	n. 합목적성, 적합성	the ( ) of things	사물의 합목적성
03	breeding	n. 번식	a ( ) site	번식지
04	survivorship	n. 생존, 잔존	nonbreeding ( )	비번식기 생존(율)
05	specific	a. 특정한, (~에) 독특한	a ( ) area	특정한 지역
06	straightforward	a. 간단한	seemingly a ( ) process	외견상 간단한 과정
07	reproductive	a. 번식의	satisfy its ( ) needs	번식의 필요를 충족하다
08	as opposed to	~와는 달리	( ) ( ) ( ) resident birds	텃새들과는 달리

✚ 본문 문장 속에서 단어들을 확인해 보세요.

Resident-bird habitat selection is seemingly a straightforward process / in which a young dispersing individual moves / until it finds a place / where it can compete successfully to satisfy its needs.

텃새들의 서식지 선택은 외견상 간단한 과정이다 / 흩어지는 어린 개체가 옮겨 다니는 / 그것이 장소를 찾을 때까지 / 자신의 필요를 충족시키기 위해 성공적으로 경쟁할 수 있는.

01	confront	✎ 마주하다, 직면하다	be confronted with change	변화와 (마주하다)
02	fitness		the fitness of things	사물의 ( )
03	breeding		a breeding site	( )지
04	survivorship		nonbreeding survivorship	비번식기 ( )
05	specific		a specific area	( ) 지역
06	straightforward		seemingly a straightforward process	외견상 ( ) 과정
07	reproductive		satisfy its reproductive needs	( ) 필요를 충족하다
08	as opposed to		as opposed to resident birds	텃새들과는 ( )

➕ 본문 문장 속에서 단어의 의미를 우리말로 해석해 보세요.

Resident-bird habitat selection is seemingly a straightforward process / in which a young dispersing individual moves / until it finds a place / where it can compete successfully to satisfy its needs.

➔ 텃새들의 서식지 선택은   이다 /   / 그것이 장소를 찾을 때까지 / 자신의 필요를 충족시키기 위해 성공적으로 경쟁할 수 있는.

91

글의 흐름으로 보아, 주어진 문장이 들어가기에 가장 적절한 곳은?

> Thus, individuals of many resident species, confronted with the fitness benefits of control over a productive breeding site, may be forced to balance costs in the form of lower nonbreeding survivorship by remaining in the specific habitat where highest breeding success occurs.

Resident-bird habitat selection is seemingly a straightforward process in which a young dispersing individual moves until it finds a place where it can compete successfully to satisfy its needs. (①) Initially, these needs include only food and shelter. (②) However, eventually, the young must locate, identify, and settle in a habitat that satisfies not only survivorship but reproductive needs as well. (③) In some cases, the habitat that provides the best opportunity for survival may not be the same habitat as the one that provides for highest reproductive capacity because of requirements specific to the reproductive period. (④) Migrants, however, are free to choose the optimal habitat for survival during the nonbreeding season and for reproduction during the breeding season. (⑤) Thus, habitat selection during these different periods can be quite different for migrants as opposed to residents, even among closely related species.

*disperse: 흩어지다 **optimal: 최적의

정답과 해설 p.83

01　Resident-bird habitat selection is seemingly a straightforward process / [in which
선행사　　　　　　　　　　　　　　　　　　　「전치사 + 관계대명사」
a young dispersing individual moves / until it finds a place / {where it can compete
선행사　　관계부사절
successfully to satisfy its needs}].

02　Initially, / these needs include only food and shelter. // However, eventually, /
the young must locate, identify, and settle in a habitat / [that satisfies not only
선행사　　　주격 관계대명사절
survivorship but reproductive needs as well].

03　In some cases, / the habitat / [that provides the best opportunity for survival] / may
주어　　　주격 관계대명사절　　　　　동사
not be the same habitat / as the one / [that provides for highest reproductive capacity]
선행사　　　주격 관계대명사절
/ because of requirements specific to the reproductive period. // Thus, / individuals
전치사(~ 때문에)　　　형용사구　　　　　　　주어
of many resident species, / (confronted with the fitness benefits of control / over
삽입구(분사구문)
a productive breeding site), / may be forced to balance costs / in the form of lower
동사구(be forced + to부정사: 어쩔 수 없이 ~하게 되다)
nonbreeding survivorship / by remaining in the specific habitat / [where highest
「by + 동명사: ~함으로써」　　　　　　관계부사절
breeding success occurs].

04　Migrants, / however, / are free to choose the optimal habitat / for survival during the
「be free + to부정사: 자유롭게 ~하다」　　　전치사구 병렬
nonbreeding season / and for reproduction during the breeding season. // Thus, /
habitat selection during these different periods / can be quite different for migrants /
as opposed to residents, / even among closely related species.
「as opposed to + (동)명사: ~와는 달리」

01　텃새들의 서식지 선택은 외견상 간단한**straightforward** 과정이다 / 흩어지는 어린 개체가 옮겨 다니는 / 그것이 장소를 찾을 때까지 / 자신의 필요를 충족시키기 위해 성공적으로 경쟁할 수 있는.

02　처음에는, / 이러한 필요에 음식과 은신처만 포함된다. // 그러나 궁극적으로, / 그 어린 새는 서식지를 찾고, 확인하고, 그곳에 정착해야 한다 / 생존뿐만 아니라 번식의**reproductive** 필요도 충족시켜 주는.

03　일부의 경우, / 서식지가 / 생존을 위한 최고의 기회를 제공하는 / 동일한 곳이 아닐 수도 있다 / 서식지와 / 최고의 번식 능력을 제공해주는 / 번식기에만 특별히 요구되는 조건들 때문에. // 따라서 / 많은 텃새 종의 개체들은 / 장악하고 있다는 이점의 적합성에 직면했을 때**confronted with the fitness benefits** / 다산에 유리한 번식지**breeding site**를 / 대가의 균형을 어쩔 수 없이 맞춰야 할 수도 있다 / 더 낮은 비번식기 생존율**survivorship**의 형태로 / 특정**specific** 서식지에 머물러 있음으로써 / 가장 높은 번식 성공이 일어나는.

04　철새들은 / 그러나 / 최적의 서식지를 자유롭게 선택한다 / 번식기가 아닌 동안에는 생존을 위한 / 그리고 번식기 동안에는 번식을 위한. // 이에 따라 / 서로 다른 시기 동안의 서식지 선택은 / 철새들에게 있어서 상당히 다를 수 있다 / 텃새들과는 달리**as opposed to residents** / 심지어 밀접하게 관련이 있는 종들 사이에서조차도.

구문 Check up	
① However, eventually, the young must locate, identify, and settle in a habitat **that / where** satisfies not only survivorship but reproductive needs as well.	② In some cases, the habitat may not be the same habitat as the one that provides for highest reproductive capacity **because / because of** requirements specific to the reproductive period.
a habitat이 장소 명사이지만 뒤에 주어가 없는 불완전한 문장이 나오므로 where가 아닌 that이 적절하다.	뒤에 명사 requirements가 나오므로 전치사 because of가 적절하다. 'specific ~'은 requirements를 꾸미는 형용사구이다.

정답 ① that ② because of

92

STEP 1 • 수능에 *진짜* 나오는 *단어*

✔ **문제에 나오는 단어들을 확인하세요.**

01	document	v. 기록하다	under-(✔ document)ed ordinary people	문서로 덜 기록된 보통 사람들
02	portray	v. 묘사하다	(　　　　) everyday situations	일상 상황을 묘사하다
03	recreate	v. 재창조하다	(　　　　) the historical context	역사적 맥락을 재창조하다
04	flesh	n. 살	add (　　　) to the bones	뼈대에 살을 붙이다
05	uncover	v. 밝히다	(　　　　) a plot	음모를 밝히다
06	account	n. 설명	provide an (　　　　　)	설명을 제공하다
07	indication	n. 시사, 조짐	a clearer (　　　　) of past events	과거 사건을 더 명확히 시사하는 것
08	archive	n. 기록 (보관소)	lack of (　　　)s	기록의 부족
09	challenging	a. 도전적인, 도전 의식을 북돋우는	a (　　　　　) representation of the past	과거에 대한 도전적 표현
10	reconstruct	v. 재구성하다	(　　　　　) the past	과거를 재구성하다
11	insignificant	a. 사소한	(　　　　　) details	사소한 디테일
12	insufficient	a. 불충분한	(　　　　　) time	불충분한 시간
13	enrich	v. 풍부하게 하다	(　　　) our lives	우리 삶을 풍요롭게 하다
14	concrete	a. 구체적인	(　　　　) proof	구체적인 증거

⊕ **본문 문장 속에서 단어들을 확인해 보세요.**

Fiction helps portray everyday situations, feelings, and atmosphere / that recreate the historical context.

소설은 일상 상황, 감정, 분위기를 묘사하는 데 도움이 된다 / 역사적 맥락을 재창조하는.

01	document	🖉 기록하다	under-documented ordinary people	문서로 덜 (기록된) 보통 사람들
02	portray		portray everyday situations	일상 상황을 ( )
03	recreate		recreate the historical context	역사적 맥락을 ( )
04	flesh		add flesh to the bones	뼈대에 ( )을 붙이다
05	uncover		uncover a plot	음모를 ( )
06	account		provide an account	( )을 제공하다
07	indication		a clearer indication of past events	과거 사건을 더 명확히 ( ) 하는 것
08	archive		lack of archives	( )의 부족
09	challenging		a challenging representation of the past	과거에 대한 ( ) 표현
10	reconstruct		reconstruct the past	과거를 ( )
11	insignificant		insignificant details	( ) 디테일
12	insufficient		insufficient time	( ) 시간
13	enrich		enrich our lives	우리 삶을 ( )
14	concrete		concrete proof	( ) 증거

➕ 본문 문장 속에서 단어의 의미를 우리말로 해석해 보세요.

Fiction helps portray everyday situations, feelings, and atmosphere / that recreate the historical context.

➔ 소설은 일상 상황, 감정, 분위기를 [   ] 데 도움이 된다 / [   ].

92

다음 글의 내용을 한 문장으로 요약하고자 한다. 빈칸 (A), (B)에 들어갈 말로 가장 적절한 것은?

Research for historical fiction may focus on under-documented ordinary people, events, or sites. Fiction helps portray everyday situations, feelings, and atmosphere that recreate the historical context. Historical fiction adds "flesh to the bare bones that historians are able to uncover and by doing so provides an account that while not necessarily true provides a clearer indication of past events, circumstances and cultures." Fiction adds color, sound, drama to the past, as much as it invents parts of the past. And Robert Rosenstone argues that invention is not the weakness of films, it is their strength. Fiction can allow users to see parts of the past that have never — for lack of archives — been represented. In fact, Gilden Seavey explains that if producers of historical fiction had strongly held the strict academic standards, many historical subjects would remain unexplored for lack of appropriate evidence. Historical fiction should, therefore, not be seen as the opposite of professional history, but rather as a challenging representation of the past from which both public historians and popular audiences may learn.

While historical fiction reconstructs the past using ____(A)____ evidence, it provides an inviting description, which may ____(B)____ people's understanding of historical events.

(A)	(B)	(A)	(B)
① insignificant ...... delay		② insufficient ...... enrich	
③ concrete ...... enhance		④ outdated ...... improve	
⑤ limited ...... disturb			

정답과 해설 **p.85**

01 Research for historical fiction / may focus on under-documented ordinary people, events, or sites. // Fiction helps portray everyday situations, feelings, and atmosphere / [that recreate the historical context].

「help + (to) 동사원형: ~하는 데 도움이 되다」
주격 관계대명사절
목적격 관계대명사절

02 Historical fiction adds "flesh to the bare bones / [that historians are able to uncover] / and by doing so provides an account / [that while not necessarily true / provides a clearer indication of past events, circumstances and cultures."] // Fiction adds color, sound, drama to the past, / as much as it invents parts of the past.

동사
it is
동사2
주격 관계대명사
동사(선행사에 수 일치)
~할 정도로

03 And Robert Rosenstone argues / that invention is not the weakness of films, / it is their strength. // Fiction can allow users to see parts of the past / [that have never — for lack of archives — been represented].

선행사(복수)
현재완료 수동태

04 In fact, / Gilden Seavey explains / that if producers of historical fiction had strongly held the archives academic standards, / many historical subjects would remain unexplored for lack of appropriate evidence. // Historical fiction should, therefore, not be seen as the opposite of professional history, / but rather as a challenging representation of the past / [from which both public historians and popular audiences may learn].

「if + 주어 + had p.p. ~ 주어 + would + 동사원형: 혼합가정법(과거에 ~했더라면 현재 …할 텐데」
「not A but (rather) B: A가 아니라 B인(as + 명사구 병렬)」
선행사
「전치사 + 관계대명사」

05 → While historical fiction reconstructs the past using insufficient evidence, / it provides an inviting description, / which may enrich people's understanding of historical events.

접속사(~이긴 하지만)
선행사
계속적 용법(= and it)

01 역사 소설을 위한 연구는 / 문서로 덜 기록된document 보통 사람이나 사건 또는 장소에 아마 초점을 맞출 것이다. // 소설은 일상 상황, 감정, 분위기를 묘사하는portray 데 도움이 된다 / 역사적 맥락을 재창조하는recreate.

02 역사 소설은 '뼈대에 살flesh을' 붙이고, / '역사가들이 밝혀낼uncover 수 있는 / 그렇게 해서 설명account을 제공한다 / 반드시 사실이 아니더라도 / 과거의 사건, 상황, 문화를 더 명확히 시사indication하는'. // 소설은 과거에 색채, 소리, 드라마를 더한다 / 과거의 부분들을 지어내는 정도까지.

03 그리고 Robert Rosenstone은 주장한다 / 지어내는 것은 영화의 약점이 아니고 / 그것은 강점이라고. // 소설은 사용자들이 과거의 일부를 보도록 해 준다 / 역사 자료archive가 없어 표현된 적이 없는.

04 실제로 / Gilden Seavey가 설명하기로, / 역사 소설 제작자들이 엄격한 학술적 기준을 고수했다면, / 많은 역사적 주제는 적절한 증거가 없어서 여전히 탐구되지 못했을 것이라고 한다. // 따라서 역사 소설은 전문적 역사와 정반대된다고 여겨져서는 안 되며, / 대신에 과거에 대한 도전적인challenging 표현으로 여겨져야 한다 / 대중 역사학자와 대중 관객이 모두 그것으로부터 배울 수도 있는.

05 → 역사 소설은 불충분한insufficient 증거를 사용하여 과거를 재구성하지만reconstruct, 그것은 매력적인 설명을 제공하는데, / 이는 역사적 사건에 대한 사람들의 이해를 풍부하게 할enrich 수도 있다.

Check up

① Fiction helps to portray / portray everyday situations, feelings, and atmosphere that recreate the historical context.

help는 to부정사와 원형부정사를 모두 목적어로 취할 수 있으므로 둘 다 정답이다.

② Fiction adds color, sound, drama to the past, as much / many as it invents parts of the past.

셀 수 있는 대상이 아닌, '정도'를 가리키고 있으므로 as much as(~한 정도로)가 적절하다.

정답 ① to portray, portray ② much

93 STEP 1 • 수능에 *진짜* 나오는 *단어*

✔ 문제에 나오는 단어들을 확인하세요.

01	craftsmanship	n. 장인정신, (훌륭한) 솜씨	the definition of (✔ craftsmanship)	장인정신의 정의
02	decline	v. 쇠퇴하다	( ) with industrialization	산업화와 함께 쇠퇴하다
03	misleading	a. 오해의 소지가 있는	a ( ) statement	오해의 소지가 있는 진술
04	enduring	a. 지속적인	an ( ) effect	지속적인 효과
05	impulse	n. 충동	a basic human ( )	인간의 기본적인 충동
06	manual labor	육체 노동	skilled ( ) ( )	숙련된 육체 노동
07	parenting	n. 양육	effective ( )	효과적인 양육
08	objective	a. 객관적인	( ) standards of excellence	탁월함에 대한 객관적 기준
09	in itself	그 자체	focus on something ( ) ( )	어떤 것 그 자체에 초점을 두다
10	stand in the way of	~을 방해하다, 훼방놓다	( ) ( ) ( ) ( ) ( ) our friendship	우리 우정을 방해하다
11	discipline	n. 수련, 단련, 훈련	the craftsman's ( )	장인의 수련
12	commitment	n. 전념, 헌신	our ( ) to human rights	인권에 대한 우리의 헌신
13	obsession	n. 집착, 강박	our ( ) with perfection	완벽에 대한 우리의 집착
14	encounter	v. 마주하다, 맞닥뜨리다	( ) a problem	문제에 맞닥뜨리다

✚ 본문 문장 속에서 단어들을 확인해 보세요.

Social and economic conditions, / however, / often stand in the way of the craftsman's discipline and commitment.

사회 및 경제적 조건은 / 그러나 / 흔히 장인의 수련과 전념을 방해한다.

01	craftsmanship	장인정신, (훌륭한) 솜씨	the definition of craftsmanship	(장인정신)의 정의
02	decline		decline with industrialization	산업화와 함께 ( )
03	misleading		a misleading statement	( ) 진술
04	enduring		an enduring effect	( ) 효과
05	impulse		a basic human impulse	인간의 기본적인 ( )
06	manual labor		skilled manual labor	숙련된 ( )
07	parenting		effective parenting	효과적인 ( )
08	objective		objective standards of excellence	탁월함에 대한 ( ) 기준
09	in itself		focus on something in itself	어떤 것 ( ) 초점을 두다
10	stand in the way of		stand in the way of our friendship	우리 우정을 ( )
11	discipline		the craftsman's discipline	장인의 ( )
12	commitment		our commitment to human rights	인권에 대한 우리의 ( )
13	obsession		our obsession with perfection	완벽에 대한 우리의 ( )
14	encounter		encounter a problem	문제에 ( )

➕ 본문 문장 속에서 단어의 의미를 우리말로 해석해 보세요.

Social and economic conditions, / however, / often stand in the way of the craftsman's discipline and commitment.

➡ 사회 및 경제적 조건은 / 그러나 / 흔히 장인의 ▨▨▨▨▨▨▨▨.

93

다음 글의 내용을 한 문장으로 요약하고자 한다. 빈칸 (A), (B)에 들어갈 말로 가장 적절한 것은?

"Craftsmanship" may suggest a way of life that declined with the arrival of industrial society — but this is misleading. Craftsmanship names an enduring, basic human impulse, the desire to do a job well for its own sake. Craftsmanship cuts a far wider swath than skilled manual labor; it serves the computer programmer, the doctor, and the artist; parenting improves when it is practiced as a skilled craft, as does citizenship. In all these domains, craftsmanship focuses on objective standards, on the thing in itself. Social and economic conditions, however, often stand in the way of the craftsman's discipline and commitment: schools may fail to provide the tools to do good work, and workplaces may not truly value the aspiration for quality. And though craftsmanship can reward an individual with a sense of pride in work, this reward is not simple. The craftsman often faces conflicting objective standards of excellence; the desire to do something well for its own sake can be weakened by competitive pressure, by frustration, or by obsession.

*swath: 구획

⬇

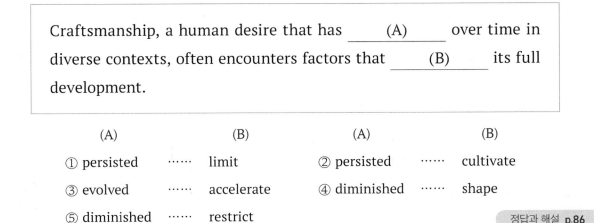

Craftsmanship, a human desire that has ____(A)____ over time in diverse contexts, often encounters factors that ____(B)____ its full development.

(A)		(B)		(A)		(B)
① persisted	......	limit		② persisted	......	cultivate
③ evolved	......	accelerate		④ diminished	......	shape
⑤ diminished	......	restrict				

정답과 해설 **p.86**

01 "Craftsmanship" may suggest a way of life / [that declined with the arrival of industrial society] / — but this is misleading. // Craftsmanship names an enduring, basic human impulse, / the desire to do a job well for its own sake. // Craftsmanship cuts a far wider swath than skilled manual labor; / it serves the computer programmer, the doctor, and the artist; / parenting improves when it is practiced as a skilled craft, / as does citizenship.

02 In all these domains, / craftsmanship focuses on objective standards, / on the thing in itself. // Social and economic conditions, / however, / often stand in the way of the craftsman's discipline and commitment: / schools may fail to provide the tools to do good work, / and workplaces may not truly value the aspiration for quality.

03 And though craftsmanship can reward an individual / with a sense of pride in work, / this reward is not simple. // The craftsman often faces conflicting objective standards of excellence; / the desire to do something well for its own sake / can be weakened / by competitive pressure, by frustration, or by obsession.

04 → Craftsmanship, / a human desire [that has persisted over time in diverse contexts], / often encounters factors / that limit its full development.

01 '장인정신craftsmanship'은 삶의 방식을 나타낼지도 모르지만 / 산업 사회의 도래와 함께 쇠퇴한decline / 이는 오해의 소지가 있다misleading. // 장인정신은 지속적enduring이고 기본적인 인간의 충동impulse을 말한다 / 즉 일 그 자체를 위해 일을 잘하고 싶은 욕망. // 장인정신은 숙련된 육체 노동manual labor보다 훨씬 더 넓은 구획을 가른다 / 그것은 컴퓨터 프로그래머, 의사, 예술가에게 도움이 된다 / 양육parenting은 그것이 숙련된 기술로서 실행될 때 향상된다 / 시민 정신이 그렇듯.

02 이 모든 영역에서 / 장인정신은 객관적인objective 기준에 초점을 맞춘다 / 즉 그 자체의in itself 것에. // 사회 및 경제적 조건은 / 그러나 / 흔히 장인의 수련과 전념을 방해한다stand in the way of craftsman's discipline and commitment / 학교는 일을 잘하기 위한 도구를 제공하지 못할 수 있고, / 직장은 품질에 대한 열망을 진정으로 가치 있게 여기지 않을 수 있다.

03 그리고 비록 장인정신이 개인에게 보상을 줄 수 있지만 / 일에 대한 자부심으로 / 이 보상은 간단하지 않다. // 장인은 흔히 탁월함에 대한 상충되는 객관적 기준에 직면한다 / 일 그 자체를 위해 어떤 일을 잘하려는 욕망은 / 약화될 수 있다 / 경쟁에서 오는 압박, 좌절, 또는 집착obsession으로 인해.

04 → 장인정신은 / 오랜 시간에 걸쳐 다양한 상황에서 존속된 인간의 욕망인 / 흔히 요소들을 마주한다encounter / 그 완전한 발전을 제한하는.

구문 Check up

① Parenting improves when it is practiced as a skilled craft, as is / does citizenship.

문맥상 앞에 나온 일반동사 improves를 대신하는 대동사로 does를 써야 한다.

② Craftsmanship, a human desire that has persisted over time in diverse contexts, often encounters / encountering factors that limit its full development.

주어 Craftsmanship 뒤로 동사가 필요하므로 encounters가 적절하다.

정답 ① does ② encounters

94 STEP 1 • 수능에 *진짜* 나오는 *단어*

✔️ 문제에 나오는 단어들을 확인하세요.

01	mobility	n. 이동성, 유동성	social (✔️ mobility)	사회적 이동성
02	transit	n. 통행, 수송, 교통	take public ( )	대중교통을 이용하다
03	discipline	n. 학과, (학문) 분야	be explored by different ( )s	다양한 학과에 의해 탐구되다
04	faculty	n. (대학의) 학부, 교수단	the ( ) of law	법학부
05	humanities	n. 인문학	major in ( )	인문학을 전공하다
06	acceleration	n. 가속	the ( ) of social change	사회 변화의 가속
07	artefact	n. (역사·문화적 의미가 있는) 인공물, 유물	learn the age of an ( )	유물의 연대를 알아내다
08	load up with	~로 가득 채우다	his car ( )ed ( ) ( ) camping gear	캠핑 장비로 가득 찬 그의 차
09	terminal	a. 불치병에 걸린, 말기 환자의	( ) creatures	불치병에 걸린 존재
10	disproportion	n. 불균형	the ( ) of motion and rest	운동과 휴식 간의 불균형
11	victim	n. 희생자, 피해자	the ( ) of a hate crime	증오 범죄의 피해자
12	exclusion	n. 배제, 제외	social ( )	사회적 배제

➕ 본문 문장 속에서 단어들을 확인해 보세요.

Mobilities in transit **offer a broad field** / **to be explored by** different disciplines in all faculties, / in addition to the humanities.

통행의 이동성은 광범위한 분야를 제공한다 / 모든 학부의 여러 다른 학과에서 탐구할 수 있는 / 인문학뿐만 아니라.

01	mobility	✏ 이동성, 유동성	social mobility	사회적 (이동성)
02	transit		take public transit	대중( )을 이용하다
03	discipline		be explored by different disciplines	다양한 ( )에 의해 탐구되다
04	faculty		the faculty of law	법( )
05	humanities		major in humanities	( )을 전공하다
06	acceleration		the acceleration of social change	사회 변화의 ( )
07	artefact		learn the age of an artifact	( )의 연대를 알아내다
08	load up with		his car loaded up with camping gear	캠핑 장비로 ( ) 그의 차
09	terminal		terminal creatures	( ) 존재
10	disproportion		the disproportion of motion and rest	운동과 휴식 간의 ( )
11	victim		the victim of a hate crime	증오 범죄의 ( )
12	exclusion		social exclusion	사회적 ( )

➕ 본문 문장 속에서 단어의 의미를 우리말로 해석해 보세요.

Mobilities in transit **offer a broad field** / **to be explored by** different disciplines in all faculties, / in addition to the humanities.

➡ ⬜⬜⬜⬜ 은 광범위한 분야를 제공한다 / ⬜⬜⬜⬜⬜ 에서 탐구할 수 있는 / ⬜⬜⬜⬜ .

94

다음 글의 내용을 한 문장으로 요약하고자 한다. 빈칸 (A), (B)에 들어갈 말로 가장 적절한 것은?

Mobilities in transit offer a broad field to be explored by different disciplines in all faculties, in addition to the humanities. In spite of increasing acceleration, for example in travelling through geographical or virtual space, our body becomes more and more a passive non-moving container, which is transported by artefacts or loaded up with inner feelings of being mobile in the so-called information society. Technical mobilities turn human beings into some kind of terminal creatures, who spend most of their time at rest and who need to participate in sports in order to balance their daily disproportion of motion and rest. Have we come closer to Aristotle's image of God as the immobile mover, when elites exercise their power to move money, things and people, while they themselves do not need to move at all? Others, at the bottom of this power, are victims of mobility-structured social exclusion. They cannot decide how and where to move, but are just moved around or locked out or even locked in without either the right to move or the right to stay.

In a technology and information society, human beings, whose bodily movement is less _____(A)_____ , appear to have gained increased mobility and power, and such a mobility-related human condition raises the issue of social _____(B)_____ .

	(A)		(B)		(A)		(B)
①	necessary	⋯⋯	inequality	②	necessary	⋯⋯	growth
③	limited	⋯⋯	consciousness	④	desirable	⋯⋯	service
⑤	desirable	⋯⋯	divide				

정답과 해설 p.86

01 Mobilities in transit offer a broad field / to be explored by different disciplines in all faculties, / in addition to the humanities.
형용사적 용법
전치사(~에도 불구하고)

02 In spite of increasing acceleration, / (for example in travelling through geographical or virtual space), / our body becomes more and more a passive non-moving container, / which is transported by artefacts / or loaded up with inner feelings of being mobile / in the so-called information society. // Technical mobilities turn human beings / into some kind of terminal creatures, / who spend most of their time at rest / and who need to participate in sports / in order to balance their daily disproportion of motion and rest.
명사구 / 삽입구 / 주어 동사 주격보어(선행사) / 계속적 용법 / turn A into B: A를 B로 바꾸다 / 선행사(복수) / 계속적 용법1 / 계속적 용법2 / 부사적 용법(= so as to balance ~)

03 Have we come closer to Aristotle's image of God / as the immobile mover, / when elites exercise their power / to move money, things and people, / while they themselves do not need to move at all? // Others, (at the bottom of this power), / are victims of mobility-structured social exclusion. // They cannot decide how and where to move, / but are just moved around or locked out or even locked in / without either the right to move or the right to stay.
전치사(~로서) / 재귀대명사(강조) / 주어 삽입구 동사(복수) / 의문사 + to부정사: ~할지 / 과거분사 병렬(are에 연결) / either A or B: A 또는 B 둘 중 하나

04 → In a technology and information society, / human beings, (whose bodily movement is less necessary), / appear to have gained increased mobility and power, / and such a mobility-related human condition / raises the issue of social inequality.
선행사 소유격 관계대명사 / 완료부정사(appear보다 과거) / such a(n) + 형 + 명: (형용사)한 그런 (명사)

01 통행transit의 이동성mobility은 광범위한 분야를 제공한다 / 모든 학부faculty의 여러 다른 학과discipline에서 탐구할 수 있는 / 인문학humanities뿐만 아니라.

02 속도가 증가하고 있음increasing acceleration에도 불구하고 / 예를 들어, 지리적 공간이나 가상의 공간을 이동하는 데 있어 / 우리의 몸은 점점 수동적이고 움직이지 않는 컨테이너가 되는데, / 그것은 인공물artefact에 의해 운송되거나 / 이동한다는 내적 느낌으로 가득 채워진다load up with / 이른바 정보 사회에서. // 기술적 이동성은 인간을 바꾸는데 / 일종의 불치병에 걸린terminal 존재로 / 그는 대부분의 시간을 쉬면서 보내고 / 스포츠에 참여할 필요가 있다 / 그들의 운동과 휴식 간 일상적인 불균형disproportion을 맞추기 위해.

03 우리는 아리스토텔레스의 신의 이미지에 더 가까워진 것인가 / 움직일 수 있지만 움직이지 않는 존재로서의 / 엘리트가 힘을 행사할 때 / 돈, 사물, 사람을 움직이는 / 자신은 전혀 움직일 필요가 없는 한편? // 이 권력의 밑바닥에 있는 또 어떤 사람들은 / 이동성으로 구조화된 사회적 배제exclusion의 희생자victim들이다. // 그들은 어떻게 어디로 이동해야 할지 결정할 수 없지만, / 그저 이리저리 옮겨지거나, 내쳐지거나, 심지어 갇히기도 한다 / 이동할 권리도 머무를 권리도 없이.

04 → 기술과 정보 사회에서, / 인간은 신체의 움직임이 덜 필요해져 / 이동성과 권력의 증가를 이룬 것처럼 보이는데, / 이동성과 관련된 그러한 인간의 상태는 / 사회적 불평등이라는 문제를 제기한다.

구문 Check up

① Others, at the bottom of this power, is / are victims of mobility-structured social exclusion.

주어 Others가 복수대명사이므로 are가 적절하다. at the bottom of this power는 문장 구조에 영향을 주지 않는 삽입구이다.

② In a technology and information society, human beings, whom / whose bodily movement is less necessary, appear to have gained increased mobility and power.

뒤에 관사 없는 명사로 시작하는 완전한 절이 나오므로 소유격 관계대명사 whose를 쓴다. whom 뒤에는 목적어가 없는 불완전한 절이 와야 한다.

정답 ① are ② whose

95 STEP 1 • 수능에 *진짜* 나오는 *단어*

✔ 문제에 나오는 단어들을 확인하세요.

01	political	*a.* 정치적인	a (✔ political) position	정치적 입장
02	significance	*n.* 의미, 중요성	have a social or political ( )	사회적 또는 정치적인 의미를 갖다
03	spread	*v.* 퍼지다	( ) widely	널리 퍼지다
04	hardwood	*n.* 활엽수, 경재(단단한 목재)	plant ( ) trees	활엽수를 심다
05	declare	*v.* 선언하다	( ) the right	권리를 선언하다
06	property	*n.* 재산, 부동산	the extent of the ( )	재산의 정도(범위)
07	permanence	*n.* 영속성	the ( ) of their claim	그들의 권리의 영속성
08	bound	*n.* 경계(선)	the ( )s and limits	경계와 한계
09	preserve	*v.* 보존하다	( ) the property	재산을 보존하다
10	testimony	*n.* 증언	give ( )	증언을 하다
11	witness	*n.* 목격자, 증인	a ( ) to the killing	살인의 목격자
12	severe	*a.* 심각한	a ( ) shortage of the hardwood	경재의 심각한 부족

⊕ 본문 문장 속에서 단어들을 확인해 보세요.

The idea / that *planting* trees could have a social or political significance / appears to have been invented by the English, / though it has since spread widely.

생각은 / 나무를 '심는 것'이 사회적 또는 정치적인 의미를 가질 수 있다는 / 영국인들에 의해 고안된 것처럼 보인다 / 비록 그것이 이후에 널리 퍼져나가기는 했지만.

문제를 풀기 전에 단어들을 **30초** 동안 다시 확인하세요.

01	political	✎ 정치적인	a political position	(정치적)입장
02	significance		have a social or political significance	사회적 또는 정치적인 ( )를 갖다
03	spread		spread widely	널리 ( )
04	hardwood		plant hardwood trees	( )를 심다
05	declare		declare the right	권리를 ( )
06	property		the extent of the property	( )의 정도
07	permanence		the permanence of their claim	그들의 권리의 ( )
08	bound		the bounds and limits	( )와 한계
09	preserve		preserve the property	재산을 ( )
10	testimony		give testimony	( )을 하다
11	witness		a witness to the killing	살인의 ( )
12	severe		a severe shortage of the hardwood	경재의 ( ) 부족

➕ **본문 문장 속에서 단어의 의미를 우리말로 해석해 보세요.**

The idea / that *planting* trees could have a social or political significance / appears to have been invented by the English, / though it has since spread widely.

➡️ 생각은 / 나무를 '심는 것'이 ▓▓▓▓▓▓▓▓▓▓▓▓▓▓▓▓ 를 가질 수 있다는 / 영국인들에 의해 고안된 것처럼 보인다 / 비록 그것이 ▓▓▓▓▓▓▓▓▓▓▓▓▓ 했지만.

95

다음 글의 내용을 한 문장으로 요약하고자 한다. 빈칸 (A), (B)에 들어갈 말로 가장 적절한 것은?

The idea that *planting* trees could have a social or political significance appears to have been invented by the English, though it has since spread widely. According to Keith Thomas's history *Man and the Natural World*, seventeenth- and eighteenth-century aristocrats began planting hardwood trees, usually in lines, to declare the extent of their property and the permanence of their claim to it. "What can be more pleasant," the editor of a magazine for gentlemen asked his readers, "than to have the bounds and limits of your own property preserved and continued from age to age by the testimony of such living and growing witnesses?" Planting trees had the additional advantage of being regarded as a patriotic act, for the Crown had declared a severe shortage of the hardwood on which the Royal Navy depended.

*aristocrat: 귀족 **patriotic: 애국적인

For English aristocrats, planting trees served as statements to mark the _____(A)_____ ownership of their land, and it was also considered to be a(n) _____(B)_____ of their loyalty to the nation.

	(A)		(B)		(A)		(B)
①	unstable	⋯⋯	confirmation	②	unstable	⋯⋯	exaggeration
③	lasting	⋯⋯	exhibition	④	lasting	⋯⋯	manipulation
⑤	official	⋯⋯	justification				

정답과 해설 **p.87**

01 The idea / [that *planting* trees could have a social or political significance] / appears
　　주어　　　　접속사(동격)　　　　　　　　　　　　　　　　　　　　　　　　　　　　　동사(단수)
to have been invented by the English, / though it has since spread widely.
완료부정사(appears보다 과거)　　　　　　　　접속사(비록 ~이지만)

02 According to Keith Thomas's history *Man and the Natural World*, / seventeenth- and
　　　　　　　　　　　　　　　　　　　　　　　　　　　　　　　　　　　　주어
eighteenth-century aristocrats began planting hardwood trees, / usually in lines, /
　　　　　　　　　　　　　　　　　동사　　　목적어
to declare the extent of their property and the permanence of their claim to it. // "What
부사적 용법(목적)　　　　　　　　　　　　　　　　　　　　　　　　　　　　　　　　　　　　의문사(무엇)
can be more pleasant," / (the editor of a magazine for gentlemen asked his readers), /
　　　　「비교급 +than: ~보다 …한」　　　　　　　　　삽입절
"than to have the bounds and limits of your own property / preserved and continued
　　　　사역동사　　　목적어　　　　　　　　　　　　　　　　　　목적격보어(과거분사구)
from age to age / by the testimony of such living and growing witnesses?"

03 Planting trees had the additional advantage of being regarded as a patriotic act, / for
　　　　　　　　　　　　　　　　　　　　동명사의 수동태(being p.p.)　　　　　　　　등위접속사(왜냐하면 ~이다)
the Crown had declared a severe shortage of the hardwood / [on which the Royal Navy
　　　　　　　　　　　　　　　　　　　　　　　　선행사　　　　　　「전치사 + 관계대명사」
depended].

04 → For English aristocrats, / planting trees served as statements / to mark the lasting
　　　　　　　　　　　　　　　　　　　　　　　　　　　　　　　형용사적 용법
ownership of their land, / and it was also considered to be an exhibition of their loyalty
　　　　　　　　　　　　　　　　　「be considered + to부정사: ~한 것으로 여겨지다」
to the nation.

---

01 생각은 / 나무를 '심는 것'이 사회적 또는 정치적인 의미political significance를 가질 수 있다는 / 영국인들에 의해
　　　고안된 것처럼 보인다 / 비록 그것이 이후에 널리 퍼져나가기는spread 했지만.

02 Keith Thomas의 역사서인 <Man and the Natural World>에 따르면, / 17세기와 18세기의 귀족들은 활엽수hardwood
　　　tree를 심기 시작했다 / 대개 줄지어 / 자신의 재산property 정도와 그것에 대한 권리의 영속성permanence을
　　　선언하기declare 위해. // "무엇이 더 즐거울 수 있겠는가"라고 / 그 신사 대상 잡지 편집자는 자신의 독자들에게 물었다
　　　/ "여러분 자신의 재산 경계bound와 한계가 ~하게 하는 것보다 / 대대로 보존되고preserve 지속되게 / 그런 살아 있고
　　　성장하는 증인witness들의 증언testimony에 의해?"

03 나무를 심는 것은 애국적인 행동으로 여겨지는 추가적인 이점을 가졌는데, / 왜냐하면 군주가 경재의 심각한severe 부족을
　　　선포했기 때문이었다 / 영국 해군이 의존하는.

04 → 영국의 귀족들에게, / 나무를 심는 것은 진술의 역할을 했고 / 자신의 땅에 대한 지속적인 소유권을 표시하는 / 그것은
　　　또한 국가에 대한 그들의 충성심의 표현으로 여겨졌다.

구문 Check up

① The idea that / which *planting* trees could have a social or political significance appears to have been invented by the English, though it has since spread widely.

앞에 추상명사 The idea가 있고, 뒤에 나오는 'planting trees could have a ~ significance'가 '생각'의 내용을 설명하는 완전한 3형식 문장이므로 동격의 접속사 that이 적절하다.

② The Crown had declared a severe shortage of the hardwood which / on which the Royal Navy depended.

뒤에 자동사 depended를 포함한 완전한 1형식 문장이 나오므로, 관계부사와 마찬가지로 완전한 절을 이끄는 on which가 적절하다. which 앞의 on은 depend on(~에 의존하다)에서 나왔다.

정답 ① that ② on which

STEP 1 • 수능에 *진짜* 나오는 *단어*

✔ 문제에 나오는 단어들을 확인하세요.

01	cross-cultural	*a.* 비교 문화적인, 여러 문화가 섞인	from a (✔ cross-cultural) perspective	비교 문화적 관점에서
02	equation	*n.* 방정식, 문제	the ( ) between benefits and costs	편익과 비용 사이의 방정식
03	dominance	*n.* 지배, 우월	( ) over others	다른 사람들에 대한 지배
04	conceivably	*ad.* 아마도, 생각건대	( ) neither	아마도 둘 다 아닌
05	bothersome	*a.* 성가신	a ( ) idea	성가신 생각
06	fond	*a.* 좋아하는, 즐기는	( ) of their independence	그들의 독립을 좋아하는
07	allergic	*a.* (~을) 몹시 싫어하는, (~에) 알레르기가 있는	( ) to housework	집안일을 몹시 싫어하는
08	conception	*n.* 개념	the ( ) of political power	정치적 권력이라는 개념
09	fixation	*n.* 고착, 고정 (관념)	a Western ( )	서양의 고정 관념
10	universal	*n.* 보편적인 것 *a.* 보편적인	a ( ) truth	보편적 진리
11	shaky	*a.* 불안정한, 불확실한	a ( ) business	불안정한 사업
12	remark	*v.* 말하다, 언급하다 *n.* 언급	( ) that it is a fact	그것이 사실이라고 언급하다
13	obsession	*n.* 강박 (관념)	cultural ( )s of our own	우리 자신의 문화적 강박 관념

➕ **본문 문장 속에서 단어들을 확인해 보세요.**

The conception of political power / as a *coercive* force, / while it may be a Western fixation, / is not a universal.

정치 권력이라는 개념은 / '강제적인' 힘으로서의 / 서양의 고정관념일지 모르겠지만, / 보편적인 것이 아니다.

01	cross-cultural	✏ 비교 문화적인	from a cross-cultural perspective	(비교 문화적) 관점에서
02	equation		the equation between benefits and costs	편익과 비용 사이의 ( )
03	dominance		dominance over others	다른 사람들에 대한 ( )
04	conceivably		conceivably neither	( ) 둘 다 아닌
05	bothersome		a bothersome idea	( ) 생각
06	fond		fond of their independence	그들의 독립을 ( )
07	allergic		allergic to housework	집안일을 ( )
08	conception		the conception of political power	정치적 권력이라는 ( )
09	fixation		a Western fixation	서양의 ( )
10	universal		a universal truth	( ) 진리
11	shaky		a shaky business	( ) 사업
12	remark		remark that it is a fact	그것이 사실이라고 ( )
13	obsession		cultural obsessions of our own	우리 자신의 문화적 ( )

✚ 본문 문장 속에서 단어의 의미를 우리말로 해석해 보세요.

The conception of political power / as a *coercive* force, / while it may be a Western fixation, / is not a universal.

➔ ▓▓▓▓▓▓▓▓▓▓ 은 / '강제적인' 힘으로서의 / ▓▓▓▓▓▓▓▓ 일지 모르겠지만, / ▓▓▓▓▓▓▓▓ 이 아니다.

96

다음 글의 내용을 한 문장으로 요약하고자 한다. 빈칸 (A), (B)에 들어갈 말로 가장 적절한 것은?

From a cross-cultural perspective the equation between public leadership and dominance is questionable. What does one mean by 'dominance'? Does it indicate coercion? Or control over 'the most valued'? 'Political' systems may be about both, either, or conceivably neither. The idea of 'control' would be a bothersome one for many peoples, as for instance among many native peoples of Amazonia where all members of a community are fond of their personal autonomy and notably allergic to any obvious expression of control or coercion. The conception of political power as a *coercive* force, while it may be a Western fixation, is not a universal. It is very unusual for an Amazonian leader to give an order. If many peoples do not view political power as a coercive force, *nor as the most valued domain*, then the leap from 'the political' to 'domination' (as coercion), *and from there* to 'domination of women', is a shaky one. As Marilyn Strathern has remarked, the notions of 'the political' and 'political personhood' are cultural obsessions of our own, a bias long reflected in anthropological constructs.

*coercion: 강제 **autonomy: 자율 ***anthropological: 인류학의

| It is _____(A)_____ to understand political power in other cultures through our own notion of it because ideas of political power are not _____(B)_____ across cultures. |

	(A)		(B)		(A)		(B)
①	rational	......	flexible	②	appropriate	......	commonplace
③	misguided	......	uniform	④	unreasonable	......	varied
⑤	effective	......	objective				

정답과 해설 p.88

01 From a cross-cultural perspective / the equation between public leadership and dominance / is questionable. // What does one mean by 'dominance'? // Does it indicate coercion? // Or control over 'the most valued'?

02 'Political' systems may be about both, either, or conceivably neither. // The idea of 'control' / would be a bothersome one for many peoples, / as for instance / among many native peoples of Amazonia / [where all members of a community are fond of their personal autonomy / and notably allergic to any obvious expression of control or coercion].

03 The conception of political power / as a *coercive* force, / (while it may be a Western fixation), / is not a universal. // It is very unusual / for an Amazonian leader / to give an order.

04 「view A as B: A를 B로 여기다」
If many peoples do not view political power as a coercive force, / *nor as the most valued domain*, / then the leap from 'the political' to 'domination' (as coercion), / *and from there* to 'domination of women', / is a shaky one. // As Marilyn Strathern has remarked, / the notions of 'the political' and 'political personhood' / are cultural obsessions of our own, / a bias long reflected in anthropological constructs.

05 → It is misguided / to understand political power in other cultures / through our own notion of it / because ideas of political power are not uniform across cultures.

01 비교 문화적cross-cultural 관점에서 / 대중적인 지도력과 지배력dominance 사이의 방정식equation은 / 의심스럽다. // '지배력'이 의미하는 바는 무엇인가? // 그것은 강제를 나타내는 것인가? // 아니면 '가장 가치 있는 것'에 대한 통제인가?

02 '정치적' 시스템은 둘 다 혹은 둘 중 하나에 관한 것이거나, 아니면 아마도conceivably 둘 다 관련이 없을 수도 있다. // '통제'라는 생각은 / 많은 부족에게는 성가신bothersome 것일 것이다 / 예를 들어 / 아마존의 많은 원주민 부족 사이에서 / 공동체의 모든 구성원이 개인의 자율성을 좋아하고fond / 통제나 강제가 명백하게 표현되는 어떤 것이든 몹시 싫어하는allergic.

03 정치 권력이라는 개념conception은 / '강제적인' 힘으로서의 / 서양의 고정관념fixation일지 모르겠지만, / 보편적인 것universal이 아니다. // 매우 이례적이다 / 아마존의 지도자에게 있어 / 명령을 내리는 것이.

04 많은 부족이 정치 권력을 강제적인 힘으로 여기지 않는다면 / 또한 '가장 가치 있는 영역으로도' / '정치적인 것'에서 (강제로서의) '지배'로 비약하는 것은 / 그리고 그로부터 '여성에 대한 지배'로 / 불안정shaky하다. // Marilyn Strathern이 말한remark 것처럼, / '정치적인 것'과 '정치적 개성'이라는 개념은 / 우리 자신의 문화적 강박 관념obsession으로, / 인류학적 구성 개념에 오랫동안 반영된 편견이다.

05 → 잘못된 것인데 / 다른 문화에서의 정치 권력을 이해하는 것은 / 그것에 대한 우리의 개념을 통해 / 왜냐하면 정치 권력에 관한 생각은 여러 문화에 걸쳐 보편적이지 않기 때문이다.

구문 Check up

① It is very unusual for / of an Amazonian leader to give an order.

to부정사의 의미상 주어는 사람의 성격을 나타내는 형용사가 나올 때를 제외하고는 「for + 목적격」으로 표시한다.

② The notions of 'the political' and 'political personhood' are cultural obsessions, a bias long reflected / was reflected in anthropological constructs.

문맥상 콤마 뒤는 cultural obsessions와 동격을 이루는 명사구인데, a bias는 '반영되는' 대상이므로 과거분사 reflected를 사용해 꾸며야 한다.

정답 ① for ② reflected

✔ 문제에 나오는 단어들을 확인하세요.

01	reunite	v. 재결합하다	break up and (✔ reunite)	헤어지고 재결합하다
02	availability	n. 이용 가능성	variation in food ( )	먹이의 이용 가능성의 변화
03	primate	n. 영장류	among ( )s	영장류 사이에서
04	elaborate	a. 정교한	( ) greeting behaviors	정교한 인사 행동
05	long-standing	a. 오래된	a ( ) friendship	오래된 우정
06	close	a. 친한, 가까운	hug a ( ) friend	친한 친구를 껴안다
07	tear up	눈물이 핑 돌다	( ) ( ) at the sight of a close friend	친한 친구의 모습에 눈물이 핑 돌다
08	trunk	n. (코끼리의) 코	elephants greeting with their ( )s	코로 인사하는 코끼리들
09	equivalent	a. 같은, 동등한 n. 동등한 것	( ) to a greeting	인사와 같은
10	theatrical	a. 극적인	( ) displays	극적인 모습
11	intensity	n. 강렬함, 강도	the ( ) of a friendship	우정의 강렬함
12	intimacy	n. 친밀함	the level of ( )	친밀함의 수준
13	strike a chord	심금을 울리다, 뭔가 생각나게 하다	( ) ( ) ( ) in our hearts	우리의 심금을 울리다
14	endangered	a. 멸종 위기에 처한	( ) species	멸종 위기에 처한 종

⊕ 본문 문장 속에서 단어들을 확인해 보세요.

Because elephant groups break up and reunite very frequently / — for instance, in response to variation in food availability — / reunions are more important in elephant society / than among primates.

코끼리 집단은 매우 자주 헤어지고 재결합하기 때문에 / 예컨대 먹이의 이용 가능성 변화에 대한 대응으로 / 재결합은 코끼리 사회에서 더 중요하다 / 영장류들 사이에서보다도.

문제를 풀기 전에 단어들을 **30초** 동안 다시 확인하세요.

01	reunite	✎ 재결합하다	break up and reunite	헤어지고 (재결합하다)
02	availability		variation in food availability	먹이의 ( )의 변화
03	primate		among primates	( ) 사이에서
04	elaborate		elaborate greeting behaviors	( ) 인사 행동
05	long-standing		a long-standing friendship	( ) 우정
06	close		hug a close friend	( ) 친구를 껴안다
07	tear up		tear up at the sight of a close friend	친한 친구의 모습에 ( )
08	trunk		elephants greeting with their trunks	( )로 인사하는 코끼리들
09	equivalent		equivalent to a greeting	인사와 ( )
10	theatrical		theatrical displays	( ) 모습
11	intensity		the intensity of a friendship	우정의 ( )
12	intimacy		the level of intimacy	( )의 수준
13	strike a chord		strike a chord in our hearts	우리의 ( )
14	endangered		endangered species	( ) 종

➕ **본문 문장 속에서 단어의 의미를 우리말로 해석해 보세요.**

Because elephant groups break up and reunite very frequently / — for instance, in response to variation in food availability — / reunions are more important in elephant society / than among primates.

➡ 코끼리 집단은 매우 자주   때문에 / 예컨대   변화에 대한 대응으로 / 재결합은 코끼리 사회에서 더 중요하다 /   보다도.

제한시간 80초
난이도 ★★★★★

STEP **2** • 수능 기출 제대로 **풀기**

97

다음 글의 내용을 한 문장으로 요약하고자 한다. 빈칸 (A), (B)에 들어갈 말로 가장 적절한 것은?

Because elephant groups break up and reunite very frequently — for instance, in response to variation in food availability — reunions are more important in elephant society than among primates. And the species has evolved elaborate greeting behaviors, the form of which reflects the strength of the social bond between the individuals (much like how you might merely shake hands with a long-standing acquaintance but hug a close friend you have not seen in a while, and maybe even tear up). Elephants may greet each other simply by reaching their trunks into each other's mouths, possibly equivalent to a human peck on the cheek. However, after long absences, members of family and bond groups greet one another with incredibly theatrical displays. The fact that the intensity reflects the duration of the separation as well as the level of intimacy suggests that elephants have a sense of time as well. To human eyes, these greetings strike a familiar chord. I'm reminded of the joyous reunions so visible in the arrivals area of an international airport terminal.

*acquaintance: 지인 **peck: 가벼운 입맞춤

> The evolved greeting behaviors of elephants can serve as an indicator of how much they are socially ____(A)____ and how long they have been ____(B)____ .

	(A)		(B)		(A)		(B)
①	competitive	·····	disconnected	②	tied	·····	endangered
③	responsible	·····	isolated	④	competitive	·····	united
⑤	tied	·····	parted				

정답과 해설 **p.89**

01 Because elephant groups break up and reunite very frequently / — (for instance, in response to variation in food availability) — / reunions are more important in elephant society / than among primates.
「비교급 + than: ~보다 …한」
삽입구

02 And the species has evolved elaborate greeting behaviors, / the form of which reflects the strength of the social bond between the individuals / (much like [how you might merely shake hands with a long-standing acquaintance / but hug a close friend / {(whom) you have not seen in a while}, / and maybe even tear up]).
선행사 계속적 용법
간접의문문(전치사 like의 목적어)
선행사
목적격 관계대명사절

03 Elephants may greet each other / simply by reaching their trunks into each other's mouths, / (which is) possibly equivalent to a human peck on the cheek. // However, / after long absences, / members of family and bond groups / greet one another with incredibly theatrical displays.
선행사(동명사구)
계속적 용법 주격보어

04 The fact / [that the intensity reflects the duration of the separation / as well as the level of intimacy] / suggests / [that elephants have a sense of time as well]. // To human eyes, / these greetings strike a familiar chord. // I'm reminded of the joyous reunions / so visible in the arrivals area of an international airport terminal.
주어 접속사(동격)
「A as well as B: B뿐만 아니라 A도」
동사(단수) 목적어
형용사구

05 → The evolved greeting behaviors of elephants / can serve as an indicator / of [how much they are socially tied] / and [how long they have been parted].
전치사
간접의문문1 간접의문문2

01 코끼리 집단은 매우 자주 헤어지고 재결합하기reunite 때문에 / 예컨대 먹이의 이용 가능성food availability 변화에 대한 대응으로 / 재결합은 코끼리 사회에서 더 중요하다 / 영장류들primate 사이에서보다도.

02 그래서 이 종은 정교한elaborate 인사 행동을 진화시켜 왔는데, / 그 형태는 개체들 사이의 사회적 유대감의 강도를 반영한다 / (마치 여러분이 오래된long-standing 지인들과는 단지 악수만 하지만 / 친한close 친구는 껴안는 것처럼 / 여러분이 한동안 보지 못했던 / 그리고 어쩌면 눈물까지 핑 돌 수도tear up 있는 것처럼).

03 코끼리는 서로 인사를 할 수도 있는데 / 단순히 코trunk를 서로의 입 안으로 갖다 대면서 / 이것은 아마도 사람들이 뺨에 가볍게 입 맞추는 것과 같을equivalent 것이다. // 그러나 / 오랜 공백 후에 / 가족이나 유대 관계 집단의 구성원들은 / 믿을 수 없을 정도로 극적인theatrical 모습으로 서로에게 인사한다.

04 사실은 / 강렬함intensity이 떨어져 있었던 시간의 길이도 반영한다는 / 친밀도intimacy뿐만 아니라 / 암시한다 / 코끼리들에게도 시간적 감각이 있다는 것을. // 사람들의 눈에 / 이런 인사 행위는 공감을 불러일으킨다strike a familiar chord. // 나는 즐거운 상봉 장면이 생각난다 / 국제공항 터미널 도착 구역에서 흔히 볼 수 있는.

05 → 코끼리의 진화된 인사 행동은 / 지표 역할을 할 수 있다 / 그들이 얼마나 사회적으로 유대감을 갖고 있으며 / 얼마나 오랫동안 헤어져 있었는지의.

구문 Check up

① And the species has evolved elaborate greeting behaviors, the form of them / which reflects the strength of the social bond between the individuals.

앞뒤로 절을 연결하면서 선행사 greeting behaviors를 대신할 수 있는 관계대명사 which가 적절하다.

② The fact that / which the intensity reflects the duration of the separation as well as the level of intimacy suggests that elephants have a sense of time as well.

주어 The fact 뒤로 '사실'의 내용을 보충 설명하는 동격 명사절이 이어지는 것이므로 that이 적절하다.

정답 ① which ② that

98 STEP 1 • 수능에 *진짜* 나오는 *단어*

✔ 문제에 나오는 단어들을 확인하세요.

01	conference	n. 회의	an environmental (✔ conference)	환경 회의
02	sustainability	n. 지속 가능성	the ( ) of economic growth	경제 성장의 지속 가능성
03	intend	v. 의도하다	( ) to change their behavior	행동을 바꾸려고 의도하다
04	public relations	홍보	a ( ) ( ) term	홍보 용어
05	widespread	a. 널리 퍼진	save our planet from ( ) harm	널리 퍼진 해악으로부터 지구를 구하다
06	institution	n. 기관, 제도	educational ( )s	교육 기관
07	corporation	n. 기업, 회사	a number of large ( )s	많은 대기업들
08	appoint	v. 임명하다, 지정하다	( ) a vice president	부사장을 임명하다
09	efficient	a. 효율적인	make the company more ( )	회사를 더 효율적으로 만들다
10	emission	n. 배출(량)	reduce the carbon ( )s	탄소 배출량을 줄이다

➕ 본문 문장 속에서 단어들을 확인해 보세요.

It became a public relations term, / an attempt to be seen as abreast / with the latest thinking of what we must do / to save our planet from widespread harm.

그것은 홍보 용어가 되었는데, / 보조를 맞추고 있는 것으로 보이려는 시도였다 / 우리가 무엇을 해야 하는가에 관한 최신의 생각과 / 널리 퍼진 해악으로부터 지구를 구하기 위해.

01	conference	회의	an environmental conference	환경 (회의)
02	sustainability		the sustainability of economic growth	경제 성장의 ( )
03	intend		intend to change their behavior	행동을 바꾸려고 ( )
04	public relations		a public relations term	( ) 용어
05	widespread		save our planet from widespread harm	( ) 해악으로부터 지구를 구하다
06	institution		educational institutions	교육 ( )
07	corporation		a number of large corporations	많은 대( )들
08	appoint		appoint a vice president	부사장을 ( )
09	efficient		make the company more efficient	회사를 더 ( ) 만들다
10	emission		reduce the carbon emissions	탄소 ( )을 줄이다

➕ **본문 문장 속에서 단어의 의미를 우리말로 해석해 보세요.**

It became a public relations term, / an attempt to be seen as abreast / with the latest thinking of what we must do / to save our planet from widespread harm.

➔ 그것은   가 되었는데, / 보조를 맞추고 있는 것으로 보이려는 시도였다 / 우리가 무엇을 해야 하는가에 관한 최신의 생각과 /   .

98 다음 글의 내용을 한 문장으로 요약하고자 한다. 빈칸 (A), (B)에 들어갈 말로 가장 적절한 것은?

After the United Nations environmental conference in Rio de Janeiro in 1992 made the term "sustainability" widely known around the world, the word became a popular buzzword by those who wanted to be seen as pro-environmental but who did not really intend to change their behavior. It became a public relations term, an attempt to be seen as abreast with the latest thinking of what we must do to save our planet from widespread harm. But then, in a decade or so, some governments, industries, educational institutions, and organizations started to use the term in a serious manner. In the United States a number of large corporations appointed a vice president for sustainability. Not only were these officials interested in how their companies could profit by producing "green" products, but they were often given the task of making the company more efficient by reducing wastes and pollution and by reducing its carbon emissions.

*buzzword: 유행어 **abreast: 나란히

While the term "sustainability," in the initial phase, was popular among those who _____(A)_____ to be eco-conscious, it later came to be used by those who would _____(B)_____ their pro-environmental thoughts.

(A)	(B)	(A)	(B)
① pretended	⋯⋯ actualize	② pretended	⋯⋯ disregard
③ refused	⋯⋯ realize	④ refused	⋯⋯ idealize
⑤ attempted	⋯⋯ mask		

정답과 해설 **p.90**

01 After the United Nations environmental conference / in Rio de Janeiro in 1992 / made the term "sustainability" widely known around the world, / the word became a popular buzzword by those / [who wanted to be seen as pro-environmental] / but [who did not really intend to change their behavior]. // It became a public relations term, / (which was) an attempt to be seen as abreast / with the latest thinking of [what we must do / to save our planet from widespread harm].

02 But then, / in a decade or so, / some governments, industries, educational institutions, and organizations / started to use the term in a serious manner.

03 In the United States / a number of large corporations / appointed a vice president for sustainability. // Not only were these officials interested / in how their companies could profit / by producing "green" products, / but they were often given / the task of making the company more efficient / by reducing wastes and pollution / and by reducing its carbon emissions.

04 → While the term "sustainability," (in the initial phase), was popular / among those [who pretended to be eco-conscious], / it later came to be used by those / [who would actualize their pro-environmental thoughts].

01 국제 연합 환경 회의conference가 / 1992년에 리우데자네이루에서의 / '지속 가능성sustainability'이라는 용어를 전 세계적으로 널리 알려지게 만든 후에 / 그 단어는 사람들에 의해 인기 있는 유행어가 되었다 / 친환경적으로 보이기를 원하는 / 하지만 자신의 행동을 진짜 바꾸려 의도하지는intend 않았던. // 그것은 홍보public relations 용어가 되었고, / 이것은 보조를 맞추고 있는 것으로 보이려는 시도였다 / 우리가 무엇을 해야 하는가에 관한 최신의 생각과 / 널리 퍼진widespread 해악으로부터 지구를 구하기 위해.

02 그러나 그런 다음 / 십여 년이 지난 후, / 일부 정부, 산업, 교육 기관educational institution, 그리고 조직이 / 그 용어를 진지한 방식으로 사용하기 시작했다.

03 미국에서 / 많은 대기업large corporation이 / 지속 가능성 담당 부사장을 임명했다appoint. // 이 임원들은 관심이 있을 뿐만 아니라 / 회사가 어떻게 이익을 얻을 수 있는가에 / '친환경' 제품을 만들어서 / 그들은 흔히 받기도 했다 / 회사를 더 효율적으로efficient 만들라는 과제를 / 쓰레기와 오염을 줄임으로써, / 그리고 그 회사의 탄소 배출량emission을 줄임으로써.

04 → 비록 '지속 가능성'이라는 용어는 초기 단계에서 인기가 있었지만 / 친환경 의식이 있는 체했던 사람들 사이에서, / 나중에 그것은 사람들에 의해 사용되었다 / 자신의 친환경주의적 생각을 실현하고자 하는.

구문 Check up

① It became a public relations term, an attempt to be seen as abreast with the latest thinking of that / what we must do to save our planet from widespread harm.

앞에 of의 목적어 역할을 할 선행사가 없고 뒤에 must do의 목적어가 없는 불완전한 절이 나오므로 선행사를 포함한 관계대명사 what이 적절하다.

② Not only these officials were / were these officials interested in how their companies could profit by producing "green" products, ~

Not only가 부정어구이므로 의문문 어순의 도치 구문을 써야 한다. 따라서 were these officials가 적절하다.

정답 ① what ② were these officials

99 STEP 1 • 수능에 *진짜* 나오는 *단어*

✔️ 문제에 나오는 단어들을 확인하세요.

01	negotiation	n. 협상	(✔️ negotiation) skills	협상 능력
02	integrative	a. 통합의	an ( ) agreement	통합적 합의
03	mythical	a. 허구의	the ( ) fixed pie	허구의 고정된 파이
04	settlement	n. 합의	a peace ( )	평화 합의
05	mutually beneficial	상호 이익이 되는	a ( ) ( ) trade-off	상호 이익이 되는 절충안
06	suppress	v. 억누르다, 억제하다	( ) efforts to seek joint benefits	공동의 이익을 찾으려는 노력을 억누르다
07	applicant	n. 지원자	a job ( )	일자리 지원자
08	resolution	n. 해결	the ( ) of the salary issue	급여 문제의 해결
09	simulated	a. 모의의	a ( ) negotiation	모의 협상
10	jail sentence	징역형	a three-year ( ) ( )	3년의 징역형
11	competitively	ad. 경쟁적으로	approach the situation ( )	상황에 경쟁적으로 접근하다
12	cooperatively	ad. 협조적으로	work ( )	협조적으로 일하다
13	constraint	n. 제약	due to time ( )s	시간 제약 때문에
14	misperception	n. 오해	a common ( )	흔한 오해

➕ 본문 문장 속에서 단어들을 확인해 보세요.

Stressful conditions such as time constraints / contribute to this common misperception, / which in turn may lead to less integrative agreements.

시간 제약처럼 스트레스가 많은 조건은 / 이러한 흔한 오해의 원인이 되며, / 이는 결국 덜 통합적인 합의로 이어질 수 있다.

01	negotiation	✏ 협상	negotiation skills	(협상)능력
02	integrative		an integrative agreement	( )합의
03	mythical		the mythical fixed pie	( ) 고정된 파이
04	settlement		a peace settlement	평화( )
05	mutually beneficial		a mutually beneficial trade-off	( )절충안
06	suppress		suppress efforts to seek joint benefits	공동의 이익을 찾으려는 노력을 ( )
07	applicant		a job applicant	일자리( )
08	resolution		the resolution of the salary issue	급여 문제의 ( )
09	simulated		a simulated negotiation	( )협상
10	jail sentence		a three-year jail sentence	3년의 ( )
11	competitively		approach the situation competitively	상황에 ( ) 접근하다
12	cooperatively		work cooperatively	( ) 일하다
13	constraint		due to time constraints	시간 ( ) 때문에
14	misperception		a common misperception	흔한 ( )

➕ 본문 문장 속에서 단어의 의미를 우리말로 해석해 보세요.

Stressful conditions such as time constraints / contribute to this common misperception, / which in turn may lead to less integrative agreements.

➔ 　　　　　처럼 스트레스가 많은 조건은 / 　　　　　　의 원인이 되며, / 이는 결국 　　　　　　합의로 이어질 수 있다.

99 다음 글을 읽고, 물음에 답하시오.

Many negotiators assume that all negotiations involve a fixed pie. Negotiators often approach integrative negotiation opportunities as zero-sum situations or win-lose exchanges. Those who believe in the mythical fixed pie assume that parties' interests stand in opposition, with no possibility for integrative settlements and mutually beneficial trade-offs, so they (a) suppress efforts to search for them. In a hiring negotiation, a job applicant who assumes that salary is the only issue may insist on $75,000 when the employer is offering $70,000. Only when the two parties discuss the possibilities further do they discover that moving expenses and starting date can also be negotiated, which may (b) block resolution of the salary issue.

The tendency to see negotiation in fixed-pie terms (c) varies depending on how people view the nature of a given conflict situation. This was shown in a clever experiment by Harinck, de Dreu, and Van Vianen involving a simulated negotiation between prosecutors and defense lawyers over jail sentences. Some participants were told to view their goals in terms of personal gain (e.g., arranging a particular jail sentence will help your career), others were told to view their goals in terms of effectiveness (a particular sentence is most likely to prevent recidivism), and still others were told to focus on values (a particular jail sentence is fair and just). Negotiators focusing on personal gain were most likely to come under the influence of fixed-pie beliefs and approach the situation (d) competitively. Negotiators focusing on values were least likely to see the problem in fixed-pie terms and more inclined to approach the situation cooperatively. Stressful conditions such as time constraints contribute to this common misperception, which in turn may lead to (e) less integrative agreements.

*prosecutor: 검사 **recidivism: 상습적 범행

[99-1] 윗글의 제목으로 가장 적절한 것은?

① Fixed Pie: A Key to Success in a Zero-sum Game
② Fixed Pie Tells You How to Get the Biggest Salary
③ Negotiators, Wake Up from the Myth of the Fixed Pie!
④ Want a Fairer Jail Sentence? Stick to the Fixed Pie
⑤ What Alternatives Maximize Fixed-pie Effects?

[99-2] 밑줄 친 (a)~(e) 중에서 문맥상 낱말의 쓰임이 적절하지 <u>않은</u> 것은?

① (a)
② (b)
③ (c)
④ (d)
⑤ (e)

정답과 해설 p.92

01 Many negotiators assume / [that all negotiations involve a fixed pie]. // Negotiators
명사절(목적어)
often approach integrative negotiation opportunities / as zero-sum situations or win-
전치사(~로서)
lose exchanges.

02 Those who believe in the mythical fixed pie assume / that parties' interests stand in
주격 관계대명사절
opposition, / with no possibility for integrative settlements and mutually beneficial
trade-offs, / so they suppress efforts to search for them. // In a hiring negotiation, / a
= integrative ~ trade-offs
job applicant who assumes that salary is the only issue / may insist on $75,000 / when
주격 관계대명사절
the employer is offering $70,000. // Only when the two parties discuss the possibilities
도치를 유도하는 부정어(오로지 ~할 때만)
further / do they discover / that moving expenses and starting date can also be
도치 구문(조동사 + 주어 + 동사원형)   선행사(문장)
negotiated, / which may block resolution of the salary issue.
계속적 용법

03 The tendency to see negotiation in fixed-pie terms / varies / depending on how people
주어   형용사적 용법   동사(단수)   ~에 따라
view the nature of a given conflict situation. // This was shown in a clever experiment
by Harinck, de Dreu, and Van Vianen / involving a simulated negotiation between
전치사구   현재분사구
prosecutors and defense lawyers over jail sentences.

04 Some participants were told to view their goals in terms of personal gain / (e.g.,
「some ~ others ~ still others ~: 어떤 사람들 ~ 다른 사람들 ~ 또 다른 사람들 ~」
arranging a particular jail sentence will help your career), / others were told to view
their goals in terms of effectiveness / (a particular sentence is most likely to prevent
recidivism), / and still others were told to focus on values / (a particular jail sentence
is fair and just).

05 Negotiators focusing on personal gain / were most likely to come under the influence
현재분사구   가장 ~할 가능성이 높다
of fixed-pie beliefs / and approach the situation competitively. // Negotiators focusing
to부정사 병렬   현재분사구
on values / were least likely to see the problem in fixed-pie terms / and more
가장 ~할 가능성이 낮다
inclined to approach the situation cooperatively. // Stressful conditions such as time
constraints / contribute to this common misperception, / which in turn may lead to
계속적 용법(콤마 앞 보충)
less integrative agreements.

01 많은 협상가는 가정한다 / 모든 협상이 고정된 파이를 수반한다고. // 협상가들은 흔히 통합 협상integrative negotiation 기회에 접근한다 / 제로섬 상황이나 승패 교환으로.

02 허구의mythical 고정된 파이를 믿는 사람들은 가정한다 / 당사자들의 이해관계가 반대 입장에 있다고 / 통합적인 합의settlement와 상호 이익이 되는mutually beneficial 절충안의 가능성이 없는 / 그래서 그들은 이를 찾으려는 노력을 억누른다suppress. // 고용 협상에서 / 급여가 유일한 문제라고 생각하는 구직자job applicant는 / 7만 5천 달러를 요구할 수 있다 / 고용주가 7만 달러를 제시할 때. // 두 당사자가 가능성에 대해 더 자세히 논의할 때만 / 그들은 발견하게 된다 / 이사 비용과 시작 날짜 또한 논의될 수 있다는 것을 / 이것은 급여 문제의 해결resolution을 방해할(→ 촉진할) 수 있을 것이다.

03 협상을 고정된 파이 관점에서 보는 경향은 / 달라진다 / 사람들이 주어진 갈등 상황의 본질을 어떻게 보느냐에 따라. // 이는 Harinck, de Dreu와 Van Vianen에 의한 기발한 실험에서 밝혀졌다 / 징역형jail sentence에 대한 검사와 피고측 변호인 간의 모의simulated 협상을 포함하는.

04 어떤 참가자들은 개인적 이득의 관점에서 그들의 목표를 보라는 말을 들었고, / (예를 들어, 특정 징역형을 정하는 것이 당신의 경력에 도움이 될 것이다) / 다른 참가자들은 그들의 목표를 효과성의 관점에서 보라는 말을 들었으며, / (특정 형은 상습적 범행을 방지할 가능성이 가장 크다) / 그리고 또 다른 참가자들은 가치에 초점을 맞추라는 말을 들었다 / (특정 징역형은 공정하고 정당하다).

05 개인적 이득에 초점을 맞춘 협상가들은 / 고정된 파이에 대한 믿음의 영향을 받을 가능성이 가장 컸다 / 그리고 상황에 경쟁적으로competitively 접근할. // 가치에 초점을 맞춘 협상가들은 / 문제를 고정된 파이 관점에서 볼 가능성이 가장 낮았고 / 상황에 협조적으로cooperatively 접근하려는 경향이 더 컸다. // 시간 제약time constraint처럼 스트레스가 많은 조건은 / 이러한 흔한 오해misperception의 원인이 되며, / 이는 결국 덜 통합적인 합의로 이어질 수 있다.

DAY 15
100 STEP 1 · 수능에 *진짜* 나오는 *단어*

✔ 문제에 나오는 단어들을 확인하세요.

01	outperform	v. 능가하다	(✔ outperform) all others	다른 모두를 능가하다
02	prediction	n. 예측, 예견	an accurate ( )	정확한 예측
03	commit	v. (범죄 등을) 저지르다	( ) another crime	또 다른 범죄를 저지르다
04	candidate	n. 후보자	a potential ( )	유력한 후보자
05	formula	n. 공식	use a simple ( )	간단한 공식을 쓰다
06	tie	n. 무승부, 동점	end in a ( )	무승부로 끝나다
07	consistent	a. 일관성 있는	remain ( )	일관성 있는 상태를 유지하다
08	irrelevant	a. 관련이 없는	( ) considerations	관련 없는 고려사항
09	intensive	a. 집중적인	( ) care	집중 치료(실)
10	crucial	a. 매우 중요한	miss a ( ) step	매우 중요한 단계를 놓치다
11	infection	n. 감염	prevent ( )s at home	집에서의 감염을 예방하다

⊕ 본문 문장 속에서 단어들을 확인해 보세요.

There is evidence / that even very simple algorithms can outperform expert judgement / on simple prediction problems.

증거가 있다 / 매우 간단한 알고리즘조차도 전문가의 판단을 능가할 수 있다는 / 간단한 예측 문제에 대한.

01	outperform	✎ 능가하다	outperform all others	다른 모두를 (능가하다)
02	prediction		an accurate prediction	정확한 ( )
03	commit		commit another crime	또 다른 범죄를 ( )
04	candidate		a potential candidate	유력한 ( )
05	formula		use a simple formula	간단한 ( )을 쓰다
06	tie		end in a tie	( )로 끝나다
07	consistent		remain consistent	( ) 상태를 유지하다
08	irrelevant		irrelevant considerations	( ) 고려사항
09	intensive		intensive care	( ) 치료(실)
10	crucial		miss a crucial step	( ) 단계를 놓치다
11	infection		prevent infections at home	집에서의 ( )을 예방하다

➕ **본문 문장 속에서 단어의 의미를 우리말로 해석해 보세요.**

There is evidence / that even very simple algorithms can outperform expert judgement / on simple prediction problems.

→ 증거가 있다 / 매우 간단한 알고리즘조차도 ▮▮▮▮ 수 있다는 / ▮▮▮▮에 대한.

100 다음 글을 읽고, 물음에 답하시오.

There is evidence that even very simple algorithms can outperform expert judgement on simple prediction problems. For example, algorithms have proved more (a) accurate than humans in predicting whether a prisoner released on parole will go on to commit another crime, or in predicting whether a potential candidate will perform well in a job in future. In over 100 studies across many different domains, half of all cases show simple formulas make (b) better significant predictions than human experts, and the remainder (except a very small handful), show a tie between the two. When there are a lot of different factors involved and a situation is very uncertain, simple formulas can win out by focusing on the most important factors and being consistent, while human judgement is too easily influenced by particularly salient and perhaps (c) irrelevant considerations. A similar idea is supported by further evidence that 'checklists' can improve the quality of expert decisions in a range of domains by ensuring that important steps or considerations aren't missed when people are feeling (d) relaxed. For example, treating patients in intensive care can require hundreds of small actions per day, and one small error could cost a life. Using checklists to ensure that no crucial steps are missed has proved to be remarkably (e) effective in a range of medical contexts, from preventing live infections to reducing pneumonia.

*parole: 가석방 **salient: 두드러진 ***pneumonia: 폐렴

[100-1] 윗글의 제목으로 가장 적절한 것은?

① The Power of Simple Formulas in Decision Making
② Always Prioritise: Tips for Managing Big Data
③ Algorithms' Mistakes: The Myth of Simplicity
④ Be Prepared! Make a Checklist Just in Case
⑤ How Human Judgement Beats Algorithms

[100-2] 밑줄 친 (a)~(e) 중에서 문맥상 낱말의 쓰임이 적절하지 <u>않은</u> 것은?

① (a)
② (b)
③ (c)
④ (d)
⑤ (e)

정답과 해설 p.93

01 There is evidence / [that even very simple algorithms can outperform expert
동격 명사절(= evidence)
judgement / on simple prediction problems]. // For example, / algorithms have proved
동사
more accurate than humans / in predicting [whether a prisoner released on parole will
주격보어(비교급 형용사)   동명사 관용표현(~하는 데 있어)   과거분사구
go on to commit another crime], / or in predicting [whether a potential candidate will
주어
perform well in a job in future].
동사구   [ ]: 명사절(~인지 아닌지)

02 In over 100 studies across many different domains, / half of all cases show /that simple
                                                    주어1(부분 + of + 전체)   동사1(복수)
formulas make better significant predictions than human experts, / and the remainder
                                                                    주어2
(except a very small handful), / show a tie between the two. // When there are a lot of
                          과거분사   동사2
different factors involved / and a situation is very uncertain, / simple formulas can win
out / by focusing on the most important factors and being consistent, / while human
        동명사 관용표현(~함으로써)   접속사(~한 반면)
judgement is too easily influenced / by particularly salient and perhaps irrelevant
considerations.

03 A similar idea is supported by further evidence / [that 'checklists' can improve the
                                                동격 명사절(= further evidence)
quality of expert decisions / in a range of domains / by ensuring that important steps
or considerations aren't missed / when people are feeling relaxed]. // For example, /
treating patients in intensive care / can require hundreds of small actions per day, /
and one small error could cost a life. // Using checklists to ensure that no crucial steps
                                    주어(동명사구)   부사적 용법(목적)
are missed / has proved to be remarkably effective / in a range of medical contexts, /
            동사(단수)
from preventing live infections to reducing pneumonia.
「from A to B: A부터 B까지(동명사구 병렬)」

01 증거가 있다 / 매우 간단한 알고리즘조차도 전문가의 판단을 능가할outperform 수 있다는 / 간단한 예측prediction
문제에 대한. // 예를 들어, / 알고리즘이 인간보다 더 정확하다는 것이 입증되었다 / 가석방으로 풀려난 죄수가 계속해서
다른 범죄를 저지를commit 것인지 예측하거나, / 잠재적 (입사) 후보자candidate가 장차 직장에서 일을 잘할 것인지를
예측하는 데.

02 많은 다른 영역에 걸친 100개가 넘는 연구에서, / 모든 사례의 절반은 보여준다 / 간단한 공식formula이 인간 전문가보다
중요한 예측을 더 잘한다는 것을 / 그리고 (아주 적은 소수를 제외한) 나머지는 / 둘 사이의 무승부tie를 보여준다. //
관련된 많은 다른 요인이 있고 / 상황이 매우 불확실할 때, / 간단한 공식은 승리할 수 있다 / 가장 중요한 요소에 초점을
맞추고 일관성consistent을 유지함으로써 / 인간의 판단은 너무 쉽게 영향을 받는 반면에 / 특히 두드러지고 아마도
관련이 없는irrelevant 고려 사항에 의해.

03 비슷한 관념이 추가적 증거로 뒷받침된다 / '체크리스트'가 전문가의 결정의 질을 향상할 수 있다는 / 다양한 영역에서 /
중요한 조치나 고려 사항이 놓쳐지지 않도록 함으로써 / 사람들이 편안하다고(→ 일이 너무 많다고) 느낄 때. // 예를 들어, /
집중 치료intensive care 중인 환자를 치료하는 것은 / 하루에 수백 가지의 작은 조치를 요구할 수 있다 / 그리고 작은 실수
하나가 목숨을 앗아갈 수 있다. // 어떠한 중요한crucial 조치라도 놓치지 않기 위해 체크리스트를 사용하는 것은 / 현저히
효과가 있다는 것이 입증되었다 / 다양한 의학적 상황에서 / 활성 감염infection의 예방부터 폐렴 감소에 이르기까지.

101

STEP 1 • 수능에 *진짜* 나오는 *단어*

✔ 문제에 나오는 단어들을 확인하세요.

01	companion	n. 친구, 동반자	a traveling (✔ companion)	여행 친구
02	pound	v. (가슴이) 두근거리다	( ) with hope	희망으로 두근거리다
03	excitement	n. 흥분	hurry with ( )	흥분하여 서두르다
04	lose hope	실망하다, 낙담하다	Don't ( ) ( ) yet!	아직 실망하지 마!
05	exhibition	n. 전시(회)	the day of the special ( )	특별 전시회 날
06	relieved	a. 안도한	feel ( )	안도한 기분이 들다
07	masterpiece	n. 걸작	see his ( ) in person	그의 걸작을 직접 보다
08	grab	v. 쥐다, 잡다	( ) me by the hand	내 손을 잡다
09	drag	v. 끌다	( ) the chair	의자를 끌다
10	hurriedly	ad. 서둘러	run ( )	서둘러 달리다
11	inspire	v. 영감을 주다	( ) me to become a painter	내가 화가가 되도록 영감을 주다
12	isolation	n. 고립	( ) and loneliness	고립과 고독
13	eagerly	ad. 잔뜩 기대하며, 열심히	( ) look for another job	다른 직장을 열심히 구하다

⊕ **본문 문장 속에서 단어들을 확인해 보세요.**

"It'll be amazing to see / how he communicated the feelings of isolation and loneliness in his work," / she said eagerly.

"보면 놀라울 거야 / 그가 자기 작품에서 고립과 고독의 감정을 어떻게 전달했는지."라고 / 그녀는 잔뜩 기대하며 말했다.

01	companion	🖉 친구, 동반자	a traveling companion	여행 (친구)
02	pound		pound with hope	희망으로 ( )
03	excitement		hurry with excitement	( )하여 서두르다
04	lose hope		Don't lose hope yet!	아직 ( ) 마!
05	exhibition		the day of the special exhibition	특별 ( ) 날
06	relieved		feel relieved	( ) 기분이 들다
07	masterpiece		see his masterpiece in person	그의 ( )을 직접 보다
08	grab		grab me by the hand	내 손을 ( )
09	drag		drag the chair	의자를 ( )
10	hurriedly		run hurriedly	( ) 달리다
11	inspire		inspire me to become a painter	내가 화가가 되도록 ( )
12	isolation		isolation and loneliness	( )과 고독
13	eagerly		eagerly look for another job	다른 직장을 ( ) 구하다

➕ **본문 문장 속에서 단어의 의미를 우리말로 해석해 보세요.**

"It'll be amazing to see / how he communicated the feelings of isolation and loneliness in his work," / she said eagerly.

→ "보면 놀라울 거야 / 그가 자기 작품에서   의 감정을 어떻게 전달했는지."라고 / 그녀는   말했다.

2023학년도 9월 43~45번
제한시간 140초
난이도 101-1 ★★☆☆☆
101-2 ★☆☆☆☆
101-3 ★☆☆☆☆

STEP **2** • 수능 기출 제대로 풀기

101 다음 글을 읽고, 물음에 답하시오.

(A) Walking out of Charing Cross Station in London, Emilia and her traveling companion, Layla, already felt their hearts pounding. It was the second day of their European summer trip. They were about to visit one of the world's most famous art galleries. The two of them started hurrying with excitement. Suddenly, Emilia shouted, "Look! There it is! We're finally at the National Gallery!" Layla laughed and responded, "(a) Your dream's finally come true!"

(B) "Don't lose hope yet! Which gallery is the special exhibition at?" Layla asked. Emilia responded, "Well, his *Sunflowers* is still in England, but it's at a gallery in Liverpool. That's a long way, isn't it?" After a quick search on her phone, Layla stated, "No! It's only two hours to Liverpool by train. The next train leaves in an hour. Why don't we take it?" After considering the idea, Emilia, now relieved, responded, "Yeah, but (b) you always wanted to see Rembrandt's paintings. Let's do that first, Layla! Then, after lunch, we can catch the next train." Layla smiled brightly.

(C) However, after searching all the exhibition rooms, Emilia and Layla couldn't find van Gogh's masterpiece anywhere. "That's weird. Van Gogh's *Sunflowers* should be here. Where is it?" Emilia looked upset, but Layla kept calm and said, "Maybe (c) you've missed a notice about it. Check the National Gallery app." Emilia checked it quickly. Then, she sighed, "*Sunflowers* isn't here! It's been lent to a different gallery for a special exhibition. (d) I can't believe I didn't check!"

(D) Upon entering the National Gallery, Emilia knew exactly where to go first. (e) She grabbed Layla's hand and dragged her hurriedly to find van Gogh's *Sunflowers*. It was Emilia's favorite painting and had inspired her to become a painter. Emilia loved his use of bright colors and light. She couldn't wait to finally see his masterpiece in person. "It'll be amazing to see how he communicated the feelings of isolation and loneliness in his work," she said eagerly.

[101-1] 주어진 글 (A)에 이어질 내용을 순서에 맞게 배열한 것으로 가장 적절한 것은?

① (B) — (D) — (C)　　② (C) — (B) — (D)
③ (C) — (D) — (B)　　④ (D) — (B) — (C)
⑤ (D) — (C) — (B)

[101-2] 밑줄 친 (a)~(e) 중에서 가리키는 대상이 나머지 넷과 다른 것은?

① (a)　② (b)　③ (c)　④ (d)　⑤ (e)

[101-3] 윗글에 관한 내용으로 적절하지 않은 것은?

① Emilia와 Layla는 유럽 여행 중이었다.
② Layla는 Emilia에게 Liverpool로 가자고 제안했다.
③ Emilia는 기차를 점심 식사 전에 타자고 말했다.
④ National Gallery에는 van Gogh의 *Sunflowers*가 없었다.
⑤ Emilia는 van Gogh의 *Sunflowers*를 좋아했다.

정답과 해설 p.94

01 Walking out of Charing Cross Station in London, / Emilia and her traveling companion, Layla, / already felt their hearts pounding. // It was the second day of their European summer trip. // They were about to visit one of the world's most famous art galleries. // The two of them started hurrying with excitement. // Suddenly, Emilia shouted, / "Look! There it is! We're finally at the National Gallery!" // Layla laughed and responded, / "Your dream's finally come true!"

02 Upon entering the National Gallery, / Emilia knew exactly where to go first. // She grabbed Layla's hand / and dragged her hurriedly to find van Gogh's *Sunflowers*. // It was Emilia's favorite painting / and had inspired her to become a painter. // Emilia loved his use of bright colors and light. // She couldn't wait to finally see his masterpiece in person. // "It'll be amazing to see / how he communicated the feelings of isolation and loneliness in his work," / she said eagerly.

03 However, / after searching all the exhibition rooms, / Emilia and Layla couldn't find van Gogh's masterpiece anywhere. // "That's weird. / Van Gogh's *Sunflowers* should be here. / Where is it?" // Emilia looked upset, / but Layla kept calm and said, / "Maybe you've missed a notice about it. / Check the National Gallery app." // Emilia checked it quickly. // Then, she sighed, / "*Sunflowers* isn't here! / It's been lent to a different gallery for a special exhibition. / I can't believe I didn't check!"

04 "Don't lose hope yet! / Which gallery is the special exhibition at?" / Layla asked. // Emilia responded, / "Well, his *Sunflowers* is still in England, / but it's at a gallery in Liverpool. / That's a long way, isn't it?" // After a quick search on her phone, / Layla stated, / "No! It's only two hours to Liverpool by train. / The next train leaves in an hour. / Why don't we take it?" // After considering the idea, / Emilia, now relieved, responded, / "Yeah, but you always wanted to see Rembrandt's paintings. / Let's do that first, Layla! / Then, after lunch, we can catch the next train." // Layla smiled brightly.

---

01 런던의 Charing Cross 역에서 걸어 나오면서, / Emilia와 그 여행 친구companion Layla는 / 벌써 가슴이 두근거리는pound 기분이었다. // 그들의 유럽 여름 여행 둘째 날이었다. // 그들은 세계에서 가장 유명한 미술관 중 하나를 방문할 계획이었다. // 두 사람은 흥분excitement하여 서두르기 시작했다. // 문득 Emilia가 소리쳤다 / "봐! 저기 있네! 드디어 우리가 내셔널 갤러리에 도착했어!"라고. / Layla는 웃으며 답했다 / "네 꿈이 드디어 이루어졌네!"라고.

02 내셔널 갤러리에 들어가자마자, / Emilia는 어디로 제일 먼저 갈지 정확하게 알았다. // 그녀는 Layla의 손을 꼭 잡고grab 반 고흐의 <Sunflowers>를 찾으려고 서둘러hurriedly 그녀를 끌었다drag. // 그것은 Emilia가 가장 좋아하는 그림이었고, / 그녀가 화가가 되도록 영감을 준inspire 것이었다. / Emilia는 그의 밝은 색상과 빛의 사용을 아주 좋아했다. // 그녀는 그의 걸작을 마침내 보기를 몹시 고대하고 있었다. // "보면 놀라울 거야 / 그가 자기 작품에서 고립isolation감과 고독감을 어떻게 전달했는지."라고 / 그녀는 잔뜩 기대하며eagerly 말했다.

03 그러나, / 모든 전시실을 찾아봐도, / Emilia와 Layla는 반 고흐의 걸작masterpiece을 어디에서도 찾을 수가 없었다. // "이상하네. / 반 고흐의 <Sunflowers>는 여기 있어야 하는데. / 어디에 있지?" // Emilia는 속상해 보였지만, / Layla는 침착함을 유지하며 말했다 / "아마 네가 작품에 대한 공지를 놓쳤나 봐. / 내셔널 갤러리 앱을 확인해 봐."라고. // Emilia는 재빨리 그것을 확인했다. // 이후 그녀는 한숨을 쉬었다. / "<Sunflowers>가 여기 없네! / 그것은 특별 전시회 때문에 다른 미술관에 대여됐대. / 내가 확인을 안 해봤다니 믿을 수 없네!"

04 "아직 실망하지lose hope 마! / 특별 전시회exhibition는 어느 미술관에서 한대?"라고 / Layla는 물었다. // Emilia는 대답했다 / "음, <Sunflowers>는 여전히 잉글랜드에 있긴 한데, / 그것은 리버풀에 있는 미술관에 있어. / 거긴 멀잖아, 안 그래?"라고. // 전화로 재빨리 검색한 뒤, / Layla는 말했다. / "아냐! 리버풀까지 기차로 겨우 두 시간이야. / 다음 기차가 한 시간 뒤에 출발해. / 그걸 타면 어때?" // 그 생각을 고려해본 뒤, / 이제 안도한relieved Emilia는 답했다. / "그래, 근데 넌 늘 렘브란트의 그림들을 보고 싶어 했잖아. / 그거부터 보자, Layla! / 그런 다음 점심 먹고 그다음 기차를 타면 돼."라고 // Layla가 밝게 웃었다.

102 STEP 1 • 수능에 *진짜* 나오는 *단어*

✔ 문제에 나오는 단어들을 확인하세요.

01	crisis	n. 위기	tackle the climate (✔ crisis)	기후 위기에 대처하다
02	take on	~에 관해 이야기하다, ~을 떠맡다	( ) ( ) the relationship between the two	둘 사이의 관계성에 관해 이야기하다
03	believably	ad. 믿을 만하게	( ) represent climate change	기후 위기를 믿을 만하게 표현하다
04	improbable	a. 있을 것 같지 않은	too ( ) to belong in stories about everyday life	너무 있을 것 같지 않아 일상생활에 속할 수 없는
05	extraordinary	a. 놀라운, 대단한, 보기 드문	an ( ) achievement	보기 드문 성취
06	imperceptible	a. 감지할 수 없는	( ) changes in temperature	감지할 수 없는 온도 변화
07	occasionally	ad. 이따금, 가끔	come ( )	이따금 오다
08	spectacular	a. 극적인, 장관의	explosive and ( ) events	폭발적이고 극적인 사건들
09	confront	v. 직면하게 하다	( )ed with unexpected situations	예기치 못한 상황에 직면한
10	accumulate	v. 축적하다	( )d impacts of climate change	기후 변화의 축적된 영향
11	pose a challenge	문제[도전]을 제기하다	( ) ( ) significant ( )	중대한 문제를 제기하다

➕ 본문 문장 속에서 단어들을 확인해 보세요.

Ghosh explains / that climate change is largely absent from contemporary fiction / because the cyclones, floods, and other catastrophes / it brings to mind / simply seem too "improbable" / to belong in stories about everyday life.

Ghosh는 설명한다 / 기후 변화는 현대 소설에 대체로 존재하지 않는다고 / 사이클론, 홍수, 그리고 다른 큰 재해들이 / 그것이 상기시키는 / 그야말로 너무 '있을 것 같지 않아' 보여서 / 일상생활 이야기에 속할 수 없기 때문에.

문제를 풀기 전에 단어들을 30초 동안 다시 확인하세요.

01	crisis	✎ 위기	tackle the climate crisis	기후 (위기)에 대처하다
02	take on		take on the relationship between the two	둘 사이의 관계성에 관해 ( )
03	believably		believably represent climate change	기후 위기를 ( ) 표현하다
04	improbable		too improbable to belong in stories about everyday life	너무 ( ) 일상생활에 속할 수 없는
05	extraordinary		an extraordinary achievement	( ) 성취
06	imperceptible		imperceptible changes in temperature	( ) 온도 변화
07	occasionally		come occasionally	( ) 오다
08	spectacular		explosive and spectacular events	폭발적이고 ( ) 사건들
09	confront		confronted with unexpected situations	예기치 못한 상황에 ( )
10	accumulate		accumulated impacts of climate change	기후 변화의 ( ) 영향
11	pose a challenge		pose a significant challenge	중대한 ( )

➕ **본문 문장 속에서 단어의 의미를 우리말로 해석해 보세요.**

Ghosh explains / that climate change is largely absent from contemporary fiction / because the cyclones, floods, and other catastrophes / it brings to mind / simply seem too "improbable" / to belong in stories about everyday life.

➡ Ghosh는 설명한다 / 기후 변화는 현대 소설에 대체로 존재하지 않는다고 / 사이클론, 홍수, 그리고 다른 큰 재해들이 / 그것이 상기시키는 / 그야말로 ▇▇▇▇▇▇▇▇▇▇▇▇ / ▇▇▇▇▇▇▇▇▇▇ 때문에.

102 다음 글을 읽고, 물음에 답하시오.

Climate change experts and environmental humanists alike agree that the climate crisis is, at its core, a crisis of the imagination and much of the popular imagination is shaped by fiction. In his 2016 book *The Great Derangement*, anthropologist and novelist Amitav Ghosh takes on this relationship between imagination and environmental management, arguing that humans have failed to respond to climate change at least in part because fiction (a) fails to believably represent it. Ghosh explains that climate change is largely absent from contemporary fiction because the cyclones, floods, and other catastrophes it brings to mind simply seem too "improbable" to belong in stories about everyday life. But climate change does not only reveal itself as a series of (b) extraordinary events. In fact, as environmentalists and ecocritics from Rachel Carson to Rob Nixon have pointed out, environmental change can be "imperceptible"; it proceeds (c) rapidly, only occasionally producing "explosive and spectacular" events. Most climate change impacts cannot be observed day-to-day, but they become (d) visible when we are confronted with their accumulated impacts.

Climate change evades our imagination because it poses significant representational challenges. It cannot be observed in "human time," which is why documentary filmmaker Jeff Orlowski, who tracks climate change effects on glaciers and coral reefs, uses "before and after" photographs taken several months apart in the same place to (e) highlight changes that occurred gradually.

*anthropologist: 인류학자 **catastrophe: 큰 재해 ***evade: 피하다

[102-1] 윗글의 제목으로 가장 적절한 것은?

① Differing Attitudes Towards Current Climate Issues
② Slow but Significant: The History of Ecological Movements
③ The Silence of Imagination in Representing Climate Change
④ Vivid Threats: Climate Disasters Spreading in Local Areas
⑤ The Rise and Fall of Environmentalism and Ecocriticism

[102-2] 밑줄 친 (a)~(e) 중에서 문맥상 낱말의 쓰임이 적절하지 않은 것은?

① (a)
② (b)
③ (c)
④ (d)
⑤ (e)

정답과 해설 p.96

01 Climate change experts and environmental humanists alike / agree / [that the climate crisis is, at its core, a crisis of the imagination / and much of the popular imagination is shaped by fiction].

02 In his 2016 book *The Great Derangement*, / anthropologist and novelist Amitav Ghosh / takes on this relationship / between imagination and environmental management, / arguing [that humans have failed to respond to climate change / at least in part because fiction fails to believably represent it]. // Ghosh explains / [that climate change is largely absent from contemporary fiction / because the cyclones, floods, and other catastrophes / [it brings to mind] / simply seem too "improbable" / to belong in stories about everyday life].

03 But climate change does not only reveal itself / as a series of extraordinary events. // In fact, / as environmentalists and ecocritics from Rachel Carson to Rob Nixon have pointed out, / environmental change can be "imperceptible"; / it proceeds rapidly, / only occasionally producing "explosive and spectacular" events. // Most climate change impacts cannot be observed day-to-day, / but they become visible / when we are confronted with their accumulated impacts.

04 Climate change evades our imagination / because it poses significant representational challenges. // It cannot be observed in "human time," / which is why / documentary filmmaker Jeff Orlowski, / (who tracks climate change effects on glaciers and coral reefs), / uses "before and after" photographs / taken several months apart in the same place / to highlight changes [that occurred gradually].

01 기후 변화 전문가들과 환경 인문주의자들 모두 / 인정한다 / 기후 위기climate crisis가 근원적으로 상상력의 위기이며, / 대중적 상상력의 많은 부분이 소설에 의해 형성된다는 것을.

02 그의 2016년도 책 'The Great Derangement'에서 / 인류학자이자 소설가인 Amitav Ghosh는 / 이러한 관계를 다룬다take on / 상상과 환경 관리 사이의 / 인간은 기후 변화에 대응하는 데 실패했다고 주장하면서 / 최소한 부분적으로는 소설이 그것을 믿을 수 있게believably 표현하지 못하기 때문에. // Ghosh는 설명한다 / 기후 변화는 현대 소설에 대체로 존재하지 않는다고 / 왜냐하면 사이클론, 홍수, 그리고 다른 큰 재해들이 / 그것이 상기시키는 / 그야말로 너무 '있을 것 같지 않아improbable' 보여서 / 일상생활 이야기에 속할 수 없기 때문에.

03 하지만 기후 변화는 자신을 드러내는 것은 아니다 / 일련의 놀라운extraordinary 사건들로만. // 사실, / Rachel Carson에서 Rob Nixon에 이르는 환경론자들과 생태 비평가들이 지적했듯이, / 환경 변화는 '감지할 수 없을imperceptible' 가능성이 있다 / 그것은 빠르게(→ 점진적으로) 진행되며, / 단지 이따금occasionally '폭발적이고 극적인spectacular' 사건들을 만들어 낼 뿐이다. // 대부분의 기후 변화의 영향은 매일 관찰될 수는 없지만, / 그것들은 가시화된다 / 우리가 그것들의 축적된accumulate 영향에 직면할confront 때.

04 기후 변화는 우리의 상상에서 벗어난다 / 그것이 중요한 표현상의 문제를 제기하기pose significant representational challenges 때문에. // 그것은 '인간의 시간' 동안에는 관찰될 수 없는데, / 그것이 ~한 이유이다 / 다큐멘터리 영화 제작자 Jeff Orlowski가 / 빙하와 산호초에 미치는 기후 변화의 영향을 추적하는 / '전후' 사진을 이용하는 / 수개월 간격으로 같은 장소에서 찍힌 / 점차 일어난 변화를 강조하기 위해.

103 STEP 1 • 수능에 *진짜* 나오는 *단어*

✔ 문제에 나오는 단어들을 확인하세요.

01	supplement	*n.* 보충(제)	receive a vitamin C (✔ supplement)	비타민 C 보충제를 받다
02	inherent	*a.* 내재하는	errors (　　　) in an experiment	실험에 내재한 오차
03	assign	*v.* 배정하다, 할당하다	(　　　) them to the experimental group	실험 집단에 배정하다
04	randomization	*n.* 임의 추출	use (　　　　) in research	연구에 임의 추출을 사용하다
05	flip	*v.* (동전 등을) 던지다, 튀기다	(　　) a coin	동전을 던지다
06	chance	*n.* 우연	methods involving (　　　)	우연이 포함된 방법들
07	with respect to	~에 관하여	(　　) (　　　　) (　　) colds	감기에 관하여
08	rule out	배제하다	(　　) (　　　) the possibility	가능성을 배제하다
09	severity	*n.* 심각성	differences in the (　　　) of colds	감기의 심각성에서의 차이
10	apparent	*a.* 분명한	(　　　) effects	분명한 효과

⊕ 본문 문장 속에서 단어들을 확인해 보세요.

The following discussion describes some of the pitfalls / inherent in an experiment of this kind / and ways to avoid them.

이어지는 논의는 함정 중 일부를 설명한다 / 이러한 종류의 실험에 내재한 / 그리고 이를 피하는 방법을.

문제를 풀기 전에 단어들을 **30초** 동안 다시 확인하세요.

01	supplement	✏ 보충(제)	receive a vitamin C supplement	비타민 C (보충제)를 받다
02	inherent		errors inherent in an experiment	실험에 (　　) 오차
03	assign		assign them to the experimental group	실험 집단에 (　　　)
04	randomization		use randomization in research	연구에 (　　　)을 사용하다
05	flip		flip a coin	동전을 (　　)
06	chance		methods involving chance	(　　)이 포함된 방법들
07	with respect to		with respect to colds	감기에 (　　)
08	rule out		rule out the possibility	가능성을 (　　　)
09	severity		differences in the severity of colds	감기의 (　　　)에서의 차이
10	apparent		apparent effects	(　　) 효과

➕ **본문 문장 속에서 단어의 의미를 우리말로 해석해 보세요.**

The following discussion describes some of the pitfalls / inherent in an experiment of this kind / and ways to avoid them.

→ 이어지는 논의는 함정 중 일부를 설명한다 /   / 그리고 이를 피하는 방법을.

103 다음 글을 읽고, 물음에 답하시오.

In studies examining the effectiveness of vitamin C, researchers typically divide the subjects into two groups. One group (the experimental group) receives a vitamin C supplement, and the other (the control group) does not. Researchers observe both groups to determine whether one group has fewer or shorter colds than the other. The following discussion describes some of the pitfalls inherent in an experiment of this kind and ways to (a) avoid them. In sorting subjects into two groups, researchers must ensure that each person has an (b) equal chance of being assigned to either the experimental group or the control group. This is accomplished by randomization; that is, the subjects are chosen randomly from the same population by flipping a coin or some other method involving chance. Randomization helps to ensure that results reflect the treatment and not factors that might influence the grouping of subjects. Importantly, the two groups of people must be similar and must have the same track record with respect to colds to (c) rule out the possibility that observed differences in the rate, severity, or duration of colds might have occurred anyway. If, for example, the control group would normally catch twice as many colds as the experimental group, then the findings prove (d) nothing. In experiments involving a nutrient, the diets of both groups must also be (e) different, especially with respect to the nutrient being studied. If those in the experimental group were receiving less vitamin C from their usual diet, then any effects of the supplement may not be apparent. *pitfall: 함정

[103-1] 윗글의 제목으로 가장 적절한 것은?

① Perfect Planning and Faulty Results: A Sad Reality in Research
② Don't Let Irrelevant Factors Influence the Results!
③ Protect Human Subjects Involved in Experimental Research!
④ What Nutrients Could Better Defend Against Colds?
⑤ In-depth Analysis of Nutrition: A Key Player for Human Health

[103-2] 밑줄 친 (a)~(e) 중에서 문맥상 낱말의 쓰임이 적절하지 <u>않은</u> 것은?

① (a)
② (b)
③ (c)
④ (d)
⑤ (e)

정답과 해설 p.97

01 In studies examining the effectiveness of vitamin C, / researchers typically divide the subjects into two groups. // One group (the experimental group) receives a vitamin C supplement, / and the other (the control group) does not. // Researchers observe both groups / to determine whether one group has fewer or shorter colds than the other.

02 The following discussion describes some of the pitfalls / inherent in an experiment of this kind / and ways to avoid them. // In sorting subjects into two groups, / researchers must ensure / [that each person has an equal chance of being assigned / to either the experimental group or the control group]. // This is accomplished by randomization; / that is, / [the subjects are chosen randomly from the same population / by flipping a coin or some other method involving chance]. // Randomization helps to ensure / [that results reflect the treatment / and not factors {that might influence the grouping of subjects}].

03 Importantly, / the two groups of people must be similar / and must have the same track record with respect to colds / to rule out the possibility / [that observed differences in the rate, severity, or duration of colds / might have occurred anyway].

04 If, for example, / the control group would normally catch twice as many colds / as the experimental group, / then the findings prove nothing. // In experiments involving a nutrient, / the diets of both groups must also be different, / especially with respect to the nutrient being studied. // If those in the experimental group were receiving less vitamin C from their usual diet, / then any effects of the supplement may not be apparent.

---

01 비타민 C의 효과를 조사하는 연구에서, / 연구원들은 일반적으로 실험 대상자들을 두 집단으로 나눈다. // 한 집단(실험 집단)은 비타민 C 보충제supplement를 받고 / 다른 집단(통제 집단)은 비타민 C 보충제를 받지 않는다. // 연구원들은 두 집단 모두를 관찰한다 / 한 집단이 다른 집단보다 감기에 더 적게 또는 더 짧게 걸리는지를 알아내기 위해.

02 이어지는 논의는 함정 중 일부를 설명한다 / 이러한 종류의 실험에 내재한inherent / 그리고 이를 피하는 방법을. // 실험 대상자를 두 집단으로 분류할 때, / 연구원들은 반드시 ~하도록 해야 한다 / 각 개인이 배정될assign 확률이 동일하도록 / 실험 집단 또는 통제 집단 둘 중 한 곳에. // 이는 임의 추출randomization에 의해 달성되는데 / 즉 / 실험 대상자는 동일 모집단에서 임의로 선정된다 / 동전 던지기flip나 우연chance이 포함된 어떤 다른 방법에 의해. // 임의 추출은 반드시 ~하는 데 도움이 된다 / 결과가 처리를 반영하도록, / 그리고 실험 대상자의 분류에 영향을 줄지도 모르는 요인은 반영하지 않도록.

03 중요한 것은, / 두 집단의 사람들이 비슷하고 / 감기와 관련하여with respect to colds 동일한 기록을 가지고 있어야 한다는 것이다 / 가능성을 배제하기rule out 위해 / 감기의 비율, 심각성severity, 또는 지속 기간에서 관찰된 차이가 / 어떤 식으로든 일어났을지도 모른다는.

04 만일 예를 들어, / 통제 집단이 보통 감기에 무려 두 배나 많이 걸린다면 / 실험 집단보다 / 연구 결과는 아무것도 입증하지 못한다. // 영양분을 포함하는 실험에서는 / 두 집단의 식단 또한 달라야(→ 비슷해야) 하며, / 특히 연구 중인 영양분에 관련해서 그래야 한다. // 실험 집단에 속한 사람들이 평소 식단에서 비타민 C를 적게 섭취하고 있었다면, / 보충제의 어떤 효과도 분명하지apparent 않을 수 있다.

104 STEP 1 · 수능에 *진짜* 나오는 *단어*

✔ 문제에 나오는 단어들을 확인하세요.

01	sufficient	a. 충분한	provide (✔ sufficient) context	충분한 문맥을 제공하다
02	well-crafted	a. 잘 만들어진	a ( ) text	잘 만들어진 텍스트
03	approximation	n. 근접한 것, 근사치	an ( ) of the author's intention	작가의 의도와 근접한 것
04	novelist	n. 소설가	great ( )s	위대한 소설가들
05	vanish	v. 사라지다	( ) overnight	하룻밤 사이에 사라지다
06	fictive	a. 허구의, 상상의	the ( ) world	허구의 세계
07	correspondence	n. 관련성, 일치, 상응	bear close ( )	밀접한 관련성을 지니다
08	out-of-date	a. 시대에 뒤떨어진, 구식의	an ( ) translation	시대에 뒤떨어진 번역
09	bring ~ up to date	~을 최신으로 하다	( ) the language ( ) ( ) ( )	언어를 최신의 것으로 하다
10	at the price of	~을 대가로, 희생하여	( ) ( ) ( ) ( ) my reputation	내 명성을 대가로
11	intense	a. 격렬한, 강렬한	an ( ) struggle	격렬한 분투
12	frame of reference	(판단과 이해에 근간이 되는) 준거 틀	supply the right ( ) ( ) ( )	적절한 준거 틀을 제공하다

✚ 본문 문장 속에서 단어들을 확인해 보세요.

An out-of-date translation will give us this experience; / as we read, / we must bring the language up to date, / and understanding comes / only at the price of a fairly intense struggle with the text.

시대에 뒤떨어진 번역은 우리에게 이런 경험을 줄 것인데, / 우리가 읽을 때, / 우리는 언어를 최신의 것으로 해야 하고 / 이해는 오기 때문이다 / 오로지 텍스트와의 꽤 격렬한 분투의 대가로.

01	sufficient	✎ 충분한	provide sufficient context	(충분한) 문맥을 제공하다
02	well-crafted		a well-crafted text	( ) 텍스트
03	approximation		an approximation of the author's intention	작가의 의도와 ( )
04	novelist		great novelists	위대한 ( )들
05	vanish		vanish overnight	하룻밤 사이에 ( )
06	fictive		the fictive world	( ) 세계
07	correspondence		bear close correspondence	밀접한 ( )을 지니다
08	out-of-date		an out-of-date translation	( ) 번역
09	bring ~ up to date		bring the language up to date	언어를 ( )
10	at the price of		at the price of my reputation	내 명성을 ( )
11	intense		an intense struggle	( ) 분투
12	frame of reference		supply the right frame of reference	적절한 ( )을 제공하다

➕ **본문 문장 속에서 단어의 의미를 우리말로 해석해 보세요.**

An out-of-date translation **will give us this experience;** / as we read, / we must bring the language up to date, / and understanding comes / only at the price of a fairly intense struggle **with the text.**

➜ ▨▨▨▨▨▨▨▨▨ 은 우리에게 이런 경험을 줄 것인데, / 우리가 읽을 때, / 우리는 ▨▨▨▨▨▨▨▨▨▨ 하고 / 이해는 오기 때문이다 / 오로지 텍스트와의 ▨▨▨▨▨▨▨▨▨.

104 다음 글을 읽고, 물음에 답하시오.

To the extent that sufficient context has been provided, the reader can come to a well-crafted text with no expert knowledge and come away with a good approximation of what has been intended by the author. The text has become a public document and the reader can read it with a (a) minimum of effort and struggle; his experience comes close to what Freud has described as the deployment of "evenly-hovering attention." He puts himself in the author's hands (some have had this experience with great novelists such as Dickens or Tolstoy) and he (b) follows where the author leads. The real world has vanished and the fictive world has taken its place. Now consider the other extreme. When we come to a badly crafted text in which context and content are not happily joined, we must struggle to understand, and our sense of what the author intended probably bears (c) close correspondence to his original intention. An out-of-date translation will give us this experience; as we read, we must bring the language up to date, and understanding comes only at the price of a fairly intense struggle with the text. Badly presented content with no frame of reference can provide (d) the same experience; we see the words but have no sense of how they are to be taken. The author who fails to provide the context has (e) mistakenly assumed that his picture of the world is shared by all his readers and fails to realize that supplying the right frame of reference is a critical part of the task of writing.

*deployment: (전략적) 배치   **evenly-hovering attention: 고르게 주의를 기울이는 것

[104-1] 윗글의 제목으로 가장 적절한 것은?

① Building a Wall Between Reality and the Fictive World
② Creative Reading: Going Beyond the Writer's Intentions
③ Usefulness of Readers' Experiences for Effective Writing
④ Context in Writing: A Lighthouse for Understanding Texts
⑤ Trapped in Their Own Words: The Narrow Outlook of Authors

[104-2] 밑줄 친 (a)~(e) 중에서 문맥상 낱말의 쓰임이 적절하지 <u>않은</u> 것은?

① (a)
② (b)
③ (c)
④ (d)
⑤ (e)

정답과 해설 **p.98**

01 To the extent that sufficient context has been provided, / the reader can come
to a well-crafted text with no expert knowledge / and come away with a good
approximation / of [what has been intended by the author].

02 The text has become a public document / and the reader can read it with a minimum of
effort and struggle; / his experience comes close to [what Freud has described / as the
deployment of "evenly-hovering attention]." // He puts himself in the author's hands
/ (some have had this experience with great novelists / such as Dickens or Tolstoy) /
and he follows where the author leads. // The real world has vanished / and the fictive
world has taken its place.

03 Now consider the other extreme. // When we come to a badly crafted text / [in which
context and content are not happily joined], / we must struggle to understand, / and
our sense of what the author intended / probably bears close correspondence to his
original intention. // An out-of-date translation will give us this experience; / as we
read, / we must bring the language up to date, / and understanding comes / only at the
price of a fairly intense struggle with the text.

04 Badly presented content with no frame of reference / can provide the same experience;
/ we see the words / but have no sense of how they are to be taken. // The author [who
fails to provide the context] / has mistakenly assumed / [that his picture of the world
is shared by all his readers] / and fails to realize / [that supplying the right frame of
reference / is a critical part of the task of writing].

01 충분한sufficient 문맥이 제공된 경우에 / 독자는 전문적 지식 없이도 잘 만들어진well-crafted 텍스트에 다가와 / 아주
근접한 것approximation을 가지고 떠날 수 있다 / 작가가 의도한 바와.

02 텍스트는 공문서와 같은 것이 되어서 / 독자는 최소한의 노력과 분투로 그것을 읽을 수 있는데 / 그의 경험이 프로이트가
설명한 것과 가까워지기 때문이다 / '고르게 주의를 기울이는 것'의 (전략적인) 배치라고. // 그는 작가의 손에 자신을
맡기고 / (어떤 사람들이 위대한 소설가novelist와 이런 경험을 했던 것처럼 / 디킨스나 톨스토이와 같은) / 그는 작가가
이끄는 곳으로 따라간다. // 현실 세계는 사라지고vanish / 허구의fictive 세계가 그것을 대신했다.

03 이제 그 반대 극단의 경우를 생각해 보자. // 우리가 조악한 텍스트에 다가갈 때 / 문맥과 내용이 적절하게 결합되지 않은 /
우리는 이해하려고 애써야 하고, / 작가가 의도한 바에 대한 우리의 이해는 / 아마도 그의 본래 의도와 밀접한(→ 거의 없는)
관련성correspondence을 지닐 것이다. // 시대에 뒤떨어진out-of-date 번역은 우리에게 이런 경험을 줄 것인데, /
우리가 읽을 때, / 우리는 언어를 최신의 것으로 해야 하고bring the language up to date / 이해는 오기 때문이다 /
오로지 텍스트와의 꽤 격렬한 분투의 대가로at the price of a fairly intense struggle.

04 준거 틀frame of reference이 없는 잘못 제시된 내용도 / 같은 경험을 제공할 수 있는데, / 우리는 단어를 보지만 /
그것들이 어떻게 받아들여져야 하는지를 이해하지 못하기 때문이다. // 문맥을 제공하지 못한 작가는 / 잘못 가정한 것이고
/ 모든 독자가 세상에 대한 자신의 그림을 공유한다고 / 깨닫지 못한다 / 적절한 준거 틀을 제공하는 것이 / 글을 쓰는 일의
중대한 부분임을.

105 STEP 1 • 수능에 *진짜* 나오는 *단어*

✔ 문제에 나오는 단어들을 확인하세요.

01	soul-stirring	*a.* 심금을 울리는	waves of (✓ soul-stirring) sound	심금을 울리는 소리의 물결
02	talent	*n.* 재능	a natural ( )	천부적인 재능
03	admiration	*n.* 감탄	with ( )	감탄하며
04	underestimate	*v.* 과소평가하다	( ) the power of music	음악의 힘을 과소평가하다
05	permission	*n.* 허락	get ( )	허락을 받다
06	confidence	*n.* 자신(감)	without ( )	자신 없이
07	pull out of	~에서 빠지다, 손을 떼다	( ) ( ) ( ) practice	연습에서 빠지다
08	dislike	*n.* 싫어함, 반감 *v.* 싫어하다	the ( ) of crossover music	크로스오버 음악에 대한 반감

⊕ 본문 문장 속에서 단어들을 확인해 보세요.

When Master Brooks played a Mozart piece on the violin / for his class to learn, / the room was filled with waves of beautiful, soul-stirring sound.

거장 Brooks가 바이올린으로 모차르트 곡을 연주했을 때 / 학급 학생들이 배우도록 / 교실은 아름답고 심금을 울리는 소리의 물결로 가득했다.

01	soul-stirring	✎ 심금을 울리는	waves of soul-stirring sound	(심금을 울리는) 소리의 물결
02	talent		a natural talent	천부적인 ( )
03	admiration		with admiration	( )하며
04	underestimate		underestimate the power of music	음악의 힘을 ( )
05	permission		get permission	( )을 받다
06	confidence		without confidence	( ) 없이
07	pull out of		pull out of practice	연습에서 ( )
08	dislike		the dislike of crossover music	크로스오버 음악에 대한 ( )

➕ **본문 문장 속에서 단어의 의미를 우리말로 해석해 보세요.**

When Master Brooks played a Mozart piece on the violin / for his class to learn, / the room was filled with waves of beautiful, soul-stirring sound.

➡️ 거장 Brooks가 바이올린으로 모차르트 곡을 연주했을 때 / 학급 학생들이 배우도록 / 교실은 ▓▓▓▓▓▓▓▓▓▓로 가득했다.

2020학년도 6월 43~45번
제한시간 150초
난이도 105-1 ★★★☆☆
105-2 ★★★☆☆
105-3 ★★☆☆☆

STEP 2 · 수능 기출 제대로 풀기

105 다음 글을 읽고, 물음에 답하시오.

(A) When Master Brooks played a Mozart piece on the violin for his class to learn, the room was filled with waves of beautiful, soul-stirring sound. The class tried to emulate the music played by this renowned guest musician. Among the students in the class, Joe Brooks was by far the best. In fact, Joe was the master's son. His father had placed a baby violin in his hands at the age of four, and Joe was a natural talent. Now, just twelve years later, he was already on (a) his way to becoming a virtuoso like his father.

*emulate: 열심히 배우다 **virtuoso: 거장

(B) When they finished practicing, Joe noticed his father standing in the corner. "Wow, that was quite wonderful," he said with admiration. Master Brooks came toward his son. "I love the way you created those unique sounds while keeping the spirit of the violin. I underestimated the power that crossover music can create," said Master Brooks to (b) him. Joe and his father returned home, both humming the melody that the band had been practicing.

(C) "Well, did you get permission?" asked Brian as soon as Joe entered the practice room the following day. "Um, I'm not sure," answered Joe without confidence. "(c) You can tell us about it after practice," Brian said as he placed his fingers on the keyboard. Beside him, Nick was tuning his guitar. Joe thought that he would play just one last time before telling them that (d) he might pull out of the concert. The trio swung into their routine, as easily as only a group that had practiced long and hard together could.

(D) After the class, Joe was alone with his father. He had something important to talk about. Joe took a deep breath and said, "I have been asked to play in a concert, and I would like your permission first. It is a crossover concert." Master Brooks looked surprised. Indeed, the master's dislike of crossover music was no secret. "Father," Joe took a deep breath and continued, "I respect your views, but it is not what (e) you think. Why don't you come and listen to our practice tomorrow? If you don't like it, I will cancel."

[105-1] 주어진 글 (A)에 이어질 내용을 순서에 맞게 배열한 것으로 가장 적절한 것은?

① (B) — (D) — (C)　　② (C) — (B) — (D)
③ (C) — (D) — (B)　　④ (D) — (B) — (C)
⑤ (D) — (C) — (B)

[105-2] 밑줄 친 (a)~(e) 중에서 가리키는 대상이 나머지 넷과 다른 것은?

① (a)　② (b)　③ (c)　④ (d)　⑤ (e)

[105-3] 윗글에 관한 내용으로 적절하지 않은 것은?

① Joe는 바이올린에 천부적인 재능이 있었다.
② Master Brooks는 Joe가 속한 밴드의 연습을 보러 갔다.
③ Master Brooks는 크로스오버 음악에 대한 자신의 견해를 바꾸었다.
④ Joe가 속한 밴드는 두 명의 연주자로 구성되었다.
⑤ Joe는 수업이 끝난 후에 아버지와 단둘이 대화를 나눴다.

정답과 해설 p.100

01 When Master Brooks played a Mozart piece on the violin / for his class to learn, / the room was filled with waves of beautiful, soul-stirring sound. // The class tried to emulate the music / played by this renowned guest musician. // Among the students in the class, / Joe Brooks was by far the best. // In fact, Joe was the master's son. // His father had placed a baby violin in his hands at the age of four, / and Joe was a natural talent. // Now, just twelve years later, / he was already on his way / to becoming a virtuoso like his father.

02 After the class, / Joe was alone with his father. // He had something important to talk about. // Joe took a deep breath and said, / "I have been asked to play in a concert, / and I would like your permission first. / It is a crossover concert." // Master Brooks looked surprised. // Indeed, the master's dislike of crossover music was no secret. // "Father," Joe took a deep breath and continued, / "I respect your views, / but it is not what you think. / Why don't you come and listen to our practice tomorrow? If you don't like it, I will cancel."

03 "Well, did you get permission?" / asked Brian / as soon as Joe entered the practice room / the following day. // "Um, I'm not sure," / answered Joe without confidence. // "You can tell us about it after practice," / Brian said / as he placed his fingers on the keyboard. // Beside him, Nick was tuning his guitar. // Joe thought / [that he would play just one last time / before telling them that he might pull out of the concert]. // The trio swung into their routine, / as easily as only a group [that had practiced long and hard together] could.

04 When they finished practicing, / Joe noticed his father standing in the corner. // "Wow, that was quite wonderful," / he said with admiration. // Master Brooks came toward his son. / "I love the way [you created those unique sounds / while keeping the spirit of the violin]. / I underestimated the power / [that crossover music can create]," / said Master Brooks to him. // Joe and his father returned home, / both humming the melody / [that the band had been practicing].

01 거장 Brooks가 바이올린으로 모차르트 곡을 연주했을 때 / 학급 학생들이 배우도록 / 교실은 아름답고 심금을 울리는soul-stirring 소리의 물결로 가득했다. // 학급 학생들은 곡을 열심히 배우려고 노력했다 / 이 유명한 초빙 음악가가 연주한. // 학급 학생 중에 / Joe Brooks가 단연 최고였다. // 사실 Joe는 그 명연주자의 아들이었다. // 그의 아버지는 그가 네 살 때 유아용 바이올린을 그의 손에 쥐어 주었고 / Joe는 천부적인 재능talent이 있었다. // 이제 겨우 12년 후에, / 그는 이미 자신의 길을 가고 있었다 / 자신의 아버지처럼 거장이 되는.

02 수업 후에 / Joe가 아버지와 단둘이 있게 되었다. // 그는 뭔가 중요한 할 말이 있었다. // Joe는 심호흡을 하고 말했다. / "저는 콘서트에서 연주해 달라는 요청을 받았는데, / 먼저 아버지의 허락을 받고 싶어요. / 그것은 크로스오버 콘서트예요." // 명연주자 Brooks는 놀란 표정이었다. // 진정, / 크로스오버 음악에 대한 그 명연주자의 반감dislike은 공공연한 일이었다. // "아버지," Joe가 심호흡을 하고 계속 말했다. / "저는 아버지의 견해를 존중하지만, / 아버지가 생각하시는 그런 게 아니에요. / 내일 우리 연습에 오셔서 들어 보지 않으시겠어요? / 아버지 마음에 안 드시면 전 취소할게요."

03 "저, 허락permission받았니?" / Brian이 물었다 / Joe가 연습실에 들어서자마자 / 다음 날. // "음, 잘 모르겠어." / Joe가 자신 없게without confidence 말했다. // "넌 연습 후에 우리에게 말해 줘도 돼." / Brian이 말했다 / 키보드에 손을 얹으며. // 그의 옆에서 Nick이 기타를 조율하고 있었다. // Joe는 생각했다 / 마지막으로 딱 한 번만 연주하겠다고 / 자신이 그 콘서트에서 빠질지도pull out of the concert 모른다는 것을 그들에게 말하기 전에. // 그 3인조는 일상적인 연주에 들어갔다 / 오랫동안 함께 열심히 연습한 그룹만이 할 수 있을 만큼 쉽게.

04 그들이 연주를 마쳤을 때, / Joe는 자신의 아버지가 구석에 서 있는 것을 알아차렸다. // "와, 정말 멋진 연주야." / 그가 감탄하며with admiration 말했다. // 명연주자 Brooks는 아들 쪽으로 다가갔다. / "나는 네가 그런 독특한 소리를 만들어내는 방식이 좋구나 / 바이올린의 정신을 지키면서. / 내가 힘을 과소평가했어underestimate / 크로스오버 음악이 창조할 수 있는." / 명연주자 Brooks가 그에게 말했다. //
Joe와 그의 아버지는 집으로 돌아갔다 / 둘 다 그 멜로디를 흥얼거리며 / 그 밴드가 연습해 왔던.

☑ **종합 성적표**

구분	공부한 날 ❶	결과 분석			
		출처	풀이 시간 ❷	채점 결과 (O, ✕)	틀린 이유 ❸
Day 13 주어진 문장 넣기	월 일	2024학년도 대수능 38번	분 초		
		2024학년도 9월 39번	분 초		
		2023학년도 6월 39번	분 초		
		2022학년도 9월 38번	분 초		
		2021학년도 대수능 38번	분 초		
		2021학년도 9월 39번	분 초		
		2020학년도 대수능 38번	분 초		
Day 14 문단 요약	월 일	2024학년도 9월 40번	분 초		
		2023학년도 대수능 40번	분 초		
		2023학년도 6월 40번	분 초		
		2022학년도 6월 40번	분 초		
		2021학년도 대수능 40번	분 초		
		2020학년도 대수능 40번	분 초		
		2020학년도 6월 40번	분 초		
Day 15 장문의 이해	월 일	2024학년도 6월 41~42번	분 초		
		2023학년도 대수능 41~42번	분 초		
		2023학년도 9월 43~45번	분 초		
		2023학년도 9월 41~42번	분 초		
		2022학년도 9월 41~42번	분 초		
		2021학년도 9월 41~42번	분 초		
		2020학년도 6월 43~45번	분 초		

3일간 공부한 내용을 다시 보니, ……

❶ **매일 지문을 하루 계획에 맞춰 풀었다. vs. 내가 한 약속을 못 지켰다.**

<매3영 수능기출>은 단순 문제풀이를 위한 책이 아니라, 매일 규칙적으로 영어를 공부하는 습관을 잡는 책입니다. 따라서 푸는 문제 개수는 상황에 따라 다르더라도 '매일' 학습하는 것이 중요합니다.

❷ **주어진 시간을 자꾸 넘긴다?**

풀이 시간이 계속해서 권장 시간을 넘긴다면 실전 훈련이 부족하다는 신호이므로, 매일의 훈련을 실전처럼 긴장감 있게 해야 합니다. 한편으로, 오답의 이유를 철저히 분석하고 맞춤 공부법을 찾아갑니다.

❸ ⭐**틀린 이유 맞춤 솔루션**: 오답 이유에 따라 다음 해결책을 참고하세요.

(1) 해석이 잘 안 돼서
▶ <STEP 1 단어>, <STEP 3 지문 복습>을 정독하며 단어/구문 실력을 길러보세요.

(2) 해석은 되는데, 지문 이해가 안 돼서
▶ [정답 및 해설]의 <지문 자세히 보기>를 정독하며 수능 지문의 논리 전개 방식을 익혀보세요.

(3) 이해는 했는데, 선택지로 연결을 못 해서
▶ [정답 및 해설]의 <오답풀이>, <유형플러스>를 통해 함정에 주의하는 방법을 숙지하세요.

❗ **결론적으로**, 내가 **취약한 부분**은 [   ] 이다.
취약점을 보완하기 위해서 나는 [   ] 을/를 해야겠다.

복습 때 다시 봐야 할 문항과, 다시 점검할 사항이 있는 페이지는 지금 바로 접어 두세요.

매일

고3

매3

단계로
푸는

영어독해

수능기출

정답 및 해설

매일 **3**단계로 푸는 **영**어독해

수능기출 고3

정답 및 해설

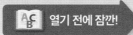

열기 전에 잠깐! 지문 자세히 보기 읽는 법

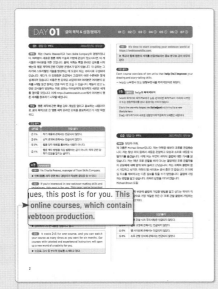

녹색 하이라이트는

정답의 결정적 근거가 되는
주제 또는 핵심 표현을 표시해요.
글 전체에 걸쳐 핵심 표현이
어떻게 반복되는지 확인해 보세요.

회색 하이라이트는

주제와 반대되거나
지문 이해에 도움이 되는
보조적 내용을 표시해요.

01 정답 ① 95%   *2024학년도 대수능*

해석 저는 **Charlie Reeves**이고 **Toon Skills Company**의 경영자입니다. 여러분이 새로운 웹툰 제작 기술과 기법에 관심이 있으시다면, 이 게시물은 여러분을 위한 것입니다. 올해, 저희는 특별 온라인 강좌를 시작했는데, 웹툰 제작에 관한 다양한 콘텐츠가 담겨 있습니다. 각 강좌는 그리기와 스토리텔링 기술을 향상하는 데 도움이 되는 10차시로 구성되어 있습니다. 게다가, 이 강좌들은 초급에서 고급까지 어떤 수준에든 맞게 설계되어 있습니다. 비용은 한 강좌당 45달러이며 여러분은 여러분의 강좌를 6개월 동안 원하는 만큼 여러 번 보실 수 있습니다. 재능이 있고 노련한 강사들이 담당하는 저희 강좌는 여러분에게 창의력의 새로운 세계를 열어줄 것입니다. 이제 **https://webtoonskills.com**에서 여러분의 웹툰 세계를 창조하기 시작할 때입니다.

해설 웹툰 제작에 관한 특별 강좌 개설을 알리고 홍보하는 내용이므로, 글의 목적으로 ① '웹툰 제작 온라인 강좌를 홍보하려고'가 가장 적절하다.

오답 풀이

선택률	오답 풀이
② 1%	작가 채용에 관해서는 언급되지 않았다.
③ 0%	신작 공개에 관해서는 언급되지 않았다.
④ 2%	웹툰 창작 대회를 홍보하는 내용이 아니다.
⑤ 1%	웹툰 제작 방법을 직접 설명하는 글이 아니라, 제작 관련 강좌가 있음을 알리는 글이다.

지문 자세히 보기

01 I'm Charlie Reeves, manager of Toon Skills Company.
▶ 만화(웹툰) 제작 관련 회사 경영자가 작성한 글임을 알 수 있다.

02 If you're interested in new webtoon-making skills and techniques, this post is for you. This year, we've launched special online courses, which contain a variety of contents about webtoon production.
▶ 웹툰 제작 기술에 관한 특별 온라인 강좌가 개설됐다는 핵심 내용이 제시된다.

03 Each course consists of ten units that help improve your drawing and story-telling skills. Moreover, these courses are designed to suit any level, from beginner to advanced.
▶ 강좌에서 다루는 내용을 설명하고 있다.

04 It costs $45 for one course, and you can watch your course as many times as you want for six months. Our courses with talented and experienced instructors will open up a new world of creativity for you.
▶ 수강료, 강사 등 부수적 정보를 소개하고 있다.

05 It's time to start creating your webtoon world at https://webtoonskills.com.
▶ 특강과 함께 웹툰의 세계를 만들어보라는 홍보 문구로 글이 마무리된다.

구문 풀이

Each course consists of ten units that **help (to) improve** your drawing and story-telling skills.
→ help는 to부정사 또는 원형부정사를 목적격보어로 취한다.

구문 플러스⁺ help의 목적격보어

help의 목적어와 목적격보어가 능동 관계이면 목적격보어 자리에 to부정사 또는 원형부정사를 쓴다. 동명사는 쓰이지 않는다.

Ella is the one who helped me **(to) adjust** (adjusting) to a new lifestyle here.
Ella는 내가 여기서의 새로운 생활방식에 적응하게 도와줬던 사람이다.

02 정답 ① 99%   *2023학년도 대수능*

해석 담당자 귀하,
제 이름은 **Michael Brown**입니다. 저는 어렸을 때부터 조류를 관찰했습니다. 저는 항상 저의 뜰에서 새들을 관찰하고 모습과 소리로 새들을 식별하기를 즐겼습니다. 어제 저는 우연히 귀하의 클럽에 대한 기사를 읽었습니다. 저는 매년 조류 관찰을 하러 다니는 열정적인 조류 관찰자들의 공동체에 대해 알게 되어 놀라고 신났습니다. 저는 귀하의 클럽에 몹시 가입하고 싶지만, 귀하의 웹 사이트는 공사 중인 것 같습니다. 이 이메일 주소를 제외하고는 다른 정보를 찾을 수가 없었습니다. 클럽에 가입하는 방법을 알고 싶습니다. 귀하의 답장을 기다리겠습니다.
Michael Brown 드림

해설 글 마지막 부분에 클럽에 가입할 방법을 알고 싶다는 목적이 직접 제시되므로, 답으로 가장 적절한 것은 ① '조류 관찰 클럽에 가입하는 방법을 문의하려고'이다.

오답 풀이

선택률	오답 풀이
② 0%	조류 관찰 시의 주의사항은 언급되지 않았다.
③ 0%	협회 규정에 관해서는 언급되지 않았다.
④ 0%	웹 사이트에 관해서는 언급되지 않았다.
⑤ 0%	조류 관찰 장비에 관해서는 언급되지 않았다.

01 To whom it may concern,
My name is Michael Brown. I have been a bird-watcher since childhood. I have always enjoyed watching birds in my yard and identifying them by sight and sound.

▶ 필자가 어린 시절부터 조류 관찰을 즐겼했다며 자신을 소개하고 있다.

02 Yesterday, I happened to read an article about your club. I was surprised and excited to find out about a community of passionate bird-watchers who travel annually to go birding.

▶ 편지 상대방의 '클럽'에 관해 언급하고 있다.

03 I would love to join your club, but your website appears to be under construction. I could not find any information except for this contact email address.

▶ 필자는 그 클럽에 가입하고 싶었지만 클럽 웹 사이트가 보수 중인 것으로 보였으며 이메일 외 다른 정보는 찾을 수 없었다고 언급한다.

04 I would like to know how to sign up for the club. I look forward to your reply.
Sincerely,
Michael Brown

▶ 'I would like to know how ~'가 '방법을 알려달라'는 목적을 직접 드러내고 있다. 답장을 기다린다는 말로 이메일이 마무리된다.

구문 풀이

I was **surprised and excited to find out** about a community of passionate bird-watchers who travel annually to go birding.

→ 감정의 형용사구인 surprised and excited 뒤에 to부정사가 나와 감정의 원인을 설명한다.

구문 플러스⁺ 감정의 원인을 설명하는 to부정사

감정 형용사 뒤에 to부정사가 나오면 '~해서 (…하다)'라고 해석한다.

I'm **glad to see you here**. 당신을 여기서 만나서 기뻐요.
We're **happy to let you know** that our daughter's getting married.
우리 딸이 결혼한다는 것을 알려드리게 되어 기쁩니다.

유형 플러스⁺ 글의 목적

주로 편지글, 안내문, 홍보문의 내용과 목적을 파악하는 유형이다.

• 문제 해결 Tip
① 도입부에서 필자-독자의 관계, 핵심 소재 등을 파악한다.
② 글의 흐름을 따라가며 필자의 상황을 이해한다.
③ 글의 중후반부에서 목적을 드러내는 명확한 표현을 찾는다.

• 목적과 관련된 표현
I'm writing to ~: ~하려고 글을 씁니다
I'd like to[want to] ~: ~하고 싶습니다
We hope ~: ~하기를 바랍니다
Would you (please) ~?: ~해 주실래요?
Please ~: ~해 주세요

---

03 정답 ① 96% *2023학년도 6월 모평*

해석 Jessica가 타고 있는 섬 관광버스는 바다에 면한 절벽 쪽으로 천천히 움직이고 있었다. 바깥에서는 하늘이 점점 어두워지고 있었다. Jessica는 "나는 교통 때문에 일몰을 놓치게 될 거야."라고 말하며 걱정스럽게 한숨지었다. 버스가 절벽의 주차장에 도착했다. 다른 승객들이 가방을 챙기는 동안, Jessica는 재빨리 버스에서 내렸고 바다 전망으로 유명한 그 절벽으로 뛰어 올라갔다. 꼭대기에 도달했을 때 그녀는 막 포기하려 했다. 바로 그때 그녀는 지는 해를 보았는데, 그것은 여전히 하늘에서 밝게 빛나고 있었다. Jessica는 "노을이 너무 아름다워. 내가 기대했던 것보다 훨씬 더 좋아."라고 혼잣말을 했다.

해설 일몰을 놓칠까 봐 걱정했던 Jessica가 절벽에서 밝게 빛나는 일몰을 마주하고 기뻐했다는 내용의 글이다. 따라서 Jessica의 심경 변화로 가장 적절한 것은 ① '걱정한 → 기쁜'이다.

오답 풀이

선택률	선지 해석 & 오답 풀이
② 2%	지루한 → 자신 있는 ▶ 글과 무관한 내용이다.
③ 1%	안도한 → 짜증 난 ▶ 전반부의 concern을 안도한 기분으로 연결 짓기 어렵다.
④ 1%	즐거운 → 무관심한 ▶ 노을을 보고 감탄하여 말한 마지막 문장을 무관심의 단서로 보기 어렵다.
⑤ 1%	후회되는 → 우울한 ▶ 글과 무관한 내용이다.

지문 자세히 보기⁺

01 The island tour bus Jessica was riding on was moving slowly toward the ocean cliffs. Outside, the sky was getting dark. Jessica sighed with concern, "I'm going to miss the sunset because of the traffic."

▶ Jessica가 교통 때문에 일몰을 볼 수 있는 시간을 놓칠까 봐 걱정했다(concern)는 상황이 제시된다.

02 The bus arrived at the cliffs' parking lot. While the other passengers were gathering their bags, Jessica quickly got off the bus and she ran up the cliff that was famous for its ocean views.

▶ 절벽에 도착한 Jessica가 풍경을 보기 위해 부랴부랴 뛰어갔다는 내용이 이어진다.

03 She was about to give up when she got to the top. Just then she saw the setting sun and it still shone brightly in the sky.

▶ Jessica가 포기하려던 순간 하늘에 밝게 빛나는 일몰이 보였다는 묘사와 함께 흐름이 반전된다.

04 Jessica said to herself, "The glow of the sun is so beautiful. It's even better than I expected."

▶ 일몰의 아름다움에 Jessica가 혼잣말로 감탄했다는 결말로 글이 마무리된다.

구문 풀이

She was about to give up when she got to the top.

→ 「**be about to** + 동사원형」은 '막 ~할 참이다'라는 뜻으로, 미래의 의미를 내포한다.

구문 플러스' 미래시제 대용 표현

be about to-V: 막 ~할 참이다
be going to-V: ~할 예정이다
be supposed to-V: ~하기로 되어 있다. ~할 예정이다

We are about to leave. 우리는 막 가려는 참이야.
The audition is supposed to be held next Thursday.
오디션은 다음 주 목요일에 열릴 예정이야.

---

04 정답 ⑤ 93%   *2022학년도 대수능*

해석 캐나다 전역에서 수많은 공룡 화석으로 유명한 앨버타주의 **Badlands**를 탐험하는 것이 Evelyn에게는 처음이었다. 젊은 아마추어 뼈 발굴자로서 그녀는 기대감으로 가득 차 있었다. 그녀는 흔한 공룡 종의 뼈 때문에 이렇게 멀리까지 이동해본 적이 없었다. 희귀한 공룡 화석을 발견하고자 하는 평생의 꿈이 막 실현될 참이었다. 그녀는 열심히 그것들을 찾기 시작했다. 하지만 황량한 땅을 여러 시간 배회하고 난 후에도, 그녀는 성과를 얻지 못했다. 이제 해는 지기 시작하고 있었고, 그녀의 목표는 여전히 손 닿지 않는 먼 곳에 있었다. 천천히 어두워지는 눈앞의 땅을 바라보며, 그녀는 혼자 한숨을 쉬며 말했다. "이렇게 멀리 와서 아무 성과도 못 내다니 믿을 수가 없네. 이게 무슨 시간 낭비야!"

해설 글 후반부의 **however**를 기점으로 글의 흐름이 바뀐다. 앞은 희귀한 화석을 발견할 꿈을 품은 Evelyn이 기대감에 설렜다는 내용인데, 뒤에서는 아무 성과도 내지 못한 Evelyn이 실망했다는 내용이다. 따라서 Evelyn의 심경 변화로 가장 적절한 것은 ⑤ '기대하는 → 실망한'이다.

오답 풀이

선택률	선지 해석 & 오답 풀이
① 1%	혼란스러운 → 겁에 질린 ▶ 글과 무관한 내용이다.
② 2%	낙담한 → 자신감에 찬 ▶ '긍정적 정서 → 부정적 정서'로 나아가는 글의 흐름과 반대된다.
③ 1%	여유로운 → 짜증난 ▶ 글과 무관한 내용이다.
④ 1%	무관심한 → 우울한 ▶ 전반부의 anticipation은 '무관심'과 반대되는 내용이다.

지문 자세히 보기'

01 It was Evelyn's first time to explore the Badlands of Alberta, famous across Canada for its numerous dinosaur fossils.

▶ Evelyn의 첫 화석 탐사라는 상황적 배경을 소개하고 있다.

02 As a young amateur bone-hunter, she was overflowing with anticipation. She had not travelled this far for the bones of common dinosaur species. Her life-long dream to find rare fossils of dinosaurs was about to come true. She began eagerly searching for them.

▶ Evelyn이 희귀한 공룡 화석을 찾고자 하는 꿈이 곧 실현될 것이라는 기대(anticipation)로 열심히(eagerly) 탐사에 나섰다는 이야기가 전개된다.

03 After many hours of wandering throughout the deserted lands, however, she was unsuccessful.

▶ Evelyn의 시도가 성공하지 못했다(unsuccessful)는 내용과 함께 글의 흐름이 반전된다.

04 Now, the sun was beginning to set, and her goal was still far beyond her reach. Looking at the slowly darkening ground before her, she sighed to herself, "I can't believe I came all this way for nothing. What a waste of time!"

▶ 목표가 아직 멀었다는 것을 깨닫고 모든 게 시간 낭비였다(a waste of time)고 혼잣말하며 한숨을 쉬는(sighed) Evelyn의 모습에서 실망을 느낄 수 있다.

구문 풀이

It was Evelyn's first time to explore the Badlands of Alberta, (which is) famous across Canada for its numerous dinosaur fossils.

→ 주격 관계대명사 which와 be동사 is가 함께 생략되었다.

구문 플러스' 주격 관계대명사의 생략

주격 관계대명사는 be동사와 함께 생략되며, 원칙적으로 단독 생략은 불가능하다. 생략이 이뤄지면 be동사의 보어인 형용사/분사/전치사구가 남아 선행사를 꾸미게 된다.

The car (that is) parked in front of the house is mine.
　　　　　　　과거분사
집 앞에 주차된 그 차는 내 차예요.
The dog (that is) barking in the backyard belongs to our neighbor.
　　　　　　　현재분사
뒷마당에서 짖고 있는 개는 우리 이웃의 개다.

---

05 정답 ① 89%   *2022학년도 6월 모평*

해석 Natalie는 첫 온라인 상담 시간에 접속하면서, "내가 컴퓨터 화면을 통해 상담사에게 어떻게 나의 마음을 열 수 있을까?"라는 의문을 가졌다. 상담 센터가 차로 오래 가야 하는 곳에 있었기 때문에, 그녀는 이것이 자신에게 많은 시간을 절약해 줄 것임을 알고 있었다. 다만 Natalie는 그것이 상담사를 직접 만나는 것만큼 도움이 될지 확신할 수 없었다. 하지만 일단 (상담) 시간이 시작되자, 그녀의 걱정은 사라졌다. 그녀는 실제로 그것이 예상했던 것보다 훨씬 더 편리하다고 생각하기 시작했다. 그녀는 마치 상담사가 함께 방 안에 있는 것처럼 느꼈다. 상담 시간이 끝났을 때, 그녀는 미소를 지으며 그에게 말했다. "온라인에서 꼭 다시 만나요!"

해설 글의 전반부에서는 Natalie가 온라인 상담에 대해 반신반의했다는 내용이 전개되지만, 'Once the session began, however, ~' 이후로는 Natalie가 온라인 상담의 편리성을 느끼고 만족해했다는 내용이 제시된다. 따라서 Natalie의 심경 변화로 가장 적절한 것은 ① '의심하는 → 만족한'이다.

오답 풀이

선택률	선지 해석 & 오답 풀이
② 1%	후회하는 → 혼란스러운 ▶ 글의 내용과 무관하다.
③ 1%	자신감 있는 → 부끄러운 ▶ 글의 내용과 무관하다.
④ 6%	지루한 → 신난 ▶ wondered나 wasn't sure를 '지루함'의 단서로 보기는 어렵다.
⑤ 0%	황홀한 → 실망한 ▶ '꼭 다시 만나자'고 약속하는 마지막 문장 내용은 실망감과 정반대된다.

지문 자세히 보기'

01 As Natalie was logging in to her first online counseling session, she wondered, "How can I open my heart to the counselor through a computer screen?"

▶ 온라인 상담을 앞둔 Natalie가 컴퓨터상에서 만나는 상담자에게 어떻게 마음을 열지 고민했다(wondered)는 내용이 제시된다.

02 Since the counseling center was a long drive away, she knew that this would save her a lot of time. Natalie just wasn't sure if it would be as helpful as meeting her counselor in person.

▶ 위의 wondered가 wasn't sure로 재진술되었다. Natalie가 온라인 상담의 효과에 대해서 확신하지 못했다는 내용이 반복된다.

03 Once the session began, however, her concerns went away. She actually started thinking that it was much more convenient than expected. She felt as if the counselor were in the room with her.

▶ however를 기점으로 글의 흐름이 바뀐다. 막상 온라인 상담에 임한 Natalie가 편리함(convenient)을 느끼며 걱정이 사라졌고(her concerns went away), 상담사와 함께 있는 듯한 인상도 받았다는 내용이 전개된다.

04 As the session closed, she told him with a smile, "I'll definitely see you online again!"

▶ 상담이 끝날 때 Natalie가 웃음 지으며(with a smile) 꼭 다시 만나자고 말할 만큼 상담에 만족했다는 내용으로 마무리된다.

구문 풀이

She felt **as if** the counselor **were** in the room with her.

→ as if 가정법 과거 구문은 주절과 종속절의 시제가 같을 때 쓴다. '(실제로 ~이지 않지만) 마치 ~인 것처럼'이라는 뜻이다.

구문 플러스⁺ as if 가정법

as if 가정법은 주절과 종속절의 시제가 같은지 다른지에 따라 가정법 과거와 가정법 과거완료를 구분한다.

She talks **as if** she **knew** the truth.
그녀는 그 사실을 아는 듯이 말한다. (가정법 과거)

She talks **as if** she **had known** the truth back then.
그녀는 그때 그 사실을 알았던 듯이 말한다. (가정법 과거완료)

---

06 정답 ② 91% *2021학년도 6월 모평*

해석 Sharon은 자신의 친구로부터 다가오는 탱고 콘서트 표를 받았다. 인터넷을 검색하던 중 그녀는 그 콘서트에 관한 리뷰를 우연히 발견하게 되었다. 리뷰를 쓴 사람은 그것을 '끔찍한 공연'이라며 혹평했다. 그로 인해 Sharon의 마음속에 과연 그것이 갈 만한 가치가 있을까 하는 의문이 생겼지만, 결국 그녀는 마지못해 콘서트에 참석하기로 마음먹었다. 구시가지에 있는 홀은 아주 오래되고 황폐했다. 주위를 둘러보며 Sharon은 어떤 쇼를 기대할 수 있을지 또다시 궁금했다. 그러나 탱고가 시작되자마자 모든 것이 바뀌었다. 피아노, 기타, 플루트, 바이올린이 마법처럼 조화를 이루며 흘러나왔다. 청중은 환호성을 질렀다. "어머나! 얼마나 환상적인 음악인가!" Sharon은 소리쳤다. 리듬과 박자가 너무 활기차고 환상적이어서 그녀의 몸과 마음을 뒤흔들었다. 그 콘서트는 그녀의 예상을 훨씬 뛰어넘었다.

해설 글의 전반부에서는 탱고 공연 표를 얻은 Sharon이 우연히 공연에 대한 혹평을 읽고 공연이 괜찮을 것인지 의심했다는 내용이 전개된다. 하지만 'But as soon as the tango started, ~' 이후로 막상 공연이 시작되자 멋진 연주와 관객의 열기에 매혹된 Sharon이 예상을 뛰어넘는 공연에 감탄했다는 내용이 이어진다. 따라서 Sharon의 심경 변화로 가장 적절한 것은 ② '의심하는 → (감탄하여) 놀란'이다.

오답 풀이

선택률	선지 해석 & 오답 풀이
① 2%	신난 → 지루한 ▶ '부정적 정서 → 긍정적 정서'로 나아가는 글의 흐름과 상반된다.
③ 1%	평온한 → 속상한 ▶ 글의 내용과 무관하다.
④ 3%	부끄러운 → 고마운 ▶ 글의 내용과 무관하다.
⑤ 1%	부러운 → 무관심한 ▶ 글의 내용과 무관하다.

지문 자세히 보기'

01 Sharon received a ticket to an upcoming tango concert from her friend. While surfing the Internet, she came across a review for the concert. The reviewer was harsh, calling it "an awful performance."

▶ 친구에게 탱고 공연 표를 받은 Sharon이 공연에 대한 혹평을 보게 되었다는 내용이 소개된다.

02 That raised in Sharon's mind the question of whether it was worthwhile to go, but in the end, she reluctantly decided to attend the concert.

▶ 공연에 대한 의문이 생겼지만(raised ~ the question ~) 마지못해(reluctantly) 공연에 가기로 했다는 내용으로 보아, Sharon이 의심 또는 회의감을 느꼈음을 알 수 있다.

03 The hall located in the old town was ancient and run-down. Looking around, Sharon again wondered what kind of show she could expect.

▶ 홀에 도착한 Sharon이 어떤 공연이 펼쳐질지 다시금 의문을 가졌다(wondered)는 내용이 제시된다.

04 But as soon as the tango started, everything changed. The piano, guitar, flute, and violin magically flew out in harmony. The audience cheered.

▶ But부터 글의 흐름이 반전되며(everything changed), 모든 악기가 조화를 이루는 멋진 공연에 관객이 환호했다는 묘사가 이어진다.

05 "Oh my goodness! What fantastic music!" Sharon shouted. The rhythm and tempo were so energetic and sensational that they shook her body and soul. The concert was far beyond her expectations.

▶ 관객들과 마찬가지로 Sharon도 환호하며(What fantastic music!), 기대를 뛰어넘는 공연에(far beyond her expectations) 즐거워했다는 내용으로 마무리된다.

구문 풀이

That **raised in Sharon's mind the question of whether it was worthwhile to go**, but in the end, she reluctantly decided to attend the concert.

→ raised의 목적어인 the question이 「of + whether절」의 수식을 받아 길어지자, 부사구인 in Sharon's mind를 목적어 앞에 삽입하고, 목적어를 뒤로 보냈다.

구문 플러스' 긴 목적어의 후치

목적어가 수식어구를 동반해 길어지면 목적어를 맨 뒤로 보낼 수 있다. 이때 본래 목적어 뒤에 쓰는 보어나 부사구가 동사와 목적어 사이에 나온다.

The wireless network **makes** possible the connection between any two devices. (동사 + 목적격보어 + 목적어)
그 무선 네트워크는 그 어떤 두 장치 간의 연결도 가능하게 한다.

---

07 정답 ③ 90%　　　　　　　　　　　*2020학년도 6월 모평*

해석 논문 제출 2시간 전이었다. 마감 시간이 눈앞에 닥쳤는데, Claire는 여전히 자신의 글로 고심하고 있었다. 시간적 압박을 받고 막다른 상태에 처해, 그녀는 그 논문을 어떻게 끝마쳐야 할지 몰랐다. 그녀는 심지어 그것을 제때 제출할 수 있을지조차 확신하지 못했다. 그녀가 자신의 논문에서 발견한 것은 휘갈겨 쓴 단어, 불완전한 문장, 겉보기에 이상하고 일관성이 없는 생각의 무더기였다. "어느 것도 의미가 통하지 않아."라고 그녀는 혼잣말했다. 그녀는 자신의 글을 살펴보고 그것을 반복해서 읽기 시작했다. 문득 예기치 않게 그 생각의 무더기에서 뭔가가 발견되

었는데, 그녀가 쓰는 동안에는 고려하지 않았던 생각의 흐름과 연결이었다. 이때부터 시계의 똑딱거리는 소리는 그녀에게 힘을 북돋아 주는 것처럼 들렸다. "그래, 난 할 수 있어!" Claire는 다시 연필을 움켜쥐며 말했다.

해설 글의 전반부에서는 Claire가 논문 제출을 얼마 안 남겨놓고 시간 압박 속에 글이 잘 풀리지 않아 고심 중이었다는 내용이 전개된다. 하지만 All of a sudden and unexpectedly 이후로는 문득 뭔가 떠올린 Claire가 시계 소리에 힘을 얻으며 의욕을 찾았다는 내용이 이어진다. 따라서 Claire의 심경 변화로 가장 적절한 것은 ③ '긴장한 → 자신감에 찬'이다.

오답 풀이

선택률	선지 해석 & 오답 풀이
① 2%	기쁜 → 부끄러운 ▶ 글의 내용과 무관하다.
② 1%	안도한 → 걱정하는 ▶ '부정적 정서 → 긍정적 정서'로 나아가는 글의 흐름과 상반된다.
④ 4%	무관심한 → 신난 ▶ 전반부의 struggling과 Pressed를 '무관심'의 단서로 보기는 어렵다.
⑤ 1%	지루한 → 당황한 ▶ 글의 내용과 무관하다.

지문 자세히 보기'

01 It was two hours before the paper submission. With the deadline close at hand, Claire was still struggling with her writing.

▶ 논문 제출을 눈앞에 둔 Claire가 글쓰기로 고전 중이었다(struggling)는 상황이 제시된다.

02 Pressed for time and stuck in a deadlock, she had no idea how to finish the paper. She wasn't even sure whether she could submit it on time. What she found in her paper was scribbled words, half sentences, and a pile of seemingly strange and disjointed ideas. "Nothing makes sense," she said to herself. She looked at her writing and began reading it over and over.

▶ 시간 압박 상태에서 글이 막히자(Pressed ~ and stuck ~) Claire가 글에 확신을 갖지 못했다는 내용이 전개된다. had no idea, wasn't ~ sure, strange and disjointed 등이 Claire의 불안과 긴장을 반영한다.

03 All of a sudden and unexpectedly, something was found in that pile of thoughts: the flow and connection of ideas she had not considered while she was writing.

▶ All of a sudden and unexpectedly가 흐름을 전환한다. Claire가 문득 새로운 것을 떠올렸다는 내용이 제시된다.

04 From this moment, the ticking of the clock sounded encouraging to her. "Yes, I can do it!" Claire said as she grabbed her pencil again.

▶ 시계 소리마저도 힘을 주는 것처럼(encouraging) 들렸다는 표현을 통해 Claire가 다시 글을 잘 써볼 의지를 되찾았음(Yes, I can do it!)을 알 수 있다.

Pressed for time and **stuck** in a deadlock, she had no idea how to finish the paper.

→ 문장의 주어이자 분사구문의 주어인 **she**가 '압박감을 받고' 막다른 상태에 '갇힌' 대상이므로 과거분사로 시작하는 분사구문이 쓰였다.

구문 플러스⁺ 과거분사로 시작하는 분사구문

수동태 동사를 포함한 부사절을 분사구문으로 전환하면 be동사가 being 또는 having been으로 바뀌며 흔히 생략된다. 결국 과거분사로 시작하는 분사구문이 만들어진다.

(Being) Praised by her teacher, she felt proud.
(=**As she was praised** ~)
선생님께 칭찬받아서, 그녀는 뿌듯한 기분이었다.

유형 플러스⁺ 심경/분위기

글 전반의 분위기 또는 필자의 심경 (변화)을 추론하는 유형으로, 문학적 이야기 글이 많이 사용된다.

· **문제 해결 Tip**.
① 글의 도입부에서 주요 인물과 상황을 파악한다.
② 상황을 묘사하는 형용사, 부사 중심으로 이야기의 흐름을 파악한다.
③ 심경 변화 유형의 경우, 중간에 보통 역접 연결어(**however**, **but**, **suddenly**, **(un)fortunately** 등)가 있어 글의 흐름이 반전된다. 따라서 전반부와 후반부에서 각각 핵심적인 단서를 따로 찾아야 한다.

· **선택지 빈출**(1): 심경 형용사

delighted	기쁜	anxious	불안한
worried	걱정되는	nervous	긴장한
grateful	고마운	indifferent	무관심한
confused	혼란스러운	frustrated	좌절한
jealous	질투하는	furious	분노한
disappointed	실망한	relieved	안도한

· **선택지 빈출**(2): 분위기 형용사

peaceful	평화로운	urgent	다급한
monotonous	단조로운	joyful	즐거운
festive	축제 같은	sorrowful	슬픈

08 정답 ⑤ 86%   *2024학년도 6월 모평*

해석 인터넷에 관한 한, (많이는 아니어도) 약간 편집적이 되는 것이 이득이 될 따름이다. 인터넷에 있는 모든 것의 익명성 수준을 고려할 때, 여러분이 받을지도 모르는 어떤 데이터든 그것의 타당성에 대해 의문을 제기하는 것이 합리적이다. 일반적으로 우리가 인도를 따라 내려오는 누군가를 만날 때, 특히 너무 놀랍게도 그들이 여러분을 알고 있었다고 자신을 소개할 때, 여러분이 스스로 일종의 방어적인 자세를 취하는 것은 우리의 자연스러운 본능이다. 일부러 우리는 그 사람이 시나리오나, 이름이나, 지인이나, 혹은 (우리를 안다는 것을) 입증할 증거(사진 같은 것)를 제시해서 우리를 어떻게 아는지 입증해야만 하는 과제를 설정한다. 일단 우리가 그 정보를 받고 그것이 인지적 검증을 통과하면, 우리는 그 사람을 더 믿을 만하다고 받아들인다. 이 모든 것은 몇 분 안에 일어나지만, 우리가 현실 세계에서 수행하는 자연스러운 방어 기제이다. 하지만, 가상 세계에서는 우리의 안녕에 물리적인 위협이 없는 것처럼 보이기 때문에 우리는 덜 방어적인 경향이 있다.

해설 첫 두 문장과 마지막 문장을 종합하면 주제를 알 수 있다. 인터넷 상에서는 우리가 덜 방어적이 되기 때문에 그곳에 실린 정보가 타당한지에 대해 더 의문을 가질 필요가 있다는 것이다. 따라서 글의 요지로 가장 적절한 것은 ⑤ '방어 기제가 덜 작동하는 가상 세계에서는 신중한 정보 검증이 중요하다.'이다.

오답 풀이

선택률	오답 풀이
① 5%	표현의 자유에 관한 내용은 없다.
② 1%	정보의 신뢰도 검증은 글의 핵심 소재가 맞지만, 검증의 기술은 언급되지 않았다.
③ 5%	가상 공간과 현실 세계를 비교하는 내용은 있지만, 정보 공유의 자유로움이 주제는 아니다.
④ 1%	보안 프로그램은 언급되지 않았다.

지문 자세히 보기

01 When it comes to the Internet, it just pays to be a little paranoid (but not a lot). Given the level of anonymity with all that resides on the Internet, it's sensible to question the validity of any data that you may receive.

▶ '편집적이 되는 것 = 인터넷상의 모든 데이터가 타당한지 의문을 제기하는 것'이다. 즉 두 문장은 '인터넷상의 데이터에 더 철저한 검증이 필요하다'는 동일한 내용이다.

02 Typically it's to our natural instinct when we meet someone coming down a sidewalk to place yourself in some manner of protective position, especially when they introduce themselves as having known you, much to your surprise.

▶ protective position 또한 paranoid와 같은 의미다. 길가에서 우리를 알은체하는 사람과 마주치면 우리는 자연스럽게 '방어 태세'를 취하게 된다는 예시이다.

03 By design, we set up challenges in which the individual must validate how they know us by presenting scenarios, names or acquaintances, or evidence by which to validate (that is, photographs). Once we have received that information and it has gone through a cognitive validation, we accept that person as more trustworthy. All this happens in a matter of minutes but is a natural defense mechanism that we perform in the real world.

▶ '방어 태세' 속에 우리는 그 사람이 우리를 어떻게 아는지 '검증'하며, 이 검증이 무사히 끝나면 그 사람을 믿게 된다고 한다. 이것은 실생활의 우리에게 '자연스러운 방어 기제'라는 설명이 뒤따른다.

04 However, in the virtual world, we have a tendency to be less defensive, as there appears to be no physical threat to our well-being.

▶ However와 함께, 가상 공간에서는 이러한 '방어와 검증' 절차가 덜 작동한다는 우려가 제시된다. 이러한 이유로 '약간 편집적이 될(= 검증을 더 열심히 할 = 방어 태세를 더 취할)' 필요가 있다는 것이 글의 요지이다.

구문 풀이

Given the level of anonymity with all that resides on the Internet, it's sensible to question the validity of any data that you may receive.
→ '~을 고려하면'의 의미로 쓰인 given은 숙어처럼 굳어진 분사구문 관용표현이다.

구문 플러스 분사구문 관용표현

형태가 숙어처럼 굳어진 분사구문 관용표현을 기억해둔다.

considering, given	~을 고려하면
judging from	~로 판단컨대
generally speaking	일반적으로 말해서
compared to/with	~와 비교하면
frankly speaking	솔직히 말해서

Considering his temper, it's best to avoid any conflicts.
그의 성미를 고려할 때, 그 어떤 갈등이든 피하는 것이 가장 좋다.
Generally speaking, Ms. Cho is a good teacher.
일반적으로 말해서, Cho 선생님은 좋은 교사이다.

09 정답 ① 49%   *2023학년도 6월 모평*

해석 흔히 간과되지만 못지않게 중요한 이해관계자는 개인정보 역설이라는 개념에서 큰 역할을 하는 소비자이다. 모든 방식의 디지털 경험과 공동체에서 소비자의 참여 수준은 그야말로 폭발적으로 증가해 왔으며, 둔화될 기미가 거의 또는 전혀 보이지 않는다. 소비자들 사이에서는 이러한 회사들이 제공하는 풍부한 경험을 추진하는 데 자신들의 개인정보가 도움이 된다는 것뿐만 아니라, 이 정보를 공유하는 것이 전체로든 부분으로든, 이러한 경험에 대해 지불하는 대가이기도 하다는 인식이 있다. 정보 수집 및 이용의 내용과 시기, 이유를 더 잘 이해하지 못할 경우, 소비자는 흔히 취약하고 갈등을 겪는다는 느낌을 받게 된다. '내 전화기에 있는 이 식당 검색 앱이 마음에 드는데, 그 앱이 내 현재 위치를 이용할 수 있느냐고 물을 때 'ok'를 누르면 내 정보는 어떻게 되는 걸까?' 그들에게 선택권을 제공할 수 있는 도구로 무장한 소비자는 수동적 방관자에서 능동적 참여자로 이동한다.

> **해설** 개인정보 제공에 있어 소비자가 중요한 이해관계자임을 설명하는 글이다. 오늘날 소비자들은 개인정보를 공유하는 것이 다양한 경험을 제공받기 위한 대가임을 인식하고 있지만, 이 정보 제공의 속성을 이해해야 능동적인 소비자가 될 수 있다는 것이 글의 주된 내용이다. 따라서 글의 요지로 가장 적절한 것은 ① '개인정보 제공의 속성을 심층적으로 이해하면 주체적 소비자가 된다.'이다.

오답 풀이

선택률	오답 풀이
② 10%	앱 활용의 필요성에 관한 내용은 언급되지 않았다.
③ 13%	디지털 데이터가 아닌, 개인정보에 관한 글이다.
④ 21%	단순히 대가가 따른다는 내용을 넘어, 대가로서의 개인정보가 제공되는 이유, 시기 등을 소비자가 알아야 한다는 것이 글의 주제이다.
⑤ 7%	개인정보 유출에 관해서는 언급되지 않았다.

지문 자세히 보기

01 Often overlooked, but just as important a stakeholder, is the consumer who plays a large role in the notion of the privacy paradox. Consumer engagement levels in all manner of digital experiences and communities have simply exploded — and they show little or no signs of slowing.

▶ 개인정보 역설이라는 개념에서 소비자가 큰 역할을 담당한다는 내용과 함께, 디지털 경험 또는 공동체에서 소비자 참여가 늘고 있다는 배경 설명이 제시된다.

02 There is an awareness among consumers, not only that their personal data helps to drive the rich experiences that these companies provide, but also that sharing this data is the price you pay for these experiences, in whole or in part.

▶ 소비자에게 개인정보 제공은 다양한 경험을 누리기 위한 대가로 인식되고 있다는 설명이 이어진다.

03 Without a better understanding of the what, when, and why of data collection and use, the consumer is often left feeling vulnerable and conflicted. "I love this restaurant-finder app on my phone, but what happens to my data if I press 'ok' when asked if that app can use my current location?"

▶ 개인정보 수집의 내용, 시기, 목적을 소비자가 더 잘 알아야 정보가 어떻게 될까에 대한 걱정에서 벗어날 수 있다는 핵심 내용이 제시된다.

04 Armed with tools that can provide them options, the consumer moves from passive bystander to active participant.

▶ 'Armed with tools ~ options'는 소비자가 개인정보 제공의 속성을 더 잘 이해하고 있는(a better understanding ~ of data collection and use) 상황을 비유적으로 나타낸다. 이러한 이해가 선행돼야 소비자가 능동적 참여자로 성장할 수 있다는 결론으로 글이 마무리된다.

구문 풀이

Often overlooked, but just as important a stakeholder, is the consumer who plays a large role in the notion of the privacy paradox.

→ 「보어 + 동사 + 주어」 어순의 도치 구문이다.

구문 플러스⁺ 보어 도치

보어를 문장 맨 앞에 써서 강조하면 뒤따르는 주어와 동사는 「동사 + 주어」 어순으로 도치된다. 단, 「so ~ that …(너무 ~해서 …하다)」 구문 속 보어가 문장 앞으로 나오면 의문문 어순 도치가 일어난다.

Happy are those who work for peace.
평화를 위해 노력하는 사람은 행복하다.

So tired did I become that I had to take a break.
나는 너무 피곤해져서 쉬어야 했다.

---

10 정답 ③ 83% 　　　　　　　　　*2022학년도 대수능*

> **해석** 조직이 소셜 미디어로 실험하는 것을 처음 고려할 때 범하는 가장 일반적인 실수 중 하나는 소셜 미디어 도구와 플랫폼에 너무 지나치게 중점을 두고 조직의 사업 목표에는 충분히 중점을 두지 않는다는 것이다. 기업을 위한 소셜 웹에서의 성공의 실제는 소셜 미디어 프로그램을 고안하는 것이 최신 소셜 미디어 도구와 채널에 대한 통찰력이 아니라 조직 자체의 목적과 목표에 대한 철저한 이해와 더불어 시작된다는 것이다. 소셜 미디어 프로그램은 그저 '다른 모든 이가 하고 있다'는 이유로 인기 소셜 네트워크상에서 '존재'를 관리해야 할 막연한 필요를 이행하는 것이 아니다. '소셜 미디어에 있다는 것' 자체로는 아무 쓸모도 없다. 조금이라도 어떤 쓸모가 있으려면, 소셜 미디어상의 존재는 조직과 고객을 위해 문제를 해결하거나 어떤 종류의 개선이라는 결과(될 수 있으면 측정 가능한 결과)를 가져와야 한다. 어떤 일이든, 목적이 성공을 이끌어낸다. 소셜 미디어의 세계도 다르지 않다.

> **해설** 기업을 위한 소셜 웹에서의 성공은 조직 목표를 철저히 이해하는 것으로 시작된다는 내용의 글로, 두 번째 문장과 마지막 두 문장이 주제를 잘 제시한다. 따라서 필자가 주장하는 바로 가장 적절한 것은 ③ '기업은 소셜 미디어를 활용할 때 사업 목표를 토대로 해야 한다.'이다.

오답 풀이

선택률	오답 풀이
① 5%	기업 이미지나 소셜 미디어의 개발에 관해서는 언급되지 않았다.
② 5%	사회적 가치와 요구라는 소재가 글과 무관하며, 사업 목표의 이해가 아닌 '수립' 또한 글과 무관하다.
④ 2%	제품 홍보에 관해서는 언급되지 않았다.
⑤ 4%	소비자의 의견 수렴에 관해서는 언급되지 않았다.

01 One of the most common mistakes made by organizations when they first consider experimenting with social media is that they focus too much on social media tools and platforms and not enough on their business objectives.

▶ 소셜 미디어 도구 또는 플랫폼과 사업 목표를 대비시키고 있다. 전자에 집중하느라 후자에 덜 신경 쓰는 행위를 가리켜 '실수'라고 했으니, 뒤에서는 해결책이 나올 것이다.

02 The reality of success in the social web for businesses is that creating a social media program begins not with insight into the latest social media tools and channels but with a thorough understanding of the organization's own goals and objectives.

▶ 「not A but B」 구문을 통해, 소셜 미디어의 도구나 채널보다는 조직의 목표에 집중해야 한다는 주장을 제시한다. 첫 문장의 social media tools와 objectives가 반복되며 내용상 계속 대비된다.

03 A social media program is not merely the fulfillment of a vague need to manage a "presence" on popular social networks because "everyone else is doing it." "Being in social media" serves no purpose in and of itself.

▶ 단지 소셜 미디어상에 '존재하는(presence, Being in social media)' 것, 즉 소셜 미디어라는 도구를 쓰는 것만으로는 기업에 도움이 되지 않는다는 부연이 이어진다.

04 In order to serve any purpose at all, a social media presence must either solve a problem for the organization and its customers or result in an improvement of some sort (preferably a measurable one).

▶ 소셜 미디어가 도움이 되려면 문제 해결 또는 개선이 이루어져야 한다는 주장이 나온다. 여기서 solve a problem, result in an improvement가 바로 조직의 '목표'와 맞닿는 구체적인 행위이다.

05 In all things, purpose drives success. The world of social media is no different.

▶ 목적(purpose)이 중요하다는 결론으로 글이 마무리된다.

구문 풀이

The reality of success in the social web for businesses is that creating a social media program begins **not** with insight into the latest social media tools and channels **but** with a thorough understanding of the organization's own goals and objectives.
→ 「not A but B」 구문의 A, B는 병렬구조를 이룬다. 여기서도 A, B 자리에 모두 「with + 명사」구가 나왔다.

구문 플러스' not A but B

「not A but B(A가 아니라 B인)」 구문의 A, B는 병렬구조를 이룬다.

I'm **not** nervous **but** scared.
나는 긴장한 것이 아니라 겁이 난다.

Love looks **not** with the eyes, **but** with the mind.
사랑은 눈으로 보는 것이 아니라, 마음으로 보는 것이다.

해석 역사적으로 전문직과 사회는 그들의 관계의 조건을 규정하고자 의도된 협상 과정에 참여해 왔다. 이 과정의 핵심에는 전문직의 자율성 추구와 책임성에 대한 공공의 요구 사이의 긴장이 있다. 사회가 전문직에 권한과 특권을 부여한 것은 사회 복지에 기여하고 더 넓은 사회적 가치와 일치하는 방식으로 자기 일을 수행하려는 그들의 자발성과 능력을 전제로 한다. 오랫동안 전문직의 전문지식과 특권적 지위는 그들이 봉사하는 사람들을 희생시키고서 그들 자신의 이익을 향상시키기 위해 쉽게 이용될 수 있는 권위와 권한을 준다고 인식되었다. Edmund Burke가 두 세기 전에 말했듯이, "인간은 자신의 욕구를 도덕적으로 구속하는 성향에 정확히 비례해서 시민적 자유를 누릴 자격이 부여된다." 자율성은 일방통행로였던 적이 없었으며 결코 절대적이고 뒤집을 수 없게 주어지지 않는다.

해설 두 번째 문장에서 전문직의 자율성 추구와 그들의 책임성에 대한 공공의 요구 사이에 긴장이 있다는 핵심 내용을 제시한다. 뒤이어 전문직의 전문지식과 특권은 이들이 사회적 가치에 합하는 일을 할 수 있도록 부여된 것이며, 책임 없이 자율성만 일방적으로 부여된 것은 아니라는 주장이 이어진다. 따라서 글의 요지로 가장 적절한 것은 ① '전문직에 부여되는 자율성은 그에 상응하는 사회적 책임을 수반한다.'이다.

오답 풀이

선택률	오답 풀이
② 20%	'It has long been recognized ~' 문장만 보면 답처럼 보이지만, 마지막 두 문장을 읽으면 결국 전문직의 권한은 책임을 수반한다는 내용이 요지임을 알 수 있다.
③ 5%	전문직의 사회적 책임은 글의 핵심 소재가 맞지만, 제도 정비는 글의 내용과 무관하다.
④ 7%	전문직의 자격 요건은 언급되지 않았다.
⑤ 23%	전문직의 업무 성과는 언급되지 않았다.

01 Historically, the professions and society have engaged in a negotiating process intended to define the terms of their relationship. At the heart of this process is the tension between the professions' pursuit of autonomy and the public's demand for accountability.

▶ 전문직의 자율성(autonomy)과 책임(accountability) 사이의 긴장이 핵심 소재이다.

02 Society's granting of power and privilege to the professions is premised on their willingness and ability to contribute to social well-being and to conduct their affairs in a manner consistent with broader social values.

▶ 전문직에 부여된 권한과 특권은 이들이 사회와 합하는 방향으로 일을 수행하려는 의지와 능력에 근간을 둔다는 내용이 제시된다. 'to contribute ~'와 'to conduct ~'가 '책임'의 내용을 보충 설명한다.

03 It has long been recognized that the expertise and privileged position of professionals confer authority and power that could readily be used to advance their own interests at the expense of those they serve. As Edmund Burke observed two centuries ago, "Men are qualified for civil liberty in exact proportion to their disposition to put moral chains upon their own appetites."

▶ 인간의 시민적 자유는 얼마나 자신의 욕구를 도덕적으로 구속하는가에 따라 결정된다는 설명을 통해, 전문직의 자율권 또한 '도덕적 구속', 즉 책임에 비례해 정해진다는 내용을 유추할 수 있다.

04 Autonomy has never been a one-way street and is never granted absolutely and irreversibly.

▶ 자율권은 결코 일방적이고(a one-way street) 절대적으로(absolutely and irreversibly) 부여된 적이 없다(never)는 결론을 비유적으로 정리한다.

구문 풀이

At the heart of this process is the tension between the professions' pursuit of autonomy and the public's demand for accountability.

→ 「장소 부사구 + 동사 + 주어」 어순의 도치 구문이다. 주어가 동사 뒤에 나오므로 수일치에 주의해야 한다.

구문 플러스⁺ 장소 부사구 도치

장소 부사구가 강조되기 위해 문장 맨 앞에 나오면 주어와 동사가 도치된다.

On the hill stands a pine tree. 언덕 위에 소나무가 서 있다.

---

12 정답 ② 73%
2021학년도 9월 모평

해석 적절한 환경이 주어지면, 기업가 정신은 캠퍼스 생활의 구조로 완전히 짜여 들어가 그것의 교육적 범위를 크게 확장할 수 있다. 한 연구가 보여주기로, 직장 내에서 동료들은 기회를 포착하고 그에 따라 행동하도록 서로에게 영향을 미친다. 즉, 사무실에서 함께 일하는 기업가들이 많을수록, 그들의 동료들이 병에 걸릴(기업가 정신에 전염될) 가능성이 더 크다는 것이다. 스탠퍼드대학교 졸업생들을 대상으로 한 연구에서 '다양한 업무 및 교육 배경을 가진 사람들이 직장에서 한 가지 역할에 집중했거나 학교에서 한 가지 과목에 집중한 사람보다 자기 자신의 사업을 시작할 가능성이 훨씬 더 크다'는 것을 발견했다. 기업가적 문화를 배양하기 위해, 단과대학과 종합대학에서는 학생들에게 폭넓은 경험의 선택지와 다양한 아이디어를 널리 접할 기회를 제공할 필요가 있다. 대학들은 학업 프로그램 기획, 주거 생활, 학생 집단, 동창회 네트워크를 결합하여 그렇게 할 수 있는 독특한 위치에 있다.

해설 마지막 두 문장에서 대학은 기업가 정신을 배양하기 적합한 환경을 학생들에게 제공할 필요가 있다는 핵심 내용이 제시된다. 당위의 **need to**가 주장을 잘 드러낸다. 따라서 필자의 주장으로 가장 적절한 것은 ② '대학은 학생들이 기업가 정신을 함양하도록 환경을 조성해야 한다.'이다.

오답 풀이

선택률	오답 풀이
① 2%	훌륭한 기업가가 되기 위한 조언은 글과 무관하다.
③ 3%	좋은 직장을 얻는 방법에 관한 조언은 글과 무관하다.
④ 6%	소모임 활동에 관해서는 언급되지 않았다.
⑤ 13%	학업 성취에 관해서는 언급되지 않았다.

지문 자세히 보기⁺

01 Given the right conditions, entrepreneurship can be fully woven into the fabric of campus life, greatly expanding its educational reach.

▶ 기업가 정신(entrepreneurship), 캠퍼스 생활(campus life) 등 글의 키워드가 제시된다.

02 One study showed that, within the workplace, peers influence each other to spot opportunities and act on them: the more entrepreneurs you have working together in an office, the more likely their colleagues will catch the bug.

▶ 직장에서 주변에 기업가가 많다면 기업가 정신이 전염될 수 있다는 내용의 연구를 소개한다.

03 A study of Stanford University alumni found that those "who have varied work and educational backgrounds are much more likely to start their own businesses than those who have focused on one role at work or concentrated in one subject at school."

▶ 연구가 추가로 열거된다. 업무 배경 또는 교육 배경이 다양한 사람들은 자기 사업을 시작할 확률이 더 높다는 이야기를 통해 역시 '배경, 환경'의 중요성을 뒷받침한다.

04 To cultivate an entrepreneurial culture, colleges and universities need to offer students a broad choice of experiences and wide exposure to different ideas. They are uniquely positioned to do this by combining the resources of academic programming, residential life, student groups, and alumni networks.

▶ 위의 두 사례에 비추어 볼 때 기업가 정신을 배양하려면 대학에서 적절한 환경을 만들어줘야 한다는 주장이 제시되고 있다.

구문 풀이

Given the right conditions, entrepreneurship can be fully woven into the fabric of campus life, **greatly expanding** its educational reach.

→ given은 수동분사구문으로, '~이 주어지면'이라는 뜻이다.

→ 'greatly expanding ~'은 문맥상 'and it can greatly expand ~'로 바꿀 수 있다. 이는 연속동작을 나타내는 분사구문이다.

앞에 나오는 주절에 이어 '그리고 ~하다'라는 의미를 나타내는 분사구문이다.

The couple welcomed us into their home, serving us a large dinner.
= The couple welcomed us into their home, **and they served us a large dinner.**
그 부부는 우리를 집으로 맞아들이고 푸짐한 식사를 대접해 주었다.

---

13 정답 ④ 80% 2021학년도 6월 모평

해석 스포츠에 대한 공식적인 정의는 중요한 함의를 갖는다. 정의가 규칙, 경쟁, 높은 기량을 강조할 때, 많은 사람이 참여에서 배제되거나 '이류'로 정의되는 다른 신체 활동을 피하게 될 것이다. 예를 들어 12세의 선수가 상위 클럽 축구팀에서 잘리면 그 선수는 지역 리그에서 뛰고 싶지 않을 수도 있는데, 그 이유는 그 선수가 그것을 진정한 스포츠가 아닌, '오락 활동'으로 보기 때문이다. 이것은 소수의 사람이 많은 수의 팬을 위해 상대적으로 높은 수준의 시합을 하는 동시에 대부분의 사람이 신체적으로 활동적이지 않은 상황을 만들 수 있는데, 이것은 건강에 부정적인 영향을 주고 사회나 지역 사회에 의료비를 증가시키는 상황이다. 스포츠가 즐거움을 위해 행해지는 광범위한 신체 활동을 포함하도록 정의되고 사회생활의 지역적인 표현들로 융합될 때 신체 활동 비율이 높을 것이고 전반적인 건강상의 이점이 있을 수 있다.

해설 스포츠에 대한 정의가 갖는 중요한 의미를 설명하는 글이다. 스포츠가 규칙, 경쟁, 높은 기량만을 강조한다면 사람들의 스포츠 참여가 저조해지고 이에 따른 사회적 비용이 증가한다는 내용 뒤로, 즐거움을 목적으로 하는 다양한 신체 활동을 스포츠의 정의 안에 포함시켜야 한다는 주장이 이어지고 있다. 따라서 글의 요지로 가장 적절한 것은 ④ '스포츠의 정의는 신체 활동 참여와 건강에 영향을 미친다.'이다.

오답 풀이

선택률	오답 풀이
① 6%	운동선수의 기량 향상에 관해서는 언급되지 않았다.
② 2%	공정한 승부에 관해서는 언급되지 않았다.
③ 7%	스포츠의 정의가 어떻게 내려지는가에 따라 스포츠의 대중화가 이루어질 수도 있다는 영향 관계를 반대로 기술한 선택지이다.
⑤ 3%	대인관계 유지에 관해서는 언급되지 않았다.

지문 자세히 보기⁺

01 Official definitions of sport have important implications. When a definition emphasizes rules, competition, and high performance, many people will be excluded from participation or avoid other physical activities that are defined as "second class."

▶ 스포츠에 대한 정의가 중요한 의미를 갖는다는 일반적인 설명 뒤로, 두 번째 문장에서 내용이 구체화된다. 스포츠가 규칙, 경쟁, 높은 기량을 강조하는 방향으로 정의되면 많은 사람들이 스포츠 참여에서 배제되는 결과가 뒤따를 것이라고 한다.

02 For example, when a 12-year-old is cut from an exclusive club soccer team, she may not want to play in the local league because she sees it as "recreational activity" rather than a real sport.

▶ 위의 정의에 따르면, 상위 축구팀에서 배제된 12살짜리 선수는 지역 리그에서의 경기를 '오락 활동'으로 치부해 참여하고 싶지 않아 할 것이라는 예시가 이어진다. recreational은 위의 second class와 문맥적 의미가 같다.

03 This can create a situation in which most people are physically inactive at the same time that a small number of people perform at relatively high levels for large numbers of fans — a situation that negatively impacts health and increases health-care costs in a society or community.

▶ 위의 결과로 많은 사람들이 스포츠에 참여하지 않아(inactive) 사회에 부정적 영향(negatively ~ health-care costs)이 미칠 것이라는 설명이 뒤따른다.

04 When sport is defined to include a wide range of physical activities that are played for pleasure and integrated into local expressions of social life, physical activity rates will be high and overall health benefits are likely.

▶ 스포츠를 정의하는 방향에 대한 최종적 결론이 도출되고 있다. 스포츠가 즐거움을 목적으로 행해지는 많은 형태의 활동을 포함하는 방향으로 정의되어야 스포츠 참여가 촉진되고, 긍정적 영향이 뒤따를 것이라는 예측이 제시된다.

구문 풀이

When a definition emphasizes rules, competition, and high performance, many people will be excluded from participation or (will) avoid other physical activities that are defined as "second class."

→ When이 이끄는 부사절은 시간 부사절이므로, 주절이 미래시제이지만 부사절의 동사가 현재시제로 쓰였다.

시간과 조건의 부사절에서는 현재시제가 미래시제를 대신한다.

All of us will miss him when he leaves.
그가 떠나면 우리 모두가 그를 그리워할 것이다.

cf. **I don't know when she will come.** (when: 의문사)
나는 그녀가 언제 돌아올지 모른다.

Let's see if it will work. (if: 명사절 접속사)
그게 효과가 있을지 보자.

---

14 정답 ① 78% 2020학년도 대수능

해석 돌이켜 보면 양의 수를 세고자 하는 욕구만큼 세속적인 것이 문자 언어처럼 근본적인 진보의 원동력이었다는 것은 놀라운 일로 보일지도 모른다. 그러나 문자 기록에 대한 욕구는 언제나 경제 활동을 수반해 왔는데, 그 이유는 누가 무엇을 소유하고 있는지 명확하게 기억할 수 없는 한 거래는 무의미하기 때문이다. 따라서 인간의 초기 글쓰기는 내기, 계산서, 계약서의 모음과 같이 목적을 위해서는 수단을 가리지 않는 것에 의해 지배된다. 우리가 예언자들에 관한 기록을 갖기 훨씬 이전에 우리는 이익에 대한 기록을 가졌다. 사실, 많은 문명이 우리가 흔히 문화의 역사와 연관 짓는 그런 종류의 위대한 문학 작품을 기록하고 후세에 남기는 단계에 결코 이르지 못했다. 이런 고대 사회에서 살아남은 것은 대부분 영수증 더미이다. 만약 그런 기록을 만들어냈던 상업적 기업이 없다면 우리는 그런 기록이 생겨난 문화에 대해 아주 훨씬 더 적게 알 것이다.

두 번째 문장에서 문자 기록의 욕구는 늘 경제 활동을 수반했다는 핵심 내용을 제시하므로, 글의 요지로 가장 적절한 것은 ① '고대 사회에서 경제 활동은 문자 기록의 원동력이었다.'이다. 마지막 두 문장에서도 고대 사회의 기록 중 살아남은 것이 결국 '영수증 더미'였음을 언급하며 문자 기록과 경제 활동의 밀접한 연관성을 뒷받침하고 있다.

오답 풀이

선택률	오답 풀이
② 14%	글에서는 경제 활동을 주로 기록하고 문학 작품을 남기는 수준까지는 이르지 못했던 문자 발달 초기를 설명하고 있다. 따라서 문학으로 경제 활동을 알 수 있다는 내용은 글과 무관하다.
③ 4%	경제 활동이 아닌 발전은 무관한 소재이다.
④ 1%	종교에 관해서는 언급되지 않았다.
⑤ 1%	작가 배출에 관해서는 언급되지 않았다.

지문 자세히 보기

01 In retrospect, it might seem surprising that something as mundane as the desire to count sheep was the driving force for an advance as fundamental as written language. But the desire for written records has always accompanied economic activity, since transactions are meaningless unless you can clearly keep track of who owns what.

▶ 문자 기록에 대한 욕구는 늘 경제 활동과 연관되어 있었다는 핵심 내용이 제시된다. 첫 문장의 **the desire to count sheep**은 **economic activity**의 예시이다.

02 As such, early human writing is dominated by wheeling and dealing: a collection of bets, bills, and contracts. Long before we had the writings of the prophets, we had the writings of the profits. In fact, many civilizations never got to the stage of recording and leaving behind the kinds of great literary works that we often associate with the history of culture.

▶ 위의 **economic activity**가 **a collection of bets, bills, and contracts**로 재진술된다. 인간의 초기 글쓰기는 각종 내기, 계산서, 계약서 등과 연관된 이익의 기록(**the writings of the profits**)이었음이 언급된다.

03 What survives these ancient societies is, for the most part, a pile of receipts. If it weren't for the commercial enterprises that produced those records, we would know far, far less about the cultures that they came from.

▶ 비유적 표현인 **a pile of receipts**를 통해, 고대 문서 기록이 경제 활동의 결과였다는 결론을 함축적으로 드러내고 있다.

구문 풀이

If it weren't for the commercial enterprises that produced those records, **we would know** far, far less about the cultures that they came from.

→ **if it weren't for**는 **without** 또는 **but for**와 마찬가지로 '~이 없다면'이라는 뜻이다. 이 표현이 종속절에 나오면 주절에는 「주어 + 조동사 과거형 + 동사원형」이 나온다.

구문 플러스⁺ if 없는 가정법

without과 **but for**는 '~이 없다면[없었다면]'이라는 뜻으로, if 없이도 가정법 과거 또는 과거완료 동사와 어울려 가정법 문장을 구성할 수 있다. 이때 주절의 시제에 따라 if it weren't for 또는 if it hadn't been for로 바꿀 수 있다.

Without you, I would feel so alone.
(= **If it weren't for you, ~**)
네가 없으면, 난 무척 외로울 거야.

But for your help, we couldn't have finished the project.
(= **If it hadn't been for your help, ~**)
네 도움이 없었다면, 우리는 그 프로젝트를 끝낼 수 없었을 거야.

유형 플러스⁺ 필자의 주장 & 글의 요지

과거에는 지문 속에 주제문이 명확히 제시되고, 이를 거의 그대로 번역한 선택지가 흔히 정답이었다. 최근에는 이러한 경향이 약해져 여러 문장 내용을 종합해 결론을 내려야 할 때가 많다.

· **문제 해결 Tip.**
  ① 도입부에서 핵심 소재를 파악한다.
  ② 명확한 주제문이 있다면, 이를 우리말로 옮긴 선택지가 정답이다.
  ③ 한 문장으로 응축된 주제문이 없다면, 결론에 주목하자. 핵심 소재에 관한 주된 의견이나 설명을 정리한 후, 내용을 종합해 답으로 연결시킨다.

· **주제문을 찾는 Tip.**
  ① 명령문/의무 표현(**must, should, need to**): ~해야 한다
  ② **It's important[essential, crucial, vital]** ~: ~이 중요하다
  ③ 「**the** + 비교급 ~, **the** + 비교급 …」: ~할수록 더 …하다
  ④ 「**it is[was]** ~ **that** …」 강조구문: …한 것은 바로 ~이다[였다]
  ⑤ **however** 뒤 → 대비로 주제 강조
  ⑥ **thus[therefore], in short**를 포함한 문장 → 핵심 요약
  ⑦ **for example** 앞의 문장 → 예시 앞의 일반적 내용, 즉 주제

15 정답 ④ 51% *2024학년도 대수능*

해석 여러분이 주의 집중하는 방식은 여러분이 스트레스에 대처하는 방식에 중요한 역할을 한다. 주의가 분산되면 스트레스를 해소하는 능력이 손상되는데, 왜냐하면 여러분의 주의가 분산되더라도, 여러분은 경험 가운데 스트레스가 많은 부분에만 집착할 수 있기에, 그것이 좁게 집중되기 때문이다. 여러분의 주의 초점 범위가 넓어지면, 여러분은 스트레스를 더 쉽게 해소할 수 있다. 여러분은 어떤 상황이라도 그 상황의 더 많은 측면을 균형 있는 시각으로 볼 수 있으며, 피상적이고 불안을 유발하는 주의 수준에 여러분을 옭아매는 어느 한 부분에 갇히지 않을 수 있다. 초점이 좁으면 각 경험의 스트레스 수준이 높아지지만, 초점이 넓으면 여러분은 각 상황을 더 넓은 시각으로 더 잘 볼 수 있기 때문에 스트레스 수준이 낮아진다. 불안감을 유발하는 하나의 세부 사항이 더 큰 그림(전체 상황)보다 덜 중요하다. 그것은 스스로를 (음식이) 눌어붙지 않는 프라이팬으로 변모시키는 것과 같다. 여러분은 여전히 달걀을 부칠 수 있지만, 그 달걀은 팬에 들러붙지 않을 것이다.

해설 글에서 반복되는 핵심 내용은 주의 집중의 범위를 넓혀서 작은 디테일보다 큰 그림을 바라볼 때 스트레스를 덜 받게 된다는 것이다. 따라서 밑줄 친 부분의 의미로 가장 적절한 것은 ④ '스트레스가 되는 측면을 넘어 경험을 더 넓게 바라보는 것'이다.

오답 풀이

선택률	선지 해석 & 오답 풀이
① 9%	일상생활에서 스트레스가 되는 그 어떤 경험도 절대 맞닥뜨리지 않는 것 ▶ 스트레스가 되는 경험 자체를 피하라는 내용은 언급되지 않았다.
② 17%	시각을 넓혀 스트레스의 원인을 찾아내는 것 ▶ 글에 따르면 시각을 넓혀야 하는 까닭은 스트레스의 원인을 찾기 위해서가 아니라, 스트레스를 덜 받기 위해서이다.
③ 8%	경험의 긍정적인 측면에만 주의를 좀처럼 국한시키지 않는 것 ▶ 긍정적인 것에만 주의 집중하는 것과 관련된 내용은 없다.
⑤ 16%	스트레스를 넓은 시각을 키우는 원천으로 생각하는 것 ▶ '스트레스', '넓은 시각' 등 핵심어는 다 들어가 있지만 주제와 관련이 없다.

지문 자세히 보기

01 How you focus your attention plays a critical role in how you deal with stress.

▶ 글의 주제문이다. 주의 집중의 방식을 스트레스 대처 방식과 연관시키고 있다.

02 Scattered attention harms your ability to let go of stress, because even though your attention is scattered, it is narrowly focused, for you are able to fixate only on the stressful parts of your experience.

▶ 주의력 분산, 즉 '좁은 주의 집중'은 '스트레스가 되는 것에만 집착하게' 해서 스트레스 해소에 '해를 끼친다'는 내용이다.

03 When your attentional spotlight is widened, you can more easily let go of stress. You can put in perspective many more aspects of any situation and not get locked into one part that ties you down to superficial and anxiety-provoking levels of attention.

▶ 대신 주의 집중을 '넓혀야' 불안과 스트레스를 낮출 수 있다는 요지가 제시된다.

04 A narrow focus heightens the stress level of each experience, but a widened focus turns down the stress level because you're better able to put each situation into a broader perspective. One anxiety-provoking detail is less important than the bigger picture.

▶ 'A narrow focus = One anxiety-provoking detail'이며, 'a widened focus = the bigger picture'이다. 즉, 좁은 시야로 스트레스가 되는 작은 요소 하나에 집중하기보다, 시야를 키워 전체 그림을 바라보라는 것이다.

05 It's like transforming yourself into a nonstick frying pan. You can still fry an egg, but the egg won't stick to the pan.

▶ '달걀이 부쳐지기는 해도 눌어붙지는 않는 프라이팬'은 '주의 집중 범위를 넓혀 스트레스를 덜 받는 상태'를 뜻하는 비유다.

구문 풀이

Scattered attention harms your ability to let go of stress, because even though your attention is scattered, it is narrowly focused, **for** you are able to fixate only on the stressful parts of your experience.

→ 문장 중간에서 또 다른 「주어 + 동사」를 연결하는 for는 등위접속사로, 앞의 이유를 설명한다.

구문 플러스 전치사 for vs. 접속사 for

• for + 명사(구): 전치사 for (~ 동안에, ~을 위해 등)
• for + 주어 + 동사: 접속사 for (~ 때문에)

She worked abroad **for a year**. → 전치사
그녀는 1년 동안 해외에서 일했다.

He worked hard. **for he aimed at the moon**. → 접속사
그는 열심히 일했는데, 그가 큰 꿈을 품었기 때문이었다.

16 정답 ② 29% *2024학년도 9월 모평*

해석 프로젝트에서 금도금이란 예상되는 결과를 불필요하게 향상하는 것으로, 즉 비용이 많이 들면서 필수적이지는 않고 목표와 관련해서는 부가 가치가 낮은 특성을 더하는 것이다. 다시 말해, (작업자) 본인의

재능을 입증한다는 것 외에는 실질적인 명분이 없이 더 많이 주는 것을 뜻한다. 금도금은 특히 프로젝트 팀원들에게 있어 흥미로운데, 이는 전문적 요소가 뚜렷한 프로젝트, 즉 검증된 경험과 폭넓은 전문적 자율성을 갖춘 전문가가 참여하는 프로젝트에서 흔하기 때문이다. 이런 환경에서 전문가들은 흔히 프로젝트가 자신의 다양한 기술을 테스트하고 강화할 기회라고 본다. 따라서 전적으로 선의에서 금도금에 참여하려는 유혹, 즉 전문가는 만족시키지만 고객의 요청에는 가치를 더하지 않으면서, 동시에 프로젝트의 귀중한 자원을 없애는, 더 많고 더 질 높은 성과를 달성하려는 유혹이 있다. 속담에서 말하듯이, '최고는 좋음의 적'이다.

해설 전문가가 자기 능력을 보여주고 시험하려는 목적으로 작업의 퀄리티와 양을 높일 때 '금도금'으로 이어질 수 있다는 내용이다. 즉 금도금이란 고객 입장에서는 부가 가치가 크지 않고 '불필요하지만' 전문가 입장에서는 자기 능력을 입증할 수 있는 특징을 더하는 관행인 것이다. 따라서 '최고가 좋음의 적'이라는 밑줄 부분은 ② '오로지 자기 자신(의 실력)을 입증하기 위해서 작업의 질을 높이는 것은 바람직하지 않다.'의 의미이다.

오답 풀이

선택률	선지 해석 & 오답 풀이
① 9%	직장에서 완벽을 추구하다 보면 팀원들 간의 갈등이 생긴다. ▶ 팀원 간의 갈등은 언급되지 않았다.
③ 28%	필요 이상의 자격을 갖춘 전문가를 프로젝트에 초빙하는 것은 나쁜 결과로 이어진다. ▶ 전문가의 자격 자체가 필요 이상 수준이라는 내용은 언급되지 않았다.
④ 17%	(계속) 바뀌는 고객의 요구에 응대하는 것은 불필요하다. ▶고객의 요구가 바뀌는지는 언급되지 않았다.
⑤ 16%	한 프로젝트를 위해 다양한 기술을 배운다고 해서 성공을 보장하지는 않는다. ▶ 기술과 성공의 연관 관계는 언급되지 않았다.

지문 자세히 보기

01 Gold plating in the project means needlessly enhancing the expected results, namely, adding characteristics that are costly, not required, and that have low added value with respect to the targets — in other words, giving more with no real justification other than to demonstrate one's own talent.

▶ '금도금'의 개념을 설명하는 'needlessly enhancing ~', 'adding ~', 'giving ~'이 모두 같은 말이다. 즉 '자기 능력을 보여주려는' 목적으로 목표에는 별로 크게 기여하지 않는 특징을 덧붙이는 게 금도금이라는 것이다.

02 Gold plating is especially interesting for project team members, as it is typical of projects with a marked professional component — in other words, projects that involve specialists with proven experience and extensive professional autonomy. In these environments specialists often see the project as an opportunity to test and enrich their skill sets.

▶ 'an opportunity ~ sets'에서, 전문가가 프로젝트를 '자기 기술을 시험해보는 장'으로 여길 때 금도금이 발생한다고 설명한다.

03 There is therefore a strong temptation, in all good faith, to engage in gold plating, namely, to achieve more or higher-quality work that gratifies the professional but does not add value to the client's requests, and at the same time removes valuable resources from the project. As the saying goes, "The best is the enemy of the good."

▶ 주제가 결론에서 반복된다. 첫 문장의 to demonstrate one's own talent가 마지막 문장에서 gratifies the professional로 바뀌었고, 'adding characteristics ~ low added value'는 'does not add value ~ from the project'로 바뀌었다.

구문 풀이

In these environments specialists often see the project as an opportunity to test and enrich their skill sets.

→ to부정사가 an opportunity를 수식한다.

구문 플러스⁺ to부정사의 형용사적 용법

to부정사구는 명사 뒤에서 명사를 수식할 수 있다.

You have the ability to make it work.

넌 그걸 해낼 수 있는 능력을 지니고 있어.

The only way to conquer a fear is to face it.

두려움을 극복하는 유일한 방법은 그것에 맞서는 것이다.

17 정답 ③ 47% *2024학년도 6월 모평*

해석 변호사들은 때때로 소유권을 '막대 다발'로 묘사한다. 이 비유는 약 1세기 전에 도입되어 법학 교육과 실무를 극적으로 변화시켰다. 그 비유는 유용한데, 우리가 소유권을 분리되고 또 다시 합쳐질 수 있는 대인 관계적인 권리의 모음으로 보는 것을 도와주기 때문이다. 어떤 자원에 관해 '그건 내 거다'라고 말할 때, 흔히 그것은 여러분이 전체 다발을 구성하는 많은 막대, 즉 판매 막대, 임대 막대, 저당잡히고 허가하고 증여하고 심지어 그것을 파괴할 권리를 소유한다는 뜻이다. 그러나 우리는 흔히 그 막대들을 쪼개는데, 토지 한 면에 대해서 보자면 이렇다. 땅 주인, 저당권을 가진 은행, 임대차 계약을 맺은 임차인, 토지 진입 면허를 가진 배관공, 광물에 대한 권리를 가진 석유 회사가 있을 수 있다. 이 당사자 각각은 그 다발의 막대 하나를 소유한다.

해설 소유권은 '막대 다발'과 같아서 판매, 임대, 저당, 허가 등 많은 권리 양상을 포함한다는 내용이다. 토지를 사례로 보면, 땅 주인, 저당권자, 세입자, 출입 허가를 받은 자 등 많은 이들이 얽혀 있다고 한다. 이들은 모두 토지를 '부분적으로 사용할' 수 있는 사람들이므로, 밑줄 친 부분의 의미로 가장 적절한 것은 ③ '재산의 한 측면을 사용할 수 있는 권리'이다.

오답 풀이

선택률	선지 해석 & 오답 풀이
① 8%	자원을 개발해야 한다는 법적 의무 ▶ 자원 개발 의무는 언급되지 않았다.
② 12%	법적으로 부동산 소유권을 주장할 우선권 ▶ 우선권에 관해서는 언급되지 않았다.

④ 13%	세입자들에 의해 동등하게 공유되는 빌딩 ▶ '동등하게 나눈다'는 표현이 '권리를 나눈다'는 내용과 관련 있어 보이지만, 글에서 '특정 건물'의 사례는 언급되지 않았다.
⑤ 20%	누구도 자기 것이라고 주장할 수 없는 토지 한 면 ▶ 땅에 관해 여러 당사자가 권리를 갖고 있다는 말을 어느한 사람도 '온전히' 자기 권리를 주장할 수 없다는 의미로 비약시키면 안 된다. 소유권의 각종 세부적 권리가 뭉친 것이 '막대 다발'이므로, '막대 하나'는 그 세부적 권리를 다시 나눈 것으로 이해해야 한다.

지문 자세히 보기

01 Lawyers sometimes describe ownership as *a bundle of sticks*. This metaphor was introduced about a century ago, and it has dramatically transformed the teaching and practice of law.

▶ 소유권을 '막대 다발'로 보는 비유가 있음을 언급한다.

02 The metaphor is useful because it helps us see ownership as a grouping of interpersonal rights that can be separated and put back together.

▶ 이 비유는 '소유권이 여러 개로 나눠지고 다시 또 조합될 수 있는' 권리임을 잘 보여준다는 내용이다.

03 When you say *It's mine* in reference to a resource, often that means you own a lot of the sticks that make up the full bundle: the sell stick, the rent stick, the right to mortgage, license, give away, even destroy the thing.

▶ 예시가 이어지고 있다. 어떤 것을 '소유한다'는 말은 그것을 판매하고 대여하는 등등 다양한 권리를 포괄한 것이라고 한다. 각각의 권리를 가리켜 '막대(the sticks)'라고 언급하고 있으며, 소유권은 그 막대의 다발(the full bundle)이라고 지칭하고 있다.

04 Often, though, we split the sticks up, as for a piece of land: there may be a landowner, a bank with a mortgage, a tenant with a lease, a plumber with a license to enter the land, an oil company with mineral rights. Each of these parties owns a stick in the bundle.

▶ 앞의 예시를 '토지 한 면'이라는 더 구체적인 대상에 적용하며, 권리를 다 쪼개는(split ~ up) 경우를 생각해보자고 한다. 토지 주인, 저당권자, 세입자 등등 매우 다양한 이해 당사자가 있고, 이들은 모두 '막대 하나'를 가진 것이라고 한다. 즉 각자가 권리의 '어느 한 면'만 가지고 있다는 의미로 이해할 수 있다.

구문 풀이

When you say *It's mine* in reference to a resource, often **that** means you own a lot of the sticks **that** make up the full bundle: the sell stick, the rent stick, the right to mortgage, license, give away, even destroy the thing.

→ 첫 번째 **that**은 문장 전체의 주어인 지시대명사이고, 두 번째 **that**은 the sticks를 꾸미는 주격 관계대명사이다.

구문 플러스 that의 다양한 용법

- 지시대명사(그것), 지시형용사(그, 저)
- 접속사: 명사절(~것), 부사절(so ~ that …: 결과의 의미)
- 관계대명사(주격, 목적격), 관계부사(방법, 이유)

He's sick. That means he won't be able to attend the meeting.
그는 아파. 그것은 그가 회의에 오지 못할 거란 의미지.

She told us that she would leave for London soon.
그녀는 우리에게 자신이 곧 런던으로 갈 거라고 말했다.

The cello that she plays is worth over a million dollars.
그녀가 연주하는 첼로는 값이 백만 달러를 넘는다.

The reason that he failed was lack of preparation.
그가 낙제한 이유는 준비 부족 때문이었다.

---

18 정답 ① 40% 　　　　2023학년도 9월 모평

해석 여러분은 여러분이 좋아할지도 모를 것을 판단하는 알고리즘에 대해 뭔가 무서운 것이 있다고 느낄 수도 있다. 그것은 컴퓨터가 여러분이 뭔가를 좋아하지 않을 것이라고 결론 짓는다면 여러분에게 그것을 볼 기회가 영영 없을 수도 있다는 뜻일까? 개인적으로, 나는 혼자서는 발견하지 못했을 새로운 음악 쪽으로 안내받는 것을 정말 좋아한다. 나는 같은 노래를 계속 반복해서 틀어놓는 틀에 빨리 갇힐 때가 있다. 그래서 나는 항상 라디오를 즐겨 듣는다. 그러나 지금 뮤직 라이브러리를 통해 나를 밀고 당기는 알고리즘은 내가 좋아할 보석을 찾는 데 완벽하게 적합하다. 원래 그런 알고리즘에 대한 나의 걱정은 모든 사람을 라이브러리의 특정 부분으로 몰아넣고 나머지 부분은 듣는 이가 없는 채로 남겨둘지도 모른다는 것이었다. 그것은 취향의 수렴을 일으킬 것인가? 그러나 일반적으로 그 배후에 있는 비선형적이고 불규칙한 수학 덕분에 이런 일은 발생하지 않는다. 여러분이 좋아하는 것과 비교해 내가 좋아하는 것이 작게 갈라져 있다는(조금 차이가 난다는) 점이 우리를 뮤직 라이브러리의 저 멀리 떨어진 구석으로 보낼 수 있다.

해설 본래 필자는 알고리즘이 추천해주는 음악을 듣다보면 특정 곡에 사람들의 선호가 쏠릴지도 모르겠다고 우려했었지만, 사람들의 선호가 조금씩 다르다는 점 때문에 '그런 일'이 생기지 '않는다'는 것을 깨달았다고 한다. 이를 토대로 밑줄 친 부분의 의미를 추론하면, ① '우리를 각자 자기 취향에 맞게 선택된 음악으로 이끌다'가 가장 적절하다.

오답 풀이

선택률	선지 해석 & 오답 풀이
② 15%	우리가 다른 청취자들과 관계를 맺게 하다 ▶ 다른 청취자들과의 관계 맺음은 언급되지 않았다.
③ 16%	우리가 알고리즘 업데이트를 자주 요구하도록 권하다 ▶ 알고리즘 업데이트는 언급되지 않았다.
④ 15%	우리가 재능이 있지만 알려지지 않은 음악가들을 찾도록 동기를 주다 ▶ 음악가 발굴에 관해서는 언급되지 않았다.
⑤ 14%	우리가 특정 음악 장르에 대한 우리의 선호를 무시하게 만들다 ▶ 우리의 개별적 선호가 '무시되는' 것이 아니라 '반영되기' 때문에 어느 한 곡에 청취자가 몰리지 않고 고루 분산될 수 있다는 내용이 글의 주제이다.

01 You may feel there is something scary about an algorithm deciding what you might like. Could it mean that, if computers conclude you won't like something, you will never get the chance to see it?

▶ 선호를 판단하는 알고리즘이 핵심 소재로 언급된다. 알고리즘이 판단하기로 우리가 어떤 것을 좋아하지 않을 것 같다면 그것을 접할 기회가 주어지지 않을 수도 있다는 우려가 들 수 있다고 한다. 그리고 이것이 알고리즘의 '무서운 점'이라고 한다.

02 Personally, I really enjoy being directed toward new music that I might not have found by myself. I can quickly get stuck in a rut where I put on the same songs over and over. That's why I've always enjoyed the radio.

▶ 필자는 개인적으로 새로운 음악을 즐겨 들어서 라디오도 즐겨 듣는다는 보충 설명이 제시되고 있다.

03 But the algorithms that are now pushing and pulling me through the music library are perfectly suited to finding gems that I'll like. My worry originally about such algorithms was that they might drive everyone into certain parts of the library, leaving others lacking listeners. Would they cause a convergence of tastes?

▶ 원래 필자가 알고리즘에 관해 지녔던 '걱정'이 다시 언급된다. 이 worry는 첫 문장의 something scary를 달리 표현한 것이다. 필자는 본디 뮤직 라이브러리의 특정 부분에만 사람들이 쏠리는 현상, 즉 '취향의 수렴'이 일어나지는 않을까 하는 의문이 있었다고 한다.

04 But thanks to the nonlinear and chaotic mathematics usually behind them, this doesn't happen. A small divergence in my likes compared to yours can send us off into different far corners of the library.

▶ 앞서 언급된 '취향의 수렴'이 this로 요약되며, 이런 현상이 일어나지 '않았다'고 한다. 모든 사람들의 취향에는 약간씩 차이(divergence)가 있기에, 사람들이 라이브러리 곳곳으로, 즉 자기 취향에 조금이라도 더 맞는 다른 곡들로 흩어지게 된다는 결론이 소개된다.

구문 풀이

My worry originally about such algorithms was that they might drive everyone into certain parts of the library, leaving others **lacking** listeners.

→ 분사구문 'leaving ~'이 「leave + 목적어 + 현재분사」 형태의 5형식 구조로 쓰였다.

구문 플러스' 현재분사 목적격보어

5형식의 목적어와 목적격보어가 능동 관계일 때 현재분사가 목적격보어로 나올 수 있다.

We saw the couple **dancing** together.
우리는 그 커플이 함께 춤추는 것을 보았다. → the couple이 '춤추는' 주체

---

19 정답 ② 28%   2022학년도 대수능

해석 과학자들은 도덕적 혹은 윤리적 결정에 대한 특별한 강점이 없으며, 기후 과학자가 의료 개혁에 대해 견해를 밝힐 자격이 없는 것처럼 물리학자도 꿀벌 집단의 붕괴 원인을 판단할 자격이 없다. 전문화된 영역에서의 전문지식을 만들어내는 바로 그 특징이 여러 다른 영역의 무지로 이어진다. 어떤 경우에는, 농부, 어부, 환자, 토착민 등 전문가가 아닌 사람들이 과학자들이 배울 수 있는 관련 경험을 지니고 있을 수 있다. 실제로, 최근 들어 과학자들은 이 점을 인식하기 시작하여, 북극 기후 영향 평가는 지역 토착 집단에게서 수집된 관찰을 포함한다. 그러므로 우리의 신뢰는 한정되고 초점이 맞춰질 필요가 있다. 그것은 매우 '특정할' 필요가 있다. 맹목적 신뢰는 최소한 신뢰가 전혀 없는 것만큼이나 우리를 문제에 봉착하게 할 것이다. 하지만 우리의 지정된 전문가들, 즉 우리가 사는 자연 세계에 관한 어려운 질문들을 처리하는 데 생애를 바친 사람들에 대한 어느 정도의 신뢰가 없으면 우리는 마비되고, 사실상 아침 통근을 위해 준비해야 할지 말아야 할지도 모를 것이다.

해설 So 이하에서 과학자들에 대한 신뢰가 특정하고 한정적일 필요가 있음을 언급한 뒤, 밑줄이 포함된 마지막 문장에서 '신뢰가 없을 때'의 위험성을 지적하며 신뢰의 필요성을 역으로 강조하고 있다. 특히 과학자들은 우리가 속한 세계의 어려운 문제들을 해결하는 사람들이라는 설명으로 보아, 마지막 문장의 'not knowing ~'은 이들이 밝혀낸 '지식'을 믿지 않으면 '아침 통근 준비'와 같은 일상적인 상황에까지 지장이 생긴다는 의미임을 알 수 있다. 따라서 밑줄 친 부분의 의미로 가장 적절한 것은 ② '특화된 전문가들에 의해 제공되는 바로 적용 가능한 정보'이다.

오답 풀이

선택률	선지 해석 & 오답 풀이
① 17%	비전문가에 의해 보급된 의심스러운 사실 ▶ 비전문가가 의심스러운 사실을 보급한다는 내용은 언급되지 않았다. 오히려 비전문가의 경험이 좋은 데이터가 된다는 점이 언급되었다.
③ 14%	중대한 결정에 거의 영향을 주지 않는 상식 ▶ 상식의 영향에 관해서는 언급하지 않았다.
④ 29%	전문가와 비전문가가 모두 만들어낸 실용적 지식 ▶ 비전문가의 경험이 전문가의 연구에 참고가 된다는 내용은 있지만, 이를 통해 전문가와 비전문가가 '함께' '실용적' 지식을 생산하는지 여부는 알 수 없다.
⑤ 12%	지역 공동체에 널리 퍼져 있는 편향된 지식 ▶ 공동체 내 편향된 지식에 관해서는 언급되지 않았다.

지문 자세히 보기'

01 Scientists have no special purchase on moral or ethical decisions; a climate scientist is no more qualified to comment on health care reform than a physicist is to judge the causes of bee colony collapse. The very features that create expertise in a specialized domain lead to ignorance in many others.

▶ 과학자는 전문 영역에 한정된(specialized) 전문지식을 지니고 있으며 다른 분야에는 무지할 수 있다는 내용이 제시된다.

02 In some cases lay people — farmers, fishermen, patients, native peoples — may have relevant experiences that scientists can learn from. Indeed, in recent years, scientists have begun to recognize this: the Arctic Climate Impact Assessment includes observations gathered from local native groups.

▶ 때때로 비전문가들이 오히려 연구와 관련된 경험을 지니고 있어 과학자들이 도움을 받을 수 있다는 설명이 이어진다. 이는 과학자들의 전문지식에 한계가 있다는 앞 내용을 뒷받침한다.

03 So our trust needs to be limited, and focused. It needs to be very *particular*. Blind trust will get us into at least as much trouble as no trust at all.

▶ 따라서, 과학자들에 대한 신뢰는 한정되어야 한다는 주장이 전개된다. 이들의 지식이 전적이지 않기에 신뢰 또한 제한되어야 한다는 것이다. limited, focused, *particular*가 모두 같은 의미이다.

04 But without some degree of trust in our designated experts — the men and women who have devoted their lives to sorting out tough questions about the natural world we live in — we are paralyzed, in effect not knowing whether to make ready for the morning commute or not.

▶ 하지만 과학자들은 우리 세계 속 질문거리를 '해결해주는' 이들이고, 그래서 이들을 어느 정도 '믿지' 않으면 우리는 마비된다(paralyzed)는 결론이 제시된다. paralyzed를 풀어 설명하는 말이 'not knowing ~'이다. 즉 우리가 '아침 통근 같은 일상에 바로 적용할 수 있도록 과학자들이 마련해둔 지식'을 우리가 믿지 않고 활용하지도 않으면 어려움이 닥친다는 의미를 비유적 표현으로 나타냈다.

구문 풀이

But without some degree of trust in **our designated experts — the men and women** who have devoted their lives to sorting out tough questions about the natural world we live in — we are paralyzed, in effect not knowing whether to make ready for the morning commute or not.

→ **our designated experts**와 동격을 이루는 **the men and women**이 2개의 줄표(—) 사이에 삽입되었다.

→ 'who ~ live in'은 **the men and women**을 꾸미는 주격 관계대명사절이다.

구문 플러스⁺ 동격 구문

앞에 나오는 특정 어구와 동격을 이루는 말을 쓰고 싶을 때 콤마(,), 줄표(—), 콜론(:) 등을 이용한다.

Jess, an old friend of mine, is a doctor.
내 오랜 친구 **Jess**는 의사이다.
Here's a list of groceries we need: a loaf of bread, some apples, and a stick of butter.
우리가 필요한 식품 목록은 이거야. 빵 한 덩이, 사과 몇 개, 그리고 버터 한 덩이.

---

20 정답 ② 49% *2021학년도 대수능*

해석 '사자가 자신의 역사가를 둘 때까지, 사냥 이야기는 항상 사냥꾼을 미화한다'라는 아프리카 속담이 있다. 이 속담은 권력과 통제와 법 제정에 관한 것이다. 환경 저널리스트들은 '사자의 역사가' 역할을 해야 한다. 그들은 법을 만드는 사람들에게 환경의 관점을 이해시켜야 한다. 그들은 인도 야생 자연의 목소리가 되어야 한다. 현재 인간 소비의 비율은 완전히 지속 불가하다. 숲, 습지, 황무지, 해안 지대, 환경 민감 지역, 이것들은 모두 인류의 가속화되는 필요를 위해 마음대로 쓰일 수 있다고 여겨진다. 하지만 소비를 줄이는 것이든, 생활 방식을 바꾸는 것이든, 인구 증가를 줄이는 것이든, 인간의 행동에 그 어떤 변화라도 요구하는 것은 인권 침해로 간주된다. 그러나 어느 지점에 이르면 인권은 '잘못된 것'이 된다. 인간의 권리와 나머지 환경의 권리 사이에 차이가 없도록 우리가 우리 생각을 바꿔야 할 때이다.

해설 밑줄이 포함된 문장 뒤에서 **have to**를 통해, 환경 저널리스트들은 환경의 입장을 대변하고 입법자들을 이해시키는 역할을 담당해야 한다고 피력하고 있다. 또한 마지막 문장에서 자연의 권리와 인간의 권리 사이에 차이가 없도록 인간의 의식 변화가 촉구된다고 언급하는데, 이는 현재의 지속 불가한 행동을 지속 가능한 쪽으로 변화시켜야 한다는 말과 같다. 따라서 밑줄 친 부분의 의미로 가장 적절한 것은 ② '자연을 위해 지속 가능한 인간 행동으로의 변화를 촉구하는 것'이다.

오답 풀이

선택률	선지 해석 & 오답 풀이
① 4%	한 종의 생물학적 진화의 역사를 밝혀내는 것 ▶ 생물학적 진화에 관해서는 언급되지 않았다.
③ 21%	만연한 인권 침해에 맞서 싸우는 것 ▶ 인간의 행동 변화를 요구하여 발생하는 인권 침해보다 환경적 과제를 걱정해야 한다는 것이 글의 주제이다.
④ 8%	더 부당하게 서술된 사람들을 위해서 역사를 다시 쓰는 것 ▶ 역사에서 부당하게 서술된 사람들에 관해서는 언급되지 않았다.
⑤ 19%	환경법 제정자들의 권한을 제한하는 것 ▶ 법 제정자들에게 환경의 입장을 이해시켜야 한다는 내용은 언급되었지만, 이들의 권한 자체를 제한해야 한다는 내용은 언급되지 않았다.

지문 자세히 보기¹

01 There is an African proverb that says, 'Till the lions have their historians, tales of hunting will always glorify the hunter'. The proverb is about power, control and law making.

▶ '사자의 입장을 대변해주는 역사가가 나타날 때까지 이야기는 사냥꾼의 편'이라는 속담을 소개하며, 이것이 권력, 통제, 법 제정에 시사하는 의미가 있음을 밝히고 있다.

02 Environmental journalists have to play the role of the 'lion's historians'. They have to put across the point of view of the environment to people who make the laws. They have to be the voice of wild India.

▶ 당위의 **have to**가 환경 저널리스트의 역할을 설명한다. **put across the point of view of the environment**와 **be the voice of wild India**가 모두 밑줄 부분과 동의어이다. 즉 환경 저널리스트는 환경의 입장을 대변하고 이를 입법자들에 이해시키는 역할을 담당한다는 것이다.

03 The present rate of human consumption is completely unsustainable. Forest, wetlands, wastelands, coastal zones, eco-sensitive zones, they are all seen as disposable for the accelerating demands of human population. But to ask for any change in human behaviour — whether it be to cut down on consumption, alter lifestyles or decrease population growth — is seen as a violation of human rights.

▶ 현재 인간의 (자원) 소비는 지속 불가한(unsustainable) 수준이지만 인간에게 행동 변화를 촉구하는 것은 인권 침해처럼 여겨지기에 제대로 이루어지지 않았음이 시사된다.

04 But at some point human rights become 'wrongs'. It's time we changed our thinking so that there is no difference between the rights of humans and the rights of the rest of the environment.

▶ 흐름 반전의 But 뒤로, (현재의 자원 소비를 묵인하며) 인권을 생각하면 '잘못될' 수도 있기에, 인간과 자연의 권리가 다르지 않다는 의식 변화가 일어나야 한다는 주장이 나온다. 이 생각은 우리가 현재의 지속 불가한 소비 패턴을 '지속 가능한' 쪽으로 바꾸게 해줄 것이다.

구문 풀이

It's time we changed our thinking so that there is no difference between the rights of humans and the rights of the rest of the environment.

→ 「it is (high) time + 주어 + 과거 동사」는 현재 사실의 반대를 나타내는 가정법 과거 표현의 일종이다. 즉 현재 행해지지 않은 일에 대해 '~할 시간'임을 촉구하는 표현이다.

구문 플러스' it is (high) time 가정법

it is (high) time (that) 주어 + 과거 동사
= it is (high) time (that) 주어 + should + 동사원형
: ~이 …해야 할 시간이다

It is time that you **got** back to work. 다시 일할 시간입니다.
= It is time that you **should get** back to work.

---

21 정답 ⑤ 42%　　　　*2020학년도 6월 모평*

해석 많은 회사가 활동과 성과를 혼동한다. 그 결과, 그들은 판매 주기 동안 수행해야 하는 활동의 형태로 획기적인 일을 제시하는 과정을 기획하는 실수를 범한다. 판매원들은 효과적인 일보다는 보상받는 일을 하는 데 비범한 재능이 있다. 만약 당신의 과정에 '제안 제출하기'나 '임의의 권유 전화 걸기'와 같은 활동이 있다면, 그것이 바로 당신의 아랫사람들이 할 일이다. 전화가 잘못된 고객에게 갔거나 아무 성과를 보지 못했어도 문제가 아니다. 제안이 구매 결정의 적절한 시점에 제출되지 않았거나 부적절한 정보를 포함했더라도 문제가 아니다. 과정이 활동을 요구했을 뿐이고, 활동은 그 결과였다. 판매원들은 요구받은 일을 한 것이다. 그들은 "쓰레기를 넣으니 쓰레기가 나오지요(콩 심은 데 콩 나고 팥 심은 데 팥 나지요). 그것은 우리의 문제가 아니라 이 바보 같은 과정 때문이에요."라고 당신에게 말하기를 즐길 것이다.

해설 밑줄 앞뒤에서 과정이 (성과가 아닌) 활동을 요구했으니 직원들

은 활동을 했을 뿐이며, 따라서 직원들은 성과 부족에 대해 본인들이 아닌 과정을 탓한다는 내용이 제시된다. 이러한 흐름으로 보아, 밑줄 친 부분의 의미로 가장 적절한 것은 ⑤ '활동에 초점을 둔 (업무) 과정은 결국 효과적이지 못하다.'이다.

오답 풀이

선택률	선지 해석 & 오답 풀이
① 9%	성과를 추구하는 데 있어서 보상이 질의 핵심이다. ▶ 영업사원들은 '성과가 있을' 일보다 '보상받을' 일을 한다는 내용이 언급되기는 하지만, 이를 근거로 보상이 곧 업무 성과의 질까지 좌우한다는 결론을 내릴 수는 없다.
② 19%	판매원들이 의사 결정 과정에 참여해야 한다. ▶ 의사 결정 참여에 관해서는 언급되지 않았다.
③ 10%	공유된 이해가 항상 성공으로 이어지지는 않는다. ▶ 공유된 이해에 관해서는 언급되지 않았다.
④ 19%	잘못된 정보에서 도출된 활동은 실패를 낳는다. ▶ 잘못된 과정이 아닌, 잘못된 정보에 근거한 활동과 그 결과에 관해서는 언급되지 않았다.

지문 자세히 보기'

01 Many companies confuse activities and results. As a consequence, they make the mistake of designing a process that sets out milestones in the form of activities that must be carried out during the sales cycle.

▶ 많은 회사가 성과와 활동을 혼동하여 업무 과정 안에 성과가 아닌 '활동(activities)'을 짜 넣는데, 이것은 실수(mistake)임을 지적하고 있다.

02 Salespeople have a genius for doing what's compensated rather than what's effective. If your process has an activity such as "submit proposal" or "make cold call," then that's just what your people will do.

▶ 영업 사원들은 '성과가 있는' 일보다는 '보상이 주어질' 일을 하기에, 업무 과정에서 활동(submit proposal, make cold call)을 요구하면 그저 활동을 수행할 것이라는 내용이 서술된다. 여기서 what's compensated는 결국 첫 문장의 activities이고, what's effective는 results이다.

03 No matter that the calls were to the wrong customer or went nowhere. No matter that the proposal wasn't submitted at the right point in the buying decision or contained inappropriate information. The process asked for activity, and activity was what it got. Salespeople have done what was asked for.

▶ 수행한 활동(the calls, the proposal)이 성과를 내지 못하더라도 상관없고, 업무 과정이 활동을 요구했으니 그 활동이 이루어진 것이라는 설명이 이어진다.

04 "Garbage in, garbage out" they will delight in telling you. "It's not our problem, it's this dumb process."

▶ 위의 'The process asked for activity, and activity was what it got.'을 비유적으로 나타낸 말이 밑줄 부분이다. this dumb process라는 표현에서 '활동'을 요구하는 과정을 비효율적으로 보는 시각이 드러난다.

As a consequence, they make the mistake of designing **a process** that **sets out** milestones in the form of activities that must be carried out during the sales cycle.

→ 선행사 **a process**를 꾸미는 **that**절에서, 단수명사인 선행사에 맞춰 단수동사 **sets out**이 쓰였다.

 플러스⁺ 주격 관계대명사절 속 동사의 수일치

주격 관계대명사절의 동사는 선행사에 수일치시킨다.

I ran across some plants that eat insects.
나는 곤충을 먹는 몇몇 식물을 우연히 접했다.

 플러스⁺ 함축 의미

밑줄 친 비유적 표현의 의미를 주제에 비추어 추론하는 유형이다. 2019학년도 6월 모의평가부터 어휘 또는 지칭을 대신해 출제되었으며, 고난도 문항에 속한다.

• 문제 해결 Tip.
　① 글의 중심 내용을 먼저 파악한다.
　② 밑줄 친 부분의 문자적 의미를 파악한다.
　③ 중심 내용과 앞뒤 문맥에 근거해 밑줄 친 부분의 숨은 의미를 추론한다. 주로 이 의미는 주제의 재진술이다.

22 정답 ⑤ 44%　　　　2024학년도 9월 모평

해석 민영 음악 라디오 방송의 주된 목적은 청취자를 광고주와 후원자 집단으로 인도하는 것이다. 상업적 성공을 달성하려면, 그 청취자는 가능한 한 대규모여야 한다. (인구 통계학적 또는 심리 통계학적 개요, 구매력, 관심 수준, 만족도, 주목의 질, 또는 정서 상태 등) 다른 어떤 특성보다도, 집단으로 모인 청취자의 크기는 음악 라디오가 수익 목적에 맞게 만들려는 방송 진행자에게 가장 중요한 측정 기준이다. 결과적으로 방송 진행자는 인기 있는 음악, 또는 적어도 청취자가 라디오를 끄거나 채널을 바꾸게 하지 않을 거라고 여겨지는 음악을 틀어 청취자의 규모를 극대화하려고 애쓴다. 청취자 보유는 많은 음악 프로그램 제작자와 라디오 방송국 경영진에 (유일한 핵심 가치까지는 아니더라도) 하나의 핵심 가치이다. 그 결과 높은 수준의 모험 회피는 흔히 '성공한' 라디오 음악 프로그램 제작자를 구분 짓는다. 방송 목록은 제한적이고, 흔히 매우 적다.

해설 민영 라디오 방송은 상업적 목적에 따라 청취자 보유와 확대에 주목하고, 그에 따라 청취율을 유지하기 위한 인기 음악을 주로 내보내며, 모험을 회피하려는 성향을 보이게 된다는 내용이다. 마지막 문장에서는 결과적으로 방송 목록이 제한적이고 적어지게 된다고 한다. 따라서 글의 주제로 가장 적절한 것은 ⑤ '음악 사업체들이 대규모 청중을 모으려고 시도한 결과'이다.

오답 풀이

선택률	선지 해석 & 오답 풀이
① 6%	국제적 청중의 관심을 끄는 음악 방송 목록의 특징 ▶ '국제적 청중'의 관심을 끈다는 내용은 없다.
② 18%	광고주가 라디오 청중의 음악적 선호에 미치는 영향 ▶ 광고주에 따라서 청중의 선호가 영향받을 수 있다는 내용은 언급되지 않았다. 첫 문장에서 '청중, 광고주'만 보고 고르지 않도록 한다.
③ 17%	라디오 음악 프로그램에서 청중 규모를 확대할 때의 어려움 ▶ 청중 규모를 확대하기 위해 노력한다는 내용은 있지만, 이것이 어렵다는 내용은 언급되지 않았다.
④ 16%	라디오 사업에서 청취자의 다양한 요구를 충족시킬 필요성 ▶ 다양한 요구 충족보다는 청취자 규모 확대에 관해 언급한다.

지문 자세히 보기

01 The primary purpose of commercial music radio broadcasting is to deliver an audience to a group of advertisers and sponsors.

▶ 민영 음악 라디오 방송이 글의 소재이다.

02 To achieve commercial success, that audience must be as large as possible. More than any other characteristics (such as demographic or psychographic profile, purchasing power, level of interest, degree of satisfaction, quality of attention or emotional state), the quantity of an audience aggregated as a mass is the most significant metric for broadcasters seeking to make music radio for profitable ends.

▶ 이런 라디오 방송은 '최대한 청중이 많아야' 상업적으로 이득을 보기에, '청중 규모가 제일 중요한 기준'이 된다는 내용이다.

03 As a result, broadcasters attempt to maximise their audience size by playing music that is popular, or — at the very least — music that can be relied upon not to cause audiences to switch off their radio or change the station. Audience retention is a key value (if not the key value) for many music programmers and for radio station management.

▶ 역시 '청중 수를 최대화하는' 것이 중요하다는 내용이다. 인기 있는 음악, 혹은 적어도 청중이 듣다가 채널을 돌리지 않을 음악 위주로 방송이 진행된다고 한다.

04 In consequence, a high degree of risk aversion frequently marks out the 'successful' radio music programmer. Playlists are restricted, and often very small.

▶ '청취자 보유'를 위한 노력의 결과(In consequence)를 소개한다. '위험을 가급적 피하며' 방송하다 보니 방송의 목록도 '제한되고 적어진다'고 설명하고 있다. 마지막 두 문장의 내용이 ⑤의 outcome으로 요약된다.

구문 풀이

To achieve commercial success, that audience must be as large as possible.

→ 문장 맨 앞의 to부정사가 주절과 콤마로 분리되면 흔히 목적(~하기 위해)을 나타낸다.

구문 플러스⁺ 목적을 나타내는 to부정사

to부정사구가 부사구 역할을 할 때 가장 흔히 나타내는 뜻은 목적(~하기 위해, ~하려면)이다. 목적의 to부정사구는 문장 앞, 뒤, 중간에 자유롭게 위치한다.

She went to the store **to buy some groceries**.
그녀는 장을 보러 마트에 갔다.

To improve your skills, you should practice the piano every day.
네 실력을 키우려면, 너는 피아노를 매일 연습해야 해.

23 정답 ② 53%　　　　2023학년도 대수능

해석 공개의 중요한 이점은 더 공격적인 형태의 규제와는 반대로 자유 시장의 작용에 대한 유연성과 존중이다. 규제하는 명령은 무딘 칼과 같아서, 이것들은 다양성을 무시하는 경향이 있으며, 의도치 않은 심각한 역효과를 발생시킬 수도 있다. 예를 들어, 가전제품에 대한 에너지 효율 요건은 덜 잘 작동하거나 소비자가 원하지 않는 특성을 가진 제품을 만들어 낼 수도 있다. 반대로 정보 제공은 선택의 자유를 존중한다. 자동차 제조업체가 자동차의 안전 특성을 측정하고 공개해야 한다면, 잠재적인 자동차 구매자는 가격과 스타일 같은 다른 속성과 안전에 대한 우려를 맞바꿀 수 있다. 식당 손님들에게 식사에 들어 있는 칼로리를 알려주면,

살을 빼고 싶은 사람들은 그 정보를 이용할 수 있고, 칼로리에 신경 쓰지 않는 사람들은 영향을 받지 않은 채로 있게 된다. 공개는 개인 의사 결정의 자율성(과 품질)을 방해하지 않으며, 심지어 촉진할 것이다.

해설 by contrast가 포함된 글 중반부 문장에서 정보 제공, 즉 '공개'가 선택의 자유를 존중할 수 있다고 언급한 데 이어, 마지막 문장에서는 결국 정보 공개가 개인의 의사 결정을 방해하는 것이 아니라 오히려 촉진할 수 있다고 결론 짓고 있다. 따라서 글의 주제로 가장 적절한 것은 ② '자유로운 선택을 보장하기 위한 정보 공개의 이점'이다.

오답 풀이

선택률	선지 해석 & 오답 풀이
① 9%	공공의 정보를 소비자가 이용할 수 있게 하는 절차 ▶ 정보 이용을 돕는 절차는 언급되지 않았다.
③ 12%	기업들이 자유 시장에서 이윤을 늘리는 전략들 ▶ 이윤 확대 전략은 언급되지 않았다.
④ 9%	현재 산업 동향을 파악하고 분석할 필요성 ▶ 산업 동향 분석이 필요하다는 내용은 언급되지 않았다.
⑤ 18%	다양화된 시장이 합리적인 고객 선택에 미치는 영향 ▶ '고객의 선택'은 글의 키워드가 맞지만, '다양화된 시장의 영향'은 글과 무관한 소재이다.

지문 자세히 보기

01 An important advantage of disclosure, as opposed to more aggressive forms of regulation, is its flexibility and respect for the operation of free markets.

▶ 정보 공개의 이점을 자유 시장 체제의 작용과 관련지어 설명한 글이다.

02 Regulatory mandates are blunt swords; they tend to neglect diversity and may have serious unintended adverse effects. For example, energy efficiency requirements for appliances may produce goods that work less well or that have characteristics that consumers do not want.

▶ '정보 공개'와 상반된 소재로 '규제 명령'이 언급되고 있다. 이것은 다양성을 무시하며 심각한 역효과를 발생시킬 수 있다는 내용과 함께, 에너지 효율 요건이 사례로 언급된다.

03 Information provision, by contrast, respects freedom of choice. If automobile manufacturers are required to measure and publicize the safety characteristics of cars, potential car purchasers can trade safety concerns against other attributes, such as price and styling. If restaurant customers are informed of the calories in their meals, those who want to lose weight can make use of the information, leaving those who are unconcerned about calories unaffected.

▶ by contrast로 흐름이 전환되며, 정보 공개의 장점(respects ~ choice)을 설명하고 있다. 'If ~로 시작하는 두 문장이 모두 관련된 예를 제시한다.

04 Disclosure does not interfere with, and should even promote, the autonomy (and quality) of individual decision-making.

▶ 글의 주제문이다. 정보 공개는 (자유 시장 경제 속) 개인의 의사 결정을 방해하는 것이 아니라, 오히려 도와줄 수 있다는 결론으로 글이 마무리된다.

구문 풀이

If restaurant customers are informed of the calories in their meals, those who want to lose weight can make use of the information, **leaving those who are unconcerned about calories unaffected.**

→ leaving의 목적격보어로 과거분사 unaffected가 왔다. 이 보어는 목적어인 'those who ~ calories'를 보충 설명한다.

구문 플러스' 과거분사 목적격보어

5형식의 목적어와 목적격보어가 수동 관계일 때 과거분사가 목적격보어로 나올 수 있다.

I had my keyboard fixed yesterday.
나는 어제 내 키보드를 고쳤다. → my keyboard가 '고쳐지는' 대상

24 정답 ④ 46%　　　　　*2022학년도 6월 모평*

해석 아이들은 (역할) 놀이와 이야기로의 몰입이 같은 활동의 형태인 것처럼 쉽게 그 둘 사이를 이동한다. 이야기식 구조의 해적 게임에서 역할을 맡는 것은 영화를 감상할 때 등장인물과 동일시하며 역할을 맡는 것과 크게 다르지 않다. 사람들이 청소년기로 성장하면서 아동기의 놀이를 그만둔다고 여겨질 수도 있겠지만, 이는 그렇지 않다. 대신에, 이런 활동의 기반과 흥미가 스포츠 활동과 관람으로, 연극, 소설, 영화의 허구로, 그리고 최근에는 비디오 게임으로 바뀌고 발전한다. 허구에서 사람들은 있을법한 세계로 들어갈 수 있다. 그런 세계에서 감정들을 경험하면, 이는 우리가 일관되지 않다거나 퇴행하고 있다는 신호가 아니다. 그것은 새로운 방식으로, 새로운 세계에서, 우리에게 감동적이고 중요할 수 있는 방식으로 우리 자아의 은유적 변신을 시도하는 것에서 기인한다.

해설 사람들은 자라면서 아동기의 (역할) 놀이를 포기하는 것 같지만, 사실은 형태가 달라질 뿐 놀이 같은 활동을 지속한다는 내용의 글이다. 중반부의 Instead 앞뒤 두 문장에서 핵심 내용이 잘 드러난다. 따라서 글의 주제로 가장 적절한 것은 ④ '아동기 이후 변화된 형태의 놀이에의 지속적 참여'이다.

오답 풀이

선택률	선지 해석 & 오답 풀이
① 12%	놀이 유형과 정서적 안정 간의 관계 ▶ 정서적 안정에 관한 내용은 없다.
② 23%	아동기에 가상의 등장인물과 동일시하는 이유 ▶ 첫 두 문장에서 아동이 해적 게임이나 영화 속 인물과 자신을 동일시한다고 언급하지만, 그 이유를 설명하지는 않는다.
③ 9%	청소년이 좋은 독서 습관을 개발하도록 돕는 방법 ▶ 독서 습관은 언급되지 않았다.
⑤ 9%	이야기 구조가 독자의 상상력에 미치는 영향 ▶ 본문의 narratively structured를 거의 그대로 따와 만든 함정 선택지로, 글에서 이야기 구조의 영향은 언급되지 않았다.

지문 자세히 보기

01 Children can move effortlessly between play and absorption in a story, as if both are forms of the same activity. The taking of roles in a narratively structured game of pirates is not very different than the taking of roles in identifying with characters as one watches a movie.

▶ 역할 놀이(play, The taking of roles)가 화제로 소개된다.

02 It might be thought that, as they grow towards adolescence, people give up childhood play, but this is not so. Instead, the bases and interests of this activity change and develop to playing and watching sports, to the fiction of plays, novels, and movies, and nowadays to video games.

▶ 사람들은 성장해가며 아동기의 역할 놀이를 포기해 갈 것이라는 통념이 있지만, 실상은 이 놀이의 기반이 바뀌는 것일 뿐 놀이 그 자체는 지속된다는 반박이 전개된다.

03 In fiction, one can enter possible worlds. When we experience emotions in such worlds, this is not a sign that we are being incoherent or regressed. It derives from trying out metaphorical transformations of our selves in new ways, in new worlds, in ways that can be moving and important to us.

▶ 우리가 허구의 세계에서 (어떤 역할과 동일시되어 그 역할의) 감정을 경험할 때 이는 우리가 아동기로 퇴행했다는 의미가 아니며, 우리 자아의 은유적 변신이 시도된 것이라는 설명이 이어진다. metaphorical transformations of our selves가 play를 재진술한다.

구문 풀이

When we experience emotions in such worlds, this is not **a sign that** we are being incoherent or regressed.

→ a sign 뒤에 '신호'의 내용을 설명하는 완전한 동격 명사절이 이어진다.

구문 플러스⁺ 동격의 접속사 that

fact, idea, rumor, news, evidence 등의 추상명사 뒤에 완전한 절을 수반하는 that이 나오면 동격의 접속사로 본다.

The rumor that our boss is resigning is not confirmed.
우리 상사가 사직한다는 소문은 확인되지 않았다.

25 정답 ③ 46%　　　　*2021학년도 대수능*

해석 사람과 기계를 협업 시스템으로 생각하지 않고, 자동화될 수 있는 작업은 무엇이든 기계에 할당하고 그 나머지를 사람들에게 맡길 때 어려움이 발생한다. 이것은 결국 사람들에게 기계와 똑같이, 즉 인간의 능력과는 다른 방식으로 행동할 것을 요구하게 된다. 우리는 사람들이 기계를 감시하기를 기대하는데, 이는 오랫동안 경계를 게을리하지 않는다는 뜻으로, 우리가 잘하지 못하는 것이다. 우리는 사람들에게 기계에 의해 요구되는 수준으로 몹시 정확하고 정밀하게 반복적인 작업을 할 것을 요구하는데, 이 또한 우리가 잘하지 못하는 것이다. 우리가 이런 식으로 어떤 과제의 기계적 구성요소와 인간적 구성요소를 나눌 때, 우리는 인간의 강점과 능력을 이용하지 못하고, 그 대신 유전적으로, 생물학적으로 부적합한 영역에 의존하게 되는 것이다. 하지만, 사람들이 실패할 때, 그들은 비난을 받는다.

해설 첫 두 문장에서 사람과 기계의 업무를 분리하면 결국 사람이 기계 같은 작업을 요구받는 어려움이 발생한다고 언급한다. 이어서 중반부에서 사람은 기계처럼 오랫동안 경계 상태를 유지하며 고도로 정밀하게 작업할 수 없다고 설명하고, 후반부에서는 그렇기 때문에 인간 특유의 장점과 능력을 살리기 어려워진다는 결론을 내린다. 따라서 글의 주제로 가장 적절한 것은 ③ '자동화 시스템에서 인간에게 부적합한 과제를 주는 것의 문제'이다.

오답 풀이

선택률	선지 해석 & 오답 풀이
① 7%	실패를 피하기 위해 인간의 약점을 극복하는 것의 어려움 ▶ 인간의 약점 극복에 관해서는 언급되지 않았다.
② 17%	기계와 인간이 함께 일하게 하는 것의 이점 ▶ 첫 문장에서 인간과 기계가 '협업'하지 않을 때의 문제점을 언급하며 협업의 중요성을 시사하지만, 이러한 협업의 이점을 글에서 언급하지는 않았다.
④ 17%	인간이 기계 자동화를 계속 추구하는 이유 ▶ 인간이 기계 자동화를 추구한다는 내용보다는, 기계와 인간의 분업으로 인한 인간의 기계화를 우려하는 내용이 주를 이룬다.
⑤ 13%	인간의 행동이 기계의 성능에 미치는 영향 ▶ 기계의 성능에 관해서는 언급되지 않았다.

지문 자세히 보기

01 Difficulties arise when we do not think of people and machines as collaborative systems, but assign whatever tasks can be automated to the machines and leave the rest to people. This ends up requiring people to behave in machine-like fashion, in ways that differ from human capabilities.

▶ 인간과 기계를 '협업'시키지 않고 역할을 나눠 맡기다 보면 결국 인간이 기계화되기를 요구받는 문제(Difficulties)가 발생한다는 것이 주제이다.

02 We expect people to monitor machines, which means keeping alert for long periods, something we are bad at. We require people to do repeated operations with the extreme precision and accuracy required by machines, again something we are not good at.

▶ 인간은 기계 같은 작업을 '잘하지 못한다'는 내용이 주를 이룬다. monitor machines, 'do repeated operations with ~ accuracy'가 '기계는 잘하지만 인간은 잘 못하는' 작업을 묘사하는 표현이다.

03 When we divide up the machine and human components of a task in this way, we fail to take advantage of human strengths and capabilities but instead rely upon areas where we are genetically, biologically unsuited. Yet, when people fail, they are blamed.

▶ 첫 문장의 'assign ~ to people'이 'divide up ~ a task'로, Difficulties가 'fail to ~ capabilities'로, machine-like가 genetically, biologically unsuited로 재진술된다. 인간과 기계의 작업 분리가 결국 인간을 부적합한 영역에 배치시킨다는 주제가 반복된다.

구문 풀이

Difficulties arise when we do not think of people and machines

23

as collaborative systems, but assign **whatever** tasks can be automated to the machines and leave the rest to people.

→ **assign**의 목적어인 명사절을 이끄는 **whatever**는 바로 뒤의 명사 **tasks**를 꾸미는 복합관계형용사로, '어떤 ~이든지'라고 해석된다.

구문 플러스⁺ 복합관계형용사

whatever 또는 whichever가 '어떤 ~이든지'의 의미로 뒤에 나오는 명사를 꾸밀 때, 이를 복합관계형용사라 부른다. 이 whatever 또는 whichever는 명사절 또는 부사절을 이끈다.

I'll do whatever job I'm asked to do. (명사절)
나는 내게 요구되는 어떤 일이든 할 것이다.
Whatever job you do, you should do your best. (부사절)
네가 무슨 일을 하든, 너는 최선을 다해야 한다.

---

26 정답 ① 70%　　　　　*2021학년도 9월 모평*

해석 플라톤에서 데카르트에 이르는 철학자들의 영향을 받은 서양의 일반 통념은 개인, 특히 천재들에게 창의력과 독창성이 있다고 믿는다. 사회적, 문화적 영향과 원인은 최소화되거나 무시되거나 고려로부터 완전히 배제된다. 사상은 독창적이든 종래의 것이든 개인과 동일시되며, 개인이라는 특별한 존재와 개인이 하는 특별한 것은 그 사람의 유전자와 두뇌에서 그 기원을 찾는다. 여기서 '요령'은 개개의 인간이 사회적 구성 그 자체로, 그들이 생애 동안 접해온 사회적, 문화적 영향의 다양성을 구현하고 반영한다는 것을 인식하는 것이다. 우리의 개인성이 부인되는 것이 아니라, 특정한 사회적, 문화적 경험의 산물로 여겨지는 것이다. 뇌 그 자체가 사회적인 것이며, 구조적으로, 그리고 그것의 사회 환경에 의한 연결성 수준에서 영향을 받는다. '개인'은 '나'가 문법적 환상인 것과 마찬가지로 법적, 종교적, 그리고 정치적 허구이다.

해설 전반부에서 창의력과 독창성은 개인의 것으로 여겨진다는 서양의 통념을 제시한다. 이어서 'The "trick" here ~' 이후로 개인은 사회적 존재이며, 개인의 특성 또한 사회문화적 경험을 토대로 만들어지는 것이라는 반박을 전개하고 있다. 따라서 글의 주제로 가장 적절한 것은 ① '개인성에 내재한 사회적 속성의 인식'이다.

오답 풀이

선택률	선지 해석 & 오답 풀이
② 3%	개인성과 집단성의 간격을 채우는 방법 ▶ 간격에 관해서는 언급되지 않았다.
③ 6%	독창적인 사상과 종래의 사상을 구분하는 것과 관련된 문제 ▶ 사상을 구별 짓는다는 내용은 언급되지 않았다. 본문의 **original and conventional**을 따온 함정 선택지이다.
④ 14%	인간 유전자에 구현된 진정한 개인성의 인정 ▶ 유전자보다도 사회문화적 영향이 개인성 형성에 영향을 미친다는 것이 글의 주제이다.
⑤ 4%	개인주의에서 상호의존으로 전환할 필요성 ▶ 개인주의, 상호의존 모두 언급되지 않았다.

지문 자세히 보기⁺

01 Conventional wisdom in the West, influenced by philosophers from Plato to Descartes, credits individuals and especially geniuses with creativity and originality.

▶ 창의력과 독창성을 개인에게 귀속시키는 서양의 통념을 소개하고 있다.

02 Social and cultural influences and causes are minimized, ignored, or eliminated from consideration at all. Thoughts, original and conventional, are identified with individuals, and the special things that individuals are and do are traced to their genes and their brains.

▶ 이 통념에 따르면 사회문화적 영향은 거의 무시되고, 사상은 개인과 개인의 특성(**their genes and ~ brains**)으로부터 비롯된 것으로 여겨진다는 부연 설명이 이어진다.

03 The "trick" here is to recognize that individual humans are social constructions themselves, embodying and reflecting the variety of social and cultural influences they have been exposed to during their lives.

▶ "trick"과 함께 흐름이 전환된다. 개인 그 자체가 사회적 구성체(**social constructions**)이며, 사회문화적 영향(**social and cultural influences**)을 반영한다는 내용이 제시된다.

04 Our individuality is not denied, but it is viewed as a product of specific social and cultural experiences. The brain itself is a social thing, influenced structurally and at the level of its connectivities by social environments. The "individual" is a legal, religious, and political fiction just as the "I" is a grammatical illusion.

▶ 개인과 개인의 뇌는 사회문화적 경험의 산물로서 사회적 속성을 지니며(**a social thing**), '개인'이라는 것이 어쩌면 허구에 불과할 수 있다는 결론으로 글이 마무리된다.

구문 풀이

The "trick" here is to recognize that **individual humans** are social constructions **themselves**, embodying and reflecting the variety of social and cultural influences they have been exposed to during their lives

→ that절의 주어인 **individual humans**를 강조하기 위해 주절 끝에 **themselves**라는 재귀대명사를 썼다.

구문 플러스⁺ 재귀대명사 강조 용법

재귀대명사는 주어, 목적어, 보어를 강조할 수 있다. 이때 재귀대명사의 위치는 강조하는 말 바로 뒤 또는 문장 끝이다.

The brain itself is a social thing. (주어 강조)
뇌 자체가 사회적인 것이다.

---

27 정답 ⑤ 50%　　　　　*2020학년도 대수능*

해석 인간은 유능한 도덕적 행위자로서 세상에 들어오지 않는다. 또한 모든 이가 그 상태로 세상을 떠나지도 않는다. 하지만 (태어나서 죽는) 그 사이 어딘가에서, 대부분의 사람들은 그들에게 도덕적 행위자 공동체의 구성원 자격을 주는 얼마간의 예의를 습득한다. 유전자, 발달, 그리고 학습은 모두 예의 바른 인간이 되는 과정에 기여한다. 하지만 천성과 양육 사이의 상호 작용은 매우 복잡하며, 발달 생물학자들은 그저 그것이 얼마나 복잡한지를 간신히 이해하기 시작하고 있을 뿐이다. 세포, 유기체, 사회 집단, 그리고 문화에 의해 제공되는 맥락이 없으면, **DNA**는 비활성이다. 사람들은 도덕적이도록 '유전적으로 프로그램이 짜여 있다'고 말하는 누구든 유전자가 작동하는 방식에 대해 지나치게 단순화된 견해를 가지고 있다. 유전자와 환경은 아이들의 도덕적 발달 과정 또는 다른 어떤 발달 과정이든 천성 '대' 양육이라는 견지에서 논의될 수 있다고 생각하는 것을 무의미하게 만드는 방식으로 상호 작용한다. 발달 생물학자들은 이제 그것이 진정 둘 다, 즉 양육을 '통한' 천성이라는 것을 안다. 인간 종의 도덕적 진화와 발달에 대한 완전한 과학적 설명은 까마득히 멀다.

해설 however가 포함된 글 중반부 문장에서 도덕성 발달에 관한 천성과 양육 사이의 상호작용은 매우 복잡하다고 언급한다. 이어서 마지막 세 문장에서는 천성과 양육은 서로 대립하지 않고 엮여서 작용하므로, 인간의 도덕성 발달을 과학적으로 완벽히 규명하기는 아직 어렵다고 한다. 이러한 흐름으로 보아, 글의 주제로 가장 적절한 것은 ⑤ '도덕적 발달에 있어서 유전-환경의 복잡한 상호 작용'이다.

오답 풀이

선택률	선지 해석 & 오답 풀이
① 10%	문화적 관점에서 보는 인간 도덕성의 진화 ▶ '천성, 유전자' 등 생물학적 요소에 대한 내용도 포함되어야 하기에 주제로 부적합하다.
② 9%	유전자 진화 과정 연구의 어려움 ▶ 유전자 진화 연구의 어려움은 언급되지 않았다.
③ 7%	도덕적 행위자로서 아이들을 교육해야 할 필요성의 증가 ▶ 교육의 필요성보다는 천성과 양육의 관계를 밝히는 것이 글의 초점이다.
④ 25%	발달 생물학에서의 천성 대 양육 논쟁 ▶ 글의 또 다른 키워드인 '도덕성'을 포함하지 않아 주제로 보기에 너무 포괄적이다.

지문 자세히 보기⁺

01 Human beings do not enter the world as competent moral agents. Nor does everyone leave the world in that state.

▶ 도덕적 행위자(moral agents)로서의 인간이라는 화제가 제시된다.

02 But somewhere in between, most people acquire a bit of decency that qualifies them for membership in the community of moral agents. Genes, development, and learning all contribute to the process of becoming a decent human being.

▶ 인간의 도덕성에는 유전자, 발달, 학습이 모두 관여한다는 설명이 이어진다.

03 The interaction between nature and nurture is, however, highly complex, and developmental biologists are only just beginning to grasp just how complex it is. Without the context provided by cells, organisms, social groups, and culture, DNA is inert. Anyone who says that people are "genetically programmed" to be moral has an oversimplified view of how genes work.

▶ 역접의 **however**와 함께, 도덕성 발달에 관한 천성과 양육의 상호작용은 대단히 복잡하다는 주제가 나온다. 'people ~ moral'은 nature. 즉 천성의 영향력을 중시하는 견해로, 글에 따르면 '지나치게 단순화된' 견해이다.

04 Genes and environment interact in ways that make it nonsensical to think that the process of moral development in children, or any other developmental process, can be discussed in terms of nature *versus* nurture. Developmental biologists now know that it is really both, or nature *through* nurture.

▶ 천성 '대' 양육, 즉 두 요소가 대립적으로 작용한다는 시각은 무의미하며, 사실은 두 요소가 모두 도덕성 발달에 이바지하는 것(**nature** *through* **nurture**)임이 서술된다.

05 A complete scientific explanation of moral evolution and development in the human species is a very long way off.

▶ 도덕성 발달을 완전하게 설명하려면 멀었다(a ~ long way off)는 결론은 천성과 양육의 상호작용이 그만큼 복잡하다는 뜻이다. 즉 'The interaction ~ is, however ~ complex'와 마지막 문장은 문맥상 같은 의미이다.

구문 풀이

Anyone who says that people are "genetically programmed" to be moral has an oversimplified view of how genes work.

→ anyone who를 한 단어로 바꾸면 복합관계대명사 whoever(~하는 누구든)이다.

구문 플러스⁺ 복합관계대명사

복합관계대명사의 종류와 의미를 잘 정리해 둔다.

종류	의미① : 명사절	의미② : 부사절
whoever	~하는 누구든 (=anyone who)	누가 ~하든 간에 (=no matter who)
whichever	~하는 어떤 것이든 (=anything that)	어떤 것이[어떤 것을] ~하든 간에 (=no matter which)
whatever	~하는 무엇이든 (=anything that)	무엇이[무엇을] ~하든 간에 (=no matter what)

Do whatever she asks you to. (명사절)
그녀가 네게 요청하는 무엇이든 해라.
Whatever she says, I will go my own way. (부사절)
그녀가 뭐라 말하든 간에, 나는 내 길을 갈 것이다.

해석 12세기부터 13세기에 귀족의 자녀에게 '식탁 예절'을 가르치는 최초의 교범이 등장했다. 그것은 그 이후 Baldassare Castiglione가 쓴 <The Courtier>, Monsignor Della Casa가 쓴 <The Galateo> 및 다양한 유럽 국가에서 제작된 많은 다른 책들과 함께 근대 초기에 큰 성공을 거둔 장르였다. 다양한 방식과 의미로, 이 책들은 모두 식탁에 참여하는 자들을 식탁에서 추방되는 자들로부터 분리하면서, 누가 '내부자'이고 '외부자'인지를 규정하거나 구별하기 위하여 의도된 도구들이다. 바로 이런 이유에서 귀족 계층을 대상으로 한 '좋은 예절'의 교범은 예의범절이 좋지 않은 소작농을 항상 부정적으로 언급하는데, 이들은 규칙이 무엇인지를 '알지 못하며', 이런 이유로 귀족의 식탁에서 배제된다. 음식 예절은 사회적 장벽, 그리고 그 장벽 타파의 불가능성에 대한 표시가 되어 버렸다.

해설 귀족들의 식탁 예절은 귀족과 귀족이 아닌 계층을 구별하는 사회적 장벽으로 자리 잡았다는 내용의 글로, 마지막 문장이 핵심 내용을 잘 요약한다. 따라서 글의 주제로 가장 적절한 것은 ① 계층 구별 표시로서의 식탁 예절'이다.

오답 풀이

선택률	선지 해석 & 오답 풀이
② 3%	계층 간의 평등을 가져오기 위한 출판물 ▶ 식탁 예절에 관한 책이 계층 간의 평등이 아닌 '분리'를 가져왔다는 것이 글의 주제이다.
③ 10%	내부자와 외부자 구별의 의도되지 않은 영향 ▶ 글에 따르면 내부자와 외부자의 구별이 의도되었듯(intended) 그 영향 또한 의도되었다.
④ 10%	교육적 목적을 위해 음식 예절을 정교화하려는 시도 ▶ 단순한 교육 목적이 아니라 계층을 구별하려는 목적이 투영된 결과가 식탁 예절이었다.
⑤ 18%	다양한 배경 출신의 사람들을 단결시키는 데 있어서 예절의 역할 ▶ 일반적 예절이 아닌 '식탁 예절'이 사람들을 단결시키지 않고 '분리'시켰다는 것이 글의 주된 내용이므로 답으로 부적절하다.

지문 자세히 보기

01 In the twelfth to thirteenth centuries there appeared the first manuals teaching "table manners" to the offspring of aristocrats. It was a genre that subsequently had a great success in the early modern period with *The Courtier* by Baldassare Castiglione, *The Galateo* by Monsignor Della Casa, and many others produced in different European countries.

▶ 귀족 자녀를 대상으로 한 식탁 예절 교육을 핵심 소재로 언급하고 있다.

02 In a variety of ways and meanings, these are all instruments intended to define or distinguish who is *in* from who is *out*, separating the participants from the ostracized.

▶ 식탁 예절 교육은 결국 누가 (귀족 사회의) '내부자'이고 '외부자'인지를 구별할(distinguish, separating) 목적이었다는 내용이 제시된다.

03 It is for this reason that manuals of "good manners" addressed to the aristocracy always have a negative reference to the peasant who behaves badly, who "doesn't know" what the rules are, and for this reason is excluded from the lordly table.

▶ who is *out*의 예로 '소작농'이 언급되고 있다. 이들은 식탁 예절을 모르고 바로 그 이유로 귀족의 식탁에서 배제당한다는 설명이 이어진다.

04 Food etiquette had become a sign of social barriers and of the impossibility of breaking them down.

▶ 결국 식탁 예절은 귀족과 귀족이 아닌 사람들을 구별하는 사회적 장벽이 되었다는 주제가 정리된다. a sign of social barriers를 재진술한 표현이 ①의 a marker for class distinction이다.

구문 풀이

It is for this reason **that** manuals of "good manners" addressed to the aristocracy always have a negative reference to the peasant who behaves badly, who "doesn't know" what the rules are, and for this reason is excluded from the lordly table.

→ for this reason을 강조하는 「it is[was] ~ that …」 강조구문이다.

구문 플러스 it is[was] ~ that … 강조구문

「it is[was] ~ that …」 강조구문은 it is[was]와 that 사이에 명사(구·절) 또는 부사(구·절)를 넣어 강조하는 문장 형태이다.

It was my daughter that woke me up. (명사구 강조)
나를 깨운 것은 다름 아닌 내 딸이었다.

It was at school that I met my husband. (부사구 강조)
내가 내 남편을 만난 것은 바로 학교에서였다.

유형 플러스 글의 주제

글의 중심 소재 또는 그에 관한 필자의 생각을 명사구로 잘 요약한 선택지를 찾는 문제이다. 최근 5년간 생소한 학술적 용어를 설명하거나 추상적 소재를 다루는 글이 많이 등장하며 난이도가 상승했다.

· 문제 해결 Tip
① 도입부에서 글의 핵심 소재를 파악한다.
② 핵심 소재에 관한 필자의 견해가 드러나거나, 핵심 소재의 주요한 특징이 드러나는 부분에 주목한다.
③ 명확한 주제문이 있다면, 이를 적절한 핵심어와 함께 잘 요약한 선택지를 찾는다.

29 정답 ① 72%
2024학년도 6월 모평

해석 더 먼 거리를 더 빠른 속도로 더 많이 이동하는 것이 더 큰 경제적 성공을 만든다는 개념인 하이퍼 모빌리티는 도시 지역의 두드러진 특징인 것으로 보이는데, 도시에는 현재 세계 인구의 절반을 넘는 사람이 산다. 2005년까지 전 세계 도시에서 매일 대략 75억 건의 이동이 이루어졌다. 2050년에는 사회 기반 시설 및 에너지 가격이 허락하는 한 2000년보다 서너 배 더 많은 인킬로미터를 이동할지도 모른다. 화물 이동도 같은 기간 세 배 넘게 증가할 수 있다. 이동성 흐름은 관련 사회 기반 시설이 변함없이 도시 형태의 중추를 구성하면서 도시화의 핵심 동력이 되었다. 그러나 전 세계적으로 증가하는 도시 이동성 수준에도 불구하고, 장소, 활동 및 서비스에 대한 접근은 점점 더 어려워졌다. 시간, 비용 및 편안함 측면에서 보면, 도시에서 장소에 접근하는 것은 덜 편리할 뿐만 아니라, 도시에서 돌아다니는 바로 그 과정은 많은 부정적인 외부 효과를 발생시킨다. 그에 따라 세계의 많은 도시는 전례 없는 접근성 위기에 직면해 있으며, 지속 불가능한 이동성 시스템을 특징으로 한다.

해설 하이퍼 모빌리티로 도시의 이동량은 엄청나게 늘었지만, 오히려 접근성 위기와 각종 부정적 외부 효과 또한 초래되었다는 내용이다. 따라서 글의 제목으로 가장 적절한 것은 ① '하이퍼 모빌리티가 항상 도시에 좋은 걸까?'이다.

오답 풀이

선택률	선지 해석 & 오답 풀이
② 5%	접근성: 도시 지역망 가이드 ▶ 지역망 가이드에 관한 내용이 아니다.
③ 4%	경제적 성공으로 가는 길고 구불구불한 길 ▶ 하이퍼 모빌리티라는 핵심 개념이 빠졌으며, '경제적 성공으로 향한다'는 내용도 글과 무관하다.
④ 8%	하이퍼 모빌리티로 인한 불가피한 지역 갈등 ▶ 지역 갈등은 언급되지 않았다.
⑤ 9%	사회 기반 시설: 하이퍼 모빌리티의 필수 요소 ▶ 글의 주제는 Yet 이후에 나오는데, 이 제목은 글의 전반부 내용만 담고 있어 포괄적이지 못하다.

지문 자세히 보기'

01 Hyper-mobility — the notion that more travel at faster speeds covering longer distances generates greater economic success — seems to be a distinguishing feature of urban areas, where more than half of the world's population currently reside.

▶ '도시의 하이퍼 모빌리티'에 관한 내용이다.

02 By 2005, approximately 7.5 billion trips were made each day in cities worldwide. In 2050, there may be three to four times as many passenger-kilometres travelled as in the year 2000, infrastructure and energy prices permitting. Freight movement could also rise more than threefold during the same period. Mobility flows have become a key dynamic of urbanization, with the associated infrastructure invariably constituting the backbone of urban form.

▶ '이동성 흐름이 도시의 핵심 동력'이라는 내용을 뒷받침하기 위해 사람과 화물의 이동량을 보여주는 숫자적 근거를 제시하고 있다.

03 Yet, despite the increasing level of urban mobility worldwide, access to places, activities and services has become increasingly difficult.

▶ Yet으로 글의 흐름이 반전된다. 이동량 증가(the increasing ~ mobility)에도 불구하고 도시의 활동이나 서비스는 점점 더 어려워진다(increasingly difficult)는 것이다.

04 Not only is it less convenient — in terms of time, cost and comfort — to access locations in cities, but the very process of moving around in cities generates a number of negative externalities. Accordingly, many of the world's cities face an unprecedented accessibility crisis, and are characterized by unsustainable mobility systems.

▶ less convenient, 'generates ~ externalities'가 모두 'an ~ crisis', 'unsustainable ~ systems'를 뒷받침하는 표현이다. 즉 하이퍼 모빌리티로 불편함과 외부 효과가 증대됐으며, 이것이 오히려 이동성 위기를 야기한다는 점으로 볼 때, 하이퍼 모빌리티가 '과연 도시에 좋은지' 의문을 제기한다고 볼 수 있다.

구문 풀이

Not only is it less convenient — in terms of time, cost and comfort — **to access locations in cities, but the very process of moving around in cities generates a number of negative externalities.**

→ 「not only A but (also) B(A뿐만 아니라 B도)」의 not only가 문장 맨 앞에 나오자 A 자리의 「주어 + 동사」가 의문문 어순으로 도치되었다.

구문 플러스⁺ 부정어구의 도치 (1)

부정어구가 문장 맨 앞에 나와 강조되면 뒤따르는 주어와 동사는 의문문 어순으로 도치된다.

Never have I seen such a creative boy.
나는 그토록 창의적인 아이를 본 적이 없다.

Under no circumstances should you open the door.
어떤 상황에서도 문을 열어서는 안 된다.

Not a word did I say. 나는 한 마디도 하지 않았다.

30 정답 ⑤ 63%
2023학년도 대수능

해석 뇌 시각 체계의 다양한 부분들은 필요할 때 필요한 것만 알려주는 방식으로 정보를 얻는다. 여러분의 손 근육이 어떤 물체에 닿을 수 있도록 돕는 세포들은 그 물체의 크기와 위치를 알아야 하지만 색깔에 대해 알 필요는 없다. 그것들은 모양에 대해 약간 알아야 하지만, 매우 자세히는 아니다. 여러분이 사람의 얼굴을 인식하도록 돕는 세포는 모양의 세부 사항에 극도로 예민해야 할 필요가 있지만, 위치에는 신경을 덜 쓸 수 있다. 어떤 물체를 보는 사람이라면 모양, 색깔, 위치, 움직임 등 그것에 관한 모든 것을 보고 있다고 추정하는 것은 당연하다. 하지만, 여러분

뇌의 한 부분은 그것의 모양을 보고, 다른 한 부분은 색깔을 보며, 또 다른 부분은 위치를 감지하고, 또 다른 한 부분은 움직임을 인식한다. 따라서 국부적 뇌 손상 후 물체의 특정한 측면은 볼 수 있으면서 다른 측면은 보지 못하는 것이 가능하다. 수 세기 전, 사람들은 누군가 물체가 무슨 색깔인지 못 보면서 어떻게 그 물체를 볼 수 있는지 상상하기 어려워했다. 심지어 오늘날에도, 여러분은 물체가 어디에 있는지 못 보면서 그 물체를 보거나, 또는 물체가 움직이고 있는지 보지 못하면서 물체를 보는 사람들에 대해 알게 되면 놀라워할 수 있다.

해설 시각 체계의 각 부분은 '각자 필요할 때 필요한 정보만' 알려주기 때문에, 물체의 다양한 측면 중 어느 하나를 인식하지 못해도 그 물체를 '보는' 것이 가능하다는 내용이다. 따라서 글의 제목으로 가장 적절한 것은 시각 체계 각 부분의 '독립성'을 잘 설명하는 ⑤ '개별적이고 독립적이다: 뇌세포의 시각적 인지'이다.

오답 풀이

선택률	선지 해석 & 오답 풀이
① 7%	시각 체계는 절대 우리 신뢰를 저버리지 않는다! ▶ 신뢰에 관해서는 언급되지 않았다.
② 15%	색에 예민한 뇌세포의 비밀 임무 ▶ 색상만을 지각하는 부분이 따로 있을 수 있다는 내용은 언급되지만, 비밀 임무는 언급되지 않았다.
③ 9%	맹점: 뇌에 관해 아직 알려지지 않은 것 ▶ 맹점에 관해서는 언급되지 않았다.
④ 7%	왜 뇌세포는 자연의 회복 과정을 전형적으로 보여주는가 ▶ 자연의 회복 과정은 언급되지 않았다.

지문 자세히 보기

01 Different parts of the brain's visual system get information on a need-to-know basis.

▶ 글의 주제문이다. 시각 체계의 각 부분은 '필요한 정보만 필요할 때 알려준다'는 내용을 뒤에서 어떻게 풀어 설명하는지 살펴보자.

02 Cells that help your hand muscles reach out to an object need to know the size and location of the object, but they don't need to know about color. They need to know a little about shape, but not in great detail. Cells that help you recognize people's faces need to be extremely sensitive to details of shape, but they can pay less attention to location.

▶ 어떤 물체의 크기와 위치는 알더라도 색상은 모르거나, 모양은 잘 알아도 위치는 모르는 예시가 나온다. 이는 '필요할 때 필요한 것만 아는' 시각 체계의 작동 방식 때문에 가능한 사례이다.

03 It is natural to assume that anyone who sees an object sees everything about it — the shape, color, location, and movement. However, one part of your brain sees its shape, another sees color, another detects location, and another perceives movement.

▶ 우리는 어느 하나를 '볼' 수 있다면 모양, 색상, 위치 등 모든 측면을 본다고 가정하지만, 실상은 그렇지 않다는 내용이 However 뒤에 나온다. 시각 체계의 각기 다른 부분 중 어느 하나는 모양만, 어느 하나는 색상만, 어느 하나는 움직임만 보는 등 '개별적으로' 정보를 처리한다는 것이다.

04 Consequently, after localized brain damage, it is possible to see certain aspects of an object and not others. Centuries ago, people found it difficult to imagine how someone could see an object without seeing what color it is. Even today, you might find it surprising to learn about people who see an object without seeing where it is, or see it without seeing whether it is moving.

▶ 이러한 특성 때문에 어느 한 측면만 보고 나머지는 못 보는(see ~ others) 일이 가능하다는 결론이 제시된다. 이 결론은 첫 문장의 주제와 결국 같다.

구문 풀이

However, **one** part of your brain sees its shape, **another** sees color, **another** detects location, and **another** perceives movement.
→ '뇌의 여러 부분' 중 하나를 처음 언급하고자 부정대명사 one을 썼다. 추가로 '또 다른 부분'을 언급하기 위해 부정대명사 another를 썼다.

구문 플러스 부정대명사 one, another, the other

one: (여럿 중) 하나
another: (추가로 또 다른) 하나
the other: (다른 대상을 다 언급하고 마지막 남은) 나머지 하나

I have three aunts. **One** works as a nurse, **another** runs a small shop, and **the other** is a college student.
나는 이모가 셋 있어. 한 명은 간호사로 일하고, 다른 이모는 작은 가게를 운영하고, 나머지 이모는 대학생이야.

31 정답 ② 87%   *2023학년도 9월 모평*

해석 음악가와 심리학자뿐만 아니라, 열성적인 음악 애호가와 전문가도 흔히 음악의 아름다움은 정확히 정해진 악보로부터 표현상 벗어나는 데 있다는 의견을 표한다. 콘서트 공연은 악보에 인쇄된 정보를 훨씬 뛰어넘는다는 사실에서 흥미로워지고 매력을 얻는다. 음악 연주에 관한 초기 연구에서, Carl Seashore는 음악가가 같은 두 음을 정확히 똑같이 연주하는 경우가 거의 없다는 것을 발견했다. 같은 미터 구조 내에서, 박자, 음량, 음질 및 인토네이션에 있어 광범위한 변주 가능성이 있다. 이러한 변주는 작품에 기초하지만 그로부터 개별적으로 갈라진다. 우리는 일반적으로 이것을 '표현성'이라고 부른다. 이것은 우리가 서로 다른 예술가가 같은 음악을 연주하는 것을 들을 때 흥미를 잃지 않는 이유를 설명해 준다. 이것은 또한 다음 세대가 같은 레퍼토리를 반복하는 것이 가치 있는 이유이기도 하다. 새롭고 영감을 주는 (음악) 해석은 우리가 이해를 넓히는 데 도움을 주는데, 이 이해는 음악계를 풍부하게 하고 활기를 불어넣는 역할을 한다.

해설 같은 곡과 음을 연주하더라도 누가 연주하는가에 따라 완벽히 똑같지는 않으며, 바로 이 점 때문에 음악이 매력적임을 설명하는 글이므로, 제목으로 가장 적절한 것은 ② '절대 똑같지 않다: 음악 연주에서 변주의 중요성'이다.

선택률	선지 해석 & 오답 풀이
① 2%	음악 비평에서 성공적인 커리어를 구축하는 방법 ▶ 음악 비평에서의 커리어 구축은 언급되지 않았다.
③ 8%	음악 치료에서 개인적 표현의 중요성 ▶ '개인적 표현'은 글과 관련되어 보이지만, 음악 '치료'가 글에서 전혀 언급되지 않으므로 오답이다.
④ 2%	냉정을 유지하라: 음악 연주 시 무대공포증을 극복하기 ▶ 무대 공포증에 관해서는 언급되지 않았다.
⑤ 1%	클래식 음악계에서 새로운 것은 무엇인가? ▶ 클래식 음악계의 새로운 점을 언급하기보다, 음악 연주 또는 표현상의 다채로움에 관해 설명하는 글이다.

지문 자세히 보기

01 Not only musicians and psychologists, but also committed music enthusiasts and experts often voice the opinion that the beauty of music lies in an expressive deviation from the exactly defined score. Concert performances become interesting and gain in attraction from the fact that they go far beyond the information printed in the score.

▶ 음악은 악보에 표기된 정보를 훨씬 뛰어넘어 다채로운 표현으로 연주될 수 있다는 내용의 글이다. expressive deviation과 go far beyond가 문맥상 같은 의미이다.

02 In his early studies on musical performance, Carl Seashore discovered that musicians only rarely play two equal notes in exactly the same way. Within the same metric structure, there is a wide potential of variations in tempo, volume, tonal quality and intonation.

▶ 같은 음도 완벽히 동일하게 연주되는 경우는 드물며, 말 그대로 변주 가능성이 무궁무진하다는 점이 언급되고 있다.

03 Such variation is based on the composition but diverges from it individually. We generally call this 'expressivity'. This explains why we do not lose interest when we hear different artists perform the same piece of music.

▶ 'diverges ~ individually'는 variations와 의미 같다. 음악의 다채로운 변주 가능성, 즉 표현성 때문에 똑같은 곡을 각기 다른 연주자의 버전으로 듣는 것이 지루하지 않다는 설명이 계속된다.

04 It also explains why it is worthwhile for following generations to repeat the same repertoire. New, inspiring interpretations help us to expand our understanding, which serves to enrich and animate the music scene.

▶ variations가 다시 New, inspiring interpretations로 재진술되고, 이것이 우리의 음악적 이해를 확장시키고 풍부하게 하는 데 일조한다는 결론이 제시된다.

구문 풀이

This explains (the reason) why we do not lose interest when we hear different artists perform the same piece of music.

→ 관계부사 why 앞에 일반적인 선행사 the reason이 생략되었다. 거꾸로 the reason을 남기고 why를 생략해도 된다.

구문 플러스 관계부사의 선행사 생략

the time, the place, the reason 등 일반적인 선행사는 관계부사 앞에서 흔히 생략된다.

This beach is (the place) where we first met.
이 해변가는 우리가 처음 만난 곳이다.
We had a big fight, and that's (the reason) why he left early this morning.
우리는 크게 싸웠고, 그것이 그가 오늘 아침 일찍 떠난 이유다.

---

32 정답 ① 40% — 2022학년도 대수능

해석 물건을 고치고 복원하는 것에는 흔히 최초 제작보다 훨씬 더 많은 창의력이 필요하다. 산업화 이전의 대장장이는 가까이에 사는 마을 사람들을 위해 주문에 따라 물건을 만들었기에, 제품을 주문 제작하는 것, 즉 사용자에게 맞게 그것을 수정하거나 변형하는 일이 일상적이었다. 고객들은 뭔가 잘못되면 물건을 다시 가져다주곤 했고, 따라서 수리는 제작의 연장이었다. 산업화와 결국 대량 생산이 이루어지면서, 물건을 만드는 것은 제한된 지식을 지닌 기계 관리자의 영역이 되었다. 그러나 수리에는 설계와 재료에 대한 더 큰 이해, 즉 전체에 대한 이해와 설계자의 의도에 대한 이해가 계속 요구되었다. 1896년의 <Manual of Mending and Repairing>의 설명에 따르면, "제조업자들은 모두 기계나 방대한 분업으로 일하고, 말하자면 수작업으로 일하지는 않는다. 그러나 모든 수리는 손으로 '해야 한다'. 우리는 기계로 손목시계나 총의 모든 세부적인 것을 만들 수 있지만, 기계는 그게 고장 났을 때 고칠 수 없으며, 시계나 권총은 말할 것도 없다!"

해설 산업화 이전과 이후의 수리 개념을 제품의 제작과 대비하여 설명한 글이다. 산업화 이전에는 수리가 제품 제작의 연장선으로 취급되었지만, 산업화 이후에는 제작이 기계에 넘겨진 반면 수리는 계속 인간의 일로 남았다는 내용이다. 글 중반부의 'But repair continued to require ~'와 후반부의 'But all repairing must be done by hand.'가 사실상 같은 의미로, 수리는 '제품에 대한 폭넓은 이해를 요구하는 인간의 작업'임을 설명한다. 따라서 글의 제목으로 가장 적절한 것은 ① '현대 대장장이에게 여전히 남아있는 것: 수리의 기술'이다.

오답 풀이

선택률	선지 해석 & 오답 풀이
② 13%	수리 기술이 어떻게 발전했는가에 관한 역사적 개괄 ▶ 글에 preindustrial, industrialization 등 시대 표현이 나와 '역사적 개괄'처럼 보이지만, 수리 기술의 발전 과정은 글과 무관하다.
③ 9%	창의적 수리공이 되는 방법: 조언과 아이디어 ▶ 조언과 아이디어로 볼 내용은 언급되지 않았다.
④ 24%	수리의 과정: 만들고, 수정하고, 변형하라! ▶ 수리의 구체적인 업무 과정은 언급되지 않았다. 본문에 나온 단어(creativity, modifying or transforming)를 짜깁기해 혼동을 유발하는 선택지이다.
⑤ 14%	산업화가 우리의 망가진 과거를 고칠 수 있을까? ▶ 과거를 수리한다는 내용은 언급되지 않았다.

01 Mending and restoring objects often require even more creativity than original production.

▶ 중심 소재로 수리(Mending and restoring ~)를 제시하고, 보조 소재로 제작을 언급한다.

02 The preindustrial blacksmith made things to order for people in his immediate community; customizing the product, modifying or transforming it according to the user, was routine. Customers would bring things back if something went wrong; repair was thus an extension of fabrication.

▶ 산업화 이전에는 주문 제작이 주를 이루었으며 수리가 제작의 연장 선이었다는 내용이 제시된다. 즉, 수리와 제작은 같은 맥락의 작업이었다는 것이다.

03 With industrialization and eventually with mass production, making things became the province of machine tenders with limited knowledge. But repair continued to require a larger grasp of design and materials, an understanding of the whole and a comprehension of the designer's intentions.

▶ 산업화 이후에는 제작이 제한된 지식을 지닌 직원과 기계에게로 넘어가고, 수리는 제품에 대한 폭넓은 이해를 계속 필요로 하는 행위로 남았음이 언급된다. 수리를 설명하는 a larger grasp, 'an understanding ~ and a comprehension ~'은 제작을 설명하는 limited knowledge와 반대된다.

04 "Manufacturers all work by machinery or by vast subdivision of labour and not, so to speak, by hand," an 1896 *Manual of Mending and Repairing* explained. "But all repairing must be done by hand. We can make every detail of a watch or of a gun by machinery, but the machine cannot mend it when broken, much less a clock or a pistol!"

▶ 제작은 기계와 분업에 의지하지만, 수리는 사람의 손으로 행해져야 한다는 내용이 계속된다. machinery와 vast subdivision of labour가 by hand와 반대된다.

구문 풀이

We can make every detail of a watch or of a gun by machinery, but the machine cannot mend it **when broken**, much less a clock or a pistol!"

→ 시간, 조건, 양보의 부사절에서는 「대명사 주어＋be동사」를 동반 생략할 수 있다. 여기서도 원래 문장 **when it is broken**에서 **it is**를 함께 생략하고 「접속사＋분사」만 남겼다. 생략된 **it**은 앞에 나온 **a watch or a gun**을 가리킨다.

구문 플러스+ 부사절 축약

시간, 조건, 양보의 부사절에서 「대명사 주어＋be동사」는 함께 생략할 수 있다. 생략된 대명사 주어는 주절의 주어와 일치하는 경우가 보통이지만 다를 수도 있다.

We have to leave if **(it is)** possible. (We ≠ it)
가능하면 우리는 떠나야 한다.

---

33 정답 ② 40%   2021학년도 대수능

해석 사람들은 보통 촉각을 시간의 현상으로 생각하지 않지만, 그것은 공간적인 만큼 전적으로 시간에 기반을 두고 있다. 직접 알아보려면 실험을 해볼 수 있다. 친구에게 손바닥이 위로 향하게 해서, 손을 컵 모양으로 동그랗게 모아 쥐고, 눈을 감으라고 요청해 보라. 그의 손바닥에 작은 평범한 물건을 올려놓고 — 반지, 지우개, 무엇이든 괜찮다 — 손의 어떤 부분도 움직이지 말고 그것이 무엇인지 알아맞혀 보라고 요청해 보라. 그는 무게와 아마 전체적인 크기 외에 아무것도 모를 것이다. 그런 다음 그에게 눈을 감은 채로 그 물건 위로 손가락을 움직여보라고 말하라. 그는 거의 틀림없이 그것이 무엇인지 즉시 알아낼 것이다. 손가락이 움직이게 함으로써 촉각이라는 감각적 지각에 시간을 더했다. 망막의 중심에 있는 중심와(窩)와 손가락 끝 사이에 직접적인 유사함이 있는데, 둘 다 몹시 예민하다는 것이다. 어둠 속에서 셔츠 단추를 잠그거나 현관문을 여는 것과 같이 촉각을 복잡하게 사용하는 능력은 지속적이고도 시간에 따라 달라지는 촉각의 패턴에 의존한다.

해설 촉각은 시간적 현상으로 이해될 수 있다는 첫 문장 이후, 마지막 문장까지 이에 대한 보충 설명이 이어지고 있다. 따라서 글의 제목으로 가장 적절한 것은 ② '시간이 정말 중요하다: 촉각의 숨겨진 본질'이다.

오답 풀이

선택률	선지 해석 & 오답 풀이
① 15%	촉각과 움직임: 인간의 두 가지 주요 요소 ▶ 예시에서 손가락을 움직이는 상황을 언급하기는 하지만, 이는 촉각을 사용하기 위한 부수적 행위이다. 움직임 자체가 글의 중심 소재는 아니다.
③ 9%	오감을 적시에 사용하는 방법 ▶ 오감 중 '촉각'에 한정된 글이다.
④ 23%	시간 개념 형성에서 촉각의 역할 ▶ 첫 문장에 시간 관련(temporal) 단어가 나오기는 하지만 이는 촉각의 특성만을 설명한다. 시간 개념 형성에 관한 내용은 없다.
⑤ 14%	지식의 촉진제로서 촉각의 놀라운 기능 ▶ 촉각이 지식의 촉진제라는 내용은 언급되지 않았다.

01 People don't usually think of touch as a temporal phenomenon, but it is every bit as time-based as it is spatial. You can carry out an experiment to see for yourself.

▶ 촉각은 시간적 현상(touch as a temporal phenomenon)으로 이해될 수 있다는 주제가 제시된다.

02 Ask a friend to cup his hand, palm face up, and close his eyes. Place a small ordinary object in his palm — a ring, an eraser, anything will do — and ask him to identify it without moving any part of his hand. He won't have a clue other than weight and maybe overall size.

▶ 눈을 감고 물건을 만져보지 못한 채로 물건을 알아맞히게 하면 답이 나오기 어렵다는 예가 제시된다.

03 Then tell him to keep his eyes closed and move his fingers over the object. He'll most likely identify it at once. By allowing the fingers to move, you've added time to the sensory perception of touch.

▶ 하지만 물건을 만지게 하면 쉽게 답이 나오는데, 이 '만져보는' 행위는 촉각이라는 감각에 시간을 더하는(added time to ~ touch) 행위임을 설명하고 있다.

04 There's a direct analogy between the fovea at the center of your retina and your fingertips, both of which have high acuity. Your ability to make complex use of touch, such as buttoning your shirt or unlocking your front door in the dark, depends on continuous time-varying patterns of touch sensation.

▶ 촉각을 복잡하게 사용하는 능력은 시간에 따라 달라지는(time-varying) 촉각 패턴에 좌우된다는 말을 통해, 촉각과 시간의 연관성을 반복 강조한다.

구문 풀이

There's a direct analogy between the fovea at the center of your retina and your fingertips, **both of which** have high acuity.
→ both of which는 「수량표현 + of + 관계대명사」 형태로, 이때 which는 'the fovea ~ and your fingertips'를 선행사로 받는 계속적 용법의 관계대명사이다.

구문 플러스' 수량표현 + of + 관계대명사

「수량표현 + of + 관계대명사」는 계속적 용법으로만 쓰이며, of 뒤에는 목적격 관계대명사 whom, which가 나온다. who, that, what은 사용하지 않는다.

I have **two laptops**, **one of which** I hardly use.
나는 노트북이 두 대 있는데, 그중 한 대는 내가 거의 안 쓴다.
We have **foreign students**, **some of whom** are Japanese.
우리는 외국인 학생이 있는데, 그중 일부는 일본인이다.

---

34 정답 ① 40%　　　*2021학년도 9월 모평*

해석 인간의 지식이 완벽하게 정확하지 않고, 그랬던 적이 '결코 없다'는 발견은 현대 인간의 영혼이 겸손해지고 아마도 진정되는 효과를 가져다주었다. 우리가 목격했듯이, 19세기는 세계가 부분들뿐만 아니라 전체로서 언제나 완벽하게 알려질 수 있다고 믿은 마지막 시기였다. 우리는 이제 이것이 불가능하며, 언제나 불가능했다는 것을 깨닫는다. 비록 한계가 보통 우리의 필요를 충족시키기 위해 조정될 수 있을지라도, 우리는 한계 내에서 알며, 완전히 아는 것은 아니다. 의아스럽게도 이 새로운 수준의 불확실성으로부터 훨씬 더 위대한 목표가 나타나고 달성 가능해 보인다. 비록 우리가 세계를 절대적으로 정확하게 알 수 없을지라도, 우리는 여전히 그것을 제어할 수 있다. 심지어 우리의 본질적으로 불완전한 지식조차도 그 어느 때만큼이나 강력하게 작동하는 듯 보인다. 간단히 말해, 우리는 가장 높은 산이 얼마나 높은지 결코 정확하게 알 수 없을 테지만, 우리는 그런데도 우리가 정상에 도달할 수 있다는 것을 계속 확신한다.

해설 첫 문장에서 인간의 지식은 완벽하지 않다는 화제가 제시된 후, 이렇듯 불완전한 지식에도 불구하고 인간은 다음 목표를 세우며 계속해서 나아간다는 내용이 Curiously 이하로 이어지고 있다. 따라서 글의 제목으로 가장 적절한 것은 ① '아직 이르지 못한 정상: 지식을 향해 나아가는 여정'이다.

오답 풀이

선택률	선지 해석 & 오답 풀이
② 24%	산을 넘어: 성공으로 향하는 단 한 걸음이지만 위대한 발걸음 ▶ 마지막 문장의 '산'은 우리가 구체적 사실을 정확히 모를 수 있다는 것을 예로 들기 위해 등장했다. 성공으로 향하는 여정과 관련된 비유적 표현이 아니다.
③ 13%	부분들을 하나의 전체로 통합하기: 완벽으로 가는 길 ▶ 부분의 통합에 관해서는 언급되지 않았다. 본문의 a whole과 parts를 이용해 혼동을 유발하는 선택지이다.
④ 15%	불확실성의 시대에 함께 사는 방법 ▶ 함께 사는 방법으로 볼 내용은 언급되지 않았다.
⑤ 8%	지식 기반 사회의 두 얼굴 ▶ 지식 기반 사회는 글과 무관한 소재이다.

지문 자세히 보기'

01 The discovery that man's knowledge is not, and *never has been*, perfectly accurate has had a humbling and perhaps a calming effect upon the soul of modern man.

▶ 인간의 지식은 정확하지 않고 그랬던 적도 없다는 사실이 제시된다.

02 The nineteenth century, as we have observed, was the last to believe that the world, as a whole as well as in its parts, could ever be perfectly known. We realize now that this is, and always was, impossible. We know within limits, not absolutely, even if the limits can usually be adjusted to satisfy our needs.

▶ 세상을 완전하게 이해할 수 있다고 믿었던 19세기 상황과 지식에 한계가 있음을 받아들인 현재 상황을 대비하고 있다. **within limits, not absolutely**가 '한계'를 잘 설명한다.

03 Curiously, from this new level of uncertainty even greater goals emerge and appear to be attainable. Even if we cannot know the world with absolute precision, we can still control it.

▶ 지식의 한계를 지식의 불확실성(uncertainty)으로 정리하며, 바로 여기서 세상에 대한 '제어(control)'라는 새로운 목표가 생겨난다는 핵심 내용을 언급한다.

04 Even our inherently incomplete knowledge seems to work as powerfully as ever. In short, we may never know precisely how high is the highest mountain, but we continue to be certain that we can get to the top nevertheless.

▶ 위의 we can still control it이 we can get to the top nevertheless로 재진술되며, 우리가 지식의 불완전성(inherently incomplete)에도 불구하고 계속해서 '정상'을 향해 나아갈 수 있음을 설명한다. the top이 ①의 Summits로 연결된다.

구문 풀이

Even if we cannot know the world with absolute precision, we can still control it.
→ even if는 '비록 ~일지라도'라는 의미의 부사절을 이끈다.

---

35 정답 ④ 49%　　　　2020학년도 9월 모평

해석 19세기 후반부터 줄곧, 노쇠한 이들에게서 발견되는 활기 부족, 그들의 고립과 위축, 과거에 대한 연연, 그리고 세상사에 대한 관심 결여는 노쇠의 '증상', 즉 뇌의 필연적인 노화의 사회적 수치로서 특징적으로 기술되었다. 제2차 세계 대전 후에 노화에 대한 학술적 담론은 이것들을 전형적으로 노쇠의 '원인'으로 기술했다. 노쇠한 이들의 정신적 노화의 장소는 더 이상 노화한 뇌가 아니라 비자발적 퇴직, 사회적 고립, 그리고 전통적인 가족 유대감의 해체를 통해 노인들로부터 삶에서 의미를 유지했던 역할을 빼앗아 버린 사회였다. 노인들이 이 의미 있는 사회적 역할을 박탈당했을 때, 그들이 점점 더 고립되고 예전에 그들의 마음을 사로잡았던 흥미와 활동으로부터 단절되었을 때, 당연하게도 그들의 정신이 노화했다. 노인들은 그들의 정신을 잃었다기보다는 그들의 위치를 잃었다.

해설 세 번째 문장부터 노인은 뇌의 노화 때문이 아니라 그들의 역할을 앗아간 사회로 인해 정신의 노화를 겪게 된다는 내용이 이어지고 있다. 따라서 글의 제목으로 가장 적절한 것은 ④ '노인들을 쇠하게 만드는 것: 사회적으로 배제되는 것'이다.

오답 풀이

선택률	선지 해석 & 오답 풀이
① 8%	나이 든 신체와 함께하는 나이 든 정신: 틀림없는 진리 ▶ 신체 또는 뇌 노화가 아니라 사회적 역할의 박탈이 정신적 노화를 이끈다고 하였다.
② 16%	과거에서 현재까지 변함없다: 노령에 대한 사회적 이미지 ▶ 두 번째 문장에서 2차 세계 대전 후 노화에 대한 학술적 담론이 변했다고 하였다.
③ 17%	노인들을 위한 나라는 없다: 더 심해진 나이 차별 ▶ 나이에 따른 차별은 언급되지 않았다.
⑤ 9%	장애가 있는 것이 아니라 능력이 다른 것이다: 노령의 새로운 얼굴 ▶ 노년층의 다른 능력에 관해서는 언급되지 않았다.

지문 자세히 보기¹

01 From the late nineteenth century on, the dullness found in the senile, their isolation and withdrawal, their clinging to the past and lack of interest in worldly affairs were characteristically represented as the *symptoms* of senility — the social shame of the inevitable deterioration of the brain. Following World War II, academic discourse on aging typically represented these as the *causes* of senility.

▶ 노인의 활기 부족, 고립과 위축, 과거에 대한 집착, 세상사에 대한 무관심 등은 과거에는 노화의 증상처럼 여겨졌지만 2차 세계 대전 이후 노화의 '원인'으로 이해되고 있다는 화제가 소개된다.

02 The location of senile mental deterioration was no longer the aging brain but a society that, through involuntary retirement, social isolation, and the loosening of traditional family ties, stripped the elderly of the roles that had sustained meaning in their lives.

▶ 노화의 원인은 노인에게서 사회적 역할을 박탈하는 사회(a society)에 있음을 지적하고 있다.

03 When elderly people were deprived of these meaningful social roles, when they became increasingly isolated and were cut off from the interests and activities that had earlier occupied them, not surprisingly their mental functioning deteriorated.

▶ 위의 mental deterioration이 their mental functioning deteriorated로, 'stripped ~'가 'deprived ~'로 재진술되었다. 역시 노화의 원인이 사회에 있음을 지적하고 있다.

04 The elderly did not so much lose their minds as lose their place.

▶ lose their place는 'stripped ~', 'deprived ~'와 문맥상 같은 의미이다. 사회적 고립이 정신적 기능의 쇠퇴를 낳는다는 논지가 반복된다.

구문 풀이

The elderly did not so much lose their minds as lose their place.
→ 「the + 형용사(~한 사람들)」가 주어로 쓰였다.
→ 「not so much A as B(A라기보다 B인)」 구문을 기억해 둔다. A와 B는 병렬구조를 이룬다.

유형 플러스¹ 글의 제목

글의 중심 내용을 파악해야 한다는 점에서 주제와 비슷하지만, 선택지 표현이 더 함축적이므로 주의가 필요한 유형이다.

· **문제 해결 Tip.**
① 도입부에서 글의 핵심 소재를 파악한다.
② 명확한 주제문 또는 결론을 통해 핵심 소재에 관한 주된 설명, 필자의 견해 등을 파악한다.
③ 글의 중심 내용을 너무 넓지도 좁지도 않게 나타낸 선택지를 찾는다. 특히 비유적 표현이 있거나, 글의 중심 내용을 답으로 유도할 수 있는 질문 형태의 선택지가 정답일 가능성이 크다.

36 정답 ④ 97% *2024학년도 6월 모평*

해석 프랑스 영화감독인 Jean Renoir(1894~1979)는 프랑스 파리에서 태어났다. 그는 유명 화가 Pierre-Auguste Renoir의 아들이었다. 그와 나머지 Renoir 일가 사람들은 아버지의 그림 중 다수의 모델이었다. 제1차 세계대전이 발발했을 때, Jean Renoir는 프랑스 군에서 복무하다가 다리에 부상을 입었다. 1937년에 그는 그의 더 잘 알려진 영화 중 하나인 <La Grande Illusion>을 만들었다. 그것은 엄청나게 흥행했지만, 독일에서는 상영이 허용되지 않았다. 제2차 세계대전 중, 1940년에 나치가 프랑스를 침공했을 때 그는 미국 할리우드로 가서 거기서 경력을 이어갔다. 그는 영화계에서 평생의 업적을 인정받아 1975년 아카데미 공로상을 받은 것을 포함해 경력 내내 수많은 명예상과 상을 받았다. 전반적으로, 영화 제작자이자 예술가로서 Jean Renoir의 영향력은 지속되고 있다.

해설 '*During World War II, when the Nazis invaded France in* 1940, *he went to Hollywood in the United States ~*'에서 제2차 세계대전 당시 Renoir는 미국 할리우드로 건너갔다고 한다. 따라서 그가 프랑스에 계속 있었다고 잘못 진술한 ④ '제2차 세계대전 내내 프랑스에 머물렀다.'가 글의 내용과 일치하지 않는다.

오답 풀이

선택률	오답 풀이
① 0%	He was the son of the famous painter Pierre-Auguste Renoir.
② 1%	At the outbreak of World War I, Jean Renoir was serving in the French army ~
③ 0%	In 1937, he made *La Grande Illusion*, ~
⑤ 0%	He was awarded ~ the Academy Honorary Award in 1975 ~

지문 자세히 보기

01 Jean Renoir (1894–1979), a French film director, was born in Paris, France. He was the son of the famous painter Pierre-Auguste Renoir. He and the rest of the Renoir family were the models of many of his father's paintings.

▶ Jean Renoir 감독은 파리 태생으로, 아버지가 유명 화가였다는 내용이다.

02 At the outbreak of World War I, Jean Renoir was serving in the French army but was wounded in the leg.

▶ 제1차 세계대전 중 Renoir는 프랑스 군에 참전했었다는 내용이다.

03 In 1937, he made *La Grande Illusion*, one of his better-known films. It was enormously successful but was not allowed to show in Germany.

▶ 1937년에 제작된 그의 유명작 중 하나인 <La Grande Illusion>이 언급된다.

04 During World War II, when the Nazis invaded France in 1940, he went to Hollywood in the United States and continued his career there.

▶ 제2차 세계대전 중 Renoir는 프랑스에 있지 않고 미국으로 이동해 할리우드에서 커리어를 지속했다는 내용이다.

05 He was awarded numerous honors and awards throughout his career, including the Academy Honorary Award in 1975 for his lifetime achievements in the film industry. Overall, Jean Renoir's influence as a film-maker and artist endures.

▶ Renoir가 경력 내내 많은 상을 받았으며 특히 1975년에는 아카데미 공로상을 수상하기도 했다는 내용이다.

구문 풀이

He **was awarded numerous honors and awards** throughout his career, ~

→ 「be p.p. + 직접목적어」 형태의 4형식 수동태이다.

구문 플러스 4형식 문장의 수동태

4형식 동사는 본래 목적어를 2개 취하므로, 동사가 수동태로 바뀌어도 be p.p. 뒤에 목적어가 1개 남을 수 있다.

He **was given a new book** for his birthday.
그는 생일에 새 책을 받았다.

We **were told that she had left an hour before**.
우리는 그녀가 한 시간 전에 떠났다고 들었다.

37 정답 ③ 98% *2023학년도 9월 모평*

해석 Leon Festinger는 미국의 사회 심리학자였다. 그는 1919년 뉴욕에서 러시아인 이민자 가정에서 태어났다. 아이오와대학교의 대학원생이었던 Festinger는 선도적인 사회 심리학자 Kurt Lewin의 영향을 받았다. 그곳을 졸업한 후, 그는 1945년에 매사추세츠 공과대학의 교수가 되었다. 이후 그는 스탠퍼드대학교로 옮겨 그곳에서 사회 심리학 연구를 계속했다. 그는 사회 비교 이론으로 훌륭한 명성을 얻었다. Festinger는 국제 학술 협력에 적극적으로 참여했다. 1970년대 후반, 그는 역사 분야로 관심을 돌렸다. 그는 20세기에 가장 많이 인용된 심리학자 중 한 명이었다. Festinger의 이론은 현대 심리학에서도 여전히 중요한 역할을 한다.

해설 '*~ Stanford University, where he continued his work in social psychology.*'에서 Leon Festinger는 스탠퍼드대학교에서 사회 심리학 연구를 그만두지 않고 계속했다고 하므로, 내용과 일치하지 않는 것은 ③ 'Stanford University에서 사회 심리학 연구를 중단했다.'이다.

선택률	오답 풀이
① 0%	He was born in New York City in 1919 to a Russian immigrant family.
② 0%	~ Festinger was influenced by Kurt Lewin, a leading social psychologist.
④ 1%	Festinger actively participated in international scholarly cooperation.
⑤ 0%	In the late 1970s, he turned his interest to the field of history.

지문 자세히 보기

01 Leon Festinger was an American social psychologist. He was born in New York City in 1919 to a Russian immigrant family.

▶ Leon Festinger가 러시아계 미국 이민자 가정에서 출생했다는 내용이 언급된다.

02 As a graduate student at the University of Iowa, Festinger was influenced by Kurt Lewin, a leading social psychologist. After graduating from there, he became a professor at the Massachusetts Institute of Technology in 1945.

▶ Festinger는 아이오와대 대학원 재학중 사회 심리학자 Kurt Lewin의 영향을 받았으며, 졸업 후 매사추세츠 공과 대학에 교수로 부임했다는 설명이 제시되고 있다.

03 He later moved to Stanford University, where he continued his work in social psychology. His theory of social comparison earned him a good reputation.

▶ 스탠퍼드대로 이직한 Festinger가 사회 심리학 연구를 계속하여 사회 비교 이론으로 명성을 얻었다는 내용이 이어진다.

04 Festinger actively participated in international scholarly cooperation.

▶ Festinger가 국제 학술 협력에도 적극 참여했다는 점이 추가로 언급된다.

05 In the late 1970s, he turned his interest to the field of history. He was one of the most cited psychologists of the twentieth century.

▶ 1970년대 후반부터 Festinger는 역사 분야로 관심을 돌렸다는 내용이 언급된다. Festinger가 20세기 심리학 분야에서 가장 많이 인용된 학자 중 한 명이 될 만큼 입지를 다졌다는 내용도 제시된다.

06 Festinger's theories still play an important role in psychology today.

▶ 그의 연구가 오늘날 심리학 연구에도 중요한 영향을 미치고 있다는 설명으로 글이 마무리된다.

구문 풀이

In the late 1970s, he turned his interest to the field of history.
→ 과거시제 동사 turned가 명백한 과거 표현(in + 연도)과 함께 쓰였다.

구문 플러스⁺ 과거 vs. 현재완료

과거: in + 연도, last night, yesterday 등 과거 표현과 함께 사용
현재완료: over the years, for(~동안), since(~한 이후로) 등 기간 표현과 함께 사용

It **rained a lot last year**. 작년에 비가 많이 왔다.
It **has rained for a week straight**. 일주일 연속으로 비가 왔다.

---

38 정답 ④ 92%　　　　　　　*2022학년도 대수능*

해석 위의 그래프들은 2015년 지역별 세계 중산층의 점유율과 2025년의 예상 점유율을 보여준다. 아시아 태평양 지역의 세계 중산층 점유율은 2015년에 46퍼센트로부터 2025년에는 60퍼센트로 증가할 것으로 예상된다. 2025년의 아시아 태평양 지역의 예상 점유율은 여섯 개의 지역 중에서 가장 크며, 같은 해 유럽의 예상 점유율의 세 배보다 더 많다. 유럽과 북미 지역의 점유율은 둘 다 감소할 것으로 예상되어, 유럽은 2015년 24퍼센트에서 2025년 16퍼센트로, 북미 지역은 2015년 11퍼센트에서 2025년 8퍼센트로 떨어질 것이다. 중남미 지역은 세계 중산층 점유율에 있어서 2015년에서 2025년까지 변하지 않을(→ 변할) 것으로 예상된다. 2015년에 그랬듯이, 2025년에 중동 및 북아프리카의 점유율은 사하라 사막 이남의 아프리카의 점유율보다 더 클 것이다.

해설 도표에 따르면 중남미 지역의 세계 중산층 점유율은 2015년에 9%이지만 2025년에는 7%로 떨어질 것으로 예상된다고 한다. 따라서 도표와 일치하지 않는 것은 ④이다.

선택률	오답 풀이
① 0%	아시아 태평양 지역의 중산층 점유율이 2015년 46%, 2025년 60%로 정확하게 제시되었다.
② 2%	2025년 아시아 태평양의 중산층 점유율이 지역 중 가장 크고(60%), 유럽의 예상 점유율(16%)의 세 배를 넘는다는 내용이 정확하게 제시되었다.
③ 1%	유럽과 북미의 중산층 점유율이 모두 하락할 것으로 예상된다는 내용이 수치와 함께 정확히 제시되었다.
⑤ 3%	2025년 중동 및 북아프리카 지역의 중산층 예상 점유율(6%)은 사하라 사막 이남 아프리카의 예상 점유율(4%)보다 크다는 내용이 정확하게 제시되었다.

지문 자세히 보기

01 The above graphs show the percentage share of the global middle class by region in 2015 and its projected share in 2025.

▶ 도표의 성격이 명시된다. 2015년과 2025년의 세계 중산층 점유율을 지역별로 분석한 자료라는 것이다.

02 It is projected that the share of the global middle class in Asia Pacific will increase from 46 percent in 2015 to 60 percent in 2025. The projected share of Asia Pacific in 2025, the largest among the six regions, is more than three times that of Europe in the same year.

▶ 아시아 태평양 지역의 중산층 점유율 변화를 분석한 후, 유럽과 비교하고 있다.

03 The shares of Europe and North America are both projected to decrease, from 24 percent in 2015 to 16 percent in 2025 for Europe, and from 11 percent in 2015 to 8 percent in 2025 for North America.

▶ 유럽 및 북미 지역의 중산층 점유율 변화에 관해 전망하고 있다.

04 Central and South America is not(→ is) expected to change from 2015 to 2025 in its share of the global middle class.

▶ 도표에서 중남미 지역의 점유율은 2015년 9%에서 2025년 7%로 '변할' 것으로 전망하므로, 변화가 예측되지 '않는다'는 설명은 부적합하다.

05 In 2025, the share of the Middle East and North Africa will be larger than that of sub-Saharan Africa, as it was in 2015.

▶ 중동 및 북아프리카 지역과 사하라 이남 아프리카의 중산층 점유율을 비교 분석하고 있다.

구문 풀이

The projected share of Asia Pacific in 2025, **the largest among the six regions**, is more than three times that of Europe in the same year.

→ 「the + 최상급(가장 ~한)」 구문이 주어를 보충 설명한다.

구문 플러스˚ 최상급

「the + 최상급」은 in, of, among, ever 등 범위를 나타내는 표현과 함께 쓰여 '~에서 가장 …한'의 의미를 나타낸다.

Lotte World Tower is **the tallest** buliding in South Korea.
롯데월드타워는 한국에서 가장 높은 건물이다.

She is **the smallest** person among us.
그녀는 우리 중 가장 작은 사람이다.

유형 플러스˚ 도표 불일치

주어진 도표나 그래프가 제시하는 정보를 파악하고, 이를 본문과 대응시키는 문제이다.

- **문제 해결 Tip.**
  ① 도표의 제목과 첫 문장을 함께 보며 무엇에 관한 도표인지 확인한다.
  ② 증감 또는 비교 표현에 주목하며 도표와 본문의 일치 여부를 확인한다.
  ③ 도표의 항목, 단위 표현을 잘못 보지 않도록 주의한다.

- **주의할 표현 Tip.**
  A outweigh B = B be outweighed by A
  : A가 B보다 더 중요하다[더 무겁다]
  A outnumber B = B be outnumbered by A
  : A가 B보다 수가 더 많다
  A follow B = B be followed by A
  : A가 B를 따르다(A가 B보다 더 뒤에 있다, B가 A를 앞서다)

---

39 정답 ⑤ 92%

해석 Marc Isambard Brunel(1769~1849)은 Thames Tunnel의 설계와 건설로 가장 잘 알려져 있다. 원래 프랑스에서 태어난 Brunel은 프랑스 혁명 중에 미국으로 달아났다. 그는 후에 런던으로 거처를 옮겼다. 나폴레옹 전쟁이 한창일 때, 그는 부츠를 만드는 기계를 발명했다. 나폴레옹 전쟁 중에, Brunel의 공장은 영국 군대에 부츠를 공급했다. 그러나 전쟁이 끝난 후, 정부는 그의 부츠를 더 이상 사지 않았고 그는 폐업했다. 몇 년 후, Brunel은 빚 때문에 몇 달 동안 감옥에 수감되었다. 그 당시, 런던은 템스강에 의해 상당히 나뉘어 있었고 사람과 상품이 강을 가로질러 건널 더 많은 방법이 필요했다. 1825년, Brunel은 강 밑의 터널을 설계했다. Thames Tunnel은 1843년 3월 25일에 정식으로 개통했고, Brunel은 건강이 좋지 않았음에도 불구하고 개통식에 참석했다.

해설 마지막 문장에 따르면 Brunel은 건강이 좋지 않은데도 불구하고 터널 개통식에 참가했다고 하므로, 내용과 일치하지 않는 것은 ⑤ 'Thames Tunnel 개통식에 아파서 참석하지 못했다.'이다.

오답 풀이

선택률	오답 풀이
① 2%	~ Brunel escaped to the United States during the French Revolution.
② 1%	~ he invented machines for making boots.
③ 2%	~ Brunel's factory supplied British troops with boots.
④ 2%	~ Brunel was imprisoned for several months because of his debt.

지문 자세히 보기˚

01 Marc Isambard Brunel (1769–1849) is best known for the design and construction of the Thames Tunnel. Originally born in France, Brunel escaped to the United States during the French Revolution. He later moved to London.

▶ Marc Isambard Brunel의 생애에 관한 글이다. 프랑스 태생인 Brunel은 프랑스 대혁명 때 미국으로 달아났다가 런던으로 이주했다는 내용이 언급된다.

02 When the Napoleonic Wars were at their height, he invented machines for making boots. During the Napoleonic Wars, Brunel's factory supplied British troops with boots.

▶ 나폴레옹 전쟁 당시 Brunel은 부츠를 만드는 기계를 발명해 영국 군대에 부츠를 공급했다는 설명이 이어진다.

03 After the Wars ended, however, the government stopped buying his boots and he went out of business. A few years later, Brunel was imprisoned for several months because of his debt.

▶ 전쟁 후 정부가 부츠를 사들이지 않으면서 Brunel의 사업이 기울었고, 그가 빚 때문에 몇 달 동안 수감되기도 했다는 내용이 이어진다.

04 At that time, London was very much divided by the River and needed more ways for people and goods to move across it. In 1825, Brunel designed a tunnel under the river.

▶ Brunel이 템스강 밑을 지나는 터널(Thames Tunnel)을 설계했음이 언급된다.

> **05** The Thames Tunnel officially opened on 25 March 1843, and Brunel, despite being in ill health, attended the opening ceremony.
>
> ▶ 터널 개통 당시 Brunel은 몸이 좋지 않았음에도 개통식에 참석했다는 점이 언급된다.

구문 풀이

At that time, London was very much divided by the River Thames and needed more ways **for people and goods** to move across it.

→ **more ways**를 꾸미는 **to move across it** 앞에 「for + 목적격」 형태의 의미상 주어가 삽입되었다.

구문 플러스' to부정사의 의미상 주어

to부정사의 의미상 주어는 to부정사 앞에 「for + 목적격」으로 표시되는 것이 일반적이다. 단, 사람의 성격을 묘사하는 형용사가 앞에 나오면 「of + 목적격」으로 표시된다.

It is important for you to have a positive mindset. (일반적 경우)
여러분이 긍정적인 사고방식을 갖는 것은 중요합니다.
It is thoughtful of you not to interrupt. (사람 성격: 사려 깊은)
끼어들지 않다니 당신은 사려 깊군요.

---

40 정답 ③ 92%　　　　　　*2021학년도 6월 모평*

해석

노래하는 Tommy

축하합니다! 이제 **Tommy**는 여러분의 노래하는 친구입니다. 그와 함께 놀고 그를 돌보는 방법을 배우기 위해 이 사용 설명서를 읽으세요. **Tommy**는 언제 어디서나 여러분에게 노래를 불러 줍니다. 노래를 재생하기 위해 인터넷 연결은 필요 없습니다!

사용 전
1. **Tommy**의 눈을 덮고 있는 보호 필름을 제거하세요.
2. 배터리 칸에 **AA** 건전지 두 개를 넣고 전원 단추를 누르세요.
3. 소리 크기 설정을 선택하세요: '낮음' 또는 '높음'

작동
1. 재생
- **Tommy**의 오른쪽 귀를 건드리면 노래를 시작합니다.
2. 중지
- **Tommy**의 모자를 누르면 노래를 멈춥니다.
3. 조절
- 다섯 곡의 노래 중에 선택하세요.
- **Tommy**의 배지를 누르면 다음 노래로 건너뜁니다.

주의사항
Tommy는 방수가 되지 않습니다. **Tommy**가 물에 젖지 않게 조심하세요!

해설 Operation의 Stop 항목에서 Tommy의 모자를 누르면 노래가 멈춘다고 하므로, 내용과 일치하지 않는 것은 ③ '모자를 누르면 노래가 시작된다.'이다.

오답 풀이

선택률	오답 풀이
① 1%	An Internet connection is not required ~
② 2%	Insert two AA batteries into the battery box ~
④ 1%	Choose from five songs.
⑤ 1%	Tommy is not waterproof.

지문 자세히 보기'

01 Singing Tommy

Congratulations! Tommy is now your singing friend. Read these instructions to learn how to play with and care for him. Tommy sings to you anytime, anywhere. An Internet connection is not required to play the songs!

▶ 인터넷 연결 없이 어디서든 작동할 수 있는 노래 인형 **Tommy**를 소개하고 있다.

02 Before Use
1. Remove the protective film covering Tommy's eyes.
2. Insert two AA batteries into the battery box and press the power button.
3. Choose your volume setting: LOW volume or HIGH volume.

▶ 사용 전에 눈에 붙은 보호 필름을 떼고 **AA** 건전지를 두 개 넣은 뒤 볼륨을 조정하라는 내용이 언급된다.

03 Operation
1. Play
- Touch Tommy's right ear to start a song.
2. Stop
- Press Tommy's hat to stop the song.
3. Control
- Choose from five songs.
- Push Tommy's badge to skip to the next song.

▶ **Tommy**의 구체적인 작동법을 설명하고 있다. 오른쪽 귀를 누르면 노래가 시작되고, 모자를 누르면 노래가 꺼지며, 선택할 수 있는 곡은 다섯 곡이라는 점이 언급된다.

04 Caution
Tommy is not waterproof. Be careful not to get Tommy wet!

▶ **Tommy**는 방수가 아니므로 젖지 않게 조심하라는 주의사항이 언급된다.

구문 풀이

Be careful **not to get** Tommy wet!

→ 「not + to부정사」가 부사적 용법으로 쓰여 '~하지 않도록, ~하지 않기 위해'라고 해석된다.

41 정답 ④ 95% *2020학년도 대수능*

해석

2019 자선 배드민턴 경기

Cliffield 커뮤니티 센터가 주최하는 자선 토너먼트 경기에 참가하세요! 이 행사는 Salke 아동병원을 지원합니다.

시간 및 장소
· 11월 23일 토요일 오후 2시
· Cliffield 스포츠 센터

토너먼트에 참가하는 방법
· 두 명이 한 팀을 구성하세요.
· 팀 참가비 100달러를 기부금으로 내세요.

활동
· 작년 우승팀과의 3점 내기 시합에 도전하세요.
· 20달러 추가 기부 시 프로 선수들에게서 배드민턴 기술을 배울 수 있습니다.

※ 라켓과 셔틀콕은 제공됩니다.

'여기를 클릭하셔서 지금 등록하세요!'

해설 'With an additional $20 donation, ~'에서 20달러를 추가 기부하면 프로 배드민턴 선수들로부터 기술을 배울 수 있다고 하므로, 내용과 일치하는 것은 ④ '20달러 추가 기부 시 배드민턴 기술을 배울 수 있다.' 이다.

오답 풀이

선택률	오답 풀이
① 1%	~ hosted by Cliffield Community Center!
② 0%	Make a two-member team.
③ 1%	your team's $100 entry fee
⑤ 1%	Rackets and shuttlecocks will be provided.

지문 자세히 보기⁺

01 2019 Badminton Challenge for Charity
Join the charity tournament event hosted by Cliffield Community Center! This event supports Salke Children's Hospital.

▶ 자선 배드민턴 경기의 주최처(Cliffield Community Center)와 후원처가 언급된다.

02 When & Where
· Saturday, November 23, 2:00 p.m.
· Cliffield Sports Center

▶ 경기가 열리는 시간과 장소가 언급된다.

03 How to Join the Tournament
· Make a two-member team.
· Pay your team's $100 entry fee as a donation.

▶ 팀은 2명으로 구성되며, 참가비는 팀 단위로 책정되어 있음이 언급된다.

04 Activities
· Challenge last year's champion team to a 3-point match.
· With an additional $20 donation, you can learn badminton skills from professional players.

▶ 활동 내용이 언급된다. 20달러를 추가 기부하면 전문 선수들로부터 레슨을 받을 수 있다는 내용이 나온다.

05 ※ Rackets and shuttlecocks will be provided.
Click here to register now!

▶ 라켓과 셔틀콕은 제공된다는 점이 추가로 제시된다.

구문 풀이

Make a two-member team.
→ 「수사 + 명사」 형태의 복합형용사가 명사 team을 수식한다.

해석 British Columbia의 해안가를 따라서 짙은 황록색과 반짝이는 파란색 지대가 위치한다. 이 지대는 Great Bear Rainforest인데, 면적이 640만 헥타르, 즉 Ireland나 Nova Scotia 정도의 크기이다. 그것은 매우 다양한 야생 동물의 서식지이다. 그 지역에 서식하는 독특한 동물 중 하나는 Kermode 곰이다. 그것은 British Columbia의 공식 포유류로 알려져 있는 희귀종 곰이다. 연어 또한 이곳에서 발견된다. 인간뿐만 아니라 매우 다양한 동물들이 그것을 먹기 때문에 그것은 이 지역의 생태계에서 매우 중요한 역할을 한다. Great Bear Rainforest는 또한 수백 년 동안 살 수 있는 나무인 Western Red Cedar의 서식지이기도 하다. 그 나무의 목재는 가볍고 방부성이 있어 건축물을 짓고 가구를 만드는 데 사용된다.

해설 '~ about the size of Ireland or Nova Scotia.' 문장에서 Great Bear Rainforest의 면적은 Ireland '또는' Nova Scotia 정도의 크기라고 하므로, 내용과 일치하지 않는 것은 ② 'Ireland와 Nova Scotia를 합친 크기이다.'이다.

오답 풀이

선택률	오답 풀이
① 3%	Along the coast of British Columbia lies a land of forest green and sparkling blue. This land is the Great Bear Rainforest, ~
③ 1%	One of the unique animals living in the area is the Kermode bear.
④ 2%	Salmon are also found here. They play a vital role in this area's ecosystem ~
⑤ 1%	The Great Bear Rainforest is also home to the Western Red Cedar ~

지문 자세히 보기

01 Along the coast of British Columbia lies a land of forest green and sparkling blue. This land is the Great Bear Rainforest, which measures 6.4 million hectares — about the size of Ireland or Nova Scotia.

▶ Great Bear Rainforest의 위치와 면적이 언급된다. 이곳은 British Columbia 해안가에 위치하며, 크기는 Ireland 또는 Nova Scotia와 비슷하다는 내용이 제시된다.

02 It is home to a wide variety of wildlife. One of the unique animals living in the area is the Kermode bear. It is a rare kind of bear known to be the official mammal of British Columbia.

▶ 이곳에 사는 야생 동물의 예로 the Kermode bear가 언급된다.

03 Salmon are also found here. They play a vital role in this area's ecosystem as a wide range of animals, as well as humans, consume them.

▶ 연어가 이곳 생태계에 매우 중요한 역할을 한다는 점이 언급된다.

04 The Great Bear Rainforest is also home to the Western Red Cedar, a tree that can live for several hundred years. The tree's wood is lightweight and rot-resistant, so it is used for making buildings and furniture.

▶ 이곳에 서식하는 나무로 Western Red Cedar를 언급하며, 목재의 특징에 관해 덧붙인다.

구문 풀이

One of the unique animals living in the area **is** the Kermode bear.
→ 「one of the + 복수명사」 주어는 단수 취급한다(is). living in the area는 the unique animals를 꾸미는 현재분사구이다.

구문 플러스⁺ one of the + 복수명사

「one of the + 복수명사(~중 하나)」 주어와 단수동사 사이에 수식어가 삽입될 때 주의가 필요하다.

One of the robbers who were arrested **was** released.
　　　　　　　(the robbers 수식)
체포된 강도들 중 한 명이 석방되었다.

유형 플러스⁺ 내용 불일치

주로 특정 인물의 생애나 동물의 특징에 관해 설명하는 글을 읽고 본문과 일치하지 않는 선택지를 찾는 유형이다.

· 문제 해결 Tip.
① 첫 문장에서 무엇에 관한 설명문인지 파악한다.
② 선택지를 먼저 읽고, 글의 내용을 예측한다.
③ 선택지의 근거가 되는 문장을 본문에서 찾고, 정보의 일치/불일치 여부를 검토한다.

43 정답 ③ 48%　　　　　2024학년도 9월 모평

해석　스트레스 반응을 자원으로 보는 것은 두려움이라는 생리 기능을 용기라는 생명 작용으로 바꿀 수 있다. 그것은 위협을 도전으로 바꿀 수 있고, 여러분이 압박감 속에서도 최선을 다하도록 도울 수 있다. 불안감의 경우처럼 스트레스가 도움이 되지 않는다고 느껴질 때조차도, 그것을 기꺼이 받아들이면 그것을 더 많은 에너지, 더 많은 자신감, 더 기꺼이 행동을 취하려는 의지 등 유용한 것으로 바꿀 수 있다. 스트레스의 징후를 알아차릴 때마다 이 전략을 여러분의 삶에 적용할 수 있다. 심장이 두근거리거나 숨이 가빠지는 것을 느낄 때, 그것은 여러분의 몸이 더 많은 에너지를 주려고 노력하는 방식임을 깨달으라. 여러분의 몸에서 긴장을 감지한다면 스트레스 반응이 여러분의 힘을 이용할 기회를 준다는 점을 상기하라. 손바닥에 땀이 나는가? 첫 데이트에 나갔을 때 어떤 기분이었는지 기억해 보라. 여러분이 원하는 것에 가까이 있을 때 손바닥에 땀이 난다.

해설　③ 앞에는 부사절, 뒤에는 명사절이 나오므로 문장에 술어가 빠져 있다. 따라서 Realizing을 Realize로 바꾸어 명령문으로 만들어야 한다.

오답 풀이

선택률	오답 풀이
① 9%	help의 목적격보어인 원형부정사 do이다.
② 14%	can transform의 주어가 welcoming it(=the stress)이고, 목적어는 문맥상 the stress이므로, 두 대상은 완벽히 동일하지 않다. 따라서 itself가 아닌, it이 알맞게 쓰였다.
④ 16%	「remind + 사람 + that S′ V′ ~」 구문이다. that 뒤에 완전한 문장이 나왔다.
⑤ 13%	가주어 it에 이어 진주어 to go가 쓰였다.

지문 자세히 보기

01　Viewing the stress response as a resource can transform the physiology of fear into the biology of courage. It can turn a threat into a challenge and can help you do your best under pressure.

▶ 준사역동사 can help의 목적격보어로는 원형부정사 또는 to부정사가 올 수 있다. 따라서 do는 적절하고, 이 do를 to do로 바꿔도 된다.

02　Even when the stress doesn't feel helpful — as in the case of anxiety — welcoming it can transform it into something that is helpful: more energy, more confidence, and a greater willingness to take action.

▶ the stress를 받는 단수대명사로 it을 썼다. 동사 can transform 앞에 it이 또 있어 재귀대명사 자리가 아닌지 헷갈릴 수 있지만, 정확한 주어는 welcoming it이다. 즉 the stress와 완벽히 동일한 대상이 아니므로 재귀대명사를 쓰지 않아도 된다.

03　You can apply this strategy in your own life anytime you notice signs of stress. When you feel your heart beating or your breath quickening, realizing(→ realize) that it is your body's way of trying to give you more energy.

▶ 동사 앞에는 접속사 When, 뒤에는 접속사 that이 있는 것으로 보아, ④가 유일한 술어 자리이다. 접속사로 연결된 동사는 문장 전체의 술어 역할을 할 수 없기 때문이다. 따라서 realizing 대신 realize를 써야 하고, 이때 문장은 주어 없이 원형으로 시작하는 명령문(~하라)이 된다.

04　If you notice tension in your body, remind yourself that the stress response gives you access to your strength.

▶ remind는 「remind A of B」 형태로 주로 쓰는데, B 자리에 that절이 오면 전치사 of를 뺀다.

05　Sweaty palms? Remember what it felt like to go on your first date — palms sweat when you're close to something you want.

▶ it은 '그것'으로 해석되지 않는 가주어이고, to go가 what절의 진짜 주어이다. felt like 뒤에 명사가 빠져 있다.

구문 풀이

Viewing the stress response as a resource can transform the physiology of fear into the biology of courage.
→ 동명사구가 문장의 주어로 쓰였다.

구문 플러스' 명사구 주어

동명사구, to부정사구가 문장의 주어로 쓰이면 단수 취급한다.

Singing in the shower makes me happy.
샤워하며 노래하는 것은 나를 행복하게 한다.
To become a teacher is to study forever.
교사가 되는 것은 평생 공부하는 것이다.

44 정답 ② 43%　　　　　2023학년도 9월 모평

해석　윤리적 문제를 인식하는 것은 비즈니스 윤리를 이해하는 데 가장 중요한 단계이다. 윤리적 문제는 옳거나 그르다고, 즉 윤리적 또는 비윤리적이라고 평가될 수 있는 여러 가지 행동들 중에서 한 사람이 선택하기를 요구하는 식별 가능한 문제, 상황 또는 기회이다. 대안 중에서 선택하고 결정을 내리는 방법을 배우는 것은 훌륭한 개인적 가치관뿐만 아니라 관심 사업 영역에 대한 지식 역량도 필요로 한다. 또한 직원들은 언제 자신이 속한 조직의 정책과 윤리 강령에 의존할지, 혹은 언제 동료나 관리자와 적절한 행동에 대해 논의할지를 알아야 한다. 윤리적 의사결정이 항상 쉬운 것은 아닌데, 왜냐하면 어떤 결정이 내려지든 딜레마를 만들어내는 애매한 영역이 늘 있기 때문이다. 예를 들어, 직원은 시간 절도를 하는 동료에 대해 보고해야 하는가? 판매원은 고객에게 프레젠테이션을 할 때 어떤 제품의 안전 상태가 좋지 않다는 기록에 대한 사실을 생략해야 하는가? 그러한 질문은 의사결정자가 자신이 선택한 윤리를 평가하여 지침을 요청할 것인지 여부를 결정하도록 요구한다.

해설 단수동사 requires 앞에 주어가 필요하므로, ②의 Learn을 동명사인 Learning으로 고쳐야 한다.

오답 풀이

선택률	오답 풀이
① 6%	관계대명사 that이 받는 선행사 several actions가 '평가되는' 대상이므로 수동태 be evaluated가 바르게 쓰였다.
③ 17%	'when + to부정사'의 to rely on과 병렬 연결되는 have가 바르게 쓰였다.
④ 16%	선행사 gray areas를 받으면서 뒤에 불완전한 절을 연결하는 관계대명사 that이 바르게 쓰였다.
⑤ 18%	decide 뒤에서 '~인지 아닌지'의 의미를 나타내는 whether가 바르게 쓰였다.

지문 자세히 보기

01 Recognizing ethical issues is the most important step in understanding business ethics. An ethical issue is an identifiable problem, situation, or opportunity that requires a person to choose from among several actions that may be evaluated as right or wrong, ethical or unethical.

▶ 주격 관계대명사절의 동사는 선행사를 기준으로 단수-복수, 능동-수동 여부를 결정한다. 여기서 several actions라는 선행사가 '평가되는' 행위의 대상이고, 밑줄 뒤에 목적어도 없으므로 be evaluated를 수동태로 알맞게 썼다.

02 Learn(→ Learning) how to choose from alternatives and make a decision requires not only good personal values, but also knowledge competence in the business area of concern.

▶ 문두의 동사원형에 밑줄이 있을 때에는 주어 자리인데 원형이 잘못 쓰인 것인지, 혹은 문장이 명령문인지 판단해야 한다. 여기서는 뒤에 단수동사 requires가 나오는 것으로 보아 밑줄 부분이 주어 자리이므로, Learn을 명사구인 Learning으로 바꾸어야 문장이 성립한다.

03 Employees also need to know when to rely on their organizations' policies and codes of ethics or have discussions with co-workers or managers on appropriate conduct.

▶ 동사 need to know의 목적어가 'when + to부정사' 형태로 제시되었다. 등위접속사 or 앞뒤로 2개의 부정사구가 병렬 연결되어 'to rely on ~ or (to) have ~'의 구조가 완성된다.

04 Ethical decision making is not always easy because there are always gray areas that create dilemmas, no matter how decisions are made. For instance, should an employee report on a co-worker engaging in time theft? Should a salesperson leave out facts about a product's poor safety record in his presentation to a customer?

▶ 앞에 선행사 gray areas가 있고, 뒤에 나오는 create dilemmas가 주어 없이 동사로 시작하는 불완전한 문장이므로, 주격 관계대명사 that을 썼다.

05 Such questions require the decision maker to evaluate the ethics of his or her choice and decide whether to ask for guidance.

▶ 'whether + to부정사'는 '~할지 말지'라는 의미를 나타내는 명사구이다. 이는 be not sure, ask, check, decide, see 등의 동사구와 흔히 어울려 쓰인다.

구문 풀이

Learning how to choose from alternatives and make a decision requires **not only** good personal values, **but also** knowledge competence in the business area of concern.
→ 상관접속사 구문인 「not only A but also B(A뿐만 아니라 B도)」이다.

구문 플러스' not only A but also B

「not only A but also B(A뿐만 아니라 B도)」의 A, B는 병렬구조를 이룬다. only는 just, merely 등으로 대체할 수 있으며, also는 생략되기도 한다.

This bag is **not only** stylish **but also** eco-friendly.
이 가방은 멋스러울 뿐 아니라 친환경적이다.

Leadership requires **not only** insight **but (also)** courage and dedication.
리더십은 통찰력뿐 아니라 용기와 헌신을 필요로 한다.

---

45 정답 ③ 63% *2022학년도 9월 모평*

해석 다른 사람들이 전달하고 있는 어떤 것이든 받아들이는 것은 그들의 관심사가 우리의 관심사와 일치할 때에만 성공하는데, 체내의 세포, 벌집 속의 벌을 생각해 보라. 인간 사이의 의사소통에 관한 한, 관심사의 그런 공통성은 좀처럼 이루어지지 않는데, 심지어 임산부도 태아가 보내는 화학적 신호를 믿지 못할 이유가 있다. 다행히도, 가장 적대적인 관계에서도 의사소통이 이루어지게 할 수 있는 방법이 있다. 먹잇감은 포식자에게 자신을 쫓지 말도록 설득할 수 있다. 그러나 그러한 의사소통이 일어나기 위해서는, 신호를 받는 자가 그것을 믿는 것이 더 좋을 것이라는 강력한 보장이 있어야 한다. 메시지는 전체적으로 정직한 상태로 유지되어야 한다. 인간의 경우, 정직성은 전달된 정보를 평가하는 일련의 인지 기제에 의해 유지된다. 이러한 기제는 우리가 가장 유익한 메시지를 받아들이며(개방적이면서), 반면에 가장 해로운 메시지를 거부할(경계할) 수 있게 해준다.

해설 ③ which 뒤에 나오는 'those ~ will be better off ~'가 앞의 추상명사 guarantees를 설명하는 완전한 문장인 것으로 보아, 관계대명사 which 대신 동격 접속사인 that을 써야 한다.

오답 풀이

선택률	오답 풀이
① 3%	주어 such commonality가 불가산명사이므로 is가 알맞게 쓰였다.
② 9%	주어 A prey를 받기 위해 단수대명사 it이 알맞게 쓰였다.
④ 15%	5형식의 keep이 수동태인 be kept로 바뀐 후, 목적격보어였던 형용사 honest가 동사 뒤에 알맞게 연결되었다.
⑤ 8%	information이 '전달되는' 대상이므로 communicated가 과거분사로 알맞게 쓰였다.

지문 자세히 보기

01 Accepting whatever others are communicating only pays off if their interests correspond to ours — think cells in a body, bees in a beehive. As far as communication between humans is concerned, such commonality of interests is rarely achieved; even a pregnant mother has reasons to mistrust the chemical signals sent by her fetus.

▶ such commonality는 불가산명사로서 단수형으로 쓰였기에 is가 동사로 쓰였다. 주어를 수식하는 말의 일부인 interests에 속지 않도록 주의한다.

02 Fortunately, there are ways of making communication work even in the most adversarial of relationships. A prey can convince a predator not to chase it.

▶ A prey를 지칭하고자 not to chase의 목적어 자리에 it을 썼다. not to chase의 의미상 주어는 A prey와 다른 존재인 a predator이기 때문에, 목적어 자리에 itself가 아닌 it을 썼다.

03 But for such communication to occur, there must be strong guarantees which(→ that) those who receive the signal will be better off believing it.

▶ 앞에 명사가 있으므로 관계대명사가 적절해 보이지만, 뒤에 나오는 절이 완전하다. 이때는 추상명사 뒤에서 명사를 보충할 수 있는 동격 접속사 that을 떠올려야 한다.

04 The messages have to be kept, on the whole, honest.

▶ 본래 이 문장은 '~ keep the messages honest'이다. 여기서 목적어 The messages를 주어로 삼고, 동사를 수동태로 바꾼 뒤, 목적격보어였던 형용사 honest를 이어서 써줬다. 동사와 보어 사이에 on the whole이 삽입되어 혼동을 유발하므로 주의가 필요하다.

05 In the case of humans, honesty is maintained by a set of cognitive mechanisms that evaluate communicated information. These mechanisms allow us to accept most beneficial messages — to be open — while rejecting most harmful messages — to be vigilant.

▶ 명사를 수식하는 분사의 태를 판단할 때는 수식받는 명사를 기준으로 생각한다. 여기서 information은 '전달되는' 대상이므로, 수식어로 과거분사 communicated를 썼다.

구문 풀이

The messages have to be kept, on the whole, honest.
→ keep은 형용사를 목적격보어로 취하는 5형식 동사의 일종이다. 이 keep이 수동태로 바뀐 후, honest는 목적격보어에서 주격보어가 되었다.

구문 플러스 — 형용사를 목적격보어로 취하는 5형식 동사

keep, find, consider, make, call, leave, think 등

This coat will keep you warm.
이 코트가 너를 따뜻하게 해줄 거야.

Your degree doesn't make you smart.
학위가 당신을 똑똑하게 만들지는 않는다.

---

46 정답 ⑤ 42% 2022학년도 6월 모평

해석 대부분의 과학 역사가들은 별과 행성에 대한 연구, 즉 우리가 현재 천문학이라 부르는 것에 대해 배우고자 하는 동기로 농업 활동을 규제하기 위한 신뢰할 만한 달력의 필요성을 지적한다. 초기 천문학은 언제 작물을 심어야 하는지에 대한 정보를 제공했고 인간에게 시간의 흐름을 기록하는 최초의 공식적인 방법을 제공했다. 영국 남부에 있는, 4,000년 된 고리 모양의 돌들인 스톤헨지는 아마도 우리가 살고 있는 세계의 규칙성과 예측 가능성을 발견한 데 대한 가장 잘 알려진 기념비일 것이다. 스톤헨지의 커다란 표식은 우리가 계절의 시작을 표시하기 위해 여전히 사용하는 날짜인 지점(하지, 동지 등)과 분점(춘분, 추분 등)에 태양이 뜨는 지평선의 장소를 가리킨다. 그 돌들은 심지어 (해·달의) 식(蝕)을 예측하는 데 사용되었을지도 모른다. 글이 없던 시절 사람들이 세운 스톤헨지의 존재는 자연의 규칙성뿐만 아니라, 눈앞에 보이는 모습의 이면을 보고 사건에서 더 깊은 의미를 발견할 수 있는 인간의 정신적 능력을 말없이 증언해 준다.

해설 마지막 문장에서 the ability를 꾸미는 to see behind와 병렬을 이루도록 ⑤ discovers를 (to) discover로 고쳐야 한다.

오답 풀이

선택률	오답 풀이
① 12%	humans의 소유격을 받는 대명사 their가 알맞게 쓰였다.
② 11%	Stonehenge는 고유명사 주어이므로 동사로 is가 알맞게 쓰였다.
③ 16%	뒤에 rises가 포함된 완전한 1형식 문장이 나오므로 where가 알맞게 쓰였다.
④ 18%	주어인 The stones가 '사용된' 대상이므로 been used가 알맞게 쓰였다.

지문 자세히 보기

01 Most historians of science point to the need for a reliable calendar to regulate agricultural activity as the motivation for learning about what we now call astronomy, the study of stars and planets. Early astronomy provided information about when to plant crops and gave humans their first formal method of recording the passage of time.

▶ 문맥상 초기 천문학이 '인간들의' 시간 기록 도구를 마련해주었다는 의미이므로, 복수명사 humans의 소유격을 나타내는 their를 썼다.

02 Stonehenge, the 4,000-year-old ring of stones in southern Britain, is perhaps the best-known monument to the discovery of regularity and predictability in the world we inhabit.

▶ 고유명사인 Stonehenge는 단수 취급하므로, 뒤따르는 동사 자리에 is를 썼다. 'the 4,000-year-old ring ~ Britain'은 주어를 보충 설명하는 동격 명사구로, 역시 단수이다.

03 The great markers of Stonehenge point to the spots on the horizon where the sun rises at the solstices and equinoxes — the dates we still use to mark the beginnings of the seasons.

▶ 선행사 the spots가 장소 명사이고, 'the sun rises ~'는 1형식 문장이다. 따라서 관계부사 where를 사용했다. 참고로 선행사를 꾸미는 전명구(on the horizon)에 의해 선행사와 형용사절이 분리된 구조이다.

04 The stones may even have been used to predict eclipses.

▶ 주어인 The stones가 '사용되었을' 수도 있는 대상이고, 동사 뒤에 목적어 없이 부사구(to predict ~)가 나오므로 been used라는 수동태 표현이 나왔다. 태는 주어-동사의 관계를 이르는 말임을 명심한다.

05 The existence of Stonehenge, built by people without writing, bears silent testimony both to the regularity of nature and to the ability of the human mind to see behind immediate appearances and discovers(→ (to) discover) deeper meanings in events.

▶ discovers가 The existence of Stonehenge에 연결되는 동사라면 '스톤헨지의 존재'가 '발견하는' 행위의 주체처럼 해석되어 의미가 어색하다. 문맥으로 보아, the ability를 꾸미는 to see behind와 연결되어 '눈에 보이는 것의 이면을 보고 더 깊은 의미를 발견해내는 능력'이라고 해석될 to부정사구가 필요하다.

구문 풀이

The great markers of Stonehenge point to the spots on the horizon where the sun **rises** at the solstices and equinoxes — the dates we still use to mark the beginnings of the seasons.

→ rise는 '(~이) 오르다'라는 뜻의 1형식 동사이다. 비슷한 형태의 타동사 raise(올리다, 키우다)와 혼동하지 않도록 한다.

구문 플러스' 혼동하기 쉬운 자동사-타동사

형태가 유사한 자동사-타동사 묶음을 함께 기억해 둔다.

자동사	타동사
rise-rose-risen (오르다)	raise-raised-raised (올리다)
lie-lay-lain (눕다)	lay-laid-laid (놓다)
sit-sat-sat (앉다)	seat-seated-seated (앉히다)
fall-fell-fallen (넘어지다)	fell-felled-felled (넘어뜨리다)
arise-arose-arisen (발생하다, 유발되다)	arouse-aroused-aroused (불러일으키다, 자극하다)

Smoke **rises** from the chimney. 굴뚝에서 연기가 난다.
Parents **raise** their kids with love. 부모는 자녀를 사랑으로 키운다.
Problems **arise** in any minute. 문제는 언제든 발생한다.
Anger **arouses** anger. 화는 화를 부른다.

47 정답 ① 30%　　　　2021학년도 9월 모평

해석 경쟁을 벌이는 활동은 최고는 인정받고 나머지는 무시되는, 단지 수행 기량을 보여주는 공개 행사 그 이상일 수 있다. 참가자에게 수행 기량에 대한 시기적절하고 건설적인 피드백을 제공하는 것은 일부 대회와 경연이 제공하는 자산이다. 어떤 의미에서는, 모든 대회가 피드백을 제공한다. 많은 경우에, 이것은 참가자가 상을 받는지에 관한 정보에 국한된다. 그런 유형의 피드백을 제공하는 것은 꼭 탁월함은 아니더라도 우월한 수행 기량을 보여주는 것으로 강조점을 옮긴다고 해석될 수 있

다. 최고의 대회는 단순히 이기는 것 또는 다른 사람을 '패배시키는 것'만이 아니라, 탁월함을 장려한다. 우월성에 대한 강조는 우리가 일반적으로 유해한 경쟁 효과를 조장한다고 간주하는 것이다. 수행 기량에 대한 피드백은 프로그램이 '이기거나, 입상하거나, 또는 보여주는' 수준의 피드백을 넘어설 것을 요구한다. 수행 기량에 관한 정보는 우승 또는 입상하지 못하는 참가자뿐만 아니라 그렇게 하는(우승 또는 입상하는) 참가자에게도 매우 도움이 될 수 있다.

해설 ① which 다음으로 2개의 수동태 동사를 포함한 완전한 절이 나오므로, 관계대명사 which 대신 관계부사 where를 써야 한다.

오답 풀이

선택률	오답 풀이
② 5%	주어 The provision이 단수명사이므로 단수동사 is가 알맞게 쓰였다.
③ 22%	not necessarily(반드시 ~하지는 않은)의 일부인 necessarily가 문맥에 맞게 쓰였다.
④ 20%	전치사 as 뒤에 동명사 fostering이 알맞게 쓰였다.
⑤ 23%	앞에 나온 일반동사구 win or place를 대신하기 위해 대동사 do가 알맞게 쓰였다.

지문 자세히 보기

01 Competitive activities can be more than just performance showcases which(→ where) the best is recognized and the rest are overlooked.

▶ 뒤에 「주어 + be p.p.」의 완전한 문장이 연결되는 것으로 보아 관계대명사 which를 관계부사로 바꿔주어야 한다. 이때 performance showcases가 공간 명사이므로, where를 쓰면 자연스럽다.

02 The provision of timely, constructive feedback to participants on performance is an asset that some competitions and contests offer.

▶ 주어 The provision에 맞추어 is를 썼다. 'of ~ performance'는 주어를 보충 설명한다.

03 In a sense, all competitions give feedback. For many, this is restricted to information about whether the participant is an award- or prizewinner. The provision of that type of feedback can be interpreted as shifting the emphasis to demonstrating superior performance but not necessarily excellence.

▶ 부정어 not과 어울려 '반드시 ~하지는 않은'의 의미를 나타내는 부사로 necessarily를 썼다. 뒤에 나오는 명사 excellence 때문에 기계적으로 형용사를 쓰지 않도록 주의한다.

04 The best competitions promote excellence, not just winning or "beating" others. The emphasis on superiority is what we typically see as fostering a detrimental effect of competition.

▶ 「see A as B(A를 B로 여기다)」 구문의 as는 전치사이므로, B 자리에 동명사 fostering을 썼다. 이때 B는 의미상 목적어 A를 설명하는 목적격 보어처럼 취급되므로, B 자리에 (동)명사뿐 아니라 형용사가 나오기도 한다.

05 Performance feedback requires that the program go beyond the "win, place, or show" level of feedback. Information about performance can be very helpful, not only to the participant who does not win or place but also to those who do.

▶ 일반동사를 대신할 때는 **do/does/did**를 쓰므로, 여기서도 **win or place**를 대신하고자 **do**를 활용했다. **who**의 선행사 **those**가 복수대명사이므로 **do** 또한 복수형으로 쓰였음을 기억해 둔다.

구문 풀이

Performance feedback **requires** that the program **(should) go** beyond the "win, place, or show" level of feedback.
→ 주장, 요구, 명령, 제안 등의 의미를 갖는 동사 뒤로, '~해야 한다'라는 의미의 **that**절이 목적어로 나올 때, **that**절의 동사 자리에는 「**(should) +** 동사원형」이 나온다.

구문 플러스 that 목적절의 should 생략 (1)

주장 - insist	
요구 - request, ask, demand	
명령 - command, order	**+ that S (should) V**
제안 - suggest, propose	~해야 하다
충고 - recommend, advise	

He **insisted** that she **leave** immediately.
그는 그녀가 즉시 떠나야 한다고 주장했다.

She **suggested** that he **practice** more.
그녀는 그가 더 연습해야 한다고 제안했다.

---

48 정답 ④ 43%　　　*2020학년도 9월 모평*

해석 심리적인 이유부터 시작하자면, 다른 사람의 개인적인 일에 대해 아는 것은 이 정보를 가진 사람이 그것을 뒷공론으로 반복하도록 부추길 수 있는데, 왜냐하면 숨겨진 정보로서는 그것이 사회적으로 비활동적인 상태로 남기 때문이다. 그 정보를 소유한 사람은 그 정보가 반복될 때만 자신이 무언가를 알고 있다는 사실을 사회적 인지, 명성, 악명 등 사회적으로 가치 있는 어떤 것으로 바꿀 수 있다. 자신의 정보를 남에게 말하지 않는 동안은, 그는 그것을 알지 못하는 사람들보다 자신이 우월하다고 느낄 수도 있다. 그러나 알면서 말하지 않는 것은 '말하자면 그 비밀 속에 보이지 않게 들어 있다가 폭로의 순간에만 완전히 실현되는 우월함'의 감정을 그에게 주지 못한다. 이것이 유명한 인물들과 윗사람들에 대해 뒷공론을 하는 주요 동기이다. 뒷공론을 만들어 내는 사람은 자신이 그의 '친구'라고 소개하는 그 뒷공론 대상의 '명성' 일부가 자신에게 옮겨질 것이라고 생각한다.

해설 ④가 포함된 문장에서 **superiority**를 꾸미는 주격 관계대명사 **that** 뒤로 동사가 나와야 하므로 **actualizing**을 **actualizes**로 고쳐야 한다.

오답 풀이

선택률	오답 풀이
① 4%	**tempt**는 목적격보어로 **to**부정사를 취하는 5형식 동사이므로, **to repeat**이 알맞게 쓰였다.
② 23%	**only**가 포함된 부사절이 맨 앞에 나오면 뒤따르는 주어와 동사는 의문문 어순으로 도치된다. 따라서 「조동사 + 주어 + 동사원형」의 **turn**이 알맞게 쓰였다.
③ 6%	'정보를 말하지 않는' 주체와 대상이 모두 **he**이므로 목적어 자리에 재귀대명사 **himself**가 알맞게 쓰였다.
⑤ 23%	뒤에 관사 없는 명사로 시작되는 완전한 문장이 나오므로 소유격 관계대명사 **whose**가 알맞게 쓰였다.

지문 자세히 보기

01 To begin with a psychological reason, the knowledge of another's personal affairs can tempt the possessor of this information to repeat it as gossip because as unrevealed information it remains socially inactive.

▶ 「**tempt** + 목적어 + **to**부정사(~이 …하도록 부추기다)」의 5형식 구문이므로, 목적격보어 자리에 **to repeat**을 썼다.

02 Only when the information is repeated can its possessor turn the fact that he knows something into something socially valuable like social recognition, prestige, and notoriety.

▶ **only**를 포함하는 부사(구, 절)는 부정어구와 마찬가지로 의문문 어순의 도치 구문을 유도한다. 여기서도 'Only when ~' 뒤로 조동사 **can**, 주어 **its possessor** 뒤에 동사원형 **turn**을 썼다.

03 As long as he keeps his information to himself, he may feel superior to those who do not know it.

▶ **keep ~ to oneself**(~을 말하지 않다, 비밀로 하다)에 맞춰 **himself**를 썼다. 이 **himself**는 주어 **he**와 동일인이다.

04 But knowing and not telling does not give him that feeling of "superiority that, so to say, latently contained in the secret, fully actualizing(→ actualizes) itself only at the moment of disclosure." This is the main motive for gossiping about well-known figures and superiors.

▶ 주격 관계대명사 **that** 뒤에 동사가 필요하므로, **actualizing**은 적절하지 않다. 이때 선행사 **superiority**가 불가산명사이므로 동사를 단수형인 **actualizes**로 고친다. 참고로 **that**과 **actualizes** 사이의 **so to say**나 **latently contained in the secret**은 문장 구조에 영향을 미치지 않는 삽입구이다.

05 The gossip producer assumes that some of the "fame" of the subject of gossip, as whose "friend" he presents himself, will rub off on him.

▶ 선행사 **the subject of gossip**의 소유격을 나타내면서, 뒤에 나오는 관사 없는 명사 "**friend**"를 꾸미기 위해 소유격 관계대명사 **whose**를 썼다. 이 **whose** "**friend**"가 한꺼번에 전치사 **as**의 목적어 역할을 한다.

구문 풀이

~ feeling of "superiority that, **so to say, latently contained in the secret, fully actualizes** itself only at the moment of disclosure."
→ 주어 **feeling of superiority**와 동사 **actualizes** 사이에 의미를 보충하는 삽입구가 왔다.

구문 플러스⁺ 삽입 구문

앞말의 내용을 자세히 풀어쓰거나 내용을 덧붙이고 싶을 때 콤마(,)나 줄표(—)를 이용해 내용을 추가할 수 있다.

They are, **as far as I know,** unreliable people. → 부사처럼 중간에 삽입
내가 알기로, 그들은 못 미더운 사람들이다.

---

49 정답 ⑤ 32% *2020학년도 6월 모평*

해석 인간 심리의 흥미로운 일면은, 우리가 처음으로 어떤 것을 경험할 때 그것에 관한 모든 것이 분명하지 않다면 그것들을 더 좋아하고 더 매력적으로 여기는 경향이 있다는 것이다. 이것은 음악에 있어서 분명히 사실이다. 예를 들어 우리는 라디오에서 우리의 관심을 끄는 노래를 처음 듣고, 그 노래가 마음에 든다고 판단할 수 있다. 그러고 나서 다음에 그것을 들을 때, 우리는 처음에 알아차리지 못한 가사를 듣거나, 배경에서 피아노나 드럼이 무엇을 하고 있는지 알아챌 수 있다. 우리가 전에 놓쳤던 특별한 화음이 나타난다. 매번 들으면서 우리는 점점 더 많은 것을 듣고 이해하게 된다. 때때로 예술 작품이 우리에게 그것의 중요한 세부 요소들을 모두 드러내는 데 걸리는 시간이 길어질수록, 그것이 음악이든, 미술이든, 춤이든, 또는 건축이든 간에 우리는 그것을 더 좋아하게 된다.

해설 ⑤가 포함된 문장은 「the + 비교급 ~, the + 비교급 …(~할수록 더 …하다)」 구문인데, 첫 번째 「the + 비교급」에 「it takes + 시간 + to부정사(~하는 데 …의 시간을 들이다)」가 포함되어 있다. 이때 대명사 it은 다른 대명사로 바꿀 수 없으므로, that 대신 it을 써야 한다.

오답 풀이

선택률	오답 풀이
① 7%	find의 목적격보어 자리이므로 형용사 appealing이 알맞게 쓰였다.
② 24%	and 앞의 동사 might hear와 병렬을 이루는 동사로 (might) decide가 알맞게 쓰였다.
③ 26%	앞에 선행사가 없고 뒤에 동사의 목적어가 없는 불완전한 절이 나오는 것으로 보아 what이 알맞게 쓰였다.
④ 9%	단수명사 주어 A special harmony 뒤로 단수동사 emerges가 알맞게 쓰였다. emerge는 수동태로 쓸 수 없는 1형식 동사이기도 하다.

지문 자세히 보기

01 An interesting aspect of human psychology is that we tend to like things more and find them more appealing if everything about those things is not obvious the first time we experience them.

▶ 5형식 동사 find의 목적격보어로 비교급 형용사 more appealing을 썼다.

02 This is certainly true in music. For example, we might hear a song on the radio for the first time that catches our interest and decide we like it.

▶ 조동사 might 뒤의 hear와 병렬을 이루는 동사원형으로 decide를 썼다. a song을 꾸미는 that절의 동사 catches와 병렬구조로 보지 않도록 주의한다.

03 Then the next time we hear it, we hear a lyric we didn't catch the first time, or we might notice what the piano or drums are doing in the background.

▶ might notice의 목적어 역할과 뒤에 나오는 관계대명사절의 동사 are doing의 목적어 역할을 겸하도록 관계대명사 what을 썼다. what은 선행사를 포함하므로 앞에 명사가 없고 뒤에도 불완전한 절이 나온다.

04 A special harmony emerges that we missed before. We hear more and more and understand more and more with each listening.

▶ 주어 A special harmony가 단수명사이자 '나타나는' 주체이므로, 단수형이면서 능동태 동사인 emerges를 썼다.

05 Sometimes, the longer that(→ it) takes for a work of art to reveal all of its subtleties to us, the more fond of that thing — whether it's music, art, dance, or architecture — we become.

▶ 「it takes + 시간 + to부정사(~하는 데 …의 시간을 들이다)」 구문의 it은 this, that 등 다른 대명사로 대체될 수 없다. 이 it은 진주어 'to reveal ~'을 대신하는 가주어로 보기도 하고, 시간을 나타내는 비인칭 주어로 보기도 한다.

구문 풀이

Sometimes, **the longer it takes for a work of art to reveal** all of its subtleties to us, **the more fond** of that thing whether it's music, art, dance, or architecture we become.

→ 「it takes + 시간 + to부정사(~하는 데 …의 시간을 들이다)」 구문의 시간 표현 long이 「the + 비교급 ~, the + 비교급 …」 구문으로 강조되었다.

구문 플러스⁺ it takes + 시간 + to부정사

it takes + 사람[행위 주체] + 시간 + to부정사
= it takes + 시간 + for + 사람[행위 주체] + to부정사

It took him six years to finish college.
= **It took six years for him to finish college.**
그가 대학 공부를 마치는 데 6년이 걸렸다.

유형 플러스⁺ 어법성 판단

어법상 적절한 것 또는 적절하지 않은 것을 찾는 문제로, 최근에는 후자의 유형이 주로 출제된다. 시험에 자주 나오는 어법 사항을 미리 정리해 두어야 제대로 대비할 수 있다.

• 문제 해결 Tip
① 밑줄 부분에서 묻는 문법 사항을 파악한다.
② 밑줄 주변의 단서 중심으로 어법의 적절성을 검토한다.
③ 어법성을 판단할 때 의미가 중요한 선택지(병렬구조 등)는 반드시 앞뒤 문맥도 함께 살펴본다.

50 정답 ④ 58%　　*2024학년도 대수능*

해석　상점가 경제는 공유되는 문화라는 더 지속적인 유대 위에 자리 잡은, 겉으로 보기에 유연한 가격 설정 메커니즘을 특징으로 한다. 구매자와 판매자 둘 다 서로의 제약을 알고 있다. 델리의 상점가에서, 구매자와 판매자는 대체로 다른 행위자들이 일상생활에서 가지는 재정적인 제약을 평가할 수 있다. 특정 경제 계층에 속하는 각 행위자는 상대방이 무엇을 필수품으로 여기고 무엇을 사치품으로 여기는지를 이해한다. 비디오 게임과 같은 전자 제품의 경우, 그것들은 식품과 같은 다른 가정 구매품과 동일한 수준의 필수품이 아니다. 따라서 델리의 상점가에서 판매자는 비디오 게임에 대해 직접적으로 매우 낮은(→ 높은) 가격을 요구하지 않으려 주의하는데, 구매자가 비디오 게임의 소유를 절대적인 필수 사항으로 볼 이유가 전혀 없기 때문이다. 이러한 유형의 지식에 대한 접근은 비슷한 문화 및 경제 세계에 속하여 생기는 서로의 선호와 한계를 관련지어 가격 일치를 형성한다.

해설　비디오 게임이 구매자에게 식료품처럼 중대한 필수품으로 여겨지지 않음을 안다면, 판매자는 비디오 게임에 대해 '높은' 값을 부르지 않으려 할 것이라는 의미로, ④의 **low**를 **high**로 고쳐야 한다.

오답 풀이

선택률	선지 해석 & 오답 풀이
① 3%	**restrictions**(제약)　▶ 판매자와 구매자가 서로의 '재정적 제약'을 안다는 뒷 내용으로 보아 restrictions는 적절하다.
② 5%	**assess**(평가하다)　▶ 상대가 무엇을 필수품 또는 사치품으로 여기는지 이해한다(understands)는 설명과 같은 의미로 assess를 썼다.
③ 8%	**necessity**(필수품)　▶ 사치품과 달리, 식료품처럼 '필수로' 여겨지는 품목을 나타내고자 necessity를 썼다.
⑤ 27%	**similar**(비슷한)　▶ 하나의 특정 경제 계층(a specific economic class)에 속하는 주체들끼리 서로의 제약을 이해할 수 있다는 설명으로 보아 similar은 적합하다.

지문 자세히 보기

01　Bazaar economies feature an apparently flexible price-setting mechanism that sits atop more enduring ties of shared culture. Both the buyer and seller are aware of each other's restrictions.

▶ 판매자와 구매자가 서로의 제약 사항을 잘 이해하고 있는 '상점가 경제'에 관해 설명하는 글이다.

02　In Delhi's bazaars, buyers and sellers can assess to a large extent the financial constraints that other actors have in their everyday life. Each actor belonging to a specific economic class understands what the other sees as a necessity and a luxury.

▶ 특정 경제 계층에 속하는 경제 주체들끼리는 서로에게 무엇이 필수품이고 사치품인지를 구별할 수 있기에, 서로의 재정적 제약 상황을 잘 이해하고 있다는 부연 설명이다.

03　In the case of electronic products like video games, they are not a necessity at the same level as other household purchases such as food items. So, the seller in Delhi's bazaars is careful not to directly ask for very low(→ high) prices for video games because at no point will the buyer see possession of them as an absolute necessity.

▶ '비디오 게임'이 예시로 나온다. 게임은 식료품 같은 필수품이 아니기 때문에, 이러한 구매자의 한계나 선호를 아는 판매자가 비디오 게임에 '높은' 가격을 매길 수 없다는 흐름이다.

04　Access to this type of knowledge establishes a price consensus by relating to each other's preferences and limitations of belonging to a similar cultural and economic universe.

▶ 비슷한 경제문화적 환경 속에 속하여 서로의 니즈와 한계를 잘 알고 있다는 점 때문에 가격 일치도 가능하다는 결론이다.

구문 풀이

Each actor belonging to a specific economic class understands what the other sees as a necessity and a luxury.

→ 여기서 **what**은 의문사로, '무엇을'이라는 의미다.

구문 플러스' what의 용법

의문사 또는 관계사로 쓰일 때 what이 어떻게 해석되는지 기억해 둔다.

① 의문대명사 what: 무엇
No one knows what he does.
아무도 그가 뭘 하는지 모른다.
② 의문형용사 what: 어떤
I know what method he used.
난 그가 어떤 방법을 썼는지 알아.
③ 관계대명사 what: ~한 것
What she said turned out to be a lie.
그녀가 말했던 것은 거짓말로 드러났다.
④ 관계형용사 what: ~한 모든
She gave me what little money she had.
그녀는 자기가 가진 얼마 안 되는 모든 돈을 내게 줬다.

51 정답 ④ 41%　　*2023학년도 6월 모평*

해석　최근 몇 년 동안 전 세계적으로 도시 교통 전문가들은 도시의 자동차 수요에 부응하기보다는 그것을 관리해야 한다는 견해를 대체로 따랐다. 소득 증가는 필연적으로 자동차 보급의 증가로 이어진다. 기후 변화로 인한 불가피성이 없다 하더라도, 인구 밀도가 높은 도시의 물리적 제약과 그에 상응하는 접근성, 이동성, 안전, 대기 오염, 그리고 도시 거주

적합성에 대한 요구 모두가 단지 이러한 증가하는 수요에 부응하기 위해 도로망을 확장한다는 선택권을 제한한다. 결과적으로, 도시가 발전하고 도시의 거주자들이 더 부유해짐에 따라, 사람들이 자동차를 사용하지 '않기로' 결정하도록 설득하는 것이 점점 더 도시 관리자와 계획 설계자들의 핵심 중점 사항이 된다. 걷기, 자전거 타기, 대중교통과 같은 대안적인 선택 사항의 질을 높이는 것이 이 전략의 핵심 요소이다. 하지만 자동차 수요에 부응하는(→ (수요를) 관리하는) 가장 직접적인 접근 방법은 자동차 여행을 더 비싸게 만들거나 행정 규정으로 그것을 제한하는 것이다. 자동차로 하는 이동이 기후 변화의 원인이 된다는 점이 이런 불가피성을 강화한다.

해설 늘어나는 도시 내 자동차 수요에 '맞추는' 것이 아니라 이 수요를 제한 또는 통제하고 '관리하는' 것에 관해 설명하는 글이다. ④가 포함된 문장 또한 자동차로 하는 이동의 비용을 증가시키거나 행정 규정으로 이를 통제하는 구체적 방법을 소개하는 것으로 보아, 자동차의 수요를 '관리한다'는 의미가 되도록 accommodating 대신 managing을 써야 한다.

오답 풀이

선택률	선지 해석 & 오답 풀이
① 12%	**limit**(제한하다) ▶ 도시의 물리적 제약 등 여러 요인 때문에, 순전히 자동차 수요 증가에 응대하고자 도로망을 확장하기는 어렵다는 의미의 문장이다. 따라서 도로망 확장이라는 선택권이 '제한된다'는 의미의 limit은 적절하다.
② 11%	**persuading**(설득하는 것) ▶ 자동차 수요를 관리하기 위해 사람들에게 차를 이용하지 말아달라고 '설득하는 것'을 예로 드는 문맥이므로 persuading은 적절하다.
③ 13%	**alternative**(대안의) ▶ 도보, 자전거 등은 자동차의 '대안'이 맞으므로 alternative는 적절하다.
⑤ 23%	**reinforces**(강화하다) ▶ 자동차가 기후 변화에 기여한다는 사실 또한 자동차 수요를 관리해야 할 당위성을 '강화한다'는 의미로 reinforces가 알맞게 쓰였다.

지문 자세히 보기'

01 In recent years urban transport professionals globally have largely acquiesced to the view that automobile demand in cities needs to be managed rather than accommodated.

▶ 자동차 수요에 '부응하는' 행위와 이를 '통제, 관리'하는 행위가 대비되어 언급된다. 최근에는 '관리'가 필요하다는 견해가 주류였다는 점도 함께 언급된다.

02 Rising incomes inevitably lead to increases in motorization. Even without the imperative of climate change, the physical constraints of densely inhabited cities and the corresponding demands of accessibility, mobility, safety, air pollution, and urban livability all limit the option of expanding road networks purely to accommodate this rising demand.

▶ 기후 변화 때문이 아니더라도 도시의 물리적 한계로 인해 도로망을 확장해 자동차 수요에 대응하기는 어려워졌다(limit)는 내용이다.

03 As a result, as cities develop and their residents become more prosperous, persuading people to choose *not* to use cars becomes an increasingly key focus of city managers and planners. Improving the quality of alternative options, such as walking, cycling, and public transport, is a central element of this strategy.

▶ 'persuading ~'과 'Improving ~'은 모두 자동차 수요를 '관리'하기 위한 구체적 조치의 예시이다.

04 However, the most direct approach to accommodating (→ managing) automobile demand is making motorized travel more expensive or restricting it with administrative rules. The contribution of motorized travel to climate change reinforces this imperative.

▶ 앞에 언급된 조치보다도 더 직접적인 자동차 수요 '관리' 조치를 소개하는 부분이다. 자동차로 하는 이동을 더 비싸게 하거나 행정 규칙으로 제한하는 것은 모두 자동차 수요를 '통제, 관리'하려는 목적과 맞닿는다.

구문 풀이

As a result, as cities develop and their residents become more prosperous, **persuading** people **to choose** *not* to use cars becomes an increasingly key focus of city managers and planners.
→ 동명사 persuading의 목적격보어로 'to choose ~'라는 to부정사구가 나왔다.

구문 플러스' to부정사를 목적격보어로 취하는 동사

allow, ask, cause, encourage, enable, force, persuade, order, tell, teach 등

They generously **allowed** me **to stay**.
그들은 관대하게도 내가 머물도록 허락해 주었다.

She told me **to leave** immediately.
그녀는 나더러 즉시 떠나라고 말했다.

52 정답 ③ 38%   *2022학년도 대수능*

해석 천연 제품들만 투입물로 사용될 수 있는 방식이라 정의되는 '유기농' 방식은 생물권에 해를 덜 끼칠 것이라는 점이 시사되어 왔다. 그러나 '유기농' 경작 방식의 대규모 채택은 많은 주요 작물의 산출량을 감소시키고 생산비를 증가시킬 것이다. 무기질 질소 공급은 많은 비(非)콩과 작물 종의 생산성을 중상 수준으로 유지하는 데 필수적인데, 그것은 질소성 물질의 유기적 공급이 무기 질소 비료보다 흔히 제한적이거나 더 비싸기 때문이다. 게다가, '친환경 거름' 작물로 거름이나 콩과 식물을 광범위하게 사용하는 것에는 이점(→ 제약)이 있다. 많은 경우, 화학 물질이 사용될 수 없으면 잡초 방제가 매우 어렵거나 많은 손일이 필요할 수 있는데, 사회가 부유해짐에 따라 이 작업을 기꺼이 하려는 사람이 더 적을 것이다. 그러나 윤작의 합리적인 사용과 경작과 가축 경영의 특정한 조합과 같이, '유기농' 경작에서 사용되는 몇몇 방식들은 농촌 생태계의 지속 가능성에 중요하게 기여할 수 있다.

해설 ③이 포함된 문장 뒤에서 화학 물질을 사용하지 않고 농사를 지으면 잡초 방제가 어렵고 사람의 일거리가 늘어난다는 말로 유기농 농법의 한계를 설명하고 있다. 따라서 ③에는 benefits 대신 constraints가 들어가야 한다.

오답 풀이

선택률	선지 해석 & 오답 풀이
① 7%	reduce(감소시키다) ▶ 뒤에 '생산비가 증가한다'는 내용이 and로 연결되는 것으로 보아, ①에도 유기농 농법이 생산에 이롭지 못함을 뒷받침하는 단어가 나와야 한다. 따라서 산출량을 '감소시킨다'라는 뜻의 reduce는 적절하다.
② 8%	essential(필수적인) ▶ 'because organic supplies ~'에서 유기 비료의 한계를 언급하며 무기 비료의 '필요성'을 뒷받침하고 있다. 따라서 essential은 적절하다.
④ 36%	fewer(더 적은) ▶ 맥락상 유기 비료를 쓰면 일거리는 더 많아지는데 일을 하려는 사람은 '적어져서' 문제가 있다는 의미이다. 따라서 fewer는 적절하다.
⑤ 12%	contributions(기여) ▶ however로 흐름이 반전되며, 유기농 농법이 그 한계에도 불구하고 '기여'하는 바가 있음을 말하는 문장이다. 따라서 contributions는 적절하다.

지문 자세히 보기

01 It has been suggested that "organic" methods, defined as those in which only natural products can be used as inputs, would be less damaging to the biosphere. Large-scale adoption of "organic" farming methods, however, would reduce yields and increase production costs for many major crops.

▶ 중심 소재로 유기농 농법("organic" methods)을 제시한 뒤, 이것이 환경에는 좋을지라도 생산에는 좋지 않을 수 있다(reduce yields and increase production costs)는 점을 언급하고 있다.

02 Inorganic nitrogen supplies are essential for maintaining moderate to high levels of productivity for many of the non-leguminous crop species, because organic supplies of nitrogenous materials often are either limited or more expensive than inorganic nitrogen fertilizers.

▶ 유기 비료는 공급이 제한적이거나 더 비싸기에 사실상 무기 비료의 사용은 생산량 유지에 필수적이라는 설명이 이어진다. 즉 유기농 농법만으로는 생산에 한계가 있다는 것이다.

03 In addition, there are benefits(→ constraints) to the extensive use of either manure or legumes as "green manure" crops. In many cases, weed control can be very difficult or require much hand labor if chemicals cannot be used, and fewer people are willing to do this work as societies become wealthier.

▶ 첨가의 In addition 뒤로, 앞과 마찬가지로 유기농 농법의 '이점'이 아닌 '한계점'이 언급된다. 화학 물질을 안 쓰면 잡초를 막기도 어렵고 손이 많이 간다는(weed control ~ much hand labor) 부연 설명이 이어진다.

04 Some methods used in "organic" farming, however, such as the sensible use of crop rotations and specific combinations of cropping and livestock enterprises, can make important contributions to the sustainability of rural ecosystems.

▶ 위와 같은 한계에도 불구하고 생태계를 위해서는 유기농 농법이 유의미할 수 있다는 결론으로 글이 마무리된다.

구문 풀이

It **has been suggested** that "organic" methods, defined as those **in which** only natural products can be used as inputs, would be less damaging to the biosphere.

→ has been suggested는 '~되어 왔다'라는 의미의 현재완료 수동태 동사이다.

→ in which는 「전치사 + 관계대명사」 형태로, 뒤에 완전한 절을 수반한다.

구문 플러스 현재완료 수동태

수동을 나타내는 be p.p.의 be동사에 현재완료 시제를 적용하면 「have been p.p.」가 만들어진다.

Since the late 19th century, dogs **have been used** in police work.
19세기 후반부터, 개들은 (계속) 경찰 업무에 사용되어 왔다.

53 정답 ④ 46%　　　　　　　　2022학년도 6월 모평

해석 스포츠는 소비자에게 다른 제품이 좀처럼 일으키지 못하는 종류의 정서적 반응을 촉발시킬 수 있다. 은행 고객이 은행에 대한 충성심을 보여주기 위해 기념품을 구입하거나, 고객이 자동차 보험 회사에 매우 강한 동질감을 가져서 회사 로고로 문신을 한다고 상상해 보라. 우리는 일부 스포츠 추종자들이 선수, 팀, 그리고 그 스포츠 자체에 매우 열정적이어서 그들의 관심이 집착에 아주 가깝다는 것을 알고 있다. 이런 중독은 팬을 팀과 묶어주는 정서적 접착제를 제공하고, 구장에서 일어나는 실패에도 불구하고 충성심을 유지하게 한다. 대부분의 관리자는 스포츠 팬만큼 그들 제품에 열정적인 고객을 가지기를 오직 꿈꾸지만, 스포츠로 인해 촉발되는 감정은 또한 부정적인 영향을 미칠 수 있다. 스포츠의 정서적 격렬함은 조직이 향수와 클럽 전통을 통해 과거에 대한 강한 애착을 가지고 있다는 것을 의미할 수 있다. 그 결과, 조직은 효율성, 생산성 및 변화하는 시장 상황에 신속하게 대응해야 할 필요성을 늘릴(→ 무시할) 수도 있다. 예를 들어, 더 매력적인 이미지를 투사하기 위해 클럽 색깔을 바꾸자는 제안은 그것이 전통과의 관계를 끊기 때문에 무산될 수도 있다.

해설 스포츠의 강한 정서적 반응은 조직이 과거에 대한 애착이 강하다는 뜻일 수도 있다는 내용 뒤로, 마지막 문장에서 전통을 깨는 제안에 동의하지 않는 경우를 예로 들고 있다. 이를 종합할 때, ④가 포함된 문장은 조직이 과거에 대한 애착 때문에 변화의 필요성을 '낮게 평가'할 수도 있다는 의미여야 한다. 따라서 ④의 increase를 ignore로 고쳐야 한다.

선택률	선지 해석 & 오답 풀이
① 6%	**identifying**(동질감을 갖는) ▶ 회사 로고로 문신을 할 만큼 회사에 '동질감'을 갖는다는 뜻으로서 identifying은 적절하다.
② 8%	**passionate**(열정적인) ▶ 뒤의 **that**절에서 선수, 팀, 스포츠 자체에 대한 추종자들의 관심이 집착에 가까워진다고 설명하는 것으로 보아, 이들이 매우 '열정적'이라는 뜻의 passionate는 적절하다.
③ 28%	**failure**(실패) ▶ 경기 중 '실패'에도 불구하고 팬들이 충성심을 유지한다는 의미로 failure를 적절하게 썼다.
⑤ 12%	**defeated**(무산된) ▶ 조직이 과거에 대한 애착과 향수를 느낀다는 말로 보아, 전통과의 단절을 뜻하는 제안이 '무산될' 수도 있다는 의미의 defeated는 적절하다.

지문 자세히 보기'

01 Sport can trigger an emotional response in its consumers of the kind rarely brought forth by other products. Imagine bank customers buying memorabilia to show loyalty to their bank, or consumers identifying so strongly with their car insurance company that they get a tattoo with its logo.

▶ 스포츠가 일으키는 독특한 정서적 반응(an emotional response)을 화제로 언급한 후, Imagine 이하로 예를 든다.

02 We know that some sport followers are so passionate about players, teams and the sport itself that their interest borders on obsession. This addiction provides the emotional glue that binds fans to teams, and maintains loyalty even in the face of on-field failure.

▶ 선수, 팀, 스포츠 자체에 대한 스포츠 팬들의 강한 열정을 설명하는 내용이 이어진다. passionate, obsession, the emotional glue, loyalty가 모두 스포츠 팬들의 열정 또는 충성심을 묘사한다.

03 While most managers can only dream of having customers that are as passionate about their products as sport fans, the emotion triggered by sport can also have a negative impact. Sport's emotional intensity can mean that organisations have strong attachments to the past through nostalgia and club tradition. As a result, they may increase(→ ignore) efficiency, productivity and the need to respond quickly to changing market conditions.

▶ While 이후로 이러한 열정의 부작용(a negative impact)이 언급된다. 강한 열정이 과거에 대한 강한 애착(strong attachments)을 불러일으켜 변화하는 시장 상황에 제대로 대처하지 '못하게' 한다는 것이다. 흐름상 효율성과 생산성을 '높여준다'는 말보다 '무시한다'는 설명이 적합하다.

04 For example, a proposal to change club colours in order to project a more attractive image may be defeated because it breaks a link with tradition.

▶ 위에서 언급한 대로 변화에 대처할 필요성을 '무시하는' 태도로 인해 전통을 깨는 제안이 무산될 수도 있다는 예가 제시된다.

구문 풀이

While most managers can only dream of having customers that are as passionate about their products as sport fans, the emotion triggered by sport can also have a negative impact.

→ 접속사 while은 여기서 '~한 반면에'라는 의미이다.

구문 플러스 접속사 while의 의미

while의 의미: 1) ~하는 동안 2) ~한 반면에

I watched TV **while** I was having lunch.
나는 점심을 먹는 동안 TV를 보았다.

While we'd like to help you, we don't have much time available.
우리도 너를 돕고 싶지만, 여유 시간이 별로 없어.

---

54 정답 ⑤ 54%   *2021학년도 대수능*

해석 편승 효과가 어떻게 발생하는지는 빛의 속도 측정의 역사로 입증된다. 이 속도는 상대성 이론의 기초이기 때문에, 과학에서 가장 자주 면밀하게 측정된 물리량 중 하나이다. 우리가 아는 한, 그 속도는 시간이 흐르는 동안 변함이 없었다. 하지만 1870년부터 1900년까지 모든 실험에서 너무 빠른 속도가 발견되었다. 그러고 나서, 1900년부터 1950년까지는 반대되는 현상이 일어났다 — 모든 실험에서 너무 느린 속도를 발견했다! 결과가 항상 실제 값의 어느 한쪽에 있는 이런 오류는 '편향'이라 불린다. 그것은 아마 시간이 지나면서 실험자들이 자신들이 발견하리라 예상했던 것과 일치하도록 결과를 잠재의식적으로 조정했기 때문에 생겨났을 것이다. 결과가 그들이 예상한 것과 부합하면, 그들은 그것을 취했다. 결과가 부합하지 않으면, 그들은 그것을 버렸다. 그들은 고의로 부정직했던 것이 아니고, 그저 통념에 영향을 받았을 뿐이다. 그 패턴은 누군가가 예상된 것 대신에 실제로 측정된 것을 보고할 용기가 부족했을(→ 있었을) 때에야 바뀌었다.

해설 실험자들은 빛의 속도 값에 대한 통념에 영향을 받았기 때문에 무의식적으로 측정 결괏값을 조정했다는 내용이 마지막 문장 앞까지 전개된다. 이어서 마지막 문장은 이 패턴이 '변화한' 이유를 설명하고 있다. 즉 누군가 실제 결괏값을 보고할 용기를 '지녔을' 때 이러한 패턴이 깨졌다는 의미가 되도록 ⑤의 lacked를 had로 고쳐야 한다.

선택률	선지 해석 & 오답 풀이
① 6%	**quantities**(양) ▶ 빛의 속도는 측정 가능한 양의 일종이므로 quantities는 적절하다.
② 13%	**opposite**(정반대) ▶ 값이 너무 높았던 앞 상황과 반대로 값이 너무 낮았던 때도 있었음이 언급되므로 opposite는 적절하다.
③ 15%	**match**(부합하다) ▶ 뒤에서 결과가 예상과 맞으면 취하고 맞지 않으면 버렸다는 내용이 나오는 것으로 보아, 예상에 '부합하게' 결과를 조정했다는 의미의 match는 적절하다.
④ 12%	**influenced**(영향받은) ▶ 예상되는 값에 맞추어 결과를 조정한 이유가 통념에 '영향을 받았기' 때문이라는 뜻이므로 influenced는 적절하다.

01 How the bandwagon effect occurs is demonstrated by the history of measurements of the speed of light. Because this speed is the basis of the theory of relativity, it's one of the most frequently and carefully measured quantities in science.

▶ 편승 효과를 설명하고자 빛의 속도 측정(measurements of the speed of light)의 예를 언급하고 있다.

02 As far as we know, the speed hasn't changed over time. However, from 1870 to 1900, all the experiments found speeds that were too high. Then, from 1900 to 1950, the opposite happened — all the experiments found speeds that were too low!

▶ 빛의 속도는 변한 적이 없지만, 시대에 따라 측정 결괏값은 너무 높은(too high) 값과 너무 낮은(too low) 값을 오간 적이 있다는 설명이 이어진다.

03 This kind of error, where results are always on one side of the real value, is called "bias." It probably happened because over time, experimenters subconsciously adjusted their results to match what they expected to find.

▶ 결괏값이 왔다 갔다 했던 이유가 언급되고 있다. 실험자들이 '예상되는' 값에 맞추어 실험 결과를 조정했기(adjusted their results) 때문이라는 것이다.

04 If a result fit what they expected, they kept it. If a result didn't fit, they threw it out. They weren't being intentionally dishonest, just influenced by the conventional wisdom.

▶ 실험 결과의 조정이 일어난 이유가 제시된다. 실험자들이 부정직해서가 아니라, 이들이 단지 통념에 영향을 받았기(influenced ~) 때문이라고 한다.

05 The pattern only changed when someone lacked(→ had) the courage to report what was actually measured instead of what was expected.

▶ changed에서 글의 흐름이 반전된다. 누군가 기대되는 값이 아닌 실제 값을 보고할 용기를 '냈을' 때 상황의 전환이 일어났다는 것이다. 따라서 용기가 '부족했다'라는 표현 대신 용기가 '있었다'라는 표현이 적절하다.

구문 풀이

How the bandwagon effect occurs is demonstrated by the history of measurements of the speed of light.

→ 명사절 주어(How ~ occurs)는 단수 취급한다(is).

구문 플러스+ 구 또는 절인 주어의 수일치

주어가 구 또는 절이면 단수 취급한다.

Sleeping well is important to be healthy. (주어=동명사구)
잘 자는 것은 건강해지는 데 중요하다.

That she will pass the test is certain. (주어=명사절)
그녀가 시험을 통과할 것이 확실하다.

---

55 정답 ③ 69%　　　　　　　　　　2021학년도 6월 모평

해석 덩어리로 나누는 것은 음악의 인식에서 필수적이다. 만일 우리가 그것을 한 음 한 음 우리의 뇌에서 부호화해야 한다면 우리는 가장 간단한 동요보다 더 복잡한 것은 어느 것이든 악전고투 끝에 이해하게 될 것이다. 물론, 기량이 뛰어난 대부분의 음악가들은 한 음도 틀리지 않고 수천 개의 음을 포함하는 작품을 완전히 외워서 연주할 수 있다. 그렇지만 겉보기에는 굉장한 것 같은 이러한 기억의 성취는 보통 말하는 그런 개별적인 음을 기억하는 것이 아니라 음악적인 '과정'을 기억함으로써 일어날 것 같지 않게(→ 가능하게) 되는 것이다. 만일 피아니스트에게 모차르트 소나타를 41번 마디로부터 시작해 달라고 요청하면, 그녀는 아마도 그 음악을 처음부터 머릿속으로 재생해서 그 마디까지 와야 할 것이다. 그 악보는 그저 그녀의 머릿속에 펼쳐져 있어서 어떤 임의의 지점부터 읽힐 수 있는 것이 아니다. 그것은 흡사 여러분이 어떻게 운전해서 직장까지 가는지 설명하는 것과 같다. 여러분은 추상적인 목록으로 길의 이름을 열거하는 것이 아니고, 마음속에서 그것을 되짚어감으로써 여러분의 경로를 구성해야 한다. 음악가들이 리허설 중에 실수한다면, 그들은 한 악구의 시작부로 되돌아간 뒤 다시 시작한다('2절부터 다시 합시다').

해설 ③이 포함된 문장 뒤에서 음악가들은 특정 지점부터 연주를 해야 하면 처음부터 머릿속에서 음악을 되짚어본다고 했다. 즉 음악은 한 음 한 음이 아닌 과정으로 기억되기에, 비록 개별적인 음이 몇천 개에 달하는 곡이어도 음악가들이 외워서 연주할 수 '있다'는 것이다. 따라서 ③의 improbable을 possible로 고쳐야 한다.

오답 풀이

선택률	선지 해석 & 오답 풀이
① 4%	**struggle**(악전고투하다) ▶ 음악은 음 단위가 아닌 '덩어리' 단위로 인식된다는 설명으로 보아, 한 음 한 음 이해하는 것은 '고생스럽다'는 의미의 **struggle**은 적절하다.
② 4%	**memory**(기억) ▶ 뒤에서 '놀라운 기억(recall)의 성취'를 언급하는 것으로 보아 온전히 '기억'해서 곡을 연주해낸다는 의미의 **memory**는 적절하다.
④ 12%	**mentally**(머릿속으로) ▶ 자동차로 출근하는 길을 설명할 때 머릿속으로 길을 되짚어보듯이(mentally retracing it) 음악 또한 혼자 기억해보는 과정을 묘사하고자 **mentally**를 적절하게 썼다.
⑤ 9%	**start**(시작) ▶ 'If you ask a pianist ~'에서 피아니스트는 특정 마디로부터 연주해야 할 때 '처음부터' 음악을 되짚어본다고 한다. 공연 리허설의 경우도 비슷함을 언급하고자 **start**를 적절하게 썼다.

01 Chunking is vital for cognition of music. If we had to encode it in our brains note by note, we'd struggle to make sense of anything more complex than the simplest children's songs.

▶ 음악의 인식(cognition of music)이 주요 화제이다. 음악은 음 단위가 아니라 일정한 덩어리(Chunking)로 나뉘어 인식된다는 내용이 제시된다.

02 Of course, most accomplished musicians can play compositions containing many thousands of notes entirely from memory, without a note out of place. But this seemingly awesome accomplishment of recall is made improbable(→ possible) by remembering the musical *process*, not the individual notes as such.

▶ 위의 Chunking이 the musical *process*로 재진술되며, 음이 많은 음악이 실수 없이 연주될 수 '있는' 까닭을 설명한다. 즉 음악가들은 한 음 한 음이 아닌 '과정'으로 음악을 기억한다는 것이다.

03 If you ask a pianist to start a Mozart sonata from bar forty-one, she'll probably have to mentally replay the music from the start until reaching that bar — the score is not simply laid out in her mind, to be read from any random point.

▶ 피아니스트는 특정 마디부터 연주해달라는 부탁을 받으면 처음부터 그 음악을 머릿속에서 죽 따라오며 그 마디를 기억하려 한다는 예시가 언급된다. mentally replay the music from the start는 음악가가 위에서 언급된 음악의 '과정'을 되살려보는 행위로 이해할 수 있다.

04 It's rather like describing how you drive to work: you don't simply recite the names of roads as an abstract list, but have to construct your route by mentally retracing it. When musicians make a mistake during rehearsal, they wind back to the start of a musical phrase ('let's take it from the second verse') before restarting.

▶ mentally retracing it과 `wind back ~`이 위의 `mentally replay ~`를 재진술한다. 즉 음악가는 어떤 덩어리의 시작부터 되돌아가 음악이 전개되는 과정을 따라가며 음악을 기억하고 연주한다는 내용이 반복된다.

구문 풀이

If we **had to encode** it in our brains note by note, **we'd struggle** to make sense of anything more complex than the simplest children's songs.

→ 「if + 주어 + 과거 동사 ~, 주어 + 조동사 과거형 + 동사원형 ~」은 가정법 과거 구문으로, 현재 사실의 반대를 가정한다.

구문 플러스⁺ 가정법 과거

가정법 과거는 과거시제를 이용해 현재 사실과 반대되는 상황을 가정한다. 문법 문제로 나오면 주로 시제 오류를 묻는다.

If I **knew** the answer, I **could tell** you.
내가 답을 안다면, 너에게 말해줄 텐데.

= As I don't know the answer, I can't tell you.
내가 답을 몰라서 네게 말해줄 수 없어.

---

56 정답 ② 31% — *2020학년도 6월 모평*

해석 때로는 신임을 얻지 못한다는 인식이 자기 성찰에 필요한 동기를 제공할 수 있다. 직장에서 동료들이 자신에게 공유된 책무를 믿고 맡기지 않고 있다는 사실을 깨달은 직원은 성찰을 통해 자신이 지속적으로 다른 사람들을 실망하게 했거나 이전의 약속들을 이행하지 못했던 분야를 찾아낼 수 있다. 그러면 그녀에 대한 다른 사람들의 불신은 그녀가 그

들의 신임을 더 받을 만하게 해 주는 방식으로 자기 몫의 직무를 수행하지 못하게 할(→ 하도록 동기부여) 수 있다. 하지만 신뢰할 만하고 믿을 만한 사람이 되려는 노력을 성실하게 하는 사람에 대한 불신은 혼란스러울 수 있고, 그 사람이 자신의 인식을 의심하고 스스로를 불신하게 할 수 있다. 예를 들어 밤에 외출할 때 부모가 의심하고 믿어주지 않는 십 대 아이를 생각해 보라. 비록 그녀가 자신의 계획에 대해 솔직해 왔고 합의된 규칙은 어떤 것도 어기고 있지 않을지라도, 존경할 만한 도덕적 주체로서의 그녀의 정체성은 속임수와 배신을 예상하는 널리 스며 있는 부모의 태도에 의해 손상된다.

해설 첫 두 문장에서 신뢰받지 못하고 있음을 알 때 사람들은 자신을 돌아보게 된다고 한다. ②가 포함된 문장은 그러한 성찰 이후 사람들이 신뢰를 더 얻을 만한 방식으로 행동하지 '않는' 것이 아니라 '기꺼이 행동하려' 한다는 의미가 되어야 한다. 따라서 ②의 forbid를 motivate로 고쳐야 한다.

오답 풀이

선택률	선지 해석 & 오답 풀이
① 5%	realizes(깨닫다) ▶ 첫 문장에서 신임을 얻지 못하고 있음을 알(awareness)' 때 자아 성찰이 이뤄진다고 하므로, 불신을 '깨달을' 때 상황을 돌아보게 된다는 의미의 realizes는 적절하다.
③ 30%	sincere(성실한) ▶ 스스로 믿을 만한 사람이 되고자 '성실히' 노력하는 사람에게는 불신이 해가 된다는 의미로 sincere를 적절하게 썼다.
④ 18%	suspicious(의심하는) ▶ and 앞뒤는 비슷한 표현이 연결되는데, 뒤에 and distrustful이 나오는 것으로 보아 suspicious는 적절하다.
⑤ 13%	breaking(깨는) ▶ 규칙을 '어기지' 않으려 노력하는데 돌아오는 것이 불신이면 도덕적 주체로서의 정체성이 손상된다는 뜻으로 breaking을 적절하게 썼다.

지문 자세히 보기⁺

01 Sometimes the awareness that one is distrusted can provide the necessary incentive for self-reflection.

▶ 신뢰받지 못한다는 인식(the awareness)과 자아 성찰(self-reflection)에 관한 글이다.

02 An employee who realizes she isn't being trusted by her co-workers with shared responsibilities at work might, upon reflection, identify areas where she has consistently let others down or failed to follow through on previous commitments. Others' distrust of her might then forbid(→ motivate) her to perform her share of the duties in a way that makes her more worthy of their trust.

▶ 동료들로부터 신뢰를 얻지 못하는 상태임을 알 때 자아 성찰(reflection)이 이루어지는 것이므로, 이 성찰 뒤에 신뢰를 얻을 만한(more worthy ~) 방식으로 행동하려는 '동기가 생긴다'는 설명이 적합하다.

03 But distrust of one who is sincere in her efforts to be a trustworthy and dependable person can be disorienting and might cause her to doubt her own perceptions and to distrust herself.

▶ 흐름 반전의 **But** 뒤로, 신뢰받지 못한다는 믿음이 부정적으로 작용하는(**cause her to doubt ~**) 경우가 언급된다.

04 Consider, for instance, a teenager whose parents are suspicious and distrustful when she goes out at night; even if she has been forthright about her plans and is not breaking any agreed-upon rules, her identity as a respectable moral subject is undermined by a pervasive parental attitude that expects deceit and betrayal.

▶ 바르게 행동하려는 자녀에게 부모가 의심과 불신을 보이면 (**suspicious and distrustful, expects deceit and betrayal**) 자녀의 도덕적 주체로서의 정체성이 약화된다는 설명으로 글이 마무리된다. 이전 문장의 'doubt ~ and ~ distrust herself'가 'her identity ~ undermined'로 바뀌어 표현되었다.

구문 풀이

An employee who realizes she isn't being trusted by her co-workers with shared responsibilities at work might, upon reflection, identify areas **where** she has consistently let others down or failed to follow through on previous commitments.

→ 장소 선행사인 **areas**를 꾸미고자 관계부사 **where**가 쓰였다.

구문 플러스 관계부사 where

where는 장소의 선행사를 수식하며, 완전한 절을 수반한다. area, region 등 물리적 공간의 명사뿐 아니라 situation, case 등 추상적 공간의 선행사도 where 앞에 나올 수 있다.

This is **the palace where** the royal family stays.
여기는 왕족이 머무는 궁전이다.
We are in **a situation where** we can't do anything.
우리는 우리가 아무것도 할 수 없는 상황에 있다.

유형 플러스 어휘 추론

문맥상 적절한 어휘 또는 적절하지 않은 어휘를 고르는 유형이다. 반의어 관계에 유의하여 어휘의 적절성을 파악하는 것이 핵심이다.

・문제 해결 Tip.
① 글의 핵심 소재 및 중심 내용을 파악한다.
② 중심 내용에 근거해 선택지 어휘의 쓰임을 검토한다.
③ 적절한 어휘를 고르는 경우, (A)~(C)에 각각 반의어 쌍이 주어진다. 사전적 의미로 반의어가 아니더라도 문맥상 반의어일 때도 많으므로 주의가 필요하다.
④ 적절하지 않은 어휘를 고르는 경우, 증가-감소, 긍정-부정 등 명확하게 반의어가 떠오르는 선택지를 눈여겨 보도록 한다. 최근 경향을 살펴보면, 밑줄 친 단어 자체는 쉽지만, 주제를 예시에 적용해야 풀 수 있도록 출제하여 난이도를 높이고 있다.

57 정답 ④ 45%   2024학년도 9월 모평

해석 1945년 이후 제2차 세계대전 이후 유례없는 경제 성장은 건축 붐과 중심 도시에서 새로운 교외 지역으로의 대규모 이주를 부추겼다. 교외 지역은 자동차에 훨씬 더 많이 의존했고, 이는 주로 대중교통에 의존하던 것에서 자가용으로의 전환을 알렸다. 이것은 곧 더 나은 고속도로와 초고속도로의 건설과 대중교통의 감소, 심지어 쇠퇴까지로 이어졌다. 이러한 모든 변화와 함께 여가의 사유화가 이뤄졌다. 더 많은 사람이 내부 공간이 더 넓어지고 아름다운 외부 정원이 딸린 자기 집을 갖게 됨에 따라, 그들의 휴양과 여가 시간은 점점 더 집, 또는 기껏해야 인근 지역에 집중되었다. 이러한 집 중심의 여가에서 주요한 활동 한 가지는 TV 시청이었다. 사람들은 더 이상 영화를 보러 전차를 타고 극장까지 갈 필요가 없었고, 유사한 오락이 텔레비전을 통해 무료로 더 편리하게 이용 가능해졌다.

해설 경제 성장으로 사람들이 집과 자가용을 갖추게 되면서 여가가 '집을 중심으로' 발달하게 되었다는 내용이다. 따라서 빈칸에 들어갈 말로 가장 적절한 것은 ④ '사유화'이다.

오답 풀이

선택률	선지 해석 & 오답 풀이
① 13%	downfall(몰락) ▶ 글에 따르면 여가는 오히려 이전과 다른 방향으로 '발전'했다.
② 18%	uniformity(획일성) ▶ 여가의 획일화는 언급되지 않았다.
③ 12%	restoration(회복) ▶ 여가가 시들해지거나 없어졌다가 '회복'되었다는 내용이 아니다.
⑤ 12%	customization(맞춤화) ▶ 여가를 집에서 따로 즐길 수 있다는 내용만 다룰 뿐, 개인마다 '맞춤화'된 선택권이 있다는 내용은 없다.

지문 자세히 보기

01 In the post-World War II years after 1945, unparalleled economic growth fueled a building boom and a massive migration from the central cities to the new suburban areas.

▶ 빈칸 앞까지는 모두 배경 상황을 설명한다. 2차 대전 이후 폭발적 경제 성장이 이뤄지면서 교외로 인구가 분산되었다는 내용이 제시된다.

02 The suburbs were far more dependent on the automobile, signaling the shift from primary dependence on public transportation to private cars. Soon this led to the construction of better highways and freeways and the decline and even loss of public transportation.

▶ 교외는 교통이 중요하기 때문에 사람들은 자가용을 구비하기 시작했고, 도로가 함께 발달하면서 대중교통은 도리어 축소되었다는 내용이다.

03 With all of these changes came a privatization of leisure. As more people owned their own homes, with more space inside and lovely yards outside, their recreation and leisure time was increasingly centered around the home or, at most, the neighborhood.

▶ 빈칸 문장에서 비로소 '여가'라는 핵심어가 등장한다. 이어서 빈칸 뒤는 여가가 '집'과 '인근 지역'에 집중되기 시작했다고 설명한다.

04 One major activity of this home-based leisure was watching television. No longer did one have to ride the trolly to the theater to watch a movie; similar entertainment was available for free and more conveniently from television.

▶ 위의 'centered around the home ~'을 this home-based leisure라는 말로 요약했다. 이 요약과 같은 말이 빈칸에도 들어가야 한다.

구문 풀이

No longer did one have to ride the trolly to the theater to watch a movie; **similar entertainment was** available for free and more conveniently from television.

→ 세미콜론(;) 앞뒤로 문장이 연결되었다. 참고로 세미콜론 앞은 「부정어구 + did + 주어 + 동사원형」 어순의 도치 구문이다.

구문 플러스 문장을 연결하는 세미콜론(;)

문장 중간의 세미콜론은 and, but, so 등의 의미로 문장과 문장을 연결한다.

Martha has gone to the library; her sister has gone to play soccer.
Martha는 도서관에 갔고, 그녀의 언니는 축구를 하러 갔어.

58 정답 ④ 51%   2023학년도 9월 모평

해석 팬은 감정 그 자체를 느낀다. 그들은 제공된다고 보이는 것 이상의 의미를 만든다. 그들은 정체성과 경험을 만들고, 다른 사람들과 공유하기 위해 그들만의 예술적 창작물을 만든다. 한 사람은 개인적인 팬이 되어, '어떤 스타와 이상적인 관계, 즉 강한 추억과 향수의 감정'을 느끼며, '자아감 형성을 위해 수집'하는 등의 활동을 할 수 있다. 그러나 더 흔히 개인적인 경험은 애착을 공유하는 다른 사람들이 그들의 애정의 대상을 중심으로 교제하는 사회적 상황에 끼워 넣어져 있다. 팬덤의 많은 즐거움은 다른 팬들과 관계를 맺는 데서 온다. 1800년대의 보스턴 사람들은 일기에 쓰기를, 콘서트에 모인 군중의 일부가 되는 것이 참석하는 즐거움의 일부라고 했다. 팬이 사랑하는 것은 그들의 팬덤의 대상이라기보다, 그 애정이 제공하는 서로에 대한 애착(그리고 서로 간의 차이)이라는 강력한 주장이 제기될 수 있다.

해설 'But, more often, ~' 문장에서 팬으로서의 사적인 경험은 팬덤을 공유하는 다른 사람들과 교제하는 사회적 상황과 맞물려 있다고 한다. 이어서 빈칸 뒤에서도 콘서트 참여의 기쁨은 군중의 일부가 된다는 데 있다는 기록을 예로 들어, 팬들 간 관계 맺음에 관해 언급하고 있다. 따라서 빈칸에 들어갈 말로 가장 적절한 것은 ④ '다른 팬들과 관계를 맺는 데서 온다'이다.

오답 풀이

선택률	선지 해석 & 오답 풀이
① 13%	세계적인 스타들 간의 협업으로 강화된다 ▶ 스타끼리 협업한다는 내용은 언급되지 않았다.
② 20%	스타와 자주 사적인 연락을 나누는 데서 기인한다 ▶ 스타와 따로 연락한다는 내용은 언급되지 않았다.
③ 11%	팬이 자신의 우상과 함께 나이 들어 가면서 깊어진다 ▶ 스타와 팬이 함께 나이 든다는 내용은 언급되지 않았다.
⑤ 5%	스타가 미디어에 등장하여 고양된다 ▶ 스타가 미디어에 나온다는 내용은 언급되지 않았다.

지문 자세히 보기

01 Fans feel for feeling's own sake. They make meanings beyond what seems to be on offer. They build identities and experiences, and make artistic creations of their own to share with others. A person can be an individual fan, feeling an "idealized connection with a star, strong feelings of memory and nostalgia," and engaging in activities like "collecting to develop a sense of self."

▶ 팬 활동이 화제로 제시된다. 팬들은 팬 활동을 통해 자기 정체성을 확립하거나, 자기만의 창작물을 만들어보기도 하고, 스타와의 관계를 상상해보기도 하면서 사적인 경험을 즐길 수 있다는 내용이 언급된다.

02 But, more often, individual experiences are embedded in social contexts where other people with shared attachments socialize around the object of their affections. Much of the pleasure of fandom comes from being connected to other fans. In their diaries, Bostonians of the 1800s described being part of the crowds at concerts as part of the pleasure of attendance.

▶ But 뒤로 팬 활동의 큰 부분을 차지하는 것이 '다른 팬들과의 사회적 관계'임이 언급된다. being part of the crowds at concerts는 social contexts의 예시이다.

03 A compelling argument can be made that what fans love is less the object of their fandom than the attachments to (and differentiations from) one another that those affections afford.

▶ 결국 팬들이 사랑하는 것은 팬덤의 대상인 스타보다도 팬들끼리의 애착 관계(the attachments to ~ one another)일 수 있다는 주장을 언급하고 있다.

구문 풀이

A compelling argument can be made that what fans love is **less** the object of their fandom **than** the attachments to (and differentiations from) one another that those affections afford.

→「less A than B」는 'A라기보다 B인'이라는 뜻이다. A, B 자리에 둘 다 명사구가 나왔다.

구문 플러스 less A than B

less A than B = not so much A as B = A라기보다 B인

Kim is **less** a scientist **than** a businessperson.
Kim은 과학자라기보다는 사업가다.
The task was **not so much** unfinished **as** unfinishable.
그 일은 미완성된 것이라기보다는, 완성할 수 없는 것이었다.

---

59 정답 ④ 34%　　　　　*2023학년도 6월 모평*

해석 형식주의의 관점에서 문학에 관해 쓰고자 하는 비평가는 먼저 글의 모든 요소를 개별적으로 검토하고 그것들이 모여서 하나의 예술 작품을 만드는 방식에 대해 질문하는 면밀하고도 주의 깊은 독자가 되어야 한다. 작품의 자율성을 존중하는 그러한 독자는 작품의 외부나 너머가 아니라 내부를 들여다봄으로써 작품에 대한 이해를 달성한다. 가령 역사적 시대, 작가의 일대기, 또는 문학적 양식을 검토하는 대신, 그 사람은 글이 자족적인 실체이며, 자신은 그 글이 스스로를 드러내도록 해주는 지배적인 원칙을 찾고 있다는 추정으로 글에 접근할 것이다. 예를 들어, James Joyce의 단편 소설인 'Araby' 속의 등장인물들과 그가 개인적으로 알았던 사람들과의 연관성은 흥미로울 수도 있겠지만, 형식주의자에게 그것들은 이야기가 어떻게 의미를 만들어내는지를 이해하는 데 있어 이야기 안에 포함된 다른 정보보다 덜 적절하다.

해설 빈칸 뒤에서 형식주의자는 문학을 읽을 때 시대상이나 작가의 일대기 등등을 고려하는 대신 글 자체가 자족적인 실체라고 보고 글 내부의 정보에 충실하려 한다는 내용이 전개되고 있다. 따라서 빈칸에 들어갈 말로 가장 적절한 것은 ④ '작품의 외부나 너머가 아니라 내부를 들여다봄'이다.

오답 풀이

선택률	선지 해석 & 오답 풀이
① 21%	자기 자신을 작품 안팎에 모두 놓음 ▶ 역사적 시대, 작가 생애, 문학적 양식 등 작품 '외부'에 있는 정보는 형식주의자가 찾는 작품의 의미와 덜 관련된 요소라고 하였다.
② 15%	작품과 세상 사이에서 중간 위치를 찾음 ▶ 형식주의자가 작품과 (현실의) 세상 사이 중간에 위치한다는 내용은 글을 통해 알 수 없다.
③ 21%	그 안에 드러난 역사적인 사실을 찾아봄 ▶ 역사적 사실이나 시대상은 형식주의자의 관심사가 아니라는 내용이 빈칸 뒤에 나온다.
⑤ 10%	작품 속 등장인물의 문화적 관련성을 탐구함 ▶ 문화적 관련성은 언급되지 않았다.

지문 자세히 보기

01 The critic who wants to write about literature from a formalist perspective must first be a close and careful reader who examines all the elements of a text individually and questions how they come together to create a work of art.

▶ 형식주의적 문학 비평에 관해 설명하는 글이다.

02 Such a reader, who respects the autonomy of a work, achieves an understanding of it by looking inside it, not outside it or beyond it.

▶ 이 관점은 작품의 '자율성'을 중시한다는 설명으로 보아, 작품 자체에 집중하는 관점임을 알 수 있다.

03 Instead of examining historical periods, author biographies, or literary styles, for example, he or she will approach a text with the assumption that it is a self-contained entity and that he or she is looking for the governing principles that allow the text to reveal itself.

▶ 시대상, 작가 생애, 문학 양식 등 작품 '외적인' 정보는 부수적으로 취급되며, 작품 자체의 내부 정보가 작품을 이해하는 데 충분한 자족적 실체로 여겨진다는 설명이 뒤따른다.

04 For example, the correspondences between the characters in James Joyce's short story "Araby" and the people he knew personally may be interesting, but for the formalist they are less relevant to understanding how the story creates meaning than are other kinds of information that the story contains within itself.

▶ 'the correspondences ~ he knew personally'는 작품 외부의 부수적 정보에 관한 구체적인 예이며, other kinds of information과 문맥상 대비된다. 즉 작품 속 인물과 작가가 실제 알았던 인물 사이의 연관성은 흥미로운 정보일 수는 있지만, 작품 '내부의' 다른 정보보다는 '덜 중요하게' 여겨진다는 설명이 일관성 있게 제시된다.

구문 풀이

For example, the correspondences between the characters in James Joyce's short story "Araby" and the people he knew personally may be interesting, but for the formalist they are **less relevant** to understanding how the story creates meaning **than are other kinds of information** that the story contains within itself.
→ 「less + 원급 + than(~보다 덜 …한)」 구문의 than 뒤로 주어와 동사가 도치되었다.

구문 플러스' as/than 도치

비교구문의 as/than 뒤로 이어지는 「주어 + 동사」는 도치되기도 한다. 단, 대명사 주어는 도치되지 않는다.

My brother plays more mobile games **than do his friends**.
내 남동생은 자기 친구들보다 더 많은 모바일 게임을 한다.

My brother plays more mobile games **than I do**. (도치 ×)
내 남동생은 나보다 더 많은 모바일 게임을 한다.

60 정답 ① 50%　　　　　　　　　　*2022학년도 대수능*

해석 유머는 실제적인 이탈뿐만 아니라 인식의 이탈을 포함한다. 어떤 것이 재미있기만 하면, 우리는 잠깐 그것이 진짜인지 허구인지, 진실인지 거짓인지에 관해 관심을 두지 않는다. 이러한 이유로 우리는 재미있는 이야기를 하는 사람들에게 상당한 여지를 준다. 만약 그들이 상황의 어리석음을 과장하거나 심지어 몇 가지 세부 사항을 꾸며서라도 추가 웃음을 얻고 있다면, 우리는 그들에게 기꺼이 희극적 허용, 일종의 시적 허용을 허락한다. 실제로, 재미있는 이야기를 듣고 있는 누군가가 '아니야, 그는 스파게티를 키보드와 모니터에 쏟은 것이 아니라 키보드에만 쏟았어.'라며 말하는 사람을 바로잡으려고 하면, 그는 아마 듣고 있는 다른 사람들에게서 방해하지 말라는 말을 들을 것이다. 유머를 만드는 사람은 사람들의 머릿속에 생각을 집어넣고 있는데, 그 생각이 가져올 재미를 위해서이지 정확한 정보를 제공하기 위해서가 아니다.

해설 'If they are getting extra laughs ~'에서 상황을 과장하거나 세부적인 내용을 일부 꾸며내서라도 웃음을 더 유발하려 한다면 희극적 허용이 용인된다고 한다. 이어서 예시에서는 이때 정보를 '정확하게' 수정하려는 사람이 오히려 가만 있으라는 요구를 받게 된다고 한다. 이러한 흐름으로 보아, 마지막 문장은 유머를 말하는 상황에서 '사실적인' 정보 전달보다 재미가 우선시된다는 의미일 것이다. 따라서 빈칸에 들어갈 말로 가장 적절한 것은 ① '정확한'이다.

오답 풀이

선택률	선지 해석 & 오답 풀이
② 29%	detailed(세부적인) ▶ 본문의 details를 이용해 만든 함정 선택지이다. 유머에서는 정보가 '사실인지' 아닌지가 중요하지 않다는 글의 요지상, 정보의 '자세함'보다는 '정확함'을 부정하는 것이 바람직하다.
③ 10%	useful(유용한) ▶ 정보의 유용성에 관해서는 언급되지 않는다.
④ 7%	additional(추가적인) ▶ 추가적 정보에 관해서는 언급되지 않는다.
⑤ 5%	alternative(다른, 대안의) ▶ 다른 정보에 관해서는 언급되지 않는다.

지문 자세히 보기'

01 Humour involves not just practical disengagement but cognitive disengagement. As long as something is funny, we are for the moment not concerned with whether it is real or fictional, true or false.

▶ 유머(Humour)의 인식적 이탈이 주된 내용으로, 'not concerned ~'가 인식적 이탈의 의미를 설명한다. 어떤 것이 웃기다면 우리는 그 내용이 사실인지 아닌지는 신경 쓰지 않는다는 것이다.

02 This is why we give considerable leeway to people telling funny stories. If they are getting extra laughs by exaggerating the silliness of a situation or even by making up a few details, we are happy to grant them comic licence, a kind of poetic licence.

▶ considerable leeway와 comic licence는 문맥상 동의어이다. 유머에서의 희극적 '허용'은 상황을 과장하거나 세부 사항을 꾸며내는 것을 가능케 한다는 보충 설명이 이어진다.

03 Indeed, someone listening to a funny story who tries to correct the teller — 'No, he didn't spill the spaghetti on the keyboard and the monitor, just on the keyboard' — will probably be told by the other listeners to stop interrupting.

▶ 예시로 주제를 뒷받침하고 있다. 유머를 듣던 누군가가 정보를 고쳐 주려고(correct) 하면 방해하는(interrupting) 것으로 여겨진다는 내용으로 보아, '사실적인' 정보 전달은 유머의 목적이 아니라는 요지를 확인할 수 있다.

04 The creator of humour is putting ideas into people's heads for the pleasure those ideas will bring, not to provide accurate information.

▶ 빈칸은 유머의 목적이 '아닌' 것에 대한 설명이므로, '사실적인, 정확한' 정보 전달에 관한 내용이어야 한다.

구문 풀이

As long as something is funny, we are for the moment not concerned with **whether** it is real or fictional, true or false.

→ whether가 이끄는 명사절이 be not concerned with(~에 관심을 두다)의 목적어 역할을 한다.

구문 플러스' 접속사 whether

whether는 '~인지 아닌지'라는 의미의 명사절 접속사이다. whether가 이끄는 절은 문장 속에서 주어, 타동사의 목적어, 전치사의 목적어, 보어 역할을 한다.

Whether she will come is a question to everyone.
= It is a question to everyone **whether** she will come.
그녀가 올지 말지는 모두에게 의문이다.

We wonder **whether(=if)** she will come.
우리는 그녀가 올 것인지 모르겠다.

We are all concerned with **whether** she will come.
우리 모두는 그녀가 올 것인지 아닌지에 관심을 두고 있다.

---

61 정답 ② 46% *2022학년도 9월 모평*

해석 TV를 보는 것처럼 평범한 행동일지라도 어떤 사람들이 주의를 딴 데로 돌려 고통스러운 자각에서 벗어나는 방법이 될 수 있다. 이 생각을 검증하기 위해, Sophia Moskalenko와 Steven Heine은 참가자들에게 시험 성적에 관한 거짓 피드백을 주었고, 그런 다음 연구의 다음 부분으로 각각 TV 앞에 앉아 비디오를 시청하게 했다. 음악 사운드트랙과 함께 자연의 장면을 보여 주는 비디오가 나오자, 실험자는 이것이 잘못된 비디오라고 소리쳤고, 아마도 제대로 된 것을 가지러 가면서, 비디오가 재생될 때 참가자를 홀로 남겨두었다. (시험 성적에 관하여) 낙제라는 피드백을 받았던 참가자들은 스스로 성공했다고 생각하는 참가자들보다 훨씬 더 오래 비디오를 시청했다. 연구자들은 텔레비전 시청을 통해 주의를 딴 데로 돌리는 것이 고통스러운 실패나 자신과 자기 안내 지침 사이의 불일치와 관련된 불편함을 효과적으로 완화할 수 있다고 결론지었다. 이와 대조적으로, 성공한 참가자들은 자기 자신과 관련된 생각에서 주의가 딴 데로 돌려지기를 거의 바라지 않았다!

해설 실험 결과에 따르면 시험 성적에 관해 부정적 피드백을 받은 사람들은 영상 시청으로 주의를 분산해 자기 자신에 관한 생각을 피하려 했다고 한다. 따라서 빈칸에 들어갈 말로 가장 적절한 것은 ② '주의를 딴 데로 돌려 고통스러운 자각에서 벗어나는'이다.

오답 풀이

선택률	선지 해석 & 오답 풀이
① 12%	가까운 동료들이 주는 불편한 피드백을 무시하는 ▶ '가까운 동료'로부터 피드백을 받는다는 내용은 언급되지 않았다.
③ 20%	매체로부터 건설적인 피드백을 받는 ▶ 매체로부터 피드백을 얻는다는 내용은 없다.
④ 11%	분산된 주의력을 특정 과업에 다시 집중시키는 ▶ 자기 자신이 아닌, 과업에 집중하는 경우에 관해서는 언급하지 않는다.
⑤ 12%	강렬한 자아 성찰에 몰입하는 ▶ 자아 성찰을 '피한다'는 말이 적합하다.

지문 자세히 보기'

01 Even as mundane a behavior as watching TV may be a way for some people to escape painful self-awareness through distraction.

▶ 예시 앞에 제시된 주제문이다. 고통스러운 자기 인식을 피할 목적으로 주의를 돌리는 상황을 설명하는 글이다.

02 To test this idea, Sophia Moskalenko and Steven Heine gave participants false feedback about their test performance, and then seated each one in front of a TV set to watch a video as the next part of the study. When the video came on, showing nature scenes with a musical soundtrack, the experimenter exclaimed that this was the wrong video and went supposedly to get the correct one, leaving the participant alone as the video played.

▶ 주제를 뒷받침하는 실험이 소개된다. 실험 참가자들은 시험 성과에 대한 거짓된 피드백을 받은 후, 비디오가 틀어진 방에 혼자 남겨졌다는 설명이 이어진다. 여기서 비디오는 distraction의 예시이다.

03 The participants who had received failure feedback watched the video much longer than those who thought they had succeeded.

▶ 시험 성과에 관해 부정적 피드백을 받았던 사람들은 좋은 피드백을 받은 사람들보다 비디오를 더 오래 시청했다는 결과가 언급된다.

04 The researchers concluded that distraction through television viewing can effectively relieve the discomfort associated with painful failures or mismatches between the self and self-guides. In contrast, successful participants had little wish to be distracted from their self-related thoughts!

▶ TV 시청을 통한 주의력 분산(distraction)이 실패로 인한 불편감을 완화해 주었다(relieve the discomfort)는 결론이 나온다. 실험의 결론과 첫 문장의 주제는 같은 내용이다.

구문 풀이

The participants who had received failure feedback watched the video **much longer** than those who thought they had succeeded.

→ 비교급 강조 부사 much가 비교급 부사 longer를 수식한다.

구문 플러스' 비교급 강조 부사

much, even, far, still, a lot(훨씬): 비교급 수식
cf. very(매우, 단연코): 원급 또는 최상급 수식

She is **very** smart on the whole.
그녀는 전반적으로 매우 똑똑하다.

She is **much** smarter than before.
그녀는 전보다 훨씬 똑똑하다.

She is **the very** smartest in the class.
그녀는 단연코 반에서 제일 똑똑하다.

해석 수메르 경제의 전형적 모델에서 사원은 상품의 생산, 수집, 그리고 재분배를 관장하는 행정 당국으로서 기능했다. **Uruk**의 사원 단지에서 행정용 (점토)판을 발견한 것은 상징의 사용, 그리고 결과적으로 글자가 중앙 집권화된 경제 지배의 도구로 발달했음을 시사한다. **Uruk** 시기 가정집의 터에서 나온 고고학적 증거가 없다는 것을 고려하면, 개인들이 <u>사적인 합의</u>를 위해서도 그 체계를 사용했는지는 명확하지 않다. 그 문제와 관련하여, 읽고 쓰는 능력이 초기에 얼마나 널리 퍼져 있었는지 명확하지 않다. 초기 판의 식별 가능한 기호와 그림 문자의 사용은 행정가들이 읽고 쓸 줄 아는 측과 읽고 쓸 수 없는 측이 서로 이해할 수 있는 어휘 목록이 필요했던 것과 일치한다. 쐐기 문자가 더욱 추상적이 되면서, 사람들이 서로 뭐에 합의했는지 안다는 것을 확실히 하기 위해 읽고 쓰는 능력이 점점 더 중요해졌음이 틀림없다.

해설 문자는 경제 지배를 위한 도구로 발달했다는 설명과 함께, 마지막 두 문장에서 문자를 읽고 쓰는 능력의 전파에 관해 추론하고 있다. 문자 초기에는 글을 알든 모르든 쉽게 이해할 수 있는 상징이나 상형 문자가 사용되었으나, 이것이 추상화된 문자로 발전하면서 개인이 서로 동의한 내용을 확인하려면 문자를 알아야 했다는 것이다. 다시 말해, 문자의 보급은 '개인이 합의한' 사항을 확인하려는 목적과 맞닿아 이루어졌을 것이라는 내용이므로, 빈칸에 들어갈 말로 가장 적절한 것은 ② '사적인 합의'이다.

오답 풀이

선택률	선지 해석 & 오답 풀이
① 16%	종교 행사 ▶ 사원(**temple**)이라는 종교적 소재가 등장하기는 하지만, 종교적 행사는 언급되지 않았다.
③ 13%	공동 책임 ▶ 공동 책임에 관해서는 언급되지 않는다.
④ 26%	역사 기록 ▶ 역사 기록에 관해서는 언급되지 않았다. 문자와 역사를 흔히 가깝게 생각하는 배경지식에 의한 오답을 유도하는 선택지이다.
⑤ 3%	권력 이동 ▶ 권력 이동에 관해서는 언급되지 않는다.

지문 자세히 보기'

01 In the classic model of the Sumerian economy, the temple functioned as an administrative authority governing commodity production, collection, and redistribution. The discovery of administrative tablets from the temple complexes at Uruk suggests that token use and consequently writing evolved as a tool of centralized economic governance.

▶ 초기 문자 체계는 중앙 집권화된 경제 지배를 위한 도구로서 발달했다는 배경 설명이 제시된다.

02 Given the lack of archaeological evidence from Uruk-period domestic sites, it is not clear whether individuals also used the system for personal agreements. For that matter, it is not clear how widespread literacy was at its beginnings.

▶ 문자 초기에 읽고 쓰는 능력이 얼마나 보급되어 있었는지는 증거가 부족하여 명확히 알 수 없다는 내용이 언급된다.

03 The use of identifiable symbols and pictograms on the early tablets is consistent with administrators needing a lexicon that was mutually intelligible by literate and nonliterate parties. As cuneiform script became more abstract, literacy must have become increasingly important to ensure one understood what he or she had agreed to.

▶ 글을 아는 사람에게든 모르는 사람에게든 통용되던 상징과 상형 문자의 시대를 지나, 문자가 추상화된 이후에는 개인이 서로 합의한 내용을 확인하려면 문자를 알아야 했을 것이라는 추론이 나온다. 'one understood ~ had agreed to'를 요약한 말이 ②의 **personal agreements**이다.

구문 풀이

As cuneiform script became more abstract, literacy **must have become** increasingly important to ensure one understood what he or she had agreed to.

→ 「**must have p.p.**」는 '~했음에 틀림없다'라는 의미로, 과거에 대한 강한 추측을 나타낸다.

구문 **플러스'** 조동사 + have p.p.

「조동사 + have p.p.」 과거에 대한 추측 표현

형태	의미
would have p.p.	~했을 것이다
could have p.p.	~할 수 있었을 것이다
may[might] have p.p.	~했을지도 모른다
must have p.p.	~했음에 틀림없다
cannot have p.p.	~했을 리가 없다
should have p.p.	~했어야 했다(안 한 일 후회)
shouldn't have p.p.	~하지 말았어야 했다(한 일 후회)

I **must have been dreaming**. 난 꿈을 꾸고 있었던 게 틀림없어.
I **cannot have deleted** the file. 내가 그 파일을 지웠을 리 없어.
We **should have left** earlier. 우린 더 일찍 떠났어야 했어.
You **shouldn't have said** so. 넌 그런 말을 하지 말았어야 했어.

해석 여러 번 반복하여 말했던 이야기를 다시 말하기 시작할 때, 기억에서 되찾는 것은 이야기 자체에 대한 지표이다. 그 지표는 다양한 방식으로 윤색될 수 있다. 시간이 흐르면서, 그 윤색된 것들조차도 표준화된다. 한 노인이 수백 번 말한 이야기는 변형을 거의 보이지 않으며, 실제로 존재하는 것이면 어떤 변형이든 그 기원과 관계없이 이야기 자체의 일부가 된다. 사람들은 일어났을 수도, 또는 일어나지 않았을 수도 있는 세부 사항을 자신들의 이야기에 덧붙인다. 그들은 지표들을 기억해 내고 세부 사항들을 재구성하고 있다. 만약, 어떤 시점에 그들이 타당성에 대해서는 정말로 확신하지 못한 채 멋진 세부 사항을 덧붙인다면, 바로 그 세부 사항을 붙여 몇 번 더 그 이야기를 말하다 보면 그것은 이야기 지표에서 영구적인 위치를 확보할 것이다. 다시 말해 우리가 되풀이해서 말하는 이야기는 그 이야기가 전달하는 사건들에 대해 우리가 가지고 있는 기억과 동일하다.

어떤 이야기를 반복하다 보면 약간 더해지고 윤색되는 내용까지 그대로 우리 머릿속 기억의 지표가 된다는 내용의 글이다. 실제 있었는지 확실하지 않은 세부 사항일지라도 계속해서 덧붙인 채로 이야기하다 보면 기억 속에서 '영구적 입지'를 갖게 된다는 내용이 In other words 앞까지 이어진다. 따라서 빈칸에 들어갈 말로 가장 적절한 것은 이야기와 기억이 결국 같아진다는 뜻의 ① '동일하다'이다.

오답 풀이

선택률	선지 해석 & 오답 풀이
② 24%	**beneficial**(유익한) ▶ 이야기가 기억에 유익한지는 글에서 다루지 않는다.
③ 19%	**alien**(이질적인) ▶ 이야기를 하다 보면 그 내용이 곧 우리 기억의 일부가 된다는 글의 주제와 충돌한다.
④ 13%	**prior**(이전인) ▶ 이야기가 우리의 기억보다 먼저 존재한다는 내용은 글의 중심 내용과 무관하다.
⑤ 8%	**neutral**(중립적인) ▶ 이야기와 기억이 서로 중립적이거나 별개이지 않고 서로 긴밀히 연관된다는 것이 글의 주제이다.

지문 자세히 보기

01 When you begin to tell a story again that you have retold many times, what you retrieve from memory is the index to the story itself. That index can be embellished in a variety of ways.

▶ 이야기를 반복해서 말할 때 우리는 이야기에 대한 지표 위주로 기억을 되살리는데, 이것은 다양하게 윤색될(embellished) 수 있다는 내용이 제시된다.

02 Over time, even the embellishments become standardized. An old man's story that he has told hundreds of times shows little variation, and any variation that does exist becomes part of the story itself, regardless of its origin.

▶ 시간이 지나며 이 윤색은 이야기 속에 고착된다는 설명이 뒤따른다. become standardized, shows little variation, 'becomes ~ the story'가 모두 이 현상을 설명한다.

03 People add details to their stories that may or may not have occurred. They are recalling indexes and reconstructing details.

▶ 실제 일어났는지 확실치 않은 세부 내용도 추가되면서 세부 사항의 재구성이 일어난다고 한다. 앞의 embellished가 add details, reconstructing details로 바뀌어 표현되었다.

04 If at some point they add a nice detail, not really certain of its validity, telling the story with that same detail a few more times will ensure its permanent place in the story index. In other words, the stories we tell time and again are identical to the memory we have of the events that the story relates.

▶ 그럴듯한 세부 사항을 추가한 후 그 내용을 반복하다 보면 이야기의 기억 지표 안에 영구히 편입(ensure its permanent place)된다는 내용으로 보아, 결국 말로 하던 이야기가 기억이 된다는 것을 알 수 있다.

구문 풀이

An old man's story that he has told hundreds of times shows little variation, and any variation that **does exist** becomes part of the story itself, regardless of its origin.

→ any variation을 꾸미는 that절의 동사 does exist는 조동사 do를 이용해 일반동사를 강조한 것이다.

구문 플러스⁺ 동사 강조

「do[does, did] + 동사원형」은 일반동사의 강조 형태이다.

I did believe in Santa Claus when I was young.
어렸을 때 나는 산타클로스를 정말로 믿었다.
You do look great today. 너 오늘 정말로 멋져 보여.

64 정답 ⑤ 16%

해석 사진 이전에는 장소들이 잘 이동하지 않았다. 화가들이 항상 특정 장소를 그 '거처'에서 벗어나게 해 다른 곳으로 이동시키기는 했지만, 그림은 제작에 시간이 많이 걸렸고, 상대적으로 운반이 어려웠으며, 단품 수주 생산이었다. 사진의 증가는 특히 신문, 정기 간행물, 광고, 책, 광고에서 사진의 기계적인 복제를 가능하게 한 1880년대 하프톤 판의 도입으로 이루어졌다. 사진은 소비자 자본주의와 결합했고, 이제 세계는 '이전에는 전혀 사용되지 않았거나 단 한 명의 고객을 위한 그림으로만 사용되었던 인물, 풍경, 사건들을 무한한 양으로' 제공받았다. 자본주의가 세계를 '백화점'으로 정리하면서 '표현물의 확산과 유통은… 극적이고 사실상 피할 수 없는 세계적 (대)규모를 달성했다'. 점차 사진은 세계를 눈에 보이고 아름답고 바람직한 것으로 만드는 값싼 대량생산품이 되었다. 경험들은 그것을 저렴한 이미지로 바꾸어서 '대중화'되었다. 가볍고 작고 대량으로 제작된 사진은 장소의 시공간적 순환을 위한 역동적인 수단이 되었다.

해설 사진의 시대가 열린 후 이미지가 대량생산품처럼 생산되고 보급되면서, 공간 또한 제약 없이 소비될 수 있는 이미지로 전 세계를 순환하게 되었다는 내용이다. 이때 빈칸은 사진 '이전' 시대를 설명하므로, 답으로 가장 적절한 것은 '유통이 그만큼 자유롭지 않았다'는 의미의 ⑤ '장소들이 잘 이동하지 않았다'이다.

오답 풀이

선택률	선지 해석 & 오답 풀이
① 17%	그림만이 자연과 연결돼 있었다 ▶ 그림 또는 사진이 자연과 연결되어 있었다는 데 중점을 두는 글이 아니다.
② 26%	그림이 예술의 주요 형태였다 ▶ 사진 이전과 이후를 대비하며 그림과 사진을 대조하는 글은 맞다. 하지만 단순히 '그림이 예술의 주요 형태였다'는 내용을 넘어서, 그림과 사진이 제작 및 유통 면에서 어떻게 달랐고, 그에 따라 이미지의 순환에도 어떤 영향이 있었는지에 관한 내용이 구체적으로 담겨야 한다.
③ 25%	예술은 세상을 비추는 거울을 떠받쳤다 ▶ 예술로 세상을 볼 수 있었다는 글이 아니다.
④ 16%	여행에 대한 욕구가 강하지 않았다 ▶ '장소의 이동'을 문자 그대로 '여행'과 연결지으면 안 된다. 장소의 이미지가 사람들에게 전파되는 과정을 '이동'이라고 표현한 것이다.

지문 자세히 보기

01 Prior to photography, places did not travel well. While painters have always lifted particular places out of their 'dwelling' and transported them elsewhere, paintings were time-consuming to produce, relatively difficult to transport and one-of-a-kind.

▶ 사진 이전의 '그림'은 제작에 시간이 오래 걸리고, 수송도 어려웠으며 하나씩 생산되었음을 언급한다.

02 The multiplication of photographs especially took place with the introduction of the half-tone plate in the 1880s that made possible the mechanical reproduction of photographs in newspapers, periodicals, books and advertisements. Photography became coupled to consumer capitalism and the globe was now offered 'in limitless quantities, figures, landscapes, events which had not previously been utilised either at all, or only as pictures for one customer'.

▶ '한 명의 고객만을' 위해 만들어지던 그림과는 달리, 사진의 시대가 되자 그림의 '기계적 복제'가 가능해졌고, 이미지는 '무한한 양으로' 만들어질 수 있었다는 내용이 전개된다.

03 With capitalism's arrangement of the world as a 'department store', 'the proliferation and circulation of representations ... achieved a spectacular and virtually inescapable global magnitude'. Gradually photographs became cheap mass-produced objects that made the world visible, aesthetic and desirable. Experiences were 'democratised' by translating them into cheap images. Light, small and mass-produced photographs became dynamic vehicles for the spatiotemporal circulation of places.

▶ 'the proliferation and circulation of representations ~ global magnitude', mass-produced, democratised, the spatiotemporal circulation이 모두 사진의 특징을 설명한다. 즉 사진은 '기계적 생산 = 대규모 생산과 유통 = 이미지의 민주화 = 시공간적 순환'이 가능한 매체라는 것이다. 사진 이전의 '그림'을 설명하는 빈칸에는 거꾸로 '대규모 생산과 유통이 어려웠다'는 말이 들어가야 한다.

구문 풀이

~ paintings were time-consuming **to produce**, relatively difficult **to transport** and one-of-a-kind.

→ to부정사가 앞에 나온 형용사를 수식하고 있다.

구문 플러스 형용사를 수식하는 to부정사

부사적 용법으로 쓰인 to부정사는 형용사를 수식할 수 있다(~하기에 …한).

a goal difficult to achieve 이루기에 어려운 목표

65 정답 ⑤ 17%

해석 우리는 우리의 의식을 현재, 과거, 미래로 분리하는 것이 허구이며, 또한 희한하게도 자기 지시적인 틀이라는 것을 이해한다. (즉) 여러분의 현재는 여러분 어머니 미래의 일부였고 여러분 자녀의 과거는 여러분 현재의 일부가 될 것이다. 시간에 대한 우리의 의식을 이러한 전통적인 방식으로 구조화하는 것에는 일반적으로 잘못된 것이 없고, 이것은 흔히 충분히 효과적이다. 그러나 기후 변화의 경우, 시간을 과거, 현재, 미래로 분명하게 구분하는 것은 심하게 (사실을) 오도해왔으며, 가장 중요하게

는 지금 살아 있는 우리들의 책임 범위를 시야로부터 숨겨왔다. 시간에 대한 우리의 의식을 좁히는 것은 사실 우리의 삶이 깊이 뒤얽혀 있는 과거와 미래의 발전에 대한 책임으로부터 우리를 단절시키는 길을 닦는다. 기후의 경우, 우리가 사실을 직면하면서도 책임을 부인한다는 것이 문제가 아니다. 문제는 시간을 나눔으로써 현실이 시야로부터 흐릿해지고, 그리하여 과거와 현재의 책임에 관한 질문이 자연스럽게 생겨나지 않는다는 것이다.

해설 글 중반부의 **however** 이후로 시간을 과거, 현재, 미래로 나눠 생각하는 것이 기후 변화 대처에 좋지 않은 이유가 언급된다. 즉 현재를 살아가는 우리가 과거와 미래에 대해 지고 있는 책임을 의식하지 못하게 만든다는 것이다. 같은 맥락에서 마지막 문장은 '현실이 시야로부터 흐려지는' 문제가 생긴다고 하므로, '문제가 아닌' 점을 설명하는 빈칸에는 '현실을 모르게 된다'와 반대되는 말이 들어가야 한다. 따라서 답으로 가장 적절한 것은 ⑤ '우리가 사실을 직면하면서도 책임을 부인한다'이다.

오답 풀이

선택률	선지 해석 & 오답 풀이
① 22%	우리의 모든 노력이 효과가 있다고 밝혀져서 장려된다 ▶ (기후 변화와 관련된) 노력의 효과에 관해서는 언급되지 않았다.
② 27%	충분한 과학적인 증거가 우리에게 제공되었다 ▶ (기후 변화에 관한) 과학적 증거의 제공 여부는 언급되지 않았다.
③ 19%	미래의 우려가 현재의 필요보다 더욱 긴급하다 ▶ 과거, 현재, 미래의 (책임에 관해) 상대적 중요성을 따지는 내용은 언급되지 않았다.
④ 16%	우리 조상들이 다른 시간적 틀을 유지했다 ▶조상들의 시간적 틀에 관해서는 언급되지 않았다.

지문 자세히 보기⁺

01 We understand that the segregation of our consciousness into present, past, and future is both a fiction and an oddly self-referential framework; your present was part of your mother's future, and your children's past will be in part your present.

▶ '시간을 과거, 현재, 미래로 쪼개어 생각하는' 인간 의식의 경향성을 소재로 제시한다.

02 Nothing is generally wrong with structuring our consciousness of time in this conventional manner, and it often works well enough. In the case of climate change, however, the sharp division of time into past, present, and future has been desperately misleading and has, most importantly, hidden from view the extent of the responsibility of those of us alive now.

▶ 이렇듯 과거, 현재, 미래를 엄격히 나눠 생각하는 것이 오해의 소지가 있고(misleading) 현재를 살아가는 우리의 책임 범위를 가리는 (hidden ~ alive now) 역효과를 낳았다는 핵심 내용이 제시된다..

03 The narrowing of our consciousness of time smooths the way to divorcing ourselves from responsibility for developments in the past and the future with which our lives are in fact deeply intertwined. In the climate case, it is not that we face the facts but then deny our responsibility. It is that the realities are obscured from view by the partitioning of time, and so questions of responsibility toward the past and future do not arise naturally.

▶ **The narrowing**은 앞의 **the segregation, the sharp division**과 문맥상 의미가 같고, '**divorcing ~ future**'는 뒤의 '**the realities ~ from view**'와 같다. 즉 '과거, 현재, 미래의 구별'이 '우리를 책임으로부터 단절시키고, 현실이 흐려지게 만드는' 원인이라는 것이다. 마지막 두 문장은 우리가 현실을 '알면서도 외면하는' 것이 문제가 아니라, 현실 자체를 모르는 것이 문제임을 지적하는 흐름이다.

구문 풀이

The narrowing of our consciousness of time smooths **the way to divorcing** ourselves from responsibility for developments in the past and the future **with which** our lives are in fact deeply intertwined.

→ **way**는 '방법'이라는 뜻일 때 주로 to부정사의 수식을 받지만, '~로 향하는 길'이라는 의미를 나타낼 경우 'to+(동)명사'의 수식을 받기도 한다.
→ **with which**는 「전치사+관계대명사」 형태로, 뒤에 완전한 절을 수반한다.

구문 플러스⁺ 전치사 + 관계대명사

「전치사 + 관계대명사」는 관계부사처럼 완전한 절을 이끈다.

The bed in which(=where) we slept last night was very comfortable.
우리가 지난밤 잤던 침대는 아주 편했다.

66 정답 ① 40%　　　　*2023학년도 대수능*

해석 흔히 댄스 플로어라고 불리는 꿀벌 군집의 입구는 군집의 상태와 벌집 밖의 환경에 관한 정보를 교환하는 시장이다. 댄스 플로어에서의 상호 작용을 연구하는 것은 국지적 정보에 반응해 행동을 바꾸는 개체들이 어떻게 군집에서 그 노동력을 조절하게 하는지에 관한 여러 분명한 사례를 제공한다. 예를 들어, 물을 모아온 꿀벌들은 벌집으로 돌아오자마자 자기 물을 넘겨줄 벌집 안의 수신자 벌을 찾는다. 만약 (받아줄 벌을) 찾는 시간이 짧으면, 그 돌아온 벌은 8자 춤을 추어서 그 물의 출처까지 갈 다른 벌들을 모집할 가능성이 더 크다. 반대로, 찾는 시간이 길다면 그 벌은 물을 가지러 가는 것을 포기할 가능성이 더 크다. 물을 받는 벌들은 자기 자신을 위해서든, 아니면 다른 벌과 애벌레에게 전해주기 위해서든, 물이 필요할 때에만 넘겨받을 것이므로, 물을 넘겨주는 데 들어가는 시간은 군집의 전반적인 물 수요와 상관관계가 있다. 따라서 (시간이 늘든 줄든 간에) 물을 넘겨주는 시간에 대한 물 조달자 개체의 반응은 군집의 수요에 맞춰 물의 수집량을 조절한다.

해설 For example 이하의 예시에 따르면, 밖에서 물을 가져온 벌은 군집의 다른 개체에게 물을 나눠주는 데 걸리는 시간을 보고 물을 더 구하러 갈지, 아니면 물 수집을 중단할지 결정한다고 한다. 이를 근거로 마지막 두 문장에서는 물을 나눠주는 데 걸리는 시간과 군집의 물 수요, 나아가 물의 수집량 사이에 관련성이 있다고 한다. 따라서 빈칸에 들어갈 말로 가장 적절한 것은 '물 수집 행위가 수요에 따라 결정된다'는 의미와 통하는 ① '군집에서 그 노동력을 조절하게 하는지'이다.

선택률	선지 해석 & 오답 풀이
② 26%	거리를 측정하여 물이 있는 곳을 찾는지 ▶ 거리를 측정한다는 내용은 언급되지 않았다.
③ 16%	필요할 때 군집의 업무량을 줄이는지 ▶ 군집 내에서 물에 대한 수요가 많아 가져온 물을 나눠주는 데 시간이 얼마 안 드는 상황이면 물을 가져오는 업무의 양은 오히려 '늘어날' 수도 있다. 따라서 '줄어드는' 상황만 언급하면 글의 내용을 충분히 담아낼 수 없다.
④ 11%	각자의 재능에 따라 일을 나누는지 ▶ 재능에 따른 분업은 언급되지 않았다.
⑤ 7%	일벌들이 기본적 의사소통 패턴을 습득하도록 훈련시키는지 ▶ 꿀벌의 8자 춤이 일종의 의사소통 수단처럼 언급되지만, 이것의 패턴과 습득에 관해서는 언급되지 않았다.

지문 자세히 보기

01 The entrance to a honeybee colony, often referred to as the dancefloor, is a market place for information about the state of the colony and the environment outside the hive. Studying interactions on the dancefloor provides us with a number of illustrative examples of how individuals changing their own behavior in response to local information allow the colony to regulate its workforce.

▶ 꿀벌이 군집 내의 국지적 정보에 따라 자신의 행동을 조절할 때 어떤 결과가 일어나는지 설명하는 글이다. 빈칸 뒤의 예시를 일반화해 주제문의 빈칸을 완성하면 된다.

02 For example, upon returning to their hive honeybees that have collected water search out a receiver bee to unload their water to within the hive. If this search time is short then the returning bee is more likely to perform a waggle dance to recruit others to the water source.

▶ 벌이 물을 구해왔을 때, 구해온 물을 군집 내의 다른 개체들에 나눠주는 시간이 적게 걸린다면 이 벌은 (물이 많이 필요한 상황임을 알고) 다른 개체들을 추가로 모집하고자 할 것이라는 예시가 나온다.

03 Conversely, if this search time is long then the bee is more likely to give up collecting water. Since receiver bees will only accept water if they require it, either for themselves or to pass on to other bees and brood, this unloading time is correlated with the colony's overall need of water.

▶ 역접의 Conversely 뒤로, 앞과는 다른 상황이 언급된다. 만일 물을 받아줄 벌을 찾는 데 시간이 오래 걸리면, 물을 가져온 벌은 (군집 내에 물이 별로 필요하지 않은 상황임을 알고) 물을 구하러 가지 않을 것이라고 한다. 이를 토대로, 'this unloading time ~ need of water'에서는 '물을 나눠주는 데 걸린 시간'과 '군집 내 물의 수요'가 서로 관련이 있다고 설명한다.

04 Thus the individual water forager's response to unloading time (up or down) regulates water collection in response to the colony's need.

▶ 예시의 최종 결론(= 주제)이 제시된다. 물을 나눠주는 시간이 길어지는지 짧아지는지에 따라 군집의 수요에 맞는 물 수집이 이뤄진다는 것이다. 이는 '(물 수집과 관련된) 노동력이 조절된다'는 말과 같다.

구문 풀이

For example, upon returning to their hive honeybees that have collected water search out a receiver bee to unload their water to within the hive.
→ 「(up)on + 동명사(~하자마자)」 구문이다.

구문 플러스' 혼동하기 쉬운 전치사 + 동명사

(up)on + 동명사: ~하자마자
in + 동명사: ~할 때, ~하는 데 있어
by + 동명사: ~함으로써

On arriving home. I found out she had gone.
집에 도착하자마자. 나는 그녀가 (이미) 간 것을 알아차렸다.
In eating breakfast. he always chooses cereal.
아침을 먹을 때, 그는 항상 시리얼을 선택한다.
Don't risk your reputation by telling such a lie.
그런 거짓말을 해서 네 명성을 위험에 빠뜨리지 마라.

---

67 정답 ② 28%   *2022학년도 대수능*

해석 정확성과 확정성은 모든 의미 있는 과학 토론을 위한 필요조건이며, 과학에서의 발전은 상당 부분, 훨씬 더 높은 정확성을 달성하는 계속 진행 중인 과정이다. 그러나 역사적 진술은 진술의 증식을 중요시하는데, 이는 한 가지 진술의 정제가 아닌, 훨씬 더 다양한 진술 집합의 생성에 중요성을 두는 것이다. 역사적 통찰은 이전에 선택한 것들을 지속해서 '좁혀 가는' 것의 문제, 즉 진리에 가까워지는 것의 문제가 아니라, 반대로 가능한 관점들의 '폭발적 증가'이다. 그러므로 그것은 이전의 진술에서 무엇이 옳고 틀렸는지에 대한 신중한 분석으로 진리를 획득하는 것이 아니라, 새롭고 대안적인 진술의 생성으로 확정성과 정확성에 대해 이전에 가졌던 환상을 드러내는 것을 목표로 한다. 그리고 이러한 관점에서 보면, 역사적 통찰의 발전은 외부인에게는 과학에서처럼 진리에 훨씬 더 많이 근접해가기보다는 훨씬 더 큰 혼란을 만들어내는 과정, 즉 이미 획득한 것처럼 보이는 확실성과 정확성에 대한 지속적인 의문 제기로 진정 여겨질 수도 있다.

해설 글에 따르면 과학은 한 번 생산된 진술을 분석하고 가다듬어 진리에 다가가려 하지만, 역사 연구에서는 이미 제시된 진술이 있어도 또 다른 가능성을 계속해서 탐구하며 진술을 확장하려 한다. 이러한 흐름으로 보아, 역사 탐구의 과정은 '정확해 보이는 진술이 이미 있어도' 이에 의문을 제기하며 오히려 더 큰 혼란을 만들어내려는 것처럼 보인다는 결론이 적절하다. 따라서 빈칸에 들어갈 말로 가장 적절한 것은 ② '이미 획득한 것처럼 보이는 확실성과 정확성'이다.

선택률	선지 해석 & 오답 풀이
① 30%	역사적 진술을 평가하는 기준 ▶ 진술의 평가 기준 자체에 의문을 제기한다는 내용은 없다. 평가 기준보다는 진술의 목표 또는 발전 방향에 관한 설명이 주를 이룬다.
③ 21%	어떤 사건에 대한 다른 해석의 가능성 ▶ 역사적 통찰에서는 다른 해석의 가능성에 이의를 제기하기보다 장려한다고 하므로 답으로 부적절하다.
④ 12%	역사 저술에서 다수의 관점 공존 ▶ 여러 관점이 공존한다는 것에 '이의를 제기하면' 다양한 진술 생산이 촉진될 수 없으므로 답으로 부적절하다.
⑤ 10%	수집된 역사적 증거의 정확성과 신뢰성 ▶ 역사적 진술이 아닌, 역사적 증거는 글과 무관한 소재이다.

지문 자세히 보기

01 Precision and determinacy are a necessary requirement for all meaningful scientific debate, and progress in the sciences is, to a large extent, the ongoing process of achieving ever greater precision.

▶ 과학적 진술은 더 높은 정확성과 확정성을 얻는 방향으로 발전해간다는 배경 설명이 제시된다. 이 문장의 'achieving ~ precision'을 아래에서 refinement로 재진술한다.

02 But historical representation puts a premium on a proliferation of representations, hence not on the refinement of one representation but on the production of an ever more varied set of representations.

▶ 진술의 '정제'를 추구하는 과학과 반대로, 역사 연구는 더 다양한 진술의 생산(production)과 확장(proliferation)을 중시한다는 핵심 내용이 제시된다.

03 Historical insight is not a matter of a continuous "narrowing down" of previous options, not of an approximation of the truth, but, on the contrary, is an "explosion" of possible points of view. It therefore aims at the unmasking of previous illusions of determinacy and precision by the production of new and alternative representations, rather than at achieving truth by a careful analysis of what was right and wrong in those previous representations.

▶ 과학에서는 기존 진술을 좁혀가는(narrowing down) 쪽으로 진리에 다가가려 하지만(approximation), 역사 분야에서는 계속 새롭고 다른 시각과 해석을 만들고 찾으려 한다(explosion, production)는 설명이 이어진다.

04 And from this perspective, the development of historical insight may indeed be regarded by the outsider as a process of creating ever more confusion, a continuous questioning of certainty and precision seemingly achieved already, rather than, as in the sciences, an ever greater approximation to the truth.

▶ 그래서 외부자들의 눈에는 역사 연구가 진리에 다가가기보다는 혼란으로 나아가는 과정처럼 보일 수 있다는 결론이 뒤따른다. '기존 진술의 확정성과 정확성'을 인정하는 대신 계속 의심하기(questioning) 때문에 혼란처럼 보인다는 것이다.

구문 풀이

It therefore aims **at the unmasking of previous illusions of determinacy and precision by the production of new and alternative representations, rather than at achieving truth** by a careful analysis of what was right and wrong in those previous representations.

→ 동사 aim에 연결되는 「at + (동)명사」구가 「A rather than B(B라기보다 A인)」에 의해 병렬구조를 이룬다.

구문 플러스 A rather than B

「A rather than B(B라기보다 A인)」의 A, B는 병렬구조를 이룬다.

The problems were situational rather than personal.
그 문제는 개인적이라기보다 상황에 따른 것이었다.

Your symptoms are caused by virus infection rather than by parasites.
귀하의 증상은 기생충보다는 바이러스 감염에 의해 생깁니다.

---

68 정답 ① 30% 2022학년도 9월 모평

해석 개별적이고 문화적으로 형성된 행동과 문화적 통합의 상태 사이의 상호의존성을 인식하는 것은 중요하다. 사람들은 아무리 모순되더라도 자신이 내면화한 문화적 패턴에 의해 제공되는 형태 내에서 일한다. 사상은 다른 수용된 사상의 논리적 영향이나 결과로 도출되고, 바로 이러한 방식으로 문화적 혁신과 발견이 가능하다. 새로운 사상은 논리적 추론을 통해 발견되지만, 그러한 발견은 개념 체계에 내재 및 내장되어 있고, 오직 그 전제를 수용하기 때문에 가능해진다. 예를 들어, 새로운 소수의 발견은 사용되고 있는 특정 숫자 체계의 '실제' 결과이다. 따라서, 문화적 사상은 이전 사상의 결과물이기 때문에 '진보'와 '발전'을 보여 준다. 많은 개인의 축적된 작업은 특정 '발견'이 가능해지거나 가능성이 높아지는 집적된 지식을 생산한다. 그러한 발견은 (시기상) '무르익었고', 더 일찍 발생할 수 없었을 것이며, 또한 다수의 개인에 의해 동시에 이루어질 가능성이 있다.

해설 새로운 사상은 이미 수용된 다른 사상의 논리적 영향 또는 결과이며 기존의 개념 체계를 전제로 한다는 내용이 주를 이룬다. 따라서 빈칸에 들어갈 말로 가장 적절한 것은 ① '이전 사상의 결과물이기'이다.

오답 풀이

선택률	선지 해석 & 오답 풀이
② 17%	추상적 추론 능력에서 비롯되기 ▶ 추상적 추론 능력은 언급되지 않았다.
③ 18%	문화적 보편성의 토대를 형성하기 ▶ 문화적 보편성은 언급되지 않았다.
④ 13%	같은 시대의 사람들 사이에서 출현하기 ▶ '(이전부터) 축적된' 작업이 (새로운) 사상을 낳는다는 내용과 부합하지 않는다.
⑤ 22%	개인들의 혁신적 사고를 촉진하기 ▶ 개인의 사고가 '모여서' 혁신이 이룩된다는 내용이 글의 요지이다. 사상이 거꾸로 새로운 사고나 혁신을 촉진한다는 내용은 없다.

01 It is important to recognise the interdependence between individual, culturally formed actions and the state of cultural integration. People work within the forms provided by the cultural patterns that they have internalised, however contradictory these may be.

▶ 사람들은 문화적 패턴이라는 틀 안에서 행동한다는 일반적 내용이 제시된다.

02 Ideas are worked out as logical implications or consequences of other accepted ideas, and it is in this way that cultural innovations and discoveries are possible.

▶ 사상, 발견, 혁신 등은 이미 수용된 다른 사상의 영향 또는 결과로 파생된다는 핵심 내용이 이어진다. 'implications or consequences of ~ ideas'를 재진술한 것이 ①의 outgrowths of previous ideas이다.

03 New ideas are discovered through logical reasoning, but such discoveries are inherent in and integral to the conceptual system and are made possible only because of the acceptance of its premises. For example, the discoveries of new prime numbers are 'real' consequences of the particular number system employed.

▶ 위의 'logical implications or consequences ~'이 'made possible only because of ~'로 재진술된다. 새로운 사상은 기존의 개념 체계에 내장되어 있으며(inherent ~ and integral ~), 그 체계를 전제로 하기 때문에 파생될 수 있다는 의미이다.

04 Thus, cultural ideas show 'advances' and 'developments' because they are outgrowths of previous ideas. The cumulative work of many individuals produces a corpus of knowledge within which certain 'discoveries' become possible or more likely. Such discoveries are 'ripe' and could not have occurred earlier and are also likely to be made simultaneously by numbers of individuals.

▶ 많은 개인의 작업이 모여 집적된 지식이 생기면 시기상 적합할 때 '발견'이라는 결과물로 이어진다는 결론이 제시된다. The cumulative work와 a corpus of knowledge는 앞의 other accepted ideas, the conceptual system과 문맥상 같다.

구문 풀이

New ideas are discovered through logical reasoning, but such discoveries are inherent in and integral to the conceptual system and **are made possible** only because of the acceptance of its premises.
→ 「be made + 형용사」는 5형식 문장인 「make + 목적어 + 형용사」의 수동태이다.

구문 플러스 5형식 문장의 수동태

5형식 동사가 수동태로 바뀌면 원래 목적격보어였던 명사 또는 형용사가 그대로 be p.p. 뒤에 나와 주어를 보충한다.

People **considered** the boy a genius.
사람들은 그 소년을 천재로 여겼다.

→ The boy **was considered** a genius.
그 소년은 천재라고 여겨졌다.

---

69 정답 ④ 30%　　　　　*2021학년도 9월 모평*

해석 프로토피아는 목적지라기보다는 생성의 상태이다. 그것은 과정이다. 프로토피아적인 방식에서는 어제보다 오늘, 비록 그저 약간이라 하더라도, 상황이 더 낫다. 그것은 점진적인 개선이나 가벼운 진보이다. 프로토피아적이라는 말에서 '프로'는 과정과 진보라는 개념에서 비롯된다. 이 미묘한 진보는 극적이지도 않고 자극적이지도 않다. 프로토피아는 거의 새로운 이점만큼 많은 새로운 문제를 발생시키기 때문에 그것을 놓치기 쉽다. 오늘의 문제는 어제의 기술적 성공이 가져온 것이고, 오늘의 문제에 대한 기술적 해결책은 내일의 문제를 유발할 것이다. 문제와 해결책의 이런 순환적 팽창은 시간이 지남에 따라 작은 순이익의 꾸준한 축적을 보이지 않게 한다. 계몽주의와 과학의 발명 이래로 줄곧, 우리는 매년 파괴해 온 것보다 조금 더 많은 것을 만들어냈다. 그러나 그 얼마 안 되는 긍정적인 차이는 수십 년에 걸쳐 우리가 문명이라고 부를 수 있는 것으로 조합된다. 그것의 장점은 영화에서 주연을 맡아 돋보이는 법이 없다.

해설 과정과 진보로서의 프로토피아 개념을 설명한 글이다. 빈칸 앞에 따르면 프로토피아는 진보의 과정으로서 새로운 이점만큼이나 문제도 파생시키기에, 과거의 성공이 오늘의 문제가 되고 오늘의 해결책은 또 미래의 문제를 낳는다고 했다. 이어서 빈칸 뒤에서는 우리가 꾸준히 어제보다 더 나은 것들을 만들어오기는 했으나 이것은 수십 년에 걸쳐서 모여야만 '문명'이라는 결과로 드러나므로 영화 속 주연처럼 눈에 띄는 법이 없다고 했다. 이러한 흐름으로 보아, 빈칸에 들어갈 말로 가장 적절한 것은 꾸준히 진보의 과정이 이루어져도 그 이득이 쉽게 눈에 보이지는 않는다는 의미의 ④ '시간이 지남에 따라 작은 순이익의 꾸준한 축적을 보이지 않게 한다'이다.

오답 풀이

선택률	선지 해석 & 오답 풀이
① 16%	현재의 혁신의 한계를 감춘다 ▶ 빈칸 뒤를 보면 혁신의 한계가 아닌 '이득'이 눈에 드러나지 않는다는 것을 중점적으로 말하고 있다.
② 19%	자신감 있게 미래를 예측하는 것을 어렵게 만든다 ▶ 미래 예측에 관한 내용은 언급되지 않는다.
③ 17%	프로토피아적인 문명을 빨리 이루도록 우리에게 동기를 부여한다 ▶ 프로토피아는 극적이지 않은 점진적 과정을 뜻하므로 이 문명을 '빨리' 이룬다는 설명은 흐름상 어색하다.
⑤ 19%	기술적 성공에서 상당한 변화를 만든다 ▶ 상당한 변화가 아니라 '작은' 변화가 몇십 년 동안 누적되어 문명이 되는데, 이것의 이점이 눈에는 잘 띄지 않는다는 것이 중심 내용이다.

01 Protopia is a state of becoming, rather than a destination. It is a process. In the protopian mode, things are better today than they were yesterday, although only a little better. It is incremental improvement or mild progress.

▶ 프로토피아는 변화(becoming)의 과정, 정확히는 점진적 변화와 가벼운 진보를 뜻한다는 정의가 제시된다.

02 The "pro" in protopian stems from the notions of process and progress. This subtle progress is not dramatic, not exciting. It is easy to miss because a protopia generates almost as many new problems as new benefits.

▶ 위의 mild progress를 subtle progress로 재진술하며, 프로토피아 과정에서 이득뿐 아니라 문제도 새로 파생된다는 내용을 전개한다.

03 The problems of today were caused by yesterday's technological successes, and the technological solutions to today's problems will cause the problems of tomorrow. This circular expansion of both problems and solutions hides a steady accumulation of small net benefits over time.

▶ 어제의 성공이 오늘의 문제가 되고, 오늘의 해결책이 또 내일의 문제가 되는 일련의 과정을 'This circular expansion ~'으로 요약한다.

04 Ever since the Enlightenment and the invention of science, we've managed to create a tiny bit more than we've destroyed each year. But that few percent positive difference is compounded over decades into what we might call civilization. Its benefits never star in movies.

▶ 우리는 매년 이전보다 아주 조금씩 발전해오고 있지만 이 얼마 안 되는 긍정적 차이(that few ~ difference)는 돋보이지 않는다(never star in movies)는 설명을 통해, '프로토피아 상태에서 쌓이는 작은 이득의 축적은 눈에 띄지 않는다'는 결론을 추론할 수 있다.

구문 풀이

In the protopian mode, things are better today than they were yesterday, **although (they are)** only a little better.
→ 양보의 접속사 although 뒤에서 「대명사 주어 + be동사」인 they are가 생략되고 보어인 only a little better가 접속사 뒤에 바로 이어졌다.

구문 플러스⁺ 접속사 vs. 전치사

전치사: 뒤에 (동)명사구
접속사: 뒤에 절, 현재분사/과거분사, 형용사, 전명구 등
　　　　분사구문　　　　　　분사구문의 being 또는
　　　　　　　　　　　　　「대명사 주어 + be동사」가 생략됨

She was good at history **despite** the fact that she found it boring.
그녀는 역사를 지겨워한다는 사실에도 불구하고 역사를 잘했다.

Although she is young, she is dependable.
= **Although** being young, she is dependable.
= **Although** young, she is dependable.
어리지만, 그녀는 믿음직하다.

---

70 정답 ① 34%　　　　　　*2020학년도 6월 모평*

해석 디지털 기술은 제품에서 서비스로의 이동을 앞당겨 비물질화를 가속한다. 서비스의 유동적인 특성은 그것들이 물질에 얽매일 필요가 없다는 것을 의미한다. 그러나 비물질화는 단지 디지털 상품에 관련된 것만은 아니다. 탄산음료 캔과 같은 고체의 물리적 상품조차도, 더 적은 양의 물질을 가지고 있으면서도 더 많은 이익을 내놓을 수 있는 이유는 그것들의 무거운 원자가 무게가 없는 비트로 대체되기 때문이다. 유형의 것들은 더 많은 알루미늄 원자들이 하던 일을 하는 무형의 것들, 즉 더 나은 설계, 혁신적인 과정, 스마트 칩, 그리고 궁극적으로 온라인 연결성 등

으로 대체된다. 따라서 지능과 같이 부드러운 것들이 알루미늄과 같은 단단한 물건에 삽입되어서, 딱딱한 물건들을 더 소프트웨어처럼 작용하게 만든다. 비트가 주입된 물질적 상품들은 점점 마치 그것들이 무형의 서비스인 것처럼 행동한다. 명사가 동사로 변한다. 하드웨어가 소프트웨어처럼 동작한다. Silicon Valley에서 사람들은 이렇게 말한다. "소프트웨어가 모든 것을 장악한다."

해설 디지털 시대에 들어 유형의 것이 무형의 것으로 대체되고, 하드웨어가 흔히 소프트웨어처럼 기능한다는 내용의 글이므로, 빈칸에 들어갈 말로 가장 적절한 것은 이러한 비물질화 경향을 잘 설명하는 ① '그것들이 무형의 서비스인'이다.

오답 풀이

선택률	선지 해석 & 오답 풀이
② 21%	그것들이 모든 디지털 상품들을 대체하는 ▶ 물질적 상품이 디지털 상품을 대체하면 '무형의' 것 대신 '유형의' 것이 남게 되므로 주제와 상반된다.
③ 19%	하드웨어가 소프트웨어보다 오래 존속할 수 있는 ▶ 하드웨어가 소프트웨어 같아진다는 빈칸 앞뒤 내용으로 보아 하드웨어가 소프트웨어보다 더 오래 남는다는 말은 어색하다.
④ 11%	디지털 서비스가 사용될 수 없는 ▶ 물질이 서비스로 바뀐다는 내용과 상충한다.
⑤ 13%	소프트웨어가 하드웨어와 충돌하는 ▶ 소프트웨어와 하드웨어의 충돌에 관해서는 언급되지 않았다.

지문 자세히 보기⁺

01 Digital technology accelerates dematerialization by hastening the migration from products to services. The liquid nature of services means they don't have to be bound to materials.

▶ 재화가 서비스로 바뀌는 과정(the migration ~ to services)인 비물질화에 관해 설명하는 글이다.

02 But dematerialization is not just about digital goods. The reason even solid physical goods — like a soda can — can deliver more benefits while inhabiting less material is because their heavy atoms are substituted by weightless bits.

▶ 비물질화는 디지털 상품뿐 아니라 단단한 물리적 상품에서도 일어난다는 보충 설명이 이어진다. 'their heavy atoms ~ weightless bits'가 비물질화를 묘사한다.

03 The tangible is replaced by intangibles — intangibles like better design, innovative processes, smart chips, and eventually online connectivity — that do the work that more aluminum atoms used to do. Soft things, like intelligence, are thus embedded into hard things, like aluminum, that make hard things behave more like software.

▶ 유형의 것이 무형의 것으로 대체되는(The tangible ~ intangibles) 과정이 곧 비물질화라는 설명과 함께, 그 결과로 하드웨어가 소프트웨어처럼 기능하게 된다는 내용이 제시된다. The tangible이 hard things와 같고, intangibles가 Soft things, software와 같다.

04 Material goods infused with bits increasingly act as if they were intangible services. Nouns morph to verbs. Hardware behaves like software. In Silicon Valley they say it like this: "Software eats everything."

▶ 뒤에서도 하드웨어가 소프트웨어처럼 기능한다는 말이 반복되는 것으로 보아, 물질적 상품이 '소프트웨어' 또는 '무형의' 서비스와 같아진다는 결론을 내릴 수 있다.

구문 풀이

The tangible is replaced by intangibles — intangibles like better design, innovative processes, smart chips, and eventually online connectivity — that do the work that more aluminum atoms **used to do.**

→ 조동사 **used to**(~하곤 했다)는 현재 계속되지 않는 과거의 습관이나 상태를 묘사한다.

구문 플러스 조동사 used to

「used to + 동사원형」: ~하곤 했다
cf. 「be used to + 동사원형」: ~하기 위해 사용되다
　　「be used to + (동)명사」: ~(하는 것)에 익숙해지다

He **used to** be a pilot but now he has a desk job.
그는 한때 조종사였지만 지금은 사무직에 있다.

유형 플러스 빈칸 추론

글의 중심 내용과 관련된 부분을 빈칸으로 두고 이에 들어갈 말을 추론하게 하는 유형이다. 독해 28문항 중 4문항이라는 가장 큰 비중을 차지하며, 순서, 삽입 유형과 함께 최고난도 유형으로 꼽힌다.

· **문제 해결 Tip.**
① 반복되는 핵심 표현에 주목한다.
② 핵심 표현을 적절히 '재진술'한 선택지가 있는지 찾는다.
③ 글의 처음 또는 마지막에 빈칸이 있을 때, 중간에 예시가 나온다면, 예시를 '일반화'한 내용이 답에 해당한다.
④ 글 후반부에 빈칸이 있을 때, 전반부에서 구체적 예시나 비유가 등장했다면, 그 예시나 비유를 토대로 '추론'되는 결론이 답에 해당한다.

71 정답 ③ 81%   *2024학년도 6월 모평*

해석   흥미롭게도, 전문가들은 복잡한 과제를 수행하거나 많은 과제를 결합할 때 초보자만큼 어려움을 겪지 않는다. 전문가는 제한된 영역 내에서 엄청난 연습을 하기 때문에, 자기 분야에서의 핵심 구성 요소 기술은 고도로 숙련되고 더 자동화되어 있는 경향이 있다. 그래서 고도로 숙련된 이러한 각각의 기술은 비교적 적은 인지 자원을 필요로 하여, 전문가가 경험하는 총 인지 부하를 효과적으로 낮춘다. 따라서 전문가는 비교적 쉽게 복잡한 과제를 수행하고 많은 과제를 결합할 수 있다. (게다가, 초보자는 과제가 분할되고 분리될 때 그것을 처리하는 데 탁월하다.) 이것은 그들이 반드시 초보자보다 더 많은 인지적 자원을 가지고 있기 때문인 것은 아니며, 오히려 핵심 기술을 수행하면서 달성한 높은 수준의 능숙함 때문에 그들은 자신들이 가지고 있는 것으로 더 많은 것을 할 수 있다. 반면에, 초보자는 각각의 구성 기술에서 동일한 수준의 능숙함과 자동성을 달성하지 못했으며, 따라서 그들은 전문가가 비교적 쉽고 효율적으로 결합하는 기술들을 결합하려고 애쓴다.

해설   전문가가 초보자보다 쉽게 일을 처리하는 이유에 관한 글인데, ③은 초보자의 작업 수행이 탁월한 상황을 언급하므로 흐름에서 벗어난다. 따라서 전체 흐름과 관계 없는 문장은 ③이다.

오답 풀이

선택률	오답 풀이
① 1%	전문가들은 고도로 숙련돼 있다는 앞 문장에 이어서, 이들의 인지 부하가 적게 들어간다는 보충 설명을 제시한다.
② 5%	인지 부하가 적게 들기 '때문에' 복잡한 일 처리가 더 쉬워진다는 주제가 다시 한 번 언급된다.
④ 8%	② 문장 내용이 **This**로 연결된다. 일 처리가 쉬운 까닭은 핵심 기술을 익히며 쌓아둔 능숙함 때문이라는 보충 설명이다.
⑤ 3%	앞에서 언급된 전문가의 상황과 초보자의 상황을 대조하는 문맥이다.

지문 자세히 보기

01   Interestingly, experts do not suffer as much as beginners when performing complex tasks or combining multiple tasks.

▶ 전문가들이 복잡한 일을 처리할 때 초보자만큼 고생하지 않는다는 내용이다. 첫 문장이 주제문이고, 나머지가 이유를 설명한다.

02   Because experts have extensive practice within a limited domain, the key component skills in their domain tend to be highly practiced and more automated. Each of these highly practiced skills then demands relatively few cognitive resources, effectively lowering the total cognitive load that experts experience. Thus, experts can perform complex tasks and combine multiple tasks relatively easily.

▶ 전문가들은 핵심 기술이 고도로 숙련돼 있고, 그렇기에 인지 자원의 필요량이 줄어서 복잡한 과제를 비교적 쉽게 수행할 수 있다는 부연 설명이다. 'the key component skills ~ highly practiced and more automated'가 these highly practiced skills로 연결되며 비슷한 설명이 반복된다.

03   Furthermore, beginners are excellent at processing the tasks when the tasks are divided and isolated.

▶ 첨가의 Furthermore가 나오므로 앞에 이어 '전문가의 숙련된 일 처리'를 이야기해야 하는데, 엉뚱하게 '초보자의 일 처리'가 언급되고 있다. 즉 흐름상 어긋나는 지점이다.

04   This is not because they necessarily have more cognitive resources than beginners; rather, because of the high level of fluency they have achieved in performing key skills, they can do more with what they have. Beginners, on the other hand, have not achieved the same degree of fluency and automaticity in each of the component skills, and thus they struggle to combine skills that experts combine with relative ease and efficiency.

▶ This에 'experts can perform complex tasks ~ relatively easily'를 넣으면 글이 자연스럽게 읽힌다. 전문가들이 쉽게 복잡한 일을 수행하는 까닭은 인지적 자원 양이 많기 때문보다는, 자기 분야에서 달성해 온 능숙함 때문이라는 것이다. 이어서 on the other hand와 함께 흐름이 반전되면서, '초보자'와 비교하는 내용이 자연스럽게 연결된다.

구문 풀이

Interestingly, experts do **not** suffer **as much as** beginners when performing complex tasks or combining multiple tasks.
→ 원급 비교 부정 표현인 「**not as** + 원급 + **as**(~만큼 …하지 않은)」이다. 이는 **less than**(덜 ~한)을 활용해 'experts suffer less than beginners when ~'으로 바꿔도 된다.

구문 **플러스⁺** **원급 비교 표현**

두 대상이 동등하거나 비슷할 때 쓰는 표현으로, 형용사/부사의 원급을 활용한다.

You're **as tall as** your brother. 넌 너희 형만큼 키가 크구나.
My grandpa is **not so healthy as** he used to be.
(= My grandpa is **less healthy than** he used to be.)
우리 할아버지는 과거만큼 건강하시지 않다.

72 정답 ③ 81%   *2023학년도 대수능*

해석   배우, 가수, 정치가, 그리고 수없이 많은 다른 사람은 사용된 단어의 단순한 해독을 넘어서는 의사소통 수단으로서의 사람 목소리의 힘을 인정한다. 따라서 여러분의 목소리를 통제하고 다양한 목적을 위해 사용하는 법을 배우는 것은 경력 초기의 교사로서 개발해야 할 가장 중요한 기술 중 하나이다. 여러분이 더 자신 있게 수업할수록, 긍정적인 학급의 반응이 나올 확률은 더 높다. 목소리를 크게 낼 수 있는 것이 학교에서 일할 때 매우 유용할 경우가 있으며, 시끄러운 교실, 구내식당이나 운동장을 (목소리로) 가를 수 있다는 것을 아는 것은 갖춰야 할 훌륭한 기술이다. (학교 내의 심각한 소음 문제에 대처하려면 학생, 학부모, 교사가 함께 해결책을 찾아야 한다.) 하지만 나는 가장 큰 목소리는 놀라울 만큼 드물게 쓰고 소리치는 것을 최대한 피하도록 늘 조언코자 한다. 조용하고도 권위 있으며 침착한 어조는 약간 당황한 고함 소리보다 훨씬 더 큰 효과를 지닌다.

해설 교사로서 목소리의 힘을 잘 이용할 필요가 있다는 내용인데, ③의 경우 학교에서의 소음 문제 대처에 관해 언급하고 있다. 따라서 전체 흐름과 관계 없는 문장은 ③이다.

오답 풀이

선택률	오답 풀이
① 2%	앞에서 교사들은 목소리를 목적에 맞게 사용하는 법을 익혀야 한다고 언급한 데 이어, 수업 때는 자신 있는 목소리가 좋다는 예시를 들고 있다.
② 2%	특히 목소리를 '크게' 내는 것이 학교 환경에서 유리한 순간이 있다는 내용으로 ①과 자연스럽게 연결된다.
④ 10%	얼핏 보면 '큰 목소리를 쓰지 말라'는 내용 때문에 흐름상 어색해 보인다. 하지만 **However**가 있기 때문에 ②와 내용상 반대되더라도 흐름이 자연스럽다.
⑤ 2%	④에 이어, 큰 목소리가 아닌 '조용한' 어조가 효과를 발휘하는 순간도 있다는 내용을 언급한다.

지문 *자세히 보기*

01 Actors, singers, politicians and countless others recognise the power of the human voice as a means of communication beyond the simple decoding of the words that are used. Learning to control your voice and use it for different purposes is, therefore, one of the most important skills to develop as an early career teacher.

▶ 학교에서 선생님들이 목소리를 다양한 목적에 맞게 조절해 사용하는 법을 알 필요가 있다는 내용의 글이다.

02 The more confidently you give instructions, the higher the chance of a positive class response. There are times when being able to project your voice loudly will be very useful when working in school, and knowing that you can cut through a noisy classroom, dinner hall or playground is a great skill to have.

▶ 'confidently ~ instructions', 'project ~ loudly'는 목소리를 비교적 크게 쓰는 것이 효과적인(useful) 상황에 해당한다. 즉 ① 앞에 제시된 주제에 대해 예를 드는 것이다.

03 In order to address serious noise issues in school, students, parents and teachers should search for a solution together.

▶ 앞 문장의 'a noisy ~ playground'에 이어 noise issues를 언급하므로, 얼핏 보면 흐름에 적합해 보인다. 하지만 '소음 문제'에 대처하기 위해 다양한 당사자의 논의가 필요하다는 내용은 주제와 무관하다.

04 However, I would always advise that you use your loudest voice incredibly sparingly and avoid shouting as much as possible. A quiet, authoritative and measured tone has so much more impact than slightly panicked shouting.

▶ **However** 뒤로, 큰 목소리가 비록 유용하더라도 가급적 '적게' 써야 한다는 조언이 이어지고 있다. 마지막 문장은 '조용한' 목소리가 효과적일 때가 있다는 예시로 이 조언을 뒷받침한다.

구문 풀이

However, I would always advise that you **(should) use** your loudest voice incredibly sparingly and **avoid** shouting as much as possible.
→ 충고의 동사 **advise** 뒤에 나온 **that** 목적절에서 **should**가 생략되었다. 동사원형인 **use**와 **avoid**만 남아 있어도 '~해야 한다'고 해석하는 것이 포인트다.

구문 플러스 that 목적절의 should 생략 (2)

that 목적절이 '~해야 한다'는 의미를 나타낼 때에만 생략이 일어난다. 만일 '~해야 한다'라는 의미로 해석되지 않으면 that절의 시제는 문장 전체의 시제에 자연스럽게 맞춘다(시제 일치).

She insisted that he **apologize** for his mistakes.
그녀는 그가 실수에 대해 사과해야 한다고 주장했다. → 의무 주장
He **insisted** that the accident **had actually happened**.
그는 사고가 진짜로 일어났다고 주장했다. → 과거의 사실 주장

73 정답 ③ 77% *2022학년도 9월 모평*

해석 다양한 이론적 관점은 이주에 대한 통찰을 제공한다. 행위자들이 효용 극대화에 참여한다고 상정하는 경제학은 하나의 틀을 제시한다. 이런 관점에서는 개인은 합리적인 행위자라고, 즉 그들은 특정한 지역을 떠나는 것의 비용 및 편익과 대비하여 남는 것의 비용과 편익 모두를 평가한 바에 근거하여 이주 결정을 내린다고 추정된다. 편익은 단기적 및 장기적인 금전적 이득, 안전, 문화적 표현의 더 큰 자유를 포함할 수도 있지만 이에 국한되지는 않는다. (더 큰 금전적 혜택이 있는 사람들은 사치품을 구입하여 자신의 사회적 지위를 과시하기 위해 돈을 쓰는 경향이 있다.) 개인적 비용은 이동 비용, 타지에서 사는 것의 불확실성, 다른 언어에 적응하는 것의 어려움, 다른 문화에 대한 불확실성, 새로운 지역에서 사는 것에 대한 큰 염려를 포함하지만 이에 국한되지는 않는다. 또한 가족, 친구와의 이별과 미지의 것에 대한 두려움과 관련된 심리적 비용도 비용-편익 평가에서 고려되어야 한다.

해설 이주에 관한 경제학적 해석을 설명한 글로, 이주를 택하는 사람들은 떠나는 것과 남아있는 것의 비용과 편익을 평가하여 결정을 내린다는 내용이다. 하지만 ③은 이주에 관한 언급 없이 사치품 소비로 지위를 과시하려는 사람들을 언급한다. 따라서 전체 흐름과 관계없는 문장은 ③이다.

오답 풀이

선택률	오답 풀이
① 2%	앞서 언급된, '이주에 관한 경제학적 관점'이 **this perspective**로 자연스럽게 이어진다.

② 5%	이민으로 인한 편익을 부연 설명하며 ①과 자연스럽게 연결된다.
④ 11%	②에 이어 이주의 개인적 비용을 설명하고 있다.
⑤ 3%	④에 이어 이주의 심리적 비용을 추가로 언급한다.

Her friends laughed at her. 친구들은 그녀를 비웃었다.
→ **She was laughed at by her friends.**
　 그녀는 친구들에게 비웃음을 당했다.

지문 자세히 보기

01 A variety of theoretical perspectives provide insight into immigration. Economics, which assumes that actors engage in utility maximization, represents one framework.

▶ '이주'를 경제학의 효용 극대화 관점에서 설명할 수 있다는 화두를 제시한다.

02 From this perspective, it is assumed that individuals are rational actors, i.e., that they make migration decisions based on their assessment of the costs as well as benefits of remaining in a given area versus the costs and benefits of leaving.

▶ 경제학적 관점에서 보면 어느 한 곳에 남거나 떠나는 것의 비용과 편익(the costs and benefits)을 따져서 이주가 결정되는 것이라고 한다.

03 Benefits may include but are not limited to short-term and long-term monetary gains, safety, and greater freedom of cultural expression.

▶ 이주의 편익(Benefits)에 관한 설명이다.

04 People with greater financial benefits tend to use their money to show off their social status by purchasing luxurious items.

▶ 위에서 언급된 monetary gains가 financial benefits로 재진술되며 자연스럽게 연결되는 듯 하지만, 지위 과시를 위한 사치품 소비는 글의 주제와 관련이 없다.

05 Individual costs include but are not limited to the expense of travel, uncertainty of living in a foreign land, difficulty of adapting to a different language, uncertainty about a different culture, and the great concern about living in a new land. Psychic costs associated with separation from family, friends, and the fear of the unknown also should be taken into account in cost-benefit assessments.

▶ 이주의 편익에 이어서 이민의 비용(Individual costs, Psychic costs)을 설명하고 있다.

구문 풀이

Psychic costs associated with separation from family, friends, and the fear of the unknown also **should be taken into account** in cost-benefit assessments.

→ be taken into account는 구동사 take into account의 수동태이다. 「by + 행위자」는 생략되었다.

구문 플러스 구동사의 수동태

타동사가 부사나 전치사와 결합하여 만들어진 구동사는 수동태로 바뀌어도 「be + p.p.」 뒤에 부사나 전치사를 그대로 쓴다. 「by + 행위자」가 명시되는 경우 그 형태에 주의한다.

---

74 정답 ④ 81% 　2022학년도 6월 모평

해석 친족 유대 관계는 오늘날에도 계속 중요하다. 사람들이 자주 가족 모임을 갖는 미국과 같은 현대 사회에서, 그들은 자기 친척에게 자주 전화하고, 아주 다양한 도움을 제공한다. Eugene Litwak은 이 행동 패턴을 '수정확대가족'이라고 언급했다. 그것은 다세대의 유대 관계가 유지되기 때문에 확대가족 구조이지만, 일반적으로 세대 간 공동 거주에 기초를 두지 않고 대부분의 확대가족이 공동 집단으로서 기능하지는 않기 때문에 수정확대가족 구조이다. 비록 수정확대가족의 구성원들이 흔히 가까이 살기는 하지만, 수정확대가족은 지리적 근접이 필요치 않으며, 유대 관계는 친척이 상당히 멀리 떨어져 있더라도 유지된다. (가족 구성원들이 서로 아무리 멀리 떨어져 살지라도, 중요한 문제에 관해서는 가족의 최고 연장자가 결정을 내린다.) 친척이 항상 아주 가까이서 사는 전통적인 확대가족과는 대조적으로, 수정확대가족의 구성원들은 친척에게서 자유로이 멀리 이주해서 직업상의 발전을 위한 기회를 추구할 수도 있다.

해설 수정확대가족의 특징을 설명한 글로, 각 구성원은 지리적으로 떨어져 살지만 친밀한 관계를 유지한다는 내용이 주를 이룬다. 하지만 ④는 가족 문제의 결정권자에 관해 언급하므로 글의 내용과 무관하다. 따라서 전체 흐름과 관계없는 문장은 ④이다.

오답 풀이

선택률	오답 풀이
① 3%	두 번째 문장에서 언급된 오늘날의 가족 형태를 '수정확대가족'이라는 용어로 정리한다.
② 4%	①에서 제시한 수정확대가족의 의미를 보충 설명한다. It이 the modified extended family를 가리킨다.
③ 7%	②와 같은 흐름에서 수정확대가족이 지리적 근접성을 필요로 하지 않는다는 내용이 제시된다.
⑤ 3%	③을 이유로 수정확대가족의 구성원은 자유롭게 먼 곳으로 옮겨갈 수 있다는 내용이 연결된다.

지문 자세히 보기

01 Kinship ties continue to be important today. In modern societies such as the United States people frequently have family get-togethers, they telephone their relatives regularly, and they provide their kin with a wide variety of services.

▶ 오늘날의 가족관계(Kinship ties)를 화두로 제시한다.

02 Eugene Litwak has referred to this pattern of behaviour as the 'modified extended family'. It is an extended family structure because multigenerational ties are maintained, but it is modified because it does not usually rest on co-residence between the generations and most extended families do not act as corporate groups.

▶ 수정확대가족의 의미를 풀이하고 있다. 기존 확대가족과 달리 수정확대가족은 세대 간 공동 거주에 기초를 두지 않고, 공동 집단으로 기능하지도 않는다는 것이다.

03 Although modified extended family members often live close by, the modified extended family does not require geographical proximity and ties are maintained even when kin are separated by considerable distances.

▶ 위의 does not usually rest on co-residence가 does not require geographical proximity로 연결된다. 수정확대가족의 구성원은 공동 거주에 기반을 두지 않기에 지리적으로 가깝지 않아도 된다는 흐름이다.

04 The oldest member of the family makes the decisions on important issues, no matter how far away family members live from each other.

▶ 위의 separated by considerable distances와 'no matter how far away ~'가 서로 연결되어 보이지만, 가족 문제의 결정권이 '최고 연장자'에게 있다는 내용은 주제와 무관하다.

05 In contrast to the traditional extended family where kin always live in close proximity, the members of modified extended families may freely move away from kin to seek opportunities for occupational advancement.

▶ 앞서 나온 does not require geographical proximity가 may freely move away from kin으로 연결된다. 지리적 근접성이 필요하지 않기에 자유롭게 멀리 이주해갈 수 있다는 설명으로 글이 마무리된다.

구문 풀이

The oldest member of the family makes the decisions on important issues, **no matter how** far away family members live from each other.

→ no matter how는 복합관계부사 however(아무리 ~할지라도)와 같은 말로, 「no matter how + 형/부 + 주어 + 동사」의 어순으로 쓴다.

구문 플러스⁺ no matter + 의문사

「no matter + 의문사」는 '~할지라도'라는 의미의 부사절을 이끈다.

종류	의미	동의어
no matter who	누가[누구를] ~할지라도	whoever
no matter which	어떤 것이[어떤 것을] ~할지라도	whichever
no matter what	무엇이[무엇을] ~할지라도	whatever
no matter when	언제 ~할지라도	whenever
no matter where	어디에서 ~할지라도	wherever
no matter how	아무리 ~할지라도	however

Be yourself **no matter what** they say.
남들이 무슨 말을 하더라도 너답게 행동해.

Try to realize your dream **no matter how** hard it is.
아무리 어렵더라도 당신의 꿈을 실현하기 위해 노력하라.

---

75 정답 ③ 81%   *2021학년도 9월 모평*

해석 미국처럼 고도로 상업화된 환경에서는 많은 경관이 상품으로 여겨지는 것이 놀랍지 않다. 다시 말해 경관은 그 시장 잠재력 때문에 가치 있게 여겨진다. 주민들은 경관이 지역 사회를 위해 어떻게 소득을 창출할 수 있는가에 부분적으로 기초하여 정체성을 발전시킨다. 이 과정에는 자연의 요소를 상품으로 전환하는 것 그 이상이 포함된다. 사람들과 그들의 자아의식을 포함하여 경관 자체가 상품의 형태를 띤다. (미국에서 경관 보호는 일반적으로 산악 지대에 있는 황무지 지역을 보호하는 데 전통적으로 초점을 두고 있다.) 시간이 흐르면서 경관 정체성은 경관에 대한 이야기를 판매하기 위해 사용될 수 있는 일종의 '로고'로 발전할 수 있다. 따라서 California의 'Wine Country(포도주의 고장)', Florida의 'Sun Coast(태양의 해변)', 혹은 South Dakota의 'Badlands(악지)'는 외지인과 거주자가 모두 장소를 인식하는 방식을 형성하며, 이런 호칭들은 그곳에 사는 사람들의 문화와 관련된 일련의 기대치를 형성한다.

해설 경관이 상품처럼 여겨지는 상황에 관해 설명한 글인데, ③의 경우 '경관 보호'라는 무관한 소재를 언급하며 주제에서 벗어난다. 따라서 전체 흐름과 관계없는 문장은 ③이다.

오답 풀이

선택률	오답 풀이
① 3%	경관이 상품처럼 여겨진다는 앞 내용에 이어, 이것이 자연 요소의 상품화 그 이상을 뜻한다는 설명이 적절히 이어진다.
② 4%	사람들(의 자의식)을 포함한 경관 자체가 상품화된다는 설명으로 ①에서 언급한 '그 이상'의 의미를 보충한다.
④ 8%	경관이 일종의 판매 '로고'처럼 되어간다는 설명으로 ②의 내용을 확장한다.
⑤ 2%	④ 내용에 해당하는 예시가 나온다.

지문 자세히 보기

01 In a highly commercialized setting such as the United States, it is not surprising that many landscapes are seen as commodities. In other words, they are valued because of their market potential.

▶ 경관이 시장 가치(market potential) 중심으로 평가되며 상품(commodities)이 되어가는 풍조를 언급한다.

02 Residents develop an identity in part based on how the landscape can generate income for the community. This process involves more than the conversion of the natural elements into commodities. The landscape itself, including the people and their sense of self, takes on the form of a commodity.

▶ 'how ~ generate income'이 위의 market potential을 부연하며, '얼마의 수익을 가져다줄 것인지'가 곧 경관의 시장 가치임을 설명하고 있다. 키워드인 a commodity가 반복된다.

03 Landscape protection in the US traditionally focuses on protecting areas of wilderness, typically in mountainous regions.

▶ Landscape protection, wilderness, mountainous regions 등 글의 다른 부분에서 등장하지 않는 소재가 열거되므로 흐름상 부자연스럽다.

04 Over time, the landscape identity can evolve into a sort of "logo" that can be used to sell the stories of the landscape. Thus, California's "Wine Country," Florida's "Sun Coast," or South Dakota's "Badlands" shape how both outsiders and residents perceive a place, and these labels build a set of expectations associated with the culture of those who live there.

▶ 경관 정체성이 경관에 관한 이야기를 파는(sell) 로고가 될 수 있다는 설명과 함께 예시(California's ~ "Badlands")가 열거된다.

구문 풀이

Over time, the landscape identity can evolve into a sort of "logo" that **can be used to sell** the stories of the landscape.
→ 「**be used to** + 동사원형」은 '~하기 위해 사용되다'라는 뜻으로, use의 수동태에 목적의 **to**부정사가 함께 쓰인 구문이다.

구문 플러스 유의할 be used to 표현

「be used to + 동사원형」: ~하기 위해 사용되다
「be used to + (동)명사」: ~(하는 것)에 익숙해지다

A hammer **is used to hit** a nail into the wall.
망치는 벽에 못을 박을 때 사용된다.

She **is used to getting** up early.
그녀는 일찍 일어나는 데 익숙하다.

---

76 정답 ③ 68%   *2020학년도 대수능*

해석 상식적 지식에는 장점이 있을 수도 있지만 약점도 있는데, 그중 중요한 것은 그것이 모순되는 경우가 많다는 것이다. 예를 들어, 우리는 비슷한 사람들이 서로 좋아하기 마련이라는 말('유유상종')을 듣지만, 닮지 않은 사람들이 서로 좋아하기 마련이라는 말('정반대되는 사람들은 서로에게 끌린다')도 듣는다. 우리는 집단이 개인보다 더 현명하고 더 똑똑하다는 말('백지장도 맞들면 낫다')을 듣지만, 집단 작업이 필연적으로 좋지 않은 결과를 만든다는 말('사공이 많으면 배가 산으로 간다')도 듣는다. 이런 모순된 말들 각각은 특정한 상황에서는 사실일 수도 있지만, 언제 적용되는지와 언제 적용되지 않는지에 관한 명확한 진술이 없으면 격언은 사람들 사이의 관계에 대한 통찰력을 거의 제공하지 못한다. (그러한 이유로 우리는 삶의 긴 여정에서 어려움과 도전에 직면할 때마다 격언에 매우 의존한다.) 그것들은 우리가 결정을 내려야 하는 상황에서는 그야말로 거의 아무런 지침도 제공하지 못한다. 예를 들어, 위험을 수반하는 선택에 직면할 때, '모험하지 않으면 아무것도 얻을 수 없다' 또는 '나중에 후회하는 것보다 조심하는 것이 낫다' 중에 우리는 어느 지침을 이용해야 하는가?

해설 상식을 말하는 격언에는 모순이 많다는 약점이 있음을 설명하는 글이다. ②에서 격언은 명확한 상황 진술이 없으면 관계에 대한 통찰력을 주지 못한다고 설명하는데, ③은 '그래서' 우리가 격언에 많이 의존한다는 부자연스러운 결과를 제시하고 있다. 따라서 전체 흐름과 관계없는 문장은 ③이다.

지문 자세히 보기

01 Although commonsense knowledge may have merit, it also has weaknesses, not the least of which is that it often contradicts itself.

▶ 상식(commonsense knowledge)에는 모순(contradicts)이 흔히 있다는 화두를 제시하고 있다.

02 For example, we hear that people who are similar will like one another ("Birds of a feather flock together") but also that persons who are dissimilar will like each other ("Opposites attract"). We are told that groups are wiser and smarter than individuals ("Two heads are better than one") but also that group work inevitably produces poor results ("Too many cooks spoil the broth").

▶ For example 뒤로, 상식을 나타내는 격언이 서로 모순되는 사례가 열거된다.

03 Each of these contradictory statements may hold true under particular conditions, but without a clear statement of when they apply and when they do not, aphorisms provide little insight into relations among people.

▶ 위의 예시를 these contradictory statements로 정리하며, 이것이 인간 관계에 대해 통찰력을 얼마 제공해주지 못하는 한계가 있음을 지적한다.

04 That is why we heavily depend on aphorisms whenever we face difficulties and challenges in the long journey of our lives.

▶ 앞의 aphorisms가 반복되지만 주제와 반대되어 흐름상 무관한 문장이다. 격언의 모순 때문에 통찰력을 얻을 수 없는데 '바로 그래서' 우리가 격언에 많이 의지한다는 진술은 어색하다.

05 They provide even less guidance in situations where we must make decisions. For example, when facing a choice that entails risk, which guideline should we use — "Nothing ventured, nothing gained" or "Better safe than sorry"?

▶ 앞서 나온 provide little insight와 비슷한 표현으로 provide even less guidance가 등장한다. 이는 모순된 격언이 결정 상황에서도 크게 도움이 되지 않음을 설명한다.

구문 풀이

Although commonsense knowledge may have merit, it also has weaknesses, **not the least of which** is that it often contradicts itself.

→ **not the least of which**(그중 가장 중요한 것은)는 계속적 용법의 관용 표현이다. **which**는 **weaknesses**를 받는다.

구문 플러스⁺ not the least of which

선행사 중에서도 '특히 가장 중요한' 요소를 뒤에서 강조하고 싶을 때 not the least of which를 사용한다.

There are many human rights, not the least of which is the right to life.
많은 인권이 있는데, 그중에서도 생명권이 가장 중요하다.

---

77 정답 ④ 85%　　　　　　　*2020학년도 9월 모평*

해석 우리가 매일 하는 일의 많은 부분은 자동적이고 습관에 의해 좌우되며, 의식적인 인식을 거의 필요로 하지 않는데, 이는 나쁜 것이 아니다. Duhigg의 설명에 따르면, 우리의 습관은 꼭 필요한 정신 에너지 절약 장치이다. 우리는 새로운 문제가 발생할 때 그것을 해결할 수 있도록 의식적인 마음의 부담을 덜어주어야 한다. 예를 들어, 사교댄스를 추는 방법에 대한 문제를 해결하고 나면, 우리는 그것을 습관적으로 할 수 있어서, 춤을 추는 동안 (춤에 집중하는) 대신에 대화에 집중할 만큼 정신적으로 자유로워진다. 하지만 탱고를 처음 배울 때 말을 하려고 해보면 엉망진창이 되며, 우리는 스텝에 집중하려면 의식적인 주의가 필요하다. (탱고 음악가는 다양한 배경의 더 다양한 청중을 끌어모으기 위해 각기 다른 장르의 음악을 한데 모은다.) 만약 우리가 모든 행동, 예를 들어 우리가 딛는 모든 스텝에서 발을 어디에 두어야 할지에 의식적으로 초점을 맞추어야 한다면 우리가 성취할 수 있는 것이 얼마나 적을지 상상해 보라.

해설 습관화되어 자동으로 처리되는 행동은 우리의 정신적 에너지를 아껴준다는 내용의 글이다. 하지만 ④는 탱고 음악가가 청중을 끌어모으는 방법에 관해 설명하므로 주제와 무관하다. 따라서 전체 흐름과 관계없는 문장은 ④이다.

오답 풀이

선택률	오답 풀이
① 2%	습관이 우리의 정신적 에너지를 아껴준다는 앞 내용에 이어, 이것이 필요함을 설명하고 있다.
② 3%	춤이 습관화된 상황에서의 정신적 자유를 예로 들고 있다.
③ 5%	②와 반대로 춤이 습관화되지 않은 상황을 언급한다.
⑤ 2%	②와 ③의 예시를 토대로 볼 때, 모든 행동에 의식적 주의를 기울여야 한다면 어떻겠는지 상상해보라는 말로 습관화의 이점을 시사한다.

지문 자세히 보기⁺

01 Much of what we do each day is automatic and guided by habit, requiring little conscious awareness, and that's not a bad thing. As Duhigg explains, our habits are necessary mental energy savers.

▶ 행동이 습관화되는(habit) 것은 우리의 정신적 에너지를 아껴준다는 면에서 나쁘지 않다는 핵심 내용이 제시된다.

02 We need to relieve our conscious minds so we can solve new problems as they come up.

▶ 위의 mental energy savers와 relieve our conscious minds가 서로 같은 의미이다. 습관이 필요하다는 부연 설명이다.

03 Once we've solved the puzzle of how to ballroom dance, for example, we can do it by habit, and so be mentally freed to focus on a conversation while dancing instead.

▶ 춤추는 상황을 예로 들어, 동작이 습관화되면 우리는 대화 등 다른 활동에 참여할 수 있을 만큼 정신적으로 자유롭다(mentally freed)는 점을 설명한다.

04 But try to talk when first learning to dance the tango, and it's a disaster — we need our conscious attention to focus on the steps.

▶ 위와 대비되는 상황으로 탱고를 처음 배울 때를 언급한다. 이 경우 모든 동작에 의식적 주의가 들어가기 때문에 다른 활동을 하지 못할 것이라는 설명이 이어진다.

05 Tango musicians bring different genres of music together to attract a more diverse audience from varying backgrounds.

▶ 위의 tango에 이어 Tango musicians가 나오기 때문에 연결되어 보이지만, 탱고 음악가들이 청중을 끌어모으는 방법은 글의 주제와 관련이 없다.

06 Imagine how little we'd accomplish if we had to focus consciously on every behavior — e.g., on where to place our feet for each step we take.

▶ 모든 행동에 주의를 기울여야 하면 많은 것을 성취할 정신적 에너지가 부족하므로, 습관화로 인한 에너지 절약이 필요하다는 결론을 간접적으로 드러내고 있다.

구문 풀이

But **try** to talk when first learning to dance the tango, **and** it's a disaster — we need our conscious attention to focus on the steps.
→ 「명령문 + and(~하라, 그러면 …)」 구조이다.

구문 플러스⁺ 명령문 + 등위접속사

명령문 + and: ~하라, 그러면 …
명령문 + or: ~하라, 그렇지 않으면 …

Be nice to others, and you'll have lots of friends.
남들에게 잘해. 그러면 친구가 많아질 거야.

Hurry up, or you'll be late for class.
서둘러. 그렇지 않으면 수업에 늦을 거야.

유형 플러스⁺ 무관한 문장 찾기

중심 내용과 어긋나는 문장을 찾는 유형으로, 난이도는 쉽다.

· **문제 해결 Tip.**
　① 선택지 앞의 도입부에서 글의 핵심 소재, 중심 내용 등을 파악한다.
　② 중심 내용을 기준으로 각 선택지 문장이 흐름상 적절한지 파악한다.
　③ 주제와 상관없는 지엽적 소재만 다루지는 않는지, 또는 주제와 반대되는 표현이 나오지는 않는지에 초점을 맞춰 독해한다.

78 정답 ③ 53%   2024학년도 6월 모평

해석 다윈은 얼굴이 붉어지는 것을 특별나게 인간적인 것으로 여겨, 이것이 사회적 환경에서 당혹감과 자의식에 의한 무의식적인 신체 반응을 나타낸다고 보았다.

(B) 우리가 혼자 있을 때는 어색하거나 부끄럽거나 창피하다고 느끼더라도 얼굴이 붉어지지 않는다. 이것은 우리가 다른 사람들이 우리를 어떻게 생각할지 염려하기 때문인 듯하다. 연구에 따르면 단지 얼굴이 붉어진다는 말을 듣는 것만으로도 그렇게 된다는 것이 확인되었다. 우리는 다른 사람들이 우리 피부를 꿰뚫어 우리 마음을 들여다볼 수 있는 것처럼 느낀다.

(C) 하지만, 우리가 때로 자신도 모르는 사이에 얼굴이 새빨개질 때 사라지고 싶어 하기는 해도, 심리학자들은 얼굴이 붉어지는 것이 실제로는 긍정적인 사회적 목적에 부합한다고 주장한다. 얼굴이 붉어질 때, 이것은 우리가 사회적 규범을 어겼음을 인정한다는 것을 다른 사람에게 알리는 신호이자 실수에 대한 사과이다.

(A) 아마도 우리가 잠깐 체면을 잃는 것이 집단의 장기적인 결속에는 도움이 되는 것 같다. 흥미롭게도 누군가가 사회적 실수를 저지른 후 얼굴을 붉히면, 우리는 그 사람을 얼굴을 붉히지 않는 사람보다 더 호의적인 시각으로 바라보게 된다.

해설 얼굴이 붉어지는 것이 '사회적 환경'에서의 반응이라는 주어진 글에 이어, (B)에서는 '혼자 있을 때'를 대비해 설명한다. 한편 (C)는 얼굴이 붉어지는 것이 긍정적인 사회적 목적에 부합한다는 내용과 함께 그 의미를 설명하고, (A) 또한 얼굴 붉힘이 집단의 결속에 도움이 된다고 말하며 (C)를 뒷받침한다. 따라서 글의 순서로 가장 적절한 것은 ③ '(B)-(C)-(A)'이다.

오답 풀이

선택률	오답 풀이
① 4%	(A)와 (C)가 모두 얼굴을 붉히는 것이 사회적으로 도움이 될 수 있다는 내용이므로, 두 단락을 (C)의 However로 연결하면 어색하다.
② 25%	(B)는 우리가 얼굴이 붉어질 때 속을 들킨 기분을 느낀다는 내용으로 끝나는데, 여기서 바로 '체면의 상실이 사회 결속 기능을 수행한다'는 (A)로 넘어가면 어색하다. (B)에서 사회적 기능에 관한 내용이 전혀 언급되지 않기 때문이다.
④ 13%	(A)의 마지막은 '얼굴을 붉히는 사람들에 대한 우리의 호감'을 언급하는데, (B)의 처음은 이와 무관하게도 '우리가 혼자 있을 때 얼굴을 붉히지 않는다'는 내용이다.
⑤ 10%	②와 동일

지문 자세히 보기

01 Darwin saw blushing as uniquely human, representing an involuntary physical reaction caused by embarrassment and self-consciousness in a social environment.

▶ 핵심 소재로 '얼굴이 붉어지는 것(blushing)'을 언급하며, 이것이 사회적 상황(a social environment)에서의 반응이라고 설명한다.

02 If we feel awkward, embarrassed or ashamed when we are alone, we don't blush; it seems to be caused by our concern about what others are thinking of us. Studies have confirmed that simply being told you are blushing brings it on. We feel as though others can see through our skin and into our mind.

▶ 사회적 상황과 대조되는 예시로 혼자 있을 때(when we are alone)가 언급된다. 혼자 있을 때는 얼굴이 붉어지지 않는 것으로 보아 이것이 '사회적 상황에서의 반응'임을 알 수 있다고 한다. 위의 embarrassment and self-consciousness가 feel awkward, embarrassed or ashamed로 이어지고 있다.

03 However, while we sometimes want to disappear when we involuntarily go bright red, psychologists argue that blushing actually serves a positive social purpose. When we blush, it's a signal to others that we recognize that a social norm has been broken; it is an apology for a faux pas.

▶ '남이 우리 피부를 뚫고 우리 마음을 관찰했다'는 느낌 때문에 얼굴이 붉어진다는 설명에 이어, 얼굴 붉힘으로 인한 '사회적 이점(a positive social purpose)'을 언급한다. However가 있어 소재가 자연스럽게 전환된다.

04 Maybe our brief loss of face benefits the long-term cohesion of the group. Interestingly, if someone blushes after making a social mistake, they are viewed in a more favourable light than those who don't blush.

▶ 위의 a positive social purpose가 benefits the long-term cohesion of the group라는 더 구체적인 표현으로 재진술된다. '사회적 기능'이란 결국 '집단의 장기적 결속'이며, 실제로 우리는 얼굴을 붉히는 사람을 더 좋게 보기도 한다는 설명이 추가된다.

구문 풀이

Studies have confirmed that **simply being told you are blushing brings it on**.

→ 생략된 의미상 주어인 you가 '듣는' 것이므로 동명사의 수동형(being p.p.)인 being told가 쓰였다.

구문 플러스⁺ 동명사의 수동태

동명사의 의미상 주어와 to부정사가 수동 관계일 때, 동명사는 being p.p. 형태로 쓴다.

He rejected **being sent** to another branch.
그는 다른 지점으로 파견되는 것을 거절했다.

79 정답 ④ 29%   2023학년도 대수능

해석 결과 기반 가격 책정 중 가장 일반적으로 알려진 형태는 '승소 시 보수 약정'이라고 불리는 관행으로, 변호사들이 이용한다.

(C) 승소 시 보수 약정은 개인 상해 및 특정 소비자 소송에 대해 비용이

청구되는 주요 방식이다. 이 방식에서 변호사는 소송이 해결될 때까지 수수료나 지불금을 받지 않는데, 이때 그들은 의뢰인이 받는 금액의 일정 비율을 받는다.

(A) 따라서 의뢰인에게 유리한 결과만 보수가 지불된다. 의뢰인의 관점에서 보면 이러한 가격 책정은 타당한데, 그 부분적인 이유는 이러한 소송의 의뢰인 대부분이 법률 사무소에 익숙지 않고 어쩌면 겁먹을 수 있기 때문이다. 그들의 가장 큰 두려움은 해결까지 몇 년이 걸릴지도 모르는 소송에 대한 높은 수수료이다.

(B) 승소 시 보수 약정을 사용하여, 의뢰인은 합의금을 받을 때까지 수수료를 지불하지 않도록 보장받는다. 이런 식의 승소 시 보수 약정 사례에서, 서비스의 경제적 가치는 서비스가 있기 전에 결정하기 어렵고, 공급자는 구매자에게 가치를 전달하는 위험과 보상을 그들이 나눌 수 있게 하는 가격을 형성한다.

해설 '승소 시 보수 약정'이라는 용어를 소개하는 주어진 글 뒤에, 이 용어를 다시 언급하며 관행의 내용을 자세히 설명하는 **(C)**가 먼저 연결된다. 특히 **(C)**의 후반부는 변호사가 소송이 다 해결된 후 보수를 지불받는다는 내용인데, **(A)**는 결과적으로(Thus) 의뢰인에 유리한 판결이 났을 때만 변호사도 보수를 가져갈 수 있다는 내용으로 연결된다. 나아가 **(A)**의 후반부에 의뢰인들이 높은 소송 수수료를 두려워한다는 내용이 언급되는데, **(B)**는 '이 두려움'이 경감될 수 있다는 내용이다. 따라서 글의 순서로 가장 적절한 것은 ④ '(C)-(A)-(B)'이다.

오답 풀이

선택률	오답 풀이
① 2%	주어진 글은 **contingency pricing**이라는 용어를 언급만 했을 뿐 개념을 자세히 설명하지 않는다. 따라서 어떤 상황의 결과(**Therefore**)를 설명하는 **(A)**와 연결되지 않는다.
② 16%	**(B)**의 첫 문장은 주어진 글과 연결되어도 자연스럽다. 하지만 두 번째 문장의 **these and other instances**는 이미 **contingency pricing**의 예시를 든 뒤 일반적인 결론으로 나아갈 때 쓰는 표현이다. 따라서 **(B)**는 글의 전반부보다는, 후반부 단락으로 적합하다.
③ 13%	
⑤ 40%	**(C)**가 '변호사-의뢰인'의 사례를 다루므로, 같은 사례를 계속 언급하는 **(A)**가 먼저 나와야만 한다. **(B)**는 첫 문장에서 사례를 마무리하고 마지막 문장에서 일반적 결론으로 나아가는 단락이기 때문에 **(A)**보다 앞에 나오면 사례의 흐름이 끊기게 된다.

지문 · 자세히 보기

01 The most commonly known form of results-based pricing is a practice called *contingency pricing*, used by lawyers.

▶ '승소 시 보수 약정'이 글의 핵심 소재이다.

02 Contingency pricing is the major way that personal injury and certain consumer cases are billed. In this approach, lawyers do not receive fees or payment until the case is settled, when they are paid a percentage of the money that the client receives.

▶ 용어를 반복 제시하며, 이 관행이 자주 적용되는 법률 사례를 언급하기 시작하는 단락이다. 승소 시 보수 약정 관행에 따를 때, 변호사들은 의뢰인이 받는 돈의 일정 비율을 보수로 책정받는다는 내용이 언급된다.

03 Therefore, only an outcome in the client's favor is compensated. From the client's point of view, the pricing makes sense in part because most clients in these cases are unfamiliar with and possibly intimidated by law firms. Their biggest fears are high fees for a case that may take years to settle.

▶ 'they are paid ~ the client receives'와 'only an outcome ~ compensated'는 사실상 같은 내용이다. '의뢰인의 합의금에서 일정 비율을 뗀다'는 말은 결국 '의뢰인이 이겨서 돈을 받아야 변호사도 돈을 받는다'는 의미라는 것이다. 나머지 두 문장은 이것이 의뢰인 입장에서 타당한 이유를 설명한다.

04 By using contingency pricing, clients are ensured that they pay no fees until they receive a settlement. In these and other instances of contingency pricing, the economic value of the service is hard to determine before the service, and providers develop a price that allows them to share the risks and rewards of delivering value to the buyer.

▶ 앞에서 의뢰인들은 높은 소송 수수료에 대해 걱정(biggest fears)한다고 언급한 데 이어, 승소 시 보수 약정 관행을 이용하면 이 걱정이 해결된다(clients are ensured ~ a settlement)는 내용이 자연스럽게 연결된다. 마지막 문장은 일반적인 공급자(providers)와 구매자(the buyer)를 언급하며 승소 시 보수 약정의 경제학적 의미를 정리하고 있다.

구문 풀이

~ the economic value of the service is hard to determine before the service, ~
→ 가주어-진주어 구문(it is hard to determine the economic value of the service ~)에서 진주어인 to부정사의 목적어를 문장 전체의 주어로 올린 형태이다.

구문 플러스 목적어 상승 구문

주로 가주어-진주어 구문에서 to부정사의 목적어를 문장 전체의 주어로 올려 문장을 다시 구성한 형태를 말한다. 문장에 difficult, easy, hard, impossible 등의 형용사가 있을 때 이런 재구성이 가능하다.

Music is easy for us to appreciate.
(= **It is easy for us to appreciate music.**)
음악은 우리가 감상하기 쉽다.

80 정답 ② 61%　　　　　*2022학년도 대수능*

해석 시장 반응 모형에 따르면, 공급자가 새로운 공급원을 찾게 하고, 혁신가가 대용하게 하고, 소비자가 아껴 쓰게 하고, 대안이 생기게 하는 것은 바로 가격의 인상이다.

(B) 특정 재화나 서비스에 과세하여 가격이 인상되면 이러한 자원의 사용이 줄거나 새로운 공급원 또는 선택 사항의 창조적 혁신이 있을 것이다. 세금을 통해 조성된 돈은 정부가 직접 서비스를 공급하거나 대안을 모색하는 데 사용할 수 있다.

(A) 그러한 '환경세'의 많은 예가 존재한다. 예를 들어, 쓰레기 매립 비용, 인건비, 쓰레기 처리를 준비하는 데 관련된 비용에 직면한 일부 도시는 가정이 모든 폐기물을 특별 쓰레기봉투에 담아서 처리하도록 요구했는

데, 이는 소비자가 직접 구입하는 것이며 흔히 한 장당 1달러 이상의 비용이 드는 것이었다.

(C) 그 결과 재활용이 크게 증가했고 소비자가 포장과 폐기물에 더 세심한 주의를 기울이게 되었다. 소비자에게 쓰레기 비용을 자기 것으로 만들게 함으로써, 가정에서 나오는 쓰레기 흐름의 감소가 관찰되었다.

해설 주어진 글에서 공급자와 소비자의 행동을 변화시키는 중대 요인으로 가격 인상을 언급한 후, **(B)**는 과세를 통해 가격 인상을 유도했을 때의 결과를 소개한다. **(A)**는 이러한 과세 중 하나로 '환경세'를 언급하며 예를 들기 시작하고, **(C)**는 예시를 마무리 짓는다. 따라서 글의 순서로 가장 적절한 것은 ② '(B)-(A)-(C)'이다.

오답 풀이

선택률	오답 풀이
① 4%	주어진 글에 '세금'에 관한 언급이 없으므로 '이러한 세금'을 언급하는 **(A)**가 바로 이어질 수 없다.
③ 15%	**(B)**에서 '과세'를 일반적으로 언급하는데 **(C)**에서는 '소비자에게 쓰레기 처리 비용이 부과된' 구체적인 상황을 다루므로 흐름이 매끄럽지 않다.
④ 12%	주어진 글에서 '가격 인상'을 화제로 꺼낸 후 중간 설명 없이 곧바로 '결과'를 제시하는 **(C)**가 이어질 수는 없다.
⑤ 9%	

지문 자세히 보기

01 According to the market response model, it is **increasing prices** that drive providers to search for new sources, innovators to substitute, consumers to conserve, and alternatives to emerge.

▶ 공급자, 소비자, 혁신가 등 다양한 경제 주체의 행동 변화를 야기하는 요소로 가격 인상(**increasing prices**)을 언급하고 있다.

02 **Taxing** certain goods or services, and so **increasing prices**, should result in either decreased use of these resources or creative innovation of new sources or options. The money raised through **the tax** can be used directly by the government either to supply services or to search for alternatives.

▶ **increasing prices**라는 표현이 반복되는 가운데, 가격 인상의 수단으로 과세(**Taxing, the tax**)를 언급하고 있다.

03 Many examples of such "green taxes" exist. Facing landfill costs, labor expenses, and related costs in the provision of garbage disposal, for example, some cities have required households to dispose of all waste in **special trash bags, purchased by consumers themselves, and often costing a dollar or more each.**

▶ 과세의 예로 **green taxes**, 나아가 **special trash bags**를 언급한다. 시민들이 직접 돈을 주고 사는 특별 쓰레기 봉투의 형태로 '환경세'를 부과한 경우를 설명한다.

04 **The results** have been **greatly increased recycling and more careful attention** by consumers to packaging and waste. By internalizing the costs of trash to consumers, there has been an observed decrease in the flow of garbage from households.

▶ 쓰레기 봉투 구매를 통한 환경세의 결과(**The results**)로 사람들이 재활용을 더 잘하고 폐기물 처리에 더 주의를 기울이게 되었다는 내용이 나온다.

구문 풀이

The money raised through the tax can be used directly by the government **either** to supply services **or** to search for alternatives.
→ 「**either A or B**(A와 B 둘 중 하나)」 구문이다. A, B 자리에 모두 목적의 **to**부정사구가 나왔다.

구문 플러스 either A or B

「either A or B(A와 B 둘 중 하나)」 구문의 A, B는 병렬구조를 이룬다.

I go to school **either** by subway **or** by bus.
나는 지하철 아니면 버스로 등교한다.

The students need to **either** take the test **or** write a report.
학생들은 시험을 치거나 아니면 보고서를 써야 한다.

81 정답 ① 20%　　　　　　2022학년도 6월 모평

해석 공간 기준점(공간적으로 기준이 되는 장소)은 자기 자신보다 더 크다. 이것은 그다지 역설적이지 않은데, 랜드마크(주요 지형지물)는 그 자체이기도 하지만, 또한 주변 지역을 (자신의 범위로) 규정하기도 한다. **(A)** 많은 대학 캠퍼스에서 반복되어 온 전형적인 예에서, 연구원들은 먼저 학생들에게서 캠퍼스 랜드마크의 목록을 수집한다. 그런 다음, 그들은 다른 학생 집단에게 쌍으로 이루어진 장소 사이의 거리를 추정하게 하는데, 일부는 랜드마크까지, 일부는 캠퍼스의 평범한 건물까지의 거리를 추정해 보라고 요청한다. **(C)** 주목할 만한 결과는 평범한 장소에서 랜드마크까지의 거리가 랜드마크에서 평범한 장소까지의 거리보다 더 짧다고 추정된다는 것이다. 그래서 사람들은 Pierre의 집에서 에펠탑까지의 거리가 에펠탑에서 Pierre의 집까지의 거리보다 더 짧다고 추정할 것이다. 블랙홀처럼, 랜드마크는 평범한 장소를 자기 방향으로 끌어들이는 것처럼 보이지만, 평범한 장소들은 그렇지 않다. **(B)** 거리 추정에 관한 이 비대칭은 A에서부터 B까지의 거리가 B에서부터 A까지의 거리와 같아야 한다는 가장 기초적인 유클리드 거리 법칙에 위배된다. 그렇다면, 거리에 관한 추정은 반드시 일관성이 있는 것은 아니다.

해설 랜드마크는 주변 공간을 규정하는 특성이 있다고 설명하는 주어진 글 뒤로, '전형적인 실험 예시'를 드는 **(A)**가 이어진다. **(C)**는 **(A)**에서 언급한 실험의 결과를 소개하고, **(B)**는 **(C)**의 결과를 바탕으로 최종적 결론을 도출한다. 따라서 글의 순서로 가장 적절한 것은 ① '(A)-(C)-(B)'이다.

오답 풀이

선택률	오답 풀이
② 20%	주어진 글에 '거리의 비대칭'으로 지칭할 만한 내용이 없으므로 **(B)**가 바로 이어지는 것은 부자연스럽다.
③ 19%	
④ 15%	실험 내용이 언급되기도 전에 '놀랄 만한 결과'를 소개하는 **(C)**부터 이어지는 것은 부자연스럽다.
⑤ 26%	

01 Spatial reference points are larger than themselves. This isn't really a paradox: landmarks are themselves, but they also define neighborhoods around themselves.

▶ 공간 기준점으로서 랜드마크는 주변 공간을 규정하는(define) 특성이 있다는 일반론이 제시된다.

02 In a paradigm that has been repeated on many campuses, researchers first collect a list of campus landmarks from students. Then they ask another group of students to estimate the distances between pairs of locations, some to landmarks, some to ordinary buildings on campus.

▶ 예시(a paradigm)로 대학 캠퍼스에서의 연구가 소개된다. 참여자들로 하여금 각각 랜드마크와 일반 건물을 도착점으로 한 거리를 측정해 보게 한다는 실험 과정이 언급된다.

03 The remarkable finding is that distances from an ordinary location to a landmark are judged shorter than distances from a landmark to an ordinary location. So, people would judge the distance from Pierre's house to the Eiffel Tower to be shorter than the distance from the Eiffel Tower to Pierre's house. Like black holes, landmarks seem to pull ordinary locations toward themselves, but ordinary places do not.

▶ 실험의 결과(The remarkable finding)로서 같은 두 지점 간의 거리 측정값이 희한하게도 어디를 도착지로 보고 가는가에 따라 달라진다는 내용이 제시된다.

04 This asymmetry of distance estimates violates the most elementary principles of Euclidean distance, that the distance from A to B must be the same as the distance from B to A. Judgments of distance, then, are not necessarily coherent.

▶ 최종적 결론이 제시되는 단락이다. 위에서 언급한 '측정값이 다른' 상황이 거리상의 비대칭(This asymmetry of distance estimates)이라는 말로 요약된다.

구문 풀이

Like black holes, landmarks seem to pull ordinary locations toward themselves, but ordinary places do not.

→ 전치사 like는 뒤에 명사구를 동반하여 '~처럼'이라는 의미를 나타낸다. 형태가 비슷한 alike(비슷한)와 비교해 둔다.

구문 플러스' like vs. alike

like ① 동사: 좋아하다 ② 전치사: ~와 같은
alike ① 형용사: 비슷한, 닮은 ② 부사: 둘 다, 똑같이

Like many other kids, he likes to be praised.
다른 많은 아이들과 마찬가지로, 그는 칭찬받기를 좋아한다.
Your family all look alike. 네 가족은 다 닮았네.

---

82 정답 ② 46% 2021학년도 9월 모평

해석 기원전 5세기에, 그리스의 철학자 Protagoras는 "인간이 만물의 척도이다."라고 선언했다. 다시 말해서, 우리는 세상을 향해 "당신은 무슨 쓸모가 있는가?"라고 물어볼 자격이 있다고 느낀다.
(B) 우리는 우리가 세상의 기준이라고, 즉 모든 것이 우리와 비교되어야 한다고 추정한다. 그런 추정은 우리로 하여금 많은 것을 간과하게 한다.
(A) 공감, 의사소통, 슬픔, 도구 만들기 등 '우리를 인간답게 만들어 준다고' 일컬어지는 능력들은 모두 우리와 세상을 공유하는, 지력을 지닌 다른 존재들에게도 다양한 정도로 존재한다. 척추동물(어류, 양서류, 파충류, 조류, 포유류)은 모두 동일한 기본 골격, 장기, 신경계, 호르몬, 행동을 공유한다.
(C) 다양한 자동차 모델들이 각각 엔진, 동력 전달 체계, 네 바퀴, 문, 좌석을 가지고 있는 것과 마찬가지로, 우리는 주로 우리의 외부 윤곽과 몇 가지 내부적인 조정 면에서 다르다. 하지만 순진한 자동차 구매자들처럼, 대부분의 사람들은 오직 동물들의 다양한 겉모습만을 본다.

해설 주어진 글에서 인간이 만물의 '척도'라는 인용구를 제시하고, (B)는 이것이 인간을 세상의 '기준'이자 '비교 대상'으로 보는 시각임을 부연한다. 한편 (B) 후반부는 이런 시각 때문에 우리가 많은 것을 놓친다고 지적하고, (A)는 소위 '인간만의' 능력이라고 여겨지는 것들이 사실은 인간만의 것이 아님을 상기시킨다. 이어서 (C)는 인간과 다른 동물이 별 차이가 없음을 자동차에 빗대 설명한다. 따라서 글의 순서로 가장 적절한 것은 ② '(B)-(A)-(C)'이다.

오답 풀이

선택률	오답 풀이
① 9%	인간이 만물의 척도라는 언급 뒤로 인간의 능력이 (기준이 될 만큼) 독보적이지 않다는 내용의 (A)가 이어지는 것은 부자연스럽다.
③ 28%	인간을 기준으로 보는 시각 때문에 간과되는 것들이 생겨난다는 (B) 뒤로, '(A) 인간은 다른 동물과 다르지 않다 → (C) 달라도 외관상에서 다를 뿐이다'라는 흐름이 더 자연스럽다.
④ 13%	인간이 만물의 기준이자 척도라는 내용 뒤로 인간과 동물이 별 차이가 없다는 내용의 (C)가 역접의 연결어 없이 바로 이어지는 것은 부자연스럽다.
⑤ 5%	

01 In the fifth century *B.C.E.,* the Greek philosopher Protagoras pronounced, "Man is the measure of all things." In other words, we feel entitled to ask the world, "What good are you?"

▶ 고대 그리스 철학자의 말을 인용해 인간을 만물의 척도로 보는 시각을 소개한다.

02 We assume that we are the world's standard, that all things should be compared to us. Such an assumption makes us overlook a lot.

▶ 위의 measure가 standard, compared로 재진술된다. 인간을 기준으로 보는 시각은 우리가 많은 것을 간과하게 한다는 내용으로, overlook이 여기서 흐름을 반전시킨다.

03 Abilities said to "make us human" — empathy, communication, grief, toolmaking, and so on — all exist to varying degrees among other minds sharing the world with us. Animals with backbones (fishes, amphibians, reptiles, birds, and mammals) all share the same basic skeleton, organs, nervous systems, hormones, and behaviors.

▶ '우리가 간과하게 되는 것들'을 구체적으로 설명한다. 우리가 '인간에게만' 있다고 여기는 많은 능력이 다른 존재에게도 다 공유되는(all exist, all share) 것임을 언급하며, 인간이 만물의 기준이라는 시각을 반박하고 있다.

04 Just as different models of automobiles each have an engine, drive train, four wheels, doors, and seats, we differ mainly in terms of our outside contours and a few internal tweaks. But like naive car buyers, most people see only animals' varied exteriors.

▶ 자동차가 각기 다르게 생겨도 내부는 비슷하듯이, 인간과 다른 존재들 또한 겉모습이 다를 뿐 내면은 큰 차이가 없는데(a few internal tweaks), 우리 대부분은 오로지 그 외관상 차이만 보고 있다는 결론이 제시된다.

구문 풀이

We assume **that** we are the world's standard, **that** all things should be compared to us.

→ 동사 assume의 목적어로 2개의 **that**절이 나왔다. 이때 두 **that**절은 콤마로 연결된 동격 관계이다.

구문 플러스' 콤마 뒤의 접속사 that

관계대명사 that과 달리 명사절 접속사 that은 삽입, 동격 구문 등에서 콤마 뒤에 나올 수 있다.

We now know **that** everything in the world is relative, **that** there is no absolute truth.
이제 우리는 세상 모든 것이 상대적임을, 즉 절대적 진리란 없다는 것을 안다.

---

83 정답 ④ 55% *2021학년도 6월 모평*

해석 중대한 건강 문제로 고생하는 사람들에 대한 연구는 대다수의 응답자가 자신이 겪은 역경에서 이익을 얻었다고 보고한다는 것을 보여준다. 스트레스를 주는 사건들은 때때로 사람들이 새로운 기술을 개발하고, 우선순위를 재평가하고, 새로운 통찰을 배우고, 새로운 강점을 얻게 한다.
(C) 다시 말해, 스트레스에 의해 시작된 적응 과정은 더 나은 쪽으로의 개인적 변화를 가져올 수 있다. 참가자들의 서른일곱 가지 주요 부정적인 사건 경험을 측정한 한 연구는 생애에서 겪은 역경과 정신 건강 사이의 곡선 관계를 발견했다.
(A) 높은 수준의 역경은 예상대로 나쁜 정신 건강을 예측했지만, 중간 수준의 역경에 직면했던 사람들은 역경을 거의 경험하지 않았던 사람보다 더 건강했는데, 이것은 적당한 양의 스트레스가 회복력을 촉진할 수 있음을 보여준다. 후속 연구는 생애에서 겪은 역경의 양과 피실험자들이 실험 중 주어진 스트레스 요인에 반응하는 것 사이에서 비슷한 관계를 발견했다.
(B) 중간 수준의 역경이 가장 큰 회복력을 예측했다. 따라서 적당한 양의 스트레스를 해결해야 하는 것은 미래에 스트레스를 직면할 때의 회복력을 기를 수도 있다.

해설 역경을 통해 이득을 얻을 수 있다는 내용의 주어진 글 뒤로, (C)는 이 이득이 '더 좋은 쪽으로의 변화'를 뜻함을 보충 설명한다. (C)의 후반부에서 연구를 예로 들고, (A)는 연구 결과를 소개하며 '회복력'을 키워드로 꼽는다. (B)는 (A)에 이어 '회복력'과 역경의 관계를 최종적으로 정리한다. 따라서 글의 순서로 가장 적절한 것은 ④ '(C)-(A)-(B)'이다.

오답 풀이

선택률	오답 풀이
① 6%	역경을 통한 '이득'을 일반적으로 언급하는 주어진 글 뒤로, 그 이득이 '정신 건강'에 관한 것임을 설명하지 않은 채 바로 (A)를 연결해 연구 결과를 제시하는 것은 자연스럽지 않다.
② 12%	(B)는 구체적인 연구 내용을 기반으로 결론을 제시하는 단락이므로, 일반적인 화제만 제시하는 주어진 글 뒤에 이어지기 부적합하다.
③ 15%	
⑤ 11%	글은 보통 일반적 진술에서 구체적 진술로 나아간다. (C)에서 '정신 건강'이라는 일반적 키워드를 언급하므로, (A)에서 '정신 건강' 중에서도 '회복력'임을 짚어주고, (B)에서 '회복력'으로 마무리하는 흐름이 적절하다. 정신 건강과 회복력을 둘 다 언급해주는 (A) 없이 (C)-(B)를 연결하기는 어렵다.

지문 자세히 보기'

01 Studies of people struggling with major health problems show that the majority of respondents report they derived benefits from their adversity. Stressful events sometimes force people to develop new skills, reevaluate priorities, learn new insights, and acquire new strengths.

▶ 역경으로부터 얻는 이득에 관해 설명하는 글이다. 'develop ~, reevaluate ~, learn ~, and acquire ~'가 benefits의 예를 보여준다.

02 In other words, the adaptation process initiated by stress can lead to personal changes for the better. One study that measured participants' exposure to thirty-seven major negative events found a curvilinear relationship between lifetime adversity and mental health.

▶ 위의 'develop ~, reevaluate ~, learn ~, and acquire ~'가 personal changes for the better로 바뀌어 표현되었다. 이어서 역경과 정신 건강(mental health)의 연관 관계가 언급된다.

03 High levels of adversity predicted poor mental health, as expected, but people who had faced intermediate levels of adversity were healthier than those who experienced little adversity, suggesting that moderate amounts of stress can foster resilience. A follow-up study found a similar link between the amount of lifetime adversity and subjects' responses to laboratory stressors.

▶ 중간 수준의 역경을 겪은 사람들이 정신적으로 더 건강했다는 내용과 함께 특히 회복력(resilience)이 촉진되었다는 점이 언급된다.

04 Intermediate levels of adversity were predictive of the greatest resilience. Thus, having to deal with a moderate amount of stress may build resilience in the face of future stress.

▶ 회복력(resilience)이라는 키워드가 반복되며, 중간 수준의 역경이 정신 건강 중에서도 회복력 요인과 관련 있다는 최종 결론이 제시된다.

High levels of adversity predicted poor mental health, **as expected**, but people who had faced intermediate levels of adversity were healthier than those who experienced little adversity, suggesting that moderate amounts of stress can foster resilience.

→ 「as + 과거분사」 형태의 as expected는 'as it was expected ~'라는 부사절에서 it was를 생략한 것이다.

구문 플러스° as + 과거분사

「as + 과거분사」는 '~된 대로, ~된 듯이'라는 의미로, 문장 맨 앞, 뒤, 중간에 자유롭게 쓰인다.

As predicted, Team Korea won the gold medal.
예측된 대로, 한국 팀이 금메달을 땄다.

Climate change, **as discussed** earlier, is leading to a series of physical changes.
이전에 논의되었듯이, 기후 변화는 일련의 물리적 변화를 초래하고 있다.

84 정답 ⑤ 44% 　　　2020학년도 대수능

해석 영화는 지배적인 문화를 지지하고 시간이 지남에 따라 그것을 재생산하는 수단의 역할을 한다고 말할 수 있다.
(C) 그러나 영화가 하는 일이 오로지 적절한 삶에 대한 문화적 지시와 처방을 전달하는 것뿐이라면, 관객들이 왜 그러한 영화가 즐겁다고 느끼는지 의문이 제기될 수도 있다. 우리 중 대부분은 그러한 교훈적인 영화에 싫증이 나게 될 것이고, 아마도 그것들을 소련과 다른 독재 사회에서 흔했던, 문화적 예술 작품과 유사한 선전으로 보게 될 것이다.
(B) 이 질문에 대한 간단한 답은 영화가 책임 있는 행동에 관한 두 시간짜리 국민 윤리 교육이나 사설을 제시하는 것 이상을 한다는 것이다. 그것들은 또한, 우리가 결국 만족스럽다고 느끼는 이야기를 한다.
(A) 나쁜 사람들은 보통 벌을 받고, 낭만적인 커플은 진정한 사랑에 이르는 길에서 만나는 장애물과 어려움에도 불구하고 거의 항상 서로를 만나게 되며, 우리가 소망하는 세상의 모습이 영화 속에서 대개 결국 세상의 모습이 된다. 우리가 왜 그렇게 많이 영화를 즐기는지를 설명해 주는 것은 바로 영화의 이 이상적인 측면임이 틀림없다.

해설 영화는 지배적 문화를 지지하고 재생산한다는 내용의 주어진 글 뒤로, **(C)**는 만일 영화가 교훈이나 선전의 역할만 담당한다면 왜 관객들이 그토록 영화를 재미있게 여기는지 의문이라고 한다. **(B)**는 영화에는 '만족스러운' 이야기가 있다는 설명으로 **(C)**의 질문에 답한다. **(A)**는 '만족스러운' 이야기 내용의 예를 들면서, 결국 영화 안에는 우리가 바라는 세상의 모습이 담겨 있다고 설명한다. 따라서 글의 순서로 가장 적절한 것은 ⑤ '(C)-(B)-(A)'이다.

선택률	오답 풀이
① 8%	영화와 지배적 문화의 관계를 일반적으로 언급하는 주어진 글 뒤로 영화 '이야기'의 구체적 사례를 제시하는 (A)를 연결하기는 부자연스럽다.
② 14%	주어진 글에서 '질문'이 제시되지 않으므로 '이 질문'에 대한 답을 제시하는 (B)를 바로 연결하는 것은 부적절하다.
③ 12%	
④ 21%	(A) 또한 '질문'을 제시하지 않으므로 '질문'을 전제하고 답을 말하는 (B) 앞에 나오기 부적절하다.

지문 자세히 보기°

01 Movies may be said to support the dominant culture and to serve as a means for its reproduction over time.

▶ 영화는 지배적 문화를 지지하고, 이러한 문화를 재생산하는 수단 역할을 한다는 내용이 제시된다.

02 But one may ask why audiences would find such movies enjoyable if all they do is give cultural directives and prescriptions for proper living. Most of us would likely grow tired of such didactic movies and would probably come to see them as propaganda, similar to the cultural artwork that was common in the Soviet Union and other autocratic societies.

▶ give cultural directives and prescriptions는 위의 'support ~', 'serve as ~'와 같은 의미이다. 영화가 지배적 문화를 지지하고 재생산하는 선전(propaganda)과 같다면 왜 관객들이 영화를 좋아하는지 궁금할 수 있다고 한다.

03 The simple answer to this question is that movies do more than present two-hour civics lessons or editorials on responsible behavior. They also tell stories that, in the end, we find satisfying.

▶ 위의 'why ~ enjoyable'을 this question으로 요약하며 답(The simple answer)을 제시하고 있다. 영화는 문화적 기능 외에도 '만족스러운' 이야기를 전달해주는 역할을 한다는 설명이 이어진다.

04 The bad guys are usually punished; the romantic couple almost always find each other despite the obstacles and difficulties they encounter on the path to true love; and the way we wish the world to be is how, in the movies, it more often than not winds up being. No doubt it is this utopian aspect of movies that accounts for why we enjoy them so much.

▶ 위의 'stories ~ satisfying'이 'the way ~ winds up being'과 this utopian aspect로 연결된다. 즉 영화는 세상을 우리가 바라는 모습대로 그려내기에 우리에게 만족감을 주고, 이러한 이상적 측면이 매력으로 작용한다는 것이다.

But one may ask why audiences would find such movies enjoyable if **all they do is (to) give** cultural directives and prescriptions for proper living.

→ 주어가 「all + 주어 ~ do」의 형태로 '오직 ~한 것이라고는'의 의미를 나타낼 때, be동사의 보어인 to부정사에서 to가 생략될 수 있다.

 **플러스⁺** 주격보어 자리의 원형부정사

주격보어인 to부정사에서 to가 생략되려면 다음 조건을 따른다.
- 주어가 what, all, the only thing 중 하나로 시작할 것
- 주어의 마지막이 do동사일 것
- 문장의 본동사가 be동사일 것

What she needs to **do** <u>is</u> **improve** her communication skills.
그녀가 해야 할 일은 의사소통 능력을 향상시키는 것이다.

All you have to **do** <u>is</u> **listen** carefully.
네가 해야 할 일은 주의 깊게 듣는 것뿐이다.

The only thing she could **do** <u>was</u> **apologize** for her mistake.
그녀가 할 수 있었던 유일한 것은 자기 잘못을 사과하는 것뿐이었다.

유형 플러스⁺ 글의 순서

주어진 글 뒤에 이어질 단락의 순서를 논리적으로 적절한 흐름대로 배열하는 고난도 유형이다. 저학년 시험에서는 문학적 이야기도 등장하지만, 고3 기출에서는 과학·환경·철학·경제 등 비문학 지문이 주로 활용된다.

- **문제 해결 Tip.**
  ① 박스 안에 주어진 글을 통해 핵심 소재나 배경 상황을 파악한다.
  ② 연결어, 지시어, 대명사, 시간 표현 등 순서 파악의 단서를 활용하여 각 단락을 위치에 맞게 배열한다.
  ③ 답을 고르기 전, 배열한 순서대로 글을 읽으며 흐름이 적절한지 검토한다. 내용상 '일반적 진술 → 구체적 진술'의 흐름이 잘 지켜져야 한다.

85 정답 ③ 37%　　*2024학년도 대수능*

해석　과학은 때때로 승자 독식 대회로 묘사되는데, 이는 2등이나 3등을 하는 데 보상이 없다는 의미이다. 이는 과학 대회의 본질에 대한 극단적인 견해이다. 과학 대회를 그렇게 설명하는 사람들조차도 그것이 다소 부정확한 설명이라고 말하는데, 반복과 입증이 사회적 가치를 지녔으며 과학에서는 일반적이라는 것을 감안할 때 그렇다. 또한 그것은 단지 소수의 대회만 존재한다고 시사하는 경우에 부정확하다. 물론, 힉스 입자의 확인 또는 고온 초전도체 개발과 같은 몇몇 대회는 세계적인 수준으로 여겨진다. 하지만 다른 많은 대회에는 다양한 부문이 있고, 그런 대회의 수는 증가하고 있을 것이다. 예를 들어, 여러 해 동안 암에는 '하나'의 치료법만 있다고 생각되었지만, 이제는 암이 여러 가지 형태를 띠고 있으며, 치료를 제공하려면 다양한 접근법이 필요하다고 인식된다. 승자는 한 명이 아니라, 여러 명이 있을 것이다.

해설　③ 앞에서 과학 대회가 소수만 있다는 점을 생각해보라고 하는데, 주어진 문장은 이 내용을 Yes로 긍정하며 한 부문에서 세계 최고로 여겨지는 몇몇 대회(some contests)의 예를 든다. 한편 ③ 뒤에서는 다른 많은 대회(many other contests)를 언급하며 흐름을 반전시킨다. 따라서 주어진 문장이 들어가기에 가장 적절한 곳은 ③이다.

오답 풀이

선택률	오답 풀이
① 4%	앞에서 과학 대회를 승자 독식으로 보는 견해가 '극단적'이라고 지적한 데 이어 뒤에서 '부정확한' 견해라는 설명을 더하고 있다.
② 10%	'부정확하다'라는 표현이 also와 함께 반복되며, 앞 내용을 보충 설명한다.
④ 38%	'승자가 하나라고 보지 않는' many other contests의 예시로 암 치료법이 언급된다. 과거에는 암 치료법도 하나라고 생각했지만 지금은 여러 치료법을 긍정하고 있는 사례에서 '승자는 여럿'이라는 결론을 확인할 수 있는 문맥이다.
⑤ 12%	실제로 '승자는 많을 수 있다'는 결론으로 예시를 마무리한다.

지문　자세히 보기"

01　Science is sometimes described as a winner-take-all contest, meaning that there are no rewards for being second or third. This is an extreme view of the nature of scientific contests.

▶ 과학 대회를 '승자 독식'으로 보는 견해는 '극단적'임을 지적하고 있다.

02　Even those who describe scientific contests in such a way note that it is a somewhat inaccurate description, given that replication and verification have social value and are common in science. It is also inaccurate to the extent that it suggests that only a handful of contests exist.

▶ 위의 extreme이 somewhat inaccurate로 재진술된다. 또한, 과학 대회가 소수라는 점을 고려해도 이 견해가 '부정확함'을 알 수 있다고 한다.

03　Yes, some contests are seen as world class, such as identification of the Higgs particle or the development of high temperature superconductors. But many other contests have multiple parts, and the number of such contests may be increasing.

▶ 위의 only a handful of contests 뒤에 some contests가 연결되어 예시를 들고, 이어서 many other contests가 연결되어 대비 관계를 이룬다. But이 나왔는데 앞에 대비되는 대상이 없으므로 논리적 단절을 확인할 수 있다.

04　By way of example, for many years it was thought that there would be "one" cure for cancer, but it is now realized that cancer takes multiple forms and that multiple approaches are needed to provide a cure. There won't be one winner – there will be many.

▶ '~ multiple approaches are needed ~'가 앞에 나온 many other contests의 예시이고, 마지막 문장은 예시의 결론이다. 즉, '과학 대회에도 승자가 많을 수 있다'는 것이 글 전체의 요지다.

구문 풀이

Even **those who** describe scientific contests in such a way **note** that it is a somewhat inaccurate description, given that replication and verification have social value and are common in science.

→ 지시대명사 **those**는 who가 이끄는 형용사절의 수식을 받아 '~한 사람들'로 해석된다. 술어는 복수동사인 **note**이다.

구문 플러스'　those의 용법

those가 수능 독해에 주로 등장하는 형태를 기억해 둔다.
- those who ~: ~한 사람들
- 원급, 비교급 구문의 those: 앞에 나온 복수의 비교대상을 가리킴

Those who stay in the race win the race in the end.
경주에 남아 있는 사람들이 결국 경주에서 이긴다.

House rents are higher here than those in my neighborhood.
(those = house rents)
여기 집세가 우리 동네 집세보다 더 비싸다.

86 정답 ③ 24%　　*2024학년도 9월 모평*

해석　예술 작품의 제작에 대해 안다는 표시를 하는 데는, 화가가 다양한 종류의 물감을 섞는 방법이나 이미지 편집 도구의 작동방식 같은 상세한 전문 지식이 필요하지 않다. 필요한 것이라고는 물감 작업과 이미징 앱을 사용한 작업의 중대한 차이에 대한 일반적인 느낌일 뿐이다. 이런 느낌은 아마도 소비자 이미징 앱을 사용하는 방법을 포함해서 컴퓨터 사용법에 대한 기본적인 친숙함뿐 아니라, 물감과 붓에 대한 기본적인

친숙함을 포함할 수도 있다. 예술 비평가와 같은 전문가의 경우, 재료와 기법에 더 친숙하다는 점은 작품에 관해 잘 알고 내린 판단에 이르는 데 흔히 유용하다. 이것은 모든 종류의 예술 재료나 도구가 예술 창작에 있어 고유한 도전과 행위유발성을 동반하기 때문이다. 비평가들은 흔히 예술가들이 특정한 예술적 효과를 위해 다양한 종류의 재료와 도구를 활용하는 방식에 관심이 있다. 그들은 또한 예술 작품 그 자체로 구현된, 특정 재료와 도구로 달성할 수 있는 것의 한계를 뛰어넘으려는 예술가의 시도가 성공적인지에 관심이 있다.

해설 ③ 앞은 예술 작품 제작을 이해하는 데 '일반적, 기초적 지식'만 있으면 된다는 내용인데, ③ 뒤는 도구나 재료마다 창작 과정에 고유한 과제가 따르기 때문에 '더 깊은 이해'가 필요할 수 있다는 내용이다. 따라서 '전문가의 깊은 이해'에 관한 내용으로 전환되는 주어진 문장은 ③에 들어가야 한다.

오답 풀이

선택률	오답 풀이
① 3%	'전문 지식이 필요하지 않다'는 설명에 이어 '일반적 감각'만 있으면 된다는 내용이 자연스럽게 이어진다.
② 7%	앞의 a general sense가 This sense로 자연스럽게 연결된다.
④ 51%	'비평가'가 갑자기 나왔다는 느낌에 고르기 쉽다. 하지만 ④ 앞이 각 재료나 소재마다 '고유한 과제'가 따른다는 내용이고, ④ 뒤는 그렇기에 비평가들이 예술가들의 소재 또는 도구 활용에 관심을 갖는다는 보충 설명이다. 따라서 ④ 앞뒤의 흐름은 끊김 없이 자연스럽다.
⑤ 16%	They로 앞 문장의 Critics를 가리키며 자연스럽게 내용을 추가한다(also).

지문 자세히 보기

01 Acknowledging the making of artworks does not require a detailed, technical knowledge of, say, how painters mix different kinds of paint, or how an image editing tool works.

▶ 예술 작품 제작을 알은체할 때는 '전문 지식이 필요하지 않다'는 의미이다.

02 All that is required is a general sense of a significant difference between working with paints and working with an imaging application. This sense might involve a basic familiarity with paints and paintbrushes as well as a basic familiarity with how we use computers, perhaps including how we use consumer imaging apps.

▶ 전문 지식 없이 '일반적인 느낌' 정도만 있으면 된다는 보충 설명이다. 일반적인 느낌은 도구에 대한 '기본적인 친숙함'이라는 표현으로 구체화된다.

03 In the case of specialists such as art critics, a deeper familiarity with materials and techniques is often useful in reaching an informed judgement about a work. This is because every kind of artistic material or tool comes with its own challenges and affordances for artistic creation.

▶ 흐름이 반전되는 지점이다. 비평가 등 전문가들은 '소재나 기법에 대한 더 깊은 이해'가 필요하다는 내용과 함께, 왜 그러한지(This is because ~)가 언급된다. 소재나 도구마다 각기 다른 창작 과제가 동반되기에 이를 이해하고 비평하려면 '더 깊은 지식'이 필요하다는 것이다.

04 Critics are often interested in the ways artists exploit different kinds of materials and tools for particular artistic effect. They are also interested in the success of an artist's attempt — embodied in the artwork itself — to push the limits of what can be achieved with certain materials and tools.

▶ 'This is because ~' 문장에 대한 뒷받침이다. 창작자가 각 소재나 도구를 어떻게 이용했는지, 그런 시도가 성공적이었는지를 비평가들(Critics, They)이 관심 있게 본다는 내용으로 글이 마무리된다.

구문 풀이

This sense might involve a basic familiarity with paints and paintbrushes as well as a basic familiarity with how we use computers, perhaps including how we use consumer imaging apps.

→ 「A as well as B(B뿐만 아니라 A도)」 앞뒤로 'a familiarity with ~'가 병렬 연결되었다.

구문 플러스 A as well as B

A as well as B가 주어 자리에 나오면 A에 수일치한다. A, B는 병렬구조를 이룬다.

Cindy as well as her siblings has a talent for music.
→ Cindy에 수일치 / Cindy와 her siblings는 명사구 병렬
Cindy의 형제자매뿐 아니라 Cindy도 음악에 소질이 있다.

---

87 정답 ③ 35% *2023학년도 6월 모평*

해석 집단적 탐지의 역학은 흥미로운 특징이 있다. 개체들은 어떤 단서를 포식자 공격의 증거로 사용하는가? 어떤 경우, 개체가 포식자를 탐지할 때 최선의 반응은 피난하는 것이다. 무리로부터의 이탈은 경계하지 않는 동물들에게 위험 신호를 보내서 먹잇감 동물이 그 구역에서 조직화되어 쏟아져 나가는 것처럼 보이게 할 수도 있다. (새의 한 종류인) 검은 눈 검은방울새에 관한 연구는 경계하지 않는 동물들이 무리 친구들의 개별적 이탈에 주목하기는 하지만, 여러 개체의 이탈은 경계하지 않는 동물에게 더 큰 도망 반응을 일으킬 수 있다는 견해를 뒷받침해준다. 이것은 정보 신뢰성의 관점에서 이치에 맞는다. 무리 구성원 하나가 이탈하는 경우, 그것은 포식 위험과 관계가 거의 없는 여러 이유로 그렇게 했을 수 있다. 경계하지 않는 동물들이 단 하나의 구성원이 무리를 떠날 때마다 도망한다면, 그것들은 포식자가 전혀 없는 (가짜 경보인) 때에도 자주 반응할 것이다. 반면에 여러 개체가 동시에 무리를 이탈할 때, 진짜 위험이 존재할 가능성이 훨씬 더 크다.

해설 여러 개체가 무리로부터 이탈하는 모습이 위험을 경고하는 신호 역할을 하여, 연쇄적으로 더 큰 도망 반응을 일으킬 수 있다는 내용의 글이다. ③ 앞에서 제시된 이 핵심 내용을 주어진 문장에서 This로 받으며, '정보 신뢰성'의 관점에서 생각해보자고 언급한다. ③ 뒤에서는 한 마리의 개체가 이탈할 때와 여러 개체가 이탈하는 경우를 나누어, 후자가 더

'믿을 만한' 위험 정보를 제시한다는 보충 설명을 이어 간다. 따라서 주어진 문장이 들어가기에 가장 적절한 곳은 ③이다.

선택률	오답 풀이
① 5%	포식자의 위험을 경고하는 신호가 무엇인지 묻는 초반부 질문에 대한 답이 아직 제시되지 않았다. 따라서 '무엇'을 정보 신뢰성의 관점에서 이해해보자는 것인지 그 대상이 불명확하다.
② 16%	개체의 무리 이탈이 위험을 경고하는 신호일 수 있다는 일반적 내용은 제시되었지만, 한 마리와 여러 마리의 이탈을 나누어서 '정보 신뢰성'을 비교할 만한 문맥이 아직 형성되지 않아 답으로 부적절하다.
④ 27%	개체 한 마리의 이탈은 포식자의 위험과 별로 연관이 없을 수도 있다는 일반적 내용 뒤로, 이를 신호 삼아 다른 개체가 도망간다면 허위 경보에 움직인 것일 수도 있다는 분석이 뒤따른다. 즉 앞 내용을 뒤에서 자연스럽게 보충하는 흐름이므로 주어진 문장을 넣기 부적절하다.
⑤ 17%	앞에서 한 마리의 이탈이 정보 신뢰성 관점에서 큰 의미가 없다는 내용을 언급한 후, On the other hand로 흐름을 뒤집으며 여러 마리의 이탈에 관해 설명하는 부분이다. 즉 역접어 앞뒤로 반대되는 두 사례가 적절히 제시되므로 주어진 문장을 넣을 만한 흐름 단절이 있다고 보기 어렵다.

01 The dynamics of collective detection have an interesting feature. Which cue(s) do individuals use as evidence of predator attack?

▶ 집단적 탐지의 역학이라는 핵심 소재를 제시하며, 각 동물이 포식자의 공격이 있음을 알아차리는 단서는 무엇일지 묻고 있다.

02 In some cases, when an individual detects a predator, its best response is to seek shelter. Departure from the group may signal danger to nonvigilant animals and cause what appears to be a coordinated flushing of prey from the area.

▶ '그룹에서의 이탈'이 위험을 알리는 단서 역할을 할 수 있다는 답이 제시된다.

03 Studies on dark-eyed juncos (a type of bird) support the view that nonvigilant animals attend to departures of individual group mates but that the departure of multiple individuals causes a greater escape response in the nonvigilant individuals.

▶ 특히, 연구에 따르면 한 개체가 도망갈 때보다도 여러 개체가 달아나는 모습을 볼 때 연쇄적인 도망 반응이 일어날 수 있다는 핵심 내용이 제시된다.

04 This makes sense from the perspective of information reliability.

▶ 위 핵심 내용이 This로 이어지며, '이것'은 '정보 신뢰성'의 관점에서 분석해볼 수 있다는 설명이 연결된다.

05 If one group member departs, it might have done so for a number of reasons that have little to do with predation threat. If nonvigilant animals escaped each time a single member left the group, they would frequently respond when there was no predator (a false alarm). On the other hand, when several individuals depart the group at the same time, a true threat is much more likely to be present.

▶ 'If one group member departs, ~'와 '~ when several individuals depart the group ~'가 서로 다른 두 상황을 제시한다. 상황별로 정보 신뢰성의 관점을 비교하는 문맥인 것이다. 한 마리 개체만이 도망갈 때보다 여러 개체가 도망갈 때 위험이 실재한다는 것을 '더 믿을 수 있기' 때문에 더 큰 도망 반응이 뒤따르게 된다는 내용이 상술된다.

If one group member departs, it might have done so for a number of reasons that **have little to do with** predation threat.

→ **have little to do with**(~와 거의 관련이 없다) 구문이다.

구문 플러스 have to do with

have (something) to do with: ~와 관련이 있다
have little[nothing] to do with: ~와 관련이 거의[전혀] 없다
have much to do with: ~와 관련이 크다
have more[less] to do with A than B: B보다 A와 더[덜] 관련이 있다

My job has something to do with books.
제 직업은 책하고 관련이 있어요.
She has nothing to do with this accident.
그녀는 이 사고와 아무 관련이 없다.
Your disease has more to do with stress than your genes.
당신의 병은 유전자보다도 스트레스와 더 관련이 있습니다.

---

88 정답 ④ 40% *2022학년도 9월 모평*

해석 초기 인류는 매우 제한된 수의 물질, 즉 돌, 나무, 찰흙, 가죽 등 자연적으로 존재하는 물질에만 접근할 수 있었다. 시간이 흐르면서 그들은 자연적인 특성의 물질보다 더 우수한 특성을 가진 물질을 만들어 내는 기술을 발견했는데, 이 새로운 물질에는 도자기와 다양한 금속이 포함되었다. 게다가, 물질의 특성이 열처리와 여타 다른 물질의 첨가로 바뀔 수 있다는 것이 발견되었다. 이 시기에, 물질 이용은 주어진 상당히 제한된 물질 집합 중에서 물질의 특성에 근거하여 용도에 가장 적합한 물질을 결정하는 것을 수반하는 전적으로 선택의 과정이었다. 과학자들이 물질의 구조적 요소와 물질 특성의 관계를 이해하게 된 것은 바로 비교적 최근에 이르러서였다. 대략 지난 100년 동안 획득된 이 지식으로 그들은 상당한 정도로 물질의 특성을 형성할 수 있게 되었다. 따라서 금속, 플라스틱, 유리, 섬유를 포함하여, 복잡한 우리 현대 사회의 요구를 충족하는 상당히 특화된 특성을 가진 수만 가지의 다양한 물질이 발달했다.

해설 ④ 앞에서 본래 물질 이용은 기존에 주어진 한정된 집합 가운데 선택하는 것이었다고 하는데, ④ 뒤에서는 갑자기 '이러한 지식'을 언급한다. ④ 앞에 '지식'으로 가리킬 대상이 없어 논리적 공백이 발생하므로, 주어진 문장이 들어가기에 가장 적절한 곳은 ④이다.

선택률	오답 풀이
① 5%	초기 인류의 물질 이용에 관한 설명 뒤로, 시간에 따른 변화에 관한 내용이 자연스럽게 이어진다.
② 16%	물질 생성 기술이 발견되었다는 내용 뒤로 특성 가공 또한(Furthermore) 발견되었다는 내용이 자연스럽게 추가된다.
③ 26%	물질을 만들고 가공할 수 있게 됐다는 내용과 물질 이용이 선택 행위에 불과했다는 내용이 대비되는 듯 보이지만, 여기서 this point는 뒤에 언급되는 최근 100년(past 100 years)에 비하면 아직 과거의 시점이다. 즉 처음부터 ③ 뒤의 문장까지 '과거'에 관한 설명이 계속되는 것이다.
⑤ 13%	최근 100년 사이 '지식'이 획득된 결과로 수만 가지의 물질이 만들어지게 되었다는 흐름이 자연스럽다.

지문 자세히 보기

01 The earliest humans had access to only a very limited number of materials, those that occur naturally: stone, wood, clay, skins, and so on.

▶ 초기 인류의 물질 이용은 자연 발생하는 몇 안 되는 물질에 한정되었음을 설명하고 있다.

02 With time, they discovered techniques for producing materials that had properties superior to those of the natural ones; these new materials included pottery and various metals. Furthermore, it was discovered that the properties of a material could be altered by heat treatments and by the addition of other substances.

▶ 시간이 지나며 물질을 생성하거나 특성을 변화시킬 수 있다는 것이 밝혀졌다는 내용이 제시된다.

03 At this point, materials utilization was totally a selection process that involved deciding from a given, rather limited set of materials, the one best suited for an application based on its characteristics.

▶ 첫 문장의 내용이 반복된다. 최근 이전의 과거(this point)에는 물질 이용이 제한된 선택 사항 중 가장 적합한 것을 고르는 행위(a selection process, deciding ~ the one ~)에 지나지 않았다는 것이다.

04 It was not until relatively recent times that scientists came to understand the relationships between the structural elements of materials and their properties.

▶ At this point와 relatively recent times가 대비를 이룬다. '최근에 들어서야' 물질의 구조적 요소와 그 특성의 관계가 이해되기 시작했다는 새로운 흐름이 이어진다.

05 This knowledge, acquired over approximately the past 100 years, has empowered them to fashion, to a large degree, the characteristics of materials. Thus, tens of thousands of different materials have evolved with rather specialized characteristics that meet the needs of our modern and complex society, including metals, plastics, glasses, and fibers.

▶ 위의 'understand ~ their properties'가 This knowledge로, relatively recent times가 approximately the past 100 years로 표현되었다. '지난 100년'이라는 '최근 시기'에 축적된, 물질의 구조적 요소와 특성의 관계에 관한 '지식' 덕분에 수만 가지에 이르는 다양한 물질이 발달했다는 결론으로 글이 마무리된다.

구문 풀이

It was not until relatively recent times **that** scientists came to understand the relationships between the structural elements of materials and their properties.

→ 「it is[was] not until A that B(바로 A하고 나서야 비로소 B하다)」 구문이다.

구문 플러스 it is[was] not until A that B

「it is[was] ~ that …」 강조구문을 이용해 「not until A B(A하고 나서야 B하다)」를 강조하면 「it is[was] not until A that B」 구문이 된다.

It was not until last year that I learned to read Spanish.
나는 바로 작년에서야 비로소 스페인어를 읽는 법을 배웠다.

89 정답 ④ 43%   *2021학년도 대수능*

해석 내가 여러분에게 Maddy가 나쁘다고 말한다고 생각해 보라. 아마 여러분은 나의 억양이나 우리가 말하고 있는 맥락으로 보아 내가 도덕적으로 나쁘다는 뜻을 의도하고 있음을 추론한다. 게다가 일반적인 언어 관행을 고려하고 내가 진심이라고 상정한다면, 여러분은 내가 Maddy를 못마땅해하고 있다고, 또는 내 생각에 여러분이 그녀를 못마땅해하든 해야 한다고 말하고 있는 것이라고 아마도 추론할 것이다. 하지만 여러분은 Maddy가 구체적으로 어떻게 나쁜 것인지와 그녀의 일반적인 성격 특성 등에 대해서는 더 자세하게 인식하지 못할 수도 있는데, 사람들은 여러 방면에서 나쁠 수 있기 때문이다. 그에 반해서, 만일 내가 Maddy는 사악하다고 말한다면, 여러분은 다른 사람들에 대한 그녀의 일반적인 행동과 태도를 더 알게 된다. '사악한'이라는 낱말은 '나쁜'보다 더 구체적이다. 사악함은 많은 형태를 띤다는 점에서 나는 여전히 Maddy의 성격을 정확하게 지적하지 않았다. 하지만 그럼에도 불구하고 더 많은 세부 사항, 아마도 Maddy가 어떤 사람인지에 관한 더 강한 함축적 의미가 있다. 게다가 다시 한번 일반적인 언어 관행을 상정하면, 우리가 여전히 그녀의 도덕적 성격을 논하고 있다고 가정할 때, 여러분은 또한 내가 Maddy를 못마땅해하고 있거나 여러분이 그녀를 못마땅해하든지 해야 한다고 말하고 있는 것임을 파악할 것이다.

해설 In contrast 앞뒤로 bad와 wicked라는 단어를 각각 사용해 사람의 성격을 묘사하는 상황을 대조하는 글이다. ④ 앞의 문장에서 wicked는 bad보다 구체적이라고 한다. 이때 ④ 뒤의 문장은 But으로 시작하므로, 앞과 자연스럽게 연결되려면 앞과 상반된 내용이 뒤에 이어져야 한다. 하지만 ④ 뒤는 앞과 마찬가지로 wicked를 쓸 때 세부사항과 함의가 더 많이 들어간다는 의미이므로 논리적 공백이 발생한다. 따라서 주어진 문장이 들어가기에 가장 적절한 곳은 ④이다.

선택률	오답 풀이
① 3%	bad라는 단어를 써서 성격 묘사를 했을 때 어떻게 나쁜지 구체적으로 파악할 수는 없다는 내용이 However 뒤로 자연스럽게 이어진다.
② 14%	앞과 대조적으로(In contrast) wicked를 사용했을 때의 상황이 적절히 제시된다.

③ 21%	wicked라는 단어를 쓰면 더 많은 의미를 추론할 수 있는 이 유로, 이 단어의 의미가 더 구체적이기 때문이라는 설명이 자연스럽게 이어진다.
⑤ 19%	wicked를 썼을 때 추론 가능한 의미에 관한 부가 설명이 자연스럽게 뒤따른다.

지문 자세히 보기

01 Imagine I tell you that Maddy is bad. Perhaps you infer from my intonation, or the context in which we are talking, that I mean morally bad. Additionally, you will probably infer that I am disapproving of Maddy, or saying that I think you should disapprove of her, or similar, given typical linguistic conventions and assuming I am sincere.

▶ Maddy라는 사람의 성격을 묘사하고자 bad라는 단어를 썼을 때, 우리가 억양이나 맥락을 단서로 추론할 수 있는 의미들(morally bad, I am disapproving of Maddy, ~ you should disapprove of her)을 열거하고 있다.

02 However, you might not get a more detailed sense of the particular sorts of way in which Maddy is bad, her typical character traits, and the like, since people can be bad in many ways.

▶ However 뒤로, 위에서 추론한 의미들이 구체적이지는 않다(not ~ detailed)는 설명이 뒤따른다.

03 In contrast, if I say that Maddy is wicked, then you get more of a sense of her typical actions and attitudes to others. The word 'wicked' is more specific than 'bad'.

▶ In contrast로 흐름이 반전되며, bad 대신 wicked를 쓰는 경우가 대비된다. 부연에 따르면 이 wicked의 의미는 bad보다 더 구체적(more specific)이다.

04 I have still not exactly pinpointed Maddy's character since wickedness takes many forms.

▶ wicked를 써서 묘사한 이 경우에도 성격에 대한 구체적인 설명은 없었다(not exactly pinpointed)는 점을 상기시키고 있다.

05 But there is more detail nevertheless, perhaps a stronger connotation of the sort of person Maddy is. In addition, and again assuming typical linguistic conventions, you should also get a sense that I am disapproving of Maddy, or saying that you should disapprove of her, or similar, assuming that we are still discussing her moral character.

▶ 흐름 반전의 But과 함께, '그렇지는 하지만' wicked라는 단어에 더 많은 함의와 세부사항이 실려 있다는 설명이 이어진다. 앞에 나온 more specific이 more detail과 a stronger connotation으로 재진술된다.

구문 풀이

However, you might not get a more detailed sense of the particular sorts of way **in which** Maddy is bad, her typical character traits, and the like, since people can be bad in many ways.

→ 방법의 선행사 way 뒤에 관계부사 how 대신 「전치사 + 관계대명사」 형태의 in which가 쓰였다.

구문 플러스 관계부사의 의무적 생략

방법을 나타내는 선행사 the way와 관계부사 how는 함께 쓰지 않고, 둘 중 하나를 반드시 생략한다. the way 뒤에 how 대신 in which나 by which를 쓰기도 한다.

The way we work has completely changed.
= **How we work has completely changed.**
= **The way in which we work has completely changed.**
우리가 일하는 방식은 완전히 변했다.

90 정답 ④ 64% *2021학년도 9월 모평*

해석 영화에는 문법이 없다. 그러나 영화 언어 사용에 관한 어렴풋이 정의된 몇 가지 규칙이 있고, 영화의 문법, 즉 그것의 체계적인 처리 방식은 이러한 규칙들을 정리하고 그것들 사이의 관계를 보여준다. 문어와 구어에서와 마찬가지로, 영화의 문법은 영화에서 사용된 결과물이지 그것의 결정 요인은 아니라는 것을 기억하는 것이 중요하다. 영화 문법에 관해 미리 정해진 것은 아무것도 없다. 오히려, 그것은 특정 방법이 실제로 운용할 수 있고 유용하다고 밝혀지면서 자연스럽게 발전했다. 문어와 구어의 문법처럼, 영화의 문법은 자연스럽게 발전한 것으로, 규범적이지 않고 기술적이며, 여러 해에 걸쳐 상당히 변화했다. '할리우드 문법'은 지금은 웃기게 들릴지 모르지만, 30년대, 40년대, 50년대 초반에는 할리우드 영화의 구성 방식의 정확한 모델이었다.

해설 영화 문법의 발전 과정에 관한 글이다. ④ 앞에서 영화 문법에 관해 미리 정해져 있던 것은 없다고 언급한 뒤, 주어진 문장은 '오히려' 영화 문법은 실용성을 인정받은 방법 위주로 자연스럽게 발전했다는 설명을 이어 간다. ④ 뒤에서는 '자연스러운 발전'이라는 주어진 문장의 설명을 반복한다. 따라서 주어진 문장이 들어가기에 가장 적절한 곳은 ④이다.

오답 풀이

선택률	오답 풀이
① 3%	영화에는 문법이 없지만(however) 어렴풋이 정의된 규칙들이 모여 문법이 된다는 내용이 자연스럽게 연결된다.
② 6%	영화의 규칙을 언급한 앞 내용에 이어 이 규칙이 '사용의 결과'로 형성되었다는 설명이 자연스럽게 이어진다.
③ 15%	영화 문법 규칙은 '결과적으로' 만들어졌다는 설명 뒤로, 이 말이 곧 '미리 정해진 것은 없다'는 뜻임을 자연스럽게 보충 설명한다.
⑤ 10%	영화 문법이 시간의 흐름에 따라 많이 변했다는 내용 뒤로, 과거와 오늘날 '할리우드 문법' 개념의 변화에 관한 설명이 적절히 이어진다.

지문 자세히 보기

01 Film has no grammar. There are, however, some vaguely defined rules of usage in cinematic language, and the syntax of film — its systematic arrangement — orders these rules and indicates relationships among them.

▶ 영화의 문법이 글의 화제이다. grammar, rules of usage in cinematic language, the syntax of film이 모두 같은 의미이다.

02 As with written and spoken languages, it is important to remember that the syntax of film is a result of its usage, not a determinant of it. There is nothing preordained about film syntax.

▶ 영화 문법은 사용의 결과(a result of its usage)로 파생된 것이며, 미리 정해져 있던 문법은 없다(nothing preordained)는 설명이 제시된다.

03 Rather, it evolved naturally as certain devices were found in practice to be both workable and useful.

▶ Rather는 여기서 앞의 nothing과 함께 「not A (but) rather B」의 대구를 이루며 주제를 반복 강조하는 연결어이다. '정해져 있던 것이 없다'는 앞 내용에 이어 '오히려' 자연스럽게 발전했다는 설명을 덧붙이는 것이다. 앞서 나온 a result of its usage가 evolved naturally로 바뀌어 표현되었다.

04 Like the syntax of written and spoken language, the syntax of film is an organic development, descriptive rather than prescriptive, and it has changed considerably over the years. "Hollywood Grammar" may sound laughable now, but during the thirties, forties, and early fifties it was an accurate model of the way Hollywood films were constructed.

▶ 위의 evolved naturally가 an organic development로 바뀌었다. 영화 문법이 자연스러운 발전의 산물이라는 내용 뒤로, 이것이 세월에 걸쳐 상당히 변화해왔다는 내용이 추가된다.

구문 풀이

"Hollywood Grammar" may **sound laughable** now, but during the thirties, forties, and early fifties it was an accurate model of the way Hollywood films were constructed.

→ 2형식 동사 sound 뒤로 형용사 laughable이 보어로 나왔다.

구문 플러스⁺ 2형식 감각동사

look, sound, smell, taste, feel 등은 감각에 관련된 2형식 동사로, 「like + 명사」 또는 형용사를 보어로 취한다.

She **looks like a model**. 그녀는 모델 같아 보인다.
What he said **sounded** absurd. 그의 말은 불합리하게 들렸다.

91 정답 ④ 69%   *2020학년도 대수능*

해석 텃새들의 서식지 선택은 흩어지는 어린 개체가 (생존을 위한) 필요를 충족시키기 위해 성공적으로 경쟁할 수 있는 장소를 찾을 때까지 옮겨 다니는, 외견상 간단한 과정이다. 처음에는, 이러한 필요에 음식과 은신처만 포함된다. 그러나 궁극적으로, 그 어린 새는 생존뿐만 아니라 번식을 위한 필요조건도 충족시켜 주는 서식지를 찾고, 확인하고, 그곳에 정착해야 한다. 일부의 경우, 번식기에만 특별히 요구되는 조건들 때문에, 생존을 위한 최고의 기회를 제공하는 서식지가 최고의 번식 능력을 가능하게 해주는 서식지와 동일하지 않을 수도 있다. 따라서 많은 텃새 종의 개체들은 다산에 유리한 번식지를 장악하고 있다는 이점의 적합성에 직면했을 때, 가장 높은 번식 성공이 일어나는 특정 서식지에 머물러 있으면서 더 낮은 비번식기 생존율의 형태로 대가의 균형을 어쩔 수 없이 맞춰야 할 수도 있다. 그러나 철새들은 번식기가 아닌 동안에는 생

존을 위한 최적의 서식지를, 번식기 동안에는 번식을 위한 최적의 서식지를 자유롭게 선택한다. 이에 따라 서로 다른 시기 동안의 서식지 선택은 심지어 (생물학적으로) 밀접하게 관련이 있는 종들 사이에서조차도, 텃새들과는 달리 철새들에게 있어서 상당히 다를 수 있다.

해설 ④ 앞은 생존에 유리한 서식지와 번식에 유리한 서식지가 다를 수 있다는 일반적인 내용인데, ④ 뒤는 however로 시작하며 철새의 서식지 선택을 설명한다. 이때 ④ 앞에 철새의 선택과 비교되는 구체적인 내용이 나오지 않기에 글의 흐름이 어색하게 끊기므로, 주어진 문장이 들어가기에 가장 적절한 곳은 ④이다.

오답 풀이

선택률	오답 풀이
① 1%	앞에 제시된 화제인 서식지 선택에 우선(Initially) 관여하는 요인으로 음식과 은신처를 적절히 언급한다.
② 5%	앞서 언급된 음식과 은신처를 '생존'적 필요로 요약하며, 이외에도 번식적 필요가 개입된다는 설명을 적절히 이어 간다.
③ 17%	앞에 나온 생존과 번식을 다시 언급하며, 두 가지 필요에 각각 적합한 서식지가 서로 다를 수 있다는 내용을 적절히 제시한다.
⑤ 6%	철새의 서식지 선택에 관한 설명 이후, 이것이 텃새의 선택과는 사뭇 다르다는 결론(Thus)을 적절히 제시한다.

지문 자세히 보기

01 Resident-bird habitat selection is seemingly a straightforward process in which a young dispersing individual moves until it finds a place where it can compete successfully to satisfy its needs.

▶ 텃새들의 서식지 선택을 화제로 제시한다.

02 Initially, these needs include only food and shelter. However, eventually, the young must locate, identify, and settle in a habitat that satisfies not only survivorship but reproductive needs as well.

▶ 서식지 선택에 관여하는 두 가지 요인으로 생존과 번식을 언급한다.

03 In some cases, the habitat that provides the best opportunity for survival may not be the same habitat as the one that provides for highest reproductive capacity because of requirements specific to the reproductive period.

▶ 생존에 최고인 서식지가 번식에 최고인 서식지와는 다른 상황이 생길 수 있다는 내용이 이어진다.

04 Thus, individuals of many resident species, confronted with the fitness benefits of control over a productive breeding site, may be forced to balance costs in the form of lower nonbreeding survivorship by remaining in the specific habitat where highest breeding success occurs.

▶ 위와 같은 이유로(Thus), 한 곳에 죽 서식하는 텃새들은 번식에 유리한 서식지를 점령하다 보면 비번식기의 생존율이 낮은 곳을 택할 수도 있다는 예시가 나온다.

05 Migrants, however, are free to choose the optimal habitat for survival during the nonbreeding season and for reproduction during the breeding season. Thus, habitat selection during these different periods can be quite different for migrants as opposed to residents, even among closely related species.

▶ 역접의 **however**로 보아, 앞에서 '텃새의 선택'을 언급하고 '철새의 선택'을 대조하는 문맥이다. 철새는 번식기, 비번식기의 서식지를 자유롭게 달리할 수 있기에, 텃새들과 달리 철새 종들끼리도 선택이 서로 다를 수 있다는 결론으로 글이 마무리된다.

구문 풀이

Thus, habitat selection during these different periods can be quite different for migrants **as opposed to** residents, even among closely related species.

→ **as opposed to** 뒤에 명사 **residents**가 목적어로 나와 '~와는 달리'라는 의미를 나타낸다.

 플러스' as opposed to + (동)명사

as opposed to 뒤에는 명사 또는 동명사가 나올 수 있다.

As opposed to dogs, wolves live in the wild.
개와는 달리, 늑대는 야생에서 산다.

He remained calm **as opposed to** her being nervous.
그녀가 긴장한 것과는 달리 그는 차분함을 유지했다.

유형 플러스' 주어진 문장 넣기

글의 논리적 공백을 포착할 수 있는지 묻는 문제로, 고난도 유형에 속한다. 순서와 마찬가지로 연결어, 지시사, 대명사로 힌트를 얻는다.

• **문제 해결 Tip.**
① 선택지가 나오기 전 도입부에서 글의 핵심 소재, 중심 내용 등을 파악한다.
② 연결어, 지시사, 대명사의 사용에 주목하며, 흐름상 단절되는 지점이 없는지 파악한다.
③ 논리적 공백이 포착되는 지점에 주어진 문장을 넣어서 읽어 보며 글의 일관성을 검토한다.

• **단서 활용 Tip.**
① 박스 안에 주어진 문장에 **however, still, but, though** 등 역접어가 나오면, 앞뒤에 서로 반대되는 내용이 연결되는 선택지를 찾아 답으로 고른다.
② 주어진 문장이 아닌 글 중간에 **however, still, but, though** 등 역접어가 나올 때, 그 역접어 앞뒤 내용이 반대되지 않고 서로 같다면 논리적 공백을 의심한다.
③ **such, this, it, they** 등 지시 표현이 나오면 지칭 대상을 앞에서 명확하게 확인하고 넘어간다. 지칭 대상을 알 수 없다면 논리적 공백을 의심한다.

92 정답 ② 36%

2024학년도 9월 모평

해석 역사 소설을 위한 연구는 문서로 덜 기록된 보통 사람이나 사건 또는 장소에 아마 초점을 맞출 것이다. 소설은 역사적 맥락을 재창조하는 일상 상황, 감정, 분위기를 묘사하는 데 도움이 된다. 역사 소설은 '역사가들이 밝혀낼 수 있는 뼈대에 살'을 붙이고, '그렇게 해서 반드시 사실이 아니더라도 과거의 사건, 상황, 문화를 더 명확히 시사하는 설명을 제공한다'. 소설은 과거에 색채, 소리, 드라마를 더하여 과거의 부분들을 지어내기까지 한다. 그리고 **Robert Rosenstone**은 지어내는 것이 (역사) 영화의 약점이 아닌 강점이라고 주장한다. 소설은 역사 자료가 없어 표현된 적이 없는 과거의 일부를 사용자들이 보도록 해 준다. 실제로 **Gilden Seavey**가 설명하기로, 역사 소설 제작자들이 엄격한 학술적 기준을 고수했다면, 많은 역사적 주제는 적절한 증거가 없어서 여전히 탐구되지 못했을 것이라고 한다. 따라서 역사 소설은 전문적 역사와 정반대된다고 여겨져서는 안 되며, 대신에 대중 역사학자와 대중 관객이 모두 그것으로부터 배울 수도 있는 과거에 대한 도전적인 표현으로 여겨져야 한다.

→ 역사 소설은 (A) 불충분한 증거를 사용하여 과거를 재구성하지만, 그것은 매력적인 설명을 제공하는데, 이는 역사적 사건에 대한 사람들의 이해를 (B) 풍부하게 할 수도 있다.

해설 글에 따르면 역사 소설은 학문적으로 적절한 증거가 없어 표현되지 못했던 사실에 살을 붙여서, 비록 '허구를 포함할지라도' 과거를 더 풍부하게 이해할 수 있도록 도와준다고 한다. 따라서 요약문에 들어갈 말로 가장 적절한 것은 ② '불충분한 - 풍부하게 할'이다.

오답 풀이

선택률	선지 해석 & 오답 풀이
① 16%	사소한 - 지연시킬 ▶ 역사 소설이 과거에 대한 이해를 '지연시키지' 않고 '도와준다'는 것이 글의 결론이므로 (B)는 부적절하다.
③ 20%	구체적인 - 강화할 ▶ '증거가 부족한' 사실에 대해 허구를 덧붙여 과거에 대한 이해를 돕는다는 내용이 핵심이므로 (A)는 부적절하다.
④ 19%	구식인 - 향상할 ▶ 증거가 '구식이라는' 내용은 없으므로 (A)는 부적절하다.
⑤ 9%	제한된 - 방해할 ▶ 역사 소설이 과거에 대한 '더 명확한' 이해를 도와준다는 내용으로 보아 (B)는 부적절하다.

지문 자세히 보기

01 Research for historical fiction may focus on under-documented ordinary people, events, or sites. Fiction helps portray everyday situations, feelings, and atmosphere that recreate the historical context.

▶ '역사 소설'의 특징이 주된 내용이다. '기록이 부족한' 과거 보통 사람들과 사건을 다루며 '역사적 맥락을 재창조해주는' 매체가 역사 소설이라는 것이다.

02 Historical fiction adds "flesh to the bare bones that historians are able to uncover and by doing so provides an account that while not necessarily true provides a clearer indication of past events, circumstances and cultures." Fiction adds color, sound, drama to the past, as much as it invents parts of the past.

▶ '맥락을 재창조한다'는 것은 결국 사실에 '살'을 붙여 '꼭 사실은 아닐지라도 과거를 더 잘 이해하게 해주는 설명'을 덧붙인다는 말과 같다. 즉 'flesh = a clearer indication = color, sound, drama'가 모두 위의 recreate the historical context를 보충 설명한다.

03 And Robert Rosenstone argues that invention is not the weakness of films, it is their strength. Fiction can allow users to see parts of the past that have never — for lack of archives — been represented.

▶ 위에서 언급한 '맥락 재창조' 작업을 invention이라고 짧게 요약했다. 이러한 '지어내기'는 우리가 '자료가 부족해서 표현하지 못하던' 과거를 볼 수 있게 해준다는 설명이 뒤따른다.

04 In fact, Gilden Seavey explains that if producers of historical fiction had strongly held the strict academic standards, many historical subjects would remain unexplored for lack of appropriate evidence. Historical fiction should, therefore, not be seen as the opposite of professional history, but rather as a challenging representation of the past from which both public historians and popular audiences may learn.

▶ 위의 lack of archives가 lack of appropriate evidence라는 비슷한 표현으로 반복된다. 결국 '정보가 부족한 사실에 대해 허구의 살을 붙여 과거를 더 풍성하게 이해할 수 있게 하는' 것이 역사 소설의 기능이라는 내용이 되풀이된다.

구문 풀이

~ if producers of historical fiction **had strongly held** the strict academic standards, many historical subjects **would remain** unexplored for lack of appropriate evidence.

→ 가정법 과거완료 종속절(if + 주어 + had p.p. ~)과 가정법 과거 주절(주어 + 조동사 과거형 + 동사원형)이 결합된 혼합가정법 문장이다.

구문 플러스⁺ 혼합가정법

과거의 원인이 달랐더라면 현재의 결과도 달랐으리라는 아쉬움과 후회를 주로 나타낸다.

If he **had saved** more money, he **wouldn't be** in debt now.
그가 (과거에) 돈을 더 모았더라면, 지금 빚을 지지 않았을 텐데.

해석 '장인정신'은 산업 사회의 도래와 함께 쇠퇴한 삶의 방식을 나타낼지도 모르지만, 이는 오해의 소지가 있다. 장인정신은 지속적이고 기본적인 인간의 충동, 즉 일 그 자체를 위해 일을 잘하고 싶은 욕망을 말한다. 장인정신은 숙련된 육체 노동보다 훨씬 더 넓은 구획을 가르는 것으로, 컴퓨터 프로그래머, 의사, 예술가에게 도움이 되며, 시민 정신과 마찬가지로 양육도 숙련된 기술로서 실행될 때 향상된다. 이 모든 영역에서 장인정신은 객관적인 기준, 즉 그 자체의 것에 초점을 맞춘다. 그러나 사회 및 경제적 조건이 흔히 장인의 수련과 전념을 방해하는데, 즉 학교는 일을 잘하기 위한 도구를 제공하지 못할 수 있고, 직장은 품질에 대한 열망을 진정으로 가치 있게 여기지 않을 수 있다. 그리고 비록 장인정신이 일에 대한 자부심으로 개인에게 보상을 줄 수 있지만, 이 보상은 간단하지 않다. 장인은 흔히 탁월함에 대한 상충되는 객관적 기준에 직면하며, 일 그 자체를 위해 어떤 일을 잘하려는 욕망은 경쟁에서 오는 압박, 좌절, 또는 집착으로 인해 약화될 수 있다.

→ 오랜 시간에 걸쳐 다양한 상황에서 (A) 존속된 인간의 욕망인 장인정신은 흔히 그 완전한 발전을 (B) 제한하는 요소들을 마주한다.

해설 첫 두 문장에서 장인정신은 산업화가 이뤄지며 쇠퇴한 삶의 방식이 아니라 '지속적인' 욕망이라고 한다. 또한 글 중간의 **however** 뒤로 장인정신의 발전을 '저해하는' 요소에 관해 언급하고 있다. 이를 종합할 때, 빈칸 (A), (B)에 들어갈 말로 가장 적절한 것은 ① '존속했다 - 제한하다'이다.

오답 풀이

선택률	선지 해석 & 오답 풀이
② 8%	존속했다 - 증진시키다 ▶ **however** 이하로 장인정신을 '방해하는' 요소에 관한 설명이 나오므로 (B)에 **cultivate**는 적절하지 않다.
③ 3%	발전했다 - 가속화하다 ▶ 장인정신을 '가속화한다'는 내용은 주제와 반대되므로 (B)에 **accelerate**는 적절하지 않다.
④ 3%	줄어들었다 - 형성하다 ▶ 첫 두 문장에서 장인정신을 쇠퇴한 생활 방식으로 여기는 것은 오해라고 하므로, (A)에 **diminished**는 부적절하다. 장인정신을 '만들어간다'는 내용 또한 **however** 뒷 내용과 모순하므로 (B)에 **shape**도 적절하지 않다.
⑤ 10%	줄어들었다 - 제한하다 ▶ ④와 같은 이유로 (A)에 **diminished**는 적절하지 않다.

지문 자세히 보기

01 "Craftsmanship" may suggest a way of life that declined with the arrival of industrial society — but this is misleading. Craftsmanship names an enduring, basic human impulse, the desire to do a job well for its own sake. Craftsmanship cuts a far wider swath than skilled manual labor; it serves the computer programmer, the doctor, and the artist; parenting improves when it is practiced as a skilled craft, as does citizenship.

▶ '장인정신'이라는 핵심 소재를 소개한다. 흔히 장인정신이 산업화의 도래와 함께 쇠퇴했다고 생각하지만, 실은 이것은 인간의 지속적인 (**enduring**) 욕망이며 다양한 분야와 관련된다는 내용이다.

02 In all these domains, craftsmanship focuses on objective standards, on the thing in itself. Social and economic conditions, however, often stand in the way of the craftsman's discipline and commitment: schools may fail to provide the tools to do good work, and workplaces may not truly value the aspiration for quality.

▶ **however**와 함께, 장인정신을 '방해하는' 요소에 관한 언급이 시작된다. 먼저 사회·경제적 상황이 언급되며, **schools**와 **workplaces**가 사례로 제시된다.

03 And though craftsmanship can reward an individual with a sense of pride in work, this reward is not simple. The craftsman often faces conflicting objective standards of excellence; the desire to do something well for its own sake can be weakened by competitive pressure, by frustration, or by obsession.

▶ 두 번째로 장인정신에 대한 보상 또한 간단치 않아서 장인정신의 발전이 '저해될' 수 있다는 내용이다. '탁월함에 대한 객관적 기준이 엇갈리는' 상황은 '장인정신에 대한 보상이 어려운 상황'의 구체적 사례다.

구문 풀이

~ parenting **improves** when it is practiced as a skilled craft, **as does citizenship**.
→ 접속사 **as**(~듯이, ~대로) 뒤로 「대동사 + 주어」 어순이 나왔다. **does**는 앞의 일반동사 **improves**를 가리킨다.

구문 플러스 대동사

앞에 나온 술어의 반복을 피하기 위해 조동사/be/do를 쓸 때 이를 대동사라고 한다.

They will not help you, but I will.
그들은 널 안 도와주겠지만, 난 도와줄게.
A: Who is going to the workshop? / B: I am.
워크숍에 누가 가죠? / 저요.
He loves to swim, and his brother does too.
그는 수영을 좋아하고, 그의 남동생도 좋아한다.

해석 통행의 이동성은 인문학뿐만 아니라 모든 학부의 여러 다른 학과에서 탐구할 수 있는 광범위한 분야를 제공한다. 예를 들어, 지리적 공간이나 가상의 공간을 이동할 때 속도가 증가하고 있음에도 불구하고, 우리의 몸은 점점 수동적이고 움직이지 않는 컨테이너가 되는데, 그것은 인공물에 의해 운송되거나 이른바 정보 사회에서 이동한다는 내적 느낌으로 가득 채워진다. 기술적 이동성은 인간을 일종의 불치병에 걸린(가련한) 존재로 바꾸는데, 그는 대부분의 시간을 쉬면서 보내고 운동과 휴식 간의 일상적인 불균형을 맞추기 위해 스포츠에 참여할 필요가 있다. 엘리트가 돈, 사물, 사람을 움직이는 힘을 행사하면서 자신은 전혀 움직일 필요가 없을 때, 우리는 아리스토텔레스의 움직일 수 있지만 움직이지 않는 존재로서의 신의 이미지에 더 가까워진 것인가? 이 권력의 밑바닥에 있는 또 어떤 사람들은 이동성으로 구조화된 사회적 배제의 희생자들이다. 그들은 어떻게 어디로 이동해야 할지 결정할 수 없지만, 이동할 권리도 머무를 권리도 없이 그저 이리저리 옮겨지거나, 내쳐지거나, 아니면 심지어 갇히기도 한다.

→ 기술과 정보 사회에서, 인간은 신체의 움직임이 덜 (A) 필요해져 이동성과 권력의 증가를 이룬 것처럼 보이는데, 이동성과 관련된 그러한 인간의 상태는 사회적 (B) 불평등이라는 문제를 제기한다.

해설 글 전반부에 따르면 오늘날 정보 사회 속 인간은 물리적 공간이든 가상 공간이든 더 빨리 이동할 수 있게 되었지만 실제로는 더 움직이지 않는 존재가 되었다고 한다. 이어서 후반부에 따르면 특히 엘리트들이 직접 움직이지 않으면서 다른 대상이나 존재를 움직일 힘을 갖게 된 한편, 자기 의지대로 이동도 머무름도 선택할 수 없는 희생자들도 생겨났다고 한다. 따라서 요약문의 빈칸 (A), (B)에 들어갈 말로 가장 적절한 것은 ① '필요한 - 불평등'이다.

오답 풀이

선택률	선지 해석 & 오답 풀이
② 21%	필요한 - 성장 ▶ 엘리트와 엘리트가 아닌 계층으로 나누어졌다는 후반부 내용을 '성장'으로 볼 수는 없으므로 (B)에 growth는 부적절하다.
③ 10%	한정된 - 의식 ▶ 정보 사회 속 인간이 더 수동적이고 움직이지 않게 되었다는 설명으로 보아, 움직임에 '덜 제한받게' 되었다는 의미를 완성하는 limited는 (A)에 부적절하다.
④ 14%	바람직한 - (사회) 복지 ▶ 이동이 '바람직한지' 가치 평가를 하는 내용은 언급되지 않으므로 (A)에 desirable은 부적절하다. 나아가 사회 복지도 글과 무관한 소재이므로 (B)에 service도 부적절하다.
⑤ 11%	바람직한 - 분열 ▶ ④와 같은 이유로 (A)에 desirable은 부적절하다.

지문 자세히 보기

01 Mobilities in transit offer a broad field to be explored by different disciplines in all faculties, in addition to the humanities.

▶ '통행의 이동성'에 관해 분석하는 글이다.

02 In spite of increasing acceleration, for example in travelling through geographical or virtual space, our body becomes more and more a passive non-moving container, which is transported by artefacts or loaded up with inner feelings of being mobile in the so-called information society. Technical mobilities turn human beings into some kind of terminal creatures, who spend most of their time at rest and who need to participate in sports in order to balance their daily disproportion of motion and rest.

▶ 정보 사회에서 이동의 속도는 증가했지만, 정작 실제로 인간은 덜 움직이는 수동적 존재로 전락했다는 내용이 제시된다. a passive non-moving container, terminal creatures, at rest, dispropotion of motion and rest가 모두 움직임이 '덜 필요해진' 인간의 모습을 묘사한다.

03 Have we come closer to Aristotle's image of God as the immobile mover, when elites exercise their power to move money, things and people, while they themselves do not need to move at all?

▶ 이렇듯 덜 움직이게 되었지만 한편으로 다른 사람이나 대상을 움직일 수 있게 된 인간, 특히 엘리트들이 과거 아리스토텔레스가 그리던 신의 모습에 근접해진 것인지 자문하는 내용이 이어진다.

04 Others, at the bottom of this power, are victims of mobility-structured social exclusion. They cannot decide how and where to move, but are just moved around or locked out or even locked in without either the right to move or the right to stay.

▶ 한편으로 엘리트가 아닌 다른 사람들(Others), 즉 이동의 힘에서 '소외된' 사람들이 생겨났다는 내용이 이어지고 있다. 'cannot decide ~'와 'without ~ the right to move ~'는 자신의 이동에 관해 스스로 결정할 수 없는 '희생자' 계층의 상황을 설명한다.

구문 풀이

They cannot decide **how and where to move**, but are just moved around or locked out or even locked in without either the right to move or the right to stay.

→ 동사구 cannot decide의 목적어로 「의문사 + to부정사」가 나왔다.

---

95 정답 ③ 41%   *2022학년도 6월 모평*

해석 나무를 '심는 것'이 사회적 또는 정치적인 의미를 가질 수 있다는 생각은 비록 이후에 널리 퍼져나가기는 했지만 영국인들에 의해 고안된 것처럼 보인다. Keith Thomas의 역사서인 <Man and the Natural World>에 따르면, 17세기와 18세기의 귀족들은 자신의 재산 범위와 그것에 대한 권리의 영속성을 선언하기 위해 대개 줄지어 활엽수를 심기 시작했다. 그 신사 대상 잡지 편집자(Thomas)는 독자들에게 묻기를, "그런 살아 있고 성장하는 증인들(나무)의 증언에 의해 여러분의 재산 경계와 한계가 대대로 보존되고 지속되게 하는 것보다 즐거울 수 있는 것이 무엇이겠는가?"라고 했다. 나무를 심는 것은 애국적인 행동으로 여겨지는 추가적인 이점을 가졌는데, 왜냐하면 군주가 영국 해군이 의존하는 경재(활엽수에서 얻은 단단한 목재)가 심각하게 부족하다고 선포했기 때문이었다.

→ 영국의 귀족들에게, 나무를 심는 것은 자신의 땅에 대한 (A) 지속적인 소유권을 표시하는 진술의 역할을 했고, 또한 국가에 대한 충성심을 (B) 표현하는 것으로 여겨졌다.

해설 두 번째 문장과 마지막 문장에서, 영국 귀족들의 나무 심기는 재산에 대한 소유권을 표시하기 위한 행위였을 뿐 아니라 애국심을 드러내는 행위였다고 설명한다. 따라서 요약문의 빈칸 (A), (B)에 들어갈 말로 가장 적절한 것은 ③ '지속적인 - 표현'이다.

오답 풀이

선택률	선지 해석 & 오답 풀이
① 20%	불안정한 - 확인 ▶ 소유권의 '영속성'을 드러내려 했다는 설명으로 보아 (A)에 unstable은 부적절하다.
② 13%	불안정한 - 과장 ▶ 충성심을 '과장'한다는 내용은 없으므로 (B)에 exaggeration은 부적절하다.

④ 19%	지속적인 - 조작	
	▶ 충성심을 '조작'한다는 내용은 없으므로 (B)에 manipulation은 부적절하다.	
⑤ 8%	공식적인 - 정당화	
	▶ 충성심을 '정당화'한다는 내용은 없으므로 (B)에 justification은 부적절하다.	

지문 자세히 보기

01 The idea that *planting* trees could have a social or political significance appears to have been invented by the English, though it has since spread widely.

▶ 영국에서 '나무 심기'가 사회적 또는 정치적으로 어떻게 이해되었는지 설명하는 글이다.

02 According to Keith Thomas's history *Man and the Natural World*, seventeenth- and eighteenth-century aristocrats began planting hardwood trees, usually in lines, to declare the extent of their property and the permanence of their claim to it.

▶ 17~18세기 영국에서 나무 심기는 재산의 범위와 소유권을 표시했다는 내용으로, 이 문장의 **permanence**가 (A)의 **lasting**으로 바뀌었다.

03 "What can be more pleasant," the editor of a magazine for gentlemen asked his readers, "than to have the bounds and limits of your own property preserved and continued from age to age by the testimony of such living and growing witnesses?"

▶ 'to have ~ preserved and continued'가 이전 문장의 'to declare ~'를 재진술하며, 나무 심기로 소유권을 표시했다는 설명을 계속한다.

04 Planting trees had the additional advantage of being regarded as a patriotic act, for the Crown had declared a severe shortage of the hardwood on which the Royal Navy depended.

▶ 나무 심기의 다른 이점(**the additional advantage**)에 관한 내용이 추가된다. 나무 심기가 애국적인 활동(**a patriotic act**)으로도 여겨졌다는 것이다.

구문 풀이

The idea that *planting* trees could have a social or political significance **appears to have been invented** by the English, though it has since spread widely.

→ 동사 **appears**보다 더 먼저 일어난 사건을 묘사하기 위해 「to have p.p.」 형태의 완료부정사가 쓰였다.

구문 플러스 to부정사의 시제

to부정사의 시제는 본동사와 같은지 다른지에 따라 형태를 결정한다.
• 본동사와 동일 → 단순부정사(to-V)
• 본동사보다 과거 → 완료부정사(to have p.p)

He appears to be sick. 그는 아픈 것 같다.
┊---- 현재 ----┊

He appears to have been sick. 그는 아팠던 것 같다.
　　현재　　　과거

해석 비교 문화적 관점에서 대중적 리더십과 지배력 사이의 방정식은 의심스럽다. '지배력'이 의미하는 바는 무엇인가? 그것은 강제를 나타내는 것인가? 아니면 '가장 가치 있는 것'에 대한 통제인가? '정치적' 시스템은 둘 다 혹은 둘 중 하나에 관한 것이거나, 아니면 아마도 둘 다 관련이 없을 수도 있다. '통제'라는 생각은 많은 부족에게는 성가신 것일 텐데, 예를 들어 공동체의 모든 구성원이 개인의 자율성을 좋아하고 통제나 강제가 명백하게 표현되는 어떤 것이든 몹시 싫어하는 아마존의 많은 원주민 부족 사이에서처럼 말이다. 서양의 고정관념일지 모르겠지만, '강제적인' 힘으로서의 정치 권력이라는 개념은 보편적인 것이 아니다. 아마존의 지도자가 명령을 내리는 것은 매우 이례적이다. 많은 부족이 정치 권력을 강제적인 힘으로도, '가장 가치 있는 영역으로도' 여기지 않는다면, '정치적인 것'에서 (강제로서의) '지배'로, 그리고 그로부터 '여성에 대한 지배'로 비약하는 것은 불안정하다. Marilyn Strathern이 말한 것처럼, '정치적인 것'과 '정치적 개성'이라는 개념은 우리 자신의 문화적 강박 관념으로, 인류학적 구성 개념에 오랫동안 반영된 편견이다.

→ 우리가 정치 권력에 관해 지닌 관념을 통해 다른 문화에서의 정치 권력을 이해하는 것은 (A) 잘못된 것인데, 왜냐하면 정치 권력에 관한 생각은 여러 문화에 걸쳐 (B) 보편적이지 않기 때문이다.

해설 글 중반부 이후로, 정치 권력을 강제력으로 이해하는 시각은 보편적이지 않고 서양에 국한된 것일 수 있으므로 이를 바탕으로 다른 부족의 정치 권력을 이해할 수는 없다는 내용이 제시된다. 따라서 요약문의 빈칸 (A), (B)에 들어갈 말로 가장 적절한 것은 ③ '잘못된 - 보편적인'이다.

오답 풀이

선택률	선지 해석 & 오답 풀이
① 23%	합리적인 - 탄력적인 ▶ 정치 권력에 대한 시각은 모든 문화에 보편적이지 않고 '우리가 지닌' 문화적 강박 관념의 일종일 수 있다는 내용으로 보아 (A)에 **rational**은 부적절하다.
② 19%	적절한 - 흔한 ▶ ①과 같은 이유로 (A)에 **appropriate**은 부적절하다.
④ 12%	불합리한 - 다양한 ▶ 정치 권력에 관한 생각이 문화마다 다르다는 것이 글의 결론이므로 (B)에 **varied**를 넣어 다양하지 '않다'는 의미를 완성해서는 안 된다.
⑤ 8%	효과적인 - 객관적인 ▶ ①과 같은 이유로 (A)에 **effective**는 부적절하다.

지문 자세히 보기

01 From a cross-cultural perspective the equation between public leadership and dominance is questionable. What does one mean by 'dominance'? Does it indicate coercion? Or control over 'the most valued'?

▶ 지배력(**dominance**)이 강제 또는 통제의 의미를 나타내는지 묻고 있다.

02 'Political' systems may be about both, either, or conceivably neither. The idea of 'control' would be a bothersome one for many peoples, as for instance among many native peoples of Amazonia where all members of a community are fond of their personal autonomy and notably allergic to any obvious expression of control or coercion.

▶ 위 질문에 대한 답과 함께(both, either, or ~ neither), 정치 체제가 꼭 어디서든 강제 또는 통제로 이해되지는 않는다는 예시(many native peoples of Amazonia)를 든다.

03 The conception of political power as a *coercive force*, while it may be a Western fixation, is not a universal. It is very unusual for an Amazonian leader to give an order.

▶ 예시를 토대로 정치 권력을 강력력으로 이해하는 것이 보편적이지 않다(not a universal)는 일반적 결론을 내린다.

04 If many peoples do not view political power as a coercive force, *nor as the most valued domain*, then the leap from 'the political' to 'domination' (as coercion), *and from there* to 'domination of women', is a shaky one. As Marilyn Strathern has remarked, the notions of 'the political' and 'political personhood' are cultural obsessions of our own, a bias long reflected in anthropological constructs.

▶ 정치 권력을 강제력으로 보는 시각이 일반적이지 않기에 이를 전제로 내린 결론은 불안정하다는 설명과 함께, '정치적인 것'에 관한 개념은 결국 우리의 문화적 강박 관념임을 정리한다. shaky와 cultural obsessions 모두 위의 not a universal과 상통한다.

구문 풀이

The conception of political power **as a coercive force**, while it may be a Western fixation, is not a universal.
→ **as**가 전치사로 쓰여 자격(~로서)의 의미를 나타낸다.

As Marilyn Strathern has remarked, the notions of 'the political' and 'political personhood' are cultural obsessions of our own, a bias long reflected in anthropological constructs.
→ **As**가 접속사로 쓰여 '~듯이, ~대로' 등으로 해석된다.

구문 플러스 as의 다양한 의미

1. 접속사 as: ~할 때, ~하면서, ~함에 따라, ~ 때문에, ~듯이 등
2. 전치사 as: ~로서

As time went by, we grew apart from each other.
시간이 가면서, 우리는 서로 멀어졌다.

As I said before, I have no idea about that.
내가 전에 말했듯이, 난 그거 몰라.

As a child, Lee used to draw a lot.
아이로서(어렸을 때), Lee는 그림을 많이 그렸었다.

---

97 정답 ⑤ 48% *2020학년도 대수능*

해석 코끼리 집단은 매우 자주, 예컨대 먹이의 이용 가능성 변화에 대한 대응으로 헤어지고 재결합하기 때문에, 재결합은 영장류들 사이에서보다도 코끼리 사회에서 더 중요하다. 그래서 이 종은 정교한 인사 행동

을 진화시켜 왔는데, 그 형태는 (마치 여러분이 오래 알고 지낸 지인들과는 단지 악수만 하지만 한동안 보지 못했던 친한 친구는 껴안고, 어쩌면 눈물까지 핑 돌 수도 있는 것처럼) 개체들 사이의 사회적 유대감의 강도를 반영한다. 코끼리는 단순히 코를 서로의 입 안으로 갖다 대면서 인사를 할 수도 있는데, 이것은 아마도 사람들이 뺨에 가볍게 입 맞추는 것과 같을 것이다. 그러나 오랜 공백 후에 가족이나 친밀 집단의 구성원들은 믿을 수 없을 정도로 극적인 모습을 보이며 서로에게 인사한다. 강렬함이 친밀도뿐만 아니라 떨어져 있었던 시간의 길이도 반영한다는 사실은 코끼리들에게도 시간적 감각이 있다는 것을 암시한다. 사람들의 눈에 이런 인사 행위는 공감을 불러일으킨다. 나는 국제공항 터미널 도착 구역에서 흔히 볼 수 있는 즐거운 상봉 장면이 생각난다.

→ 코끼리의 진화된 인사 행동은 그들이 얼마나 사회적으로 **(A)** 유대감을 갖고 있으며 얼마나 오랫동안 **(B)** 헤어져 있었는지를 보여주는 지표가 될 수 있다.

해설 마지막에서 세 번째 문장을 통해 코끼리의 인사가 강렬해지는 것은 서로 간의 친밀도뿐 아니라 공백의 기간까지 반영한다는 결론을 알 수 있다. 따라서 요약문의 빈칸 **(A)**, **(B)**에 들어갈 말로 가장 적절한 것은 ⑤ '유대감을 가진 - 헤어진'이다.

오답 풀이

선택률	선지 해석 & 오답 풀이
① 23%	경쟁적인 - 단절된 ▶ 코끼리들의 '경쟁'에 관한 내용은 없으므로 **(A)**에 **competitive**는 부적절하다.
② 12%	유대감을 가진 - 멸종 위기에 처한 ▶ 코끼리의 '멸종 위기'에 관한 내용은 없으므로 **(B)**에 **endangered**는 부적절하다.
③ 5%	책임이 있는 - 고립된 ▶ 코끼리의 '사회적 책임'에 관한 내용은 없으므로 **(A)**에 **responsible**은 부적절하다.
④ 11%	경쟁적인 - 연합된 ▶ 코끼리의 인사는 '떨어져 있었던' 기간을 반영한다는 내용으로 보아, 이와 반대로 '연합한' 기간을 반영한다는 뜻의 **united**는 **(B)**에 부적합하다.

지문 자세히 보기

01 Because elephant groups break up and reunite very frequently — for instance, in response to variation in food availability — reunions are more important in elephant society than among primates.

▶ 코끼리 사회에서 재결합(reunions)이 중요한 의미를 갖는다는 배경 설명이 제시된다.

02 And the species has evolved elaborate greeting behaviors, the form of which reflects the strength of the social bond between the individuals (much like how you might merely shake hands with a long-standing acquaintance but hug a close friend you have not seen in a while, and maybe even tear up).

▶ 재결합이 중요하기 때문에 인사 행위가 정교하게 발달했고, 이는 유대감의 강도(the strength of the social bond)를 보여준다는 점이 언급된다.

03 Elephants may greet each other simply by reaching their trunks into each other's mouths, possibly equivalent to a human peck on the cheek. However, after long absences, members of family and bond groups greet one another with incredibly theatrical displays.

▶ **However** 앞뒤로 평범한 인사와 극적인 인사가 대비된다. 특히, 상대와의 오랜 공백(**long absences**)이 있었던 상황에서 인사가 극적인 모습을 띤다는 설명이 나온다.

04 The fact that the intensity reflects the duration of the separation as well as the level of intimacy suggests that elephants have a sense of time as well. To human eyes, these greetings strike a familiar chord. I'm reminded of the joyous reunions so visible in the arrivals area of an international airport terminal.

▶ 코끼리의 인사는 친밀감의 강도(**the level of intimacy**)뿐 아니라 떨어져 있었던 시간의 길이(**the duration of the separation**)까지도 반영한다는 결론이 제시된다.

구문 풀이

I'm reminded of the joyous reunions so visible in the arrivals area of an international airport terminal.
→ 「A be reminded of B(A가 B를 상기하다)」는 「remind A of B(A에게 B를 상기시키다)」의 수동태이다.

구문 플러스 remind A of B

remind는 '~에게 …을 상기시키다'라는 의미일 때 「remind A of B」 형태로 쓴다. 단 B에 해당하는 말이 that절이면 A 뒤에 of를 쓰지 않는다.

The song **reminded** me **of** my childhood.
그 노래는 내게 어린 시절을 상기시켰다.
→ 수동태: I **was reminded of** my childhood by the song.
　　　　　나는 그 노래에 내 어린 시절이 생각났다.
Mother **reminded** me **that** we must talk to each other with kind words.
엄마는 내게 우리가 서로 친절한 언어로 이야기해야 한다는 것을 상기시켰다.

---

98 정답 ① 69%　　　　　*2020학년도 6월 모평*

해석 1992년에 리우데자네이루에서 열린 국제 연합 환경 회의가 '지속 가능성'이라는 용어를 전 세계적으로 널리 알려지게 만든 후에, 그 단어는 친환경적으로 보이기를 원하지만 자신의 행동을 진짜 바꿀 의도는 아니었던 사람들에 의해 인기 있는 유행어가 되었다. 그것은 홍보 용어가 되었고, 널리 퍼진 해악으로부터 지구를 구하기 위해 우리가 무엇을 해야 하는가에 관한 최신의 생각과 보조를 맞추고 있는 것으로 보이려는 시도가 되었다. 그러나 그런 다음 십여 년이 지난 후, 일부 정부, 산업, 교육 기관, 그리고 조직이 그 용어를 진지하게 사용하기 시작했다. 미국에서 많은 대기업이 지속 가능성 담당 부사장을 임명했다. 이 임원들은 '친환경' 제품을 만들어 회사가 어떻게 이익을 얻을 수 있는가에 관심을 둘 뿐만 아니라, 흔히 쓰레기와 오염을 줄이고 회사의 탄소 배출량을 줄여 회사를 더 효율적으로 만들라는 과제를 받기도 했다.

→ 초기 단계에서 '지속 가능성'이라는 용어는 친환경 의식이 있는 (A) 체했던 사람들 사이에서 인기가 있었지만, 나중에 그것은 친환경주의적 생

각을 (B) 실현하고자 하는 사람들이 사용하게 되었다.

해설 전반부는 '지속 가능성'이라는 용어가 친환경적인 조치를 실제로 취할 의도는 없으면서 친환경적으로 보이고 싶어 했던 사람들 사이에서 인기를 얻었다는 내용이다. 이후 'But then, ~'에서 흐름이 반전된다. 후반부에 따르면 지속 가능성이라는 용어를 많은 회사에서 진지하게 받아들이고 환경을 지키면서 효율성도 높일 방법을 고민하기 시작했다고 한다. 따라서 요약문의 빈칸 (A), (B)에 들어갈 말로 가장 적절한 것은 ① '(~한) 체했다 - 실현하다'이다.

오답 풀이

선택률	선지 해석 & 오답 풀이
② 11%	(~한) 체했다 - 무시하다 ▶ 시간이 지나며 '지속 가능성'이라는 용어가 실제로 환경을 생각하는 노력과 맞물려 쓰이기 시작했다는 내용으로 보아 (B)에 disregard는 부적절하다.
③ 9%	거부했다 - 실현하다 ▶ '지속 가능성'이라는 말을 초기에 썼던 사람들은 친환경적인 것처럼 보이기를 '원했다'는 설명으로 보아 (A)에 refused는 부적절하다.
④ 6%	거부했다 - 이상화하다 ▶ 친환경적인 생각을 '이상화했다'는 내용은 없으므로 (B)에 idealize는 부적절하다.
⑤ 3%	시도했다 - 감추다 ▶ 근래에 들어 '지속 가능성'이 '진지하게' 여겨진다는 내용으로 보아 (B)에 mask는 부적절하다.

지문 자세히 보기

01 After the United Nations environmental conference in Rio de Janeiro in 1992 made the term "sustainability" widely known around the world, the word became a popular buzzword by those who wanted to be seen as pro-environmental but who did not really intend to change their behavior.

▶ '지속 가능성'이라는 용어가 처음 퍼지던 때를 설명하고 있다. 친환경적으로 보이고자 하나 실제로 친환경적인 행동으로 나아갈 생각은 없던(**wanted ~ but ~ did not really intend to ~**) 사람들 사이에서 이 용어가 유행했다는 내용이 제시된다.

02 It became a public relations term, an attempt to be seen as abreast with the latest thinking of what we must do to save our planet from widespread harm.

▶ **a popular buzzword**가 **a public relations term**으로 바뀌어 표현되었다. 환경 보호라는 최신 주제에 보조를 맞추는 것처럼 보이기 위해 '지속 가능성'을 홍보 용어처럼 썼다는 내용이 반복된다.

03 But then, in a decade or so, some governments, industries, educational institutions, and organizations started to use the term in a serious manner.

▶ **But then**에서 흐름이 전환되며, 지속 가능성이 진지하게 사용되기 시작했다는 내용이 이어진다.

구문 풀이

Not only were these officials interested in how their companies could profit by producing "green" products, but they were often given the task of making the company more efficient by reducing wastes and pollution and by reducing its carbon emissions.

→「not only A but (also) B(A뿐만 아니라 B도)」의 not only가 문장 맨 앞에 나오자 A 자리의「주어 + 동사」가 의문문 어순으로 도치되었다.

유형 플러스˚ 문단 요약

글의 중심 내용을 근거로 주어진 요약문을 완성하는 유형으로, 쉬운 빈칸 추론 문항과 유사하다. 낯설고 추상적인 개념을 설명하거나, 서로 다른 두 소재를 대비하거나, 실험을 소개하는 글이 많이 활용된다.

· 문제 해결 Tip.
① 요약문을 통해 글의 내용을 예측한다. 가령, 요약문이 **according to research**로 시작하면 본문에 실험이 소개된다는 뜻이므로, 결론에 주목해야 한다. 또한 요약문에 **while**(~하는 반면)이 있으면 서로 다른 두 소재나 내용이 대조된다는 뜻이므로, 글에서 흐름이 반전되는 지점 앞뒤를 잘 읽어야 한다.
② 한 문장으로 응축된 주제문이 있다면, 요약문이 주제문과 같은 의미가 되도록 빈칸을 완성한다.
③ 주제문이 없다면, 결론을 중점적으로 읽고 키워드를 추려 빈칸을 완성한다.

99 정답 ③ 48%, ② 26%　　*2024학년도 6월 모평*

[해석] 많은 협상가는 모든 협상이 고정된 파이를 수반한다고 가정한다. 협상가들은 흔히 제로섬 상황이나 승패 교환으로 통합 협상 기회에 접근한다. 허구의 고정된 파이를 믿는 사람들은 당사자들의 이해관계가 통합적인 합의와 상호 이익이 되는 절충안의 가능성이 없는 반대 입장에 있다고 가정하기 때문에 이를 찾으려는 노력을 억누른다. 고용 협상에서 급여가 유일한 문제라고 생각하는 구직자는 고용주가 7만 달러를 제시할 때 7만 5천 달러를 요구할 수 있다. 두 당사자가 가능성에 대해 더 자세히 논의할 때만 이사 비용과 시작 날짜 또한 협상할 수 있다는 사실을 발견하게 되는데, 이는 급여 문제의 해결을 <u>방해할(→ 촉진할)</u> 수 있을 것이다.

협상을 고정된 파이 관점에서 보는 경향은 사람들이 주어진 갈등 상황의 본질을 어떻게 보느냐에 따라 달라진다. 이는 징역형에 대한 검사와 피고측 변호인 간의 모의 협상을 포함하는, **Harinck, de Dreu**와 **Van Vianen**의 기발한 실험에서 밝혀졌다. 어떤 참가자들은 개인적 이득의 관점에서 목표를 보라는 말을 들었고(예를 들어, 특정 징역형을 정하는 것이 당신의 경력에 도움이 될 것이다), 다른 참가자들은 효과성의 관점에서 목표를 보라는 말을 들었으며(특정 형은 상습적 범행을 방지할 가능성이 가장 크다), 그리고 또 다른 참가자들은 가치에 초점을 맞추라는 말을 들었다(특정 징역형은 공정하고 정당하다). 개인적 이득에 초점을 맞춘 협상가들은 고정된 파이에 대한 믿음의 영향을 받아 상황에 경쟁적으로 접근할 가능성이 가장 컸다. 가치에 초점을 맞춘 협상가들은 문제를 고정된 파이 관점에서 볼 가능성이 가장 낮았고, 상황에 협조적으로 접근하려는 경향이 더 컸다. 시간 제약처럼 스트레스가 많은 조건은 이러한 흔한 오해의 원인이 되며, 이는 결국 덜 통합적인 합의로 이어질 수 있다.

99-1

[해설] 협조적 협상에 방해가 될 수 있는 고정적 파이 개념을 설명하고, 여기서 벗어나야 통합적 합의가 가능해진다는 결론을 암시하는 글이다. 따라서 글의 제목으로 가장 적절한 것은 ③ '협상가들이여, 고정된 파이라는 근거 없는 믿음에서 깨어나라!'이다.

오답 풀이

선택률	선지 해석 & 오답 풀이
① 17%	고정된 파이: 제로섬 게임 성공의 비결 ▶ 고정된 파이 관념에 맞춰 협상을 '제로섬 게임'처럼 인식하는 것은 통합적 합의를 '방해하는' 요소라고 했다.
② 13%	고정된 파이는 어떻게 하면 제일 많은 급여를 받을지 여러분에게 알려준다 ▶ 고정된 파이 관념 때문에 오히려 급여 협상이 잘 안 된다는 예시 내용과 모순된다.
④ 11%	더 공정한 징역형을 원하는가? 고정된 파이를 고수하라 ▶ 공정한 징역형은 고정된 파이 관념과 정반대로 '가치'에 집중해 협상했던 상황과 관련이 있다. 따라서 글의 내용과 모순되는 선택지이다.
⑤ 11%	어떤 대안이 고정된 파이 효과를 극대화하나? ▶ 예시에 나온 가치관에 집중한 협상은 고정된 파이를 '극대화하기' 위한 방안이 아니라 '줄이기' 위한 방안이다.

99-2

[해설] 세 번째 문장에서 허구의 고정된 파이를 믿다 보면 모든 당사자가 이득을 볼 수 있는 통합적 합의가 어려워진다고 한다. 이어서 급여를 둘러싼 고용 협상의 예가 이어진다. 예시에서 구직자는 '고정된 파이' 관념에 갇혀 고용주가 제시하려는 연봉보다 훨씬 높은 액수를 고수하는 태도를 보인다. 이때 좀 더 가능성을 열어두고, 이사 비용이나 근무 시작 날짜 등 다른 문제에 관해서도 협상하다 보면 타협하기 어려워 보였던 급여 문제까지 해결하기 '더 쉬워진다'는 것이 (b)의 내용이다. 따라서 ② (b)의 **block**을 **facilitate**로 바꿔야 문맥상 적절하다.

오답 풀이

선택률	선지 해석 & 오답 풀이
① 6%	**suppress**(억누르다) ▶ 서로 입장이 반대된다고 생각해서 절충안을 찾으려는 노력을 '억누르게' 된다는 의미로 **suppress**는 적절하다.
③ 17%	**varies**(달라지다) ▶ 뒤에 나오는 실험을 보면 똑같은 징역형에 관해 논쟁하면서도 개인적 이득, 목표, 가치 중 어떤 것에 초점을 맞춰 보느냐에 따라 협상에 대한 태도가 '달라졌다'는 내용이므로 **varies**는 적절하다.
④ 23%	**competitively**(경쟁적으로) ▶ 개인적 이득에 집중하는 협상은 고정된 파이 관념에 충실한 협상이다. 이 경우 사람들은 '경쟁적으로' 협상에 임한다는 의미로 **competitively**를 썼다.
⑤ 28%	**less**(덜) ▶ 시간 제약처럼 스트레스를 키우고 협상을 고정된 파이로 인식하는 오해를 불러일으키는 상황은 통합적 합의의 가능성을 '낮춘다'는 의미로 **less**를 썼다.

지문 자세히 보기'

01　Many negotiators assume that all negotiations involve a fixed pie. Negotiators often approach integrative negotiation opportunities as zero-sum situations or win-lose exchanges.

▶ 협상의 '고정된 파이'는 어느 한쪽이 '이기거나 진다'는 태도로 협상에 임하는 것이라는 내용이다.

02　Those who believe in the mythical fixed pie assume that parties' interests stand in opposition, with no possibility for integrative settlements and mutually beneficial trade-offs, so they suppress efforts to search for them. In a hiring negotiation, a job applicant who assumes that salary is the only issue may insist on $75,000 when the employer is offering $70,000. Only when the two parties discuss the possibilities further do they discover that moving expenses and starting date can also be negotiated, which may block(→ facilitate) resolution of the salary issue.

▶ 'parties' ~ trade-offs'가 '고정된 파이' 개념을 상술한다. 즉 서로 입장이 반대된다고 믿고 서로 이득이 되는 절충안을 찾으려 하지 않는 상태라는 것이다. 예시를 고용 협상으로 보여주는데, 급여 문제를 고정된 파이로 바라보는 구직자는 마냥 높은 액수를 제시하게 되므로, 상황을 해결하려면 '가능성을 열어놓고 토의하는' 과정이 필요하다고 한다. discuss the possibilities가 곧 efforts to search for integrative settlements and mutually beneficial trade-offs의 사례이다.

03 The tendency to see negotiation in fixed-pie terms varies depending on how people view the nature of a given conflict situation. This was shown in a clever experiment by Harinck, de Dreu, and Van Vianen involving a simulated negotiation between prosecutors and defense lawyers over jail sentences.

▶ 고정된 파이 관점은 사람들이 갈등 상황의 본질을 어떻게 파악하는가에 따라 달라진다는 일반론 뒤로, 실험 연구의 사례를 든다.

04 Some participants were told to view their goals in terms of personal gain (e.g., arranging a particular jail sentence will help your career), others were told to view their goals in terms of effectiveness (a particular sentence is most likely to prevent recidivism), and still others were told to focus on values (a particular jail sentence is fair and just).

▶ 실험 집단은 세 집단으로 나뉘었으며, 개인적 이득, 처벌의 유효성, 처벌의 가치에 각각 집중해 협상에 임하게 했다는 내용이 이어진다.

05 Negotiators focusing on personal gain were most likely to come under the influence of fixed-pie beliefs and approach the situation competitively. Negotiators focusing on values were least likely to see the problem in fixed-pie terms and more inclined to approach the situation cooperatively. Stressful conditions such as time constraints contribute to this common misperception, which in turn may lead to less integrative agreements.

▶ '개인적 이득'에 집중한 집단이 가장 고정된 파이 관념의 영향을 크게 받아 '경쟁적' 태도를 보였고, 가치관에 집중한 집단이 가장 영향을 덜 받아 '협조적' 태도를 보였다는 결론이 제시된다. 또한, 스트레스가 심한 상황은 '이런 오해', 즉 '고정된 파이' 개념을 더 강화시켜 사람들이 통합적 합의에 '덜' 이르게 만들었다는 내용이 추가된다.

구문 풀이

Only when the two parties discuss the possibilities further **do they discover** that moving expenses and starting date can also be negotiated, which may facilitate resolution of the salary issue.
→ only를 포함한 부사절이 문장 맨 앞에 나오면서 주절이 「조동사 + 주어 + 동사원형」 어순으로 도치되었다.

 플러스⁴ 부정어구의 도치 (2)

only(오로지 ~인, ~밖에 없는)는 도치를 일으키는 부정어구의 일종이다.

Only by learning from your mistakes can you grow.
실수를 통해 배울 때에만 너는 성장할 수 있다.

Only when the sun sets do the stars appear.
해가 저야만 별이 나타난다.

---

100 정답 ① 43%, ④ 50%   *2023학년도 대수능*

해석 매우 간단한 알고리즘조차도 간단한 예측 문제에 대한 전문가의 판단을 능가할 수 있다는 증거가 있다. 예를 들어, 가석방으로 풀려난 죄수가 계속해서 다른 범죄를 저지를 것인지 예측하거나, 잠재적 (입사) 후보자가 장차 직장에서 일을 잘할 것인지를 예측하는 데 알고리즘이 인간보다 더 정확하다는 것이 입증되었다. 많은 다른 영역에 걸친 100개가 넘는 연구에서, 모든 사례의 절반은 간단한 공식이 인간 전문가보다 중요한 예측을 더 잘한다는 것을 보여주며, (아주 적은 소수를 제외한) 나머지는 둘 사이의 무승부를 보여준다. 많은 다른 요인이 관련돼 있고 상황이 매우 불확실할 때, 간단한 공식은 가장 중요한 요소에 초점을 맞추고 일관성을 유지하여 승리할 수 있는 반면, 인간의 판단은 특히 두드러지고 아마도 관련이 없는 고려 사항에 의해 너무 쉽게 영향을 받는다. 사람들이 편안하다고(→ 일이 너무 많다고) 느낄 때 중요한 조치나 고려 사항을 놓치지 않도록 함으로써 '체크리스트'가 다양한 영역에서 전문가의 결정의 질을 향상할 수 있다는 추가적인 증거는 비슷한 관념을 뒷받침한다. 예를 들어, 중환자실에 있는 환자를 치료하려면 하루에 수백 가지의 작은 조치가 필요할 수 있으며, 작은 실수 하나로 목숨을 앗아갈 수 있다. 어떠한 중요한 조치라도 놓치지 않기 위해 체크리스트를 사용하는 것은 활성 감염의 예방부터 폐렴 감소에 이르기까지 다양한 의학적 상황에서 현저히 효과가 있다는 것이 입증되었다.

100-1
해설 단순한 알고리즘이나 공식이 인간의 판단보다 더 나을 수 있다는 주제를 전반부에서 제시하고, 그 이유를 설명하는 글이다. 따라서 글의 제목으로 가장 적절한 것은 ① '의사 결정에 있어 간단한 공식의 힘'이다.

오답 풀이

선택률	선지 해석 & 오답 풀이
② 10%	항상 우선순위를 정하라: 빅 데이터 관리 요령 ▶ 빅 데이터에 관해서는 언급되지 않았다.
③ 12%	알고리즘의 실수: 단순함의 신화 ▶ 단순한 알고리즘의 '실수'가 아닌 '우수성'을 언급하고 있다.
④ 22%	준비하라! 만일을 대비해 체크리스트를 만들라 ▶ 글에서 체크리스트는 '무관한 고려 사항에 영향받아 중요한 단계를 놓치지 않게 해줄' 부수적인 수단으로 언급되었다. 체크리스트를 '만들어야 한다'는 조언이나 주장이 글의 주제는 아니다.
⑤ 14%	인간의 판단이 알고리즘을 이기는 방법 ▶ 글에서는 인간의 판단이 알고리즘의 예측에 못 미칠 때가 있다는 내용까지만 다룬다. 어떻게 알고리즘을 이길지는 언급되지 않는다.

100-2
해설 (d)가 포함된 문장 뒤로, **For example**과 함께 중환자실의 상황을 예로 든다. 이는 사람들이 '편안하다고' 느끼는 상황이라기보다는, 긴박감이나 업무 부담을 느끼기 쉬운 상황이다. 따라서 ④ (d)의 **relaxed**를 반의어인 **overloaded**로 고쳐야 한다.

선택률	선지 해석 & 오답 풀이
① 3%	**accurate**(정확한) ▶ 알고리즘이 '인간 전문가의 예측을 능가한다'는 첫 문장 내용으로 보아, 알고리즘의 판단이 더 '정확하다'는 의미의 **accurate**는 적절하다.
② 7%	**better**(더 잘하는) ▶ 첫 두 문장을 재진술하는 말로 간단한 공식이 인간 전문가보다 중요한 예측을 '더 잘한다'는 의미의 **better**는 적절하다.
③ 34%	**irrelevant**(관련이 없는) ▶ 인간의 예측이 덜 정확한 이유로 '관련이 없는' 고려 사항에 더 많이 영향받기 때문임을 설명하는 **irrelevant**는 적절하다.
⑤ 6%	**effective**(효과가 있는) ▶ 중요한 단계에 집중하게 해주는 체크리스트가 여러 의학 상황에서 현저히 '효과가 있다'는 의미의 **effective**는 적절하다.

지문 자세히 보기

01 There is evidence that even very simple algorithms can outperform expert judgement on simple prediction problems. For example, algorithms have proved more accurate than humans in predicting whether a prisoner released on parole will go on to commit another crime, or in predicting whether a potential candidate will perform well in a job in future.

▶ 알고리즘의 예측이 인간의 판단을 넘어선다(**outperform, more accurate**)는 주제를 제시하고 있다. **For example** 앞뒤로 같은 내용이 반복된다.

02 In over 100 studies across many different domains, half of all cases show simple formulas make better significant predictions than human experts, and the remainder (except a very small handful), show a tie between the two. When there are a lot of different factors involved and a situation is very uncertain, simple formulas can win out by focusing on the most important factors and being consistent, while human judgement is too easily influenced by particularly salient and perhaps irrelevant considerations.

▶ 다른 많은 연구 사례에서도 간단한 공식이 인간 전문가보다 예측을 잘한다(**better**)는 점이 입증되었다는 내용 뒤로, 그 이유가 제시된다. 간단한 공식은 중요 사항에 집중하는 반면(**focusing ~ consistent**), 인간은 무관한(**irrelevant**) 고려 사항에 영향을 더 쉽게 받기 때문이라는 것이다.

03 A similar idea is supported by further evidence that 'checklists' can improve the quality of expert decisions in a range of domains by ensuring that important steps or considerations aren't missed when people are feeling relaxed(→ overloaded).

▶ 같은 맥락에서 '체크리스트'를 생각해보면, 체크리스트는 인간이 중요한 단계를 놓치지 않게(**ensuring ~ aren't missed**) 해주기 때문에 업무 정확도를 높여줄 수 있다고 한다.

04 For example, treating patients in intensive care can require hundreds of small actions per day, and one small error could cost a life. Using checklists to ensure that no crucial steps are missed has proved to be remarkably effective in a range of medical contexts, from preventing live infections to reducing pneumonia.

▶ 이어서 중환자실의 환자를 돌보는(**treating ~ intensive care**) 사례가 언급되는데, 이는 사람들이 '느긋함'보다는 '피로나 부담'을 느낄 수 있는 업무 사례이다. 이런 식의 다양한 의료 상황에서 실제로 체크리스트가 유용하다(**effective**)는 것이 입증됐다는 결론으로 글이 마무리된다.

구문 풀이

In over 100 studies across many different domains, **half of all cases show** simple formulas make better significant predictions than human experts, ~

→ 「부분 + of + 전체」 형태의 「half of + 복수명사」가 주어이므로, 동사는 복수형으로 쓰였다.

구문 플러스 「부분 + of + 전체」 주어의 수 일치

주어가 「부분 + of + 전체」 형태로 제시되면, 동사는 전체 명사에 수 일치한다.

Most of the patients in the room <u>were</u> in their twenties.
그 방의 환자들 대부분은 20대였다.

Much of the region <u>is</u> covered with ice.
그 지역의 많은 부분은 얼음으로 덮여 있다.

---

101 정답 ⑤ 88%, ② 90%, ③ 92%   2023학년도 9월 모평

해석 **(A)** 런던의 Charing Cross 역에서 걸어 나오면서, Emilia와 그 여행 친구 Layla는 벌써 가슴이 두근거리는 기분이었다. 그들의 유럽 여름 여행 둘째 날이었다. 그들은 세계에서 가장 유명한 미술관 중 하나를 방문할 계획이었다. 그들 두 사람은 흥분하여 서두르기 시작했다. 갑자기 Emilia가 "봐! 저기 있네! 드디어 우리가 내셔널 갤러리에 도착했어!"라고 소리쳤다. Layla는 웃으며, "네 꿈이 드디어 이루어졌네!"라고 답했다.

(D) 내셔널 갤러리에 들어가자마자, Emilia는 어디로 제일 먼저 갈지 정확하게 알았다. 그녀는 Layla의 손을 꼭 잡고 서둘러 그녀를 끌며 반 고흐의 <Sunflowers>를 찾으러 갔다. 그것은 Emilia가 가장 좋아하는 그림이었고, 그녀가 화가가 되도록 영감을 준 것이었다. Emilia는 그의 밝은 색상과 빛의 사용을 아주 좋아했다. 그녀는 그의 걸작을 마침내 보기를 몹시 고대하고 있었다. "그가 자기 작품에서 고립감과 고독감을 어떻게 전달했는지 보면 놀라울 거야."라고 그녀는 잔뜩 기대하며 말했다.

(C) 그러나, 모든 전시실을 찾아봐도, Emilia와 Layla는 어디에서도 반 고흐의 걸작을 찾을 수가 없었다. "이상하네. 반 고흐의 <Sunflowers>는 여기 있어야 하는데. 어디에 있지?" Emilia는 속상해 보였지만, Layla는 침착함을 유지하며 말했다. "아마 네가 작품에 대한 공지를 놓쳤나 봐. 내셔널 갤러리 앱을 확인해 봐."라고 말했다. Emilia는 재빨리 그것을 확인했다. 이후 그녀는 한숨을 쉬었다. "<Sunflowers>가 여기 없네! 그것은 특별 전시회 때문에 다른 미술관에 대여됐대. 내가 확인을 안 해봤다니 난 믿을 수 없네!"

(B) "아직 실망하지 마! 특별 전시회는 어느 미술관에서 한대?"라고

Layla는 물었다. Emilia는 "음, <Sunflowers>는 여전히 잉글랜드에 있긴 한데, 리버풀에 있는 미술관에 있어. 거긴 멀잖아, 안 그래?"라고 대답했다. 전화로 빠르게 검색해 본 다음, Layla는 말했다. "아냐! 리버풀까지 기차로 겨우 두 시간이야. 다음 기차가 한 시간 뒤에 출발해. 그걸 타면 어때?" 그 생각을 고려해본 뒤, 이제 안도한 Emilia는 답했다. "그래, 근데 넌 늘 렘브란트의 그림들을 보고 싶어 했잖아. 그거부터 보자, Layla! 그런 다음 점심 먹고 그다음 기차를 타면 돼." Layla가 밝게 웃었다.

101-1

해설 런던 여행 중인 Emilia와 Layla가 내셔널 갤러리에 도착했다는 (A) 뒤로, 갤러리에 들어가자마자 Emilia가 반 고흐의 작품을 찾았다는 (D), 찾던 그림이 다른 갤러리에 대여된 것을 알고 Emilia가 실망했다는 (C), 리버풀까지 이동하기로 한 두 사람이 먼저 Layla가 보고 싶어 하던 렘브란트의 그림부터 보기로 했다는 (B)가 차례로 연결되는 흐름이다. 따라서 글의 순서로 가장 적절한 것은 ⑤ '(D)-(C)-(B)'이다.

오답 풀이

선택률	오답 풀이
① 1%	(A)에서 두 사람은 아직 기대에 부풀어 있는데 (B)는 '실망하지 말라'는 말로 시작하므로 (A)-(B)는 이어지지 않는다.
② 5%	(A)에서 두 사람은 내셔널 갤러리 앞까지 온 상태인데, (C)에서는 이미 들어가 전시실을 다 돌아본 상태이며, (D)는 '이제 막' 갤러리에 들어서는 상태이다. 따라서 (C)를 가장 먼저 배치하면 어색하다.
③ 2%	
④ 2%	(D)에서 Emilia는 아직 자기가 원하던 그림을 볼 수 있을 거라는 기대에 부풀어 있는 상태인데, (B)는 '실망 말라'는 위로로 시작하므로 (D) 뒤에 이어질 수 없다. 정황상 아무리 찾아도 그림이 없었다는 반전으로 시작하는 (C)가 먼저 나와야만 (B)가 이어질 수 있다.

101-2

해설 Emilia가 Layla를 상대로 말하는 상황이므로, (b)의 you는 Layla이다. 나머지 (a), (c), (d), (e)는 모두 Emilia를 가리킨다. 따라서 가리키는 대상이 다른 하나는 ② '(b)'이다.

오답 풀이

선택률	오답 풀이
① 2%	Layla가 Emilia를 상대로 말하는 것이므로, Your는 Emilia's이다.
③ 2%	Layla가 Emilia를 상대로 말하는 것이므로, you는 Emilia이다.
④ 2%	Emilia가 말하는 문장에서 자기 자신을 I로 가리키는 것이다.
⑤ 2%	앞 문장의 Emilia가 주어인 She로 이어진다.

101-3

해설 (B)에 따르면 Emilia는 <Sunflowers>를 보러 리버풀로 이동하자는 Layla의 제안에, 우선은 내셔널 갤러리에서 Layla가 보고 싶어 했던 렘브란트의 그림부터 보고 점심을 먹은 뒤(after lunch) 가자고 제안한다. 따라서 내용과 일치하지 않는 것은 ③ 'Emilia는 기차를 점심 식사 전에 타자고 말했다.'이다.

지문 **자세히 보기**

01 Walking out of Charing Cross Station in London, Emilia and her traveling companion, Layla, already felt their hearts pounding. It was the second day of their European summer trip. They were about to visit one of the world's most famous art galleries. The two of them started hurrying with excitement. Suddenly, Emilia shouted, "Look! There it is! We're finally at the National Gallery!" Layla laughed and responded, "Your dream's finally come true!"

▶ 내셔널 갤러리에 도착한 Emilia와 Layla가 기대감에 부푼 상황이다.

02 Upon entering the National Gallery, Emilia knew exactly where to go first. She grabbed Layla's hand and dragged her hurriedly to find van Gogh's *Sunflowers*. It was Emilia's favorite painting and had inspired her to become a painter. Emilia loved his use of bright colors and light. She couldn't wait to finally see his masterpiece in person. "It'll be amazing to see how he communicated the feelings of isolation and loneliness in his work," she said eagerly.

▶ (A)에 이어 '갤러리에 들어서자마자'의 순간을 다루고 있다. 보고 싶었던 그림을 볼 생각에 Emilia가 특히 신나 했다(couldn't wait, amazing, eagerly)는 내용이 이어진다.

03 However, after searching all the exhibition rooms, Emilia and Layla couldn't find van Gogh's masterpiece anywhere. "That's weird. Van Gogh's *Sunflowers* should be here. Where is it?" Emilia looked upset, but Layla kept calm and said, "Maybe you've missed a notice about it. Check the National Gallery app." Emilia checked it quickly. Then, she sighed, "*Sunflowers* isn't here! It's been lent to a different gallery for a special exhibition. I can't believe I didn't check!"

▶ However와 함께 상황이 반전되며, '전시장을 모두 둘러본 후'의 이야기가 이어진다. Emilia가 보려던 그림이 다른 전시장에 대여된 상태이고, 헛걸음을 하여 실망했다(upset, sighed)는 내용이다.

04 "Don't lose hope yet! Which gallery is the special exhibition at?" Layla asked. Emilia responded, "Well, his *Sunflowers* is still in England, but it's at a gallery in Liverpool. That's a long way, isn't it?" After a quick search on her phone, Layla stated, "No! It's only two hours to Liverpool by train. The next train leaves in an hour. Why don't we take it?" After considering the idea, Emilia, now relieved, responded, "Yeah, but you always wanted to see Rembrandt's paintings. Let's do that first, Layla! Then, after lunch, we can catch the next train." Layla smiled brightly.

▶ 한숨을 쉬는 Emilia를 Layla가 위로했다는 내용으로 시작되어, 이들이 여행 계획을 수정하기로 했다는 내용으로 끝난다.

구문 풀이

"No! It's only two hours to Liverpool by train. The next train **leaves** in an hour. Why don't we take it?"

→ 기차가 떠나는 시간은 일정표에 따라 정해진 미래 상황이므로 현재시제(**leaves**)를 사용해 표현했다.

구문 플러스' 현재(진행)시제로 미래 표현하기

현재시제: 기차 시간, 공식 일정 등 (예외가 없는 한) 예정된 미래
현재진행시제: 비교적 확실한 가까운 미래 (계획)

My flight **leaves** at noon tomorrow.
내 비행기는 내일 정오에 뜬다. → 시간표로 정해진 일정

I'm **meeting** your teacher tomorrow evening.
나 내일 저녁 너희 선생님 만나. → 가까운 미래의 계획

---

102 정답 ③ 56%, ③ 43%   2023학년도 9월 모평

해석 기후 변화 전문가들과 환경 인문주의자들 모두 기후 위기가 근원적으로 상상력의 위기이며, 대중적 상상력의 많은 부분이 소설에 의해 형성된다는 데 동의한다. 인류학자이자 소설가인 Amitav Ghosh는 그의 2016년도 책 'The Great Derangement'에서 상상과 환경 관리 사이의 이러한 관계를 다루면서, 인간이 기후 변화에 대응하지 못한 것은 최소한 부분적으로는 소설이 그것을 믿을 수 있게 표현하지 못하기 때문이라고 주장한다. Ghosh는 기후 변화가 상기시키는 사이클론, 홍수, 그리고 다른 큰 재해들이 일상생활 이야기에 속하기에는 그야말로 너무 '있을 것 같지 않아' 보여서 기후 변화가 현대 소설에 대체로 존재하지 않는다고 설명한다. 하지만 기후 변화는 일련의 놀라운 사건들로만 드러나는 것은 아니다. 사실, Rachel Carson에서 Rob Nixon에 이르는 환경론자들과 생태 비평가들이 지적했듯이, 환경 변화는 '감지할 수 없을' 가능성이 있는데, 즉 그것은 빠르게(→ 점진적으로) 진행되며, 단지 이따금 '폭발적이고 극적인' 사건들을 만들어 낼 뿐이다. 대부분의 기후 변화의 영향은 매일 관찰될 수는 없지만, 그것들은 우리가 그 축적된 영향에 직면할 때 가시화된다.

기후 변화는 중요한 표현상의 문제를 제기한다는 점에서 우리의 상상에서 벗어난다. 그것은 '인간의 시간' 동안에는 관찰될 수 없으며, 이런 이유로 빙하와 산호초에 미치는 기후 변화의 영향을 추적하는 다큐멘터리 영화 제작자 Jeff Orlowski는 수개월 간격으로 같은 장소에서 찍은 '전후' 사진을 이용해서 점차 일어난 변화를 강조한다.

102-1

해설 기후 변화가 근본적으로 상상력의 위기라고 언급한 첫 문장 내용으로 보아, 글의 제목으로 가장 적절한 것은 ③ '기후 변화를 표현하는 데 있어 상상력의 침묵'이다. 여기서 '침묵'이란 상상력이 기후 변화를 묘사하는 데 '제 기능을 하고 있지 못하다'는 점을 비유적으로 이른 말이다.

오답 풀이

선택률	선지 해석 & 오답 풀이
① 15%	현재의 기후 문제에 대한 다양한 태도 ▶ 기후 문제에 대한 태도가 다양하다는 내용은 언급되지 않았다.
② 14%	느리지만 중요하다: 생태 운동의 역사 ▶ 'Slow but Significant'는 기후 변화의 특징이 맞지만, 이것을 '생태 운동의 역사'라는 무관한 소재와 연관시키므로 답으로 부적절하다.
④ 11%	뚜렷한 위협: 지역에 퍼져나가는 기후 재앙들 ▶ 지역 단위로 퍼져가는 기후 재앙을 묘사하는 글이 아니다.
⑤ 4%	환경주의와 생태 비평의 흥망성쇠 ▶ 생태 비평에 관해서는 언급되지 않았다.

102-2

해설 기후 변화는 '날마다 감지하지 못할' 수준으로 일어나며, 우리 눈에 가시화될 때는 그 영향력이 축적되었을 때라는 전후 맥락으로 보아, ③ (c)의 **rapidly**는 반의어인 **gradually**로 고쳐야 한다.

오답 풀이

선택률	선지 해석 & 오답 풀이
① 9%	fails(실패하다) ▶ 첫 문장에서 기후 변화는 상상력의 위기인데, 이 상상이란 소설에 기초를 둔다고 했다. 따라서 결국 소설이 기후 변화를 제대로 묘사하지 '못한' 것이라는 의미로 **fails**를 썼다.
② 15%	extraordinary(놀라운, 보기 드문) ▶ 앞 문장에서 소설 속 기후 변화는 사이클론, 홍수, 기타 재난 등의 형태로 '있을 법하지 않게' 묘사된다고 하는데, 실제 기후 변화가 이렇게 '특별한' 형태로 일어나지는 않는다는 의미로 **extraordinary**를 썼다.
④ 24%	visible(가시화된) ▶ 기후 변화는 매일 드러나는 것이 아니라 그 영향이 축적되었을 때 비로소 '눈에 보인다'는 의미로 **visible**을 썼다.
⑤ 9%	highlight(강조하다) ▶ 몇 달에 걸쳐 똑같은 곳에서 찍은 전후 사진을 대조하여 점진적으로 일어난 변화를 '강조한다'는 의미로 **highlight**을 썼다.

지문 자세히 보기'

01 Climate change experts and environmental humanists alike agree that the climate crisis is, at its core, a crisis of the imagination and much of the popular imagination is shaped by fiction.

▶ 기후 변화가 기본적으로 상상력의 위기라는 핵심 내용이 제시된다.

02 In his 2016 book *The Great Derangement*, anthropologist and novelist Amitav Ghosh takes on this relationship between imagination and environmental management, arguing that humans have failed to respond to climate change at least in part because fiction fails to believably represent it. Ghosh explains that climate change is largely absent from contemporary fiction because the cyclones, floods, and other catastrophes it brings to mind simply seem too "improbable" to belong in stories about everyday life.

▶ '상상력의 위기'라는 말의 의미를 설명하는 부분으로, 'fails to ~ represent it'과 too improbable은 문맥상 같은 의미이다. 즉 소설에서 기후 변화는 믿을 만하지 못하게, 즉 너무 있을 법하지 않은 일처럼 그려지기 때문에 대중은 기후 변화를 올바르게 상상하지도, 이에 알맞게 대처하지도 못한다는 것이다.

03 But climate change does not only reveal itself as a series of extraordinary events. In fact, as environmentalists and ecocritics from Rachel Carson to Rob Nixon have pointed out, environmental change can be "imperceptible"; it proceeds rapidly(→ gradually), only occasionally producing "explosive and spectacular" events. Most climate change impacts cannot be observed day-to-day, but they become visible when we are confronted with their accumulated impacts.

▶ 기후 변화의 실상은 '특별하고, 폭발적이고, 극적인' 사건이 아니라, '감지할 수 없을 만큼' 점진적으로 일어나는 변화임이 언급된다. 때문에 오로지 그 결과가 축적되어야만 우리 눈에 보일 수 있다는 보충 설명이 뒤따른다.

04 Climate change evades our imagination because it poses significant representational challenges. It cannot be observed in "human time," which is why documentary filmmaker Jeff Orlowski, who tracks climate change effects on glaciers and coral reefs, uses "before and after" photographs taken several months apart in the same place to highlight changes that occurred gradually.

▶ cannot be observed in "human time" 또한 앞의 "imperceptible", cannot be observed day-to-day와 문맥상 의미가 같다. 즉 하루마다 눈으로 바로 확인할 수 있는 변화가 아니라, '점차적으로 일어나는' 변화가 곧 기후 위기의 특징임이 계속해서 언급된다.

구문 풀이

~ the cyclones, floods, and other catastrophes it brings to mind simply seem too "improbable" to belong in stories about everyday life.
→ 주어인 the cyclones, floods, and other catastrophes를 꾸미는 형용사절 it brings to mind 앞에 목적격 관계대명사가 생략되었다.

구문 플러스' 목적격 관계대명사의 생략

목적격 관계대명사는 문장에서 자유롭게 생략된다. 생략이 일어나면 '명사 + 주어 + 동사'가 바로 연결된 형태로 나타난다.

The cute boy we used to know has changed!
우리가 알던 그 귀여운 소년은 변해버렸다!

'Take care' was the last word he said to me.
'잘 지내'가 그가 내게 마지막으로 한 말이었다.

103 정답 ② 40%, ⑤ 34% *2022학년도 9월 모평*

해석 비타민 C의 효과를 조사하는 연구에서, 연구원들은 일반적으로 실험 대상자들을 두 집단으로 나눈다. 한 집단(실험 집단)은 비타민 C 보충제를 받고 다른 집단(통제 집단)은 비타민 C 보충제를 받지 않는다. 연구원들은 한 집단이 다른 집단보다 감기에 더 적게 또는 더 짧게 걸리는

지를 알아내기 위해 두 집단 모두를 관찰한다. 이어지는 논의는 이러한 종류의 실험에 내재한 함정 중 일부와 이를 피하는 방법을 설명한다. 실험 대상자를 두 집단으로 분류할 때, 연구원들은 반드시 각 개인이 실험 집단 또는 통제 집단 둘 중 한 곳에 배정될 확률이 동일하도록 해야 한다. 이는 임의 추출에 의해 달성되는데, 즉 실험 대상자는 동전 던지기나 우연이 포함된 어떤 다른 방법에 의해 동일 모집단에서 임의로 선정된다. 임의 추출은 반드시 결과에 처리가 반영되고 실험 대상자의 분류에 영향을 줄지도 모르는 요인은 반영되지 않도록 하는 데 도움이 된다. 중요한 것은, 감기의 비율, 심각성, 또는 지속 기간에서 관찰된 차이가 어떤 식으로든 일어났을지도 모른다는 가능성을 배제하기 위해, 감기와 관련하여 두 집단의 사람들이 비슷하고 동일한 기록을 가지고 있어야 한다는 것이다. 예를 들어, 통제 집단이 보통 실험 집단보다 감기에 무려 두 배나 많이 걸리는 경우, 연구 결과는 아무것도 입증하지 못한다. 영양분을 포함하는 실험에서는 두 집단의 식단 또한 달라야(→ 비슷해야) 하며, 연구 중인 영양분에 관련해서 특히 그래야 한다. 실험 집단에 속한 사람들이 평소 식단에서 비타민 C를 적게 섭취하고 있었다면, 보충제의 어떤 효과도 분명하지 않을 수 있다.

103-1

해설 집단을 나누어 실험할 때의 주의사항을 설명하는 글이다. 두 집단 중 어디에든 배정될 확률이 서로 같아야 하고, 집단의 성질 또한 동일해야 한다는 내용이 전개되고 있다. 아울러 후반부에 나오는 예시를 통해, 두 집단 간의 동질성을 보장할 수 없다면 실험 결과 또한 믿을 수 없다는 결론을 이끌어내고 있다. 따라서 글의 제목으로 가장 적절한 것은 ② '상관없는 요인이 결과에 영향을 미치지 않도록 하라!'이다.

오답 풀이

선택률	선지 해석 & 오답 풀이
① 13%	완벽한 계획과 불완전한 결과: 연구의 슬픈 현실 ▶ 계획과 결과의 불일치로 인한 연구의 현실을 지적하는 내용은 글과 무관하다.
③ 16%	실험 연구에 참여하는 인간 참가자들을 보호하라! ▶ 실험 대상자 보호 문제는 언급되지 않았다.
④ 17%	어떤 영양분이 감기를 더 잘 막을 수 있을까? ▶ 감기와 영양분은 실험의 예를 보여주면서 언급된 지엽적 소재이다. 이 예시를 바탕으로 내릴 수 있는 일반적 결론을 주제로 잡아야 한다.
⑤ 14%	영양에 대한 심층 분석: 인간 건강에 핵심적인 요소 ▶ ④와 마찬가지로 지엽적 소재인 영양분을 주제로 잘못 잡은 선택지이다.

103-2

해설 Importantly 이후로 실험 집단과 통제 집단은 본질적으로 '동질해야' 한다는 내용이 언급된다. 이를 영양분 연구에 적용하면, 실험 집단과 통제 집단의 식단이 '비슷한' 상태에서 연구를 진행해야 한다는 설명이 알맞다. 따라서 ⑤ (e)의 different를 반의어인 similar로 바꾸어야 한다.

오답 풀이

선택률	선지 해석 & 오답 풀이
① 6%	avoid(피하다) ▶ 실험의 '함정'을 언급하므로 이를 '피하는' 방법을 서술하겠다는 뜻의 avoid는 적절하다.

② 15%	equal(동일한) ▶ 뒤에서 실험 집단과 통제 집단에 각각 배정될 확률을 '같게' 만들어주는 임의 추출 기법을 설명하므로 equal은 적절하다.
③ 20%	rule out(배제하다) ▶ 실험과 관계없는 요인이 결과에 간섭할 가능성을 '배제한다'는 의미의 rule out은 적절하다.
④ 25%	nothing(아무것도 ~않다) ▶ 실험 집단과 통제 집단에 본질적인 차이가 있는 경우 '아무것도' 입증되었다고 볼 수 '없다'는 문맥이므로 nothing은 적절하다.

지문 자세히 보기

01 In studies examining the effectiveness of vitamin C, researchers typically divide the subjects into two groups. One group (the experimental group) receives a vitamin C supplement, and the other (the control group) does not. Researchers observe both groups to determine whether one group has fewer or shorter colds than the other. The following discussion describes some of the pitfalls inherent in an experiment of this kind and ways to avoid them.

▶ 실험 집단과 통제 집단을 나눠 영양소의 효능을 살펴보는 연구에서 생기는 함정(pitfalls)과 이를 피할 방법(ways to avoid them)을 소개하는 글이다.

02 In sorting subjects into two groups, researchers must ensure that each person has an equal chance of being assigned to either the experimental group or the control group. This is accomplished by randomization; that is, the subjects are chosen randomly from the same population by flipping a coin or some other method involving chance. Randomization helps to ensure that results reflect the treatment and not factors that might influence the grouping of subjects.

▶ 집단을 나눌 때, 각 실험 대상자가 두 집단에 배정될 확률은 같아야 한다(an equal chance)는 내용과 함께, 임의 추출 기법에 관해 설명한다.

03 Importantly, the two groups of people must be similar and must have the same track record with respect to cold to rule out the possibility that observed differences in the rate, severity, or duration of colds might have occurred anyway. If, for example, the control group would normally catch twice as many colds as the experimental group, then the findings prove nothing.

▶ 특히 두 집단은 동질성이 있어야 한다(similar)는 점이 언급된다. 만일 감기와 영양소에 관해 연구하고 있다면, 통제 집단과 실험 집단은 '감기'에 관련된 요인에 있어 비슷해야 한다(the same track record)는 내용이 예시와 함께 전개된다.

04 In experiments involving a nutrient, the diets of both groups must also be different(→ similar), especially with respect to the nutrient being studied. If those in the experimental group were receiving less vitamin C from their usual diet, then any effects of the supplement may not be apparent.

▶ 추가로(also), '영양소'와 관련된 요인에 있어서도 두 집단이 '비슷해야 한다는 내용이 이어지고 있다. 영양소 섭취 면에서 두 집단 간에 본질적인 차이가 있다면 연구 결과를 믿을 수 없다는 결론이 뒤따른다.

구문 풀이

If, for example, the control group would normally catch **twice as many** colds **as** the experimental group, then the findings prove nothing.
→ '~보다 … 배 더 ~한'의 의미를 나타내는 「배수사 + as + 원급 + as」 표현이다.

구문 플러스° 배수 표현

배수사 + as + 원급 + as ~ = 배수사 + 비교급 + than ~
= ~보다 … 배 더 ~한

Cats sleep **twice as much as** people.
고양이는 사람보다 두 배 더 많이 잔다.
The new building is **three times taller than** the old one.
새 건물은 예전 것보다 세 배 더 높다.

---

104 정답 ④ 48%, ③ 41%   *2021학년도 9월 모평*

해석 충분한 문맥이 제공된 경우, 독자는 전문적 지식 없이도 잘 만들어진 텍스트에 다가와 작가가 의도한 바와 아주 근접한 것을 가지고 떠날 수 있다. 텍스트는 공문서와 같은 것이 되어서 독자는 최소한으로 노력하고 분투하며 그것을 읽을 수 있는데, 그의 경험이 프로이트가 '고르게 주의를 기울이는 것'의 (전략적인) 배치로 설명한 것과 가까워지기 때문이다. 그는 작가의 손에 자신을 맡기고(어떤 사람들이 디킨스나 톨스토이와 같은 위대한 소설가와 이런 경험을 했던 것처럼) 작가가 이끄는 곳으로 따라간다. 현실 세계는 사라지고 허구의 세계가 그것을 대신했다. 이제 그 정반대 경우를 생각해 보자. 문맥과 내용이 적절하게 결합되지 않은 조악한 텍스트의 경우, 우리는 이해하려고 애써야 하고, 작가가 의도한 바에 대한 우리의 이해는 아마도 그의 본래 의도와 밀접한(→ 거의 없는) 관련성을 지닐 것이다. 시대에 뒤떨어진 번역은 우리에게 이런 경험을 줄 것인데, 우리는 읽어나가면서 언어를 새롭게 가다듬어야 하고, 이해는 텍스트와의 꽤 격렬한 분투의 대가로만 오기 때문이다. 준거 틀이 없는 잘못 제시된 내용도 같은 경험을 제공할 수 있는데, 우리는 단어를 보지만 그것들이 어떻게 받아들여져야 하는지를 이해하지 못하기 때문이다. 문맥을 제공하지 못한 작가는 세상에 대한 자신의 그림을 모든 독자가 공유한다고 잘못 가정한 것이고, 적절한 준거 틀을 제공하는 것이 글을 쓰는 일의 중대한 부분임을 깨닫지 못한다.

104-1

해설 'Now consider the other extreme.' 앞뒤로, 문맥을 적절하게 제시하는 경우와 그렇지 않은 경우를 대비하고 있다. 문맥을 적절히 제시한 텍스트는 독자로 하여금 작가의 의도대로 글을 이해할 수 있게 하는 반면, 문맥을 적절히 제시하지 못한 텍스트는 독자의 이해 과정을 힘들게 할 수 있다는 내용이 주를 이룬다. 따라서 글의 제목으로 가장 적절한 것은 ④ '글쓰기에서의 문맥: 텍스트 이해를 위한 등대'이다.

선택률	선지 해석 & 오답 풀이
① 7%	현실과 허구의 세계 사이에 벽 세우기 ▶ 문맥이 적절히 제시된 텍스트를 읽을 때는 작가가 창조한 허구가 현실을 대체하게 된다는 내용으로 보아, '벽'을 세워 두 세계를 분리한다는 제목은 글과 맞지 않다.
② 17%	창의적 글 읽기: 작가의 의도를 넘어서는 것 ▶ 작가의 의도를 넘어서는 것보다는 적절한 문맥 안에서 의도를 제대로 파악하는 것에 관한 글이다.
③ 18%	효과적인 글쓰기를 위한 독자 경험의 유용성 ▶ 독자 경험이 글쓰기에 도움이 되는지에 관해서는 언급되지 않았다.
⑤ 10%	자신의 말에 갇히다: 작가들의 좁은 견해 ▶ 작가들의 견해가 좁다는 내용은 언급되지 않았다.

104-2

해설 (c)가 포함된 문장은 'Now consider the other extreme.' 앞과 반대로, 문맥을 적절히 제시하지 못할 때 독자가 작가의 의도를 이해하기 어려워한다는 내용이다. 문맥과 내용이 적절히 조화되지 못하면 작가의 의도와 '멀어진다'는 의미가 되도록, ③ (c)의 **close**를 **little**로 고쳐야 한다.

선택률	선지 해석 & 오답 풀이
① 9%	minimum(최소한의) ▶ 문맥이 충분히 제시되면 전문 지식 없이도 글이 마치 '공문서'인 양 명확하게 이해될 수 있다는 설명으로 보아, 이해에 들어가는 노력이 '최소'가 된다는 의미의 minimum은 적절하다.
② 7%	follows(따라가다) ▶ 충분한 문맥이 있으면 독자는 작가의 의도에 '근접'할 수 있다는 첫 문장 내용으로 보아 독자가 작가의 의도대로 '따라간다'는 의미의 follows는 적절하다.
④ 30%	the same(같은) ▶ 번역이 구식일 때와 마찬가지로, 준거 틀이 없을 때에도 독자의 이해가 어려워지는 '똑같은' 상황이 생긴다는 의미이므로 the same은 적절하다.
⑤ 13%	mistakenly(잘못, 실수로) ▶ 적절한 준거 틀, 즉 문맥을 주지 못한 작가는 독자들이 자신과 똑같이 세상을 이해할 것이라고 '잘못' 가정했다는 뜻으로 mistakenly가 알맞게 쓰였다.

01 To the extent that sufficient context has been provided, the reader can come to a well-crafted text with no expert knowledge and come away with a good approximation of what has been intended by the author.

▶ 문맥이 충분하게 주어지면 독자는 작가가 의도한 바와 아주 근접한 수준으로 글을 이해할 수 있다(a good approximation of ~)는 핵심 내용이 제시된다.

02 The text has become a public document and the reader can read it with a minimum of effort and struggle; his experience comes close to what Freud has described as the deployment of "evenly-hovering attention." He puts himself in the author's hands (some have had this experience with great novelists such as Dickens or Tolstoy) and he follows where the author leads. The real world has vanished and the fictive world has taken its place.

▶ 문맥이 적절히 주어질 때 이해는 쉽게(with a minimum of effort and struggle) 달성되며, 독자는 작가가 이끄는 대로 따르게 된다(follows)는 부연 설명이 이어진다.

03 Now consider the other extreme. When we come to a badly crafted text in which context and content are not happily joined, we must struggle to understand, and our sense of what the author intended probably bears close(→ little) correspondence to his original intention. An out-of-date translation will give us this experience; as we read, we must bring the language up to date, and understanding comes only at the price of a fairly intense struggle with the text.

▶ 앞과는 반대되는 예시(the other extreme)로, 문맥과 내용이 조화를 이루지 못하는 상황과 번역이 시대에 뒤처지는 상황이 언급된다. 둘 다 독자의 고생(struggle)으로 이어진다는 설명이 뒤따른다.

04 Badly presented content with no frame of reference can provide the same experience; we see the words but have no sense of how they are to be taken. The author who fails to provide the context has mistakenly assumed that his picture of the world is shared by all his readers and fails to realize that supplying the right frame of reference is a critical part of the task of writing.

▶ 적절한 준거 틀을 주지 못할 때에도 불충분한 문맥으로 독자를 고생시키게 된다는 내용이 추가된다. 위의 struggle to understand가 'have no sense ~ to be taken'으로 바뀌어 표현되었다.

Badly presented content with no frame of reference can provide the same experience; we see the words but have no sense of how they are **to be taken**.

→ to부정사의 의미상 주어 they는 the words를 가리키는데, 이는 '(독자에 의해) 받아들여지는' 대상이다. 따라서 보어인 to부정사구가 to be p.p. 형태로 쓰였다.

to부정사의 의미상 주어와 to부정사가 수동 관계일 때, to부정사는 to be p.p. 형태로 쓴다.

I didn't expect to be invited to his wedding.
나는 그의 결혼식에 초대받을 것을 예상하지 않았다.

1~2단락의 긴 지문을 읽고 제목과 어휘 문제를 해결하는 유형이다. 두 문제 중 하나는 보통 3점으로 출제된다.

· **문제 해결 Tip.**
① 도입부에서 글의 중심 소재를 파악하고, 연결어 등을 힌트로 삼아 글을 흐름 위주로 속독한다.
② 주제문 또는 반복되는 표현을 근거로 적절한 제목을 추론한다.
③ (a)~(e) 바로 앞뒤 문맥을 단서로 밑줄 어휘의 적절성을 판단해 보고, 어색한 어휘는 반의어로 교체해 본다.

105 정답 ⑤ 79%, ⑤ 79%, ④ 83% *2020학년도 6월 모평*

해석 (A) 거장 Brooks가 학급 학생들이 배우도록 바이올린으로 모차르트 곡을 연주했을 때, 교실은 아름답고 심금을 울리는 소리의 물결로 가득했다. 학급 학생들은 이 유명한 초빙 음악가가 연주한 곡을 열심히 배우려고 노력했다. 학급 학생 중에 Joe Brooks가 단연 최고였다. 사실 Joe는 그 명연주자의 아들이었다. 그의 아버지는 그가 네 살 때 유아용 바이올린을 그의 손에 쥐어 주었고, Joe는 천부적인 재능이 있었다. 이제 겨우 12년 후에, 그는 이미 아버지처럼 거장이 되는 <u>자신</u>의 길을 가고 있었다.
(D) 수업 후에 Joe가 아버지와 단둘이 있게 되었다. 그는 뭔가 중요한 이야기가 있었다. Joe는 심호흡을 하고 말했다. "저는 콘서트에서 연주해 달라는 요청을 받았는데, 먼저 아버지의 허락을 받고 싶어요. 크로스오버 콘서트예요." 명연주자 Brooks는 놀란 표정이었다. 진정, 그 명연주자가 크로스오버 음악을 싫어하는 것은 공공연한 일이었다. "아버지," Joe가 심호흡을 하고 계속 말했다. "저는 아버지의 견해를 존중하지만, <u>아버지</u>가 생각하시는 그런 게 아니에요. 내일 우리 연습에 오셔서 들어 보지 않으시겠어요? 아버지 마음에 안 드시면 취소할게요."
(C) "저, 허락받았니?" 다음 날 Joe가 연습실에 들어서자마자 Brian이 물었다. "음, 잘 모르겠어." Joe가 자신 없게 말했다. "넌 연습 후에 우리에게 말해 줘도 돼." Brian이 키보드에 손을 얹으며 말했다. 그의 옆에서 Nick이 기타를 조율하고 있었다. Joe는 마지막으로 딱 한 번만 연주하고 나서 자신이 콘서트에서 빠질지도 모른다는 것을 말하겠다고 생각했다. 그 3인조는 일상적인 연주에 들어갔는데, 오랫동안 함께 열심히 연습한 그룹만이 할 수 있듯 그렇게 쉽게 들어갔다.
(B) 그들이 연주를 마쳤을 때, Joe는 자신의 아버지가 구석에 서 있는 것을 알아차렸다. "와, 정말 멋진 연주야." 그가 감탄하며 말했다. 명연주자 Brooks는 아들 쪽으로 다가갔다. "나는 네가 바이올린의 정신을 지키면서 그런 독특한 소리를 만들어내는 방식이 좋구나. 크로스오버 음악이 창조할 수 있는 힘을 내가 과소평가했어."라고 명연주자 Brooks가 그에게 말했다. Joe와 그의 아버지는 둘 다 그 밴드가 연습해 왔던 그 멜로디를 흥얼거리며 집으로 돌아갔다.

105-1
해설 바이올린의 거장 Brooks와 그의 아들 Joe를 소개한 (A) 뒤로, Joe가 아버지를 크로스오버 연주 연습에 초대했다는 내용의 (D), 아버지의 마음을 확신하지 못한 채로 Joe가 연습을 시작했다는 내용의 (C), 아들의 연주를 본 Brooks가 감동했다는 내용의 (B)가 연결되어야 한다. 따라서 글의 순서로 가장 적절한 것은 ⑤ '(D)-(C)-(B)'이다.

오답 풀이

선택률	오답 풀이
① 3%	(A)는 아들 Joe가 있는 반에서 Brooks가 수업을 했다는 내용이다. 이 뒤로 (B)가 이어지면 '누가' 수업이 아닌 '연습'을 마친 상황인지 분명하지 않다.
② 4%	(A)에 허락을 구한다는 내용이 없으므로 '허락을 받았는지' 묻는 (C)가 이어지면 어색하다.
③ 7%	
④ 6%	수업 중인 (A)에 이어 (D)에서는 수업이 끝난 상황을 언급하지만, '누가' '무엇을' 연습했는지는 언급하지 않는다. 따라서 (D) 뒤에 (B)가 이어지면 내용 흐름이 부자연스럽다.

105-2
해설 (a)~(d)는 Joe, (e)는 Master Brooks이므로, 가리키는 대상이 다른 하나는 ⑤ '(e)'이다.

오답 풀이

선택률	오답 풀이
① 3%	문장의 주어인 he가 Joe이므로, 주어의 소유격을 나타내는 his 또한 Joe이다.
② 4%	Master Brooks와 대화 중인 대상은 Joe이다.
③ 4%	Joe의 친구 Brian이 말을 거는 대상은 Joe이다.
④ 8%	콘서트에 빠질 수도 있는 사람은 Joe이다.

105-3
해설 (C)에 따르면 Joe 외에 Brian과 Nick이 연습 멤버로 언급된다. 즉 Joe를 포함한 연습 인원은 총 3명(The trio)이므로, 내용과 일치하지 않는 것은 ④ 'Joe가 속한 밴드는 두 명의 연주자로 구성되었다.'이다.

오답 풀이

선택률	오답 풀이
① 3%	(A) ~ Joe was a natural talent.
② 3%	(B) When they finished practicing, Joe noticed his father standing in the corner.
③ 6%	(B) "I love the way you created those unique sounds ~. I underestimated the power that crossover music can create." ~
⑤ 3%	(D) After the class, Joe was alone with his father. He had something important to talk about.

지문 자세히 보기

01 When Master Brooks played a Mozart piece on the violin for his class to learn, the room was filled with waves of beautiful, soul-stirring sound. The class tried to emulate the music played by this renowned guest musician. Among the students in the class, Joe Brooks was by far the best. In fact, Joe was the master's son. His father had placed a baby violin in his hands at the age of four, and Joe was a natural talent. Now, just twelve years later, he was already on <u>his</u> way to becoming a virtuoso like his father.

▶ 바이올린의 거장 Master Brooks가 지도하는 수업에 아들 Joe가 있었다는 배경 상황이 제시된다.

02 After the class, Joe was alone with his father. He had something important to talk about. Joe took a deep breath and said, "I have been asked to play in a concert, and I would like your permission first. It is a crossover concert." Master Brooks looked surprised. Indeed, the master's dislike of crossover music was no secret. "Father," Joe took a deep breath and continued, "I respect your views, but it is not what you think. Why don't you come and listen to our practice tomorrow? If you don't like it, I will cancel."

▶ 진행되던 수업이 끝난 후(After the class), Joe가 아버지에게 크로스오버 연주를 하는 것에 대한 허락(permission, Why don't you ~)을 구했다는 내용이 이어진다.

03 "Well, did you get permission?" asked Brian as soon as Joe entered the practice room the following day. "Um, I'm not sure," answered Joe without confidence. "You can tell us about it after practice," Brian said as he placed his fingers on the keyboard. Beside him, Nick was tuning his guitar. Joe thought that he would play just one last time before telling them that he might pull out of the concert. The trio swung into their routine, as easily as only a group that had practiced long and hard together could.

▶ 허락을 구한 다음날(the following day) 연습에 참여한 Joe에게 친구들이 허락을 받았는지(~ did you get permission?) 물었다는 내용이 연결된다. Joe를 포함해 총 3명의 멤버(The trio)가 연습을 시작했다는 묘사도 이어진다.

04 When they finished practicing, Joe noticed his father standing in the corner. "Wow, that was quite wonderful," he said with admiration. Master Brooks came toward his son. "I love the way you created those unique sounds while keeping the spirit of the violin. I underestimated the power that crossover music can create," said Master Brooks to him. Joe and his father returned home, both humming the melody that the band had been practicing.

▶ 연습이 끝났을 때(finished practicing), Joe는 자리에 와 있던 아버지를 발견했고, 부자는 함께 연습곡을 흥얼거리며 귀가했다는 결말로 글이 마무리된다.

 구문 풀이

Among the students in the class, Joe Brooks was **by far** the best.
→ **by far**(단연코)는 최상급 앞뒤에서 최상급을 강조한다.

구문 플러스¹ 최상급 강조 부사

much, by far, the very, ever 등은 최상급을 강조한다.

This has been the longest winter ever!
올해 겨울은 역대 제일 기네!

We want the very best quality.
우리는 단연코 최고의 품질을 원한다.

 유형 플러스' 장문의 이해 (2)

긴 문학적 이야기를 읽고 순서, 지칭, 불일치 문제를 해결하는 유형이다. 지문이나 문제는 쉽지만 시간 안배가 관건이다.

· 문제 해결 Tip.
① 연결어, 지시어, 대명사, 시간 표현 등에 유의하여 **(A)** 뒤에 이어질 단락의 순서부터 잡는다.
② 앞뒤 문맥에 유의하며, **(a)~(e)**의 지칭 대상을 판별한다.
③ 불일치 문제의 ①~⑤는 글의 원래 순서가 아닌, **(A)~(D)** 단락 순서대로 제시된다. 순서와 지칭을 풀며 흐름을 대략적으로 파악했다면, 선택지를 읽고 키워드 중심으로 본문 문장을 찾아 빠르게 대조한다.

Memo

Memo